Sr. Ce
Fall of 1949

SOCIAL PSYCHOLOGY OF MODERN LIFE

REVISED EDITION

SOCIAL PSYCHOLOGY OF MODERN LIFE

REVISED EDITION

STEUART HENDERSON BRITT

Manager of Research and Merchandising Department, McCann-Erickson, Inc.

Also Member of Board of Directors Richardson, Bellows, Henry & Co., Inc.

RINEHART & COMPANY, INC.

PUBLISHERS NEW YORK

▶ TO P. Y. E. ◀
(*both editions*)

DESIGNED BY STEFAN SALTER

PRINTED IN THE UNITED STATES OF AMERICA
BY J. J. LITTLE AND IVES COMPANY, NEW YORK

PREFACE TO FIRST EDITION

Three objectives are stressed in this book: (1) As a social psychology it is written for students of sociology, students of psychology, and interested laymen. (2) The social psychology of modern everyday life is emphasized rather than abstract theoretical problems. (3) Experimental and observational materials are introduced on every topic, especially those which throw the most light on problems of human interrelations in the United States. Part I explains what is meant by social psychology and describes its principal methods. Part II shows the interrelations of physiological, psychological, and sociological materials, and emphasizes the cultural aspects of human behavior.

Part III deals with some of the individual bases of social adjustment: instincts, conditioning, and motivation; traits and attitudes; language; and irrational thinking and behavior. Part IV then takes up some special problems of social behavior: prejudice, judging emotions, subliminal stimulation, stereotyping; the influence of other persons through unconscious factors, suggestion, imitation, laughter, and group influence on individual performance; behavior as influenced by crowds, audiences, booms, crazes, and fads and fashions; the relationships between sex, dominance, and prestige; and the social psychology of leadership and invention.

Part V is a psychological analysis of some representative groups and institutions and their influence on the individual, especially the family, the school, the church, the fraternity and club, the political party, and the occupational group. Part VI considers some of our most important social conflicts, including delinquency, problems of race differences, prejudices against minority groups, nationalism, and war, and suggests some possible solutions to these problems.

Three sets of study aids are provided. First, there is a list of study questions at the end of each chapter which will be helpful in reviewing. Second, suggested readings at the end of each chapter will furnish additional information on topics of special interest. Finally, there are four appendixes at the end of the book which will be useful from time to time. In these appendixes are found a list of footnotes, giving references to all materials cited in the present book; a list of textbooks on social psychology; a list of general bibliographical sources, and of sociological, psychological, and allied journals; and finally a list of dictionaries and vocabularies for the principal terms used in social psychology.

The greatest thanks go to Mr. Selden C. Menefee and Miss Audrey G. Granneberg who read the entire manuscript in its initial stages and made countless helpful suggestions. Grateful acknowledgment is also extended to Dr. Frank H. Hankins, Dr. Arthur F. Jenness, and Dr. O. H. Mowrer, each of whom read and criticized the manuscript in its final stages, and to Dr. Daniel Katz, who helped in the preparation of the last section of Chapter 23. The aid of three student assistants, Miss Alice L. Fracker, Miss Mary Jo Oslin, and especially Mr. John T. Wilson, is also sincerely appreciated.

S. H. B.

WASHINGTON, D. C.
April 1, 1941

PREFACE TO REVISED EDITION

This new edition brings *Social Psychology of Modern Life* thoroughly up to date. The book has been completely revised, for new concepts and materials have been introduced in every chapter.

Discussions of and references to over 200 new books and articles have been added. Practically all of these were published in the 1940's. Several hundred other sources have also been read and consulted.

In other words, *new* experimental and observational materials have been introduced wherever appropriate; and recent examples and illustrations of the social psychology of modern life have also been given.

The first edition went into an eleventh printing in 1948. The present revision is similar to the previous book in two significant ways. From the teacher's standpoint, and so that the transition may be easy in changing from the previous edition to the present one, the same order of chapters and sections has been retained. From the student's standpoint, the materials have been written in such a way that they will be *read* and *remembered.*

To summarize, the writer has attempted to assimilate a wealth of factual data from the literature of the social sciences and other sources—see the sixty-six pages of footnotes in Appendix A—and then to present this information in an interesting, readable style.

In addition, specific references in *Readings in Social Psychology* (edited by Newcomb, Hartley, and other members of a committee of the Society for the Psychological Study of Social Issues) have been added at the end of all but three chapters. This enables the reader to supplement the present book with a set of logically integrated outside readings.

S. H. B.

New York City
January 1, 1949

TABLE OF CONTENTS

▶ APPENDIXES

LIST OF ILLUSTRATIONS

LIST OF TABLES

PART ONE

SOCIAL PSYCHOLOGY AND ITS METHODS

1. THE SOCIAL PSYCHOLOGY OF EVERYDAY LIFE
2. THE METHODS OF SOCIAL PSYCHOLOGY

► THIS introductory section raises questions relating to the scope of social psychology and shows what other fields it cuts across. It indicates some practical problems for the student, problems which he should keep in mind during the study of social psychology. Finally, the methods of social psychology are outlined, with emphasis on objectivity and scientific materials.

CHAPTER ONE

THE SOCIAL PSYCHOLOGY OF EVERYDAY LIFE

INFORMATION, PLEASE! A Few Questions—Value of Psychology—Social Psychology—Psychological Sociology / WHAT IS SOCIAL PSYCHOLOGY? The Problem of Defining Social Psychology—Other Fields of Psychology—The Social Sciences—Interrelations in Social Psychology / THE PHYSICAL SCIENTISTS LOOK US OVER. The Scope of Social Psychology—Prediction and Control in Social Psychology—Difficulties of Exact Prediction in Physical Science—Prediction of Human Behavior—Practical Predictions.

▶ INFORMATION, PLEASE!

A FEW QUESTIONS

After reading this book, you should be able to give meaningful answers to many practical questions of everyday life.[1] * What are the psychological devices used by "rabble rousers"? What are the underlying myths and legends that cause friction between Gentile and Jew? Why do social movements that promise Utopia seek converts? Why do people like to go to motion pictures which frighten them or make them cry? Why do educational institutions constantly raise money by appealing to "school spirit" and "the old Alma Mater" instead of saying that money is needed to build laboratories and to pay professors? What are the factors that create stereotypes of the college professor, the lawyer, the family physician? Can personality be judged from the voice? How are propagandistic devices being used at the present time by all sorts of persons and organizations to influence *you?*

VALUE OF PSYCHOLOGY

Of course, you have ready answers to some of these questions now. But after a course in social psychology you should be able to give more correct and complete answers. More and more, outstanding persons are realizing the benefits to be derived from the study of psychology. Thus, the engineers who attended the Economics Conference for Engineers a few years ago specifically recommended that executives, in order to learn more about their men, take courses in psychology and human relations—courses presented on a factual, scientific basis.[2] Similarly, when a newspaper correspondent asked a former chief of the Division of Foreign

* Numbers like this [1] throughout the volume indicate references listed separately for each chapter beginning on page 605.

Service Personnel of the State Department, "What are the requirements for a young man who wishes to enter the foreign service?" he promptly replied: "A man must have a sound education. In addition to general subjects, a knowledge of social psychology and sociology is very important. A man must have an inquiring mind and the ability to analyze people and situations."[3]

SOCIAL PSYCHOLOGY

Now, answers to such questions as those presented above necessarily fall within the province of two different "disciplines." One is called sociology, the other psychology. *Social psychology,* which is the connecting link between sociology and psychology, is therefore the best approach to them.

Colleges treat the materials of social psychology both in departments of psychology and in departments of sociology.[4] Unfortunately, this has sometimes resulted in a rivalry between certain psychologists (not all) who believe that they have all the wisdom of human behavior, and certain sociologists (not all) who believe that they know all the answers. However, in the past few years an increasing number of social psychologists of both schools have realized the absurdity of this situation. Increasingly, the division is a matter of history.

PSYCHOLOGICAL SOCIOLOGY

A question for your consideration is whether there are any advantages in dealing with "social psychology" instead of "psychological sociology." Suppose this book bore the title *Psychological Sociology* instead of the label *Social Psychology*—would that make any difference? Although there is a difference in treatment of materials by "social psychologists" and "psychological sociologists," this is largely due to the growth of social psychology in two separate departments of liberal arts colleges. Perhaps also "social psychology" is easier to say—"social" is a more convenient adjective, and "psychology" is a more convenient noun. At any rate, a true social psychology is emerging to which both sociologists and psychologists adhere. This book attempts to present this scientific approach and to bridge the gap between the two camps.

▶ WHAT IS SOCIAL PSYCHOLOGY?

THE PROBLEM OF DEFINING SOCIAL PSYCHOLOGY

How can social psychology be defined? First of all, it might be said that *all* psychology is social psychology. This seems increasingly apparent as we realize that the research problems carried on in the experimental laboratory depend for their ultimate solutions upon an understanding of what people do in group situations.

> . . . However much laboratory techniques may contribute to the understanding of emotional and mental processes, these can be comprehended only if they are also studied as social phenomena. Inasmuch as every individual grows up in a culture among other people, such things as perception, memory, reasoning, and the other psychological processes are socially conditioned and can be fully understood only in their specific social setting.[5]

Many years ago Gabriel Tarde (1843-1904), a French sociologist, pointed out that "all psychological phenomena can be divided into [1] the physiological and [2] the social, and that when we have relegated elementary sensations and appetite to the former head, all that is left of our mental life, our beliefs, ideas and desires falls within the scope of social psychology."[6] It might appear presumptuous to insist on stating too strongly that all psychology is social psychology. It might seem unfair to workers in educational psychology, child psychology, and physiological psychology. However, most students of behavior would agree that probably 90 per cent of all instances of psychological behavior is social or cultural in character.[7] Social psychology, as defined in this book, will deal with those materials of psychology which are more *social* in nature, as distinguished from materials which are more *individual* in nature.

We would certainly agree with Floyd H. Allport that "Social psychology must not be placed in contradistinction to the psychology of the individual; *it is a part of the psychology of the individual,* whose behavior it studies in relation to that sector of his environment comprised by his fellows."[8] Since it is difficult to find human situations in which social factors are entirely absent, it is practically impossible to draw a hard and fast line between individual psychology and social psychology. We can say only that individual psychology is "simply that psychology in which social factors (past or present) play a *relatively small* part," while social psychology is "that psychology in which social factors play a *relatively large* part."[9]

In conclusion, then, *social psychology is the study of the behavior of individuals in their reactions to other individuals and in social situations.*[10] The word "behavior" includes not only overt conduct, but also "internal" behavior such as attitudes and consciousness.[11]

OTHER FIELDS OF PSYCHOLOGY

If social psychology is defined thus broadly, is should be apparent that it cuts across a number of other fields. Thus, it is impossible to discuss social psychology without introducing materials from *genetic* or *developmental* psychology and *child* psychology. The development and growth of a human being, especially his personality development, is a social-psychological problem. We shall find it necessary to introduce certain studies from the field of *comparative* psychology, for we may wish to make comparisons between human and infrahuman behavior; in fact, we could devote considerable attention simply to the social psychology of the vertebrates.[12] We must cut across *educational* psychology, particularly when we come to discuss that modern phenomenon called "education." It is essential to deal with certain aspects of *abnormal* psychology in order to understand the psychology of "normal" people. Finally, any course in psychology must depend on some of the techniques and findings of *experimental* psychology.

THE SOCIAL SCIENCES

Social psychology cannot be completely divorced from fields of knowledge outside the scope of psychology proper. The bulletins of colleges and universities are often deceptive in that they suggest real boundaries between departments, as if each subject were a world of knowledge to itself. Here is the department of psychology, and over there is the department of sociology; here is economics, and over there is political science; here is history, and over there is anthropology. Actually these departmental boundaries are not at all precise, for each department draws heavily on one or more of the others for both content and point of view. Scholars in such fields as economics, history, government, political science, psychology, sociology, and anthropology are all concerned with the prediction and control of human behavior in all its aspects. These subjects are interrelated. Not only is there great overlapping of ideas and materials from one of these disciplines to another, but in certain instances similar or even identical problems are handled simply with a different emphasis or a different technique.

In social psychology, we necessarily cut across many other social sciences and draw pertinent materials and attitudes from them. As an example, take the social psychology of the family. There is a wealth of *sociological* material on the family which has to be considered by any psychologist concerned with the family. Again, take the problem of individual differences; this is dealt with in detail by *economists* as well as by psychologists. Consider the problems of our particular culture, and we have to take materials from *anthropology* and then analyze them in their *historical* setting. Look at the problems that are on the front page of your newspaper this morning; you can interpret them more meaningfully if you are well grounded in *political science* as well as in social psychology. The materials presented in this book should be related to the other social sciences; otherwise group behavior cannot be satisfactorily explained.

INTERRELATIONS IN SOCIAL PSYCHOLOGY

"Well," you may say, "if social psychology draws on all these fields, isn't it a hodgepodge?" You will be right in that it does cover a "multitude of sins," but, as we shall see, order can now be produced out of what once was chaos. One author has drawn attention to the fact that during one year the *Journal of Social Psychology* published articles with such diverse titles as: "A Quantitative Comparison of the Nationality Preferences of Two Groups"; "Examinations in Familiar and Unfamiliar Surroundings"; "Voluntary Simulation of Allergic Sneezing"; "The Instability of Post-war Marriages"; "An Analysis of the Perception of Intelligence in the Face"; "Denunciation and Religious Certainty"; "A Psychoneurotic Inventory of Penitentiary Inmates."[13] You may feel that this is a strange assortment of subjects, yet every one of these investigations has a definite bearing on some larger phase of social psychology. Thus, a study of nationality preferences aids our understanding of the social psychology of prejudice; an analysis of examinations is helpful in our system of education; an investigation of postwar marriages adds to our knowledge of family relations; the question of religious certainty is important both for the social psychology of leadership and for a study of the institution of religion itself.

▶ THE PHYSICAL SCIENTISTS LOOK US OVER

THE SCOPE OF SOCIAL PSYCHOLOGY

Because of a lack of appreciation of the ultimate significance of highly specialized bits of psychological research, certain physical scientists are very critical of social psychology. They often fail to see the interrelations of the data produced. They may even point out that in physics, or in chemistry, you find certain standard topics treated in all the recognized texts, whereas if you pick up any of the textbooks in social psychology, you find overlapping on some topics, and also great gaps where matters discussed in some books are completely omitted in others. Physical scientists are apt to say, then, that there is no agreement as to exactly what is the field of social psychology because there is no agreement upon any exact set of data. The situation is not really so bad as it may seem to outsiders, for, considering the relative newness of scientific social psychology, there is remarkable agreement among the various writers concerning its scope. Granted that one author might stress rivalry, and another temperament, as important psychological problems, not a single text on social psychology of the last few years could possibly omit from consideration a discussion of such topics as attitudes, language, leadership, or propaganda. A comparison of the textbooks published since the beginning of 1936 will show enough agreement between most of the authors to deduce that social psychology is "coming of age."[14]

PREDICTION AND CONTROL IN SOCIAL PSYCHOLOGY

A second criticism by physical scientists is more drastic. A truly righteous physicist or chemist looks at the various social sciences and says, "Social science? Oh, yes, that's the stuff which isn't social, and neither is it science." His real objection is that there are no types of behavior you can predict or control as a result of studying social psychology. As you know, a chemist can put together two chemicals and can predict in advance what will happen; he can argue, however, that when you put two human beings together, no one can predict what will happen. In other words, objection number two of the physical scientist is that in *true* science accurate predictions can be made of what will happen, but that in social psychology it is anybody's guess as to what will take place under a given set of conditions.

DIFFICULTIES OF EXACT PREDICTION IN PHYSICAL SCIENCE

Now, is this a sound objection? Actually the physical scientist under certain conditions may be in just as difficult a position as the social psychologist when it comes to making exact predictions. Let us give the chemist a dozen or two solutions of chemicals and pour them into a beaker, not knowing what the chemicals are or what quantities are represented. See if he can predict what the final result will be. A chemist faced with the same problem that a social psychologist faces in human behavior, dealing at the outset with unknown materials and quantities, also finds it difficult to make predictions.

Why is this? Some social scientists are still telling us that we can never approach human relations as scientifically as a chemist can approach common table salt and sulphuric acid. The chemist knows that when he adds a solution of sodium chloride to one of sulphuric acid he gets sodium sulphate and hydrochloric acid.

But it all depends. If many other chemicals are present, the result becomes harder to predict. So, render either the chemical or the human situation complex and prediction becomes all but impossible in any specific instance. Both scientists prefer uncomplicated situations and rather simple problems concerned with masses or aggregates.

When the chemist mixes sulphuric acid and common salt together he is really working with great aggregates of molecules, atoms, electrons, and so on, not with simple individuals. He does not know just what would happen if he added a molecule of salt to a molecule of the acid. He can never tell anything about an individual molecule of anything. Maybe some individuals do not react at all.[15]

PREDICTION OF HUMAN BEHAVIOR

Is it true that you cannot tell what may happen when you put two human beings together? The next time you want your hair cut, see if you can predict what will happen when you and your barber, two human beings, get together. For one thing, you know that he will cut your hair, and not vice versa. You know just what will be the order of his acts—using the clippers, the scissors, shaving your neck, and finally snipping off the loose ends. If you know your barber, you may also be able to predict what he will talk about.

There are whole series of behavior situations where, with a little careful observation, you can predict very precisely not only what people will do but what they will say. A student rushed up to a mailbox on the corner; the mail truck had just arrived, and the postman was carrying away a sack of mail. Handing over his letters, the student asked, "What am I supposed to say?" and the postman replied without hesitation, "*Everyone* says, 'Ah, just in time!' "

The owner of a dress shop says that 99 per cent of all husbands, when brought in by their wives to see the latest style creation, will sit dejectedly and say quite glumly, "What do I know about it?" The next time you take a motor trip, try making a few inquiries about your route from filling-station operators and "natives," and note how, after the explicit directions about turning to the right at the white church a half mile beyond the third traffic light, nearly every informant will end his speech with the statement, "You can't miss it!"

A certain registrar, after only an hour or so of practice in interviewing students applying for admission, can predict rather accurately upon seeing a person enter the room what his first statement will be when he reaches the admissions desk.

> Every person who has been employed in such capacity as to meet the public expects great sameness in reactions. The same excuses are offered, the same efforts are made to trick one, the same comments made, and the same general types of behavior reappear over and over again. People do or say the same thing with such monotonous regularity as to make those who deal with the public very tired and often somewhat cross.[16]

PRACTICAL PREDICTIONS

A third answer to the objection concerning prediction in social psychology is that there are a number of people with psychological training who are making rather startling predictions as to what people will do in important situations. And a smart restaurant manager knows in advance just about how many people will eat in his dining room, even what most of them will order, while insurance companies predict quite accurately how many people will die and be injured in any given year. Consider Dr. George Gallup's American Institute of Public Opinion. By October, 1938, Dr. Gallup had predicted what the results would be in sixty-two different elections; he was correct on fifty of them—a batting average of 87 per cent.[17] The average state-by-state error of the Gallup poll in the 1940 presidential election was only 2½ per cent.[18] Although there have been instances in which public-opinion pollsters have been wrong, notably in predicting the election results in 1948, the point is that they have been right in the great majority of instances, and the margin of error normally is less than 4 per cent. In this same connection, consider the various market research surveys which serve as useful guides for many businesses as to what the market is likely to be for particular products, and what are the best ways to capture that market.

During World War II psychologists of the National Defense Research Committee developed many useful batteries of tests for predicting specific aspects of behavior of men in the armed services.[19] For example, the validity of certain tests for predicting code-learning ability was high enough so that the general use of the tests in classifying personnel for radio-code instruction would have considerably reduced man-power wastage caused by the failure of men in Radio Code Schools. Also, there is experimental evidence that indicates "that among individuals who have been delinquent in civilian life, those who are likely to be delinquent in army life can be selected with a high degree of accuracy. . . ."[20]

Then, there are the innumerable instances where psychologists predict the scholarship of college students even before they begin their first year of study. Table 1 shows quite pointedly what happened to 113 students at the University of Illinois who were in the lowest 10 per cent on an intelligence test and, by contrast, what did or did not happen to the upper 10 per cent on the same test.

TABLE 1

Records at the End of the First Semester of the Upper and Lower 10 Per Cent of the Distribution of Intelligence in a Group of Students at the University of Illinois (After F. L. Ruch)[21]

	Poorest Tenth, Per Cent	*Best Tenth, Per Cent*
Withdrew before the end of the semester	12	4
Were dropped by the university	24	0
Placed on probation	37	2
Made average grades or better	10	84

Psychologists are thus able to make predictions of human behavior in many aspects of everyday life. As our fund of research on social behavior grows, we will be able to predict more and more accurately what a human being will do in given situations, although, because of the complex nature of the beast, never as precisely as the chemist can predict the results of mixing simple chemicals in a test tube.

QUESTIONS AND PROBLEMS FOR DISCUSSION

1. *A person with no training in psychology asks you, "What is social psychology?" What will you tell him?*
2. *Make a list of topics which you think should be discussed in a course in social psychology. Underscore five which you regard as of major importance.*
3. *There might be some differences between "social psychology" and psychological sociology." What might they be?*
4. *Give some concrete examples of the "overlapping" of social psychology with other social sciences.*
5. *Give several specific examples of practical problems in social psychology.*
6. *What kinds of predictions can a trained social psychologist make that other persons are not likely to make?*

RECOMMENDED READINGS

Allport, F. H., Britt, S. H., Miles, C. C., Murphy, G., Goodenough, F. L., Katz, D., Brown, J. F., Maslow, A. H., Dashiell, J. F., Robinson, E. S., and Cantril, H., "The Subject Matter and Methods of Social Psychology," *Social Forces,* 1937, 15, 455–495.

Bray, C. W., *Psychology and Military Proficiency: A History of the Applied Psychology Panel of the National Defense Research Committee.* Princeton: Princeton University Press, 1948.

Cantril, H., and Research Associates, *Gauging Public Opinion.* Princeton: Princeton University Press, 1944.

Crowther, J. G., *The Social Relations of Science.* New York: The Macmillan Company, 1940.

Gallup, G. H., and Rae, S. F., *The Pulse of Democracy: The Public Opinion Poll and How It Works.* New York: Simon and Schuster, 1940.

Pressey, S. L., Janney, J. E., and Kuhlen, R. G., *Life: A Psychological Survey.* New York: Harper & Brothers, 1939.

Schmidt, E. P. (editor), *Man and Society: A Substantive Introduction to the Social Sciences.* New York: Prentice-Hall, Inc., 1937.

Thorndike, E. L., *Human Nature and the Social Order.* New York: The Macmillan Company, 1940.

CHAPTER TWO

THE METHODS OF SOCIAL PSYCHOLOGY

KEYNOTE I—EMPIRICISM. Recent Development of Social Psychology—Empiricism—Social Psychology for the Study of World Problems—(1) The Experimental Method of Psychological Analysis—(2) The Observational Method of Psychological Analysis—The Use of Statistical Techniques—Other Techniques / KEYNOTE II—OBJECTIVITY. Three Pairs of Magic Glasses—Difficulties of Objectivity—The Scientific Attitude / KEYNOTE III—A HEALTHY SKEPTICISM.

▶ KEYNOTE I—EMPIRICISM

RECENT DEVELOPMENT OF SOCIAL PSYCHOLOGY

How does it happen that we are now able to make some fairly accurate predictions of social behavior? We could not have done this so well 15 or 20 years ago. We are able to do this now only because social psychology has completely changed in character from the beginning of the century until now. The first textbooks to bear the name *Social Psychology* were written only about forty years ago. The late Professor William McDougall published an *Introduction to Social Psychology* in 1908, and Professor Edward Alsworth Ross's pioneering *Social Psychology,* written from a sociologist's viewpoint, appeared in the same year. If you will examine either of these books, or for that matter, some of the textbooks of the 1920's, you will find that they consisted of a great deal of "armchair" philosophizing on the part of the author as to what he thinks human behavior is like, or perhaps what he wishes it would be like. The social psychology of the past, that is, up to only a few years back, was typified by wordy arguments and discussions of points of view. A great deal of energy was put into disputations about particular "schools" and systems of sociology and psychology.

EMPIRICISM

The last few years have seen a change in all this. Recent workers have followed in the steps of Auguste Comte (1790-1857), who developed the concept of "social physics." His positivistic philosophy has been emulated, perhaps unknowingly, by many social psychologists of recent years who have been interested in both the social and physiological bases of behavior. Social psychology, particularly of the last decade, can be typified by one word—*empirical.* The empirical method is characterized principally by two steps: *experimentation* and *scientific observation.* Probably the most important development of this empirical movement has been the emphasis on an experimental approach (that is, an approach through actual experiences) to social-psychological problems, and at the same time a "dropping out" of the previous tendency to rely on the personal opinion of oneself or of others.[1]

The result is that in the last two decades we have had a tremendous number of important experimental, observational, and statistical studies, which means that we know a great deal more today about human behavior than the social psychologists of the early 1900's could possibly guess by armchair methods. Consider such monumental studies as Terman's *Genetic Studies of Genius,*[2] the classical studies by Hartshorne and May on character,[3] the analysis of *Propaganda* by Doob,[4] *The Psychology of Radio* by Hadley Cantril and Gordon W. Allport,[5] the revolutionary approach to problems of law presented by Edward S. Robinson in his *Law and the Lawyers.*[6] Even a cursory examination of studies of the last few years shows that the keynote of present-day social psychology lies in careful scientific experimentation and observation.

SOCIAL PSYCHOLOGY FOR THE STUDY OF WORLD PROBLEMS

If social psychology so consistently makes use of these exact scientific methods, you may well ask why we do not go right ahead in this chapter and make a social-psychological analysis of certain world situations. Careful empirical studies of present world events may be of much greater interest to you than the differences in points of view between two social scientists. Academic discussions may seem remote from a world full of wars, depressions, and vexing industrial situations. It is necessary, however, to postpone a concrete analysis of the pressing problems of the world today until further investigation of the foundations of individual and social behavior have been made. This is not to deny the thesis of this book, as presented in Chapter 1, that we should be vitally concerned with the psychology of everyday life. It simply means that we must truly make empirical analyses of fundamental types of behavior *before* we are in a position to arrive at really sound conclusions concerning problems national and international in scope.

Perhaps an analogy will help. Suppose this were a book on physiology or elementary psychology, and that we were attempting to learn about the psychology of audition—how it is that we hear. Before we could even begin a consideration of *how* we hear, and the theories of hearing, we would, first of all, have to go into considerable detail as to the anatomy and physiology of the entire auditory mechanism and its relation to the nervous system. We would, in the second place, have to go into a discussion of the physical characteristics of sound waves. In the third place, we would have to employ a special terminology so that we could understand each other and so that the words we used would have very specific connotations—so that when such terms as "cochlea" or "decibel" appeared, they would carry precise meanings. Only then would we be in a position to discuss theories of hearing.

In much the same way, if we are to carry on any intelligent discussion of, let us say, the social psychology of war, it is first necessary to understand the social psychology of conditioning, of dominance and leadership, of prejudices, of propaganda, and of other basic phenomena. "Why do men go to war?" is a simple enough question, but it is not simple to answer. A valid psychological answer requires a knowledge of at least five different variables: (1) man's unlearned responses, (2) the various habits he has formed, (3) the traditions of his group, (4) the social conventions he respects, and (5) the effects of agencies such as his church, school, and family upon his development.[7] We should, then, be in a position at the conclusion of a course in social psychology to have a much better understanding of the social psychology of war. Having made an analysis of the various basic problems of human behavior, we should also be in a much better position to interpret more accurately many other things we read about in our daily newspapers.

1. THE EXPERIMENTAL METHOD OF PSYCHOLOGICAL ANALYSIS

In order to understand the social psychology of any current problem, obviously we must consider how empirical methods may be applied. Psychologists, just as physical scientists, want to use the experimental method and experimental means wherever possible. A world-famous psychologist has said that anything which exists exists in some degree, and if it exists in some degree, it can be measured.

Is that true? Certainly the attempt of every psychologist has been to isolate some particular variable or causal factor and to study it independently until he understands that variable as it affects human behavior. The standard formula in any experimental situation is: Keep all your variables constant except one; then vary that one independently of the others, and you will know that any results obtained are due to that one variable and not to any of the others. For example, when Galileo wished to determine the speed of fall of a bullet compared with a feather, he put both in an air-free tube so that the conditions were constant for both. The experimental variable was the weight of the objects, and in the vacuum both fell at the same rate of speed. With air admitted to the tube, of course, the bullet fell more rapidly. Within recent years a statistical method of "factorial design" has been developed and used which makes it possible to analyze the simultaneous variation of two or more factors.[8]

Unfortunately, problems of social psychology do not always readily lend themselves to experimentation. Problems of crowd behavior, of propaganda, of the family are significant, but often they must be scientifically observed instead of being experimentally attacked. You can see why this is true. The chemist or the physicist can keep all of the variables constant except one; and he can conduct his experiment over and over again. In social psychology, on the other hand, it is extremely difficult to control all of the variables save one, and it is practically impossible ever to have a group situation where all of the variables are exactly the same as they were in the previous experimental situation.

A second difficulty in the use of the experimental method is the problem of duplicating in a laboratory situation the conditions of the world around us. If we are interested in some problem of motivation, we can see instances everywhere of people being swayed by reward and by punishment, by pleasant and by unpleasant situations. Yet, when we attempt to set up conditions in the psychological laboratory which represent reward or punishment or pleasant or unpleasant situations, we run into serious difficulties. Consider the matter of punishment. There are examples all around us in the outside world—humiliation, degradation, imprisonment, even mutilation. What is the worst punishment which can be given in the psychological laboratory? So far as most psychologists are concerned, it is an electric shock. But is that at all comparable to the punishment of the gossip of your friends, or the threat of the loss of your job? Similarly, we can see in the world around us the rewards which a "Bing" Crosby or a Roosevelt or a Joe Louis receives. What is the greatest reward which can be offered in the psychological laboratory? So far as most psychologists are concerned, it is to pay a college student 50 cents or so an hour to serve as a "guinea pig."

One of the most unpleasant situations which can be devised in a psychological experiment is to give the person who acts as subject a very bitter, foul-tasting drink. Can that possibly compare with the unpleasant situation of a "hangover"? One of the most pleasant stimuli used in psychological experiments is a bonbon, given to the experimental subject when he threads a maze successfully. But can that possibly compare in its reward value with dinner at your favorite restaurant? "The fear of the policeman, to take a prosaic everyday example, has no counterpart in laboratory technique, nor yet the passionate embrace of the adoring woman; but these are what give force and vigor to the motives of everyday life."[9]

Although the experimental method is used on social-psychological problems whenever possible, sometimes owing to laboratory limitations descriptive methods must be used instead. This does not mean that we renounce scientific approaches completely, however, for we can be objective and scientific even in applying the observational method. Social psychology is not exclusively experimental; but neither is astronomy, botany, geology, or zoology for that matter.

2. THE OBSERVATIONAL METHOD OF PSYCHOLOGICAL ANALYSIS

Perhaps there has been a tendency to make a fetish of experiment and the experimental method, when actually the method of observation is equally valuable. In all scientific discipline the method of observation has been of untold value. As Gardner Murphy has pointed out:

> . . . The history of the physical sciences bristles with important ideas which have borne only a remote relation to the existing laboratory situation, and . . . the history of biology has been much more a history of learning to observe, either in the woods or under the microscope, than of controlling every relevant variable in the manner of pure experimentation. . . . Historically, experimentation has regularly proved to be not the earliest, but one of the latest developments in the effective grappling with a tough problem. It is not the pathfinder but the crowning completion of long, arduous, and penetrating analysis. Especially is this true when the uncontrollable variables so vastly outweigh the controllable ones, as is the case in astronomy, geology, and our own field of social psychology. In establishing the age of the Grand Canyon of Arizona, experiments in uranium decomposition are critical exactly because thousands of hours of systematic observation have paved the way.[10]

It is important to realize, then, that arduous training in how to observe, followed by long, systematic hours of actual observation are essential in any science, either physical or social, before experimentation of a very meaningful sort can proceed. As an example of the observational method, we might take a group of people and simply watch what they do. When you next go to the commencement exercises of a school or college, you can make interesting observations of the ritualistic character of the commencement, the psychology of fashion and clothes, the factors of rhythm, the psychological elements of crowd behavior. And if you are well trained in social psychology, you will not make just random observations which do not tie in with each other. Mere observation is no guarantee of truth. Therefore, in making use of the scientific method of observation, it is necessary to keep four different criteria in mind: personal disinterestedness, precision, system, and verification.[11]

As a scientific observer, you must be *disinterested* in the actual results of your observations. This means that you should be completely impartial and not wish your results to come out a certain way. You must keep under complete control your own biases, your own prejudices.

Your observations must be *precise*. You must be concerned not only with the question, "What is it that I am observing?" but also with the question, "To what extent does it exist?" Your question is one not only of *what* but also of *how much*. Just as in the experimental method, there should be quantification of your data wherever possible.

Scientific observation must be *systematic.* A layman (for our purposes, a non-social-psychologist) may make observations of group behavior in the most casual way. A good social psychologist, however, knows exactly what he is looking for, and for that he looks. The result is that he does not collect a miscellaneous grab bag of trivia, but instead a set of observable data which are significant for an understanding of certain definite aspects of human behavior.

Your observations must be *verified.* Psychologists know that even after careful training in observation, they can be subject to errors, first, of perception or observation, and second, of memory. From their years of scientific education social scientists should be freer from these two errors than laymen, but—even as the best newspaper reporters—they can sometimes err. A famed war correspondent has said:

> The most important thing I learned professionally was that the truth about anything is difficult to obtain. . . . Even when I witnessed an event myself I saw it differently from others. When I questioned eyewitnesses, persons who had no reason to distort the truth, each told a somewhat different story. . . . Each one saw something different. Every man's imagination unwittingly distorted what his eyes saw.
>
> I encountered the most recent example flying the Atlantic on the Hindenburg. A trained observer describing the mass celebrated by Father Schulte wrote: "Then the candles were lighted." The feature of the mass was the fact that candles were *not* lighted because of the danger of explosion. That observer knew that lighted candles were always used at mass and his imagination supplied what his eyes did not see and unconsciously falsified an interesting point of the story.[12] *

To ask anyone without psychological training whether his observations have been verified is usually to offend him. Yet verification, either by other observers or by later observations of a similar situation, is a sound policy—indeed a necessity—in social psychology.

THE USE OF STATISTICAL TECHNIQUES

Both experiments and observations often require the use of statistical methods. In fact, statistical techniques are now employed in a majority of the investigations in social psychology. An outstanding example is the pioneering work of Floyd H. Allport in which he was concerned with the influence of the group upon the individual.[13] A statistical analysis of his data was essential to a determination of his conclusions—discussed in Chapter 11. A second instance is Rice's *Quantitative Methods in Politics,* which involved statistical study of political attitudes.[14] This was pioneering work to subject political behavior to mathematical analysis.

OTHER TECHNIQUES

Social psychologists have made use of *tests,* such as intelligence and aptitude tests; *questionnaires,* especially with relation to attitudes; *psychophysical methods,* in measuring attitudes and opinions; *genetic materials,* as in studies of children; *personality analyses,* such as personality inventories; *physiological materials,* as in studying emotional reactions; the study of *group situations,* such as crowds and audiences; *field investigations,* especially the work of anthropologists; *psychoanalytic concepts,* in those instances where they are appropriate; and all sorts of data from general psychology and sociology.[15]

▶ KEYNOTE II—OBJECTIVITY

THREE PAIRS OF MAGIC GLASSES

If the empirical methods outlined here are to be useful, one more thing must be kept in mind: *objectivity.* This is an expansion of the factor of personal disinterestedness or impartiality mentioned in connection with the observational method. This attitude is excellently illustrated by Folsom:

Let us imagine ourselves aviators from some distant world, coming without preconception or prejudice to observe human life on this earth. From a lofty altitude we catch sight of a "typical" American city. . . .

We have [three] pairs of magic glasses. Our first pair differs from the naked eye only in that it renders everything transparent. It reveals to us only those things which are tangible and concrete. The picture we see contains (1) human beings, (2) their material equipment or tools, and (3) the activities of human beings.

The whole kit of tools which these humans have made for themselves, including everything from locomotives and Masonic temples to needles and toothbrushes, is known as their *material culture.* The framework of this material culture would seem to consist of large boxes called "buildings," averaging perhaps 30 feet on a side and 30 feet high, each having many small openings. . . . The buildings are arranged in quadrangles, between which run passageways known as "streets." Along these streets human beings on foot and in various kinds of boxes on wheels move at various rates of speed. By watching from one sunrise until the next we learn that these movements of human beings follow certain time cycles. During the period of darkness and the first few hours of daylight the great majority of these human ants, as they appear from our airplane, are inside the smaller buildings which make up the large outlying areas of the city, and which are known as "residences" or "homes." They are, moreover, quite inactive, sleeping on flat soft platforms called beds.

But after sunrise these creatures become active. They arise from their cloth-covered platforms, uncover their bodies, then cover them again with more numerous and complicated garments of woven fibers, assume sitting postures on small squarish objects called "chairs," next to larger and higher flat surfaces supported by uprights. On these "table" surfaces are small masses of organic material, which humans, more delicately than other animals, load in tiny shovelsful into the openings in their faces. . . .

. . . These human inhabitants fall roughly into two classes. Class number one rises earlier in the morning, is covered with garments of denim and gingham, and commonly eats breakfast in the same room where the food is cooked. Its males and some of its females go, largely on foot, to certain very large buildings with tall smokestacks, within which huge machines operate with sometimes deafening noise. Class number two rises later, dresses in finer-woven, more accurately fitting garments, lives in larger houses and in smaller families. Most of its females remain at home all morning, while the males spend the day mostly in tall buildings near the center of the city. In these buildings are no machines, no massive piles and bins of "raw materials"; but only pieces of paper, devices to make marks upon paper, and furniture to conceal and store the paper. . . .

. . . We put on our second pair of glasses. This dims our view of material things; it enables us to see that which is more abstract and intangible. . . .

We note strong bonds of connection between all who inhabit any one of the residence buildings. . . . Almost invariably each person who leaves his home in the morning comes back to the same place at night, although there are thousands of homes to choose from. . . . Closer scrutiny reveals that some personal relationship, rather than the particular place, is the controlling factor, for whole groups are seen to change their residences, afterward behaving toward the new residence exactly as they did toward the old.

In every "office" and "factory" certain persons appear to control the movements of others. After careful observation we can pick out these leaders or "bosses." As a rule, they wear cleaner, neater clothes, they do not touch dirty or greasy materials, but spend their time talking or handling pieces of paper. . . . Goods made in a factory are carried on trucks to "stores," from which people take them little by little into their residences. . . . Our suspicion is that the mechanism of . . . general control is somehow connected with certain little pieces of green paper which people are seen to carry in their pockets. . . .

. . . Let us put on our third pair of glasses. This shuts out the rest of the picture, but reveals the nature of these connecting threads or bonds. . . .

This third pair of glasses helps to explain the first picture as well as the second. We can understand now why humans use these many varied utensils for conveying food to their mouths, when the bare hands would seem to be quite adequate, and certainly easier and quicker. To convey food to their mouths is not the only purpose of these utensils. They have also another less tangible purpose, which can be discerned only by seeing the attitudes which function in the nervous systems of those who watch the eating process. Namely, the animal method of conveyance arouses an attitude of *disgust* in the beholders. We can see that this attitude is absent in the babies, and very imperfectly formed in the children, but that in adults it functions vigorously and brings various unpleasant consequences to those who provoke it. A less disastrous attitude, called *contempt,* goes out toward the person who uses eating utensils but uses them in the wrong way. The "right way," we discover, is based on a very intricate set of rules.[16] †

DIFFICULTIES OF OBJECTIVITY

What is the point of this discussion of three pairs of magic glasses? It is intended to illustrate the second keynote of social psychology, namely, objectivity. Whether we put on three pairs of magic glasses or whether we simply look at people around us, it is absolutely essential, if we are to do a sound job of understanding human behavior, to free ourselves from our own biases and our own prejudices and adopt a "don't-give-a-hang" attitude as to how our findings actually turn out. Personal feelings about intelligence tests or sex or religion can easily obscure our vision of test results, sex differences, or religious prejudice. To be objective, we must free ourselves from whatever prejudices we may have—of our "race" and religious prejudices, for example—and simply observe scientifically the world around us. This is an extremely difficult thing to do, because we are often not even conscious of our prejudices.

An illustration of the difficulties of objectivity is that of an English course called *The Bible as Literature.* In his opening lecture the professor used to say to his students: "This course is *not* concerned with theological interpretations. It is *not* concerned with the religious values of the Bible We are simply studying the Bible in exactly the same way that we would study Shakespeare, in order to understand the Bible as a literary document." He would then continue to tell his students this same thing at the beginning of every lecture for the first two weeks of his course. Yet invariably, about halfway through the semester, some student would become emotionally disturbed and begin to argue, "But that's not the correct theological interpretation according to my church." The tired professor finally resigned himself to the fact that many people are utterly incapable of dealing with questions in an impartial, detached, objective manner; he quit offering the course. We cannot end the study of social psychology, however, simply because it is difficult for some people to be objective. Instead we are faced with the job of schooling ourselves to forget our subjective attitudes and impressions and of adopting *objectivity* as our slogan.

THE SCIENTIFIC ATTITUDE

Objectivity might be said to be almost synonymous with the scientific attitude. The scientific attitude is one in which supreme value is attached to actual truth. However, since scientists have learned from experience the very great difficulty of finding and of knowing truth and the extreme likelihood of error, they must have a thoroughgoing skepticism, plus tremendous patience and open-mindedness.[17]

> The "true" man of science . . . keeps his ears open, questions every word he hears, and endeavors to hear nothing that any other man with good ears could not also hear were he willing to listen. In short he tries his best to be objective. His hopes, his aspirations, his fears must be ruthlessly repressed, and his "will to believe" must be kept in subjection. Then, perhaps, he may get a partial answer to his question.[18]

▶ KEYNOTE III—A HEALTHY SKEPTICISM

A healthy skepticism might be considered as a third keynote of social psychology. To the skeptical person dogmatism and wishful thinking are repugnant. *Please note that "skepticism" is not synonymous with cynicism, nor does it in any way imply it.* Skepticism is a healthy, scientific attitude. It means the difference between wishful thinking and an empirical approach. It means not accepting things on a purely rationalistic basis simply because they seem to be that way or because some "authority" a long time ago said that they were that way; it means trying to find out for yourself what is true.

> Confronted by a problem the scientist begins by sorting out the pertinent factors. He discards the irrelevant, testing relevancy as critically and dispassionately as possible. Then with the relevant material in front of him he begins the painstaking tasks of describing, classifying, discovering correlations, constructing hypotheses, experimentally testing, discarding or adjusting these hypotheses—and extending them to new fields. It is of the essence of this whole process that he should suspend judgment until ponderable evidence is at hand, that he should continually reexamine underlying theories and definitions, that he should be prepared to abandon a position however attractive it may be, that he should be sanely skeptical of conclusions and that he should maintain complete dispassionate intellectual honesty.[19]

A final word of warning is necessary. Even though you understand what is meant by objectivity and agree that it is a desirable scientific goal, you may feel that it means such complete impartiality that one can have no views on anything and hence must be "wishy-washy" in his ideas. The very opposite is true. To be objective does not mean that you must forever sit on the proverbial fence.

Objectivity means impartiality and suspended judgment, yes; but only up to a certain point, and that point is when your observable "facts" are in. Objectivity means the reverse of being swayed at the outset by your particular prejudices and pet peeves of "I think" or "I believe." It means going after all the facts that you can muster by every means at your disposal. Then, *after* you have all your data arrayed before you, you can begin to draw conclusions, but not before. In other words, after you make a thorough evaluation, you are perfectly entitled to take sides. You may even wish to "do something." You may then say, "After examining the entire situation, I find that. . . ." Our primary job is to make an objective examination of the social psychology of modern life; but the very fact of having made such an examination also entitles us to some evaluation of our society (see Chapter 25).

QUESTIONS AND PROBLEMS FOR DISCUSSION

1. *"We often see things not as they are, but as we are." What does this mean? Give an example.*
2. *What are the advantages and disadvantages of the experimental method in social psychology?*
3. *What is the difference between empiricism and rationalism?*
4. *Think of some problem of group behavior. What would be a subjective interpretation? An objective interpretation?*
5. *Does objectivity prevent you from taking sides on a question of social issues?*

RECOMMENDED READINGS

Cantril, H., and Allport, G. W., *The Psychology of Radio.* New York: Harper & Brothers, 1935.

Lundberg, G. A., *Social Research: A Study in Methods of Gathering Data* (2nd edition). New York: Longmans, Green and Co., 1942.

Lynd, R. S., and Lynd, H. M., *Middletown: A Study in Contemporary American Culture.* New York: Harcourt, Brace & Company, Inc., 1929.

Lynd, R. S., and Lynd, H. M., *Middletown in Transition: A Study in Cultural Conflicts.* New York: Harcourt, Brace & Company, Inc., 1937.

Murphy, G., Murphy, L. B., and Newcomb, T. M., *Experimental Social Psychology: An Interpretation of Research upon the Socialization of the Individual.* New York: Harper & Brothers, 1937.

Odum, H. W., *Man's Quest for Social Guidance.* New York: Henry Holt & Company, Inc., 1927.

PART TWO

BIOLOGICAL AND SOCIAL FOUNDATIONS OF BEHAVIOR

▶ PART II shows how physiology, psychology, and sociology are related in *social psychology*. The biological bases of human behavior are first reviewed: the heredity-environment controversy, the nervous system, the receptors and effectors, and the cycle of activity. Both the autonomic nervous system and the endocrine glands are considered in some detail as they affect our activities.

What is human nature? In order to throw some light on this question the work of various anthropologists, particularly Malinowski, Benedict, and Mead, is summarized. After a consideration of their studies of primitive peoples, a comparison is made of civilized groups.

This leads to an analysis of what is correct behavior. An objective presentation of some of the social-psychological aspects of our own society is given. The nature of *culture* is explained, and the folkways, customs, mores, and taboos of our own culture are described.

The following examples may be useful to show how physiology, psychology, and sociology are all interrelated in the following three chapters. A physiologist may be concerned with the endocrine glands, and they are important psychologically, but the mere study of some endocrine gland *per se* is not social-psychological. At the other extreme, a sociologist may be concerned with problems of climate and of geography, and these questions necessarily involve human behavior; but the study of climate and of geography is not necessarily within the scope of social psychology. Even in the field of psychology we are concerned with questions of human personality, and there is no single instance where a question of an individual's personality is not also a social question; but the mere investigation of some phase of personality is not necessarily a study in social psychology. Following is a rough diagram of the relationship between these sciences:

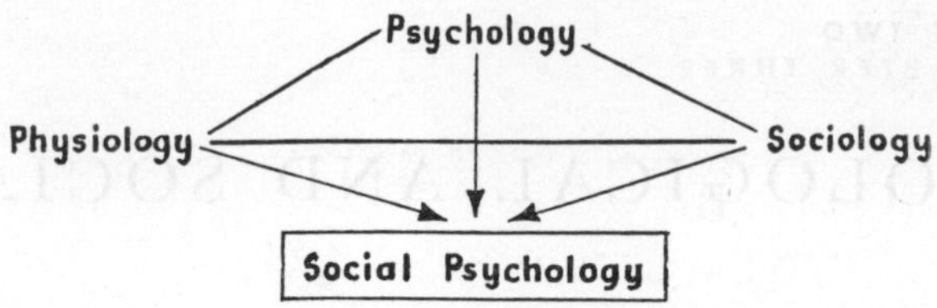

FIG. 1. RELATIONS OF SOCIOLOGY, PSYCHOLOGY, AND PHYSIOLOGY TO SOCIAL PSYCHOLOGY

Social psychology draws on all three of these fields—sociology, physiology, and (general) psychology. If you have a question the answer to which cuts across these three fields, you have a truly social-psychological question. For example, to take the same three instances of climate (sociology), endocrines (physiology), and personality (psychology), here is a truly social-psychological question: What is the result of the interplay *between* the economic and climatic factors *together with* the endocrine glands on the personality of a human being in a particular social setting? Social psychology, as indicated in Figure 1, is the study of sociological, physiological, and psychological factors so that we can better understand the functioning of individuals and of groups.

CHAPTER THREE

BIOLOGICAL BASES OF HUMAN BEHAVIOR

HEREDITY AND ENVIRONMENT. Interrelations of Heredity and Environment—Different Results from Similar Backgrounds / THE NERVOUS SYSTEM. Principal Divisions—(1) Cerebrospinal System—(2) Autonomic System—Social-Psychological Importance of the Nervous System—(1) Mediation of Activity by the Nervous System—(2) "Drives" and "Urges"—(3) Importance of Autonomic Activities—(4) Primacy of Autonomic System / RECEPTORS AND EFFECTORS. Classification of Receptors—Effectors—(1) Muscles—(2) Glands—Adrenals—Gonads—Thyroid —Parathyroids—Pituitary—Thymus—Pineal Gland—Pancreas and Liver—Interdependence of the Endocrine Glands—Endocrine Glands in Relation to Other Aspects of Behavior / THE CYCLE OF ACTIVITY. Tensions—Three Possibilities—Tissue Needs of Hunger and Sex—Management of Tensions—Cyclical Character of Internal Stresses—Biological-Cultural Conflict.

The biological bases of human behavior can be treated briefly in four different sections. After all, social psychology is concerned with physiological factors only in so far as they actually help to explain social-psychological phenomena. We must not "commit the fallacy of propinquity, and assert forthwith that man's biochemistry and anatomy are projected into his social behavior. To a great extent this belief signalizes the ideational lag that unless psychological phenomena are anchored in organic processes they float off in the great psychic ocean."[1]

However, some of the problems of (1) heredity and environment, (2) the nervous system, (3) the receptors and effectors, and (4) the cycle of activity should be discussed as a general background for the remaining portion of this book.

▶ HEREDITY AND ENVIRONMENT

INTERRELATIONS OF HEREDITY AND ENVIRONMENT

Books on psychology, sociology, education, and physiology are filled with discussions of heredity *versus* environment, often as if there were some sort of antagonism between these two concepts. Both heredity and environment should be looked upon in social psychology as extremely important for an understanding of why we behave or do not behave like human beings. To think, however, that we can determine definitely which one of these factors is *universally* more important is simply to engage in wishful thinking. If some scientist could set up an experiment in which he followed the scientific procedure of keeping all of his variables constant save one and then varying that one independently—either heredity or environment—all his fellow scientists should hail him with loud "hurrahs." No experiment has been devised in which heredity is made the variable which changes, while the environment is kept *absolutely* constant. Nor has any experiment been conducted in which environment is the experimental variable, and heredity is *absolutely* constant. Perhaps an exception is the interesting set of studies on identical twins reared apart—the differences between them not being so great as between other children reared separately.[2] Still, the problem is similar to the old question of which came first, the chicken or the egg. Not only can good points be advanced for both the chicken and the egg, but also excellent arguments can be presented in favor of both heredity and environment. Consider the following case of a college girl who has an identical twin:*

In my personal experience, besides a great physical likeness, and similarity of environment, there has always been a great similarity of mental ability. We have been constantly together, separated for only a few days in our entire life, and up until entering college had spent the entire twenty-four hours every day with each other. We have read the same books, like all the same things, including sports and clothing, and have had identically the same schooling. While in grammar school, the difference in I.Q. was zero. At the end of eight years, when averaging to see who was the highest in the class, we found that there was a difference in only one "A" in the entire eight years. So, one had to be "valedictorian," and the other "salutatorian." Similarly, in high school, the same situation was found for the four years, and history repeated itself. Similarity of ability is shown in a case where both of us had to write an essay for an American Legion essay contest. The papers were typewritten, and the identity of the writers concealed. The judges, not knowing who had written any of the great number of papers, finally could not decide between the merits of two papers, ours, and were forced to award a joint first prize.

At first glance this may seem like an argument for the importance of heredity, but note that these girls also had practically identical environments. These two factors are so intertwined that they can hardly be evaluated separately. There is, however, considerable evidence that heredity is in large measure responsible for intellectual ability, whereas environmental factors are mostly the determinants of prejudices, many "race" feelings, and the like.

* Where no footnote number appears for a quotation the material was collected by the author.

DIFFERENT RESULTS FROM SIMILAR BACKGROUNDS

Therefore, it is important to keep in mind that the heredity of individuals and their environment are *both* important. Heredity and environment are not two antagonistic processes after all, but are correlative; that is, they work together on individual organisms. Even the home environment may have different effects on children in the same family. This point is well illustrated in the following passage about two *brothers,* taken from a novel by Sinclair Lewis:

> "My father," said Ora, "was a sloppy, lazy, booze-hoisting old bum, and my mother didn't know much besides cooking, . . . and the kids I knew were a bunch of foul-mouthed loafers that used to hang around the hoboes up near the water tank . . . So naturally I've become a sort of vagabond . . . , and I suppose I'm inclined to be lazy, and not too scrupulous about the dames and the liquor. But my early rearing did have one swell result. Brought up so unconventionally, I'll always be an Anti-Puritan. . . ."
>
> "And my father," said Myron, "was pretty easy-going and always did like drinking and swapping stories with the Boys, and my mother was hard-driven taking care of us, and I heard a lot of filth from the hoboes up near the water tank. Maybe just sort of as a reaction I've become almost too much of a crank about paying debts, and fussing over my work, and being scared of liquor and women. But my rearing did have one swell result. Just by way of contrast, it made me a good, sound, old-fashioned New England Puritan."[3]†

This is a fictionalized account, of course, but it presents in striking manner a type of situation seen many times in actual life. People with the same sort of background do not necessarily respond alike to that background.

▶ THE NERVOUS SYSTEM

PRINCIPAL DIVISIONS

Probably the most important part of the internal environment, for our purposes, is that intricate network called the nervous system. This consists of (1) the *cerebrospinal* nervous system and (2) the *autonomic* nervous system. The cerebrospinal nervous system may further be subdivided into (*a*) the *central* nervous system and (*b*) the *peripheral* system. Likewise the autonomic system may be divided into its (*a*) *sympathetic* and (*b*) *parasympathetic* divisions. However, these classifications are mainly for purposes of logical analysis; no rigid distinction is made between the

† Copyright, 1934, reprinted by permission of Doubleday, Doran & Co., Inc.

various portions of the entire nervous system. When the human organism adjusts itself to any new situation, the nervous system as a whole may be involved and there is close integration of the various parts.

1. CEREBROSPINAL SYSTEM

The *cerebrospinal* system consists of (*a*) the central nervous system—which is ordinarily indicated when we speak of the "higher" thought processes—and (*b*) a peripheral portion.

The *central nervous system* consists of the *cerebrum,* which is the main division of the brain and which contains the cerebral cortex or outer bark, the latter being important in reasoning and in logical thinking; the *cerebellum,* which lies below and behind the cerebrum, and which is important in muscular coordination; the *basal ganglia,* consisting of several masses of nerve tissue which lie within the white matter of the cerebrum; the *medulla oblongata* or brain stem which adjoins the spinal cord; and the *spinal cord* itself which is made up of neurons or nerve cells within the spine or backbone.

The *peripheral* portion of the cerebrospinal system consists of an intricate network of nerves and a large number of ganglia. Most important are the twelve pairs of cranial nerves and the thirty-one pairs of spinal nerves which branch out from the central nervous system to various portions of the body.

2. AUTONOMIC SYSTEM

The central nervous system has received a great deal of attention from students of human behavior, partly because of its close relation to the various "higher" thought processes. In social psychology, however, we must be equally concerned with the *autonomic* nervous system if we are to interpret, not simply man's rational actions, but his entire gamut of behavior. The autonomic system is composed of a chain of *ganglia* on either side and slightly in front of the spinal cord, several plexuses of ganglia in the viscera of the body cavity, and three small ganglia in the head, together with the nerves connecting these ganglia with each other. The ganglia of the autonomic system are made up of nerve cells bound together by a small amount of loose connective tissue. The autonomic nerves are distributed not only to the large viscera within the body cavities but also to many of the smaller structures throughout the body. Thus, fibers run to the abdominal organs, gastrointestinal tract, liver, spleen, heart, bronchi, adrenal glands, eyes, skin, sweat glands, and so forth.

Anatomically, two sets of nerve fibers can be differentiated in the autonomic system, the *sympathetic* system, and the *parasympathetic* system. Thus, the autonomic system supplies to a great many internal organs two sets of motor fibers, the sympathetic and the parasympathetic, the reactions of which are, in general, antagonistic to each other. Figure 2 shows schematically part of this double innervation of the visceral region. As one example of this antagonistic action, impulses traveling down one set of fibers (in the vagus nerve of the parasympathetic system) will tend to slow

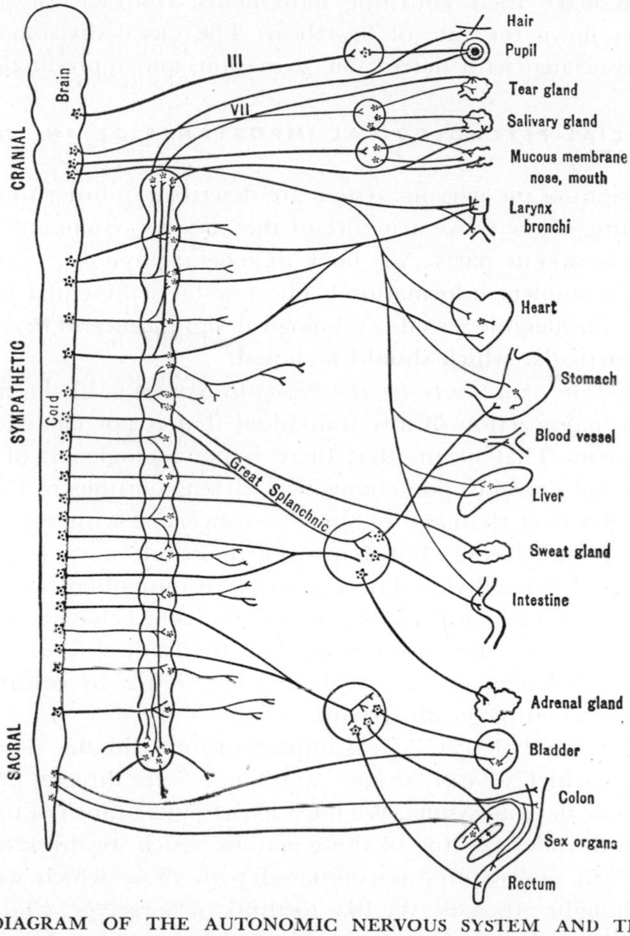

FIG. 2. DIAGRAM OF THE AUTONOMIC NERVOUS SYSTEM AND THE BODILY ORGANS EXCITED AND INHIBITED BY IT (From Guilford—Adapted from Cannon) [4]

down the rate of the heartbeat, whereas impulses conveyed by the other set (sympathetic) will tend to accelerate the rate.

Some of the principal changes produced by the sympathetic system are: dilation of the bronchial tubes; acceleration of the heart; constriction of blood vessels; the release of glycogen from the liver; inhibition of the digestive activities of the stomach, the small intestine, and the large intestine; secretion of adrenin by the adrenal glands; activation of the sweat glands.

Contrast these activities with those of the parasympathetic system, with its *cranial* and *sacral* branches. The cranial part of the parasympathetic system promotes salivation by the salivary glands, stimulates the glands of the stomach to pour out gastric juices, causes the walls of the stomach to make their churning movements, contracts the bronchial tubes, slows down the rate of heartbeat. The sacral division promotes activities associated with defecation, urination, and reproduction.

SOCIAL-PSYCHOLOGICAL IMPORTANCE OF THE NERVOUS SYSTEM

These divisions of the nervous system are described in order to give some understanding of the gross structure of the nervous system and the functions of its composite parts. Any book in general physiology will provide much more complete information.[5] The few facts presented here, however, have considerable social-psychological significance. There are four things in particular which should be noted:

1. *Mediation of Activity by the Nervous System.* In the first place, there is no major action of any individual that is not mediated by the nervous system. That means that there is not a single bit of behavior which does not depend upon changes in various portions of the nervous system. In the next chapters we shall be concerned with the social and cultural bases of behavior—but that is not the whole story. In explaining the behavior of any individual or any group of individuals, we must take into account the biological factors underlying that behavior. Perhaps in the future, when questions are raised about the leadership of a man such as Hitler, his behavior may be explained not simply by cultural factors but also by his neurological make-up.

2. *"Drives" and "Urges."* It is important to realize that a great many of the things which we call "drives" and "urges" are directly linked with the autonomic nervous system. We must look to this branch of the nervous system for an understanding of those actions which we think of as more "primitive" in our nature, as compared with those which we call the "higher" thought processes. We like to think of ourselves as rational animals. We like to believe that we are logical beings who think with our brains alone. As a matter of fact, however, we not only use our brains in thinking, but also our blood stream, our internal cellular structure, our skeletal musculature, and our "guts."

3. *Importance of Autonomic Activities.* The autonomic nervous system is intimately concerned with what we call "involuntary" activities, whereas the central nervous system is more intimately connected with what we call "voluntary" activities. This means that when we engage in such a process as multiplying two-place numbers by two-place numbers, we are doing this primarily in terms of the cerebral cortex of the central nervous system, but most of our usual, daily activities seem to be influ-

enced primarily by the autonomic nervous system. Actually very few of our daily activities can truly be called voluntary or willed. For example, you can say to yourself, "I will now do my home work," and you can proceed to do it, principally because you have a well-developed cerebral cortex. You can then say to yourself, "Heart, beat faster," or "Sweat glands, sweat," but nothing will happen. We tend to think of ourselves as being controlled primarily by our central nervous systems, and to leave out of account all such activities as sweating, heartbeat, blood circulation, and respiration, which are just as essential as is thinking in making us behave like human beings.

4. *Primacy of Autonomic System.* The notion of the central nervous system being dominant over our vegetative functions is not strictly true. During the nineteenth century many theories were developed of man as a rational animal, and authors still write today as if our central nervous systems were "dictating" most of our activities. Yet there is abundant evidence for the primacy of the autonomic system.[6] (*a*) The vegetative functions of an infant are far more advanced than those of the higher nervous system. A child at seven months of prenatal life has a complete and complex autonomic nervous system, but his central nervous functions are undeveloped. (*b*) In an idiot the central nervous system never develops adequately, and yet the individual may live a long time if someone else supplies the needs of his autonomic system. (*c*) In a case of senile dementia, the secondary system may disintegrate, and the individual will live as long as his vegetative functions remain unimpaired. (*d*) That life depends on the intactness of the autonomic system and not on the central nervous system is shown by studies of individuals with brain lesions and other accidents to the cortex—the individuals continue to live. (*e*) Urgent organic cravings such as hunger, sexual tension, and need for elimination take precedence over all other forms of activity and often defeat the "intellectual" activity of the central nervous system.

Try the following experiment: Keep constantly with you some large sheets of paper, and during the next week write down *all* your activities per day, being sure to make a complete list of everything you do. At the end of a week—or, if you prefer, at the end of one day—go through your list and divide your activities into those which were primarily controlled by your "brain" and those which were principally influenced by the autonomic nervous system. You will be struck with the fact that your cerebrum accounts for a relatively small proportion of your activities, but that your autonomic nervous system, *plus* habit patterns which you have acquired to the point of their *automatic* functioning, will account for the great preponderance of things that you do.

Indeed, it is fortunate for us that this is true. In our everyday behavior, we do not have to stop and "think" about digestive activities or routine affairs of the day. You probably always put on your left shoe before your right, or else your right shoe before your left. Nearly everyone has his own individual habit pattern in this respect, which is almost automatic. It would indeed be a sad state of affairs if every morning you had to ponder this question and decide which is the better action to pursue. Man is *not* always a rational animal. His behavior, either as an individual or in a group situation, must be understood also in terms of both his autonomic nervous system and his habit patterns which have become so automatic that the "thinking" process is not required.

▶ RECEPTORS AND EFFECTORS

CLASSIFICATION OF RECEPTORS

We learn of the world around us by means of a series of *receptors* which receive external and internal stimuli and which are intimately connected with the nervous system. These receptors are classified as exteroceptors, interoceptors, and proprioceptors. Each of these categories includes the following:

Exteroceptors:	
Contact type:	Touch; pressure; cold; heat; pain; general chemical sensibility; taste (compare below).
Distance type:	Hearing; vision; smell (compare below).
Interoceptors:	
General visceral:	Hunger; thirst; nausea; respiratory sensations; suffocation; circulatory sensations, flushing, heart panics; sexual sensations; sensations of distention of cavities; visceral pain; obscure abdominal sensations.
Special visceral:	Taste (compare above); smell (compare above).
Proprioceptors:	Muscular sensibility; tendon sensibility; joint sensibility; postural and equilibratory sensations in the labyrinth of the internal ear.

The foregoing list is presented in order to demonstrate that our understanding of our environment is not limited to the classic five senses—vision, hearing, taste, touch, and smell—but that it is also a function of kinesthetic sensations, hunger, thirst, suffocation, nausea, equilibratory sensations, and so forth.

EFFECTORS

Stimulation of the receptors results in the actions of the responding organs, known as *effectors*. Effectors are made up of both muscles and glands.

1. *Muscles.* The muscles of our bodies are of two kinds, the *striped* and the *unstriped.* Examples of striped muscles are the biceps and triceps of the upper arms, the deltoids of the shoulders, and other muscles which we use to adjust ourselves to external stimuli. Most striped muscles are referred to as "voluntary" muscles. This means that we can exercise some control over them. We have very little control over the other kind of muscles, the smooth or unstriped, such as those in the intestinal tract. These are usually called "involuntary" muscles, and are involved in digestive, circulatory, and excretory functions.

The social-psychological significance of the autonomic nervous system was stressed above, so that we would not limit our consideration of behavior to man's voluntary activities controlled by the central nervous system. Similarly, the importance of our unstriped muscles must be emphasized. We respond to the world around us not simply in terms of our striped or voluntary muscles; rather, our behavior and our attitudes at any given moment are very much dependent upon the condition of our unstriped muscles, over which we do not have a great deal of "voluntary" control.

2. *Glands.* The *glands* of the human body are another set of effector organs. They are of two types, the *duct* and the *ductless* glands—the latter often called *endocrine* glands. Examples of the duct glands are tear glands, salivary glands, and mammary (milk) glands. The ductless glands do not have special openings, but instead pour out chemical substances called hormones directly into the blood stream, and these hormones are then distributed to all parts of the body. Since the ductless or endocrine glands are of great importance in supplementing actions of the nervous system, they should be described here. Both *hyper*activity (overfunctioning) and *hypo*activity (underfunctioning) will be briefly considered, although we will concern ourselves mainly with psychological effects rather than physiological details. The principal endocrine glands are the adrenals, gonads, thyroid, parathyroids, pituitary, thymus, and pineal gland.

ADRENALS. The adrenals, which lie underneath the ends of the kidneys, are small cocked-hat affairs which weigh less than 1/4 ounce each, but have far-reaching effects on our daily behavior. Each adrenal gland is divided into two parts, one called the medulla, the other the cortex. The medulla is that portion which pours out adrenin—known commercially as adrenalin—into the blood stream. This has the effect of releasing stored sugar from the liver, speeding up the heartbeat, dilating the air passages in the lungs, constricting the arteries, inhibiting digestive activities, dilating the pupils of the eyes, causing the hairs over the body to rise, producing perspiration, and, in general, delaying the onset of fatigue. These functions are strikingly similar to those of the sympathetic branch of the autonomic nervous system, discussed above. These activities are of the utmost importance in emotional states such as fear and anger, since one can run faster or fight better when these effects are produced.

The adrenal cortex produces a hormone called cortin which is essential to life. A lack of this hormone results in general weakness, loss of appetite, lack of sex interest, and a general tired feeling. On the other hand, the hypercondition results in considerable muscular strength and general virility in both males and females.

Gonads. The gonads are directly concerned with differences in sex activities of males and females. These glands also account for the formation of the various secondary sex characteristics of both groups, such as milk production in the female, and greater hairiness in the male. (Other endocrine glands, such as the pituitary and the thymus, are also related to sex activities.)

Thyroid. The thyroid is a small gland in the neck weighing less than an ounce, often discussed by laymen as if it were some sort of mystical gland which will explain all kinds of behavior. A diseased condition of this gland, known as goiter, is in many cases rather readily recognized. The thyroid functions normally, however, in most people. In those cases where there is a hyper- or a hypocondition, the following behavior may result: In the hypocondition, sometimes due to disease, an individual may be slowed up in his movements, appear stupid and forgetful, and, in general, behave sluggishly. The hypercondition, on the other hand, results in irritability and overactivity, higher blood pressure, and a general speeding up of metabolic processes, particularly protein metabolism.

Parathyroids. The parathyroids are four tiny glands about the size of buckshot which lie in close proximity to the thyroid. Their functions are antagonistic to those of the thyroid. Thus, a hypocondition of the parathyroids may result in general irritability, tenseness, and overexcitability, whereas the hypercondition may produce lassitude, slow actions, and general sluggishness.

Pituitary. The pituitary is located at the base of the brain, just above the roof of the mouth. It consists of an anterior (front) lobe and a posterior (back) lobe. The hormone of the *anterior* lobe promotes the growth of bones and muscles, helps to develop the sex organs, aids in the formation of sugar in the system, and also stimulates the thyroid, the adrenal cortex, and the gonads. A hypocondition may result in weak muscles, a sluggish condition, and perhaps a tendency to give up and cry, whereas a hypercondition may be important to bodily strength, and may produce tendencies to aggressiveness. The *posterior* lobe, which lies nearer the brain, stimulates the unstriped or "involuntary" muscles, promotes the metabolism of fatty substances, and influences the body's chemistry, particularly so far as the bowels, blood vessels, and kidneys are concerned. The anterior and posterior lobes promote metabolism and growth. They gradually increase in size in the normal individual until about age thirty, and at that time weigh only about 1/100 ounce. In general, deficiencies may result in lack of sex development, excessive fat, slow metabolism, and sluggishness.

THYMUS. The thymus is a gland made up of two flattened lobes, a cortex and a medulla, which lies at the base of the heart, between the lungs. The thymus increases in size but gradually disappears at the age of about twenty years. It promotes calcium metabolism and growth of bony structure, and apparently has some influence on the development of sex characteristics.

PINEAL GLAND. The pineal gland was described by Descartes as the point of interaction between the soul and the body, so that it has popularly been referred to as the "seat of the soul." Descartes probably seized upon this gland as being of the utmost significance, because it consists of only one lobe which lies directly in the middle of the head at the roof of the interbrain, just above the thalamic region. Its exact effects upon behavior have never been discovered, although it is known that its functioning is intimately connected with the activities of the other glands and that it has a stimulating effect on growth.

PANCREAS AND LIVER. In addition to the foregoing seven endocrine glands the pancreas and the liver are important, for they also have a great deal to do with the general chemistry of the body. The pancreas is an elongated organ which lies back of the stomach, in close proximity to the duodenum and the spleen. Two secretions are produced by the pancreas—insulin, which enables the muscles to oxidize sugar; and a pancreatic juice which promotes intestinal activity. The functioning of the pancreas, along with other glands mentioned above, may determine to a considerable extent whether one is hungry, fatigued, tremulous, or anxious—the hyperfunction—or the reverse.

Similarly, the liver has two secretions of utmost importance. One is secretin, which stimulates activities of the pancreas and intestines. The other is bile, which has an antiseptic effect on the intestines. The liver is the largest gland in the human body. In the normal adult it often weighs 40 to 60 ounces, being heavier even than the brain.

INTERDEPENDENCE OF THE ENDOCRINE GLANDS

A proper balance of all these glands is necessary for an adequate functioning of the body. The descriptions given in the foregoing are inaccurate to the extent that they separate each gland from the others and thus fallaciously suggest that each gland has a distinct set of activities different from those of the other glands. Actually, they are all interdependent.[7] As a concrete example, take body growth, which cannot be attributed to any one gland alone. Rather, it is due—among other factors—to the interaction of the hormones produced by the thyroid, the anterior pituitary, the adrenal cortex, and the gonads. And one's social experiences and habits may influence the behavior of the glands, and vice versa.

ENDOCRINE GLANDS IN RELATION TO OTHER ASPECTS OF BEHAVIOR

The endocrine glands, together with the various receptor organs, effector muscles, various branches of the nervous system, blood stream, and, in fact, the entire bodily organism, must be taken into account in thoroughly understanding the biological bases of human behavior. We cannot explain our social behavior in terms of glands alone. It should be clear that the great majority of us do not suffer from glandular malformation or malfunctioning, that most of us are fairly "normal" so far as our glands are concerned. It is too simple a solution to say that someone is a leader of his group because he has an overactive thyroid, or that various problems of crime can be explained simply because of a hyperfunctioning of the gonads. The mere fact that a person has a high basal metabolism—a test result considered indicative of a very active individual—does not necessarily mean that he will actually behave in an active or excitable way. He may have trained himself outwardly to "take it easy" and to go slowly. In order thoroughly to understand a person's behavior in a social situation, we must have not only *physiological* data, but also information about his culture and *psychological* data on his personal history.

▶ THE CYCLE OF ACTIVITY

TENSIONS

For an understanding of the biological bases of behavior, it is important to observe how the cycle of activity works out in most organisms. A great deal has been made of S-R (stimulus-response) in psychology. Various stimuli in our internal and external environment affect us in such a way that we make responses. Tensions of various sorts build up within us. These tensions may result in general restlessness and moving about, or in a satisfaction of the tensions and release on the part of the organism.

THREE POSSIBILITIES

Three possibilities present themselves to the organism. (1) If the stimuli which demand satisfaction are actually satisfied, the general response of the organism will be one of *rest*. (2) If the stimuli are not only satisfied but there is surfeiting by the organism, *unrest* will probably result. (3) If the same stimuli demand satisfaction and the organism fails to satisfy these stimuli adequately, some sort of *substitute response* results.

TISSUE NEEDS OF HUNGER AND SEX

Take the "tissue needs" of the body as an example. Suppose that an individual is hungry. There is a bombardment of stimuli largely due to peristaltic contractions of the stomach. If he satisfies these stimuli in the usual way, by eating, he will no longer be a restless organism moving about in search of food. He will rest. Of course, if he surfeits himself, as some people constantly do and as most do on special occasions such as Thanksgiving and Christmas, he may feel considerable discomfort or unrest. If, however, he is unable to eat and to remove the tissue needs of hunger, there is a failure of adequate response and a substitute must be provided. It is for this reason that hunters and explorers may occasionally chew bits of moss, leather, or clay, even though these do not actually satisfy the organic needs of hunger.

As another example, consider the tissue needs of sex. Sexual stimuli satisfied in the normal physiological manner produce rest on the part of the organism, whether a white rat or a human being. A surfeiting of the sexual drive, however, may result in considerable unrest. A failure to satisfy the sexual drive in the usual ways permitted by society will result in some sort of a substitute response on the part of the organism.

MANAGEMENT OF TENSIONS

The problem which all individuals have before them, beginning in the cradle, is to learn to manage the tensions of their bladders, intestines, stomachs, and sex glands, and to satisfy these tissue needs only in terms of the accepted codes of their group. In certain primitive groups, it is permissible for small children publicly to take care of their processes of elimination. In our society, however, every child must learn to satisfy these tissue needs only at certain particular times and under restricted conditions. This holds true not only for the control of elimination from the bladder and the intestinal tract, but also for the control of the tissue needs of hunger, thirst, and sex. If one does not adjust his tissue needs to the standards of the group in which he lives, there will be considerable unrest on his part which may result in various sorts of substitute responses.

The organization of our lives might actually be stated in terms of physiological tensions, and the regulation of these tensions. A child must learn to sustain tensions of his bladder and anal (rectal) sphincters until the "correct" time and place for their release. He must learn to hold back his tears in public and control hunger tensions between periods of feeding. He must inhibit many sex actions, especially during adolescence. He must learn to approach other persons and their property only through the socially sanctioned "ways" of marriage, barter, purchase, contract, and persuasion, and not by raping, pilfering, stealing, slugging, and killing.[8] In fact, many of our social "ways" described in the next two chapters can be explained partly in terms of these biological bases of behavior. It has even been suggested that, "All the social virtues of courage, perseverance, strength, loyalty, virtue and chastity, and their multitudinous synonyms and derivatives are but aspects of the management of tensions."[9]

CYCLICAL CHARACTER OF INTERNAL STRESSES

Certainly we cannot answer some questions of human motivation without taking account of the rhythmical or cyclical character of these internal stresses and their cycle of activity. Hunger, for example, although it is directly traceable to the blood chemistry, also involves the periodic recurrence of hunger contractions. Most of the visceral drives are cyclical in character. However, we must also note that these cycles are extremely variable under different conditions and that they can easily be modified by training. Just as an organism can adapt itself to this or that way of satisfying the same drive, it can also adapt itself to a change in its cycle of activity produced by external circumstances.

An obvious example is the establishment, in the newborn child, of a feeding rhythm. The doctor prescribes three-hour intervals between feedings. Before long, the child's stomach (and hence his voice) proclaims the three-hour interval almost as effectively as the alarm clock. A change of schedule produces only a few days' disturbance. Now we have a four-hour and, later, a six-hour feeding rhythm; at five hours and fifty minutes perhaps, the restlessness and whimpering recommence. The rhythm is demonstrably imposed not by the unalterable characteristics of inner tissues but by neural patterns established in experience. So, too, the adult man who weighs a hundred pounds more than requirements of his life demand, nevertheless becomes desperately and miserably hungry if the one o'clock lunch time is passed. Again, individual differences in such rhythms are conspicuous. The rhythms vary from person to person, and are much more apparent in some persons than in others.[10]

BIOLOGICAL-CULTURAL CONFLICT

This does not mean, however, that all of our drives can be completely explained in terms of visceral tensions or tissue needs. The materials of the following two chapters demonstrate that human behavior cannot be reduced simply to a biological basis. Even though you eat regularly and your sex life is satisfactory, you may still have countless irritations, disgusts, and despairs based on the standards of your group. One object in discussing these biological bases of human behavior is to suggest that they be taken into account *together with* the social factors of human behavior. It is true that tissue needs are founded on physiology. But it is also true that they are influenced by social standards. Man must constantly serve two masters—one biological, the other societal. The result is conflict.[11]

It will be recognized, of course, that the internal stresses, especially as one grows older, are considerably modified. There is even a limit to how long one can continue in the same activity, or how much of a given stimulus can be absorbed. People become surfeited with food or drink or sex activity, although there is a tremendous range of individual differences as to when the feelings of satiation begin. Certainly a renewal of the same activity may often begin again very soon. As one of the old Roman poets observed, "Man is the only animal that drinks without being thirsty and makes love at all seasons."

QUESTIONS AND PROBLEMS FOR DISCUSSION

1. *"Heredity and environment are not antagonistic, but correlative." What does this mean?*
2. *Indicate the relation of personal-social stimuli to the physical functioning of the organism.*
3. *Make a complete outline of the details of the autonomic nervous system. What is the significance of the autonomic system for social psychology?*
4. *William James said, "The great thing, then, in all education, is to make our nervous system our ally instead of our enemy." How can this be accomplished?*
5. *How would you find out about the functioning of your own endocrines?*
6. *What is meant by a "drive"? Is it solely physiological?*
7. *What physiological measures might aid in analysis of personality?*
8. *Explain the "cycle of activity" and bodily tensions as related to social behavior.*
9. *"All the social virtues of courage, perseverance, strength, loyalty, virtue and chastity . . . are but aspects of the management of tensions." What does this mean? Is it true?*

RECOMMENDED READINGS

Carlson, A. J., and Johnson, V., *The Machinery of the Body*. Chicago: University of Chicago Press, revised edition, 1948.

Freeman, G. L., *Introduction to Physiological Psychology*. New York: The Ronald Press Company, 1934.

Hathaway, S. R., *Physiological Psychology*. New York: D. Appleton-Century Company, 1942.

Hoskins, R. G., *The Glands and Their Functions*. New York: W. W. Norton & Company, 1941.

Kellogg, W. N., and Kellogg, L. A., *The Ape and the Child: A Study of*

Environmental Influence upon Early Behavior. New York: McGraw-Hill Book Company, Inc., 1933.

Kempf, E. J., *The Autonomic Functions and the Personality.* New York: Nervous and Mental Diseases Publishing Co., Monograph No. 28, 1918.

Murphy, G., *Personality: A Biosocial Approach to Origins and Structures.* New York: Harper & Brothers, 1947.

Newman, H. H., Freeman, F. N., and Holzinger, K. J., *Twins: A Study of Heredity and Environment.* Chicago: University of Chicago Press, 1937.

Scheinfeld, A., *You and Heredity.* New York: Frederick A. Stokes Company, 1939.

Schwesinger, G. C., *Heredity and Environment: Studies in the Genesis of Psychological Characteristics.* New York: The Macmillan Company, 1933.

Shaffer, L. F., *The Psychology of Adjustment.* Boston: Houghton Mifflin Company, 1936.

*Newcomb, T. M., Hartley, E. L., and others (editors), *Readings in Social Psychology.* New York: Henry Holt and Company, Inc., 1947:—
Newman, H. H., "How Differences in Environment Affected Separated One-Egg Twins," pp. 1-6.

* Specific references in Newcomb, Hartley and others, *Readings in Social Psychology* are given at the very end of the chapters in the present text, and are always starred.

CHAPTER FOUR

SOCIAL ANTECEDENTS OF BEHAVIOR

SOCIAL CONTROL. Variability of Human Nature—"Ages" of Human Development—These Are Artificial Classifications—Comparison of Primitive and Civilized Peoples—Rules of Social Control / THE TROBRIAND ISLANDERS. Allegiance to the Uncle—Repression of Brother-Sister Affection —Monogamous Marriage—Violations of the Rules—Interrelations of Religion, Custom, and Law / THE ZUÑI, DOBUANS, AND KWAKIUTL. Universal Feelings of Superiority— The Zuñi— The Dobuans—The Kwakiutl—The Problem of Normal and Abnormal Behavior—Varied Patterns of "Correct" Behavior / THE SAMOANS. The Social Environment—The Samoa Islands— Differences in Samoan and American Civilization—(1) Lack of Specialization of Feeling— (2) Objective Attitudes Toward Sex—Lack of Conflicts / SEX AND TEMPERAMENT. Physiology an Incomplete Explanation of Sex Attitudes—Mead's Work in New Guinea—The Arapesh— The Mundugumor—The Tchambuli / WHAT ABOUT OURSELVES? Analysis of Our Own Society —French and American Society—Which Society Is Better?—Objective Study.

▶ SOCIAL CONTROL

VARIABILITY OF HUMAN NATURE

What is human nature? Can it be reduced to physiological factors? If physiology were the entire explanation of psychological functions, we would expect people to be much more similar in their actions than they are. Actually so-called "human nature" varies tremendously from one person to another, and from one group to another. How can we account for these variations if not on a biological basis? The answer lies in the social and historical antecedents of behavior—which may be entirely different from one group to another—and on present-day standards and customs. In the present chapter we shall see how variable human nature is in primitive societies, and even in various civilized countries. Then we can examine in Chapter 5 some of the aspects of life that make up what is called "culture."

"AGES" OF HUMAN DEVELOPMENT

Back in 1872 an economist named Walter Bagehot developed a very ingenious theory concerning the history of civilization.[1] He believed that there were three "ages" or stages of human development: (1) the custom-making age, (2) the nation-making age, and (3) the age of discussion.

He pointed out that historically the preliminary or custom-making age was one in which a "cake of custom" was the predominant means of social control. This eventually gave way to what he called the nation-making age, during which struggle and war were predominant, particularly because of conflicting "cakes of custom." Finally, Bagehot believed that we are coming into an age of discussion, in which reason, tolerance, and deliberate choice are the ways which men use to solve their problems. This analysis is somewhat similar to the theory later developed by the German psychologist, Wilhelm Wundt, who had not three but four "ages" of mankind: (1) the age of "primitive man," (2) the totemic era, with a worship of totems, (3) the age of heroes and gods, and (4) the era of humanity, which Wundt believed is "coming to be."[2]

THESE ARE ARTIFICIAL CLASSIFICATIONS

These "ages" of man are presented here not for you to remember, but merely so that you can take a quick look at them and then forget them as quickly as possible. The views of Bagehot and of Wundt are given for at least four different reasons. First of all, their outlines illustrate remarkably well the complete artificiality of any rigid threefold or fourfold classification of humanity. We cannot find any one age in the history of mankind ending sharply, and another age set up to take its place. Rather, development of civilization has been a slow, gradual process from one phase of development to another.

In the second place, these theories of Bagehot and Wundt illustrate once more the contrast between the "armchair" approach to social-psychological problems as compared with the empirical "roll-up-your-sleeves" approach. Neither Bagehot nor Wundt ever visited primitive societies. As we shall see in this chapter, this armchair philosophizing has now given way to empirical studies where anthropologists go out and live among primitive peoples to find out what they are actually like, instead of merely theorizing about them. Too many writers have been willing to discuss social-psychological problems with no factual basis. Beautiful hypotheses have been expounded, and detailed classifications built up, and these have occasionally been helpful; but the empirical attitude, involving the use of experimental, observational, and sometimes statistical approaches, is absolutely essential for actually getting at the roots of human behavior.

Third, such artificial classifications as the foregoing overlook the tremendous importance of some of the basic cultural patterns of human behavior. They fail to take account of the individual "folkways," rules of behavior, taboos, and sanctions both of primitive men and of modern peoples. Is there really any "cake of custom" which is characteristic of primitive men, differentiating them from "civilized" men? Or is the "cake of custom" found among modern Europeans and Americans as well? We have good reason to think that the latter is the case.

In the fourth place, the firsthand investigations of people in other societies which have to date been made by anthropologists serve as a means by which we can better understand our own society. In other words, we can become much more objective about the society we live in, if first of all we forget our own society completely, separate ourselves from our present surroundings, and journey, in fact or in our reading, to other countries and other cultures, to see how other people behave under conditions very different from our own.

COMPARISON OF PRIMITIVE AND CIVILIZED PEOPLES

As a matter of fact, there are certain aspects of primitive behavior strikingly similar to our own. Certain African kings are killed when they begin to show signs of physical decline.[3] Many Eskimos will eat seal only at certain seasons of the year. In some Australian groups, women are killed if they sneak in to see the "mysterious" ceremonies performed by men. In many clan-organized tribes, a man *must* marry his deceased brother's wife. Certain African tribes will permit no ordinary citizen to see their "headman" on pain of death.[4]

But are there any types of behavior in our own society which remind you of these customs? Do you not know of cases when leaders are "put on the shelf" on showing signs of slowing up? Are there not instances in our own society where certain types of food must not be eaten on certain days of the week or certain periods of the year? Do not men have their "secrets" from the women folk in their lodges and secret societies? Are not certain rules laid down whereby men must marry certain women of their own "set," so that, for example, a bank president would be unlikely to marry a ribbon clerk?

In Japan, until after World War II, the people were not allowed to see their "headman," the Emperor of Japan. Actually portraits of the Emperor were very rare; and when he traveled, even if for long distances, every window blind had to be drawn along the entire route.[5] In Argentina, dueling has gone on for a great many years. But strangely enough no one is supposed to get hurt. However, nobody is supposed to act as if he knew nobody will get hurt. One observer says:

> When I first came to Argentina and heard and read about all the dueling that goes on I thought about bullet holes in bodies, blood on the ground and maybe a corpse now and then under picturesque oaks. But that isn't the way it is . . . There hasn't been anything worse than a scratch in an Argentine duel since who can remember. Recently I asked a dueling authority why no one ever gets killed in all this shooting and cutting. He haughtily refused to answer, but

his cold stare implied that if I, too, were "a man of honor," I would understand these things.[6]

RULES OF SOCIAL CONTROL

Social control, whether it is in a primitive group or in a "civilized" society such as our own or that of another nation, involves many different types of rules.[7]

1. We have rules which we obey because they are practical. Behavior in a classroom is an example. There is no reason at all why the students in a class should not sit with their faces to the wall, except that as a practical matter in this business of education, such behavior might not achieve the purpose of the group.

2. There are also rules which are obeyed because a violation of them would make the violator appear ridiculous or clumsy, or, worse still, "not in the know." Consider, for instance, the intricate set of table manners laid down by that arbiter of "correct" society, Mrs. Emily Post. The person who violates these rules is likely to be made uncomfortable.

3. Then, there are rules which are obeyed because they are necessary to the enjoyment of all of us. Thus, we have innumerable "polite" remarks which all of us make to each other many times throughout the day: "It's so nice to see you"—"You're looking well." Did you ever go to a dinner party, have a rather boring time, and then tell your hostess, "I have had such a delightful evening!" But these rules have a certain value in contributing to the general comfort of all the actors in the human play.

4. Many rules which we follow are concerned with how to conduct ourselves toward our friends and our relatives. We can ask our relatives fairly personal questions, but not, usually, our friends and acquaintances. In American society it is permissible for a man to kiss a woman, and sometimes—if he can—even to kiss many women; but it will not do for one man to kiss another man.

5. Another set of rules is related to the attitude, "Don't tamper with the sacred." Here we have religious codes, morals, and rituals concerned with such sacred matters as birth, marriage, and death.

6. Finally, we have law. This is simply one type of custom. For us, the rules of the courts and of the legislatures are specific examples.

Now, it is interesting to note that primitive groups are likewise controlled by the same sort of rules. They, too, follow rules because they are practical, sophisticated, necessary, correct, sacred, and legal. Only the specific examples of these rules differ from those of our own society. Are the rules of modern society, then, fundamentally different from those of primitive groups? Is there any justification at all for talking about a "cake of custom" which is supposedly *typical* of primitive men? Can we say, "But we 'moderns'—we don't have any cake of custom. We are sophisticated. We have only rules which we arrive at rationally after long discussion. This is why we now have an age of humanity where such things as changes in the map of Europe are solved by discussion and rational arguments." Can we say that?

The best way to find an answer to these questions is to look at the works of a few anthropologists who have gone into the field and lived with primitive peoples. We shall refer especially to the writings of Malinowski, Benedict, and Mead.

▶ THE TROBRIAND ISLANDERS

ALLEGIANCE TO THE UNCLE

Bronislaw Malinowski, a Polish anthropologist, lived with and studied a group of dark-skinned Melanesians living in northeastern New Guinea, the Trobriand Islanders.[8] It is worth while to compare their customs with our own. Malinowski found that these Trobriand Islanders are matrilineal.

> . . . That is, they live in a social order in which kinship is reckoned through the mother only, and succession and inheritance descend in the female line. This means that the boy or girl belongs to the mother's family clan, and community: the boy succeeds to the dignities and social position of the mother's brother, and it is not from the father but from the maternal uncle . . . that a child inherits its possessions.[9]

The husband in Trobriand society is regarded as just a good friend of the family because—unless perhaps Malinowski let some of them in on the secret—he is not considered to be the father of his children. Babies are supposed to be inserted in their mothers' wombs as tiny spirits. Therefore, since a father is not a recognized kinsman of his children, but simply a beloved benevolent friend, a boy does not owe allegiance to his father but, instead, to his mother's brother. The authority over the children, in fact, is almost completely vested in the mother's brother. This brother, because of a very strict taboo, can never associate with his sister, however; he lives in a completely different village and maintains a different household. After a son's early years, he eventually moves to his uncle's village and takes up residence with him.

REPRESSION OF BROTHER-SISTER AFFECTION

Another factor about this society which is different from ours is that boys and girls, both prior to and during adolescence, are free to engage in sexual activities. There is no taboo or restriction upon sex play among children and almost none among adolescents. But there is a taboo against any sort of friendly relations—sexual or otherwise—between a brother and a sister. A strict avoidance of such relations begins to be enforced in very early childhood.

MONOGAMOUS MARRIAGE

A third important characteristic of Trobriand society is more like our own—monogamy, that is, marriage with but one person at the same time. Matrimony usually means "a permanent union, involving sexual exclusiveness, a common economic existence, and an independent household."[10]

These three factors, then, are of the utmost importance to Trobrianders— (1) allegiance of a boy to his uncle, who occupies the role which a father would occupy in our society; (2) a complete repression of any outward affection between brothers and sisters; and (3) monogamous marriage.

VIOLATIONS OF THE RULES

What about the violations of these three essential rules? Does anyone ever "get by" with a violation? A boy must live with his uncle, a boy must have nothing to do with his sister, no man can have more than one wife—these are the rules. These represent the "cake of custom" by which these people live. But these people, just like ourselves, avoid following the rules under certain circumstances.

Thus, there are many instances where men of high position are allowed to keep their sons with them, even after puberty, rather than sending the boys to live with the uncle. There are instances where the taboo between brother and sister is violated and nothing happens to the offender. There are even instances where men have several wives. But only chieftains or men of power can violate these rules with impunity. Now, does this failure to follow the "rules of the game" on the part of some primitives have any parallel at all in our own society? Do you know of any sets of rules which we *say* are custom or customary but which are not followed out if a person can "get by"? Are there instances where certain "chieftains" in our society have more sexual experiences than nonchieftains, without being condemned by "public opinion"?

In Melanesian society a sexual offense is often paid for by a person climbing to the top of the nearest bamboo tree and jumping—that is, by suicide.[11] Yet certain violators, unless the group is very much aroused, somehow never get around to jumping. Can you think of any instances at all in our society where people "fail to jump," that is, where they are not punished for their violations of our rules? Does it make any difference whether a man in our society—where, theoretically, all men are born and created equal—is black or white, rich or poor? The treatment of an offender obviously varies with persons and circumstances, both in primitive and in civilized groups.

INTERRELATIONS OF RELIGION, CUSTOM, AND LAW

Neither Malinowski nor other anthropologists have found any distinct division between religion, custom, and law in these primitive societies.[12] It is practically impossible to say which rules are simply religious, which ones are custom, and which ones are legalistic in nature, because they are so closely intertwined.[13] As indicated in the previous section, much the same thing is true of our society. If we attempt to find out what the rules are which make us "behave like human beings," we find that they are based on more than biology and that they are even more complex than the rules for certain "savages." There is, of course, enormous variation in the latitude given the individual in different groups, but in general we may observe in every society—primitive or modern—an intricately woven set of rules, well understood by the members of that society. We may also observe many cases where the rules are not obeyed; these cases are implicitly understood only by the group's members. To differentiate primitive from so-called "civilized" people on the basis of these factors, then, would be completely false.

▶ THE ZUÑI, DOBUANS, AND KWAKIUTL

UNIVERSAL FEELINGS OF SUPERIORITY

As another study in the variability of human nature, consider next the groups—Zuñi, Dobuans, and Kwakiutl—discussed by Ruth Benedict in her book, *Patterns of Culture.*[14] Because the cultural standards of Western civilization have been almost the sole basis for evaluating human behavior in terms of "normal" and "abnormal," Benedict believed that a great injustice had been done to all other culture groups whose standards are different in nature from ours. This attitude is clearly reflected not only among nations but also among inhabitants of hamlets which lie close to each other, in fact, in villages, cities, and states throughout the country. Every strongly organized group of individuals, regardless of numbers, tend to apply to themselves some title or phrase signifying that "we are *the* people," and to regard all others outside of the group as "foreigners" who are to be treated with suspicion, contempt, and hostility. *People in every group, the world over, seem to have an exaggerated belief in their own greatness, a belief that they are the salt of the earth.* We consider those people as inferior who do not behave as we and our people do. In any group we find loyalty, blind devotion, adherence to the "rules" of that group, some subordination of interests to the welfare of the group, general uniformity of actions, speech, dress, and so forth. With this goes suspicion and even abhorrence of the rules of the outside group. The "correct" rules, of course, vary entirely from one group to another.

Benedict analyzed three groups of people who were widely separated geographically. She made detailed reports on the life of the Zuñi, a Pueblo Indian group of New Mexico; of the Dobuans, a group of people living in New Guinea, fairly close to the Trobriand Islanders whom Malinowski studied; and of the Kwakiutl, a group of Indians living along the northwestern coast of North America.

THE ZUÑI

The two most important factors in Zuñi society are: (1) *lack of individualism,* and (2) prevalence of *ritualism.*

1. *Lack of Individualism.* The Zuñi are a ceremonious people whose chief interests are dances and religious observances. They value sobriety and inoffensiveness. Their ideal individual is one who possesses dignity, affability, generosity, eloquence. He is a good mixer, always coming to aid his associates; he is a good conversationalist and is very modest about himself.

Contrast this with our own society. Certainly no one can take exception to these qualities since in our own culture they are regarded as "virtues." But they are carried to extremes among the Zuñi. To them any individualism is an undesirable quality that is held in distrust; all the members of the group are expected to serve the interests of the whole group. This is carried to such a degree that individual initiative is punished by the group as a disruptive force. As an example, if any man wins consistently in foot races, he is not allowed to participate any more. Any striving for prestige or power, any kind of attempt to exercise individual control, is discouraged. Rules of marriage and separation are extremely simple.

Deviation from the "norm" of the group is the greatest offense that can be committed among the Zuñi. All forms of friction are smoothed over as quickly as they arise, and they are as quickly forgotten so that harmonious functioning of social interests can be continued. Suicide is unknown among these people and is apparently incomprehensible to them.

> The more particularly you illustrate the practice of suicide to a Zuñi audience, the more politely and smilingly incredulous they become. It is very strange the things that white people will do. But this is most laughable of all.[15]

2. *Ritualism* is also the order of the day. Ritualism from morning to night, throughout the entire year, is the chief preoccupation of the Zuñi.

"Not only those who are responsible for the ritual and those who take part in it, but all the people of the pueblo, women and families who have nothing, that is, that have no ritual possessions, center their daily conversation about it."[16] Marriage is easily arranged and occupies no position of importance as it does in most other societies. It is a matter privately contracted by the interested individuals and is not an occasion for lavish preparations. Divorce is likewise a private affair and is settled so simply that it rarely requires group intervention.

When a woman is satisfied that she will not be left husbandless (husbands are easy to get), she gathers together her husband's possessions and places them on the door sill. When he comes home in the evening, he sees the little bundle, picks it up and cries, and returns with it to his mother's house.[17]

Death is an unpleasant event but is not regarded as an occasion for excessive grief. The nearest relatives are allowed to display a reasonable amount of grief, but the entire affair is to be forgotten as quickly as possible so that normal social events can be resumed. No excess in any form, no disruptions of a moderate and peaceful way of life, no unpleasantness of any kind—these are the "rules" of the Zuñi.

THE DOBUANS

Contrast the "human nature" of the Zuñi with that of the Dobuans of New Guinea where the two outstanding factors of behavior are: (1) *competition,* including treachery and cheating, and (2) *magic*—the unexpected, as opposed to the highly standardized ritual of the Zuñi.

1. *Competition.* As distinguished from the peaceful and sober life of the Pueblo Zuñi, the Dobuans are lawless, treacherous, suspicious, and constantly fighting with each other. The tribe is divided into localities, and these are organized as war units. The dominant theme running through all their social institutions is that of possession of material goods at someone else's expense. No two individuals within the group are on really intimate terms, since one is constantly plotting or suspected of plotting the downfall of the other. Treachery and cheating are regarded as virtues, and that person is considered great who has heaped up possessions through sorcery, deceit, and slyness. The very "virtues" to which we adhere are looked upon as evils by the Dobuans; the very "virtues" to which the Dobuans adhere are looked upon as evils in our society.

Another contrast: It is customary in Dobuan society for a husband to spend one year with his wife's family when they are first married, at the end of which period his wife resides in his village for the same length of time. While in his wife's village, the husband lives under most trying circumstances. He is regarded as an alien with no status, is given the most menial tasks to perform, and is humiliated in every possible way. However, his retaliation comes when his length of service is over and his wife returns to his village, for there she is accorded the same treatment by members of his group and must patiently endure it until her position is again restored by residence in her own village.

Every activity is regarded as some form of competition—including economic exchange, food-growing, and love-making. These activities involve, wherever possible, treachery and cheating, for these are the true virtues.

2. *Magic* is of utmost importance among the Dobuans. No activity is possible without magical incantations.

> Yams cannot grow without these incantations, sex desire does not arise without love-magic, exchange of valuables in economic transactions are magically brought about, no trees are protected from theft unless malevolent charms have been placed upon them, no death occurs without the machinations of sorcery and witchcraft, no wind blows unless it is magically called.[18]

There is fierce competition for the possession of magical formulas, and deaths are commonly attributed to these sources. Malevolence and ill will toward everybody are reflected in all of the "magical" activities of these people. Personal possessions are secretly guarded from a neighbor's prying eyes, and every person has a number of different disease charms which are calculated to cause the most horrible sufferings. If a man dies, his wife is the very first one to be accused of causing his death. Also, death is a great affront that must be wiped out by retaliation on some other human being; the nearest kin to a deceased person will lie in wait for some unsuspecting victim and kill him without warning in order to "get even." All these are aspects of normal human behavior among the Dobuans.

THE KWAKIUTL

Consider now the third group, the Kwakiutl of Alaska. The two dominant themes of their life seem to be: (1) *superiority* and (2) *self-glorification.*

1. The dominating desire for *superiority* is shown in all sorts of activities, religious, social, economic, and even in matters of birth and death. These people take great pride in titles of nobility, and each time a greater title is acquired, through marriage or inheritance or gift, it is an occasion for a feast called a "potlatch." On the occasion of a potlatch, vast quantities of material possessions are distributed with the implicit understanding that they will someday be returned—with interest. Goods may be destroyed by throwing them into the blazing fire around which the people sit. Destruction and waste are signs of greatness and evoke admiration among one's fellows.

If the receiver of a gift at a potlatch is unable to repay the donor, he "loses face"; he loses all respect from the members of the group because this is equivalent to being beaten in a contest, whereas the donor is regarded with respect and admiration, and as a paragon of virtue. Feasts or potlatches are contests which are engaged in by wealthy rivals who seek to shame each other, either by distributing great amounts of wealth, or by destroying almost all of their possessions until one of the two rivals is unable to match the squanderings of the other.

2. *Self-glorification* is thus the order of the day.

> This will to superiority they exhibited in the most uninhibited fashion. It found expression in uncensored self-glorification and ridicule of all comers. Judged by the standards of other cultures the speeches of their chiefs at their potlatches are unabashed megalomania.[19]

Ridicule among the Kwakiutl is synonymous with defeat. Therefore, it behooves one to belittle and make fun of other people in order to glorify himself. Both ridicule and potlatches are employed in avenging insults and also in the most minor sorts of things, such as a false step in dancing. Many a person pays for a small error by a distribution of his property. In our society we might accuse someone who did this of having delusions of grandeur, but in the society of the Kwakiutl such a person is considered the finest possible specimen of adulthood and one worthy of emulation by all individuals.

THE PROBLEM OF NORMAL AND ABNORMAL BEHAVIOR

All this represents human behavior. Are the people in the Kwakiutl society all paranoiacs? Are they all "insane"? Or is there something wrong with *our* society? Who is right? One possible answer is that "abnormal" behavior in one society may be perfectly "normal" in another. There is no justification in social psychology for any one set of standards being regarded as the only normal set which will solve all the problems of human existence. "One man's meat is another man's poison." The fact that we label certain behavior "abnormal" in our civilization may simply mean that our patterns are hopelessly rigid; it may mean that we have taken no account of how individuals might become adjusted under modified patterns of society. Behavior of a Zuñi, Dobuan, or Kwakiutl sort would be "abnormal" in our society; but likewise many of our daily actions, which we are so apt to take for granted as natural, would be "abnormal" in any one of these three groups. We shall return to this problem in Chapter 9.

VARIED PATTERNS OF "CORRECT" BEHAVIOR

Most of us are apt to consider the standards of our own group, and all those actions which we have learned to follow automatically, as *best,* not only for us, but for everyone else. They are so much a part of us that we find it very difficult to understand that the things we consider "correct" should not be correct everywhere else. As Boas has said, "Courtesy, modesty, good manners, conformity to definite ethical standards are universal, but what constitutes courtesy, modesty, good manners, and ethical standards is not universal."[20] Neither are these differences in human nature explainable on a biological basis.

A man who is considered brave in one group may exhibit the same behavior in another group and be considered a coward. An individual who is kind and considerate to his fellows in one group may be called a "good fellow," but if he is kind and considerate in another group, he may be dubbed a fool and an idiot. The social antecedents of behavior must be understood, then, in addition to the biological bases of behavior. The results of many painstaking anthropological investigations tend to confirm the theory "that much of what we ascribe to human nature is no more than a reaction to the restraints put upon us by our civilisation."[21]

▶ THE SAMOANS

THE SOCIAL ENVIRONMENT

As a specific example of differences in human nature, let us now turn to a consideration of attitudes toward sex. Margaret Mead was greatly interested in the phenomenon of adolescence in American children, especially in girls. Apparently the question in her mind was, "Why is the period of adolescence in American girls considered such a period of storm and stress, whereas the girls of the so-called uncivilized races seem to come through this period of life with little or no trouble?" Mead realized that all girls, no matter what their group or culture, went through the same process of physical development as do American girls. They, too, cut their first teeth and lose them, cut their second teeth, grow ungainly and tall, reach puberty with their first menstruation, and gradually reach physical maturity and begin to produce the next generation. Here was a good problem for objective study. If the same processes take a different form in two different environments, we cannot make any explanation in terms of physiology alone, for that is about the same in both cases. It then seems necessary to look to social environment for an explanation.

THE SAMOA ISLANDS

In order to make her observations, Mead went to the Samoa Islands and lived there with the native people for nine months. She turned her attention to the Samoan girls. Because she was a woman she believed they would feel more at home with her than would a group of strange boys. Her work is one more illustration of the empirical method. Mead approached her problem in a practical way, by going to the Samoa Islands, by learning the customs, habits, and language of the people.[22]

What did she find? Samoan babies are nursed by the mother until they are three or four years old; except for this, the chief burden of care falls on the next older child. It is she who teaches the baby the set of avoidances he must learn, such as to keep out of the sun, not to stand upright in the house, not to tangle the strands of the weaver, not to make any noise around adults. In Samoa the precocious child is discouraged from exhibiting his talents or increasing his skill ahead of the rest of his contemporaries. The laggard is thus given an opportunity to keep abreast of his brighter brother. This, of course, makes for increased uniformity among the various age groups.

Through observation, Samoan children become familiar at an early age with the biology of birth and death. No effort is made to keep them out of the house when these events occur. The attitude of the adult is that birth and death, although frequently horrible, are nevertheless perfectly natural, and that is the attitude which the children acquire. In sex activities, the young Samoans are equally well educated through observation, although they may observe surreptitiously. With regard to sex specifically, the first attitude which a little girl learns toward boys is one of avoidance and antagonism. A brother-and-sister avoidance or "taboo" extends to all relatives of the opposite sex in her age group, and none but the most formal relations is permissible. This avoidance begins when the younger of two children is taught to feel ashamed at the elder's touch; it continues to old age. In early childhood the young girl learns to withdraw from the boys and to regard them as present enemies and future lovers. This antagonistic attitude continues up to puberty, at which time social contacts, followed shortly by sex experimentation, begin. Although sex relationships between young unmarried people are not openly countenanced, they are not actively disapproved. Girls may have several lovers before they are married without being subjected to criticism. Too great promiscuity, however, is frowned upon. Romantic love as we know it does not exist in Samoa. The youths have a flowery courtship language, but they are apt to use it on several girls at the same time—perhaps not differing in this respect from American boys. Samoan marriages are usually marriages of convenience, entered into for social and economic reasons, rather than as a result of a passionate attachment. Under such conditions adultery is not infrequent, but it does not necessarily end in divorce. "Divorce" is an easy matter, for if either spouse tires of the bargain, he or she merely returns to his or her own family.

DIFFERENCES IN SAMOAN AND AMERICAN CIVILIZATION

Since "human nature" is so different in Samoa and in America, it is possible to contrast the attitudes of American and Samoan girls at adolescence in order to determine which attitudes are due to physiological changes and which are due to the customs of the particular culture. From such a comparison it is possible then to trace the development of certain individual attitudes, ideas, and habits to the culture patterns in our civilization which are responsible for them. There are at least two differences between Samoan society and American culture which may demonstrate the *cultural,* and *not the biological,* causes of attitudes toward sex.

1. *Lack of Specialization of Feeling.* First, consider the lack of specialization of feeling, particularly sex feeling, among Samoan girls. This is perhaps the best illustration of the effect of a culture pattern—the pattern of family and social relationships—upon the thinking and behavior of the individual. Mead says that, "Samoans have a low level of appreciation of personality differences, and a poverty of conception of personal relations."[23] In their attitudes toward life and toward people the Samoans are very casual. The Samoan baby is born into a heterogeneous household, all the members of which he must obey and all of whom are responsible for his care. He forms no strong individual attachments there. In childhood he is segregated from children of the opposite sex. This prevents any social intercourse that might result in friendships and attachments which would approximate our American institution of romantic love. So, in a society where no one feels too strongly about anyone else, the adolescent Samoan girl is not tortured by poignant situations such as those she must face in our civilization where she is beset on every hand with choices to be made. Repressions or inhibitions which are so prevalent in our society, particularly with regard to sex, are not necessary in Samoan culture, and the whole pattern of sex "complexes" resulting therefrom is avoided.

2. *Objective Attitudes toward Sex.* Second, note the very objective attitudes of Samoans toward sex. The *attitudes* of Samoan adults on matters of reproduction, birth, and death are probably more influential in preventing the growth of undesirable sex attitudes in the children than is their early acquisition of the facts of life. To the Samoans these biological matters are as natural as work and play, and the children, although extremely curious about them, discuss them openly, not under the "hush-hush" conditions so characteristic of our own society. They do not have to hide their knowledge from their elders, or pretend to be surprised years later when their elders tell them the "facts of life." They are thus saved from brooding over unsolved problems and half knowledge, as well as the shock which is often attendant upon knowledge when it does not come until after adolescence has been reached.

The attitudes toward sex activity outside of marriage are also extremely important in preventing maladjustments of older unmarried women. In our civilization there are thousands of women who are unmarried, some from choice, others because they are not sufficiently appealing to any male as a life companion. Because our civilization tends to class all unmarried women who indulge in sex activity as immoral, a comparatively large percentage of these women have almost no sex life. As a consequence, they are frequently so warped in their judgments by their attempts to compensate in other ways for the deprivation, or to rationalize their "single blessedness," that maladjustments result. Also, in our civilization an older unmarried woman is "extra" socially and has a definitely limited social sphere, which often has deleterious psychological effects. In Samoa she has the same status as her married sisters.

Lack of Conflicts. The only real choices the Samoan girl must make are concerned with when she will observe the brother and sister "taboo," and when she will marry. The Samoan culture is sufficiently standardized so that girls on reaching adolescence have their several love affairs, eventually marry, have children, and continue with the work of the household. American girls, on the other hand, must literally make dozens of choices, each of which involves a conflict. As Mead says:

> Samoa's lack of difficult situations, of conflicting choice, of situations in which fear or pain or anxiety are sharpened to a knife edge will probably account for a large part of the absence of psychological maladjustment. Just as a low-grade moron would not be hopelessly handicapped in Samoa, although he would be a public charge in a large American city, so individuals with slight nervous instability have a much more favorable chance in Samoa than in America. Furthermore the amount of individualisation, the range of variation, is much smaller in Samoa. Within our wider limits of deviation there are inevitably found weak and non-resistant temperaments. And just as our society shows a greater development of personality, so also it shows a larger proportion of individuals who have succumbed before the complicated exactions of modern life.[24]

SEX AND TEMPERAMENT

PHYSIOLOGY AN INCOMPLETE EXPLANATION OF SEX ATTITUDES

There are a number of other anthropological studies which have done a great deal to discourage the assumption that attitudes toward sex are explainable simply in terms of the biology of sex. These studies are important, because one is apt to take it for granted that everything concerning sex is physiological. Social psychologists know from an examination of other cultures and from studies of their own society that, although biology may determine certain fundamental principles of behavior, attitudes toward sexual matters are largely determined by the particular culture in which we happen to be born and live, plus our own personal experiences. In certain other groups the supposed "masculine" and "feminine" attitudes toward sex which we have in our culture do not hold. The supposed dominance of the male is not something inherent in the biology of sex. This matter will be treated more fully in Chapter 13.

MEAD'S WORK IN NEW GUINEA

All cultures have definite patterns of sex differences, although these are sometimes the reverse of those in our own civilization. This is well borne out in some other studies by Margaret Mead in New Guinea.[25] In these investigations, she wished to "discover to what degree temperamental differences between the sexes were innate and to what extent they were culturally determined. . . ."[26] From her observations of various peoples she concluded that probably "many, if not all, of the personality traits that we have called masculine or feminine are as lightly linked to sex as are the clothing, the manners, and the form of headdress that a society at a given period assigns to either sex."[27] This is a startling conclusion. On what facts is it based? Mead lived with and studied three different primitive groups of New Guinea—the Arapesh, the Mundugumor, and the Tchambuli.

THE ARAPESH

The Arapesh are a mountain-dwelling people of New Guinea in which mutual trust and affection are cultural norms. Competition and aggressiveness are all but nonexistent. Even the children's games are always of a noncompetitive nature; in fact, if two Arapesh children begin to fight, they are separated, and although allowed to scream and to abuse inanimate objects, they may not "make contact" with each other. Very little emphasis is placed on age or sex differences, and there are no class differences. Perhaps the most apt expression for the Arapesh would be "one great big happy family." In this gentle, unaggressive group, *both* women and men display what we could call "feminine" characteristics.

THE MUNDUGUMOR

Mead's second group was a cannibal tribe of New Guinea, the Mundugumor, in striking contrast to the gentle Arapesh. "The Mundugumor man-child is born into a hostile world, a world in which most of the members of his own sex will be his enemies, in which his major equipment for success must be a capacity for violence, for seeing and avenging insult, for holding his own safety very lightly and the lives of others even more lightly."[28]

The Mundugumors not only do not welcome the birth of children but give them a minimum of attention after they arrive. None of the mother-child sex play that characterizes the nursing of the Arapesh baby is found; but instead the moment the child stops suckling the mother puts him away, and early weaning is accompanied by cross words and blows. Both men and women are aggressive and constantly ready to fight, and the women look upon sex activities with the same violent interest as the men. These people are ruthless in accomplishing their aims, and there are apparently few differences in the "masculine" attitudes displayed by *both* sexes.

THE TCHAMBULI

Mead's third group, the Tchambuli, is very different from either the Arapesh or the Mundugumor.

> . . . The Arapesh ideal is the mild, responsive man married to the mild, responsive woman; the Mundugumor ideal is the violent aggressive man married to the violent aggressive woman. In the third tribe, the Tchambuli, we found a genuine reversal of the sex-attitudes of our own culture, with the woman the dominant, impersonal, managing partner, the man the less responsible and the emotionally dependent person.[29]

In the Tchambuli, the woman makes the choice, and the man is chosen. The women seem to get along well with each other, while the men are "catty" about other men, eternally ready to be suspicious and distrustful. Because of their dependence on the women for security, the men are shy, sensitive, and subservient; they engage in artistic and other "feminine" activities, such as dancing and painting.

> These three situations suggest, then, a very definite conclusion. If those temperamental attitudes which we have traditionally regarded as feminine—such as passivity, responsiveness, and willingness to cherish children—can so easily be set up as the maculine pattern in one tribe, and in another be outlawed for the majority of women as well as for the majority of men, we no longer have any basis for regarding such aspects of behavior as sex-linked. And this conclusion becomes even stronger when we consider the actual reversal in Tchambuli of the position of dominance in the two sexes, in spite of the existence of formal patrilineal institutions.[30]

▶ WHAT ABOUT OURSELVES?

ANALYSIS OF OUR OWN SOCIETY

After this brief survey of certain primitive groups, you may ask, "So what?" The answer can be given in the words of G. K. Chesterton, who told how a friend walked into his apartment in London, found him packing his bags, and asked him where he was going. He replied that he was on his way to London via Paris, Belfort, Heidelberg, Frankfort. His friend then remarked that it was probably unnecessary to tell him that he was in London, to which Chesterton replied, "It is quite unnecessary, and it is spiritually untrue. . . . I cannot see any London or any England. I cannot see that door. I cannot see that chair: because a cloud of . . . custom has come across my eyes. The only way to get back to them is to go somewhere else. . . . The whole object of travel is not to set foot on foreign land; it is at last to set foot on one's own country as a foreign land."[31]

Since we are unable to embark on an ocean liner or a floating university and take a trip around the world, the next best thing is to read about other people in order to come back to our own social group and see them objectively. And we need not limit ourselves to an examination of faraway primitive peoples. Think of some of the unique patterns of behavior in our own country.

> What makes the Southern rural Negro think of Heaven as a continuous fish-fry? What makes the Sicilian immigrant pin a five-dollar bill on a standard whose center is covered with the image of his patron saint on a particular Sunday morning? Why is this Sunday specifically designated as the occasion for escorting that saint, to the tune of a brass band, up and down the streets of a "little Italy"? Why, for instance, are we ready and do we consider it the manly thing to take up arms and kill in defense of our country, but not in defense of our fraternity or sorority? Why, if we come from old Bostonian homes, are we apt to consider afternoon tea a laudatory custom and an expression of refinement?[32]

The number of forest fires each year has been a matter of grave concern to officials of the United States Forest Service. Social psychologist John P. Shea was asked to study the problem. After field trips into some of the more important timber regions and living with the "natives," Dr. Shea became convinced that most of the fires, perhaps 90 per cent, were started on purpose, and by people who live in the forests! It may seem strange that men who earn their living in the forest would want to burn them, but many unique reasons were given: "Kill snakes." "Burn out the ticks." "Get shet of the boll weevils." Some thought they were "killing" infantile paralysis germs. The *real* reasons, as distinguished from those given, were probably boredom and lack of anything very much to do. The fires were exciting and provided welcome relief to the monotonous daily existence of the people. To help solve the problem, Shea proposed that leaders in the community—and not "outsiders"—build, with the help of their neighbors, a number of recreation centers, with dance floors, horseshoe-pitching grounds, pine sticks for whittling, and plenty of brass cuspidors for the men.[33]

FRENCH AND AMERICAN SOCIETY

Suppose we make a brief comparison between American and French society. On about his second day in France, an American discovers to his amazement that the French really are not Americans. He, of course, expected them to speak a different language. But what he had not entirely expected was that they should run their railways differently, run their trains without any chair cars, have hotels which do not provide soap, maintain drugstores which do not have postage stamps for sale, publish newspapers which print the news obscurely on inside pages, charge money for theater programs, fail to put ice in ice water, regard their country as superior to the United States, and have weather which is not 78 degrees but always some unsatisfactory number called "centigrade." Is our American intrigued by all this? He is not. In fact, he finds it so shocking that he does his best to sell the French people on "up-to-date" American ways of doing things.[34]

Now, consider the impressions a Frenchman gets on first arriving in America:

> Coming from France, which to me seemed a thoroughly logical country, I was confused by the many incomprehensible contradictions of American life. . . . I could not understand why the country with the largest workers' population in the world should have no labor party; why centralization should be advocated by liberals, and States' Rights defended by big corporations; . . . why aliens should be regarded with contempt by the sons of aliens; why religion should be separated from the state, . . . why bishops should oppose child-labor regulation; why gangsters and kidnappers should grow up next door to the strange prophets and utopians of the Share the Wealth, Epic, Social Justice, and Old-Age-Pension plans. . . .[35]

WHICH SOCIETY IS BETTER?

A question sometimes asked is, "But which group is better?" Is primitive or modern society better? Is American society better, or French society? Unfortunately, no one knows the answer. The reason is a matter of simple logic—before you can say that one thing is better than something else, you have to say that it is better or worse *in some particular respect.* It is impossible to say that American or primitive or French or any other society is best for all people—although the members of every group take it for granted that their own ways are best, not only for them but for other groups as well.

If we use power as a criterion, we shall certainly regard the Western world as superior. In fact, if our notion of a superior civilization is a machine age with speed as the measure of success, the United States is far in the lead. If, however, mystical conceptions of life represent our criterion of what is best, certainly Hindu civilization would be regarded as superior.

If we shift our criterion to aesthetic values, the Chinese would be considered superior.

As Klineberg has pointed out, certain simple peoples seem to have moral standards superior to our own.[36] The Yakuts of Siberia could not understand how it was possible in our cities for some people to be starving while others had more than enough to eat. The Yakuts have the custom of sharing their food with the hungry, and a Yakut moralist might make a good case for the inferiority of our civilization. The same may be said also of the Eskimo who offered to teach white men how to live in peace with one another. We have the right to speak of our civilization as more complex than that of certain primitive peoples, but we cannot prove its complete superiority. And even its greater complexity is largely a function of the fact that it covers greater populations. "Even on the basis of our own standards it is difficult to make a clear case for the superiority of any race over another."[37]

OBJECTIVE STUDY

Your fundamental problem is to imagine yourself as having left your country, your state, your community completely and then having suddenly come back to ask, "What makes these Americans act the way they do?" It is your job to forget completely at this point that you are a Southerner "from way back" or a "damn Yankee," or a New Englander or a Westerner. It is your job to forget that you are a Catholic, Protestant, Jew, atheist, or agnostic. It is your job to forget that you are or are not a student. It is your job to forget that you are primarily a fraternity man or sorority woman or an "independent." It is your job to forget that your sympathies are essentially capitalistic or that you hold to the ideologies of labor. In other words, try to look at your own society objectively and in an unbiased manner, for the value of your study of social psychology will be seriously impaired if you insist on believing that the standards of your own group represent scientific truths or fundamentals. What you and your group do is not the only test of what is meant by "human nature."

QUESTIONS AND PROBLEMS FOR DISCUSSION

1. *Can you make any judgments as to what type of society is the most rational?*
2. *Does the history of primitive groups indicate that they are incapable of "progress" or intellectual development beyond a certain point?*
3. *Explain in detail with examples: "Courtesy, modesty, good manners, conformity to ethical standards are universal, but what constitutes courtesy, modesty, good manners, and ethical standards is not universal."*
4. *To what rules of social control do you willingly submit?*
5. *Explain: "Studies of primitive groups show that there is a wide latitude between the theoretical code and actual practice."*

6. *To what degree is your own emotional behavior influenced by the group you consider correct?*
7. *What do you think is meant by the psychosocial environment?*

RECOMMENDED READINGS

Benedict, R., *Patterns of Culture.* Boston: Houghton Mifflin Company, 1934.

Chapple, E. D., and Coon, C. S., *Principles of Anthropology.* New York: Henry Holt and Company, Inc., 1942.

Lowie, R. H., *An Introduction to Cultural Anthropology* (2nd edition). New York: Farrar & Rinehart, 1940.

Lynd, R. S., and Lynd, H. M., *Middletown: A Study in Contemporary American Culture.* New York: Harcourt, Brace and Company, 1929.

Lynd, R. S., and Lynd, H. M., *Middletown in Transition: A Study in Cultural Conflicts.* New York: Harcourt, Brace and Company, 1937.

Malinowski, B., *Crime and Custom in Savage Society.* New York: Harcourt, Brace and Company, 1926.

Malinowski, B., *Sex and Repression in Savage Society.* New York: Harcourt, Brace and Company, 1927.

Mead, M., *Coming of Age in Samoa.* New York: William Morrow & Company, 1928.

Mead, M., *Growing Up in New Guinea.* New York: William Morrow & Company, 1930.

Mead, M., *Sex and Temperament.* New York: William Morrow & Company, 1935.

*Newcomb, T. M., Hartley, E. L., and others (editors), *Readings in Social Psychology.* New York: Henry Holt and Company, Inc., 1947. (The following selections are listed according to the sequence of related discussion in the chapter you have just read.)

Mead, M., "Educative Effects of Social Environment as Disclosed by Studies of Primitive Societies," pp. 151–158.

Lee, D. D., "A Linguistic Approach to a System of Values," pp. 219–224.

Benedict, R., "Psychological Types in the Cultures of the Southwest," pp. 14–23.

Dennis, W., "Does Culture Appreciably Affect Patterns of Infant Behavior?", pp. 40–46.

Mead, M., "Adolescence in Primitive and in Modern Society," pp. 6–14.

CHAPTER FIVE

THE NATURE OF CULTURE

WHAT IS CULTURE? The Vertical Approach—Cultural Selection—Definition of Culture—Regionalism—Comparison of Cultures—Culture Not Limited to the Best—"Cultural Lag"—Prominent Aspects of American Culture—Other Patterns—Etiquette / FOLKWAYS, CUSTOMS, MORES, TABOOS. Folkways—Customs—Mores—Taboos—Taboos of Language—Interrelation of These "Ways"—Conformity Demanded—Intangible Social Forces—Easy Disintegration of Our Social "Ways"—Objections to Some Ways—A Dilemma.

▶ WHAT IS CULTURE?

THE VERTICAL APPROACH

What determines correct behavior? What are the correct standards for Americans to live by? Some of the answers to these questions were found in the preceding chapter where we made a "horizontal"—or comparative—examination of primitive and modern groups. Now we should also make a "vertical" analysis by bringing in historical factors to understand how certain ways of behaving known as "correct" ways have evolved. You should keep in mind both a horizontal or contemporary, and a vertical or historical, approach to social psychology in order to understand the society in which you live.

For instance, did it ever occur to you that the first people who used forks were called "sissies"? According to scientists of the National Geographic Society, the best etiquette up to the fifteenth century was the time-honored method of attacking food with the thumb and first two fingers; in fact, to use more fingers was bad table manners. The fork actually began to come into its own only about three hundred years ago.

Have you ever questioned the right of a university professor to walk to his office or to mow his own lawn? You would raise an eyebrow at such a sight if you were a Chinese brought up in China, for a complexity of historical factors means that today in China it is undignified for a scholar to walk, when he can be carried in a chair, or to engage in any physical exercise. In 1938 numerous Americans were amused at newspaper headlines: "King Farouk Makes Farida His Queen; Wild Fete in Cairo. 17-Year-Old Monarch of Egypt Signs Contract—His Bride Is Absent under Islamic Rite. But She Peeks at Service. Only Men Present as Ruler and Girl's Father Clasp Hands in Palace to Seal the Union." Many an American said, "How absurd." Few of them realized that an Egyptian witnessing our own modern marriage rituals would also say, "How utterly absurd!"

Still a better way to illustrate the significance of historical factors is to contrast the life of man with that of some nonhuman creature such as a lion, who is not influenced by history and tradition.

> We cannot imagine him, for example, stopping in his palpitating pursuit of a tawny female for whom he is filled with lust, because some Leo the Saint, who died perhaps a hundred lion generations before, reached the ascetic conclusion that sexual congress was, on the whole, unworthy and that burning desire might be satisfied only under very special and restricted circumstances. Nor can we visualize this same Leo aching for food because all the tissues of his body are sending frantic signals to his consciousness that they need replenishment, yet withholding his mighty paw or his cavernous jaw from either a live or a dead delicacy because that delicacy has been staked off for another lion; or because old lions assembled in a congress a thousand years before decreed private ownership in delicacies and forbade even ravenous hunger to satisfy itself except under strict rule and regulation. . . .
>
> We cannot imagine the young lion contemplating the life of some past Leo the Great and planning his entire career in emulation of the dead hero. . . . We cannot imagine him in agonies of self-condemnation because he has fallen short of an ideal which has not arisen spontaneously within himself, but has been incorporated within him by the teaching and preaching of a thousand years and of countless lions. . . .
>
> He does not foresee his own death, and knows nothing of his own birth. Sex means to him only the satisfaction that an individual of the opposite sex can give him. It does not mean parenthood, domesticity, respectability, the fulfilling of an ideal, a responsibility, and the becoming part of a great racial sweep.[1]

CULTURAL SELECTION

Human beings are constantly influenced by what countless millions of other humans prior to them have thought and done, and by what countless millions of others (not known to them) are now thinking and doing. As we saw in Chapter 3, it is essential to have some biological background in order to interpret correctly the social psychology of everyday life; but this is not the complete picture. Those who try to explain human behavior only on the basis of heredity or physiology or attempt to reduce everything to individual instincts and reflexes, overlook the tremendous force of what we call "culture patterns." Talk all you wish about instincts and reflexes, but usually the changes in attitudes which are so important in our civilization represent cultural selection only.

For example, a child born of a long line of ancestors with democratic attitudes is no more prepared *at birth* to be a good democrat than is the son of the Emperor of Japan. A Texas child born of generations accustomed to the saddle is *at birth* no better prepared to be a good horseman than a child born on New York City's "East Side." Instead, these children are born in the kind of environment that will select and encourage democratic or equestrian behavior.[2] Once more, we must turn from physiology to culture for an explanation.

DEFINITION OF CULTURE

What does this term "culture" mean? W. I. Thomas suggested that culture may be defined as "the material and social values of any group of people, whether savage or civilized (their institutions, customs, attitudes, behavior reactions) . . . ."[3] Another way of putting it is that culture consists of "standardized, group-accepted forms of habitual behavior."[4] If certain ways of behaving and of thinking are accepted by the group in which you live, they form part of your particular culture. Of course, this includes the material aspects—such as tools and machines—which may exert a directive influence over other aspects of culture.

> . . . Every individual at birth is surrounded by and very rapidly subjected to some particular pattern of norms. These norms are transmitted to him in the learning process by other individuals such as parents and teachers; by forms of architecture, music, etc.; by the methods of communication, transportation, production, distribution, monetary exchange, food habits, styles of dress, norms of punctuality, rules of play, and a thousand and one other established standards that begin to impose themselves in a more or less compelling way as the process of socialization begins. . . . Just *what* standards, values, or norms hold sway in a particular society or group the individual is born into are, obviously, not in the least determined by the new-born individual.[5]

REGIONALISM

There are not only the very obvious differences between primitives of the Trobriand Islands and civilized Americans, and between Frenchmen and Americans, but also between people from different geographical sections of the United States. Thus, cultures of the mountains of Tennessee are different from those of the plains of Kansas. As Hertzler has pointed out, the culture of a region is compounded out of a complex of such factors as topography, climate, and natural resources.[6] Thus, in spite of many uniformities of behavior, there are distinctive social patterns of the South, New England, the Middle West, and other regions. Each region gives rise to unique sentiments, wishes, interests, loyalties, attitudes, thought patterns, habit systems, and forms of public opinion. The reality of the regionally uniform behavior patterns is demonstrated by the fact that a person who migrates from one region to another finds many of his interests, attitudes, habits, and opinions at variance with the people who have lived in the other region for some time. He is for a while an "outlander"—not quite in step with the others.

For example, when a Southerner of middle or upper class migrates northward he does not easily change his attitudes toward the Negro or the sharecropper; the New Englander is surprised by the democratic ways of the prairie country; the Dust Bowl farmer finds himself a rudderless ship in the Puget Sound area, or in the California valleys; the sharecropper in Detroit must adjust himself to a new climate, new occupations, new living conditions, new class attitudes; in several regions an "outsider" is still conspicuous because of the peculiarities of his speech—the idioms, the peculiarities of pronunciation, special words and uses of words.[7]

COMPARISON OF CULTURES

Even more striking instances of differences in culture are found in comparing different regions of the world. Culture patterns in New York and Japan, for example, differ widely. If there is criticism of a public official in the United States, he usually offers an alibi of some sort and attempts to justify his behavior. Contrast this with the conduct of a Japanese police official who in the 1930's mistakenly routed the Emperor of Japan down a wrong street in a parade; instead of attempting to justify himself by an alibi, he committed suicide. The Japanese bathe nude in public bath houses, in full view of members of the opposite sex, but are shocked by public kissing or "petting."

In America if a man is in love with two women at the same time and they both know about it, he is, to say the least, in a difficult position. Yet in Nigeria a first wife encourages her husband to take a second wife in order that her domestic duties may be lightened.[8]

We believe that murder is the most atrocious crime that can be committed, and for that crime a person often pays with his own life (theoretically, at least). A grave offense of a lesser order is conspiracy against the State, for which a person may be imprisoned but ordinarily will not be executed. Contrast this code of conduct with that obtaining in Communist Russia where the offense which meets almost immediately with execution is conspiracy against the Government, but where the maximum penalty for such a thing as a private murder is ordinarily a few years' imprisonment. Americans and Russians have different culture patterns.

Examine your own society. Consider the differences between the up-to-date cooking methods of modern women and the very primitive ways which are still retained in many backwoods communities. Consider table manners. There are communities where the correct procedure for drinking coffee is out of the cup, and there are other places where the custom is to drink from the saucer; in fact, to do otherwise might offend your host and hostess. Are there any biological reasons why we should stir our coffee to cool it off, but only dip into our soup to cool it? Why not reverse the process, and stir our soup and dip our coffee? Physicians and advertisers constantly tell us we should get lots of vitamins in our food. Fruit-juices are replete with vitamins. After completing an excellent fruit salad, why shouldn't we lift up our salad plates and sip the fruit juice which remains? Are there any biological reasons, or have we simply accepted quite blithely the culture patterns of our own group?

CULTURE NOT LIMITED TO THE BEST

It should be clear that the word "culture," as used in social psychology, does not carry the dictionary connotation of cultivation and refinement. Culture is not "high-falutin' "—it does not suggest what the "best" people do. It makes no difference whether a man earns a living by manipulating tools or by manipulating his tongue—what each man does is part of his culture. We can speak as accurately of the culture in the life of the ditch digger as we can of the culture in the life of the banker. Universities are an important part of American culture, but so are hot-dog stands, movie "palaces," "swing" bands, No-Parking signs, skyscrapers, golf links, television, church services, circuses, and murder trials.

CULTURE SCHEME

Table 2 shows the culture scheme, as outlined by Wissler. The aspects of culture given there are important, no matter where you live and no matter what group you are studying. The various traits of culture may be invented, or they may be acquired or borrowed from other people, or they may grow up independently in two or more groups and later converge.

"CULTURAL LAG"

There is a division between the *material* culture, the *nonmaterial* culture, and what may be termed *adaptive* culture. Examples of material culture are raw materials, machines, manufactured products, houses, in fact, all tangible objects. Examples of nonmaterial culture are customs, beliefs, techniques in work—in other words, ways of using the material objects of culture. Adaptive culture is simply that portion of the nonmaterial culture which is adjusted to the material conditions. Various aspects of any culture change at different rates. For instance, material culture usually changes more rapidly than nonmaterial culture, and this may mean a serious time "lag" in the adaptive culture. This is ordinarily called *cultural lag,* to denote the slowness of change which sometimes

TABLE 2

The Culture Scheme (after Wissler)[9]

1. Speech
    Languages, writing systems, etc.
2. Material Traits
    a. Food habits
    b. Shelter
    c. Transportation and travel
    d. Dress
    e. Utensils, tools, etc.
    f. Weapons
    g. Occupations and industries
3. Art
    Carving, painting, drawing, music, etc.
4. Mythology and Scientific Knowledge
5. Religious Practices
    a. Ritualistic forms
    b. Treatment of the sick
    c. Treatment of the dead
6. Family and Social Systems
    a. The forms of marriage
    b. Methods of reckoning relationship
    c. Inheritance
    d. Social control
    e. Sports and games
7. Property
    a. Real and personal
    b. Standards of value and exchange
    c. Trade
8. Government
    a. Political forms
    b. Judicial and legal procedures
9. War

characterizes certain parts of human culture.[10] As a concrete example, when new ways of building houses or automobiles are devised, we usually adopt those quite readily, but when proposals are made for new techniques of education or for new ways of doing things in our courts, there is usually a long period of time before these "reforms" or changes in the nonmaterial culture catch up with those in the material culture. The problem of "cultural lag" may be studied in order to understand why it is that mechanically and technologically we in America are so tremendously advanced, and yet so utterly behind the times sociologically. In our everyday problems such as accident prevention, slum clearance, and public health, "cultural lag" is a very real factor. We shall consider this matter in greater detail in Chapter 14, in discussing leadership for social changes.

PROMINENT ASPECTS OF AMERICAN CULTURE

Wissler mentions four very prominent aspects of American culture.[11] The first is *mechanical invention.* Ours is a nation of speed and technology where a premium is placed on invention in the field of material culture, although, as we have noted above, there is often little recognition of the value of new ideas and inventions in the field of nonmaterial culture, as in our educational or legal systems. Once more, "cultural lag" is found. Second, we insist on *mass education.* We believe that in the magic formula of education lies the solution of many of our problems. Let everybody get an education—every boy and girl should have an opportunity to go to college. Then, we insist that we believe in *universal suffrage.* At least that is the theory which is written out in revered documents such as the Constitution of the United States. *Nationalism* is another significant aspect of our culture to be discussed in detail in Chapter 24. Let us adhere to patriotic ideals, let us uphold the views and tenets of our forefathers.

OTHER PATTERNS

We can easily think of many other examples of our own culture patterns, if we will really look at ourselves objectively. For example, we cling to the notion of work as a cure-all. This belief has been handed down to us from the rigorous times of the Puritans and from the days of the pioneers in the West, when an idle, able-bodied man was a drain on the community as a whole. Even though the years of the present century have changed many social and economic aspects of our national life, we still adhere to this idea.

Another example of our culture patterns is found in our belief that we should protect women, children, old people, the lame, and the blind. All of these people are put into one category. This means that women and children in many instances are treated not only in the law but by society as if they were inferior beings. Contrast this with another belief which we hold to at the very same time, the theory that men and women are really equal. Thus, although women now have the right to vote, wives do not have the same rights of contract and of property as their husbands in several States of the Union.

Another widely held notion is that what was good enough for our parents ought to be good enough for us. This is a widely accepted belief among older persons—if we could only do away with all these "new-fangled" ideas, the world would be a better and happier place.

ETIQUETTE

Then there is the matter of etiquette. Although some of the patterns of etiquette may seem superficial, they are actually of the utmost importance to most of us. A man who likes to think of himself as a gentleman ordinarily removes his hat, or at least touches the brim, when he passes a lady on the street. Of course, there is no particular efficiency in this; in fact, it is sometimes a considerable hindrance to the gentleman when his arms are full of parcels. Originally, however, in the days when men wore visors and coats of armor, to raise the visor perhaps showed that one was a friend and not an enemy.

A man who considers himself a gentleman also takes care to "tack" about gracefully when he accompanies his lady so that he will always be on the outside, next to the street. Again, this has no particular value so far as efficiency is concerned. However, in the days of mud roads when horses' hoofs let fly, probably there were advantages in the gentleman's protecting his lady from mud spatterings.

A gentleman also is careful to pick up anything which a lady drops. He will do this even though he realizes that some ladies seem to have well-developed habit patterns of letting their handkerchiefs drop at convenient times. Of course, in the days when ladies wore hoop skirts and rather large bustles, there probably were real advantages to this sort of behavior. Yet in these days of supposed equality between the sexes—when women are champion athletes and successful in business—is there any reason why the situation should not be reversed, and the woman pick up what the man drops?

However, we must not fall into the error of believing that the reasons for the continuation of certain customs are found *only* in their origins. The continued existence of any particular act is to be found, not simply in the speculative reconstruction of its origin or history, but also in the *present* motives which are satisfied. One of the outstanding motives in hat tipping, "tacking" to the outside of the sidewalk, and picking up is fairly obvious, namely, to prove that one is a gentleman; this is the principal value that still attaches to these acts.

▶ FOLKWAYS, CUSTOMS, MORES, TABOOS

We are now in a position to distinguish between certain patterns of behavior. Although this is by no means a rigid classification, we can make use of the categories: folkways, customs, mores, and taboos.

FOLKWAYS

Folkways are the "right" ways to do things, not because they are vital ways of behaving, but largely because they are traditional. "They extend over the whole of life. There is a right way to catch game, to win a wife, to make oneself appear, to cure disease, to honor guests, to treat comrades or strangers, to behave when a child is born."[12] Your particular folkways are "correct" in the group and community in which you live. Folkways often last, but they are ordinarily more susceptible to change than customs and mores. Various mannerisms grow up from time to time and distinguish one as being "in the know." The long-skirted "new look" of American women in 1947-49 was in striking contrast to the knee-level fashions which it superseded. Men fall in line and in most communities do not disregard an American folkway by wearing loose, open collars to the office. Suppose a man laid his wallet and other contents of his pockets on the table when he dined out; suppose he asked his lady to hold a mirror

He asks the lady to hold a mirror.

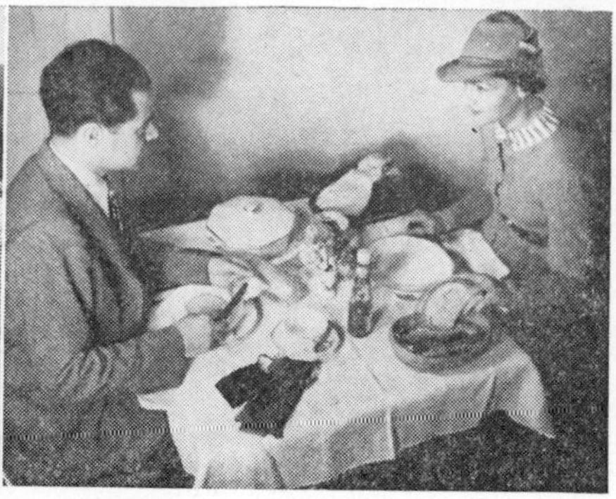

He lays his belongings on the table.

And occasionally he slips off a shoe.

When the urge comes to beautify, he does.

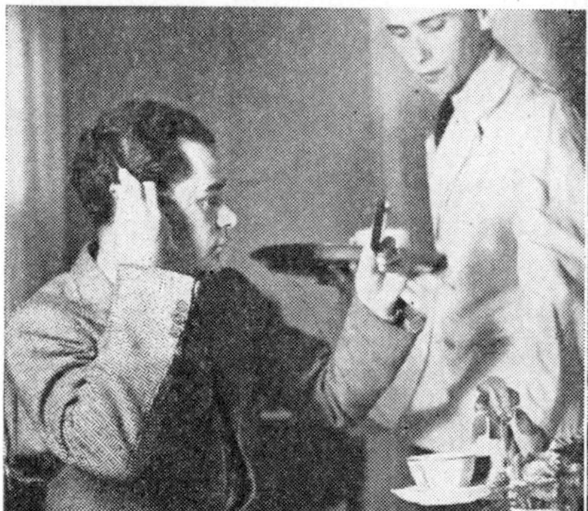

He combs his hair in a restaurant.

He tucks his foot coyly under him.

FIG. 3. IF MEN DID WHAT WOMEN DO[13]

If they did, this is how they would look!

while he adjusted his tie; suppose that at the table, when the urge came to beautify, he produced his razor; suppose he tucked his foot coyly under him against his lady's skirt; suppose that he occasionally slipped a shoe off. These things are "correct" for females to do. Why are they grossly incorrect for males? See Figure 3.

If you do not wish to follow the folkways of your group, you may "get by," but you will be considered either unsophisticated or eccentric. You may never be openly ridiculed, but—"What will people say?" See Figure 4.

CUSTOMS

Customs—closely related to folkways—are not simply proper ways of doing things; they are the "only" ways. They have usually been prevalent in a given social group over a comparatively long period of time, often so long that it seems inconceivable to the members of the group that the custom should ever be changed. When the pasteurization of milk was first proposed, it was bitterly opposed. After all, didn't our fathers, and their fathers before them, drink raw milk, and weren't they healthy? "Cultural lag" was present here.

Likewise, celebrations of festival days are so customary that many consider the exact date sacred. Until 1939 it was perfectly obvious that there was only one time to celebrate a day called Thanksgiving, and that was the last Thursday in November. Why? Because of custom. When the President of the United States suggested a change in this custom to the next to the last Thursday, people laughed openly and renewed their attacks on "that man in the White House." If you do not follow the customs of your group, you may be considered a fool and not worthy of respect. Your fellows "know" that the customs must be observed, and it will not help you any to ask naïvely who started the custom in the first place anyhow.

MORES

Finally, the *mores* must be followed even more carefully. The mores of any society involve both "thou shalts" and "thou shalt nots." Most of them are set down on bits of paper in sacred books such as the Bible, the Talmud, and the Koran, and on other bits of paper in statute books and city charters; they thus have an even greater social significance than the folkways which are simply generally understood, and not recorded in print. When ways of behaving are written down in what people call "black and white," they are indeed meaningful. The mores "are the ways of doing things which are current in a society to satisfy human needs and desires, together with the faiths, notions, codes, and standards of well living which inhere in those ways, having a genetic connection with them."[14] You cannot "get by" violating the mores as glibly as the folk-

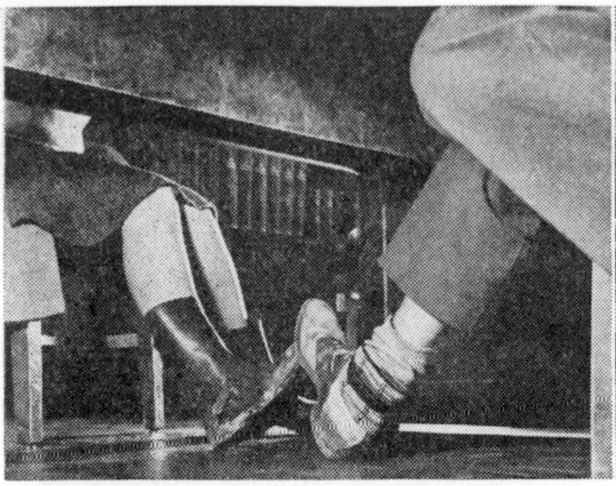

Don't play footie in library.

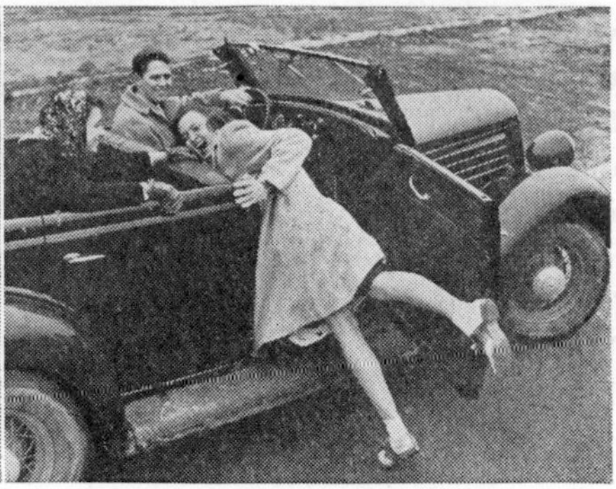

Don't break your neck rushing to get into your date's car.

Don't blow on soup.

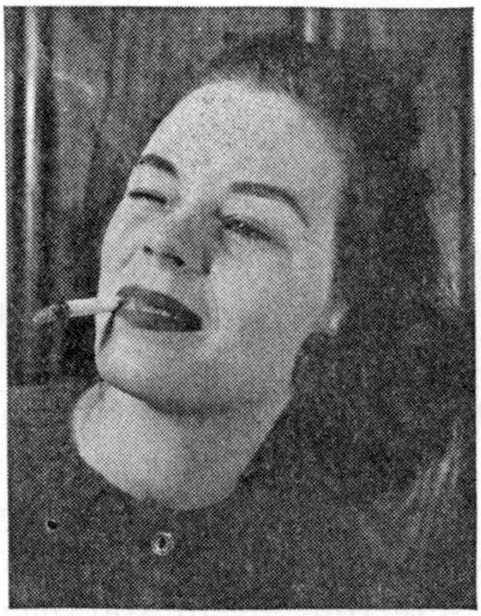

Don't dangle cigarettes in mouth.

Don't read at the table.

Don't ignore a dud blind date.

FIG. 4. DON'T'S OF CAMPUS ETIQUETTE[15]

ways, for you will be ostracized, and you may even be punished. Of course, as we have seen with primitive groups, this may depend on whether you are a "headman" or whether you know someone who knows a "headman" who "has influence."

TABOOS

The word "mores" obviously cuts across another term, namely, *taboo*. (Taboos are the negative mores.) Every society is full of "thou shalt nots" which most people follow regardless of whether they as individuals agree that those "thou shalt nots" should really be "thou shalt nots." Some taboos are recorded in print, others are simply understood without even being discussed. You don't neglect certain rules of cleanliness. You don't swear openly in the presence of certain groups, such as "ladies" or your "elders." You don't wear your hat in church if you are a Protestant man, and you don't go without it if you are a Jewish man or a Catholic woman. You don't cheat or lie, or, if you do, you confess that it is "bad" or "sinful." Such practices are taboo. We may even legislate against those practices which we think should be taboo.

In early Puritan Massachusetts both young men and young women were arrested for wearing conspicuous clothes. Devotees of fashion and of overdress became so conspicuous that in 1638 the court sent for the church elders to put a stop to the costliness of clothes, and the following of new fashions, although little could be done because so many of the elders' wives were guilty. These vanities of dress led to such flagrant flirting that in 1647 a law was passed against unauthorized courtship:

> And whereas it is a common practice in diverse places for young men irregularly and disorderly to watch all advantages for their evil purposes to insinuate into the affections of young maidens, by coming to them in places, and seasons unknown to their Parents, for such ends; whereby much evil hath grown amongst us to the dishonor of God and damage of parties, for prevention whereof for time to come it is further ordered by Authority of this Court, That whatsoever person from henceforth shall endeavor directly, or indirectly to draw away the affections of any maid in this Jurisdiction under pretence of marriage, before he hath obtained liberty and allowance from her Parents or Governours (or in absence of such) of the nearest Magistrate; he shall forfeit for the first offence five pounds, for the second towards the same party ten pounds, and be bound to forbear any farther attempt and proceedings in that unlawful design without, or against the allowance aforesaid. And for the third offence upon information, or complaint by such Parents or Governours to any Magistrate, giving *Bond* to prosecute the partie he shall be committed to prison, and upon hearing and conviction by the next Court shall be adjudged to continue in prison until the Court of Assistants shall see cause to release him.[16]

TABOOS OF LANGUAGE

Many taboos center around the use of language. Certain words must not be uttered, as we shall see in greater detail in Chapter 8 on language. And certain thoughts must never be spoken. Thus, the dogma exists among the Trobriand Islanders that children do not resemble their mothers or maternal kin. Even to hint that a child resembles his mother is a very real offense. Contrast that with our own society where to say that a child resembles anyone other than his mother may not be considered particularly polite. As another example, Trobriands hold that brothers do not resemble each other at all. When Malinowski called attention to the very striking likeness which he observed between two brothers, there came "such a hush over all the assembly that I noticed it at once. [The brother present] turned round and left us, while part of the company present, after looking away in a manner half-embarrassed, half offended, soon dispersed. I was then told by my confidential informants that I had committed a breach of custom."[17] Perhaps comparable to this in our society would be to suggest that the ancestry of a man lay in the animal kingdom.

INTERRELATION OF THESE "WAYS"

Note that there are no sharp lines which separate folkways, customs, mores, and taboos. These terms, after all, stand for closely related concepts of social ways of behaving. One of the principal values in discussing these social "ways" is to remind ourselves that our particular ways are not carried on either because of our biological make-up or owing to some "law of nature." In fact, culture is so important that what is of minor importance in one group may be of passionate concern to the members of another group. The college man's appropriation of his roommate's best necktie, or his unquestioned faith in his "right" to the use of the family automobile, are not to be explained blithely by reference to physiological needs and satisfactions. Our ways have *social* antecedents, as was stressed in the preceding chapter, and it is these social components of our everyday living which must be studied.

CONFORMITY DEMANDED

No matter where your home may be, you are dependent upon society for the means and the right to live. Owing to intricate physiological mechanisms—especially of the autonomic nervous system—you continue to live, but if you had not been born into a group with a long history back of it, it would take you and your descendants untold centuries to learn adequate adjustments to the world about you. Beginning in the cradle, you were gradually forced to learn and to assume those ways of acting and thinking which your own group considered correct. In return for being allowed to exist, the members of your group demanded that you adjust yourself to them in designated ways. Acceptance of these "ways" is the price you must pay for this business of living.[18] You must constantly conform to what is expected of you; and what is expected will vary with your age, sex, the time, and the place. The following sequences have been suggested for the growing boy in terms of the demands of his group at different periods in his development:

1. He is expected to be cute and beautiful, the idol of the family, from birth to two or three.

2. He is expected to keep out from under foot and give the adults a chance to take care of the new baby (this experience may come at any time from two to six in most families).

3. He is expected to sit still in school and learn to read and do numbers (beginning elementary school).

4. By his own age group he is expected to prove that he is male and is independent of the grownups (6 to 12).

5. The girls expect him to learn to dance and look nice and drive a car (early adolescence).

6. The school expects him to throw all his energy into winning for the ________ High School. His parents expect him to get the best marks.

7. He is expected to find a job, either to support himself or to contribute to the expenses of college or vocational school in order to prepare for a job later.

8. He is expected by his bride to love her day and night, and by the world to concentrate his energy on "making good."

This brief list is intended not to be inclusive, but merely to suggest the varieties of demands imposed upon the growing young person by a society which progressively asks him to be the center of attention, to get out of the way, to accept absolute authority, to sacrifice himself for the larger group, to be self-sustaining and independent, to love passionately and to achieve financial success.[19]

INTANGIBLE SOCIAL FORCES

As you can readily see, the ways of your society are not always tangible things which you can see or hear or smell or taste or sense through any other modality. Many of the correct ways are so intangible that we see comparatively few material bits of evidence that they exist. As an example, we are constantly controlled by forces of "law and order." Yet how many tangible evidences of law and order do you see during the week? Occasionally you see a big man in a blue uniform with brass buttons and a shiny shield who, as a police officer, is a visible symbol of law and order. You may occasionally drive by an imposing marble edifice labeled "Courthouse." Aside from such instances, most of us have little physical contact with "the law," and yet most of us are law-abiding citizens. Again, most of us are controlled very much by religious and ethical principles. Yet how many tangible signs of religion do we see about us every day? Aside from seeing an occasional individual dressed in clerical garb or a building called a church or synagogue, how much tangible evidence is there of religious forces?

So many of our social ways are not written down or even talked about that we may fail to recognize them as social forces. Yet, as the Lynds point out, "A Middletown citizen does not operate a factory, build a home, drive his car, or even take a drink of water or empty his garbage without both depending upon and being limited by these group regulations."[20] We may not realize that some of our social ways are affecting us until we stop to think about them. Consider the following incident of a few years ago:

> A crowded 4:30 bus was on its regular route between Washington, D. C., and Alexandria, Virginia—a route which becomes "Southern" once the Potomac River is crossed in that the Jim Crow law takes effect. At one stop on the Washington side of the river a light-complected, well-dressed, young Negro woman got on, holding the hand of a dark-skinned tot. She inquired about the fare and then took her place in the second seat from the front! Slowly people glanced at her, and then at the other Negroes occupying the rear seats. At the next stop the remaining seats were occupied and people were standing in the aisle. Slowly people glanced at the Negro woman, and then significantly at the other Negroes occupying the rear seats. Those who were standing glared at her.
>
> Across the Fourteenth Street Bridge went the bus. Conversation by then had lagged. What was said went on in undertones. One woman remarked to the man sitting next to her, "Why doesn't that driver do something? We're almost across the bridge." A man turned to someone who was evidently unknown to him before and said, "Hmmm. That darky certainly isn't from around these parts."
>
> Just then the bus halted—on the Virginia side. A man was earnestly talking to the operator, who was peering into the mirror trying to see behind him. With the entire bus so quiet, you could have heard a pin drop. The driver left his place, walked back to the woman and said, "I'm sorry, but the Virginia law requires that you ride in the back of the bus."

It is only when there is a flagrant violation of our accepted "ways" that we are likely to become excited about them.

EASY DISINTEGRATION OF OUR SOCIAL "WAYS"

It is largely because many of the forces which control us are so intangible that our social "ways" sometimes disintegrate quickly. After building up certain patterns of behavior over literally centuries of time, they may "slough off" completely in a great crisis. Look at the behavior of men in war. Bill Mauldin of World War II fame wrote:

> Some say the American soldier is the same clean-cut young man who left his home; others say morale is sky-high at the front because everybody's face is shining for the great Cause.
>
> They are wrong. The combat man isn't the same clean-cut lad because you don't fight a kraut by Marquis of Queensberry rules. You shoot him in the back, you blow him apart with mines, you kill or maim him the quickest and most effective way you can with the least danger to yourself. He does the same to you. He tricks you and cheats you, and if you don't beat him at his own game you don't live to appreciate your own nobleness.[21]

What we call civilization is a fairly thin veneer over the underlying biological animal. Look at any crisis and you see signs of how completely primitive we "civilized" people really are. In a certain lecture hall where a motion picture was being shown, the film suddenly caught fire. Immediately a group of supposed "intelligentsia" was transformed from civilized human beings into a group of stampeding animals. Have you ever been present in a city when a convention of some national fraternal organization was being held? Then you may have witnessed how superficial are our concepts of correct behavior when the social sanctions of the home town are removed. Or consider the effects of the news of the end of the war in Europe in 1945:

> Victory in Europe hit Halifax like a blitz. For two hysterical days, servicemen and civilians looted, burned, wrecked and smashed heads. They gutted Halifax's shopping section, destroying or stealing property valued up to $5,000,000. When order was restored, as the result of exhaustion rather than authority, two men were dead; hospitals and jails were crammed. . . .
>
> By early afternoon of V-E day a bacchic rout of men, women and even children reeled down Barrington, Hollis and Granville Streets smashing . . . windows and sacking . . . stores. Said one elderly woman: "I never had so much fun in my life."
>
> The 80-man police force was powerless. Wearing stolen fur coats and clutching pilfered dresses and shoes under their arms, drunken girls were convoyed by drunken sailors. Three sailors went through the broken window of a furniture store and climbed into bed. Typewriters were gaily smashed. One sailor kicked in a window, sheared off his toes. Another severed an artery while punching through the window of a brewery. Fires swept through a women's-wear shop, a drugstore, a jewelry shop. Firehose was uncoupled or cut as soon as it was laid.[22]

OBJECTIONS TO SOME WAYS

It is little wonder that various patterns of behavior do disintegrate so readily when you think how much you object to some of them. You feel obliged to act in certain traditional ways, but may inwardly object to doing so. College students have been asked to make lists anonymously of the social ways—especially taboos—of their particular groups which they have to follow but which they think are pointless or should be abolished. College women have listed such diversified things as: not asking men for dates, keeping your maiden name when married, not going "stag" to dances, not being able to ask a man to dance, being ostracized for the amount of inebriation considered "manly" in a man, not smoking on the street, not being able to speak to a member of the opposite sex without a "proper" introduction, not eating fried chicken by using the fingers, not being able to use "strong" language to express real feelings, not eating in public without a hat, being considered "unwomanly" for excelling in mathematics, not being able to run because it isn't "ladylike." College men have objected to the following: not speaking in a classroom without first raising your hand and obtaining recognition, not being able to share expenses with your "date," not being allowed to "dunk" in public, not being permitted to remove your coat in hot weather, not being able to ride to classes on a bicycle, not entering an automobile or house before a lady, not being able to remain seated on a crowded bus when a lady is standing (no matter how tired you are).

A DILEMMA

Students of social psychology are faced with a dilemma. The dilemma is this: If we accept the culture patterns of our society and follow them ourselves, particularly if we engage in all the "ways" of our group, we may be so caught up in these ways that we cannot stand aside and examine them objectively. On the other hand, if we attempt to stand to one side and not follow the ways of behaving of our particular group, we may not only become estranged from other members of our group and be considered peculiar people, but because of nonparticipation we may fail to understand what these ways are like and how they really function.[23]

QUESTIONS AND PROBLEMS FOR DISCUSSION

1. *What are some of your own culture patterns?*
2. *How stable are the culture patterns of your community?*
3. *In return for the means and right to live, in what ways does society demand that you adjust to other people?*
4. *To what extent is it true that human nature is simply a reaction to the restraints put upon us by our civilization?*

5. *Why are legal codes never quite in harmony with current practices in the community?*
6. *How many different explanations can you give of "cultural lag"?*
7. *Why is nonmaterial cultural lag greater than material cultural lag?*
8. *What are some of the causes of regionalism?*

RECOMMENDED READINGS

Beard, C. A., and Beard, M. R., *The Rise of American Civilization* (revised edition). New York: The Macmillan Company, 1933.

Boas, F., *Anthropology and Modern Life* (revised edition). New York: W. W. Norton & Company, 1932.

Boas, F., *The Mind of Primitive Man* (revised edition). New York: The Macmillan Company, 1938.

Chapin, F. S., *Cultural Change.* New York: Century Company, 1928.

Frazer, J. G., *The Golden Bough: A Study in Magic and Religion* (one volume, abridged edition). New York: The Macmillan Company, 1940.

Goldenweiser, A., *History, Psychology, and Culture.* New York: Alfred A. Knopf, Inc., 1933.

Kluckhohn, C., and Murray, H. A. (editors), *Personality in Nature, Society, and Culture.* New York: Alfred A. Knopf, Inc., 1948.

Linton, R., *The Cultural Background of Personality.* New York: D. Appleton-Century Company, 1945.

Merz, C., *The Great American Band Wagon.* New York: The John Day Company, 1928.

Odum, H. W., and Moore, H. E., *American Regionalism: A Cultural, Historical Approach to National Integration.* New York: Henry Holt and Company, Inc., 1938.

Ogburn, W. F., *Social Change with Respect to Culture and Original Nature.* New York: B. W. Huebsch, 1922.

Schlesinger, A. M., *Learning How to Behave.* New York: The Macmillan Company, 1946.

Sherif, M., *The Psychology of Social Norms.* New York: Harper & Brothers, 1936.

Sumner, W. G., *Folkways.* Boston: Ginn and Company, 1906 (also reprinted, 1940).

Thorndike, E. L., *Your City.* New York: Harcourt, Brace and Company, 1939.

Warner, W. L., and Lunt, P. S., *The Social Life of a Modern Community.* New Haven: Yale University Press, 1941.

Webster, H., *Taboo: A Sociological Study.* Stanford University, California: Stanford University Press, 1942.

West, J., *Plainville, U. S. A.* New York: Columbia University Press, 1945.

Wissler, C., *Man and Culture.* New York: The Thomas Y. Crowell Company, 1923.

*Newcomb, T. M., Hartley, E. L., and others (editors), *Readings in Social Psychology.* New York: Henry Holt and Company, Inc., 1947:—Linton, R., and Kardiner, A., "The Change from Dry to Wet Rice Cultivation in Tanala-Betsileo," pp. 46–55.

PART THREE

SOME INDIVIDUAL FACTORS OF SOCIAL ADJUSTMENT

Part III deals with the development of various individual factors of social adjustment.

First of all, the question of instincts is discussed, in order to show that social attitudes and behavior cannot be explained by this term. The conditioned response is then reviewed, not simply in the Pavlovian sense, but in the terms of its social implications. Case histories are introduced to illustrate some of the important mechanisms. Problems of motivation are also analyzed.

The next chapter discusses behavior, traits, and attitudes. After an explanation of covert and overt behavior, traits and attitudes are described and contrasted. Empirical studies of attitudes are then reviewed, especially the effects of covert attitudes on overt behavior, and of overt behavior on covert attitudes. The relations between desires and beliefs are analyzed. The measurement of social attitudes, together with some of the difficulties involved, is then briefly explained.

The social psychology of language is next discussed in some detail. The development of language is analyzed, and this leads to a consideration of vocal, graphic, and gesture language. Examples are used throughout. The social significance of language is then described with particular reference to the problem of meaning.

The final chapter of the section deals with man's irrational thinking and beliefs. Autistic thinking is described in detail and is contrasted with realistic thinking. This leads to a consideration of the origin and characteristics of myths and legends, with examples. The normality and abnormality of various types of behavior are analyzed.

CHAPTER SIX

UNLEARNED AND LEARNED BEHAVIOR

UNLEARNED BEHAVIOR—INSTINCTS. Dangers of Oversimplification—Lack of Agreement on List of Instincts—Use of "Instinct" by Laymen—Irrational Aspects of Behavior—Two Contrasting Views—(1) Hormic View—(2) Mechanistic View—Unlearned or Hereditary Basis of Instincts—No Fighting Instinct—No Instinct of Motherly Love—Universality of Instincts—Similarity to Reflexes—Rarity of Instincts—Instincts and Habits / LEARNED BEHAVIOR—THE CONDITIONED RESPONSE. Acquired-Behavior Patterns—The Mechanism of the Conditioned Response—Original and Conditioned Stimuli—Second-Order Conditioning—The Pavlovian Dog—Tonal Sensitivity in the White Rat—Watson's Experiment with Infants—Other Experiments with Infants—Case Histories Involving Conditioning—Constant Process of Conditioning in Everyday Life—Four Aspects of Conditioning—(1) Generalization—(2) Differentiation—(3) Traumatic Experience—(4) Ready-made Acceptance of "Ways"—All Four Mechanisms—Practical Value of Conditioning / THE PROBLEM OF MOTIVATION. Overlapping of Unlearned and Learned Behavior—Difficulties of Classifying Motives—Activity Itself as a Source of Activity—Thomas's Four Wishes—Freud and Psychoanalysis—Effects of Freud's Work—Objections to Concept of "The Unconscious"—Uniqueness of Every Social Situation.

▶ UNLEARNED BEHAVIOR—INSTINCTS

DANGERS OF OVERSIMPLIFICATION

Why do men go to war? Behold the answer, "an instinct of pugnacity." Why do men get married? Another simple answer, "the sex instinct." Why do men go to church? "The religious instinct." But are these really answers to such intricate social-psychological questions? Decidedly not. Do people even mean the same thing when they use the word "instinct"? Let us examine briefly both the history of the word as used by psychologists, and the use of the word by laymen when they talk about actions being "instinctive."

LACK OF AGREEMENT ON LIST OF INSTINCTS

Many philosophers, and more recently some psychologists and sociologists, have written rather elaborately on some particular set of "drives" which they felt were the keys which would unlock all the problems of human behavior. If you examine Adam Smith's *Wealth of Nations,* you will find that he based most of his "psychologizing" upon a supposed instinct of sympathy.[1] He seemed to think that if you could understand the sympathetic bases of human action, then you had an explanation of various economic problems. Trotter, an English sociologist, talked a great deal about the "herd instinct," as well as the supposed instincts of imitation and gregariousness.[2] Freud is well known for his discussion of the sex instinct; he also stressed in many of his writings the supposed instinct of self-preservation.

In the history of modern psychology, beginning with William James, there has been little agreement among psychologists as to what was meant by an instinct.[3] James made a list of 32 different instincts, including an "instinct of liking sugar." Warren included "clothing," "resenting," and "domineering" in his list of 26 instincts; E. L. Thorndike at one time listed about 40; according to L. L. Bernard, Woodworth once proposed as many as 110.[4] Now, when there are lists of 1, 2, 40, or 110 different instincts made up by people interested in human behavior, it looks as though something were surely amiss. Could the instincts be nothing more than hypotheses?[5]

The state of affairs was so bad that Bernard finally made an analysis of 5,684 different instances where the word "instinct" is used, and then classified these under the twenty-three headings shown in Table 3. You will observe that "sex" is listed a greater number of times than any other supposed instinct, with the "self-assertive" instinct in second place, and then in order, "gregarious or social," "family," "fear and flight," "economic," "workmanship," "intellectual," and so forth. Bernard and others have been convinced that many of these words were bandied about without any precise meaning.

TABLE 3

Analysis of 5,684 "Instincts" (from L. L. Bernard)[6]

Types	*No. of Cases*	*Types*	*No. of Cases*
Altruistic	119	Migratory and climatic	64
Antisocial	185	Play	168
Disgust or repulsion	74	Recessive and repose	36
Economic	281	Religious	83
Aesthetic	152	Retaliative	96
Ethical	48	Self-abasement	139
Family	413	Self-assertive	806
Fear and flight	287	Self-display	107
Food	228	Sex	853
Gregarious or social	697	Workmanship	266
Imitative	91	Miscellaneous	229
Intellectual	262		

USE OF "INSTINCT" BY LAYMEN

The views of a layman—the so-called "man in the street"—are of interest along with the views of psychologists. When someone has pulled the trigger of a revolver in a fit of rage he sometimes gives as an excuse, "I had a sudden *instinct* to pull the trigger." *Time* magazine reports that a baseball umpire "instinctively pulled a knife."[7] If you have ever seen a traffic accident you may have heard the driver of an automobile remark, "I *instinctively* put on the brake." It has been said that "man has a natural *instinct* of reason." One writer said of Theodore Roosevelt that he "was the born leader with an innate instinct of command."[8] Have you ever heard of the "instinct" of Turks to kill Christians, or of businessmen's "instinct" for organization?

Actually, when laymen are talking this way, what they probably mean is *automatic* or *unpremeditated* or *impulsive* behavior. When someone says that he instinctively pulled the trigger or instinctively put on the brake or instinctively did anything else, all he is saying is that he automatically or without premeditation or impulsively carried out the act. Are we in any better position to understand his behavior, then, than we were at the beginning?

IRRATIONAL ASPECTS OF BEHAVIOR

In order to answer this question satisfactorily, it may be well to leave our "man in the street" with his terminology of unpremeditated and impulsive behavior, and instead see if there is any solution to the apparently confused notions of psychologists and sociologists of the meaning of the term. Much of the confusion arose at the time when earlier psychologists and sociologists were beginning to realize that man is not altogether a rational animal. Men have always flattered themselves by thinking that their actions were deliberate, rational, and self-conscious until students of human behavior began to think that many of men's actions are not based upon reason at all, but are founded instead upon emotional urges and inner "drives." It was further realized that many of these urges and drives are not consciously recognized, even when a man deals with a rational problem. Psychologists saw that when a man "makes up his mind" to pursue a certain course, this action may be based only partially upon his thinking prior to the action, that the actual roots of his behavior may lie in activities engaged in a long time before. They also saw many instances of automatic behavior based on the autonomic nervous system.

TWO CONTRASTING VIEWS

Most of the divergent views of what is meant by instinct can be boiled down to (1) the *hormic,* and (2) the *mechanistic* views.

1. *Hormic View.* The hormic view refers to a "drive" theory of behavior. It suggests that man's behavior is purposive in character, that there is an ultimate purpose for his every act, and that this purpose is for the benefit of the organism. Philosophers would call this a *teleological* point of view. In fact, it is largely because of its teleological implications that it is contrasted with the second view, namely, the mechanistic. The mechanistic theory may be called "reflexive." According to this concept the purposive aspects of instinctive life are completely scouted; instead, attention is directed to the most primitive units of action, those bits of behavior called *reflexes,* or very closely allied with the reflexes.

The hormic or purposive view of instincts is well represented by the writings of the late William McDougall. In his *Introduction to Social Psychology* he listed twelve instincts, seven primary and five secondary.[9] In his *Outline of Psychology* he listed thirteen major and seven minor instincts, although his list varied from one edition of that book to another.[10] The list given in Table 4 is, however, fairly representative of the instincts which he insisted were found in all mankind. With each major instinct was coupled a so-called "primary emotion."

TABLE 4

McDougall's List of Major Instincts and Primary Emotions

Major Instinct	*Primary Emotion*
Parental or protective	Tender emotion
Combat	Anger
Curiosity	Curiosity
Food-seeking or hunting	Appetite (for food)
Repulsion	Disgust
Escape	Fear
Gregarious	Loneliness (not comradeship)
Self-assertion	Elation, or positive self-feeling
Submission	Subjection, or negative self-feeling
Mating or pairing	Lust
Acquisitive	Ownership
Constructive	Creativeness
Appeal	Feeling of helplessness

Of these alleged major instincts, McDougall believed that the food-seeking or hunting instinct was the strongest, and escape the second strongest drive. If you ask, "But how did McDougall know?" the only answer is that he did not, that he was actually an armchair philosopher as to instincts; and the same was true of many other writers who composed such lists. Although he made occasional references to empirical studies, McDougall's lists were based largely upon his own private views of human behavior. With each of his major instincts he linked a primary emotion. Thus, the parental or protective instinct was supposed to result in the "tender emotion," the instinct of combat was supposed to produce the emotion of anger, the instinct of curiosity the emotion of curiosity, and so on.

Not being content with a list of primary emotions, McDougall suggested that various "secondary" emotions were also of the utmost importance. These secondary emotions were said to consist of combinations of the primary emotions. Thus, the so-called secondary emotion of scorn was believed to consist of anger and of disgust, which were, in turn, based upon the "instincts" of combat and repulsion respectively. The secondary emotion of hate was based upon the primary emotions of anger + fear. Admiration was a combination of wonder + negative self-feeling; awe was a mixture of wonder + negative self-feeling + fear. One of the most complex was the secondary emotion of reverence; this was made up of wonder + negative self-feeling + fear + gratitude. In case you wonder where "gratitude" came from, it in turn was another secondary emotion, consisting of tender emotion + negative self-feeling.

This kind of analysis had far-reaching implications in the educational world of the early 1900's. Rather than scoffing at such an artificial listing, many educators were tremendously impressed. At last, here was a complete listing which looked scientifically sound and on which educational theories could be based. It seemed obvious, for instance, that if you wanted to motivate a child to learn, you simply paid attention to his primary emotion of curiosity and so tried to appeal to his instinct of curiosity. If you wished to build up a sense of personal values, you worked through the primary emotion of ownership, based on the child's acquisitive instinct. This sort of theorizing continued in vogue for many years. The whole concept of "instinct" became so misused that Bernard devoted an entire book to debunking it.[11] Even before Bernard's analysis, however, many sociologists and psychologists realized that such a classification of instincts and emotions was artificial and based not upon true empirical scientific analysis but simply upon logical constructs.

2. *Mechanistic View.* Bernard objected particularly to a teleological view of man's behavior, and suggested a more mechanistic interpretation. Why should we believe that man's complex behavior can be reduced to a simple instinct, or combination of instincts? How can war and fighting be explained simply on the basis of an instinct of combat? How can the psychology of marriage be dealt with by saying that marriages are entered into simply because of a sex instinct? Instead of such easy "explanations," we should examine more carefully our behavior patterns, particularly reflexes, random movements, tropisms, and habits. Although an exact definition of instinct might be subject to criticism, Bernard offered the following: "A specific response to a specific stimulus, the neural pattern

mediating the response being inherited."[12] This means mainly that an instinct is not to be looked upon as something mystical in character, but rather is to be considered in its physiological aspects, closely related to reflex behavior.

UNLEARNED OR HEREDITARY BASIS OF INSTINCTS

All social psychologists today agree that all instincts, by definition, are inherited. The hereditary or unlearned basis of instincts is, in fact, implied whenever the term is used. It should be obvious that it is physiologically impossible to inherit an instinct to fight or to escape or to construct things or to acquire things; in each case the *specific* behavior involved is learned. If we are to find any hereditary mechanisms, we must examine more carefully the processes connected with fertilization and birth.

Thus such terms as fighting, gregariousness, self-assertion, self-abasement, acquisition, play, imitation, and the like, are not single and definite behavior patterns. They are class terms for hundreds and thousands of concrete behavior mechanisms which are grouped together in action or in conceptual thinking because of their general similarity of function. There are almost numberless ways of fighting, playing, imitating, or of having gregarious contacts with one's fellows. Each one of these may be a unit behavior pattern and therefore entitled to be called an instinct, if it is inherited. But the whole list of activities having a common conceptual or classificatory name never occur in action together, that is, they never function as a unit behavior process as would be necessary if they were true instincts. They occur in consciousness only by a short-cut process of symbolic integration and condensation.[13]

NO FIGHTING INSTINCT

Suppose that there really were an instinct called "combat" or "fighting." In how many different ways can one fight? The answer is—with his hands, his feet, vocally, wrestling, and so forth. Suppose that we break down any one of these ways of behavior (see Figure 5). In how many ways can one employ his hands? He may use his fists, he may slap, he may pinch, he (or she) may scratch, he may use implements or weapons, and so on. Suppose we break down this last classification. What different sorts of implements or weapons can one use? He may use clubs, sticks, rocks, knives, guns, and many other weapons. Each of these may also be broken down further. Shotguns are double-barreled, single-barreled, sawed-off, double-barreled with one barrel choke and the other scatter, and so forth. Now, consider the remote possibilities of inheriting an instinct to fight in each of these different ways. No one could possibly inherit in his neurological make-up patterns of behavior which would enable him to have a "fighting" instinct to do all of these complex and intricate things.

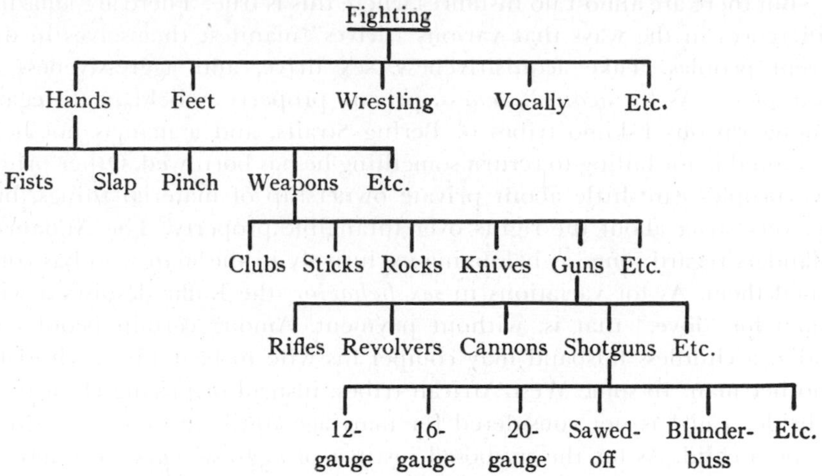

FIG. 5. A FEW OF THE POSSIBLE WAYS OF FIGHTING

NO INSTINCT OF MOTHERLY LOVE

As another example, what about maternal love? Is this instinctive? Remember that many mothers have to learn how to carry on various maternal functions.

There is no one activity or set of activities which the instinctivists have in mind when they speak of this "instinct." In different situations and on various occasions the imputed content of this so-called instinct may vary as widely as affection for the child, nursing it, spanking it to make it behave, caressing it, taking it to a baby clinic, getting it off to school, starting it in a profession and thousands of other things. Of all the possible activities and attitudes which the mother may manifest toward the child only a few are really inherited, and these are among the simplest of the whole number. They may possibly be represented by such acts as pressing the child to the breast, yielding it milk when it nurses, responding to its presence in the arms by clasping or pressure, and possibly kissing and emotional and mental disturbance when it cries or laughs.[14]

UNIVERSALITY OF INSTINCTS

This discussion of instincts is not intended simply to show the chaos and confusion which previously existed. Neither is it presented simply to contrast the hormic and mechanistic points of view. Instead, we wish to emphasize that there is a great deal of agreement at the present time as to what is meant by the word "instinct," and that most social psychologists are extremely careful not to use the term loosely. Certainly social psychologists would agree not only that instincts are hereditary—or unlearned—but also that instincts are universal; that is, when they exist at all in a member of the species they are to be found in all members of that species.

But there are almost no instances where this is true. There are amazing differences in the ways that various "drives" manifest themselves in different peoples. Take acquisitiveness, sex drive, and aggressiveness as examples.[15] As for *acquisitiveness,* private property is held in disregard among various Eskimo tribes of Bering Straits, and a man is not held accountable for failing to return something he has borrowed. Other primitive peoples care little about private ownership of material things, but are very strict about the rights over intangible property. The Andaman Islanders regard songs as belonging exclusively to the man who has composed them. As for variations in *sex behavior,* the Kaffir despises a wife taken for "love," that is, without payment. Among certain peoples of India, a childless husband may compel his wife to bear him a child by another man. In some West African tribes, instead of prizing chastity in a bride, a girl is not considered for marriage until she has successfully borne a child. As for the supposed instinct of *aggressiveness,* Eskimos of Baffinland had never engaged in warfare and could not be made to understand the meaning of battle, as contrasted with the Plains Indians who made war the center of their entire social organization.

"To describe a race or a people as innately [or instinctively] aggressive or peaceable, sedentary or nomadic, promiscuous or puritanical, overlooks the fact that culture may be entirely responsible."[16] Activities that are ordinarily spoken of so loosely as "instinctive" are usually those types of behavior which are fairly typical of our society. We mistakenly think that behavior which is fairly universal in our culture is "instinctive."

SIMILARITY TO REFLEXES

Instincts are very closely related to reflexes, so much so, in fact, that it is a matter of academic argument as to which behavior patterns may be called reflexes, and which instincts. This is quite analogous to a situation which exists in biology. We are able to say definitely that certain organisms are animals, that others are plants. At some stage in between, however, there is a point where it is extremely difficult to tell which organisms belong to the animal kingdom and which to the plant kingdom, because the organisms partake of the functions of both. In much the same way it may be difficult to say definitely which bits of behavior are instinctive and which reflexive.

RARITY OF INSTINCTS

There are probably a number of instincts at birth which are structurally determined but which have relatively less importance as one grows older. At birth, also, there are practically no habitual ways of behaving; but, owing to the individual acquisition of habit patterns, various habits become more and more important and supplant the instinctive behavior. A great deal of the instinct debate has been due to a failure to define terms. Like so many arguments the discussions have centered around the interpretation of words. If we limit the meaning of the word "instinct" to a way of acting which is ready to function the very first time an adequate stimulus is presented and without any learning, then we can say that this is very rare. There are some basic physiological activities, of course, which do seem to be of an instinctive sort; that is, they are hereditary or unlearned, universal, and reflexive in character. Obvious examples are such physiological processes as breathing, digestion, circulation of the blood, excretion, and other vegetative processes of the organism.[17] This is not an attempt to make up one more list of instincts and to say that these are the instincts which will solve all problems and explain every question of social psychology. On the contrary, these are *possible* instincts, and you may argue that they are nothing more or less than reflexes.

INSTINCTS AND HABITS

When a social scientist proposes an effective method for dealing with a social problem, a method which might destroy some "sacred cow" then in existence, he is likely to be rebuffed with the statement: "But you cannot change the basic human instincts. You can't change human nature." But what is this human nature that supposedly cannot be changed? If human nature is *only* the sum total of our instincts, and if our instincts are unlearned, hereditary reactions, then it could be concluded that human nature cannot be changed. However, if human nature also includes all those characteristics that we find in our Anglo-Saxon civilization, then obviously human nature can be changed.

The essential point of this discussion of instincts is twofold. First, it is important to realize that an explanation of behavior simply on an instinctive basis may either be untrue or at best only a half truth. The idea that men go to war because of a fighting instinct, or that men attend church because of a supposed religious instinct has never been proved. Second, *habits* largely supplant the instincts and the independent and isolated reflexes in man. Modern culture is built primarily, if not entirely, out of *acquired* behavior patterns. Our civilization in particular may be referred to as a complex of acquired characteristics. One of the principal methods of acquiring habits will be dealt with in the section that follows. However, first consider the social significance of *habit* as described by William James:

> Habit is . . . the enormous fly-wheel of society, its most precious conservative agent. . . . It . . . prevents the hardest . . . walks of life from being deserted by those brought up to tread therein. It keeps the fisherman and the deck-hand at sea through the winter; it holds the miner in his darkness, and nails the countryman to his log-cabin and his lonely farm through all the months of snow. . . . It dooms us all to fight out the battle of life upon the lines of our

nurture or our early choice, and to make the best of a pursuit that disagrees. . . . It keeps different social strata from mixing. Already at the age of twenty-five you see the professional mannerism settling down on the young commercial traveller, on the young doctor, on the young minister, on the young counsellor-at-law. You see the little lines of cleavage running through the character, the tricks of thought, the prejudices, the ways of the 'shop,' in a word, from which the man can by-and-by no more escape than his coat-sleeve can suddenly fall into a new set of folds.[18]

LEARNED BEHAVIOR —THE CONDITIONED RESPONSE

ACQUIRED-BEHAVIOR PATTERNS

We have seen that instincts are unlearned. They do not depend upon learning activity but are inherited. Accordingly, it seems undesirable to make up any exact list of instincts or to insist that one list is an all-inclusive one which will cover all forms of unlearned behavior. Actually there are comparatively few instincts, as compared with the tremendous number of habit patterns that are *learned.* Our concern is not to delimit the nature of instincts precisely but instead to be on guard against explaining human behavior by simply pinning the label "instinctive" on it. The creature called Homo sapiens is actually one of the most helpless of animal organisms at birth; he has so few instincts that he must be aided for months and even years following birth before he is able to look after himself. But from birth on, his personality is constantly being affected by experiences. New patterns of behavior are acquired which determine whether he will tend to be social or antisocial, self-assertive or retiring, and how he will behave in a variety of situations.

THE MECHANISM OF THE CONDITIONED RESPONSE

As we have previously seen, these acquired-behavior patterns may be principally *cultural* in nature, that is, patterns which are acquired because they are "correct" for the group in which the individual is born; or they may be primarily *biological,* that is, they may have an essential physiological basis. But regardless of whether these behavior patterns are mainly cultural or biological in their foundation, apparently they are acquired through the mechanism of trial-and-error learning, or by means of the conditioned response. And in learning by trial and error or by conditioning there is *integration* of the new responses.

Actually the conditioned response seems to be so basic that it is desirable to review this concept—with which you may already be familiar—and then to furnish several concrete examples. But note that *the following description of the conditioned response is purposely oversimplified.* Experimental work takes account of motivation reduction and other factors not treated here.[19] *Reward values and satisfaction* are not always explicitly discussed in the description below, although they are certainly implied. The essential point is simply to give you a basis for understanding the conditioning of attitudes.

ORIGINAL AND CONDITIONED STIMULI

In psychological experiments the terms "unconditioned" stimulus and "conditioned" stimulus are employed. The term *unconditioned* stimulus —or as we shall call it, the *original* stimulus—means the natural stimulus,

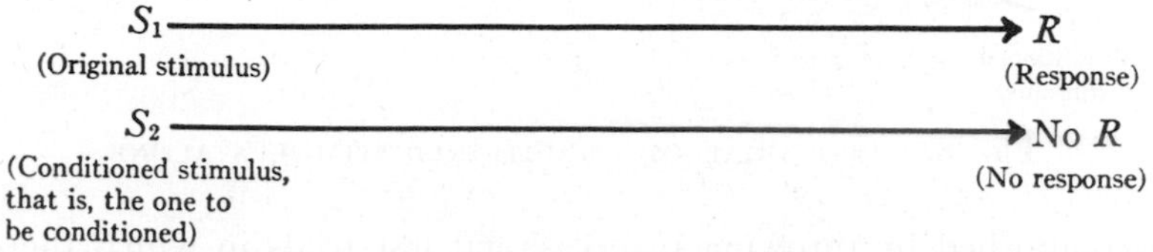

FIG. 6. THE ORIGINAL AND CONDITIONED STIMULUS

the one which ordinarily evokes a particular response. The *conditioned* stimulus is some other stimulus which ordinarily does not result in this response but which, after conditioning, will call out the same response as the original stimulus. See Figure 6.

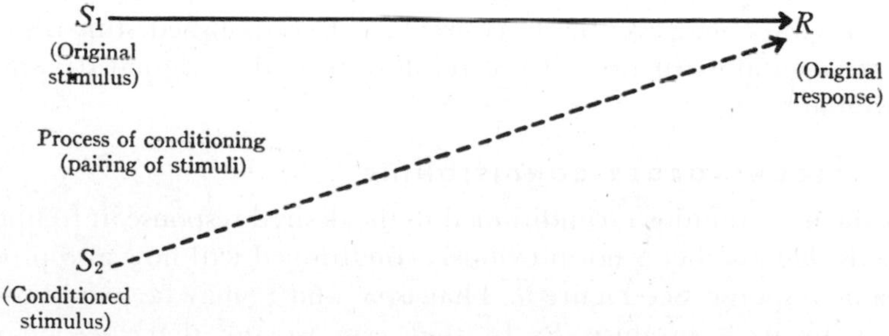

FIG. 7. REPETITION OF ORIGINAL STIMULUS AND CONDITIONED STIMULUS PRESENTED TOGETHER

How is this done? There is nothing mystical about the conditioning process, nor is it anything new and startling. As a matter of fact, Aristotle referred to the concept of conditioning over two thousand years ago when he spoke of "association of ideas." In laboratory experiments the usual process in conditioning is to present the original and the conditioned stimulus together a sufficient number of times so that the conditioned stimulus will come to evoke the response, whereas previously it had never evoked this particular response. This usually means the presentation together of the original stimulus and of the conditioned stimulus a large number of times until the reward values are sufficient for the experimental animal so that the original stimulus can be dropped out of the picture completely. The eventual result is shown in Figures 7 and 8. This

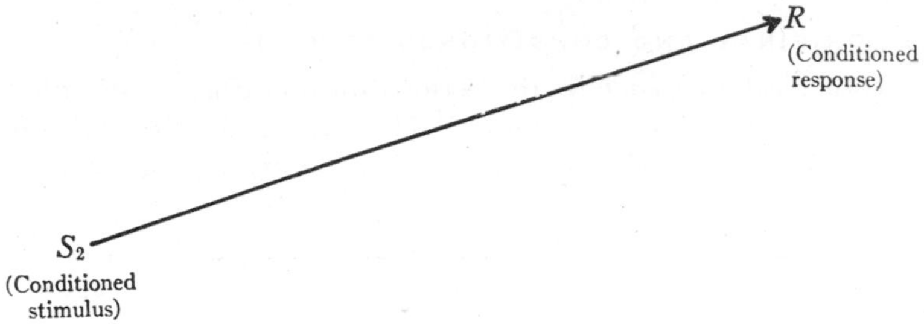

FIG. 8. TEST TRIAL OF CONDITIONED STIMULUS ALONE

is accomplished by throwing in occasional test trials in which the conditioned stimulus appears by itself, until the conditioned stimulus alone finally evokes the desired response. Following a test trial the original stimulus and conditioned stimulus are presented together again and again until another test trial is given. After many repetitions of this sort the conditioned stimulus produces the desired response (*R*), and we now say that a conditioned response has been established. That is, the stimulus to be conditioned is now associated with the desired response. The conditioned response may eventually be weakened or abolished—this is known as experimental extinction—if not reinforced by the original stimulus or one similar to it.

SECOND-ORDER CONDITIONING

After the new stimulus is conditioned to the desired response, it frequently happens that another *S* not previously conditioned will now also produce the same response. See Figure 9. That is, S_2 and S_3 may be paired so that S_3 may by itself produce *R*. In that case we say that "second-order conditioning" has taken place. Second-order conditioning is one of the fundamental bases of the integration of conditioned responses.

THE PAVLOVIAN DOG

Such is an extremely simplified account of conditioning. Take the old example of Pavlov and his salivating dogs.[20] When the original stimulus (meat) was presented, the experimental dog would respond by salivating. This is, of course, the natural response of the dog to this stimulus. On the other hand, the sound of a bell (conditioned stimulus) did not evoke *R* (salivation) in this dog. The problem, therefore, was to condition salivation to the sound of the bell. The process was that outlined above (compare Figures 7 and 8). S_1 (meat) and S_2 (bell) were presented together over and over again until S_2 was sufficient to cause the dog to drip saliva.

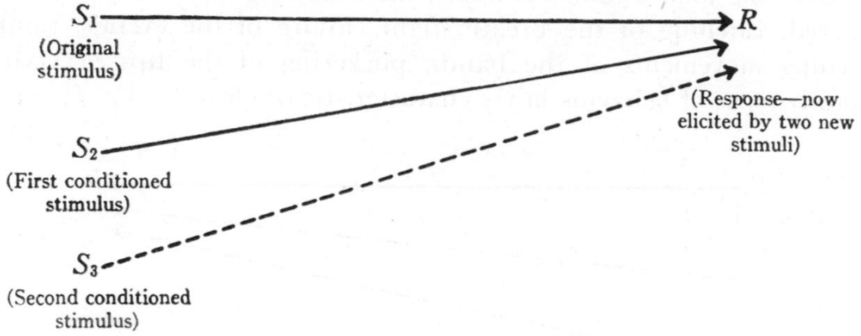

FIG. 9. SECOND-ORDER CONDITIONING

Pavlov also found that second-order conditioning could occur; thus, a differently toned bell (S_3) might also cause the dog to drip saliva. Compare Figure 9. Either of the two stimuli was now sufficient to produce the desired response.

TONAL SENSITIVITY IN THE WHITE RAT

Here is another laboratory example of conditioning. One investigator was interested in the problem of whether white rats can hear pure tones.[21] The original stimulus (S_1) was an electric shock applied to the rat's tail producing—as you might guess—a very decided change in breathing (R). The stimulus to be conditioned (S_2) was a tone of 480 double vibrations per second. After many repetitions of presenting S_1 and S_2 together, S_2 eventually came to produce R—a change in breathing—by itself. Following this, a tone of 2,048 double vibrations per second also brought out a change in the breathing response, but was later discriminated from the first tone.

WATSON'S EXPERIMENT WITH INFANTS

You may ask, "What does the salivating of dogs or the breathing in rats have to do with me?" These examples have been given simply to illustrate the mechanism of the conditioned response. Perhaps the work of Watson with human infants is of greater interest to you. In a famous Watsonian experiment, a loud noise was produced by striking a metal bar with a hammer directly back of an infant's ear.[22] Whenever this was done Watson observed a "fear" response. We cannot say unqualifiedly that this was fear, because an infant a few months old cannot introspect in words and say, "I am now experiencing a sensation of fear." In fact, Watson probably was including under the label *fear* a startle pattern, together with a mass of undifferentiated responses such as withdrawal and crying. In observing the external behavior of the baby, he found that whenever the loud sound was made, the following bits of behavior were observed: catching of the breath, tight closure of the eyelids, random clutching movements of the hands, puckering of the lips or crying—certainly types of behavior fairly characteristic of "fear."

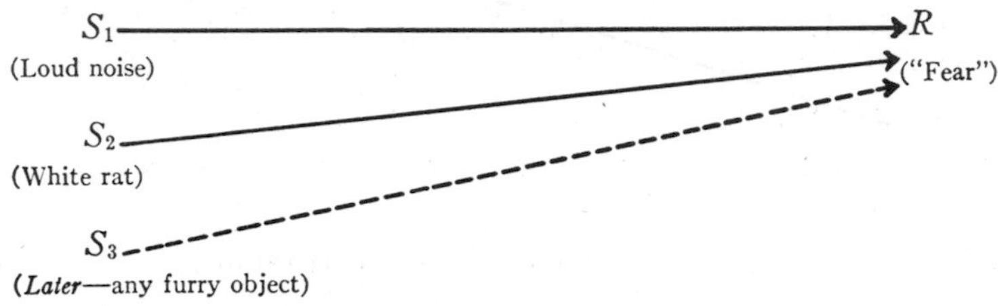

FIG. 10. THE ESTABLISHMENT OF THE "FEAR" RESPONSE TO ANY FURRY OBJECT

Watson was interested not only in building up conditioned responses in infants but also in the related problem of second-order conditioning. Thus he established the conditioned response of "fear" to what had previously been a completely innocuous stimulus, namely, a white rat. Figure 10 illustrates the mechanism. S_1 (loud noise) was the natural stimulus which resulted in the response ("fear"). Preliminary tests had indicated that S_2 (white rat) had never called forth anything similar to a fear response. In fact, the child (Albert) was used to playing with a white rat, and his normal response was petting and stroking the animal.

Watson gave Albert the white rat to play with and at the same time made a loud noise with the bar and hammer. It took only a few repetitions of rat and noise together to condition Albert so that he shrank back when the rat was presented, and the "fear" response appeared. On succeeding days all that was necessary was to present the rat, and the "fear" response was immediately evoked. Now, prior tests had also indicated that various other forms of furry objects never called for any withdrawal or fear response but instead seemed to be regarded as playthings. However, after the experiment in which the rat had been used to produce the fear response, any furry object would also produce the same response. Regardless of whether it was a Santa Claus mask, a piece of wool or cotton, or a small dog that was presented to the child, any of these furry objects now evoked the fear response.

OTHER EXPERIMENTS WITH INFANTS

This type of fear response, however, may not be universal. For example, another experimenter concluded on the basis of studies involving observation of human infants that loud sounds usually, but not inevitably, cause reactions suggesting fear.[23] He thinks that the novelty of the noise is an important factor; in fact, some novelty situations seem to call for pleasure. He found a fear response to shrill musical discords but not to lower discords; he believes, however, that loud noises in strange situations do *tend* to evoke a fear response.

English has reported some cases of the "conditioned fear response," one of which involved a little girl fourteen months old in a laboratory situation.[24] A toy duck was presented to her suspended from above, and at the same time a large metal bar was struck a resounding blow. The duck was then removed. During the trials the child was permitted to play in the laboratory, and motion pictures were taken of the child's responses. An analysis of these pictures showed that no conditioned fear was induced. The child apparently reacted separately to the noise (startle reflex) and to the duck (exploratory attention). The same child, however, at age fifteen months showed fear reactions to Daddy's shoes, newly bought. When the child saw her father's shoes, she whined nervously and looked distressed. The shoes were then placed with familiar and "friendly" house slippers (second-order conditioning). But it was three months before the shoes actually became enjoyable playthings.

As Wayne Dennis has pointed out, it is not possible to list specific stimuli for specific emotional responses.

> The child's reaction tendencies with respect to any test situation . . . can be stated, not absolutely, but only in terms of the relationship which the test situation bears to past situations and to the behavior repertoire. The child of several months of age does not react to a piece of fur, a snake, a loud noise, or a pinching of the nose, as a unique stimulus, as a thing-in-itself, but he seems to place each situation into some category of stimulation. . . . Reaction tendencies beyond the first few months cannot be said to have absolute stimuli, such as loud noises or restraint of movement but instead they have relative stimuli, such as strange objects and frustrating situations. What is strange and what is frustrating necessarily depends upon the stimulation-history of the child.[25]

In other words, the results of the early Watsonian experiments are not as clear-cut as they were first thought; but at the same time they do provide a convenient structure for understanding some elementary considerations about learning.

CASE HISTORIES INVOLVING CONDITIONING

The conditioned response is not limited to the laboratory situation. Here are two case histories where conditioning was involved.

A man suffered from a phobia [a paralyzing dread] of being grasped from behind, the disturbance appearing early in childhood and persisting to his fifty-fifth year. When walking on the street he was under the compulsion to look back over his shoulder at intervals to see if he was closely followed. In social gatherings he arranged to have his chair against the wall. It was impossible for him to enter crowded places or attend the theater.

In his fifty-fifth year he returned to the town in which he had spent his childhood. After inspecting his old home he went to the corner grocery and found that his old boyhood friend was still behind the counter. He introduced himself and they began to reminisce. Finally the grocerman said this, "I want to tell you something that occurred when you were a boy. You used to go by the store on errands and when you passed you often took a handful of peanuts from the stand in front. One day I saw you coming and hid behind a barrel. Just as you put your hand in the pile of peanuts, I jumped out and grabbed you from behind. You screamed and fell fainting on the sidewalk." The episode was remembered, and the phobia, after a period of readjustment, disappeared.[26]

A famous clinical case involves a young lady who had a phobia of church steeples. She was unable to account for this. It was eventually discovered that the young lady was with her mother at the time of her mother's death and that, as her mother was breathing her last, the church bells tolled in a neighboring church steeple. This one highly emotional experience was sufficient so that at a later time any church steeple suggested to her a very unpleasant emotional response. After adequate psychological treatment the fear gradually disappeared.

CONSTANT PROCESS OF CONDITIONING IN EVERYDAY LIFE

However, conditioning is by no means restricted to such unusual occurrences as these. Conditioning may occur in the most prosaic situations. Thus, a child given castor oil (original stimulus) mixed in orange juice (conditioned stimulus) one or two times may develop an avoidance response to orange juice. Conditioning goes on so constantly that we are likely to neglect its frequent occurrence in our everyday life. Not only do we learn to perceive the world around us in terms of association or conditioning of various elements, but we build up all kinds of social attitudes and social "ways" through the mechanism of the conditioned response. One individual outlines the basis for his prejudice against Jews—two incidents known to him, plus perhaps a number of others not consciously remembered, were sufficient to develop a very well-established prejudice.

When I was quite young, my mother read me the story of Oliver Twist. I remember quite plainly how angry I became when I learned the full extent of Fagin's operations as affecting Oliver. There was also a picture of the old Jew, showing him in all the horror imaginable—stooped, filthy, ragged, sly, sneaking, all the worst possible traits. Then I saw a few years ago Lon Chaney play the part on the screen. This performance capped the climax. Since then I have looked upon most Jews with somewhat of aversion.[27]

There is nothing instinctive about this. Here we have a *learned* pattern of behavior. In fact, conditioning begins early in life and helps to explain many specialized ways of thinking. By the age of five years most of us have developed a complex pattern of likes and dislikes which are relatively permanent. Of course, these likes and dislikes may be modified by later acquired experiences.

A man walking with a friend in the neighbourhood of a country village, suddenly expressed extreme irritation concerning the church bells, which happened to be pealing at the moment. He maintained that their tone was intrinsically unpleasant, their harmony ugly, and the total effect altogether disagreeable. The friend was astonished, for the bells in question were famous for their singular beauty. He endeavoured, therefore, to elucidate the real cause underlying his companion's attitude. Skilful questioning elicited the further remark that not only were the bells unpleasant but the clergyman of the church wrote extremely bad poetry. The causal complex was then apparent, for the man whose ears had been offended by the bells also wrote poetry, and in a recent criticism his work had been compared very unfavourably with that of the clergyman. The rivalry-complex thus engendered had expressed itself indirectly by an unjustifiable denunciation of the innocent church bells. The direct expression would, of course, have been abuse of the clergyman himself or of his works.[28]

FOUR ASPECTS OF CONDITIONING

Instance after instance of conditioning might be given, of course, but we are now in a position to describe four important aspects of the process. These are: (1) generalization, (2) differentiation, (3) traumatic experience, and (4) ready-made acceptance of "ways."

1. *Generalization.* When a conditioned response has been established to some stimulus, and when other similar stimuli will now also produce the response even though they have not been used in establishing the conditioned response, this is known as *generalization.* Here is an example from a life history:

One of the things that was instilled in me under the influence of home was that of religion. My parents not only encouraged me to accept my faith without question, but all of its doctrines without argument. This influence of home was accepted until about ten years ago. Then these parental concepts were slowly driven from my mind. It was a slow process of disintegration and a building up of a new philosophy from contacts and viewing the actions of so-called religious people.

To take just one instance of this, one summer after working extremely hard and saving my earnings, I placed them on deposit in a bank which was headed by a man who was a superintendent of my Sunday School. He was a so-called leader in the community, a man of supposedly unquestionable integrity, and above all was considered a very religious person. However, the bank failed, a large sum of money was missing, and this man was indicted and found guilty of embezzlement. This and *similar actions by numerous churchmen* started me thinking.

In this case a whole series of unfortunate experiences with people who happened incidentally to belong to the church were integrated into a dislike of churchmen and of religion. The first stimulus to be conditioned was the experience with the Sunday school superintendent, but later other stimuli (experiences) were combined with this to produce a change in religious views. Following is another instance of generalization:

I met a man named Snyder, and for some peculiar reason felt constantly suspicious of him. All his other friends liked him very much, and I could find no definite reason for disliking him, until one day it occurred to me that a number of years previously I had read a story in which a person named Snyder was a thoroughgoing villain. Having thought of this explanation, all my ill feeling departed and the real Mr. Snyder became a very good friend of mine.[29]

2. *Differentiation.* When one stimulus (or more) of a total stimulating situation later comes to stand psychologically for that total situation to such an extent that the stimulus distinguishes or sets off that situation from a closely similar situation, this is *differentiation.* In other words, the stimulus (or stimuli) is an end product or condensation of the original pattern of stimuli. Here is an example:

When I was very small I was told that "stingy" people had practically no lobes on their ears and that generosity was marked by large ears. The man who lived across the street from us was held up as an example. He was very economical, and upon inspection it was discovered that he had very small lobes. On the other hand, there was a boy who lived near by who was so generous that he was often in trouble, and he possessed very large ears. And my closest friend, a generous person, had large ears.

A family I knew annoyed me extremely by being so reticent in parting with their money that they never seemed to enjoy the things other people liked if those things cost anything; and all the people in this family had small ears. Even an old miser in our town had tiny lobes.

It seemed that the ears on all of the generous people were large and on the economical people were small. Therefore I concluded that all people with small ears must be "stingy." I even began to judge people I didn't even know just by looking at their ears.

In such instances, one or two elements are usually singled out or segregated from a total pattern of stimuli, and these come to stand *in the place of* the original total pattern. This segregation, through succeeding experience, is differentiated from similar situations. Whereas the process of generalization means a "spreading" from the original conditioned stimulus to other stimuli, one or more of which now results in the conditioned response, differentiation is the opposite, namely, a breaking down of a general pattern into discrete factors, one or more of which will now produce the original response.

3. *Traumatic Experience.* Certain actual life situations are *traumatic,* that is, intensely vivid and dramatic, such as an emotional shock.

Traumatic experience is the application of the old law of intensity or vividness in learning to personality change. . . . Abrupt shocks will bring about a new energizing of the individual, and he will rapidly acquire new attitudes and activities. . . . New adjustment is compulsory if he is to continue as a self-respecting person.[30]

The essential point is not whether the experience looks dramatic or traumatic to an outside observer, but whether or not the stimuli actually are traumatic for the individual concerned. As an example, if a small child is suddenly confronted with a large dog who barks furiously at him, this may be considered by an older person as a minor episode in the child's life. Clinical data, however, have shown that such a simple episode as this *may be* highly traumatic and have a very marked effect upon the child in his later fears and even his later permanent adjustments.

For instance, a child who is emotionally sensitive to sounds may jump in his crib at the age of two months when he hears the click of an electric light button, may be traumatized by the whistle of a steamboat at the age of two, may be easily cowed by the loud tones of an aggressive adult at three, and in the following year be disturbed by the noise of a nursery-school group of twenty children; on the basis of these early experiences he may develop a pattern of social response completely different from that developed by a child whose response to sound shows less sensitiveness.[31]

There seems to be a tendency for the conditioning process to take place more quickly—that is, with fewer repetitions of the conditioned with the original stimulus—in the traumatic than in the nontraumatic situation. In the Pavlovian-dog experiment dozens of repetitions are necessary, whereas a single experience of a highly traumatic sort may result in a well-established conditioned response. In the case of Albert, not many repetitions were required to build up a fear response toward the rat.

4. *Ready-made Acceptance of "Ways."* There is one more way in which conditioning may be significant in the acquisition of ways of thinking and acting, and that is through the *ready-made* adoption of "ways." An individual adopts certain attitudes of thinking or even overt ways of acting because of association with these attitudes or acts in other persons. The essential mechanism is one of conditioning in that there has been repetition of the conditioned stimulus to the point where it produces a response *new at that time* to the individual.

Even before he has an adequate background of appropriate experience a child may form many intense and lasting attitudes toward races and professions, toward religion and marriage, toward foreigners and servants, and toward morality and sin. A parent's tone of voice in disapproving of the ragamuffins who live along the railroad track is enough to produce an uncritical attitude in the child who has no basis in his experience for the rational adoption of the parent's point of view. It frequently happens that *subsequent* experience is fitted into the attitude thus critically adopted. . . . Few men have actually encountered "tricky Japanese" or "cruel Turks," few have known tragedy to follow a dinner party of thirteen, or the lighting of three cigarettes from the same match. And yet thousands of such attitudes and beliefs are adopted ready-made and tenaciously held against all evidence to the contrary.[32]

ALL FOUR MECHANISMS

Antireligious attitudes of 350 members of the American Association for the Advancement of Atheism were investigated by Vetter and Green, who found that the origin of their atheistic attitudes could be accounted for by all four of the mechanisms described before.[33] Thus many of the subjects developed atheistic attitudes through (1) the process of integrating *generalizations;* that is, they had read various scientific and historical documents which *cumulatively* had resulted in the gradual development of their beliefs. Again, (2) *differentiation* was found among other atheists; that is, they had developed some general point of view, perhaps a materialistic philosophy of life, and atheism had been an offshoot or by-product. Still others reported (3) a *traumatic* experience, as the rather sudden conversion to atheism after some great grief or tragedy in their lives. Finally, (4) some had adopted their view *ready-made* from some friend or other person they had known.

A study concerned with the fears of one thousand college women indicated that the things which these women were most afraid of were snakes, cancer, death, bulls, insane people, mad dogs, reckless driving, blindness, and burglars.[34] Are these fears "instinctive" or are they individually acquired? There is no evidence for any "instinctive" or unlearned fears of snakes, bulls, cancer, darkness, or any other common fears of women or men. The chemical and physiological activities of the autonomic nervous system which are an essential aspect of "fear" are probably instinctive, but the situations which actually produce fear are the result of experiences. We *learn* to be afraid. We learn on the basis of our own particular sets of experiences what things to avoid and also what things to approach, through generalization, differentiation, trauma, and adoption of ready-made attitudes—all involving the mechanism of the conditioned response. The process of conditioning will be referred to in later chapters in describing the influence of the neighborhood and the family upon the personalities of children, the social psychology of religious and "racial" prejudice, and similar matters. Further case histories and concrete examples will be introduced in connection with such problems.

PRACTICAL VALUE OF CONDITIONING

The conditioned response is also important as a basis of understanding how to remove certain phobias or how to change certain attitudes. An understanding of conditioning thus has great practical value. If we know the fears or attitudes of people, we can sometimes change these by a "reconditioning" technique. One method found effective is best described by an example. The problem was to find a quick and lasting method of dispelling certain undesirable emotional reactions.

> A girl of nineteen was much troubled by her habit of bursting into tears when with men, especially her father. The remedy lay in building strong associations of relaxation, calmness, and security, with a word regarded by the subject as particularly meaningful, in this case, the word "calm." While in a very relaxed state, the subject was instructed to think of the word "calm" and associate with it certain definite ideas of peace, security, and well-being, always with the conviction that at any future time the word "calm" would reinstate the same condition of physical and mental relaxation and composure. There were no failures by this method. Young adults were cured—no relapses after two years—after three one-hour treatments.[35]

Better still, if we can understand the basis for certain attitudes and ways of behavior, we can usually devise conditioned-response techniques for changing them. As a concrete example, Griffith made studies of football players at the University of Illinois.[36] Here is a player catching a punt, but just as he receives the ball, two ends crash into him and injure him. He develops what most football coaches call a "yellow streak," is ridiculed, and benched. The mere sight of the football coming through the air may even cause him to make flinching or protective movements. Griffith took such a man and "reconditioned" him in a period of a few days so that the "yellow streak" was overcome. First, the player was told to play catch with another man, using a football. After two or three days of practice two other men stood on either side and some distance away but did not move. Shortly the two men gradually moved into the picture, and eventually they mildly tackled the first player. He was then brought back to the squad and resumed play. This is considerably simpler, however, than the changing of more basic attitudes, as we shall see in later chapters.

▶ THE PROBLEM OF MOTIVATION

OVERLAPPING OF UNLEARNED AND LEARNED BEHAVIOR

The conditioned response is, of course, not a complete explanation of why we behave in the ways that we do. Not only is trial-and-error learning also important, but learning *by itself* is not the whole story of why men and women behave like human beings. Whereas some investigators have emphasized "drive" theories, based on *unlearned* behavior, others have stressed *learned* "motives," based largely on conditioning processes. Actually it is extremely difficult to lump all factors of motivation into these two categories of unlearned and learned, with no overlapping. For example, eating and drinking have both unlearned and learned components—basic physiological factors plus acquired mechanisms.

This illustrates why motivation is discussed at this point. The two previous sections on instincts (unlearned behavior) and on conditioning (learned behavior) involve questions of drive and incentive, and these are problems of motivation. Certain basic motives are intimately associated with both instinctive and conditioned behavior, although, as we shall see, there are a number of different ways of classifying these motives.

DIFFICULTIES OF CLASSIFYING MOTIVES

Any set of data can be classified under a number of different headings; exactly the same materials can then be rearranged by another individual and put under different headings. This is what has happened to a large extent in connection with the problem of motivation. If we attempted to divide motives into an *internal* and an *external* classification, in the first category would come homeostasis (or keeping the blood in order), sleep, hunger, thirst, sex, maternal motives based on known hormones, sensitive-zone demands; and in the second category would come exploration, curiosity, escape, fight, ascendance, submission, rivalry, competition, gregariousness, and the like. Yet there would be considerable overlapping between the two groups; actually every motive listed depends on both internal and external factors.

Another possible classification is according to the extent of known *physiological* basis.[37] (1) There are motives which have a definite physiological basis and admit of no exceptions, such as hunger, thirst, sleep, and elimination of waste products. (2) There are also motives of a definite physiological basis but which admit of exceptions in the case of some persons, such as sex, postmaternal behavior, and self-preservation. (3) Then there are motives which have an indirect physiological basis but which admit of exceptions both in groups and in individuals, such as aggressiveness, flight, and self-assertiveness. (4) Some motives have no known physiological basis, such as gregariousness, paternal and filial motives, and acquisitiveness. Note that many of these motives were formerly called "instincts," until it was discovered that they were socially produced patterns or tendencies.

The trouble with lists of motives lies not in their length but in their sharp separation of one drive from another, their sharp separation of innate from acquired need, and their sharp demarcation of focus points in the body which are supposed to underlie motion toward a goal. Nevertheless, if these limitations are kept in mind, there seems to be a distinct value in listing four groups of human motives.

Visceral Drives	*Activity Drives*	*Aesthetic Drives*	*Emotions*
hunger	exercise	color	fear
thirst	rest	tone	rage
air-getting	preservation	specific qualities	disgust
temperature	rhythm	of taste, smell,	shame
regulation	novelty	and touch	etc.
sexual	exploration	rhythm	
etc.	etc.	etc.	

It will be noted that rhythm appears twice. . . . A drive may appear under two or more categories, and conditions of unrest or striving may be so generalized as to require placement almost anywhere or nowhere. The names for drives merely indicate convenient abstractions from the infinitely complex flux of life activity.[38]

In other words, the visceral drives, activity drives, aesthetic drives, and emotions grouped in the quoted table represent a useful classification of drives or motives which are important in human behavior. These are not, however, the only possible lists, and they occur in conjunction with each other in almost infinitely complex patterns.

Gordon W. Allport has taken the position that adult motives are infinitely varied, and are self-sustaining, contemporary systems which have grown out of antecedent systems but are functionally independent of them.

> Just as a child gradually repudiates his dependence on his parents, develops a will of his own, becomes self-active and self-determining, and outlives his parents, so it is with motives. Each motive has a definite point of origin which may lie in the hypothetical instincts, or, more likely, in the organic tensions and diffuse irritability. . . . Theoretically all adult purposes can be traced back to these seed-forms in infancy. But as the individual matures the bond is broken. The tie is historical, not functional.[39]

ACTIVITY ITSELF AS A SOURCE OF ACTIVITY

Activities themselves may, and often do, become sources of drive activity. Thus, after you have once begun upon a certain type of activity, the mere fact of having started on that activity may be sufficient to lead you to continue in it, and no discoverable visceral tensions may be involved. A noted psychologist relates that when he is doing a statistical problem which may involve simply the addition of columns of figures, he finds it extremely difficult to stop adding and turn to something else, after he has once made a beginning of adding. The process of having started adding is an activity which furnishes its own motivation. In touring, you may sometime have had difficulty in stopping yourself from continuing to drive far into the night.

> . . . Any strenuous and vivid experience tends to perpetuate itself unless specific negative conditioning is present. Once thoroughly aroused, the individual maintains his orientation to that which aroused him, and does things which will bring him more stimulation of the same sort. The results may be ethically paradoxical, but psychologically simple and coherent. The same child who is utterly sympathetic to an injured playmate may turn and pummel him when a group of others have started pummeling. A boy runs to catch a bird which he loves but, failing to reach it, throws a stick which kills it. A child starts playing with his sister, a moment later is teasing her to the point of frantic squeals and tears. A man torments the one he loves, not knowing why. One shudders at a murder but must read all the details.[40]

THOMAS'S FOUR WISHES

Consider now the more complex forms of social motivation. W. I. Thomas developed a classification of motives which has been of considerable use to sociologists and anthropologists. *We recognize full well that this classification is not a complete explanation of every problem of motivation, and that it is by no means universally accepted—no such classification is —but it will prove useful for our analysis of social psychology.*

According to Thomas, there are four wishes or desires which are so fundamental that they probably include all the others—the desire (1) for new experience, (2) for security, (3) for response, and (4) for recognition.[41]

1. The desire for *new experience* expresses iself in courage, advance, attack, and pursuit. It implies, therefore, motion, change, danger, or instability. It satisfies the love of adventure, which is present in such activities as gambling. It also satisfies such curiosity as occurs when we are creating or building something or solving a problem.

2. The desire for *security* is opposed to the desire for new experience. It expresses itself in timidity, avoidance, and flight. The desire for security makes a person cautious, conservative, and apprehensive, tending to regular habits, systematic work, and the accumulation of property.

3. The desire for *response* causes people to seek intimate contacts with other people. It is the most social of the four wishes, and contains both a sexual and a gregarious (crowd) element.

4. The desire for *recognition* is expressed in the general struggle of men for position in their social group. It makes people desire a recognized and advantageous social status. The desire for recognition includes such feelings as "vanity" and "ambition."

In one study of these four wishes, made by Krout, subjects were required to keep a diary of their activities for a period of one week.[42] The time devoted to the expression of one wish was not believed to measure the intensity of the wish, but simply the extent to which an individual managed to express the wish. According to the time records of the subjects, the wish for security was found to lead the list, those for response and recognition occupied a middle position, and the desire for new experience was in last place.

It is reasonably easy to make an analysis of any bit of behavior in terms of these four wishes. Take such a simple thing as riding on a roller coaster. Why do men and women behave in this strange fashion? Possibly the desire for new experience enters the picture, since most of us do not spend very much of our lives riding roller coasters. The desire for security is not violated too drastically, in that most people come back alive. The desire for response is attained, in that most people do not go roller-coaster riding alone. The desire for recognition is achieved in that one riding a roller coaster can be looked up to as "brave" by those poor benighted creatures who are afraid to ride. Again, take such a simple act as putting into one's mouth the tip of a rolled piece of white paper containing some brown shreds, and then removing the tip and blowing out smoke.

Why do people engage in this unique pastime? Certainly many an adolescent achieves new experience. He does this, however, with a modicum of security. He achieves a certain amount of response, as used to be suggested in the cigarette advertisement, "Blow some my way." He certainly can achieve a certain amount of recognition as being "in the know" and not an outsider—no longer does he wonder what to do with his hands!

Such analyses as these, it should be clear, are merely classifications of motivated behavior. They are not even airtight classifications containing all the answers to problems of motivation. Perhaps no single set of wishes can account for the countless ways of behavior of countless people in all sorts of situations. However, we shall more than once refer to Thomas's four wishes in subsequent chapters, realizing, of course, that other analyses of motivation are also possible.

FREUD AND PSYCHOANALYSIS

Reference to *the unconscious* has been one more way of approaching the behavior of human beings. The use of this phrase, "the unconscious," comes from the work of Sigmund Freud, founder of psychoanalysis.[43] During Freud's lifetime he influenced the views not only of academic psychologists but also of the layman to such an extent that thinking about human behavior has been fundamentally changed. This influence is so strong that many people have practically forgotten to say "cruelty" instead of "sadism," or "egotism" instead of "narcissism." We read in newspapers and popular fiction about the "libido," the "Oedipus complex," "wish fulfillment," and even use these terms as though we understood them. It is small wonder that many psychologists have tended to dismiss the work of Freud as unscientific. Not only did he invent a strange terminology, but he used no brass-instrument apparatus, never set up experiments where there was an experimental and a "control" group, and did not bother with statistical procedures.

Yet as a clinician Freud forced many people to probe into the fundamental processes of the mind. He was one of the first to suggest that sleep might be analyzed for thinking processes, that dreams which we do not discuss with each other might after all represent wishful thinking, that many humorous situations are full of obscene meanings.

EFFECTS OF FREUD'S WORK

At first, such revolutionary thinking was scoffed at not only by the man in the street but also by other clinicians. Yet his work has since markedly affected our views in social psychology. First of all, it is in no small measure due to Freud that we have come to realize that the behavior of an individual cannot be understood apart from his underlying motives, and that many of these motives are so completely hidden that we ourselves cannot explain why we act as we do. When we attempt to analyze our own behavior, our introspections may not be at all valid. Freud also directed our attention to the influence of cultural pressures on the individual. Many instances of maladjustment have been traced to a lack of satisfactory adaptation to the environmental forces and the cultural pressures of the group in which one happens to be born. Delinquency—to be discussed in Chapter 21—is a case in point. Again, many a maladjusted individual in American society might find in another culture that he would be considered well adjusted.

Perhaps most important of all, Freud forced us to talk objectively about sex and sexual motives. If you look up discussions of human behavior written in the last century, you will be impressed by the almost complete omission of any material relating to sex. It is as if there had been a conspiracy among authors to pretend that, although men and women ate and slept and drank and carried on digestive activities, they were devoid of sex acts and feelings. But as a result of Freud's lifelong studies, people who are sincerely interested in human behavior—psychologists, sociologists, social workers, clergymen, lawyers, physicians, psychiatrists—have come more and more to realize that interpretations of human behavior depend to a great extent upon an understanding of the sexual life of men and women. This does *not* imply that all human activities may be explained in terms of sex. Certainly an understanding of sex *per se* gives us no magic key which will unlock and explain all problems of human behavior. Sexual activities must be studied together with physiological and social factors, as we shall see in greater detail in Chapter 13.

OBJECTIONS TO CONCEPT OF "THE UNCONSCIOUS"

Unfortunately, however, Freud's notion of repressed ideas being relegated to the so-called "unconscious" has been greatly overworked. We have seen that much of our behavior is due to factors of motivation which we do not fully understand. But Freud taught that a great deal of our motivation and, in fact, much of our behavior and many of our judgments of others were due to "the unconscious." This concept, which has been used extremely loosely, seems objectionable for several reasons. (1) The term "the unconscious" indicates that the error of *reification* is being committed—that is, unconscious activities have been reified or made into an entity or thing which can be labeled. This particular instance of reification has sometimes been referred to as "the-little-man-in-the-head" theory. It is to suggest that one's behavior is controlled at any given moment by some mystical, mythical entity which, on the basis of one's past experiences, dictates to the individual what shall or shall not be done. (2) This concept is a nonexplanatory one. It is only descriptive. To say that a given individual committed a given act because of his "unconscious" is not an explanation. To say that you have done something because of your "unconscious" (or "subconscious") is no more meaningful than to explain your behavior solely on the basis of some supposed instinct. (3) This term seems to have almost a sinister implication. Many people talk about the unconscious as though "it" (whatever *it* is) were filled with wicked, evil, and sinister thoughts. Certainly our thought processes do involve obscene and socially undesirable ideas, but they also contain many kinds of thinking which would not fall into these categories.

There can be no objection to speaking of man's unconscious activities or unconscious thinking processes if we clearly understand that we are not discussing some strange entity which exists vaguely in the nervous system or some place in space. We do not deny in the least that people are unaware of many of the thinking activities that they carry on; and it is obvious that many of the things which people do from day to day are definitely controlled by experiences which they have had in the past—either overt behavior or covert thinking in which they have engaged. Our examination of the conditioned-response mechanism has shown us to what an extent one may be influenced, even unknowingly, by past experiences. This is a far cry, however, from talking about "the unconscious," as though it were something removed from ourselves. The nervous system does not disappear from time to time and then suddenly come back into existence, resurrected by a mysterious unconscious.

UNIQUENESS OF EVERY SOCIAL SITUATION

There is no simple answer, then, to the problem of motivation. Both unlearned and learned behavior are involved, and motives and wishes may be classified in any number of ways. Although much that we do is based on unconscious activities—in the sense of being automatic or not remembered—this is only a partial explanation of motivation. Actually, every social situation is different from every other and requires a separate analysis. Each phase of social interaction is unique, and there is no such thing as a universal set of explanatory factors. Many classifications of motives may, of course, be used as a basis for studying complex forms of social motivation, and *it is with this understanding and limitation that we shall more than once in the following chapters refer to Thomas's four wishes.* We are in thorough agreement with Allport's statement, "Not four wishes, nor eighteen propensities, nor any and all combinations of these, even with their extensions and variations, seem adequate to account for the endless variety of goals sought by an endless variety of mortals."[44]

QUESTIONS AND PROBLEMS FOR DISCUSSION

1. *Why do we need empirical evidence of the existence of instincts?*
2. *What difference does it make psychologically how many instincts there are or what they are?*

3. *What are two interpretations of the term "instinct"?*
4. *Is the fixity of a certain type of behavior proof of its instinctive character?*
5. *What is the value of conditioned responses in understanding social behavior?*
6. *Can you distinguish between the processes of generalization and of differentiation of conditioned responses? Give an example of each.*
7. *What traumatic experience have you ever had which has changed your attitudes toward some object, person, event, or idea?*
8. *What factors cause you to accept ready-made attitudes? What factors cause you to reject them?*
9. *What other explanations are there of habit formation besides that of the conditioned response?*
10. *To what extent do you understand your own motivation?*
11. *Can you think of any additional desires that cannot be classified under one of Thomas's four wishes?*
12. *What is meant by Freudian psychoanalysis?*

RECOMMENDED READINGS

Bernard, L. L., *Instinct: A Study in Social Psychology.* New York: Henry Holt and Company, Inc., 1924.

Freud, S., *The Basic Writings of Sigmund Freud.* (Translated by A. A. Brill.) New York: Random House, Inc. (Modern Library, Inc.), 1938.

Guthrie, E. R., *The Psychology of Learning.* New York: Harper & Brothers, 1935.

Hilgard, E. R., and Marquis, D. G., *Conditioning and Learning.* New York: D. Appleton-Century Company, 1940.

Jones, M. C., "Emotional Development." In Murchison, C. (editor), *A Handbook of Child Psychology* (2nd edition, revised). Worcester: Clark University Press, 1933.

McGeoch, J. A., *The Psychology of Human Learning: An Introduction.* New York: Longmans, Green & Co., 1942.

Young, P. T., *Motivation of Behavior: The Fundamental Determinants of Human and Animal Activity.* New York: John Wiley & Sons, Inc., 1936.

*Newcomb, T. M., Hartley, E. L., and others (editors), *Readings in Social Psychology.* New York: Henry Holt and Company, Inc., 1947:—Bateson, G., "Social Planning and the Concept of 'Deutero-Learning,'" pp. 121–128.

CHAPTER SEVEN

BEHAVIOR, TRAITS, AND ATTITUDES

COVERT AND OVERT BEHAVIOR. Classification of Behavior—Attitudes—Difficulty of Analyzing Attitudes from Overt Behavior—Overt Behavior May Be Superficial—"Masking" of Covert Feelings—No One-to-One Relation / BEHAVIOR TRAITS. Personal Ways of Behavior—(1) Trait, No Necessary Object of Reference—(2) Trait, a Generalized Tendency toward Action—(3) Trait, Not Favorable or Unfavorable—Traits Do Not Change Much in Adult Life—Factors of Introversion-Extroversion—Measuring Behavior Traits / ATTITUDES. Covert and Overt Attitudes—Attitudinal Behavior—Classifications of Attitudes—Bases of Attitudes—Attitudes Specific and General—Attitudes Affected by the Social Situation / "COVERT" ATTITUDES AND "OVERT" BEHAVIOR AFFECT EACH OTHER. (1) "Covert" Attitudes Affect "Overt" Behavior—Some Empirical Studies of "Covert" Attitudes—Prestige Factors—Frames of Reference—(2) "Overt" Behavior Affects "Covert" Attitudes—Some Empirical Studies of "Overt" Behavior—Changing of Attitudes / ATTITUDES AND BELIEFS AS AFFECTED BY WISHES AND VALUES. Wishes and Desires—Values / THE MEASUREMENT OF SOCIAL ATTITUDES. Attitudes and Verbalized Opinions—(1) Census of Opinion—(2) A Priori Scale—(3) Psychophysical Scale—Difficulties in Measurement of Social Attitudes—Value of Attitude Measurement.

▶ COVERT AND OVERT BEHAVIOR

CLASSIFICATION OF BEHAVIOR

Things people do fall roughly into two classes: those activities which other people can observe, and those they cannot observe. Actions observable to other people, namely, *overt* behavior, can be perceived through many of the sense departments, particularly vision, hearing, touch, and smell. Other activities cannot be perceived by other individuals and fall in the classification of *covert* behavior.

Table 5 suggests a type of division between these two classifications of behavior. *Covert* behavior in general is nonobservable, for the most part internal, largely implicit, involves many anticipatory responses, and in certain respects is "attitudinal." *Overt* behavior, on the other hand, is in general observable, for the most part external, largely explicit, involves a great many consummatory or completed responses, and may be considered as more "nonattitudinal" than the reverse. It is important to note that the left-hand column is not sharply differentiated from the right-hand

TABLE 5

Classification of Behavior

Covert Behavior	*Overt Behavior*
Nonobservable	Observable
Internal	External
Implicit	Explicit
Anticipatory response	Consummatory response
"Attitudinal"	"Nonattitudinal"

column. *There is no overt behavior which does not involve both covert and overt aspects.* When you behave by talking, for example, you convey by overt openings and shuttings of your mouth and exercise of your vocal cords some indications of your covert opinions, beliefs, and attitudes. Also the terms in the left-hand column are not to be regarded as synonymous with each other, nor are the terms in the right-hand column. Instead, the words and phrases in these respective columns are listed simply to suggest that there is a great deal of similarity of meaning between the various words that appear in the same column. That is, covert behavior is not synonymous with "attitudinal" behavior but is closely identified with it. Likewise, overt behavior is not necessarily limited to explicit behavior, but much of our overt behavior seems to be explicit in nature.

ATTITUDES

Although the topic of attitudes will be treated in detail later in this chapter, a tentative definition should be presented here. "An attitude is a mental and neural state of readiness, exerting a directive or dynamic influence upon the individual's response to all objects and situations with which it is related."[1] Attitudes, then, are dealt with primarily from the standpoint of mental and neurological states of readiness, that is, as being closely related to *covert* behavior. In this way attitudes are distinguished from consummatory responses of these states of readiness, that is, from the overt behavior which results from being in a state of readiness. For example, an attitude of sympathy and agreement with the policies of the Democratic (or Republican) party may be said to be the mental and neural state of readiness which culminates in the consummatory response of voting Democratic (or Republican) at the polls. Attitudes are preliminary to the complete overt adjustment of the organism to its environment, and hence may be said to involve a minimum of muscular activity.

DIFFICULTY OF ANALYZING ATTITUDES FROM OVERT BEHAVIOR

Now, by observing the overt behavior of a particular group of individuals, can any deductions be made as to what their covert behavior or attitudes really are? Suppose, for example, that you go to a symphony concert and see all around you well-dressed women apparently listening intently to works of the great masters. Observing their overt behavior, namely, attentive listening, and also knowing that this is simply the final link in a long sequence of other overt behavior—being dressed in whatever is the latest style (for this would seem to be an aid to the listening process) and having traveled a great distance to be in this particular hall (instead of in another hall where a heavyweight bout is taking place) —can you deduce from all this overt behavior that all these listeners have basic "musical" attitudes? Hardly. As the Lynds observed, in their study of a Midwestern city, "Music seems to serve in part as a symbol that one belongs, and much of the musical activity of the woman appears as a rather self-conscious appendage of the city's club life."[2]

Even watching and listening to a person's vocal behavior or verbalizing does not necessarily mean that we know what his basic attitudes are. If you hear someone talking a great deal about a subject on which he seems informed, you cannot always reason from this that he really has attitudes which square with his talking, nor can you always predict other types of overt behavior aside from his "talking." As an example, the Lynds also point out that members of the city's women's clubs write papers on art, chiefly religious art, but that pictures and other decorations are conspicuously absent from the Protestant churches.[3]

OVERT BEHAVIOR MAY BE SUPERFICIAL

In other words, people often give lip service so superficial that it is not representative of their basic attitudes. In one empirical study the investigator used two groups of subjects, women in a reformatory and women in a college.[4] These two groups were asked to list in terms of their desirability sixteen different types of practices, which ranged from sex irregularity to dancing. It is interesting to note that there was rather close agreement by the delinquent women and the college women as to the desirability or undesirability of the various types of behavior. However, lip service to what was desirable or undesirable apparently did not square with the other behavior and attitudes of these women, in that they were in two different types of institution.

"MASKING" OF COVERT FEELINGS

Of course, you cannot observe a person's overt or external behavior and external surroundings, and then be sure that you are really "getting at" the supposed inner man. Thus, you see a man do a number of apparently foolhardy and daredevil things. If you know nothing about his life, what conclusions can you draw? Probably none—he may be either an extremely brave individual or he may be an extremely timid soul who is attempting to compensate for his feelings of timidity by showing off. When you observe a man whom you consider "masculine," can you be sure from his overt behavior that he really feels masculine? He may actually be an extremely dominant, masculine individual, or, on the other hand, he may be a person with essentially effeminate interests who has learned that our culture demands that these feelings be covered up. Similarly, an individual who is introverted or lost in himself ordinarily does not succeed as a supersalesman. Yet a person with decided introverted tendencies may take stock of himself, and, because he understands his internal, nonobservable, covert behavior and attitudes, he may control these introverted tendencies and develop into a successful salesman or a leader in social activities.[5]

NO ONE-TO-ONE RELATION

In analyzing various group situations, there is no one-to-one relation between covert and overt behavior. To study overt behavior alone, and because of this to believe that you understand the covert behavior of an individual, means that you have probably neglected a number of other significant factors. The case history of the individual enters into the picture, and data from the psychological clinic become important.

▶ BEHAVIOR TRAITS

PERSONAL WAYS OF BEHAVIOR

Everyone has a very personal and unique way of responding to his environment. In fact, our ways of behaving are usually sufficiently unique to enable other individuals to describe us fairly accurately as talkative, shy, bold, timid, or otherwise. When our friends use such adjectives in speaking about us, they are referring to our behavior traits. These traits are persistent characteristics of our reaction patterns; but they differ from our attitudes in several ways.

1. *Trait, No Necessary Object of Reference.* In the first place, a behavior trait need not have reference to a particular object or thing, whereas an attitude has a definite object of reference. People have attitudes toward religion or Chinese or drinking, but their aggressive or artistic or ascetic ways of behaving represent traits. Any number of different objects or things may arouse some particular type of behavior (trait) in us—in various circumstances we are affectionate, or argumentative, or autocratic. On the other hand, we have ways of thinking and acting with reference to specific objects and things because of attitudes.

You have specific attitudes toward your mother, and these are different from those toward your father. You have attitudes toward specific groups of people such as your fraternity or club. You also have attitudes toward various concepts, such as an attitude toward war or capital punishment.

> An attitude has a definite object of reference, while a trait has a very vague object of reference or it has none at all. Honesty, aggressiveness, and trustworthiness are traits because the object to which they refer has a very wide range and hence is very vague. Racialism, militarism, and liberalism are attitudes because they refer to definite objects, races, war, and social change, respectively.[6]

2. *Trait, a Generalized Tendency toward Action.* A second distinction between traits and attitudes is that traits are generalized tendencies toward action, whereas attitudes may be either specific or general. Thus, traits are so well ingrained in most of us that they may appear in either appropriate or inappropriate situations or both—our fundamental traits may show up in expected or unexpected ways. In fact, traits are so personal that they may be considered as qualities of behavior.[7] Attitudes, as we shall see, may be specific toward a certain person, or general toward various persons or concepts.

It has been said that traits may fall into two general classes: (1) those which are limited to the response alone, without the specific stimulus being important; and (2) those which depend upon the entire stimulus-response pattern.[8] As an example of the first, one might have a general trait of aggressiveness, not dependent upon the particular stimulus but rather upon the response. As to the second, the entire stimulus-response pattern, one might have a measure of aggressiveness toward members of another nationality.

> A general measure of nervous instability is very different from a measure of nervous instability in the presence of a social superior. . . . To put the matter in a form usable for statistical purposes, the term "trait" may refer (1) *simply to general likelihood of behaving in a defined manner, without reference to variations in a situation, or* (2) *to a given kind of behavior in a particular situation only.*[9]

3. *Trait, Not Favorable or Unfavorable.* Finally, traits do not ordinarily imply acceptance or rejection of objects or concepts, whereas attitudes are usually favorable or unfavorable, for or against something. A general tendency or trait of being outspoken or reserved is different from an attitude of friendliness or unfriendliness toward neighbors. However, some of the difficulties of distinguishing precisely between traits and attitudes, or even between certain traits, can be appreciated when it is realized that there are approximately 18,000 different English trait names representing distinctive personal forms of behavior.[10]

TRAITS DO NOT CHANGE MUCH IN ADULT LIFE

Most of our traits of which we can be reasonably cognizant do not change much in adult life. In the structure of personality, they are nodal points.

> After thirty personality changes very slowly owing to the fact . . . that by that time most individuals, unless constantly stimulated by a new environment, are pretty well settled in a humdrum way of living. Habit patterns become set. If you have an adequate picture of the average individual at thirty, you will have it with few changes for the rest of the individual's life—as most lives are lived. A quacking, gossiping, neighbor-spying, disaster-enjoying woman of thirty will be, unless a miracle happens, the same at forty and still the same at sixty.[11]

In fact, it seems extremely doubtful if there are very many fundamental changes in personality during adulthood, at least until senility is reached—unless there are really marked changes in the environmental situation. Aside from such events as marriage, the coming of children, new economic responsibilities, most of us do not change our way of life greatly after maturity. Our fundamental behavior integration is rather constant from year to year.[12] It can be described not simply by behavior traits, but by behavior *trends.* Of course, personality traits may show up differently with changes in one's associates, or with other altered social situations.[13]

FACTORS OF INTROVERSION-EXTROVERSION

Psychologists recognize the importance of traits in the various means which have been developed for measuring personality. As one example, consider the familiar concepts of introversion—being "wrapped up" in oneself—and extroversion—an expansive interest in outside objects and persons. Many people seem to assume that introversion or extroversion is a type of behavior which will enable us to "type" our friends in particular categories. However, a wealth of empirical work indicates that we cannot put ourselves or our friends in separate categories as introverts or extroverts, but that most of us are "ambivert"—that is, we have tendencies in both directions—in our activities over a period of time. The old concept of introversion-extroversion as a supposed unit trait of behavior is also disproved. Instead of speaking of an individual as introverted or extroverted, we should talk of *intellectual,* or of *emotional,* or of *social* introversion and extroversion.[14] In other words, the original concept of introversion-extroversion can be broken down into more specific traits in the intellectual, emotional, and the social field.[15] There may be as many as eighteen group factors involved in a typical test of introversion.[16]

MEASURING BEHAVIOR TRAITS

The testing movement has developed sufficiently so that certain measures of behavior are quite reliable and valid. One investigation, for example, was concerned with an analysis of personality scores of students who applied to a psychological clinic for advice and aid concerning their own problems.[17] Of 179 students, 98 were believed by the clinicians to be maladjusted cases. The remaining 81 were not considered maladjusted, but simply showed minor symptoms. *After* the clinical classification had been made, a personality test (Thurstone) was administered to these students. Table 6 reveals the high degree of relation between the clinical manifestations of maladjustment and the personality scores of maladjustment.

TABLE 6

Comparison of Clinical Classification and Personality Maladjustment Scores of 179 Students

Range of Personality Maladjustment Score	*98 Maladjusted Cases*		*81 Not Maladjusted Cases*	
	Number	*Per Cent*	*Number*	*Per Cent*
0– 29 (lowest quartile)	7	7	27	33
30– 74 (middle quartile)	53	54	44	55
75–180 (highest quartile)	38	39	10	12

Three separate judges also rated each of the 98 supposedly maladjusted cases for degree of maladjustment on a five-point scale. These ratings were then compared with the personality maladjustment scores, with the results shown in Table 7. In general, those individuals considered sufficiently maladjusted to require the services of a consulting psychologist showed far above the average scores on the personality schedule.

TABLE 7

Comparison of Maladjusted Ratings with Personality Maladjustment Scores of 98 Students

Mean Rating	*Number of Cases*	*Mean Personality Maladjustment Score*
1 (least maladjusted)	33	44.2
2	51	61.0
3	52	64.4
4	66	70.1
5 (most maladjusted)	92	75.4

This study is an indication of the kind of progress psychologists have made in the measurement of traits and attitudes. Statistical techniques now being developed will have even more important implications from the standpoint of the clinician. The following sections of the chapter deal with attitudes and their measurement.

▶ ATTITUDES

COVERT AND OVERT ATTITUDES

Our behavior involves internal, implicit, *covert* expressions and at the same time external, explicit, *overt* expression. As we have already noted, however, this is not a sharp differentiation between attitudes and behavior. Examine yourself as Exhibit *A,* and you soon realize that your attitudes are at one and the same time both overt and covert, both external and internal, both bodily and "psychic."

ATTITUDINAL BEHAVIOR

Referring to the definition given in the first section of this chapter of an attitude as a *mental and neural state of readiness,* it is perfectly apparent that you can be aware of your state of readiness—of your psychological "set"—both in its neural and its mental aspects. As an example, consider your own bodily attitudes, which are largely kinesthetic. You may have an attitude of defense against a blow, or against being pushed in a crowd. You may have an attitude of willingness to help someone in danger, or of readiness to take hold of something. These are *overt* and visually observable aspects of your attitudes. On the other hand, you—as no other person—can be aware of your *covert* attitudes. No one else so well as yourself can observe your attitude of sympathy for someone in distress, of anger toward someone who acts superior to you; yet these internal attitudes exist as part of this overt-covert continuum.[18] In fact, the term *attitudinal behavior* might be considered more accurate than the single word "attitude." And this attitudinal behavior always involves feelings and emotions.

CLASSIFICATIONS OF ATTITUDES

Attitudes have been divided in various ways for purposes of analysis. Kirkpatrick has suggested that attitudes actually involve: (1) gross somatic behavior, that is, large adjustments of the bodily organism as a whole; (2) overt verbal behavior, such as in language; and (3) internal somato-psychic patterns of thought and emotions, that is, unique and personal feelings which you have and which, even by the process of introspection, cannot be made perfectly clear to anyone else.[19] Such an analysis should clarify the general notion of what is meant by an attitude, provided you are aware of the continuous integration of these various kinds of behavior.

Here is another *conceptual* division of behavior: (1) overt-symbolic behavior; (2) overt-nonsymbolic behavior; (3) covert-symbolic behavior; (4) covert-nonsymbolic behavior.[20] This classification does not imply four different aspects of attitudes which can be set off from each other. Our intellectual-emotional-attitudinal processes can be broken down into segments only by *logical* classifications, but these do not actually exist in four different categories of this sort. For purposes of classification, however, attitudes may involve: (1) overt-symbolic behavior, which means such action as speaking, writing, gesturing; (2) overt-nonsymbolic behavior, which includes such actions as driving an automobile, shutting a door, or opening a window; (3) covert-symbolic behavior, or thought; (4) covert-nonsymbolic behavior, which refers to the processes of feeling and "emoting." The *overt* types of behavior, whether symbolic or nonsymbolic, are directly observable for the most part by other people and ordinarily can be measured. *Covert* behavior, however, whether symbolic or nonsymbolic, consists of private activities which are extremely difficult to measure accurately. Probably there are no necessary correlations among these four levels of behavior. For instance, a person might behave in such opposed and unrelated ways as driving a car cautiously down the highway (overt-nonsymbolic behavior), feeling a sense of impatience with his rate of progress (covert-nonsymbolic behavior), at the same time calculating how to rid himself of a boring companion (covert-symbolic behavior), and yet chatting gaily with him (overt-symbolic behavior).[21]

BASES OF ATTITUDES

It should be clear, then, that what we do and think constantly affects both our "behavioral" and our "mental" set. The way that you react to any particular situation in which you find yourself depends not simply upon the character of the thousands of stimuli which are bombarding you, but also upon the character of your attitudes at that particular time and place.[22] These attitudes are *learned.* They are dependent in large measure upon social conditioning, that is, on the mechanism of the conditioned response, and upon *generalization, differentiation, traumatic experiences, and acceptance of ready-made attitudes* of others. The way things taste, to take a simple example, is a function of all sorts of past experiences. Thus, it has been demonstrated experimentally that *white* sweet chocolate tastes less like chocolate than the ordinary brown kind.[23]

ATTITUDES SPECIFIC AND GENERAL

As indicated in the previous section, your attitudes may be specific in nature or they may be generalized. Thus you may have a very specific attitude of love for your mother, and you may have a very generalized attitude of affection for mothers in general and for the symbol represented by motherhood. Similarly, you may have an attitude of dislike and distrust for a particular individual, and you may also have generalized attitudes of dislike and distrust toward the whole group whom this individual symbolizes. As we shall see later in considering the social psychology of prejudice (in Chapters 10, 23, and 24), either a highly traumatic experience with one individual, or a series of events, may cause you to conclude that because one Jew or Italian or Englishman or German or banker or Communist or a member of any other group has treated you unfairly, therefore all Jews or Italians or Englishmen or Germans or bankers or Communists are likewise to be distrusted.

ATTITUDES AFFECTED BY THE SOCIAL SITUATION

What we do at any given time affects both our behavioral and our mental set. Not only does the expression of our social attitudes vary from being strongly overt or muscular—as in "taking a poke" at someone who insults us—to being highly mental or covert—as where we simply think nasty thoughts about the same person—but our overt and covert behavior are both affected by the existing social situation. Thus an individual who is in a room by himself behaves differently in an overt way than if there are other people about.[24] You may have had an opportunity to observe your own actions in this connection. Have you ever thought that you were alone and then suddenly found that there was another person present? If so, you have undoubtedly noticed distinct changes in your overt behavior, such as in facial expression or in body position.

In the same way your internal attitudes vary considerably with the social situation. You even have attitudes of "social distance" toward other individuals or groups of individuals, regardless of whether they are physically and geographically present or not. Thus you may be perfectly aware of feeling very near to persons dear to you who live a thousand miles away, and at the same time feeling very distant to the individuals who may be sitting by your side. By way of contrast, you may have feelings of nearness to people who are near to you and of distance to people who are far away. We are much more likely to be emotionally affected by the sight of a traffic accident than by newspaper accounts of the bombing of a foreign city. Our attitudes toward another economic class, a different nationality, some other religious group, or toward any people who do not think and behave as we do, are so dynamic in character that they merit special treatment in later chapters.

▶ "COVERT" ATTITUDES AND "OVERT" BEHAVIOR AFFECT EACH OTHER

1. "COVERT" ATTITUDES AFFECT "OVERT" BEHAVIOR

The interrelation of "covert" attitudes and "overt" behavior may be looked at from two different standpoints. First, we shall examine a number of empirical examples of how "covert" attitudes affect "covert" behavior. Second, we shall give some instances of how "overt" behavior affects "covert" attitudes.

Some Empirical Studies of "Covert" Attitudes. In one study, school children were asked to write out lists of three things—foods, animals, and colors.[25] Their papers were then collected. Following this they were asked to write on slips of paper those foods, animals, and colors which they liked best and also those which they disliked. Rather consistently, these children had put toward the top of the first list those foods, animals, and colors which they liked, and tended to put farther down the list those which they disliked. Although no specific instructions had been given, their already acquired attitudes ("covert") were affecting their overt behavior.

Consider the following experience while working in a large department store.

> To check up our supply of tents so that we would never unexpectedly run out of any model, we were each asked to check on a card every time we sold one. Out of curiosity I studied the checks to see how many each of us had sold, and I noticed a very interesting difference.
>
> Mr. Perry and I had sold about fifty each of a certain square and a round tent known as a palmetto design. The two models were nearly alike in all possible specifications: size, price, quality of cloth, floor-cloth, ease of setting up, etc. Yet Mr. Perry had sold about 35 of the round tents and only 15 of the others, while I had sold about 40 of the square ones and only 10 of the round tents.
>
> I asked him which of the two tents he would prefer to use if he were going on a camping trip. He said that he felt that the two tents were really about alike, and the two, rationally considered, were probably a toss-up; but at the same time he somewhat preferred the round one. I felt about the same way, but professed a leaning toward the square one. These preferences were in agreement with our proportional sales.[26]

Rice has presented information concerning interview records of social workers who had been engaged in interviewing two thousand homeless men who were applying for free lodging.[27] Since the average interviewing form used by social workers is well standardized, you might assume that the answers filled out would be completely objective. Yet Rice shows how the already formed attitudes of the social workers might affect their behavior in filling out these forms. As an example, one of the interviewers was a strong prohibitionist, while another was an ardent socialist. In analyzing the interview blanks turned in by the prohibitionist and socialist respectively, Rice found that the prohibitionist attributed 62 per cent of the cases to liquor and only 7 per cent to industrial conditions, whereas the socialist attributed 39 per cent to industrial conditions and only 22 per cent to liquor. Also, according to the information turned in by the prohibitionist, 34 per cent of the applicants themselves had mentioned liquor as a reason for their downfall, whereas the socialist reported that 60 per cent had mentioned industrial conditions as the principal reason. This study is another illustration of the way in which already acquired attitudes may affect what is done in a supposedly objective manner.

In another investigation, of children who were about to take part in a physical drill, the more popular children were carefully instructed to make rather awkward mistakes.[28] At the conclusion of the drill the teacher asked the pupils to list the names of their fellows who had interfered with the smoothness of the drill. The names listed were not those of the popular students who had actually made the errors, but were instead the names of unpopular pupils. In various social situations our attitudes affect our behavior.

Prestige Factors. Sherif conducted an interesting experiment in which he determined the preferences of his subjects for a number of authors, such as Conrad, Dickens, Poe, Scott, and Stevenson.[29] Several weeks later the same subjects were presented with literary passages, one quotation being attributed to each of the previous authors and the subjects being required to rank these in order of literary merit. Although the degree of relation between the original preference for the authors and the rating of literary passages was not very high, it did indicate that the attitudes toward the authors was very much affecting the judgments of literary merit. All the passages were quotations from Stevenson, but the experimenter had falsely attributed each of the passages to one of the authors in the first list. In other words, literary passages actually coming from the same source were judged ("overt" behavior) by subjects in accordance with their predetermined ("covert") attitudes.

A similar experiment was carried on some years ago by Saadi and Farnsworth.[30] These investigators determined the degree of liking of Stanford University students for various prominent people. At the top of the list they found such names as Mark Twain, Edison, Will Rogers, Einstein, Lindbergh; at the bottom, such people as Aimee Semple McPherson, Rudy Vallee, William Randolph Hearst. Various quotations were later submitted to the students, in each case with the name of one of these various individuals assigned to it, and the subjects were asked to rate each statement by a number which would indicate their degree of acceptance, on a five-point scale—from "1," absolute and complete agreement, to "5," absolute and complete disagreement. The names of the persons who were supposed to have said each of the quotations were coupled with various of the statements, and it was found that the amount of agreement or disagreement varied with the name of the person to whom the quotation was attributed. For example, a statement was given an average rating of 1.78 when attached to the name of Lindbergh, who was then very popular, of 1.97 when attributed to nobody, and of 2.16 when attributed to Hearst.

Frames of Reference. Sherif has dealt with this entire problem in terms of the "frames of reference"—or norms—which exist for all of us as to problems in the world about us.[31] These frames of reference are dependent upon such mechanisms as conditioning (Chapter 6) and subliminal stimulation (Chapter 10). Our own frames of reference seem real to us because they are *our own* frames. So completely do we accept their validity that we may raise an eyebrow or two at someone else who has different frames of reference. Thus, the Trobriand Islanders, who believed that sons can resemble their fathers but that sons of the same father have no fraternal resemblance, protested against the bad taste of the person who declared that two brothers resembled each other.[32] The same sort of thing is true for our frames of reference. We are apt to take it for granted that our own ways of behaving are essential and fundamental aspects of behavior for all persons, perhaps for all cultures.

In order to investigate this problem experimentally, Sherif set up a laboratory situation consisting of a dark room in which a single point of light could be moved up and down diagonally in any desired direction and located in various positions. In such a situation the outer world obviously has no organization, and the primary stimuli for the experimental subject are simply the figure-ground relationships of the spot of light on the dark wall. Sherif experimented with the judgments of various subjects concerning what they thought were different movements and locations of this spot of light. In one part of the experiment he himself, in another part a second subject working with the first subject, and in a third situation a large group of subjects, were required to state the nature and the extent of the movement perceived by them. The relative effects of having companions in this group situation and the relative prestige values of certain subjects were defined and carefully measured by him in such a way as to indicate that the judgments—that is, the frames of reference—depended very markedly upon what the frames of reference of other subjects were. After a subject had been required to make judgments in the presence of others, he would later, when working alone, continue to give the kind of judgments acquired in the group situation.

2. "OVERT" BEHAVIOR AFFECTS "COVERT" ATTITUDES

Now that some examples of how "covert" attitudes affect "overt" behavior have been presented, some instances can be given of how "overt" behavior affects "covert" attitudes.

Some Empirical Studies of "Overt" Behavior. One of the most interesting examples of this relation is shown in a rather elaborate study by Chassell.[33] Data were secured on approximately three hundred adults concerning their present personality traits and attitudes, their earlier religious and social activities, and also the personalities of their fathers, mothers, brothers, and sisters. By means of a statistical analysis, Chassell demonstrated that there was such a high degree of relation between a subject's present sex adjustment and the incidence of parental threats and punishments for sex activities in childhood, as to indicate a causal relation between the two. In other words, this investigation indicated that punishments for sex activities of children and adolescents would result to a considerable extent in lack of sex adjustment as adults. This study, along with others, also shows the desirability of fairly intimate association between children and the father, for the well-developed personality. The relation of general affection and love for the father is extremely important. This is one example, then, of how early behavior may affect present-day "covert" attitudes.

Lois B. Murphy determined sympathy scores for large numbers of children.[34] The type of measurement used was highly reliable, and the interesting thing is that the sympathy scores of the children varied decidedly in terms of the child's present situation, for example, whether the child was in a situation in which he felt himself reasonably secure. In other words, the "overt" situation determined to a great extent the "covert" sympathetic attitudes. In this connection, note the findings of Moreno.[35] Working with large numbers of children in a New York institution, he has demonstrated that when children are treated not as "bad" but as ordinary human beings, their attitudes change accordingly. He allowed children to set up groups for themselves and to have considerable voice in what activities they would engage in, both as to play and work. Their "internal" attitudes were influenced by confident encouragement of good behavior.

Another significant study is one of moral standards among college students as compared with their parents, and with their grandparents.[36] Four possible standards were presented to these three groups: (1) right as opposed to wrong, (2) prudence or intelligent judgment, (3) public opinion, and (4) aesthetic standards. It was demonstrated rather clearly that the students followed the dominant mores largely on the basis of prudence or judgment, that is, according to what they themselves felt might be the correct thing to do or not to do. At the other extreme, however, their grandparents followed the criterion of absolute right and wrong; that is, ways of behaving seemed either fundamentally right or else absolutely wrong. The parents stood someplace in between these two standards in making their judgments of moral conduct. This study is one more demonstration of the way in which "overt" behavior over a period of years tends to determine what one's "covert" attitudes will become.

In a relatively small community, Schanck investigated the attitudes of members of the Baptist Church and of the Methodist Church toward two different methods of baptism.[37] Complete immersion is considered the correct way of baptism in the Baptist Church, mere sprinkling of holy water in the Methodist Church. Table 8 illustrates the differences in attitudes between Baptists and Methodists toward these two forms of baptism, and contrasts their attitudes when they were queried as church members and when they were asked what their private feelings were.

TABLE 8

Different Attitudes Toward Baptism of the Same People

	As Church Members, Per Cent		*Private Feelings, Per Cent*	
	Methodists	*Baptists*	*Methodists*	*Baptists*
Sprinkling only	90	0	16	0
Either	9	22	71	59
Immersion only	0	67	6	17
No attitude	1	11	7	24

Note that when Methodists and Baptists were asked concerning sprinkling as contrasted with immersion in the church situation, 90 per cent of the Methodists believed that sprinkling only was the proper way and 67 per cent of the Baptists believed that immersion only was correct. But when the "overt" situation was changed so that the people were simply asked what their private feelings were, note that 71 per cent of the Methodists and 59 per cent of the Baptists said that either way was perfectly acceptable.

Another study bearing on the matter of attitudes is one by Meltzer, concerned with the experiences of anger which ninety-three college students reported during a period of one week.[38] These students kept "anger" diaries; that is, they noted down every instance when they felt angry and what the external situation was. The "outward" aspects of the "internal" anger are rather interesting. Those periods of anger which included fatigue, hunger, pain, boredom, hurry, and disappointment had a much greater frequency just before mealtimes when the biological organism needed adjustment. Also, differences were found between fraternity and sorority members on the one hand, who felt greater anger just following week ends, and unaffiliated students on the other, who had a greater frequency of anger episodes just prior to week ends. Anger was directed at everything from shoestrings to automobile tires. In fact, there are probably as many different manifestations of anger as there are different behavior patterns and social situations.

CHANGING OF ATTITUDES

A number of studies have dealt with the problem of changing attitudes by manipulating the external behavior situation. Some of these investigations have resulted in rather striking results. Robinson conducted a study during the latter part of the Hoover administration in which questionnaires were sent to several thousands of voters, and on which the subjects were asked to mark certain statements as true, probably true, undecided, probably false, or false.[39] Following this these voters listened to various radio speeches by prominent individuals on topics touched on in the questionnaire. The voters again filled out questionnaires and the results were tabulated. Robinson found that there were very few people who actually changed their attitudes as represented by their verbal opinions from the true to the false side of the ledger, or even from probably true to probably false. However, there were numerous changes from probably true to true, and from probably false to false. Robinson concluded that people had heard a phrase which gave authority to a particular predilection, and, as a result, their uncertainty was changed to certainty.

An experiment by Annis and Meier was devoted to the attitudes of seventy-five university students toward the Honorable W. Morris Hughes, Prime Minister of Australia many years ago.[40] A preliminary test showed that the name of Mr. Hughes was completely unknown to the subjects. Later on half the students read editorials "planted" in the student paper which were very critical of Hughes, while the other half read "planted" editorials which praised him. These editorials were read by the subjects at fifteen successive meetings of the class. The results indicated that these students changed from "no attitude" to attitudes of dislike on the one hand or of like on the other, depending on which type of propaganda they had read. This study, along with others of its kind, suggests that when an institution or person or question is not known to individuals, or when they have little information about it, they can be changed in their attitudes much more readily than if they already have some information about the item.

One of the most widely discussed investigations of change of attitude was conducted by Peterson and Thurstone, who were concerned with the effects of motion pictures on the attitudes of children.[41] As one example, the attitudes of children were measured with regard to the Negro. The children were then shown the moving picture, *The Birth of a Nation*, and after this their attitudes toward the Negro were again measured. Not only was there a statistically significant shift in the direction of disfavor toward Negroes, but even after a period of five months most of these prejudices remained. Peterson and Thurstone also experimented with various other motion pictures and found that attitudes of children toward the Chinese could be changed by showing them the picture, *The Son of the Gods,* a picture definitely favorable to the Chinese; that children could be made more friendly toward Germans by showing them the picture, *Four Sons;* that greater leniency toward criminals could be established by viewing *The Criminal Code;* that pacifistic attitudes could be induced by *All Quiet on the Western Front;* that attitudes of disfavor toward gambling could be brought about by seeing *The Street of Chance.*

ATTITUDES AND BELIEFS AS AFFECTED BY WISHES AND VALUES

WISHES AND DESIRES

Do you have an attitude that certain things will happen, or a belief that certain events will take place? If so, is it because the evidence actually points that way, or is it because you wish or desire that these things will take place? In other words, do your predictions of things to come simply represent wish fulfillment? Your interests and attitudes are probably very much alike, although interests primarily represent likes and dislikes and attitudes represent opinions and beliefs.

Lund presented thirty religious, political, ethical, and scientific propositions to over two hundred college students, such as: Is democracy the best form of government? Did the whale swallow Jonah? Is slander wrong?[42] Every subject not only rated each statement according to his degree of certainty or uncertainty, but also marked the extent to which he himself *wished* the statement to be true or untrue. Lund found a close relation between average belief that a thing was true or untrue, and average desire that it should be true or untrue. In other words, attitudes toward the truth of events were largely based on what people wished to be true.

Cantril attacked the same sort of problem in unique fashion by sending out a questionnaire in April, 1937, to twelve selected groups: bankers, newspaper editors, lawyers, magazine editors, life-insurance executives, public-relations counsels, Communists, historians, economists, sociologists, social psychologists, and laymen.[43] The members of these groups were asked to make predictions on various social events, such as whether or not the United States would undergo another economic depression between

1943 and 1950, whether or not there would be another general European war, whether or not President Roosevelt's Supreme Court bill (at that time very much in the newspapers) would be passed, who would win the Spanish Civil War, what would be the future of the C.I.O. The questionnaire included at the end a short attitude test in which the individuals were asked what their own views were on the Supreme Court plan, Spanish Revolution, the C.I.O., and so forth, what their own attitudes were toward Socialism and toward Fascism. Three aspects of the results are of particular interest. The first, a rather general outcome, is that those individuals whose attitudes favored a certain outcome for an event tended to forecast that desired outcome. In other words, those persons who wanted Franco to win the Spanish Civil War, tended to predict that Franco would win the Spanish Civil War, whereas those on the opposite side in terms of their attitudes made opposite predictions. The personal wishes of the subjects were also reflected in their predictions on questions such as public ownership of electric power and the outcome of the Supreme Court bill. The second finding is even more significant. The various subjects differed decidedly in the extent to which they were influenced by their wishes. The life-insurance executives, bankers, and lawyers on the one hand, the Communists on the other, were most influenced in their judgments by their attitudes. However, the historians, economists, sociologists, and social psychologists were able to make predictions without getting their wishes mixed up with their predictions to any great extent. Apparently social scientists, who are constantly dealing with problems of social value, are able to be more *objective* about their predictions than other kinds of experts. In the third place, the two groups most confident of their predictions were the bankers and the Communists, standing, as you might guess, at opposite extremes. On the other hand, social psychologists and sociologists felt the least certain about their predictions, as to whether or not they would come true.

Another study of this problem of attitudes, wishes, and knowledge was conducted by McGregor.[44] He analyzed some 3,500 predictions made by four hundred college students at Dartmouth, Bennington, and Columbia in May, 1936, about various events. These included such questions as—Will the King of England announce plans for his marriage, before May, 1937? Will Hitler be in power in May, 1937? Will Roosevelt be re-elected in November, 1936? In general, McGregor also found that the predictions were influenced by such subjective factors as wishes, opinions, and attitudes. However, he points out that when the stimulus situation is not ambiguous, wishful factors may be of negligible significance in the determination of prediction.

A closely related study deals with the relation between information and certainty with reference to the 1928 presidential campaign.[45] Each of 357 subjects was asked to indicate on a six-step scale his degree of certainty for each of several statements concerning the issues of the campaign. Following this, an information test was given. The relationship between degree of certainty and amount of information was very low; many persons who possessed inadequate knowledge were as certain in their convictions as others who had considerable understanding of the problems involved.

VALUES

E. L. Thorndike investigated a question of values, reporting his findings in his Presidential Address to the American Association for the Advancement of Science.[46] Psychologists know that attitudes are not necessarily the same thing as verbal opinions or verbal beliefs. Thorndike, of course, realized that the verbal expressions which we give either in language or in written behavior are simply possible clews to our underlying attitudes. Nevertheless, he thought it would be worth while to investigate the relations between attitudes as represented by verbal judgments and values. It would seem impossible to make a verbal judgment about any person, thing, or issue, without introducing certain values, that is, without making what are called value judgments. Thorndike was interested in the question of "values" in spending money. If you should ask any man at random whom you see on his way to lunch what is the motivation which causes him to spend money for lunch, we can predict that he would be tempted to call the nearest police officer, or else answer in relatively naïve fashion, "Why, you dope, to satisfy my hunger, of course." Likewise, if you ask yourself, "Why am I spending money on an education?" you may answer in very simple fashion, "In order to get an education." But would either of these answers really be satisfactory?

It is relatively easy to determine how much money either an individual or the total population spends for a given item. Thus, Thorndike found that in 1929 we spent in this country 17 billion dollars for food, 8 billions for clothing, 6½ billions for automobiles, and so on through such items as laundry, cleaning and dyeing, tobacco, death and burial. He wanted to know *why* we spent 17 billions for food, and the answer is not simply to satisfy our hunger. He wanted to know *why* we spent money on education, and the answer is not just to be educated. Therefore, Thorndike asked various psychologists to divide each item of our national expenses among the various wants to which it probably ministers. He then combined the results into a list of wants and their satisfaction. Among his results are the following:

Our bill for food is spent as follows: 56 per cent. to satisfy hunger; 15 per cent. to gratify the pleasures of taste and smell; 10 per cent. for the pleasures of companionship and social intercourse, including courtship; 3½ per cent. for the approval of others, and smaller percentages for protection against disease, protection against cold, enjoyment of the comfort of other and the pleasures of vision.

Our bill for clothes is spent (according to the psychologists' distribution): 41 per cent. for protection against cold, heat, and wet; 6¾ per cent. for protection against animals and disease; 12½ per cent. for the approval of others; 7 per cent. for self-approval; 10 per cent. to gain pleasure in courtship and sex activities; 8 per cent. for other social intercourse; 6 per cent. for pleasures of vision; 3½ per cent. to win mastery or domination over others, and 2 per cent. to win their affection.

The 700 million dollars for cosmetics and beauty parlors is spent about one seventh for the pleasures of sight and smell, one fourth for the pleasures of sex and courtship, one third to gain general approval from others, one eighth to have inner self-approval, and about one tenth to secure mastery or domination.

When the entire annual budget is thus transformed item by item into a budget for the satisfaction of human wants, payments for sensory pleasures, security, approval of others and the pleasures of companionship and sociability (including romance and courtship) are in each case close in magnitude to the amount paid for freedom from hunger. In fact, we pay more to maintain self-respect and the good opinion of others and avoid scorn, derision and shame than to keep our bodies fed and free from the distress of hunger.

We pay more for entertainment (including the intellectual pleasures and the sensory pleasures of sight, sound, taste and smell) than for protection against cold, heat, wet, animals, disease, criminals and other bad people, and pain.

Less than one third of what we spent went for wants which must be satisfied to keep the human species alive and self-perpetuating. The rest went chiefly to keep us amused and comfortable physically, intellectually, morally and especially socially.[47]

The values we attach to things and ideas influence our attitudes with respect to those things and ideas. In one experiment the subjects placed names of ten different occupations in rank order according to their social standing.[48] They were then told what was the characteristic response given by professional men, by businessmen, by skilled laborers, etc., to various "meaningless" (Rorschach) ink blots; but half of the subjects were given a different list of responses for the different occupations. An analysis of the responses by the subjects showed quite clearly that they were very much influenced by the type of responses to which they had been exposed. As another example of the effects of different values, this same experimenter found that in 1939-40 individuals with pro-Ally attitudes were more willing to accept pro-Ally propaganda than other people, whereas those with pro-German attitudes accepted to a significant degree pro-German propaganda.

Newcomb has published one of the most interesting studies of the effect of values on attitudes.[49] He made a careful analysis of a unique college community where "liberal" attitudes have more prestige and are considered more "proper" than conservative attitudes. Regardless of the differences in courses studied while in college, the attitudes of the students tended to shift significantly in the liberal direction during their four years. The values which become psychologically important to an individual in a group markedly affect his attitudes and his overt behavior.

▶ THE MEASUREMENT OF SOCIAL ATTITUDES

ATTITUDES AND VERBALIZED OPINIONS

Since attitudes consist of dispositions or adjustments toward certain objects or acts, this indicates that attitudes may consist of verbalized or verbalizable tendencies. It has been suggested, in fact, that an attitude "is an interrelated set of opinions organized around a point of reference."[50] Therefore, it would appear relatively simple at first blush to construct scales or other methods of measuring social attitudes. This has been done, of course, by obtaining either individual scores of individual opinions or group scores of opinions, on the assumption that these verbalized opinions come close to "mirroring" the underlying attitudes. Three different methods of attitude measurement have been rather frequently employed.[51]

1. *Census of Opinion.* The first, the *census of opinion,* consists in tabulating answers to a questionnaire. This method is ordinarily used in studying group opinions, such as in determining the percentages of persons in a particular group who believe in birth control or capital punishment or whatnot. By use of this technique Daniel Katz and F. H. Allport, in comparing student attitudes, found that those who felt maladjusted in religious faith tended also to be worried and unsettled concerning their own personalities.[52] In national surveys by the Psychological Corporation, questions have been asked such as, "Do you believe that the United States is on the way to Fascism? Yes. . . . No. . . . Don't Know. . . ." and "Do you believe the present government is helping . . . or hurting . . . business? Don't know. . . ."

2. *A Priori Scale.* The a priori scale consists of the arbitrary scoring of a set of alternative answers which are believed to be equally spaced from each other from most to least favorable. The best example is Bogardus's "social distance" test, on which subjects were asked how much intimacy they would sanction with members of various nationality groups.[53] In one form of the test, the degrees of intimacy are as follows—would admit members of a given nationality group:

1—to close kinship by marriage
2—to my club as personal chums
3—to my street as neighbors
4—to employment in my occupation in my country
5—to citizenship in my country
6—as visitors only to my country
7—would exclude from my country

3. *Psychophysical Scale.* The *psychophysical scale* differs from the *a priori* scale in that various statements have been judged and then arranged along a scale on the basis of actually discriminable differences.[54] The method, developed by Thurstone and Chave, is very time consuming, since it involves the collection of hundreds of opinions, a narrowing down of the number, submission of the smaller number to two or three hundred judges, calculation of scale values and other statistical measures, a second narrowing down of the statements, and finally the use of the scale by those whose attitudes are to be measured. This method has been criticized on a number of counts by Merton,[55] and others.[56] Also it gives approximately the same results as the second method, but, as Stagner has said, "the amount of work required to use it . . . may prove to be a blessing . . . , as it will prevent many hasty, trivial and ill-considered studies which an easier technique would allow."[57]

No matter what type of attitude scale is used, it must meet at least seven basic requirements.[58] (1) It should give results corresponding to an underlying physical order. (2) Scale values of statements chosen as landmarks should not be affected by other items in the scale. (3) Attitudes of judges who sort the statements (when scale values are determined by a sorting procedure), or attitudes of persons taking a test (when scale values are based on their responses) should not affect markedly the scale value of the statements. (4) The scale should be quite specific in content. (5) It must be valid. (6) It must be reliable. (7) It should be a measure of a linear continuum.

One of the most interesting developments for possible use in attitude measurement comes from the field of public-opinion polling. It is a special plan of question design called by George Gallup "quintamensional" because it uses five different approaches. The attempt is to obtain both qualitative as well as quantitative information. The first set of questions determines what a person knows about the issue, and whether he has really given any thought to it. The second is a "free answer" type of question, allowing the person to express his views without any limitations. Third is the "yes-or-no" type of question. In the fourth category are the questions asking the respondent to tell why he feels as he does. Finally, the problem is to find out how strongly he holds to his particular opinion or attitude.

DIFFICULTIES IN MEASUREMENT OF SOCIAL ATTITUDES

Although the various attempts at attitude measurement are significant in that they may give approximations of actual attitudes, there are a number of serious difficulties in the way of the development of any *exact* science of measurement of social attitudes.

First of all, it seems obvious that the response which is given to a question does not necessarily square with the actual attitude of the person. "Knowledge of an attitude or any other somato-psychic process in another person is always indirect and based upon inferences from various types of data."[59]

In the second place, the questionnaire for measuring attitudes represents only a symbolized situation. The measured attitude is only one type of overt-symbolic response to symbols, and this response might have been very different if the person or object or situation symbolized had actually been present. "The name 'John Jones' may provoke the disgusted response, 'What? That blathering fool! Not a brain in his head'; whereas the person, John Jones, may arouse a smile, a warm handshake, and hearty laughter at his latest joke."[60]

Yet few attitude questionnaires even present symbolizations of *actual* situations, but usually abstractions.

> The question "What would you do if you met your friend Wang Chi, the Chinese, dressed in his best and beaming with good humor, on the corner of Sacramento Street and Grant Avenue, the day before New Year, when you were alone and in no hurry?" might constitute a symbolization of an actual situation. The question, typical of "attitudinal" questionnaires, "Do you consider that Chinese make good American citizens?" presents a vague symbolization of an exceedingly vague situational abstraction. What is a Chinese? What is an American citizen? What is good?[61]

Actual changes in meanings of words or phrases from one time to another is another difficulty. Words, as symbols, may convey one meaning to a subject on one presentation of a questionnaire, a different one at a later time. Thus, in one experiment, the slogan "America First" was ranked low by one subject because it seemed to be a "jingoistic phrase," but on a second occasion was ranked high in approval because now interpreted as meaning, "America should take the lead in attempting to settle foreign affairs."[62] Again, the phrase "Balance the budget" was ranked low by a subject when he believed it to mean "abolish relief," but was later ranked high when he thought of the phrase as meaning "balance the human budget."

Another difficulty is that only attitudes that are *common* to a number of people can be measured, and there are comparatively few attitudes common enough to be profitably scaled. In fact, there is always the danger of forcing man's thinking processes into some rigid scale form, and so attitude scales should be looked upon only as rough approximations of actual attitudes.[63] These are only some of the errors against which the cautious investigator must be on guard.[64]

Deception may even occur, particularly if the investigation relates to moral or social values of the subject. Probably because of the low prestige value of the tabloids, one study of New York newspaper readers failed to show many readers of tabloids in terms of answers to a direct question as to what papers were read; it was only by disguising the study by asking who the favorite columnist or sports writer was that the information of actual newspaper-reading habits was elicited. Many studies pertaining to sexual attitudes are notoriously faulty in getting true information.

Finally, there is the problem of *ambivalence*. One may have *at the same time* contrary and opposite attitudes on some question. He feels "Yes" and "No" at once, or alternately. In other words, he has ambivalent or contradictory attitudes. These may be present to such an extent that the subject is unable to answer the question at all because of a conflict as to what his own attitudes are; or his attitudes may shift according to his environmental situation. *Note carefully the meaning of ambivalence, for the term will be employed a number of times in subsequent chapters.*

Stagner reports an interesting event which demonstrates the "flimsy" nature of supposedly strong attitudes:

> . . . A meeting of farmers was recently called to discuss the milk strike. In the afternoon, under the influence of a speaker favorably disposed toward the strike, this group voted unanimously for such action. The same group was called together in the evening to hear a speaker who was opposed to the milk strike. They then voted unanimously not to strike. Obviously the attitude involved was of a very incompletely formed sort. . . .[65]

VALUE OF ATTITUDE MEASUREMENT

These various objections do not mean that attitude measurement is of no avail at all. They simply mean that we must always be on guard against the magic of numbers. The mere fact that a problem has been reduced to figures is no guarantee of truth, and we should always inquire what lies back of the figures.

Actually a great deal of significant work is being done in the field of attitude measurement. Polls of opinion by the American Institute of Public Opinion, *Fortune* magazine, the National Opinion Research Center, the Michigan Survey Research Center, and the Psychological Corporation have been well executed and have had great practical value.[66] Such organizations as these have reduced many a problem in business and industry to a scientific study of attitudes, usually with due caution against sweeping generalizations. Carefully controlled attitude studies are often helpful in giving *approximations* of attitudes which could not otherwise be found. Instances of this will be found in succeeding chapters, in analyses of political attitudes, for example (Chapter 19).

QUESTIONS AND PROBLEMS FOR DISCUSSION

1. *In what ways do traits differ from attitudes?*
2. *What is meant by a "frame of reference"? Give an example.*
3. *What are traits? How can they be measured?*
4. *Make a list of opinions which you originally acquired at home and which have since been modified through the influence of outside elements. What was the outside influence in each case? Explain in terms of the conditioned response.*
5. *Think of several examples of* ambivalence *in your own attitudes. Why are you ambivalent in each instance?*
6. *In addition to the methods of attitude measurement described in this chapter, what other ones can you find described in the psychological literature?*
7. *Describe some instances of the influence of covert attitudes on overt behavior; and of the influence of overt behavior on covert attitudes.*
8. *How are your attitudes affected by value judgments?*

RECOMMENDED READINGS

Allport, G. W., "Attitudes." In Murchinson, C. (editor), *A Hankbook of Social Psychology*. Worcester: Clark University Press, 1935, Chapter 17.

Allport, G. W., *Personality: A Psychological Interpretation*. New York: Henry Holt and Company, Inc., 1937.

Blumer, H., *Movies and Conduct*. New York: The Macmillan Company, 1933.

Katz, D., and Allport, F. H., *Students' Attitudes*. Syracuse: Craftsman Press, 1931.

Moreno, J. L., *Who Shall Survive? A New Approach to the Problem of Human Interrelations*. Washington, D. C.: Nervous and Mental Disease Publishing Company, 1934.

Murphy, L. B., *Social Behavior and Child Personality: An Exploratory Study of Some Roots of Sympathy*. New York: Columbia University Press, 1937.

Newcomb, T. M., *Personality and Social Change*. New York: Dryden Press, 1943.

Peterson, R. C., and Thurstone, L. L., *Motion Pictures and the Social Attitudes of Children*. New York: The Macmillan Company, 1933.

Stagner, R., *Psychology of Personality*. New York: McGraw-Hill Book Company, Inc., 1937.

Thurstone, L. L., and Chave, E. J., *The Measurement of Attitude: A Psychophysical Scale and Some Experiments with a Scale for Measuring Attitude toward the Church.* Chicago: University of Chicago Press, 1929.

Young, K. (editor), *Social Attitudes.* New York: Henry Holt and Company, Inc., 1931.

Young, K., *Personality and Problems of Adjustment.* New York: F. S. Crofts & Co., 1940.

*Newcomb, T. M., Hartley, E. L., and others (editors), *Readings in Social Psychology.* New York: Henry Holt and Company, Inc., 1947. (The following selections are listed according to the sequence of related discussions in the chapter you have just read.)

Sherif, M., "Group Influences upon the Formation of Norms and Attitudes," pp. 77–90.

Levine, J. M., and Murphy, G., "The Learning and Forgetting of Controversial Material," pp. 108–115.

Information and Education Division, U. S. War Department, "The Effects of Presenting 'One Side' versus 'Both Sides' in Changing Opinions on a Controversial Subject," pp. 566–579.

Bruner, J. S., and Goodman, C. C., "Value and Need as Organizing Factors in Perception," pp. 99–108.

Maccoby, E. E., and Holt, R. R., "How Surveys Are Made," pp. 581–591.

Newcomb, T. M., "Some Patterned Consequences of Membership in a College Community," pp. 345–357.

CHAPTER EIGHT

THE SOCIAL PSYCHOLOGY OF LANGUAGE

LANGUAGE AND ITS DEVELOPMENT. Language, Thinking, and Inner Speech—Origin of Language—Language Development of the Child—Concept Formation / TYPES OF LANGUAGE. Three Kinds of Language—(1) Vocal Language (Speech)—(2) Graphic Language—(3) Gesture Language—Egocentric and Socialized Speech—Sex Differences in Conversation / THE SOCIAL SIGNIFICANCE OF LANGUAGE. Socialization—Meaning of Language—The Reality of Words—Language as a Substitute for Significant Overt Action—Problems of Definition—Emotional Terms—Words and Their Referents—The Tyranny of Words—Symbolic Value of Language.

▶ LANGUAGE AND ITS DEVELOPMENT

LANGUAGE, THINKING, AND INNER SPEECH

What percentage of your time do you spend talking to other people, reading, and in other types of language behavior? You do not need a careful introspection of your daily life to realize how important language is in enabling you to understand the society in which you live.

Although thinking is not the same as language, they are very closely related. In fact, some students of human behavior have fallen into the error of describing thinking as *inner* speech. You can, of course, note subvocal speech in your own thinking. You find that you think words to yourself, and if you put your fingers on your throat muscles during a period of intense thinking, you may be able to note slight contractions and changes in the musculature. In other words, subvocal or inner speech ordinarily accompanies the thinking process; but does this mean that thinking is nothing more than inner speech? There are at least six reasons why this is not true: (1) You may have difficulty in finding some word for a meaning which you actually have "in mind." The idea or meaning is there, but the language equivalent is not. (2) A fundamental principle of mathematics is that if A = B, then B = A. Accordingly, if thought = inner speech, it follows that inner speech = thought, but this is not true. You can recite a familiar passage with no sense of its meaning, even while thinking about something entirely different. (3) The thinking process certainly involves seeing the point, observing relationships as well as words, and sometimes physical manipulations, such as the use of a pencil in working out mathematical formulas.[1] (4) In higher forms of reasoning, speech is sometimes a handicap to the thinking process—as in using diagrams. (5) You may in silent reading cover material in half the time that would be required if you had to pronounce every individual word subvocally. (6) In thinking, you actually keep ahead of your speech organs, so that you know what you are going to say even before you say it.

In other words, language, thinking, and inner speech are very closely integrated, but this does not mean that any one of the three is synonymous with the others.

Language may be defined as "any system of communication among beings, through conventional symbols. The chief varieties of language in the human species are vocal (speech), graphic, and gesture."[2] Note that lower forms of animals and human beings both have language behavior, that is, they communicate through conventional symbols. Yerkes reports that a great deal which the captive chimpanzee hears from human lips is meaningful.[3] Every animal lover has noticed the variety of appropriate responses which pets make to various cues given by their owners.

ORIGIN OF LANGUAGE

What is the origin of language? One ingenious theory is the *onomatopoetic* notion, based on such words as *crackle, chickadee, splash, buzz,* and *bow-wow,* which are similar to the sounds made by the animals or acts they represent. The *interjectional* theory, based on such words as *ah, oh, pshaw, umm,* holds that man's original language developed from a series of automatic emotional responses. According to a third idea, the *ding-dong* theory, there were reflex associations of some particular object and a corresponding vocal response, which eventually became permanently associated. The *yo-he-ho* theory is based upon rhythmical vocalizations, supposedly used in such cooperative activities as rowing or pulling. Another ingenious theory is a phonetic one, that speech—one type of language—is a form of pantomime performed by the tongue and lips and other organs of speech instead of by the hands and body.[4] In other words, for a particular situation an individual develops characteristic movements of the speech organs which eventually are always used in that situation.

Actually, no one of these theories explains the true origin of language; although a multiplicity of these *and other* factors may account for the origin of the words or symbols we use. A child playing in the sand might invent a word for pebbles and call them "pocos." In a group of children his own age the child may continue to use the term pocos; in fact, there is no reason why pocos should not be as good a term for bits of stone as the word "pebbles." In other words, a chance vocal expression may develop certain linguistic significance. In primitive times, the opportunity for inventing new words was almost unlimited. But, in addition to an individual emitting a new sound or sequence of sounds, others had also to learn to use the new sound in a similar way.[5] In this connection Thorndike has advanced the *babble-babble* theory of the origin of language, called this because it relies on the miscellaneous vocal play of man.

> . . . A person [in a primitive group] would prattle while he worked or played much as a child of a year or two now prattles as he plays. If his making a certain sound became connected with his experiencing a certain object or act and having an image or expectation or idea of that object or act, he would have a language. That sound and the act of making it would mean that object or act to him. . . .
>
> If he did connect *ik* with his digging stick, and *ug* with his large turtle-shell container, *yum* with truffle and *kuz* with clam, he could plan an expedition to get truffles or one to get clams more easily and conveniently than he could with only pictorial memories. . . .
>
> His companions might well hear him say *kuz* as he dug up a clam or opened a clam or ate a clam, a hundred times in a week. Even if they paid no more attention to his speech than to his personal play, vocal or non-vocal, the sound *kuz* would tend to make them think of a clam more often than of any other one object. And under certain conditions they would be attentive to his speech. For example, in a group digging for clams together, if one cried *kuz* whenever he found a clam, the cry would become interesting to others.[6]

The principal conditions for language development are the isolation of a group of individuals with no simple means of communication with others.[7] In such a situation a new language is almost bound to develop. For a series of nonsense words which had arbitrary meanings assigned to them, Newman had subjects make judgments of which words denoted larger or smaller.[8] Between "glupa" and "glopa," for example, both of which had the meaning of "horse," most of the subjects chose "glopa" as signifying to them the *larger* horse. Apparently the sound of the longer vowel seemed larger.

Wherever different languages are found, certain fundamental principles can be discovered within that particular language. To illustrate this, certain words in English have taken on the same sorts of endings. The "er" and "or" endings in banker, driver, reaper, actor, confessor, professor imply someone who is doing something. Note the "ed" endings in verb forms. You know immediately from past experience that this indicates an action completed. Notice the positive and comparative forms of adjectives—big, bigger, biggest; small, smaller, smallest—and you know from the form what the word implies. "The psychological law that is here at work may be expressed by saying that words which involve the same fundamental idea tend to take on the same form."[9] This is also demonstrated in our use of plurals and in words which we use in more than one context. For example, the word "foot" does not need to be redefined when you speak of the foot of a person, of a mountain, or of a ladder;

nor do you have to redefine the word "mouth" when you speak of the mouth of a man or of a river. Colloquialisms and slang are also easily understood and frequently come into general usage, such as "o.k." or "pal."

LANGUAGE DEVELOPMENT OF THE CHILD

When you first saw the light of day, you had no language and understood none. How did you find out what it is all about? How did you learn to interpret your early environment and later the world about you?

First of all, the human infant goes through a *prelinguistic* stage, consisting of screaming and apparently random sounds. From the beginning of the birth cry—which may have had to be stimulated almost as one would start an electric clock—until a period a few months later, little indication is given of either language development or the understanding of language. After a few months, however, *babbling* begins and circular conditioned responses are established between sounds uttered and individual responses. Babbling is thus a process in which the response acts as a stimulus for its own reproduction. In contrast to the early cries, babbling carries a greater diversity of sounds and serves as a basis for the imitative process. Slightly later, this *imitation* stage appears, and the child repeats the same sounds which he hears older persons use. The acquisition of *true speech,* however, does not really begin until the child is about a year old, when he has developed one or two words. From that time on the process of speech development continues rapidly.

By the time the child is seven or eight years of age, he has developed a reasonably useful vocabulary. Although the average infant knows only about 272 words at age two, by age three he has a vocabulary of about 896 words, at four years of 1,540, at five of 2,072, and at six of 2,562 words.[10] Development of a vocabulary seems to be an easier accomplishment for infant girls than for boys. Little girls not only learn to speak at a slightly earlier age than boys but seem to develop better enunciation and grammatical forms. Although boys and girls make about the same number of sounds during their first year of life, girls outtalk boys in the second and third years.[11] They also tend to be superior to boys in the amount of verbal behavior in later years.[12]

> The first words in all infant speech are such words as "pa-pa" and "ma-ma." In all languages these words recur with some variations in the consonant elements. The interesting point for our discussion is that these words are natural only in the sense that they issue from the infant as the easier sounds to produce. The meanings attached to these early efforts of infancy are not derived from the child's intention. They come rather from the child's adult attendants. The parents have learned the value of words and urge on the child who contributes

the sounds, certain interpretations which are adopted by the whole group and turn the natural sounds into conventional words.[13]

When the baby makes a sound such as "wah-h-h," this is easily interpreted as "da-da," and this response is reinforced over and over again whenever "that man" appears on the scene. Similarly, a child may say "inc" and the mother responds by repeating to the child "drink" and giving it milk. After numerous repetitions of "inc" by the child and "drink" by the mother, plus thirst-satisfying stimuli, the child learns to reproduce the word "drink" when thirsty. In other words, the word and the object are linked together in one configuration. Watson even trained his child to say "da-da" whenever a milk bottle was given to him.[14] Instead of petting him when the sound "da-da" was uttered, Watson simply gave the baby his bottle. In other words, the bottle became "da-da," and "da-da" meant bottle. Instead of saying, "Naughty baby, now I am going to spank you!" just prior to punishment, a parent could just as easily substitute the phrase, "Nice baby, see the pretty milk bottle!" and proceed with the punishment, provided the same phrase and tone were always used.[15]

Reactions to tonal qualities and intensities are the predominant patterns which develop verbal responses. There is nothing unusually mysterious about the learning of vocal habits. Small children are learning to speak at the same time that they are learning to drink from receptacles, to eat with utensils, and to dress themselves. Learning of language by human beings is not very different from learning of tricks by animals. Any dog or horse owner knows that an animal can be trained to respond to certain intonations and word symbols, simply by rewarding him whenever he responds to certain symbols and punishing him when he responds to other symbols. Wolfe succeeded in training chimpanzees to carry out certain work activities, the reward being poker chips.[16] This type of training is analogous to that of child training, where the child must be taught to respond to verbal satisfactions of a symbolic sort.

It is four o'clock in the morning. The whole house is quiet. Baby is sleeping peacefully in his cradle, warm and dry. As the six o'clock feeding hour approaches, the rhythm of his stomach contractions speeds up. The contractions are bigger and last longer. Finally he wakes up, hungry and wet. His cries soon awaken the mother or nurse, and shortly thereafter he is changed and fed. During the process the infant is subjected to sources of gratification in addition to the food and relief from wetness. He is picked up and held. He is fondled and even caressed by the proud mother. All of this is accompanied by soft love talk. With the relief of hunger the talking stops, and the child is returned to his cradle until the next cycle of similar events. Suppose that the normal cycle should be interrupted by a pin's coming loose and pricking the baby's tender skin. Immediate howling is heard, and the mother rushes in to set things right. Again there is the association between the relief of a tension and the flood of tender phrases and loving caresses. Later the child becomes older and starts to play with other children. It will sometimes happen that the child is hurt by some plaything or is bullied by an older child [and cries]. Here again the mother sets things right and sympathizes with her child. Thus it goes throughout life—hunger, love, thirst, fear, pain are allayed in situations in which the omnipresent mother's voice plays a prominent rôle. Under these conditions the voice of the mother takes on the reward value of the purely physiological relief.[17]

In other words, not only does language behavior develop with *physiological* relief from certain tensions in the cycle of activity, but the *psychological* reward of certain word forms and their intonation becomes more and more important. In fact, the child after a time learns to respond primarily to words, which now stand as symbols of reward although no physiological reward is achieved.

The child learns to respond to the language behavior of others even before he is able to manipulate these word forms himself. This is analogous to the learning of a foreign language—if you have ever mastered conversational German or French, you undoubtedly reached some stage where you could understand what was said to you but were not able to make the proper reply. The child's own verbal habits are also sources of stimulation; the fact of hearing himself say something may tend to reinforce these word forms.

CONCEPT FORMATION

The development of language consists of something more than mastering unique word forms. It involves concept formation as well, that is, the understanding of how certain words stand for a whole set of acts or things or ideas. Concept learning—consisting of generalization and abstraction—is extremely difficult for the child until he is a few years old. In later years, however, he must learn that one single word form may stand for a variety of different ideas. He must learn such concepts as "round-ness," "table-ness," "book-ness."

A young child finds himself in a certain situation, reacts to it by approach say, and hears it called "dog." After an indeterminate intervening period he finds himself in a somewhat different situation and hears that called "dog." Later he finds himself in a somewhat different situation still, and hears that called "dog" also. Thus the process continues. The "dog" experiences appear at irregular intervals. The appearances are thus unanticipated. They appear with no obvious label as to their essential nature. This precipitates at each new appearance a more or less acute *problem* as to the proper reaction . . . ; the intervals between the "dog" experiences are filled with all sorts of other absorbing experiences which are contributing to the formation of other concepts. At length the time arrives when the child has a "meaning" for the word dog. Upon examination this "meaning" is found to be actually a characteristic more or less common to all dogs and not common to cats, dolls and "teddy-bears." But to the child the process of arriving at this meaning or concept has been largely unconscious. He has never said to himself, "Lo! I shall proceed to discover the characteristics common to all dogs but not enjoyed by cats and 'teddy-bears.'" The formation of the concept has never been an end deliberately sought for itself.[18]

The words which children first learn to hear and speak properly have a very limited meaning. The word "da-da," for example, often is applied to all men, and it is only later that the child learns to reserve it for one particular man. As the child grows older, words take on a meaning somewhat closer to that of the older persons who use them, and it is through this process that the culture patterns of the group are experienced.

Parents and older persons make use of these factors in child training, since punishment or reward is not simply on a physiological basis but may be at the verbal level. A mother may say, "If you do that, you'll hurt yourself." It is not necessary for the child actually to experience the physiological hurt; the symbolic meaning is sufficient. In much the same way social approval and disapproval of the child's actions may be transmitted to him. By a mere frown or the raising of a hand, an older person may convey to the child the meaning of a social situation. Similarly, there is the use by older persons of concepts which are completely abstract to the child, yet which serve the purpose of socializing him. Instead of telling a child to refrain from some act, a mother may simply say, "Darling, God doesn't love little boys who behave like that." In such a situation God is a nonmaterial but a psychological reality, and as such has a limited meaning for the child. This is important because, as we shall see, our adult use of words does not always differ from this childish sort of understanding.

Words may be employed by an individual which have no precise meaning for him. Thus, either child or adult may learn to use words of which the exact meanings are beyond his capacity to understand.[19] He parrots words that have little real significance for him. "I'm a bad boy, Mummy," the small child will happily announce. "I'm convinced that ours is the only correct course," may be an adult version of this same kind of meaningless verbal symbolization. Every language contains many abstractions, such as "sacrifice," "mystery," and "honor," which are difficult to reduce to precise meanings. Each person has his own ideas of their definition and application. Yet words like these may triumph over tangible things—they have tremendous social force.

▶ TYPES OF LANGUAGE

THREE KINDS OF LANGUAGE

The human species has three different types of language, namely *vocal, graphic,* and *gesture;* and all are effective instruments of social control. Vocal language is synonymous with speech. Examples of graphic language are graphs and charts, the printed matter in this book. Gesture language consists of the larger movements of the body and arms and also of the more refined changes in the fingers and the facial musculature, such as a frown or a smile. All three types have their demonstrative and emotional aspects.

1. *Vocal Language* (*Speech*). Vocal language includes more than the mere word forms of a particular language. Its symbolic nature may be illustrated by the following conversation which supposedly took place between a diner and waiter in a restaurant. Read this out loud.

F-U-N-E-X?
S-V-F-X.
N-E-M?
S-V-F-M.
L-F-M-N-X.

This illustration is not an attempt to be funny; it is given to illustrate the symbolic character of all vocal language. Word forms are simply symbols which stand for meanings of the participants. Thus, the headline in the New York *Daily News,* JUG UMP HITTER ON ROLLING RAP, was a means of conveying to several million readers that a man who had once slugged an umpire had now been arrested on a charge of picking the pockets of a sleeping citizen.[20]

Certain verbal symbols have different emotional tone. Contrast the word "stink" with the word "moonlight." You do not need to call up any olfactory or visual imagery in order to react unpleasantly to stink or pleasantly to moonlight. In this same connection, the pitch or way in which words are spoken will determine their degree of pleasantness for you. If you are a Southerner, soft-spoken and melodious speech forms seem agreeable to you. If you are a New Englander, a nasal twang may sound natural. The meaning of words may be changed by differences in pitch and accent. Consider the phrase, "What a bright idea!" If the emphasis is put on the third word, what a *bright* idea, sarcasm may be implied; whereas what a bright *idea* may imply enthusiasm, exactly the same word forms being used. Such simple words as "yes" and "no" may have different meanings according to the way in which they are said. "Yes" does not mean the same thing as "y-e-e-e-s."

Among humans there is not only a large explosive vocabulary, but the discriminations are registered in the tonal quality of words and even in the several intonations given to the same word. Thus the word "yes" may express half a dozen or more shades of tension and meaning—agreement, doubtful agreement, skeptical agreement, reluctant agreement, petulant agreement, rejection of agreement.[21]

Largely because the inflections and pitches of different languages vary so much, we often make false interpretations of cultures other than our own. Thus, because Japanese seem to Americans to say everything without much change in tone, we are likely to come to the mistaken conclusion that they are monotonous, unimaginative people. Similarly, because there is a great range in pitch in the speech of many Italians, we are likely to associate this with a volatile personality. Where we do not like the particular types of speech, this may serve as one basis of nationality prejudice. For example, if an American does not like Germans, he can talk about the awful "guttural" sound of the German language. Of course, we need to take into account the cultural factors in order to understand what the vocal behavior really means. We can make reasonably good interpretations of what the intonations mean in our own group. G. W. Allport and Cantril demonstrated experimentally that judges were able to achieve better than chance results in matching radio voices with brief descriptions of the speakers.[22]

When one individual hears another's voice, he may react to any one of four things: (*a*) the sounds that reach his ears; (*b*) the speaker himself, that is, the object emitting the sounds; (*c*) the words and sentences which are sound patterns; and (*d*) the meaning of the speaker's words. The attention of the listener may be focused upon any of these four, that is, on the loudness, pitch, and timbre of the sounds; on the kind of person emitting them; on the particular words and sentences; or on the meaning of these words and sentences.

First, subtle changes in loudness, pitch, and timbre may suggest different meanings to others. This may be illustrated where no words are even used; thus, to breathe out slowly, as in a sigh, may signify grief or boredom, whereas to breathe out suddenly, as in a snort, suggests scorn. Second, dominance and prestige are important considerations in determining the reactions to speech; exactly the same words uttered by Mr. Milquetoast and by Mr. Boldfront convey different meanings. Third, choice of words and sentences, diction, grammar, clarity, precision, and careful phraseology all influence the listeners. Which gives a more lasting impression—to say that it is a hot day, or to talk about the sizzling streets of a sweltering city? Fourth, the exact meaning of words is obviously important.

Thus, the meaning of "mandamus" would be understood by lawyers but not by laborers, while the word "mattock" would be understood by laborers but probably not by lawyers. Even more familiar words, used by almost everyone, must be handled with care. . . . The background and experiences and attitudes, of the lawyer and the laborer, of the farmer and the fisherman, may be so completely different that precisely the same word carries to each a different connotation. To use the word "Socialism" without elaboration may convey to some listeners the concept of a planned society, but to others the notion of Bolshevism and revolution. This means that the particular loyalties and peculiar prejudices of people must not be overlooked: loyalties to political party, church, lodge, profession; prejudices among Negroes and whites, Catholics and Protestants, Gentiles and Jews.[23]

2. *Graphic Language.* The second type of language is graphic. The word "graphic" sometimes means picturesque or vivid, but as employed here it refers to the printed or written word. If vocal language or speech must be simple to be intelligible, graphic language must be even more so. With the emphasis on speed that exists in our modern civilization, we even want to acquire information in the quickest possible way. We want our meanings boiled down for us and predigested. Thus, the magazine *Reader's Digest* has an enormous circulation. An article of a few thousand words is boiled down to one of a few hundred. Why should we not produce a new magazine, a *Reader's Digest of the Reader's Digest?* And from that we could go on to a *Reader's Digest of the Reader's Digest of the Reader's Digest.* The point is that we are constantly demanding oversimplification, and this means that the full connotation of words may be missed. Meaningfulness results not simply from a word itself, but from its use with other words. Likewise, the meaningfulness of phrases and even of paragraphs is in terms of their total context.

In framing graphic language, it is important, of course, to realize who the readers will be. Consider the following opening paragraph of a leaflet distributed by the National Tuberculosis Association and addressed to Southern Negroes:

> Tuberculosis is nothing like "conjur" or slow poison. Tuberculosis is real sickness and it is bad, but it can be cured.
>
> You get chickens from eggs; you get cotton from cotton seed, and potatoes from potatoes. It is just like that, and it is the same with tuberculosis. You get tuberculosis from tuberculosis bugs or germs. Nobody can give it to you by sprinkling dust on your doorstep. You cannot get it from anyone who tries to put a spell on you in any way. You can only get it from a person who is sick with the same sickness.

If this same document had been phrased in terms suitable for members of the American Association for the Advancement of Science, it would have little meaning for a great many Southern Negro readers. Note the symbolic character of printed characters as well as other forms of language. A writer does not actually convey *his* ideas to the reader. All that he does is to put on a page marks which represent his ideas and hope that these marks will be interpreted by the reader so that there will be some understanding of what the writer had in mind. Many are the inadequate and erroneous concepts obtained from a printed page. Pupils were asked to interpret the following passage: "Since there were no matches in 1763, the most primitive way of starting a fire had to be used. A piece of some very hard stone, called flint, was struck against a bit of steel. This produced a spark, which was caught in tinder or in soft, dry cloth." When they were asked what the word *primitive* in the first sentence meant, some of the replies were: *the only way, the easiest way, the most important way, the best way they could think of, the most used method, the usual way, the most dangerous way,* and *a new way.*

In a picture test representing this and three other primitive methods of fire making, many students could not identify the picture representing the method to which the selection refers. When confronted, in a personal interview, with a variety of objects, among which were those mentioned in the selection, students were found who could not select the necessary implements for making a fire; and when flint, steel, and tinder were placed before them, could not show how to strike the steel against the flint to make a spark or how to ignite the tinder. Yet some of these students did well on true-false and multiple-choice tests on the selection.[24]

Seventh-grade students read the following passage: "There were few newspapers in these early days of which we have been reading (about 1775); mail was slow and very irregular; and railroads and telegrams unheard of." The question, "What do you understand is meant by the statement that the mail was 'very irregular'?" resulted in: *It didn't always get there. Trains would get broken down. It does not come all the time. It went in a straight line. Half the time the mail would come about a week slow. The mail zigzazzed all over. No regular route. When it snowed it was stopped until the snow melted.*[25]

Simple words may be difficult, but figurative language is even more troublesome. Students were asked to explain the following passage: "Daniel Webster said of Hamilton, 'He smote the rock of national resources, and abundant streams of revenue burst forth. He touched the dead corpse of public credit and it sprang upon its feet.'" Among the responses were these:

Daniel Webster said that Hamilton a plenty of Government has burst forward. He put his hand on the dead people and free to everybody and it grew to his feet.

When he touched the dead they would spring to their feet.

Daniel Webster said of Hamilton, "He stopped mother nature and fake rivers came instead. He stopped public credit and it was returned to him."

Hamilton tried to break up the nation.[26]

Graphic language, then, is not always easy to interpret. The mere use of certain words does not even demonstrate that one has the ideas or concepts for which those words stand. So it is no mean task just to learn "what the book says." A carefully controlled experiment has indicated that a large percentage of children in the elementary grades not only did not know how to read intelligently but could not discriminate critically what they did read.[27]

3. *Gesture Language.* Gestures consist not only of large movements of the arms and legs but also of very refined and delicate facial motions to indicate to others what you have "in mind." Thus, a blinking of the eyes may mean surprise, a wrinkling of the brows, puzzlement. The *V* symbol for Allied victory—holding up the widely separated first two fingers of the hand as a greeting—which was so widely used during World War II, is an example of a gesture with tremendous social force.[28] If gestures are understood in a particular group, they have just as much social significance as vocal or graphic language. In telling young people how to behave at a dance, Mrs. Emily Post says that it is sometimes permissible for a girl to dance for a short while with her eyes closed, meaning "Please don't cut in."

The actual gesture language which you follow is simply that of the group in which you live or which you consider correct. The gestures which are "correct" for you may be extremely incorrect for people in other cultures, and vice versa. Culture determines: (*a*) the situations which will arouse certain emotional responses and not others; (*b*) the extent to which the responses are supported by custom; and (*c*) the particular forms which the expressions take.[29]

Cultural control of emotional expression is first of all *negative,* e.g., the Sioux Indian learns *not* to wince, the European soldier *not* to tremble, the Chinese gentleman *not* to snarl or shout in his rage (he may stare "with round eyes"; he may do no more). But this negative control is not the only one that reflects cultural style; one learns *when* to be angry, *when* to be ashamed, and to some degree even *how* to be angry or ashamed. One also learns the postures and gestures, the expressions of deference, embarrassment, or surprise.[30]

A contrast between Englishmen and Sicilians illustrates the correctness and incorrectness of certain gesture language. The essential reserve of some Englishmen, and lack of reserve of some Sicilians, is not a matter of "instincts" but simply a difference in training in two different cultural groups. Contrast our own behavior of embracing and kissing on the return of a loved one with that of the Maori of New Zealand with whom this is a time for tears and mournful weeping, which may continue for hours. Among the Andaman Islanders, "when two friends or relatives meet after a separation, they greet each other by sitting down, one on the lap of the other, with their arms around each other's necks, weeping and wailing for two or three minutes."[31] Japanese children are taught to smile as a social duty in the same way that they are taught to bow or to prostrate themselves. This accounts in some measure for a lack of understanding between Americans and Japanese; Americans object to the Japanese smile as insincere, whereas Japanese are often surprised at the irritated faces of Americans which reflect too closely what they actually feel.[32]

> We find it natural to stand up in the presence of a superior; the Fijians and Tongans sit down under similar circumstances. The inhabitants of the Friendly Islands would take their clothes off as a sign of respect. Among the Maori it was a sign of friendship and often of protection to double the forefinger of the right hand and place the projecting second joint to the tip of the nose. The Todas raise the open right hand to the face, resting the thumb on the bridge of the nose. To them it means respect; but almost exactly the same sign is used in our society to signify something quite different.[33]

The gestures of any culture are largely *learned* reactions. Motion-picture records have shown marked differences between gestures of immigrants and those of the next generation in this country.[34] Gestures may vary so much from one culture to another that the overt behavior of individuals in one group is almost unintelligible to members of another group. Within the same culture, of course, most of us are able to interpret rather readily what gestures mean, even the more refined and delicate kinds. Many executives and salesmen develop a certain ability to "size up" other people partly on the basis of gesture behavior. The type of gesture behavior which you adopt may even change your own attitudes. For example, if you feel irritable and cross, you can resort to the simple expedient of turning up the corners of your mouth and forcing yourself to laugh; the result is usually to dispel the irritable mood.

EGOCENTRIC AND SOCIALIZED SPEECH

Frequently a distinction is made between *egocentric* and *socialized* types of speech.[35] Egocentric speech consists primarily of a monologue about oneself.

> When a child utters phrases belonging to the [egocentric] group, he does not bother to know to whom he is speaking nor whether he is being listened

to. He talks either for himself or for the pleasure of associating anyone who happens to be there with the activity of the moment. This talk is egocentric, partly because the child speaks only about himself, but chiefly because he does not attempt to place himself at the point of view of his hearer.[36]

In socialized speech, on the other hand, a child addresses his hearer, considers his point of view, tries to influence him, or actually exchanges ideas with him. Socialized speech also includes criticism, commands, requests, threats, questions, and answers. Piaget found that about 38 per cent of the child's remarks fall in the *egocentric* category, but this finding has been criticized by others.[37] In a well-controlled experiment, McCarthy found less than 4 per cent egocentric responses.[38] Although there may be no rigid division, both children and adults have a mixture of egocentric and socialized concepts in their speech.

In one survey of 27 kindergarten children, involving the collection of over three thousand separate remarks, it was found that over 40 per cent constituted self-assertion, and a negligible part of 1 per cent contained ideas of self-depreciation.[39] This is some evidence for the egocentric nature of the conversation of kindergarten children. Goodenough collected samples of spontaneous conversations of 203 children, and found that the pronouns of the first person singular are used much more frequently during play with other children than in those situations where the child is alone with an adult.[40] But is this unique with respect to children? Certainly there is evidence that a great deal of conversation of both adolescents and adults involves egocentric beliefs and attitudes. You can demonstrate this to yourself simply by observing conversations of other persons in all sorts of social situations or by examining your own language as you talk. Observe carefully the next time you meet a friend whom you have not seen for some time. If your conversation follows the usual pattern, it will consist of a monologue on your part about yourself, followed by a second monologue by your friend concerning himself, rather than a dialogue involving a real exchange of ideas.

This problem has been investigated experimentally in the conversation of women college students.[41] The mere use of the pronoun "I" does not necessarily mean that a sentence is egocentric; for example, "I take it she went to Holyoke" is not an egocentric statement. On the other hand, "Who the Hell cares? Work don't mean nothing" is a highly egocentric statement, even though the personal pronoun does not appear. Two college women eavesdropped on other college girls in dormitory smoking rooms and wash rooms, listened to telephone conversations, even hid under beds while tea parties were being held. Their analysis of over three thousand remarks reveals that over 40 per cent of the remarks were ego-related, about the same percentage Piaget found for small children. This study indicates that egocentric speech is not something unique to any one age or pattern of life. In fact, at all ages language of various kinds is used, always involving both *covert* and *overt* aspects.

SEX DIFFERENCES IN CONVERSATION

What are the sex differences in conversation? Again, you can make your own observations. However, you are at a disadvantage in being a man and therefore not knowing what women really talk about, or else in being a woman and not being "in the know" about men's conversation.

Four interesting studies have involved the method of eavesdropping. In 1922, Moore walked down the same section of Broadway in New York City every night at 7:30 p.m. for several weeks, listening in on bits of conversation.[42] The main topics of conversation were: between men, money and business; between women, men.

In 1924, Landis and Burtt took notes on five hundred conversations in a variety of places.[43] Men were found to talk chiefly about business and money; secondly, about sports and amusements. Women's leading subjects were: first, men; second, clothes.

Baker and McGregor, who reported on conversations heard in 1936, have found marked similarities to the earlier studies.[44] However, since over the years various social changes had gone on which might influence the conversational categories used, they added one called "politics and economics," and found that this accounted for approximately one-fifth of the conversations of men to men, and about one-tenth of the conversations of women to women. These three studies are summarized in Table 9.[45]

As in many phases of social psychology, we should be concerned not simply with the findings of many years ago but with the norms of today. "Facts" concerning conversation differences may also change from one culture group to another and from one particular community to another.[46] The specific place where conversations are recorded is also important. In 1936 a study was reported of scraps of conversation, recorded at ten-minute intermissions of the Minneapolis Symphony Orchestra.[47] This meant, of course, that the conversations were influenced considerably by the types of persons present and by their psychological set. However, aside from conversations about the artists themselves, men talked to men mostly about money and business, second about men, third about women. Women talked to women first about women, second about men, and then about other subjects.

TABLE 9

Comparative Table of Conversational Topics (From Baker and McGregor)

The figures are percentages. The 1922 study is that of Moore; the 1924, Landis and Burtt; the 1936, Baker and McGregor.

		Man to Man	*Woman to Woman*	*Man to Woman*	*Woman to Man*	*Totals*
Money and Business	1922	48	3	22	12	29
	1924	49	12	19	10	27
	1936	37	6	25	19	22
Amusements	1922	14	4	25	10	14
	1924	15	11	25	24	16
	1936	9	7	19	21	14
Men	1922	13	44	13	22	20
	1924	12	22	11	14	15
	1936	4	23	4	7	9
Women	1922	8	16	10	13	10
	1924	4	15	5	10	9
	1936	17	13	11	9	11
Clothes and Decoration	1922	2	23	3	17	9
	1924	5	19	7	17	12
	1936	5	23	7	9	12
Self	1922	—	—	—	—	—
	1924	9	15	23	18	14
	1936	3	10	0	6	5
Miscellaneous	1922	15	10	27	26	18
	1924	6	6	10	7	7
	1936	7	7	10	7	8
Politics and Economics	1936	18	11	24	22	19
All		100	100	100	100	100
Number of Cases	1922	80	30	32	32	174
	1924	195	155	63	87	500
	1936	145	139	141	131	556

▶ THE SOCIAL SIGNIFICANCE OF LANGUAGE

SOCIALIZATION

The vocabulary of the child, plus his understanding of the vocal, graphic, and gesture language of older persons aids in the process of socializing him, of changing him from a mass of organic material to a human being with the culture patterns of his group. Even though he is not able to use the language symbols of older people, he may comprehend these sufficiently to be able to understand situations socially. They have some meaning for him. The *comprehension* vocabulary of an infant or an adult is only part of the total number of words in the dictionary but is much greater than the *active* vocabulary, that is, the number of words actually used in speaking and writing. Both the infant and the adult can understand words which they either do not know or cannot use. Thus culture patterns which are important for social control can be transmitted through language better than in any other way. Individuals are thus able to communicate the folkways, and the mores and taboos. The moral codes of the group are transmitted in the various social institutions of the family, the neighborhood, the play group, the gang, the community, the school, the religious sect, the fraternity, the club, the political party, the occupational group, as will be seen in greater detail in Parts V and VI. Legal codes consist of word symbols. Our abstract conceptions of philosophy and of science are transmitted through symbols. These *symbols* are stimuli which represent or suggest some object, situation, or idea.

MEANING OF LANGUAGE

This symbolic function of language is so real that the great majority of misunderstandings between individuals arise out of misinterpretations of word symbols. The old saying is, "Define your terms." You attempt to put your thoughts in symbols, and your hearer or seer in turn must interpret these symbols in his thought life. His thinking and yours may not agree because of differences in interpretation of these symbols. The social significance of language lies largely in terms of the meaningfulness of symbols.

> "There's glory for you!" said Humpty Dumpty.
>
> "I don't know what you mean by 'glory,' " Alice said.
>
> Humpty Dumpty smiled contemptuously. "Of course you don't—till I tell you. I meant 'there's a nice knock-down argument for you!' "
>
> "But 'glory' doesn't mean 'a nice knock-down argument,' " Alice objected.

"When *I* use a word," Humpty Dumpty said in rather a scornful tone, "it means just what I choose it to mean—neither more nor less."

"The question is," said Alice, "whether you *can* make words mean so many different things."

Some years ago there was a good deal of popular objection to the enrichment of bread with *nicotinic acid,* the vitamin necessary to fight pellagra. People unacquainted with chemistry had confused it with *nicotine,* the poisonous alkaloid.[48] One news release even headlined an article "Tobacco in Your Bread!" whereas it actually dealt with the fortification of white bread by nicotinic acid.[49] As a result of such misunderstanding, the Food and Nutrition Board of the National Research Council recommended the change of the name to "niacin" or "niacin amide."

Difficulties in the meaning of concepts are nowhere more apparent than in social psychology. Consider the many possible meanings of such words as "attitude," "habit," "personality," "self," "impulse," "drive," "socialization," "aggression," "character," "compensation," "inhibition," "suggestion," and "sympathy." The concepts themselves are so inclusive that they do not permit of precise identification and differentiation.[50]

Meaning of language which you hear or see depends primarily on three factors: (1) your own individual sets of experiences; (2) the time or period in which the language is used; (3) the place or location where it is used.

1. As an illustration of the first factor, that of *individual background,* it would be meaningless to talk to the average person about a "standard deviation" and to say that a standard deviation is simply the square root of the sum of the squared differences divided by the number of cases. Yet to a statistician, an economist, or a psychologist these words would be extremely meaningful.

2. The *time* or period is important as illustrated by changes in word meanings. In a famous soliloquy Hamlet said, "Thus conscience does make cowards of us all." Most people interpret conscience as the "still small voice," although at the time Shakespeare wrote, it meant conscious consideration or thoughtful meditation. Similarly, our interpretation of scientific or philosophical terms depends upon an understanding of the period at which these words were used.

3. The *place* where language symbols occur is important. Consider the following passage which appears in Earl Browder's *What is Communism?*

Whenever any form of government becomes destructive of [certain] ends, it is the right of the people . . . to institute a new government, laying its foundations on such principles and organizing its powers in such forms, as to them shall seem most likely to effect their safety and happiness. . . . When a long train of abuses and usurpations, pursuing invariably the same object, evinces a design to reduce [the masses] under absolute despotism, it is their right, it is their duty, to throw off such government and to provide new guards for their future security.[51]

If this quotation is read aloud from a book on Communism, most people will rate it as a dangerous doctrine. However, when it is pointed out that the quotation appeared originally in the Declaration of Independence, the attitude of the same persons may change—is intended by Browder to change—although exactly the same word symbols are being considered.

All three of these aspects of the meaning of words may be illustrated by such a word as "radical." (1) To a mathematician the word "radical" is simply a mathematical concept, whereas to a conservative Republican the word implies someone very dangerous. (2) The time at which the word is used may be important; the connotation of the word "radical" has changed in the twentieth century from what it was in the nineteenth. (3) The place where a word is used may determine its meaning; for example, the word "radical" used at a street meeting of a soap-box orator may be met with cheers, in Wall Street with jeers. "Radical socialist" in France means a liberal, middle-class, anti-Communist political party.

THE REALITY OF WORDS

In every culture certain words are taboo. People may think of certain concepts, even engage in inner speech about them, but they must not give a name to tabooed concepts about which everyone knows. In one group of college students, words were rated according to their freedom of use. At the bottom of the list, almost universally avoided, were the following: guts, pregnant, prostitute, whore, bastard, and most taboo, bitch.[52] Yet it is doubtful if these same students refrained from thinking about guts or prostitutes, and most adult males are familiar with a large number of "impolite" limericks which involve taboo words and concepts.[53]

Words considered taboo vary with individual background, the time, the place. "Guts" may be acceptable to a gang, indelicate in a social gathering. The words "bull" and "legs" have changed with times, considered offensive in our grandmother's time, relatively inoffensive today. The word "bloody" is fairly respectable in this country, but very taboo among Englishmen—a difference of place.

Avoidance of words is also based on ideas of what is pedantic or effeminate. Thus, another study shows that the following words, although perfectly acceptable English forms, are avoided by students as pedantic—badly, lovely, purchase, presume, and trousers (as compared with bad, swell, buy, think, and pants).[54] Similarly, college men and women avoid words which they consider "effeminate"—adorable, charming, devine, exquisite, precious, naughty, "goody," "gobs," "oodles."

Words have such reality that it is necessary to choose them carefully. Consider the hymns of the church, the precise language of the classroom, the initiation ceremony of the fraternity, and you realize that words which have all sorts of meanings to different peoples have tremendous significance in the proper atmosphere. A song of Christian soldiers in the church, an oath of allegiance in the school, a sacred and secret swearing in of a "Grand Maharajah" in the lodge, have real meaning. Words may be softened by referring to girls "in trouble," or to the "deceased" and the "departed." Even in the underworld a man is not "murdered" because that is too outspoken, but he is "knocked off," "taken for a ride," or "put on the spot."

LANGUAGE AS A SUBSTITUTE FOR SIGNIFICANT OVERT ACTION

Words have such symbolic value that they are often used as convenient substitutes for more significant overt acts. A physician may diagnose a patient's difficulty in many-syllabled words without actually telling him what to do, and the patient goes away feeling much better. A man adds up his debts without attempting to pay them, and stops worrying about them. An automobile salesman assures a prospect that a certain car is "economical" and "powerful," and these words may be accepted as substitutes for actual tests of miles per gallon or actual horsepower. Emotional tensions of a college student are relieved after an examination, not by finding out where his information is lacking, but by getting a verbal or written symbol called his "grade."

Even though surrender leaflets were not very effective in getting many Japanese to surrender in World War II, they did have a very real psychological effect on the morale of some Japanese troops. These weapons of ideas were useful substitutes for, and additions to, the convincing concreteness of steel, flame, and high explosives. Compare Figure 11.

Another example of words that may be significant *substitutes* for overt action are those used for names of perfumes: Black Panther, Chichi, Cobra, Danger, Escape, Follow Me, Forever Amber, Frenzy, Indiscrete, Innuendo, Intoxication, L'Ardente Nuite, Menace, Mistress of the Night, My Sin, Passion, Possession, Scandal, Scarlet Street, Shocking, Surrender, Tabu, Tail Spin, Tigress, Tropiques, Whirlwind, White Shoulders. What female can resist the lure of such names, especially when told that this is a perfume "to leave alone unless you can meet its challenge," or to be worn "only if you dare risk the danger and dark delight of stirring primitive emotions"?

THE BEARER HAS CEASED RESISTANCE. TREAT HIM IN ACCORDANCE WITH INTERNATIONAL LAW. TAKE HIM TO THE NEAREST COMMANDING OFFICER.

C-IN-C ALLIED FORCES

(TRANSLATION)

LIFE SAVING GUARANTEE

1. THE AMERICAN FORCES WILL AID ALL WHO USE THIS CARD.
2. USING THIS, YOU WILL RECEIVE GOOD TREATMENT.

HOW TO USE THIS CARD

1. COME SLOWLY TOWARD THE AMERICAN LINES WITH YOUR HANDS RAISED HIGH ABOVE YOUR HEAD CARRYING ONLY THIS CARD.
2. COME ONE BY ONE. DO NOT COME IN GROUPS.
3. MEN MUST WEAR ONLY LOIN CLOTHS. WE WILL PROVIDE CLOTHING.
4. YOU MUST NOT APPROACH AMERICAN POSITIONS AT NIGHT.
5. THIS CARD MAY BE USED BY ANYONE -- JAPANESE OR KOREANS, SOLDIERS OR CIVILIANS.
6. THOSE WHO DO NOT HAVE CARDS MAY COME TO US IF THEY FOLLOW THE ABOVE INSTRUCTIONS.

FIG. 11. A SURRENDER LEAFLET USED IN WORLD WAR II

PROBLEMS OF DEFINITION

If infants do not understand the words which they use, and respond to words the meanings of which they do not precisely understand, what about you? Do you use or respond to words the meanings of which you really do not comprehend? Consider such a common term as "inferiority complex." What is this supposed inferiority complex? Can you really define it? Do you really know what it means? In discussing genetics people use the word "genes" glibly. Now what is a gene? How large is it? What does it look like? Is it anything more than a concept? Many people talk about getting enough calories in their diet. How many know what a calorie is? Suppose that you have memorized that a calorie is the amount of heat required to raise the temperature of 1 gram of water 1 degree centigrade. Is this what you mean when you talk about a diet of high

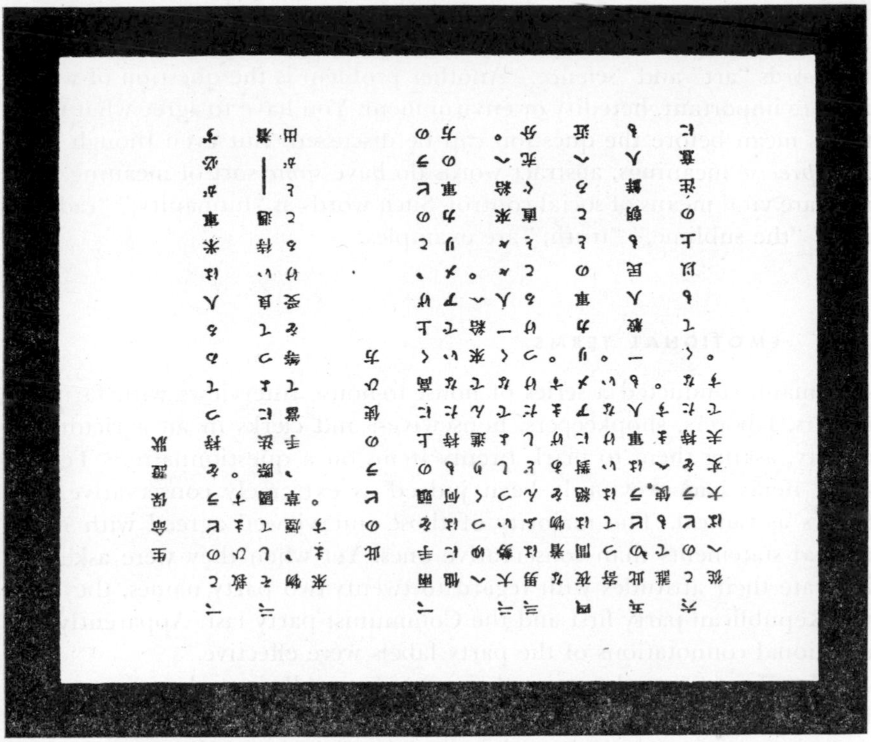

FIG. 11 (*continued*) REVERSE OF SURRENDER LEAFLET

caloric content? Advertisers sell foods because they contain vitamins. A standard brand of tomato juice is "rich in vitamins A and C." A cod-liver oil contains vitamins A and D. Yet how many of the people who buy these products because of the advertising even know what a vitamin is?

Now, if the problem of meaning exists with regard to genes, calories, and vitamins, consider the words so glibly tossed about by people on all sorts of occasions—"liberty," "morality," "individualism." When you talk about liberty, have you ever stopped to ask yourself what the word actually means to you? Can you define it? What about the word morality? Do you know what individualism is? What is unity, the soul, Fascism, Communism? Most Americans do know one thing about these last two terms, and that is that they are "agin 'em."

It is no wonder that most arguments are based on a misunderstanding of the meanings of words. There is perhaps no abstract term in any language which conveys precisely the same meaning to two different individuals. People attempt to argue the question whether art is more important than science, and the discussion is reduced to the meaning of the words "art" and "science." Another problem is the question of which is more important, heredity or environment. You have to agree what these terms mean before the question can be discussed. But even though they lack *precise* meanings, abstract words do have *some* sort of meaning, and thus are vital means of social control. Such words as "humanity," "radicalism," "the sublime," "truth," are examples.

EMOTIONAL TERMS

Hartmann conducted a series of house-to-house interviews with farmers, miners, laborers, shopkeepers, housewives, and clerks in an agricultural county, asking them to mark twenty items on a questionnaire.[55] Ten of these items had previously been judged as extremely conservative, the others as radical. The majority of those interviewed agreed with more radical statements than conservative ones. Yet when they were asked to indicate their attitudes with regard to twenty-two party names, they put the Republican party first and the Communist party last. Apparently the emotional connotations of the party labels were effective.

Menefee presented a series of statements to college students in two different forms.[56] The first form was made up of catch phrases, while the second was stripped of most of its emotional verbiage. For example, 70 per cent of the students agreed with the statement, "We should stand solidly upon the Constitution of the United States because it is the bulwark of our liberty." However, when this sentence was stripped of its catch words to read, "We should uphold the past interpretation of the United States Constitution because it guarantees certain privileges of freedom as it stands," only 53 per cent agreed with the proposition. Again, 42 per cent agreed with the classical statement, "I may not agree with what you say, but I will defend with my life your right to say it." But when this statement was reduced to its literal meaning, "One should face death rather than allow any person to be denied freedom of expression," support dropped to 16 per cent.

Emotional terms are not very helpful when we are dealing with logical materials, but they are not to be universally condemned. They have a legitimate place in poetry, for example. Keats wrote in *The Eve of St. Agnes:*

> Full on this casement shone the wintry moon,
> And threw warm gules on Madeline's fair breast.

If we replace the emotionally toned words with neutral ones, the effect is spoiled:

> Full on this window shone the wintry moon,
> Making red marks on Jane's uncolored chest.[57]

WORDS AND THEIR REFERENTS

If a word has reference to some object, event, or relation in the outside world, that thing to which the word refers is called its *referent*.[58] If all words had meaning only in terms of their referents, the psychology of meaning would be much simpler than it is. The use of one word rather than another results in a difference in meaning because something is expressed besides a reference. For example, one word may express a more emotional attitude toward the object or event referred to than another. Take such words as "firm" and "obstinate." Each refers to the same quality of character, but the first usually indicates commendation, the second condemnation. The same is true of "brave" and "foolhardy." You may call a friend levelheaded, but not a "flathead."

THE TYRANNY OF WORDS

Then there are those numerous words which do not have exact referents. They present the greatest difficulty. Although they may be mere noises, they may have far-reaching results. Here is an example of how full of noise patterns a single sentence may be:

> The Aryan Fatherland which has nursed the souls of heroes, calls upon you for the supreme sacrifice which you, in whom flows heroic blood, will not fail, and which will echo forever down the corridors of history.

With "blab" substituted for each word without an exact referent, this passage would be translated:

> The blab blab which has nursed the blabs of blabs, calls upon you for the blab blab which you, in whom flows blab blab, will not fail, and which will echo blab down the blabs of blab.[59]

These "blabs" are not attempts to be humorous. They represent blanks, where no precise meaning comes through. Many successful public speakers realize the advantages of using words which are only noises but nevertheless affect their listeners. The words produce action because of past conditioning and habituation. An outstanding Democratic politician has asserted that there are "black reactionary forces in America, blind to everything but their immediate personal profits, who do not have foresight enough to see that the preservation of democracy and human liberty demands, through necessary reforms, the solution of the human problem of the mass of the people."[60] One of the principal speakers at a Republican Convention listed various tasks to be undertaken: "First. We must restore and revitalize Liberty in America. Second. We must restore and rebuild morals in our government. Third. We must restore decent life and living to one-third of our farmers and workers, who have been chronically submerged by the New Deal. Fourth. We must restore competence to government."[61] Whether a Democrat or Republican, words of this sort have tremendous force.

Here are brief excerpts from the keynote speeches before the Democratic Convention, and before the Republican Convention, in the same year. Can you tell which is which?

> Time and again our opponents have sought to fill the minds of the people with doubt and confusion, and time and again successes have dispelled the doubts, confounded the confusers, and confused the doubters. . . . [We have] already made comprehensive plans for America to go forward now and in the postwar period.[62]

> Certainly we are not here to look for a road back to some *status quo*. There is no status to which we could or should return. The future cannot be overtaken in reverse. . . . We believe that America wants to get going and keep going. A forward-going America is what we are here for.[63]

The following sentences are taken verbatim from the radio speech of a man heard once a week by millions of Americans on the radio a few years ago. What do they really mean?

> Unintelligent forms of discontent, every time they recrudesce, are devitalized by the antiseptic power of a more intelligent social ideal. Hence, what we are witnessing today is the very procedure by which low human envy is transmuted to emulation, and low human covetousness to productive effort.[64]

Language sprinkled with vague terms may nevertheless be effective. It may have tremendous significance. It was not utterly absurd for a Securities and Exchange Commissioner to suggest to the Monopoly Committee in 1939 that a system of "wiff-waff" be applied to "agway" in "ugwug." He simply meant that a system of regulation should be applied to any "socially desirable" monopolies in industry; but he invented the new words because the old ones had become bound up in prejudices and emotional connotations.[65] Similarly, there was virtue in the proposal of the International Chamber of Commerce to eliminate the words "favorable" and "unfavorable" in discussing balances of trade, and to substitute the words "import" balances and "export" balances, which are less misleading.[66]

A former president of the American Bar Association gained attention when he demanded that breeding of "termites in the temples of justice" be halted. "Our American temples of justice are constantly being undermined by powerful and persistent assaults. Throughout the civilized world, international morality and law are giving ground to international lawlessness and anarchy."[67]

On the New York Post Office there is carved in stone the following phrase: "Neither snow nor rain nor heat nor gloom of night stays these couriers from the swift completion of their appointed rounds." Of course, all this means is that the mail will be delivered even in bad weather. Yet if the material should be translated in this way, it would not only spoil the building but also would fail to support the morale of postmen. The post office in Washington, D. C., reveals a much more elaborate motto, the sum and substance of which is that mail is sent only to nice people for laudable purposes.[68]

SYMBOLIC VALUE OF LANGUAGE

This discussion is in no sense intended to poke fun at language or at any of our social institutions. Language has a valuable symbolic and ritualistic function. Although words do not necessarily carry precise meanings, they are of tremendous importance as a means of social control. They are the foundation stones not only of etiquette, but also of flag drills in schools, hymns sung in churches, patriotic speeches, parades, badges, fraternity pins, and all other ritualistic types of behavior. Language is, in fact, a foundation stone of all social interaction.

QUESTIONS AND PROBLEMS FOR DISCUSSION

1. *What are the relations between language, thought, and social reality?*
2. *What is the importance* psychologically *of the systematization of language?*
3. *What is a concept?*

4. *In philosophy, what is the difference between nominalism and realism? Does this have any application to problems of language behavior?*
5. *Give examples of the sacredness of words.*
6. *What is the importance of verbal symbols in law and in government? Explain, giving specific examples.*
7. *What evidence can you find for any one theory of the origin of language?*
8. *To what extent are adults egocentric in their use of language?*

RECOMMENDED READINGS

Britton, K., *Communication: A Philosophical Study of Language.* London: K. Paul, Trench Trubner, 1939.

Chase, S., *The Tyranny of Words.* New York: Harcourt, Brace and Company, 1938.

Efron, D., *Gesture and Environment.* New York: King's Crown Press, 1941.

Eisenson, J., *The Psychology of Speech.* New York: F. S. Crofts & Co., 1938.

Gray, L. H., *Foundations of Language.* New York: The Macmillan Company, 1939.

Hayakawa, S. I., *Language in Action.* New York: Harcourt, Brace and Company, 1941.

Jespersen, O., *Language: Its Nature, Development, and Origin.* New York: Henry Holt and Company, Inc., 1928.

Johnson, W., *People in Quandaries: The Semantics of Personal Adjustment.* New York: Harper & Brothers, 1946.

Lee, I. J., *Language Habits in Human Affairs.* New York: Harper & Brothers, 1941.

McCarthy, D., *The Language Development of the Pre-School Child.* Minneapolis: University of Minnesota Press, 1930, Institute of Child Welfare Monograph Series, No. 4.

Mencken, H. L., *The American Language.* New York: Alfred A. Knopf, Inc., 1937.

Ogden, C. K., and Richards, I. A., *The Meaning of Meaning: A Study of the Influence of Language upon Thought and of the Science of Symbolism* (revised edition). New York: Harcourt, Brace and Company, 1930.

Philbrick, F. A., *Understanding English: An Introduction to Semantics.* New York: The Macmillan Company, 1942.

Sapir, E., *Language: An Introduction to the Study of Speech.* New York: Harcourt, Brace and Company, 1921.

Walpole, H. R., *Semantics: The Nature of Words and Their Meanings.* New York: W. W. Norton & Company, 1941.

Zipf, G. K., *The Psycho-Biology of Language: An Introduction to Dynamic Philology.* Boston: Houghton Mifflin Company, 1935.

*Newcomb, T. M., Hartley, E. L., and others (editors), *Readings in Social Psychology.* New York: Henry Holt and Company, Inc., 1947. (The following selections are listed according to the sequence of related discussion in the chapter you have just read.)

Mead, G. H., "Language and the Development of the Self," pp. 179–189.

Efron, D., and Foley, J. P., "Gestural Behavior and Social Setting," pp. 33–40.

Whorf, B. L., "Science and Linguistics," pp. 210–218.

CHAPTER NINE

THE PSYCHOLOGY OF IRRATIONALITY

AUTISTIC THINKING. Behavior and Thinking—Classification of Thinking—(1) Realistic Thinking—(2) Autistic Thinking—Music and Movies—Radio and Reading—Other Examples of Autistic Thinking—Universality of Autistic Thinking—(1) Autistic Thinking as Escape—(2) Autistic Thinking as Relaxation—(3) Autistic Thinking as a Basis for Realistic Thinking—Irrationality of Much of Our Thinking—Automatic Behavior—Autistic Thinking in Social Behavior—Propaganda Devices / MYTHS AND LEGENDS. A Test of Truth and Falsity—Examples of Myths and Legends—Bases of Legends—Experiments in Legend Making—Popular Myths and Legends—A Test of Historical Stereotypes—Historical Myths and Legends—The Millennial Hope—Economic and Political Mythology—Purposeful Distortion—Myths and Legends of the First World War—False Reports and Propaganda of the Second World War—Rumors—Necessity of Myths and Legends / BEHAVIOR—NORMAL OR ABNORMAL? Samples of Abnormal Behavior—Borderline Cases—"Abnormal" Beliefs—"Normal" Beliefs and Behavior—The Faith Ladder—Normality and Rationality—Meanings of "Abnormal"—The Psychological Meaning of Abnormality.

▶ AUTISTIC THINKING

BEHAVIOR AND THINKING

Almost any behavior involves some kind of thinking. Most thinking seems to result in behavior of one kind or another. Which, then, is the more inclusive term? Should we even attempt to differentiate between behavior and thinking?

Behavior may be said to include thinking, for thinking, after all, is one type of behavior. Actually we make an arbitrary division between behavior and thinking activities only for purposes of simplification. That is, behavior and thinking are not two separate activities of man but occur simultaneously.

CLASSIFICATION OF THINKING

Even though most of our thinking does result in overt, observable, external behavior, thinking may be dealt with as *primarily covert,* nonobservable, and internal. For purposes of analysis, the thinking process may be divided into (1) *realistic* and (2) *autistic* thinking.

1. *Realistic Thinking.* Most of us prefer to believe that we are realistic thinkers. Unless we have analyzed our own lives pretty carefully, we are convinced that we are rational human beings who decide our activities day by day on a logical basis and certainly on a conscious basis. The term "realistic," in fact, may be used as practically synonymous with directive, logical thinking, associated with the activities of the cerebral cortex. Realistic thinking implies rational processes as contrasted with snap judgments or emotional prejudices. In general, realistic thinking can be verified by others.

2. *Autistic Thinking.* On the other hand, autistic thinking means phantastic thinking—it is pleasure thinking which serves the imaginary gratification of wishes and longings. The associations are free-ranging and uncontrolled. Autistic thinking has been carefully studied in the mental processes of psychopathic individuals, in whom it is most developed. Paranoids, schizophrenics, paretics, all have various types of delusions, some of persecution and some of grandeur, which other people say are silly and absurd. They are illogical, they are false, and, therefore, they are assigned to the category of autistic thinking. However, most of us fail to recognize what a tremendous proportion of our own thinking is of this general sort. Unless we have made careful introspections of our own conscious activities, we may neglect the fact that a large percentage of our thinking is autistic in nature. Daydreams, night dreams, poetry, humor, and all sorts of phantasy life are common. The movies, the radio, newspapers, magazines, gossip, jokes, and many of our daily activities are based on thinking which is *not* of a "hard," realistic sort. Instead, a great many of these activities center around autistic or infantile ways of thinking. Note that the use of the word "infantile" as somewhat synonymous with autistic is not to condemn autistic thinking. The term is introduced, not as a value judgment, but simply to indicate that here is a level of thinking engaged in by the majority of adults which is similar to that of children. You may provide your own autistic thinking or may enjoy the phantasies produced by others, as in movies, books, and music.

MUSIC AND MOVIES. Consider, for example, the most popular types of songs: *She'll Be Comin' Round the Mountain When She Comes, The Dipsy Doodle Will Get You Yet, The Music Goes 'Round and 'Round, Flat-Foot Floogie, Pistol Packin' Mama, The Too Fat Polka.* Are these a very far cry from the nursery rhymes and other play talk which entertain little children? On December 30, 1944, a famous band leader played over the radio what he regarded as the twelve "hits" of 1944. The words of every single one represent phantasy and autistic thinking; and all but the fourth in the list that follows have *love* as their primary theme:

Come With Me, My Honey
Time Waits for No One

I Love You
Swinging on a Star
Sweet Dreams, Sweetheart
A Little on the Lonely Side
San Fernando Valley
It's a Cryin' Shame
Where You Are
I Walk Alone
Dance with the Dolly
Goodnight, Wherever You Are

What have been the most popular movies of recent years? While the so-called "psychological" or problem pictures have had quite a run, the pictures that have had greatest general appeal have been light, laugh-provoking ones—varying from *Snow White and the Seven Dwarfs* to *Going My Way*. Who have been the most popular film stars? They have included a mythical animated mouse (Mickey), a raucous, scatterbrained duck (Donald), formerly a little girl with long curls (Shirley Temple), and more recently another little girl with a wistful smile (Margaret O'Brien). Every movie producer realizes that to have a good box office he must produce pictures that will amuse and entertain at the infantile level, and that he cannot long stay in business if he brings out too many pictures that force people to engage in hard, realistic thinking. He should offer happy, carefree escape! Blumer has found distinct evidence of phantasy and daydreaming in most grade-school and high-school students as a result of attendance at the movies.[1]

RADIO AND READING. Who have been the most popular radio stars? Again we find a mythical character who exists in the form of a dummy (Charlie McCarthy), plus gentlemen such as Jack Benny, Bob Hope, and Fred Allen who amuse and entertain us. Make an estimate of what percentage of your own radio listening encourages autistic thinking and how much of it forces you to think realistically. How much do you actually know about the present international situation as compared with your detailed information about Li'l Abner, Blondie, Dick Tracy, and Little Orphan Annie in the daily comic strip? If your own life becomes dull, if your work seems boring, if your love grows stale, there is always that wonderful moment when you open the paper to find what is new in the life of Toots, Boots, Secret Agent X-9, the Phantom, or—hold your breath—Superman! Consider the type of literature which interests most of us. Millions of Americans never buy even one book per year. We prefer *short* short stories, and *short* magazine articles. Entire books are even condensed and then spliced together as *Omnibooks*. A "blurb" advertises "100 World's Best Novels Condensed," all for one dollar; within the covers of one book you can get the gist of *David Copperfield, Les Misérables, Don Quixote, Anna Karenina,* and ninety-six other classics!

OTHER EXAMPLES OF AUTISTIC THINKING. What about education? Here we have that phenomenal social institution which takes more time and energy and money of more individuals in this country than does any other. Yet many of the students who (judging from their overt behavior) are supposedly engaged in the process of education, attempt on every hand to avoid being educated! Autistic thinking is also apparent in many types of religious activities. This is not to say that religion is nothing but autistic thinking, but certainly a great deal of autistic thinking is involved in many forms of worship. The amazing alacrity with which Americans join anything and everything which someone asks them to join is also an indication of the functions of autistic thinking in the fraternity, the club, and the lodge. Aside from scientific and related types of thought, we usually try to avoid being forced to think for ourselves. It is too easy to accept someone else's ideas. It is much simpler to be entertained than educated.

During 1939, "World's Fairs" were held in two of our leading cities, to be visited by people supposedly hungry for knowledge and information. Yet the principal attraction at San Francisco was Sally Rand's "Nude Ranch" and at New York the General Motors Exhibit with its entertainment "panorama," and Billy Rose's Aquacade of girlies. We like to think of ourselves as logical people who are information-seeking; but unless our information is dressed up with a good deal of entertainment, we may not want it. Our pills must be sugar-coated.

UNIVERSALITY OF AUTISTIC THINKING

Now, this discussion does *not* mean that autistic thinking is bad. Autistic thinking is not a sign in itself of abnormality or of childishness. In fact, normal, everyday, "run-of-the-mine" adults do not differ so very much in some of their thinking from psychopathic individuals or children. In other words, a universally rational Homo sapiens is just a straw man whom we talk about. This straw man we usually identify as ourself. In fact, it is easy to think of yourself as being always a logical, realistic individual, but as for other people—well, poor fellows!

1. *Autistic Thinking as Escape.* Not only is autistic thinking nothing to be scoffed at, but it may even be praised. In the first place, autistic thinking serves as a release from the humdrum of our daily lives. After working at jobs or studies over a period of time, having perhaps driven ourselves to be logical and realistic, it seems very desirable for the human organism to have an "escape" and to be free for a while of the rigorous demands of the job.

2. *Autistic Thinking as Relaxation.* Closely related to this, autistic

thinking or undirected daydreaming is often desirable as a means of relaxation. You can lean back in your chair, put your feet up on the desk, literally or figuratively light your pipe, and let the world go by. It does not require very much effort, and may be as much fun as going to the movies or listening to the radio. In fact, one of the great appeals of radio and movies, as noted above, is that they stimulate autistic thinking in us. They are aids to relaxation, and thus are of tremendous psychological importance.

3. *Autistic Thinking as a Basis for Realistic Thinking.* Then, too, autistic thinking may serve as a basis for objective, realistic thinking. Sometimes an answer to a question you have puzzled over "just comes" to you during sleep. As was indicated above, phantasy is not sharply removed from realistic thinking, for these are two different aspects of the same fundamental thinking process. Autistic thinking may promote imaginative ideas which serve as a meaningful foundation for logical thinking. Scientific experiments in their culmination represent a great deal of logical, objective thinking, but they could scarcely be carried on unless the originator of the investigation at some time engaged in a great deal of autistic thinking or free association of ideas. For example, a study was made of the great French mathematician, Henri Poincaré:

> In carrying forward even his professional tasks, Poincaré was restless and impatient. He was unable to remain in one position long and he was also unable to stay by one task. Whenever his work failed to go along smoothly, whenever voluntary effort was demanded, he gave up for the time. Poincaré often began on a mathematical memoir with no clear idea of where he expected to come out. He would sometimes write out a set of formulas automatically in the hope that they would suggest ideas which might be put into some coherent form. In other words, he sought solutions without knowing what his problem was. Yet, with all of this lack of systematic effort, Poincaré produced great mathematical results.[2]

Investigations of other inventors and scientists indicate that the great majority go through early stages of incubating their ideas in terms of free association of ideas. In other words, they set out not to solve a specific problem but simply to engage in creative imagination, and yet end up by solving a problem. This whole matter of invention and creative production will be discussed more fully in Chapter 14.

IRRATIONALITY OF MUCH OF OUR THINKING

The crux of this entire discussion concerning autistic and realistic thinking is that too many observers of human behavior have tended to stress man's rational character and objective thought processes, and have thus overlooked the tremendous importance of unconscious factors and of free association of ideas. Although man is called Homo sapiens, probably very little logical reasoning goes on with the great majority of people if they can possibly avoid it. We tend in a great number of our activities to be irrational and not to think things through in logical steps. We certainly are so lazy that we will take the short cuts if we can. We rely whenever possible upon well-integrated responses which have occurred so many times that they are practically automatic.

If one takes himself as a specimen and counts the completed acts of reasoning within each day, he will be struck by their infrequency. Here and there we shall find some features of the rational process occurring. We may temporarily suspend our judgment on some matter, we may seek a clearer definition of a problem, we may consider alternative solutions, we may even engage in an experiment, but rarely do we find all of these features of reasoning tied together in a single, systematic, and serial process.[3]

AUTOMATIC BEHAVIOR

In the discussion of the nervous system in Chapter 3, it was suggested that you use yourself as a guinea pig and actually check up on the number of instances where you have reasoned things out objectively step by step. Examine every detail of your behavior during a single day and see what a large percentage of activities are carried on primarily on the basis of the autonomic nervous system or through sheer habit, and how few of your decisions are actually determined by reasoning and sound logic. Again, note the importance of fairly automatic types of behavior over which we have little or no control. The kinds of behavior mediated by the autonomic nervous system are just as significant psychologically as those controlled by the cerebral cortex.

We may get up in the morning, dress ourselves in the way we have learned, eat our breakfast in the routine fashion, repeat the customary phrases that go with the various activities in which we are engaged, do our work in the way we learned to do it, talk as we hear others talk, eat the food we see others eating, repeat the stories we have heard, draw the conventional inferences from the facts about us, attend a motion picture in which all the situations are trite and all the captions platitudes, read the newspaper editorials which merely repeat the notions which we already believe, go to a party of religious meeting where we are again told the "old, old story."[4]

AUTISTIC THINKING IN SOCIAL BEHAVIOR

Look about you, at all sorts of social behavior. Consider the great number of instances of hysterical behavior of large groups of people in both peace and wartime. Think of the irrational activities of any large crowd or mob. Look at the national and religious prejudices which sway people in many of their attitudes and activities. Consider how in the world of business and of politics a clever businessman or a politician understands perfectly well that if he is to succeed he must pretend to appeal to "reason," but how he actually promotes autistic thinking. Look in any newspaper or magazine at the advertising and ask yourself whether the appeals to buy cigarettes, candy bars, or automobiles are designed to reach you as a hardheaded, logical person or as a person thinking in autistic ways. How many political speeches have you ever analyzed logically? Try it and see whether they represent appeals to logic or whether they depend upon ready-made, stereotyped devices. We have already seen some indication of this in Chapter 8 on *Language,* and we shall have occasion to refer to this problem again in Chapter 10 in dealing with the *stereotyping* process.

PROPAGANDA DEVICES

There are a number of propaganda devices based on autistic appeals which are far-reaching in their effects. Seven of these are relatively simple to explain but comprehensive in scope.[5] (1) *Name calling* consists in giving a person, group, or idea a bad label, so that we reject him or it without examining the evidence. "Red," "foreigner," and "sissy," are examples. "Give a dog a bad name and hang him." (2) *Glittering generality* means, on the other hand, the association of a person, group, or idea with a "virtue word," so that we accept it without probing deeper. "Civilization," "patriotism," "motherhood," and "love" are examples. (3) *Transfer* carries the authority and prestige of someone who is respected over to something else, in order to make the latter acceptable or unacceptable. For example, one famous radio speaker carried on his campaign by identifying his program with Christ and "His Cross," his enemies with "international bankers." (4) The *testimonial* device is similar in that someone loved or hated says that a given idea is good or bad. Contrast "our minister said . . ." with "the Communists favor. . . ." (5) By the *plain-folks* device an idea is made acceptable because it is "homey" or the person presenting it is "of the people." Many a Presidential candidate has been photographed fishing or pitching hay, for reasons that are obvious. (6) *Card stacking* involves the selection and use of ideas, true or false, logical or illogical, on one side of the picture only. Every political campaign furnishes numerous instances. The heads of warring nations stack the cards when they allow the censors to present only one set of ideas about the war. (7) The *band-wagon* technique is that "everybody's doin' it" and you had better jump on the wagon, too. Whatever the program, "follow the crowd."

These devices, of course, overlap to some extent and are descriptive only. Although they do not completely answer the question of *how* and *why,* they have proved useful in analyzing everything from newspapers to politics. There are a number of other propaganda devices as well, such as the use of slogans and stereotyped phrases (see the discussion of the practical use of stereotypes in the next chapter).

▶ MYTHS AND LEGENDS

A TEST OF TRUTH AND FALSITY

Here are ten statements. Before reading further, mark each one either *true* or *false.*

1. A particularly good way to treat a black eye is to cover it with a slice of raw beefsteak.	True	False
2. A contract is unenforceable if it is signed with a pencil.	True	False
3. Cigarette smoking tends to stunt the height of growing boys.	True	False
4. Being stuck by a rusty nail or pin is more dangerous than being stuck by a nail or pin that is not rusty.	True	False
5. If you stare at a person's back, you can make him turn around.	True	False
6. Man has just five senses.	True	False
7. In the United States a contract which is signed on Sunday is illegal.	True	False
8. To sign a check in pencil invalidates the check.	True	False
9. In most jurisdictions there is a fine in money for striking someone in the face who wears glasses.	True	False
10. The Constitution of the United States guarantees trial by jury in all cases.	True	False

You have probably marked several of these statements as true. Actually every one is false. In other words, you probably believe a number of myths and legends although you do not recognize their mythical or legendary character as such. That is, your own attitudes are normally based in part upon beliefs and attitudes which are not logical or rational. This does not mean, however, that you are "abnormal" to believe some of the above statements. As a matter of fact, the great majority of people believe most of them, although in a college population the percentage of belief will be less than in a random sample of the population at large. The mere fact that these statements are untrue, irrational, or illogical does not mean that you are an irrational or illogical person. That you agree with many other people as to the truth of some of these false statements makes belief in them a perfectly normal phenomenon.

"If men define situations as real, they are real in their consequences."[6] This applies not only to institutional patterns such as traditions, conventions, customs, and rituals, but also to noninstitutional patterns such as beliefs, attitudes, booms, crazes, fads, and fashions. Beliefs and attitudes, in fact, often grow into myths and legends of social significance. Many of these are the result of autistic thinking.

EXAMPLES OF MYTHS AND LEGENDS

If you go to a lecture and then compare notes with a friend, you may be surprised to find that he did not interpret the lecture in the same way that you did. He in turn may be equally nonplused concerning you. Nearly every professor has had the experience of having a supposed quotation from his lecture thrown at him outside of class, which he is unable to recognize as even approaching anything which he had thought—let alone said. Courtrooms are also interesting places to examine the development of myths and legends where two or more observers of the same event will honestly state opposite things to be so. After Abraham Lincoln's murder, with a large theater audience in attendance, there were all sorts of different versions as to what actually occurred. Because of what William James called the "will to believe" we often fail to recognize that what other people tell us or what we read may not be true.

Myths and legends may be differentiated in that *myths* have little or no factual origin—they "are made out of the whole cloth"—whereas *legends* have some sort of factual basis; but through the process of exaggeration and retelling, "angles" have been developed which were not originally there. Myths and legends sometimes develop into folklore and tales of historical, religious, or political significance. We have the myths of St. George and the dragon, Beowulf, King Arthur and the Knights of the Round Table, and the legendary tales of Robin Hood, Helen of Troy, St. Joan of Arc, and the boyhood exploits of the latest political candidate. All of us have myths and legends which we believe; only we do not recognize them as myths and legends because we believe them to be true, especially those in our family, our school, our church, our fraternity, and our political party. Practically, the terms "myth" and "legend" may be used almost interchangeably.

BASES OF LEGENDS

Kimball Young summarizes as follows the factors which are significant in the development of legends about an observed event:

1. The *emotional state* of the observers. This is usually increased at the time of observation, if the situation is dramatic.

2. *Errors of perception* at the time of observation. If the event is spectacular or unfamiliar, it is more difficult to perceive it accurately. Attention will be limited to a few details.

3. *Errors in recall.* These are especially evident when the event is later being described to others.

4. *Predispositions* . . . of the observers. These predispositions are made of old stereotypes, prejudices and legends still persisting in the observers.

5. *False interpretation* by the observers. As far as they imagine the characteristics of the observed individuals, the observers will err in interpreting their acts.

6. The *time elapsing* between perception and recall. After a very brief interval, the event as recalled differs from the actual event. As the time elapsing between the event and its recall increases, observers begin to add or change or forget innumerable details. (Italics ours.) [7]

To these, three more factors may be added:

7. The *stereotyping* process. It is much simpler to telescope the actual details into conveniently recognized stereotypes.

8. *Autistic thinking.* Legends represent a convenient type of phantasy.

9. *Purposeful distortion.* Sometimes there is deliberate misrepresentation and spreading of a legend.

EXPERIMENTS IN LEGEND MAKING

Try an old parlor game and see how easy it is for myths and legends to develop. Whisper to your neighbor some rather commonplace statement of fact. Let him in turn whisper it to his neighbor, and so on around a group of eight or ten persons. Then compare what the last person says he has heard with the original statement. The game will reveal the ways in which changes come about even in simple factual statements.

Kirkpatrick studied this phenomenon in connection with news accounts; newspaper items beginning with the words, "It is rumored that," usually had this preface drop out very early in the retelling.[8] Dashiell conducted an experiment in which subjects looked at objects in a room and also observed the actions of the experimenter; each told what he had seen to another person, who in turn told this to another.[9] Those in the second group showed a reduction of approximately 40 per cent in "testimony capacity" as compared with the original observers, those in the third group about 20 per cent more reduction.

Written narratives have also been presented to subjects who would afterward write down a summary of what they had read, which would in turn be read by others who would attempt to reproduce it, and so on through as many as twenty reproductions.[10] In all of the experiments there was a tendency away from deductions and opinions, and instead biases toward concrete "facts." For example, when exactly the same story was given to English and Hindu students to be reproduced by members of their own group, the Englishmen developed a very typical story of English life, whereas the Hindus developed a much more imaginative story with a great deal of adornment. The autistic thinking of the two groups was different.

POPULAR MYTHS AND LEGENDS

Many myths and legends grow up without intent and are believed. Civilized individuals are apt to feel sorry for the poor primitive peoples who believe in animism and magic and live in a world of demons and devils. They fail to take into account the myths and legends of civilized men. Everyone has heard of the Indian rope trick in which a rope is tossed into the air, a boy climbs up and vanishes into thin air. Yet this is a myth; it has never happened, except in an indoor situation where a magician can produce the illusion. A group of magicians in London called the Magic Circle made a standing offer of five hundred pounds for its performance in the open air, but with no takers.[11]

Another example is a legend widely circulated some years back. Many a person told that some friend or relative was driving along the street when an old lady asked for a lift. When she got into the car she looked over the occupants very carefully and then solemnly announced, "Someone will die in this car today." As soon as possible the driver got rid of her, but at the following intersection was hailed by a policeman who put an injured man into the car and said, "Drive to the nearest hospital." On the way the badly injured man died.

Even more far fetched but widely believed—both in Russia and the United States—is the story of the physician who was visited by a little girl who asked him to come and see her sick mother. When he arrived at the house an hour or so later, he found the woman critically ill and suggested to her that she should have a nurse, as her daughter was too small to care for her properly. "Daughter?" said the woman, "I have no daughter now. She died two days ago and is behind that screen." The doctor looked behind the screen and saw lying there the little girl, obviously dead for days.

Stories of this sort grow up in our folklore and gain wide credence. Some drop out; others remain. Rather than talk about the unique folklore of the peasants of Europe, it is more interesting to discover some common folk tales which exist in our own culture. Along with our beliefs in "hoodos" and "jinxes" we have endless superstitions of what happened to someone after walking under a ladder or breaking a mirror. Apparently most Americans believe the following myths:

That every time a man spends one dollar he keeps nine other people employed.

That the pari-mutuel system gives everybody a chance to make a profit on horse races.

That the politicians are to blame for the weaknesses of our government.

That America never fought a war of aggression—or persecuted people for religious beliefs.

That all Chinese are as saintly as Confucius, while all Japanese are full of treachery.

That because a man has done something outstanding in one field, he is therefore capable of making profound observations upon all other subjects.

That the way to inspire peace is to talk about the horrors of war.[12]

These commonly accepted beliefs have superseded other myths and legends which existed ten and twenty years ago. Some of these in turn will drop out of the picture and be replaced by others.

A TEST OF HISTORICAL STEREOTYPES

Although myths and legends are occasionally found in the realm of science, they occur much more frequently in such fields as history, religion, and politics. Try the following simple experiment. In the five blank spaces below, write down the first word or phrase which you think of in response to each of the five persons whose names appear opposite:

Miles Standish ....

Captain John Smith ....

John Brown ....

William Jennings Bryan ....

Robert E. Lee ....

The chances are that opposite the name Miles Standish you have written one of the following words—"Puritan," "Priscilla," "John Alden," "Captain," or "soldier." For Captain John Smith you have written "Indians," "Pocahontas," "Jamestown," or "Powhatan"; for John Brown—"Harper's Ferry," "raid," "body," "song," or if you are cantankerous, "had a cold upon his chest"; for Bryan—"orator," "great commoner," or "cross of gold"; for Robert E. Lee—"Southern gentleman" or "Southern general." Now stop and think how much you really know of any of these characters. They are important in American history, but you may be surprised at how little factual knowledge you have about the gentlemen.

HISTORICAL MYTHS AND LEGENDS

Similarly, if you examine the facts of history, you may be surprised to learn how legendary many of your "facts" are. Many Americans believe that C. C. Pinckney once said, "Millions for defense, but not one cent for tribute." They believe that Wellington exclaimed, "Up, Guards, and at them." Nearly all believe that George Washington warned the country against "entangling alliances." Yet no one of these three individuals ever said any of these things.[13] As for the warning against entangling alliances, that statement was actually made by Jefferson. The tale of Washington and the cherry tree is another instance, the story originating with a clergyman who reported that he heard it from an "aged lady" who as a "distant relative" had sometimes visited the Washington family.[14] It is commonly believed that a great deal of witch burning occurred in early New England. Although "witches" were hanged and one was pressed to death, no woman was ever burned. On the day of the coronation of George VI as King of England, many cases of drunkenness were reported; yet recorded observations made that day revealed no apparent drunkenness in pubs or restaurants, illustrating the tendency of most people to remember the unusual or the extraordinary.[15] Following is an explanation of how the legend grew up about Captain John Smith and Pocahontas:

In his volume *A True Relation,* written in Virginia and published in England in 1608, he [Smith] recounted his early exploits and adventures. He told how, making an excursion to the Chickahominy, he was surrounded by two hundred hostile Indians, and after bemiring himself in a swamp, was captured. They carried him before an Indian king. Smith showed this monarch his compass, and so won his favor. Thence taken before the "emperor" Powhatan, he was in danger of being killed by certain Indians whose relatives he had slain, but was saved by his guards. After he had treated Powhatan to a long discourse on the greatness of the British king, the mightiness of his navy, and the "noyes of Trumpets and terrible manner of fighting" in Europe, he was sent back to Jamestown. In this book he barely mentions Pocahontas, then a maiden of perhaps twelve. But in 1616, about the time that John Rolfe brought Pocahontas as a bride to England, he wrote a letter to King James' queen, Anne of Denmark, in which he asserted: "After some ix weeks fatting among these salvage countries, at the minute of my execution, she hazarded the beating out of her own brains to save mine." And he soon went still further.

In 1624, in his *General Historie,* Smith rewrote his early narrative of Virginia adventures. This time the two hundred hostile Indians became three hundred. This time he recalled a picturesque detail, the exhibition by the Indians of a bag of gunpowder which they proposed to plant the following spring. Above all, he recounted in more dramatic form the tale of Pocahontas' gallantry. He described the grim and dusky Powhatan in the centre of the stage, himself in the fore ground fettered but undaunted, and the lovely Pocahontas suddenly emerging at the climactic instant:

"A long consultation was held, but the conclusion was two great stones were brought before Powhatan; then as many as could layd hands on him, dragged him to them, and thereon layd his head, and being ready with their clubs, prepared to beate out his braines. Pocahontas, the King's dearest daughter, when no entreaty could prevaile, got his head in her armes, and layd down her own upon his to save him from death; whereat the Emperour was contented he should live."[16]

Every historian is faced with an extremely difficult problem in deciding what events he will record as "facts" and which he will attribute to legend.

The firm establishment of strict rules for historical editing dates in America from the controversies which attended Jared Sparks' editions of the writings of Washington (1834–37) and Franklin (1836–40). . . . Observing that Washington in his old age completely rewrote his early letters, he felt it proper to revise the later letters, of which he had only rough drafts, not the final form, when they seemed to need it. He softened or omitted harsh criticisms of men and policies. Thus when Washington wrote of the "dirty, mercenary spirit" of the Connecticut troops, Sparks left out "dirty"; when Washington wrote of "rascally privateersmen," he deleted "rascally." He changed "Old Put" into "General Putnam," and Washington's statement that a certain sum "will be but a fleabite to our demands" into the statement it would be "totally inadequate."[17]

The modern newspaperman is faced with a similar problem of deciding what his public wants to read. Some years ago a foreign correspondent was instructed by his managing editor to send "a daily picture of some phase of Parisian life."

This meant that I was expected to paint a picture of Paris which conformed to the popular American notion of French mores: gay abandon and a riotous morality. *Midinettes* could never be anything but sunny creatures who filled the boulevards with laughter and song. . . . To have shown that the average French family follows an almost puritan code of morals . . . , or that the Parisian puts up his shutters at seven and retires earlier than New England villagers, would have stamped you as an ignoramus or a fool. That was not the "gay Paree" the American newspaper reader had been led to imagine. Hollywood and the popular magazines had given him a different idea, and that idea was not to be disturbed: the apache, long since vanished from the stage, had to be resuscitated; . . . the students of the Sorbonne were always shown in the act of rioting, and

American visitors endlessly astonishing the white-aproned waiters in the terrace cafés with the size of their tips.[18]

THE MILLENNIAL HOPE

Religion and politics are also good fields for the growth of myths and legends. Protestant hymns are based in fairly large measure on a notion of return to a state of infantile bliss.[19] This idea has also been carried out in many brands and kinds of religious activities, particularly with reference to a future life. According to the religious idea of the "millennial hope," in the near future our activities will suddenly be halted by divine intervention, all evil will be abolished, the earth will be completely renovated, and Christ will establish upon earth a new kingdom of blessedness to endure exactly one thousand years—hence the designation "millennial."[20]

In the last century a group of people—calling themselves Millerites—knew the exact day when the end of the world was coming, gave away all their material possessions, and went up on a hillside to pray. When the end of the world did not arrive, they set another date. An evangelist used to hold forth in Washington, D. C., on the subject, "Hell—Where Is It?" somewhat as follows:

> About all most people know about hell is that it is down, and reputed to be very hot. Some evangelists would try to make us believe that it is so jammed full of people that there is hardly standing room left. John Ford will tell you exactly how many people are in hell at the present time, just where hell is located, if the devil is in charge, if the fires burn the meanness out of people or must they go on burning forever![21]

A Bible lecturer announced in Chicago what the exact location of heaven is, what the inhabitants look like, whether children grow up or not, and why heaven will never grow tiresome.[22]

ECONOMIC AND POLITICAL MYTHOLOGY

Many are the illusions in economic and political ideologies. Numerous myths and legends of an economic Utopia are trustingly believed. Dr. Francis E. Townsend was responsible for an old-age pension plan which was popular among elderly people because it promised them security. People have been swayed again and again politically by the slogan, "Balance the Budget," when only a small percentage of financial experts really understand what the phrase means. The idea of "progress" is constantly used by politicians; the stock expression is, "Let us then go onward and upward." Obviously the persons who use these words do not know where onward and upward is, but this sounds much better than to say, "Let us go downward and backward."

Myths and legends about a political figure may be more useful than specific facts. Calvin Coolidge was "sold" to the American public by astute press agents as "Silent Cal," a quiet, honest, cautious, shrewd, plain man of the people.[23] In the spring of 1940 a handsome platinum-haired man who wanted to be President was transformed by his manager into a plain man of the people with baggy trousers and unshined shoes.[24] Another presidential aspirant was made over from a "mamma's boy" into a big, bad sort of he-man who shot wild turkeys and went fishing.

PURPOSEFUL DISTORTION

Purposeful distortion accounts for large numbers of myths and legends. Deliberate invention of stories to discredit the other party is familiar to most politicians. Every political campaign contains deliberate misrepresentations of what prominent members of the other group have done or are about to do, and this is not limited to campaign years. In 1936 after the closing of the "Quoddy Dam" project in Maine, a false rumor was widely circulated that truckloads of pies and loaves of bread were pouring into the abandoned project daily only to be fed to the hogs, because the government had a contract to buy the food.

An interesting example occurred in 1938 when two Republicans in Omaha made a bet concerning a current campaign to clean up the courthouse. One bet the other that, if fifty $1 bills were dropped in the streets from an airplane, enough people would be interested in the clean-up campaign to turn the bills in to the campaign chest. The stunt did not attract much attention and only a few bills were returned. However, a newspaper in Germany published the following version:

> When it rained dollar bills; bet of two American fliers; four weeks in jail for such a dumb stunt.
>
> Two young persons coming from a certain group who usually finds much time on its hands entered into a bet. Both of them purchased an airplane and they were arguing which one could cover a distance of 200 miles faster. They decided to have a race and that was the first sensation which these two young men created for their home town. . . .
>
> However, since money did not mean much to these snobs they made an agreement that the person who lost the race should take the sum of the bet in $1 bills and throw them from an airplane over the market place in Omaha. Naturally this unusual bet soon spread throughout the city and early in the morning of that day in which the dollar notes were to rain over Omaha the entire population was on its feet.
>
> The police were greatly surprised, because from the market place to the banks of the Missouri River tens of thousands were packed. Traffic stopped and even the police were powerless with such a mob. . . .
>
> Pandemonium reigned among the people on the streets. The mob rushed

after the money that was falling from heaven. Many people had sticks and some had butterfly nets to catch these dollar bills as they fell. Quite a number of fights ensued; practically a fight for every dollar bill. Women were knocked over. Children were stepped upon. Clothes were torn from some people, and not less than 87 persons were injured in attempts to get a share of this gold that was falling from heaven. The health authorities were kept busy.

Close to one-third of the dollar bills were no longer usable because they were practically torn to shreds during the fights.[25]

MYTHS AND LEGENDS OF THE FIRST WORLD WAR

Some of the best examples of myths and legends come from World Wars I and II. A deliberate myth was invented in the first World War, that at the Battle of Mons angels appeared before the British lines who bore a strange likeness to the bowmen who had fought for Henry V at Agincourt, and that these phantom bowmen showered arrows upon the Germans.[26] This false story not only was commonly believed by English soldiers but was picked up among French and American soldiers. Many a soldier reported that during the Franco-Prussian War thirty thousand German soldiers had been stabbed in the back while in the embraces of French prostitutes; always the same number appeared—thirty thousand.[27]

The most famous story of the first World War was the sensational one that fifty Belgian boy scouts had had both hands cut off at the wrists by the Germans so that these Belgian boys never could bear arms against the Fatherland when they grew up. In the United States the story took the form of little Belgian girls being the victims of this atrocity; posters were even circulated representing the gory situation. Lord Northcliffe had a standing offer of two hundred pounds for an authentic photograph to prove that any child had been so treated, but there were never any takers. Yet the story was commonly believed. The Germans were less successful in getting Americans to believe that Allied nurses were gouging out the eyes of wounded German prisoners, although some did accept this story.[28]

FALSE REPORTS AND PROPAGANDA OF THE SECOND WORLD WAR

Similar myths and legends grew up in 1939 at the beginning of the second World War. Polish refugees reported that a Nazi had shot a young Polish priest just after he had administered extreme unction. As he fell, so went the report, his hands with holy oil on them struck a wall and a clear impression of the hands materialized on the wall which the Nazis were unable to paint out.[29] Propaganda devices were resorted to by forces on both sides and were particularly successful when religious appeals were introduced.

Most Americans became familiar with the propaganda devices of the Nazi organization, yet many failed to realize that the English also carried on propaganda services, so successfully, in fact, as not to be recognized as propaganda. Since nearly all Americans were pro-English and anti-Nazi, even before the United States entered the war, it was not surprising to find newspaper editors and publishers printing stories and headlines which bolstered the already formulated attitudes of readers. A United Press dispatch in 1939 read: "A British radio broadcast received here early today said that a Russian broadcast intercepted in London stated that the German offensive is broken on the line of the River Bugge in Poland." This received the headline in one newspaper, "Nazis Reported Checked."[30] The opening paragraph in a story in *The New York Times* the same year read: "The British Government has ordered a naval blockade of Germany, according to information reaching officials here tonight. This government has not been informed officially of this fact, however." Nevertheless, the headline read: "British Navy Acts."[31] In neither of these cases did the headlines take account of the unofficial character of the report.

When Hitler made a speech in September, 1940, in warning to Britain and France, one news service reported that he had said that for every bomb dropped on a German city five would be dropped in return, whereas another service said that five hundred bombs would be dropped for every one.[32] The early days of the war in particular were full of dispatches that certain sources have "said that" or that a "report had been picked up that" or that "an unidentified radio station is reporting that."

. . . Frederick C. Oechsner, United Press staff correspondent, . . . visited the front. He went there with the permission of the German Ministry of Propaganda and Public Enlightenment to watch the Germans under fire.

Mr. Oechsner was at the front on September 26, 27, 28, and 29 [1939]. He didn't see any fighting. Neither did Louis P. Lochner, of the Associated Press, who accompanied him on his four-day tour of the German lines. On September 28, in fact, they didn't hear one shot. Along the Rhine, said Mr. Oechsner, the soldiers idled away the day by washing clothes and casting nets.

Maybe so; but on September 26 the Associated Press reported from Paris that French guns were hurling shells across the Rhine. On September 27, the United Press reported from Paris that German field guns were hammering the French position. On September 28, the Paris bureau of the A.P. said that "French artillery was reported to have wiped out parts of the German Siegfried line between Merzig and Saarbrucken as the entire Western Front blazed with heavy cannonading." On September 29, the Paris bureau of the U.P. said that fifty German towns and four-fifths of the industrial plants in the Saar Valley were in French hands; and, later that day, International News Service, again from Paris, told of the capture of three more German villages.

Apparently the reporters in France and those in Germany [were] covering two different wars.[33]

RUMORS

The war years of the 1940's were times when all sorts of unfounded rumors spread quickly and were readily accepted. People were jittery and willing to believe almost anything. For example, in the spring of 1940 people in the United States began to become excited about "Fifth Column" activities.

> . . . In Baltimore, a man parked his car across the street from a German restaurant. . . . A passerby threw a lighted cigarette butt into the car. The butt set fire to the cushions. Somebody saw the smoke and called for help. The restaurant owner ran over with a fire extinguisher and put out the blaze. Police radio cars arrived. The restaurant owner chatted for a few minutes with some of the policemen. They left and he went back to his restaurant. . . .
>
> Within forty-eight hours rumors had spread about the city that the restaurant had been raided as a center of Fifth Column activities. It was said that a police patrol backed up to the place and officers brought out no less than twenty-four big, square boxes, each containing a huge bomb. It was whispered that the restaurant owner had been subjected to a severe cross-examination in the local F.B.I. offices. People claimed to have heard these stories from eye-witnesses. One woman phoned a columnist on a Baltimore daily and asked in great fury: "Why do the Baltimore newspapers conceal the fact that the F.B.I. discovered a Fifth Column nest? Are they sympathetic to the Fifth Columnists?"[34]

A few months after the United States entered the war, a story went around the country which everybody who told it swore was true—everyone had got it from a friend of a friend of a friend. The story was:

> Riding on a bus, a woman passenger was heard to say: "Well, my husband has a better job than he ever had and he's making more money, so I hope the war lasts a long time."
>
> Another woman got up and slapped her face. "That is for my boy who was killed at Pearl Harbor. And this"—another slap—"is for my boy in the Philippines." At the next stop, the woman who was slapped got off.[35]

When *Time* magazine published this as nothing but a rumor, there were spontaneous and heated denials from all sorts of readers; and people claimed that the incident had actually occurred in such widely separated places as Toronto, Canada; York, Pennsylvania; and Wichita, Kansas.[36] The Harrisburg, Pennsylvania, *Telegraph* reported, however, that the same general story had appeared in a Harrisburg newspaper in 1898; and that one man remembered having been told the story by his grandmother in a Civil War setting.

Here is an example from Henry J. Taylor of how quickly a rumor may develop on an *international* basis:

When I left New York, only a few days ago, Archbishop Francis J. Spellman entrusted to me, as a convenient air messenger en route to Rome, a bulky package containing a gift for His Holiness the Pope.

On arrival in Rome I delivered the package to the reception desk at Vatican City. Printed on the upper side was the identification: "From Archbishop Francis J. Spellman, New York, to Holy See, Vatican City."

A rumor that Archbishop Spellman had arrived in Rome started within an hour. . . . That evening the Italian newspapers said that the Archbishop had arrived secretly in Rome to see the Pope. They speculated that his mission concerned the highest diplomatic purpose, probably related to the Yalta conference.

Other papers picked it up—French, Spanish, Balkan and others. From those it spread to England, the United States and South America, to the British dominions, to Africa and to China.

Berlin caught it on the radio, amplified it in Germany and sent it on to Japan. . . . It takes only a package at the right place and the right time with the right words on it to start a world-wide rumor. . . .[37]

It is small wonder that people readily accepted any stories of bureaucratic bungling in wartime Washington. One of the favorites concerned a New York bank vice-president who was hired for an important post in a government agency; some weeks later, while on a short visit to New York, he received a letter from his Washington agency telling him that he was unqualified for the job for which he had applied. According to the rumor—and to illustrate supposed government inefficiency—he suddenly noticed that he had signed the letter himself![38] Then, there was the story of the man who worked in the War Department who reputedly wore a picture of Hitler, instead of himself, on his identification badge for several weeks before any of the guards noticed it. During this same period, front-page stories and photographs in the newspapers, about white markers discovered on the ground to guide enemy bombers to an airplane plant and air base, were immediately accepted as authentic;[39] but within twenty-four hours it turned out that one set of "markers" was only some fertilizer bags which had been put out in the sun to dry, and that the other consisted of a clearing made as a feeding ground for birds.[40]

Probably one of the most widely believed stories of World War II concerned an American mother (or father, wife, or sweetheart) who received a letter from her (or his) son (or husband, or fiancé) from a Japanese (or German) prison. He said he was being treated very well and asked her (or him) to save the stamp on the envelope for his collection. Underneath the stamp the mother (or father, wife, or sweetheart) later found written, "They have cut out my tongue" (or, "They have cut off my ears," or, "They have pierced my eyes").

Many rumors were vicious, and were actively circulated as a means of weakening the morale of the American people. They might be called *wedge-driving* rumors because they were designed to foster disunity and suspicion. Many of them were means of attacking "racial" and religious groups, government leaders and policies, and the Allied nations. Some rumor spreaders were sent to jail for violation of the Wartime Sedition Act, because they had circulated rumors about bodies of soldiers rotting in holds of American ships, and of insane soldiers being shipped to secret concentration camps.[41] Here are some of the most widely believed rumors during World War II:

Anti-British Rumors:

Churchill and Roosevelt could end the war soon, but don't want to.

England is fighting for the most part, using her native troops.

England is waiting for the Americans to come so she will not have to suffer any casualties in invading Europe.

England is planning to fight with our boys while she keeps her own troops at home.

Anti-Semitic Rumors:

Roosevelt's intimate advisers are Jews; and they are unwilling to make peace with Hitler under any circumstances.

The Jews are evading the draft by inducing high blood pressure with drugs.

The Jews are getting out of the draft by bribing Jewish doctors on draft boards.

Jews are cashing in their war bonds after sixty days.

Anti-Negro Rumors:

"Eleanor" (after Mrs. Eleanor Roosevelt) Clubs are being formed all over the country among Negro domestics; their slogan is, "Every white woman in her own kitchen by Christmas."

Negroes have been buying up all ice picks in preparation for a big uprising.

Peace Rumors:

Wall Street is betting that the war will be over in a year.

Lloyd's of London is betting that the war will be over by Christmas.

Peace will come as soon as "big business" ceases to make money out of the war.

Rumors on Rationing:

Sugar rationing is unnecessary—warehouses are jammed with sugar.

Rationing is due to the inefficiency and lust for power of such men as Roosevelt and Ickes.

There is plenty of gas, rubber, and sugar; rationing is just a lot of nonsense.

Anti-Administration Rumors:

Roosevelt brought about the war for personal gains.

The United States will not be able to pay off the war bonds.

We are losing more men through accidents in defense plants than on the battlefields.

England has returned the last shipment of our tanks because of a faulty reverse gear.

Why were such rumors so widely believed? Why were they accepted almost unquestioningly even by extremely intelligent people? These rumors had several things in common; they are characteristic of most rumors that travel *widely and rapidly.*

A successful rumor is usually *brief,* often can be said in a single sentence. It is *simple* enough for anyone to understand it. It is *concrete* and *explicit,* not abstract. It deals with *familiar persons, places,* and *situations.* Usually it *cannot be verified,* or could be verified only with great difficulty. The rumor appears to be a sort of *forbidden knowledge,* and therefore is tantalizing. Such rumors usually thrive best when people share in common the same sorts of wishes, fears, and frustrations. A rumor is especially successful if it purports to come from an "inside" or authoritative source.

NECESSITY OF MYTHS AND LEGENDS

Myths, legends, and rumors are a necessary part of any culture. This discussion is not an attempt to "debunk" them or to suggest that they are useless. In fact, myths and legends play an interesting social role in our culture. It would be a mythical notion to believe that myths and legends could be eliminated. Whenever a false belief is explained away, such as the Captain John Smith or the Washington cherry-tree incident, other myths and legends bob up to take their places. This is one more bit of evidence that man is not always a logical, rational animal. Usually it is more fun to believe than not to believe. Autistic thinking is fairly easy.

Many a myth and legend which exists for other people, of course, does not exist for you. It is difficult for any of us to recognize as myths and legends those ideas which we ourselves believe. We cannot discover them for the very reason that we believe them. *If people believe things to be true, then they are true for them and have social consequences.*

▶ BEHAVIOR—NORMAL OR ABNORMAL?

SAMPLES OF ABNORMAL BEHAVIOR

You think of your own beliefs, opinions, and attitudes as perfectly normal. But consider the following examples of abnormal and borderline cases which probably do not cut across your own attitudes and beliefs. One sample is reproduced in Figure 12. Please read this carefully.

Apre 8-1937

Hon

Senator from

Washington DC

On account of the Codes of Time of this year 193
and other Codes of numbered Letters of English and
Spanish of the Yaqui mission Irrigation Language
of the temple of the Sun causing the word Law to
be Called U-all-and Union is Called Tequila
mexican alcohol and other Key words like Un-one
una-one meaning-word-and Decimal Point =
Medicine Evidentley like the Hopi Nevinoa Indian and
Yaqui Indian Doctor

I take the liberty of writing you this as
the known world including the United States Government
Has become almost devoid of intelligence and the
about half-organized drunkin murder ^{11}U.S.^{24}a^{14} D C2 H9
The Edgar Allen Poe-Pope of Perry Lake Erie and
mount Ranier washington codes are cropping out in
alcohol this year as L is opposite A and the Pope
is 79 years old meaning hp in the year E J ^{20}W-U^{21} ^{3}C-A^{14} ^{19}X-T^{23} ^{8}G-J^{9}
I do not use liquor and found out who was running
the world at the time of the Worlds war 1917 and 1918 and
have had much grief and trouble since
J5-19X is the Red Cross meaning JXN mississippi with
Rio-Pearl called the Challice in code always with
the Apache traitor attached meaning MIO and Sonia Mch
where I was born in 1876 means Arizona Mch 17
my father served 4 years in the 9th Mississippi Civil war days

FIG. 12. LETTER WRITTEN BY PSYCHOPATHIC INDIVIDUAL

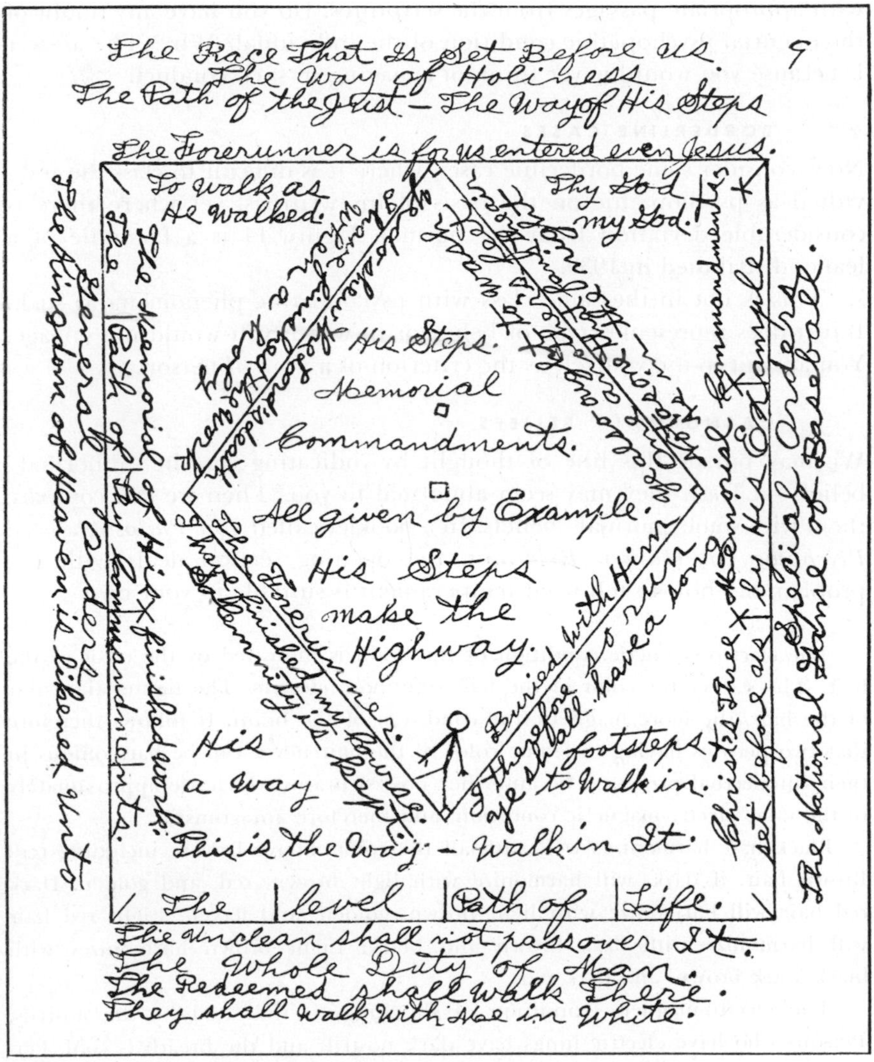

FIG. 13. A BASEBALL DIAMOND ADORNED WITH SCRIPTURAL QUOTATIONS

Do you doubt the psychological abnormality of the individual who wrote this? Probably not, because it is certainly not the sort of letter which you would be likely to write.

Consider the graphic representation of Figure 13—a baseball diamond with appropriate passages from the scriptures. Do you have any doubt of the essential psychopathic condition of the individual? Why? The answer is because you would never think of engaging in such conduct.

BORDERLINE CASES

Now, consider some borderline cases, where it is difficult to class the individual as psychopathic on the basis of his writings, yet where there is considerable deviation from the normal. Figure 14 is a facsimile of a leaflet distributed in 1939.

This is not in the same class with psychopathic phenomena as such. But it does represent a type of behavior in which you would not engage. You are apt to use yourself as the criterion of a *normal* person.

"ABNORMAL" BELIEFS

We may pursue this line of thought by indicating certain "abnormal" beliefs—at least, they may seem abnormal to you. Then we can compare them with some "normal" beliefs. In a booklet called *The Philosophy and Psychology of Human Relations,* the opening section deals with the problem of "how to tell what temperament is suitable to your own":

> The electro-magnetic condition of the brain is indicated by the color of the hair. The darker the color of the hair, the more electric. The lighter the color of the hair, the more magnetic the condition of the brain. It follows therefore that two persons having the same color of the hair never can be harmonious in their intellectual processes, because they possess brains which are approximately in the same electro-magnetic condition, and therefore antagonistic.
>
> Black hair harmonizes well with all the colors above brown, including red. Brown hair, if dark, will harmonize with light brown, red, and golden. Dark red hair will harmonize with light brown, golden, and flaxen. Light red hair will harmonize with dark brown and black. Light brown harmonizes with black, dark brown, and dark red.
>
> The electro-magnetic condition of the lungs is indicated by the nostrils. Persons who have electric lungs have dark nostrils and the breath is cool. Persons who have magnetic lungs have wide and red nostrils and the breath is usually warm. The pleasure of sexual companionship is greatly enhanced by a correct condition of harmonious association in this particular.[42]

These are abnormal beliefs only to those who do not happen to believe in these particular myths and legends. The wide sale of this booklet, plus the similarity to other psychological myths and legends, indicates that it is

- BULLETIN -

"Come - Get ready - Let's Go - Help others to get ready - To Go". Its "Leaven 100-C" - Its going - It can't be stopped.

"An influence working silently and strongly within man, that causes changes in things or opinions."

Its like Lava - you can't stop it - you can't control it - you can't buy it. Like molton volcanic matter burning its way - pushing in all directions, everything which might stand in its way - It will push its way through homes, villages, towns, counties, cities, states, still on to the Nation's Capital and then over our borders to our friendly neighbors - It can't be stopped. It has started on its way - It will not harm you. If you let it take you, it will carry you on its way to the happiest life, to a life of <u>real</u> and lasting prosperity - Don't be left behind.

It will push the Nazis out of America.

It will shove the Facists out of America.

It will drive the Communists out of America.

Every industry, mill, factory, manufacturing plant, department store, hotel, business house, lodge, association, college, school, church, or other organizations working for the Good of our land, should join this great movement. Join now - Get your membership card - Get your number. Its real - Its strong - Its courageous - Its brave - Its bold - Its mighty - Its colossal - For its convention it will need a colosseum greatly exceeding "The Flavian Amphitheater of the ancients". It must be built for 100,000 seats - Lets start to build it now - build it of materials and construction for all time -

"Let the Nation's Best People Rule."

Leaven 100-C Voter Units

Washington, D. C.

FIG. 14. A LEAFLET DISTRIBUTED IN 1939

a perfectly normal phenomenon for large numbers of people. You would probably not go to a palmist to ask seriously, "How many times will I marry?" or "How can I hold my sweetheart's love?" or "How soon will my lover propose?" Nor are you apt to subscribe to a service which sells "vitality products" and will give you new life, particularly sex vitality. Yet the fact that such activities are carried on with financial success indicates how normal such ideas are for great numbers of people.

Popular lecturers abound who talk on "The Secret Art of Successful Living," or "The Science Beyond the Radio" which involves getting in touch with the great Life Principle in order to understand the "basic laws of life." A mail-order business called *Psychiana* which was carried on successfully for years would, for a given sum of money, enable you to get in touch with the "God realm." Thousands of people with both dark and white skins have hailed as God a Negro who calls himself Father Divine. Yogi "research" is always popular with certain women's groups. Institutes of "Metaphysics" abound. Mr. and Mrs. G. W. Ballard founded the great *I Am* movement, claiming thousands of followers all over the country who studied a mythical St. Germain and the teachings of the "Great Divine Rector, the Great White Brotherhood, the Brotherhood of the Royal Teton, the Brotherhood of Mount Shasta, the Great Ones from Venus, and those other Ascended Masters whose loving help has been direct and without limit." Among other things, the leader of the movement claimed that he had destroyed with a sword of flame a number of foreign submarines in the Atlantic which were bent on the destruction of America, and that ascended spirits had successfully routed a flight of Japanese bombers who were attacking a Chinese city.

Look back over the various samples of "abnormal" beliefs and ask yourself why you call them abnormal. Not knowing the individuals responsible for these beliefs and perhaps not knowing any of their thousands of followers, you are apt to dismiss the leaders as "crackpots" and their followers as "gone with the wind." Can you tell, however, from an examination of the materials what is the character of the person who produced the materials, or whether the followers are abnormal?

"NORMAL" BELIEFS AND BEHAVIOR

Does the following set of beliefs seem abnormal or normal?

People with large or popping eyes, which are gray-blue, and which are reinforced by a strong nose and sizable ears, are often shrewd, good-natured, quick in observation, and successful in business. . . .

Blue eyes of certain shades also have an enviable reputation. When they are large, full, and really blue, they indicate optimism, enthusiasm, understanding, warmth, and a sympathetic insight into other people, plus a love of pleasure and luxury. But there is a light blue eye which is usually shifty and not deeply set in its socket that denotes the sensualist and beauty lover. Particularly does this person, if a man, love feminine beauty. Women whom he invites to tea require chaperons.[43]

In case you rate this as a set of "abnormal" beliefs, note that the quotation is taken from a very popular publication, *The American Magazine,* probably believed to be true by many thousands of persons. In nearly every community, lecturers speak on such subjects as "Your Secret Dream and How to Make It Come True." The lecturers propound completely unscientific but widely accepted notions that represent normality for people not unlike yourself.

In *Middletown* the Lynds found that a group of men and women came together weekly to study a book called *The Master Key,* their meeting beginning always with the prescribed ritual:

Leader: "How are you?"

Group: "Fine and dandy, why shouldn't I be?"

Leader: "Now we have started vibrations which have lifted us already to a higher plane."

Group, in unison: "I am relaxing, relaxing, relaxed. . . . I am wholly passive—Universal mind has taken possession of me. . . . Knowledge is Power. I desire Knowledge. I have Knowledge."[44]

Thousands of Americans believe whatever they see in print, especially if the print says in effect that "a great authority has proved." They may believe that blondes are shy and self-conscious in social gatherings, that brunettes have to work harder than blondes to attract men, that redheads are likely to be brilliant but unstable. One of the best sellers of the 1930's included a whole series of irrational beliefs which are fairly representative for many people. In the book are statements that levitation, divine healing, clairvoyance, telepathy, and spiritism are facts; that white men are the hardiest of all groups, have superior brains, and a natural immunity to fatigue and fear; that athletes are not very intelligent; that diseases are not entities but that love and hate are realities.[45] These false beliefs are perfectly normal for large numbers of people.

Drugstores are interesting places to observe the myths and legends which most people believe. Look at the advertising of patent-medicine companies. One company lists ninety-nine different remedies which will cure fevers, congestions, inflammations, heart pain, fevers of children, bilious fever, roundworms, worm fevers, itching, emaciation, sleeplessness, colic, crying of infants, teething, diarrhea, nausea, vomiting, bronchitis, neuralgia, toothache, weak stomach, bilious complaints, croup, hoarse coughing, oppressed breathing, eczema eruptions, erysipelas, rheumatic pains, and so forth, *ad nauseam*.

If you say that you do not "fall for this stuff," remember again that these are common beliefs for millions of people. After all, most people believe that lightning never strikes twice in the same place, and that birds are faultlessly kind to their young. Here are some of the "remedies" in use in certain parts of rural America: "putting a spider web on a wound to stop bleeding; . . . smoking coffee for toothache; a tobacco quid on a baby's stomach to cure 'worms'; . . . salt and vinegar poultices on the back for kidney trouble; gunpowder and cream ointment for ringworm; . . . application of a mixture of coal tar, turpentine, and camphor to the right side to cure appendicitis; and carrying a buckeye or a lump of sulphur in the pocket to cure or prevent rheumatism."[46]

Think of the number of people you know who believe in the prophetic character of dreams. Think of the number of individuals whom you know who believe in telling fortunes by means of cards, numbers, and tea leaves. Remember that "mediums" and astrologers have made millions of dollars because of the gullibility of millions of people. Consider how widespread is the belief in numerology among Americans, and the number of books written on this subject. One movie actress was induced to separate from her husband because the letters in her name and in his did not vibrate correctly. What about the send-a-dime craze—did you ever send a dime or otherwise become involved in continuing a chain letter? The majority of Americans bet and gamble, even though they recognize the irrational character of the procedure. Get-rich-quick schemes are everywhere. Victims of stock and bond manipulation are well known to everyone.

People were not unusually surprised when a congresswoman from Indiana suggested in 1937 that the Japanese cherry trees around the Tidal Basin in Washington, D. C., be destroyed because they had developed "into a symbol of traitorism and disloyalty" on the part of the Japanese government.[47] This was seriously suggested as a partial solution to the problem of American relations with Japan. When the Women's Department of the Knights of the Ku Klux Klan presented a silk Christian flag to a church organization, few people saw any inconsistency in the notion of Christianity which preaches "brotherhood of man" and a K.K.K. organization which breeds intolerance.[48]

THE FAITH LADDER

Now, what is the meaning of psychological abnormality? Certainly those types of behavior, both covert and overt, which are adequate for you may be entirely inadequate for somebody else, and beliefs and "ways" of another individual may be foreign to you. Judgments of normality and abnormality cannot be said to square with the concepts of adequacy and inadequacy. Normality-abnormality is a statistical concept and does *not* represent a value judgment. At the beginning of this section you probably marked certain false statements as true. They represented truth to you. Other individuals, such as the followers of Father Divine or the person who interprets personality in terms of eye color, also have beliefs which are true for them. There is no essential difference in the character of these beliefs. Many people cling to beliefs because of their psychological value—they are happier to believe than to doubt. Perhaps they have climbed what William James called "the faith ladder" with its seven steps:

1. There is nothing absurd in a certain view of the world being true, nothing self-contradictory;
2. It *might* have been true under certain conditions;
3. It *may* be true even now;
4. It is *fit* to be true;
5. It *ought* to be true;
6. It *must* be true;
7. It *shall* be true, at any rate true for me.[49]

NORMALITY AND RATIONALITY

The question of normality-abnormality, then, cuts across that of rationality-irrationality. Is there any relation between normality and rationality? Is there any connection between abnormality and irrationality? In other words, for the various types of behavior examined here, does it follow that abnormal behavior in a statistical sense is necessarily irrational? The answer is no. There is no necessary connection between normality and rationality. By way of example, think of any set of beliefs which you and most of your group hold. They are normal for *you.* Some of them may be demonstrated to be logical and rational, others irrational on the basis of pure logic. Deviations from the normal, on the other hand, may also be either rational or irrational.

MEANINGS OF "ABNORMAL"

Can a satisfactory definition be offered of the word "abnormal"? The term has been used in at least six different senses:[50] (1) The word has often been used to represent that which is *unusual.* In the field of morals, for instance, behavior different from your own mores may be called abnormal. (2) Abnormal also means *extreme.* A child with a very low (or very high) intelligence quotient is an example. (3) Abnormal is sometimes used as synonymous with the word *mysterious.* Dream material is often called abnormal because the nature of dreams is not exactly understood. (4) Abnormal is sometimes confused with the word *sexual.* Certain sex practices are classed as abnormal. (5) The word "abnormal" has been used to mean *pathological.* Thus, people in mental institutions are called abnormal. (6) Many people confuse the word abnormal with the word *criminal.* The view seems widespread not only that all criminals are rats, but that criminals are abnormal.

THE PSYCHOLOGICAL MEANING OF ABNORMALITY

The word normal has too frequently been used to imply those things which should be, that is, those things which *you* think should be. If certain values are dear to you and yours, then you are likely to believe that those values are normal and that anyone who deviates from them is abnormal and, therefore, inferior.

Instead of limiting yourself to these value judgments, it is much more useful to deal with abnormality in a *quantitative* sense. The only meaning of abnormality, *psychologically,* is a statistical one. The essential question is whether the behavior is typical of most people of a given group. If a type of behavior is truly representative of most members of a certain group, then that behavior is normal *for that group.* The words "normal" and "abnormal" should not in any sense imply either subjective approval or disapproval.

If we share the delusions of our fellows, we are regarded as perfectly normal; that is, if we believe as truths those myths and legends which other people believe, we are normal. We are considered abnormal by others only if we develop private delusions or beliefs which are not characteristic of our fellows. It is for this reason that normal behavior in one society may be considered abnormal in another. For the Kwakiutl the ritual of giving away all their possessions is a completely normal manifestation *in their culture.* Among the Dobuans where cheating, sorcery, and magic are regarded as virtues, this is perfectly normal *for these people.* For an Australian native to go about unclothed is no proof of exhibitionism or abnormality.

In our own culture certain types of behavior are regarded as abnormal because they are not typical. Murder, prostitution, homosexual behavior, forgery, feeble-mindedness, and disease are obviously abnormal in the statistical sense that they do not represent usual behavior. The word "normal" implies a culturally sanctioned way of behavior, and "abnormal" indicates a departure from the mode or norm of behavior. Neither term represents any sort of subjective valuation of whether or not the behavior is best for society.

QUESTIONS AND PROBLEMS FOR DISCUSSION

1. *List in two columns the advantages and disadvantages of autistic thinking.*
2. *In what instances in your own life has autistic thinking served as a basis for logical, directive thinking?*

3. *What is* not *propaganda?*
4. *How does censorship differ from propaganda?*
5. *How can you develop a resistance to purposeful propaganda?*
6. *Find some specific examples of propaganda in the second World War for* (a) *totalitarianism;* (b) *democracy;* (c) *militarism;* (d) *pacifism.*
7. *Plan an experiment to test the accuracy of perception and observation of some emotional event.*
8. *Make your own list of the ways in which legends develop.*
9. *In what ways may myths and legends be said to consist of adult extensions of the infantile world of phantasy and make-believe?*
10. *Does "debunking" of history tend to make us more rational or not?*
11. *Explain: "Modern psychiatry does not sharply distinguish between the pathological and the normal. It is only a matter of degree."*
12. *Make a list of those ways in which your own behavior is statistically normal. Make another list of those ways in which it is statistically abnormal.*
13. *"If people believe things to be true, they are true for them." Explain.*

RECOMMENDED READINGS

Allport, G. W., and Postman, L., *The Psychology of Rumor.* New York: Henry Holt and Company, Inc., 1947.

Bartlett, F. C., *Remembering: A Study in Experimental and Social Psychology.* Cambridge: University Press, 1932.

Cantril, H., with the assistance of Gaudet, H., and Herzog, H., *The Invasion from Mars: A Study in the Psychology of Panic.* Princeton: Princeton University Press, 1940.

Clarke, E. L., *The Art of Straight Thinking.* New York: D. Appleton Company, Inc., 1929.

Dewey, J., *How We Think.* Boston: D. C. Heath and Company, 1910.

Dimnet, E., *The Art of Thinking.* New York: Simon and Schuster, 1929.

Doob, L. W., *Propaganda: Its Psychology and Technique.* New York: Henry Holt and Company, Inc., 1935.

Evans, B., *The Natural History of Nonsense.* New York: Alfred A. Knopf, Inc., 1946.

Fisher, S. G., *The Legendary and Myth Making Process in Histories of the American Revolution.* Philadelphia: (Reprinted from *Proceedings of the American Philosophical Society,* Vol. 51, April-June, 1912), 1912.

Freeman, E., *Conquering the Man in the Street: A Psychological Analysis of Propaganda in War, Fascism, and Politics.* New York: The Vanguard Press, 1940.

Guthrie, E. R., *The Psychology of Human Conflict: The Clash of Motives within the Individual.* New York: Harper & Brothers, 1938.

Irwin, W., *Propaganda and the News.* New York: McGraw-Hill Book Company, Inc., 1936.

Jacobson, D. J., *The Affairs of Dame Rumor.* New York: Rinehart & Company, Inc., 1948.

Jastrow, J., *Fact and Fable in Psychology.* Boston: Houghton Mifflin Company, 1900.

Jastrow, J., *Wish and Wisdom: Episodes in the Vagaries of Belief.* New York: D. Appleton-Century Company, 1935.

Lumley, F. E., *The Propaganda Menace.* New York: D. Appleton-Century Company, 1933.

Mackay, C., *Extraordinary Popular Delusions and the Madness of Crowds.* Boston: L. C. Page & Co., 1932.

MacDougall, C. D., *Hoaxes.* New York: The Macmillan Company, 1940.

Nevins, A., *The Gateway to History.* New York: D. Appleton-Century Company, 1938.

Ponsonby, A., *Falsehood in War Time: Containing an Assortment of Lies Circulated throughout the Nations during the Great War.* New York: E. P. Dutton & Company, Inc., 1929.

Spearman, C., "Normality." In Murchison, C. (editor), *Psychologies of 1930.* Worcester: Clark University Press, 1930, Chap. 24.

Steiner, L. R., *Where Do People Take Their Troubles?* Boston: Houghton Mifflin Company, 1945.

Thouless, R. H., *How to Think Straight: The Technique of Applying Logic Instead of Emotion.* New York: Simon and Schuster, Inc., 1939.

*Newcomb, T. M., Hartley, E. L., and others (editors), *Readings in Social Psychology.* New York: Henry Holt and Company, Inc., 1947. (The following selections are listed according to the sequence of related discussions in the chapter you have just read.)

Herzog, H., "Psychological Gratifications in Daytime Radio Listening," pp. 561–566.

Cantril, H., "The Invasion from Mars," pp. 619–628.

Bartlett, F. C., "Social Factors in Recall," pp. 69–76.

Allport, G. W., and Postman, L. J., "The Basic Psychology of Rumor," pp. 547–558.

PART FOUR

BEHAVIOR IN THE PRESENCE OF OTHERS

PART IV deals with the more *social* bases of adjustment.

Our judgments of other persons depend upon our prejudices, emotional factors, stimulation that is subliminal (below the conscious threshold), and stereotyping. These factors are analyzed in terms of empirical studies and illustrative materials.

The influence of other persons is considered, first of all, in terms of "unconscious" factors of compensation, rationalization, identification, regression, and projection. Both suggestion and imitation are then analyzed in some detail, leading to explanations of uniformity of action. Various theories of laughter are presented, together with some empirical studies. Finally, there is given a brief summary of experimental work on the influence of groups on individual performance.

The behavior of people in groups is discussed under the general headings of crowd behavior and the psychology of the audience. This is followed by a consideration of booms, crazes, fads, and fashions, as illustrative of irrational group behavior.

Sex is dealt with largely in terms of masculinity and femininity rather than on a biological basis. Studies of dominance in animals, primitives, and children are reviewed because of their bearing on social behavior. Analyses are also made of dominance and prestige in various situations.

The psychology of leadership is considered from the standpoint of both the leaders and the "led." Considerable attention is then given to the problem of leadership for social change. Finally, the social psychology of invention and creative production is explained.

CHAPTER TEN

OUR JUDGMENTS OF OTHER PERSONS

THE NATURE OF PREJUDICE. The Problem of Open-mindedness—Definition of Prejudice—Growth of Prejudices—Deliberate Fostering of Prejudices—Stereotyping—The Four Mechanisms of Conditioning—The Permanence of Prejudices / JUDGING EMOTIONS. The Problem—Sherman's Experiments—Significance of Sherman's Work—Other Experimental Studies—Summary of Experimental Conclusions / SUBLIMINAL STIMULATION. "Sizing up" People—Definition of Subliminal Stimulation—Some Experimental Studies—Significance of Subliminal Stimulation—Integration of Subliminal Stimuli / THE STEREOTYPING PROCESS. The Word "Stereotype"—Individual Differences—The Type Fallacy—Judging Intelligence, as an Example of the Type Fallacy—Other Instances of the Typing Fallacy—Inconsistencies in the Stereotyping Process—The Kretschmer Hypothesis—Some Empirical Studies of Stereotyping—Reality of Stereotypes—Predictions from Stereotypes—The Individual Basis of Stereotyping—The Practical Use of Stereotypes.

What are the bases of our attitudes toward other persons? Besides the mechanism of conditioning and the general factors of motivation (Chapter 6), what social factors determine our attitudes toward other individuals and toward social situations? There are at least four answers: (1) prejudice; (2) our judgments of feelings and emotions; (3) subliminal stimulation; and (4) the stereotyping process.

▶ THE NATURE OF PREJUDICE

THE PROBLEM OF OPEN-MINDEDNESS

You probably feel that since you are an intelligent person and have been exposed to education, you are free of prejudices. After all, don't "they" say that education and intelligence are guarantees of correct thinking?

If you think you have no prejudices, try the following simple experiment:[1] First of all, select some belief of yours which you know can be either proved or disproved through a careful study of facts now published in scientific works. Next, write down immediately what your exact opinion is. Then put down all the evidence you possibly can think of which will support your belief, without looking up any references. At this point you will probably be amazed at your lack of factual information on something which you believe to be true. Now, begin the process of gathering further evidence both for and against the belief, and arrange your materials under two headings. Finally, compare the pros and cons.

Many an American thinks it is terrible the way the Nazis treated the Jews, yet he worries not at all about his own attitudes. It is the *other* people who have the prejudices, not us!

DEFINITION OF PREJUDICE

The word "prejudice" actually means a premature or biased opinion. Ogburn defines prejudice as "a hasty judgment or an opinion formed without due examination."[2] This does not mean that the formation of a prejudice is a deliberate process. On the contrary, prejudices come into being without the knowledge of most of the individuals concerned. One does not stop in the middle of his mental "tracks" and deliberately, rationally, decide to develop an unfavorable or favorable attitude toward this, that, or the other thing for this, that, or the other reason. Rather, by the unconscious workings of the processes of conditioning, subliminal stimulation, stereotyping, suggestion, imitation, and the like, in conjunction with his personal experiences and with the precipitates of his native culture, he comes to possess, all unknowingly, bias in regard to specific objects and concepts. It is also quite possible for a person to become aware of prejudice, just as he may become aware of a phobia or unreasonable fear, and yet feel helpless to overcome it. He may be exasperated by the knowledge that this very prejudice was almost none of *his* making.

GROWTH OF PREJUDICES

We get our prejudices largely through our own direct personal experiences.

> Someone is victimized by an unscrupulous lawyer; thereafter he has no use for any of the profession. . . . Someone has an unhappy experience while traveling through a certain town; thereafter he hates not only the town but everything in it; nothing good can come from such a place. Or one buys an article of merchandise only to find he has been thoroughly cheated, and dislikes in consequence the store which sold it and the firm which made it. A child, offended or pleased by a certain teacher, subsequently dislikes or likes the subject she teaches. A youth, embittered by the excessive dominance of an elder, perhaps acquires thereby a hatred for the whole principle of authority.[3]

The influence of our associates is particularly great in early childhood. In the family, the schoolroom, the church, the play group, the gang, and the club, children are constantly acquiring prejudices which represent absolute truths for them. In social psychology, of course, we are not so much concerned with the truth or falsity of these prejudices as with the ways in which they affect behavior. Nationality prejudices are found even in the jumping-rope rhymes of young schoolgirls:[4]

A tisket, a tasket,
Hitler's in his casket;
Eenie, meenie, Mussolini,
Six feet underground.

Red, white, and blue,
Your father is a Jew,
Your mother is a Japanese,
And so are You!

Many attitudes toward nationality groups develop in the school situation; teachers are often responsible for fostering prejudices which have a lasting effect on their students.[5] An examination of textbooks used in high schools and colleges shows that oftentimes nationality prejudices are fostered (compare Chapter 24).[6]

Prejudices grow up where vivid experiences are involved, where there are few counterinfluences giving the other side of the picture, and where those who hold prejudiced views are individuals with considerable prestige.[7] It is not surprising to find boys and girls growing up believing that the people on the other side of the railroad tracks—no matter which side—are not only different but inferior, that those who worship differently are inferior, that those with different-colored skins are inferior, that those whose language behavior is different are inferior. There are very few, if any, "natural" prejudices. Even though you have had certain prejudices as long as you can remember, this is no guarantee that you were born with them. After all, how much of your life can you remember before age five? Your prejudices and biases exist because of your own conditioning, largely owing to the beliefs and mores of the culture in which you live. One man says:

> My grandfather was a man who had three convictions, three first-class hatreds. He hated Democrats, he hated liquor in all its forms, and he hated Catholics. One afternoon in the Boston paper there was a story about a big fire. A Presbyterian church had burned to the ground. . . . The cause of the fire was not known. I can remember yet my grandfather pounding the table to emphasize his words. The old gentleman said in measured syllables: "Let me tell you that when they discover the cause of that fire, they'll find that the person who did it was a low, dirty, sneaking rum-drinking Catholic Democrat."[8]

We learn to be prejudiced against people who dress differently, speak differently, or behave at all differently from the way we behave ourselves. We learn to be repelled by differences in skin color, facial contour, physique, odor, touch, language, ornamentation. A man with Negro servants says, "I don't want to feel the touch of their hands against my skin." An individual who murders the king's English is looked upon as inferior by those who value correct English. In other words, we have learned to look very much askance at those who differ from us and to think that by this very token they must be inferior. Even though we may live almost side by side, we develop "social distance" toward each other.

If, in addition to appearing physically different from us and behaving differently, people have ideas and thoughts which do not square with our own, we somehow feel superior to them. Anti-Semitic prejudice is an example of this tendency, as we shall see more fully in Chapter 23. Because of an emphasis on scholarship to a greater extent in Jewish than in Gentile culture, a high percentage of Jewish people in America tend to be well educated and to hold progressive or liberal ideas. Yet this is offensive to many non-Jews.

DELIBERATE FOSTERING OF PREJUDICES

Prejudices may also be built up purposefully by the technique of the conditioned response. For example, the stimulus word "Communist" usually results in a response of dislike. On the other hand, the word "Jew" may result in no such response. Now, it becomes a simple matter for some anti-Semite to pair these two words over and over again and to talk about "Communist Jews" until the conditioned stimulus "Jew" tends by itself to produce the response of dislike formerly produced by the original stimulus "Communist." The conditioned response is established after constant repetition. The process of generalization may result in Jewish religious practices being mistakenly identified with Communism. We shall return to this point in Chapter 23 in discussing minority groups.

In every culture, children are taught that their own group is superior to all others. This is true in Germany, Italy, Russia, England, Japan, and every other country. It seems characteristic of man the world over, after looking at customs and practices different from his own, to say that people who exhibit these ways of acting are inferior. My business methods, my home, my car, my wife, my kiddies are better than anybody else's. An old Quaker is supposed to have said, "Everyone is queer but me and thee, and sometimes I think that even thee is a little bit queer."

It is difficult for people to believe that those who talk, act, think, and live in very different fashion from themselves can be quite as human as they. The greater the difference, the more emphatic this difficulty. Primitive peoples take a similar attitude, which often is so deeply rooted that they are unconscious of it. Thus the Eskimo call themselves *Inuit,* which means "People," or "Human Beings," and refer to Indians as "Children of a Louse's Egg." Neighboring tribes call the Hopi *Moki,* which means "Cowards," whereas their name for themselves, Hopi, means "Men." Bushmen call themselves Khoi-Khoi, which means "Men of Men," or, as we say, "We the People." The name which many Australian tribes apply to themselves means "Men." Generally speaking, preliterate people have about the same measure of contempt for us as we have for them, each group being ignorant of the language, ways of life, ethical standards, pleasures, trials, and hardships of the other.[9]

STEREOTYPING

Prejudice, then, involves very much the stereotyping process (discussed in detail in the last section of this chapter). If we find a fairly substantial number of people in a given group behaving or thinking differently from ourselves, we can easily stereotype and say that all individuals in that group are of a particular "type." Thus we find that certain Japanese, let us say, have been treacherous and we then come to the erroneous conclusion that all Japanese are treacherous. The stereotyping process saves us time and prevents us from doing too much "hard" thinking. So far as attitudes toward people in different occupations are concerned, you can determine rather readily how to behave toward them. In the United States people become alarmed at how these "foreigners" put on airs when it is perfectly apparent that American ways of acting are the only correct ways.

> Our lodge, our fraternity, our labor group, is superior to others. Our nation is the best, the greatest, the wealthiest, the most powerful. We identify ourselves with these stereotypes, and in the crisis of a crowd situation we act as if they were true. *They are true for us.*[10]

THE FOUR MECHANISMS OF CONDITIONING

A group of college students was given the assignment, "Write down the details and origin of some prejudice which you are conscious of having had for some time." Some of the prejudices described were directed toward Negro men, very black Negroes only, the Jewish race, the Northern Negro, enlisted men of the Army and Navy, people of a higher social status, Chinese, the white race (written by an American Indian), the Finnish people, women who smoke, royalty, and business people. One student, formerly a Protestant, indicated "a negative attitude toward all churches following Christ and all persons connected with such churches." Two of the students in this experiment had been assigned seats next to each other. One was a young lady from New England, who wrote a paper describing her prejudice against people with Southern accents. The other was a girl from Georgia, who described in considerable detail a prejudice against individuals with a Yankee nasal twang. These views and the ways they grew up were not necessarily rational. How did these people "get that way"?

A study of prejudices is a specialized examination of the social psychology of attitudes. The same four mechanisms are involved which were previously discussed (Chapter 6): (1) generalization of conditioned responses, (2) differentiation of responses, (3) traumatic experience, and (4) the acceptance of ready-made attitudes. Examples will be given of each. However, the social psychology of prejudice is so complex that *it is difficult to find examples to illustrate one only of these four points. Instead, two or more of the mechanisms usually work together,* as the following examples taken from personal histories show.

1. Here is an example of prejudice against Negroes, largely due to the *generalization* of various factors, through a combination of things and events:

During my entire life none of my family have ever had negro help. From my early childhood I can remember hearing Mother say that she didn't like negro maids or cooks because they weren't clean and weren't careful with children, and that they would often steal things from around the house.

Living in the Southern part of Texas all of my life, until the last two years, the only opportunity I had to observe negroes was during the cotton picking season when crowds of them, men, women and children, would drift across the State. They lived in the fields under trees or pitched tents, and each time they moved they carried with them all their earthly possessions. The conditions under which they lived were most unsanitary and really dirty. Negroes were looked upon as hired labor or servants and a necessary evil.

In the small town where I lived for eight years not a single negro lived there. Several times some white people would bring a negro in for a servant but they never stayed for more than a week, because there were no other negroes there for them to associate with. The Mexicans would have nothing to do with them either.

2. A second way in which prejudices grow up is by the mechanism of *differentiation;* that is, one stimulus stands for a whole group of stimuli and thus differentiates or distinguishes these stimuli from closely similar ones. This is illustrated by a young woman who reports a prejudice against Negroes, but only the *very black* ones:

To me, there is a distinct difference between the lighter members of the negro race with their smaller lips, their less kinky hair, and their lighter complexions, and the more ebony members with their hulky frames, their thick, protruding lips, and their black, coarse skin. My contacts with the lighter group have all been pleasant ones, as instanced by our two very good maids, both of whom have light skins. But my memories of the darker group have been unpleasant since I was barely 5 years old. . . .

This prejudice all began with an influx of the negro population into homes which proved to be uncomfortably near mine. Everything was fine until I was knocked down on skates by two negro bullies for no apparent reason. . . . Every time I saw these two negroes, trouble of some sort ensued.

A few years later, after I entered high school, I met hordes of negroes, also coming home from their school. The sidewalk being rather narrow, and these negroes traveling in crowds of five or six, I was almost daily knocked out into the street by a slap, accompanied by rude remarks, swearing, and much raucous laughter. . . . One day I was knocked in front of a truck and barely escaped being killed. . . .

Perhaps the most outstanding memory of a comparison between these two types of negroes—the lighter and the darker skinned—is due to the fact that the day when I was pushed in front of the truck, a very light skinned negro girl, with almost blonde hair, was the only one among the whole motley crew who failed to see the humor of my situation. I feel as though I will ever owe her a debt of gratitude.

3. A prejudice due partly to a *traumatic experience* can be illustrated by the description of a prejudice against people with red hair:

Once when I was a very small child, I was playing in my sandpile with a little red-haired boy. A controversy arose between us as to who should play with a certain little iron kettle, which belonged to me. . . .

Well, he did give it to me, with one spontaneous and impulsive gesture. He hit me over the head with it. . . . I screamed names at him which were really quite advanced for any vocabulary. A neighbor came to the rescue, and although I was the one she was having to hold back, she exclaimed, "That's just like a red-head's temper."

4. A fourth example is the prejudice of a college girl against Mrs. Franklin D. Roosevelt. Her *acceptance of ready-made attitudes* from older people with reference to drinking had been carried over and generalized to include Mrs. Roosevelt:

I have been prejudiced against Mrs. Roosevelt ever since she became First Lady. I now think she does wonderful things, is very active and does a lot of good, but I still don't like her.

I am sure the reason for this is: I have been brought up to believe that drinking of any kind is terrible, nice girls in the part of the country in which I live just don't drink, (we don't have cocktails of course). Along at the first of the Roosevelt administration, Mrs. Roosevelt wrote an article on "A Girl Should Learn Her Capacity and Drink That and No More." I remember then my estimation of her went away down and no matter what she has done since then, I don't like her. Also I now think nothing about drinking, and see no harm in a cocktail—but my prejudice against Mrs. Roosevelt remains.

THE PERMANENCE OF PREJUDICES

Note in the last example given that the writer says that she realizes that Mrs. Roosevelt is a nice person, but that she still doesn't like her. In other words, a mere examination or understanding of her prejudice does not mean that it will be eradicated. One student, after making a very thorough analysis of the pros and cons of her attitudes toward Negroes, said, "When I try to think why I believe as I do, I can think of no reasons. While I know I am wrong, I still believe this way. I apparently have no objectivity." Another described a belief that stingy people have practically no lobes on their ears and that generosity is marked by large ears (see Chapter 6). Hence, she avoided people with small ear lobes, and said, "I realize how idiotic this conclusion is, but I still catch myself judging people by it." Another wrote, "Although I am not at all proud to admit it, I entertain a strong prejudice against Jewish people." The interesting thing about all of these descriptions is that the prejudices are not based on logical reasons, yet they still hold true.

▶ JUDGING EMOTIONS

THE PROBLEM

What is there about your feelings that can be understood by someone else, an outside observer, so that he can interpret the bases of your particular attitudes? To what extent can you correctly interpret someone's feelings and emotions, on the basis of his observable behavior? In a great many situations most of us learn to conceal rather carefully our actual feelings and emotions. As healthy young animals, we rapidly learned to conform to the culture patterns of our particular group. We learned through childhood not only what is done but also what is said in polite society. All of us have necessarily developed a set of taboos not only as to what we may do, but as to what we may speak or how we may look in social situations. We conform to the standards of our group. No one leaves a dinner party telling his hostess that the steak was tough, the conversation boring, and the evening dull. Instead, we learn politely to say, "Such marvelous food! Such stimulating conversation! And I hope you will ask me to come again!"

We also learn to conceal those feelings and emotions which might be offensive to other individuals. There are limits to the extent to which one can speak of his headache, his indigestion, or of domestic difficulties which confront him. We try not to go about with worried, harassed expressions on our faces. Therefore, the problem of judging true internal feelings and emotions from facial expressions and from language behavior is a very difficult one.

SHERMAN'S EXPERIMENTS

A whole series of experiments have been conducted to determine whether or not the overt responses of a subject can be interpreted correctly by observers. One of the most interesting studies was conducted by Sherman, who was concerned with the ability of observers to name and differentiate the emotional reactions of infants below eight days of age.[11] We shall consider the details of this experiment because it dealt with emotional expressions in infants before they could have learned to inhibit or control them to any great extent, and also because the general methodology is typical of similar experiments with adults. The problem was threefold: (1) whether the observers could agree as to the emotional characteristics of these responses; (2) whether the judgments were based upon observable differences in the infants' responses or upon knowledge of the stimuli employed; and (3) whether the previous training and experience of the observers were factors in the judgments they made.

The stimuli for the babies were (*a*) hunger: infants who had not been fed were observed fifteen minutes after their proper feeding time; (*b*) dropping: infants were suddenly dropped two or three feet toward the table; (*c*) restraint: the face of the baby was held down fairly firmly on the table; and (*d*) sticking with a needle. One group of observers was presented with motion-picture views of the foregoing circumstances and the ensuing responses, and was asked to write down the names of the emotions elicited. With a second group of observers, the stimulus situations were deleted from the pictures and the observers were asked to name the emotions on the basis of the responses alone. They were also asked to give their judgments as to the nature of the stimuli used to produce the various reactions. With a third group of observers, the stimuli were paired with the wrong responses in the film, and the subjects were required to name the emotional character of each response. Finally, the infants were stimulated behind a screen, which was immediately removed; the subjects were then required to name the emotion on the basis of direct observation of the infants' responses.

There was considerable lack of agreement within each group, as well as between the various groups of observers. Instead of the four possible types of response which were known to have been elicited, the observers listed as many as twenty-five different types. Incidentally, knowledge of psychology and previous work on the emotions of infants apparently did not aid graduate students in differentiating between the reactions.

In the second part of the study Sherman was interested in ". . . the ability of a group of observers to judge the emotional characteristics of the voice of a trained vocalist when he attempts to convey a certain emotion; the ability of observers to judge the emotional characteristics of the cries of infants below twelve days of age; and the influence of the quantitative aspect of the stimulus, that is, the intensity, suddenness, and duration of the application of the stimulus, upon the character of the cries of infants."[12] The same four stimuli were used for calling out the cries of the infants, and babies varied in age from three to seven days. The twenty-three observers were graduate students in psychology, medical students, and student nurses. Many factors influenced the cries of infants, the character of the cry being in part a function of conditions other than the qualitative character of the specific stimuli. This probably accounts for the fact that the observers were unable to give judgments of the emotional character of the cries. As to judgments of the emotional character of the adult voice, these were obtained from five rapid presentations by a vocalist of single notes lasting 1½ seconds, with intensity and pitch held constant. The vocalist behind a screen presented surprise; fear and pain; sorrow; and anger and hate. Yet the observers' judgments of the intended emotions varied widely.

Significance of Sherman's Work. The significance of these two related experiments is, first of all, that subjective judgments cannot be depended upon in the laboratory situation. In the second place, we should not rely too heavily upon our judgments of another individual's behavior in social conditions. In the third place, the number of correct responses in these experiments was much greater when the stimuli were shown than when they were not shown. Judgments of other persons cannot be made accurately on the basis of facial expressions or voice or other overt manifestations; it is necessary also to know precisely what the exact stimulating conditions are.

OTHER EXPERIMENTAL STUDIES

This last point has been borne out in experiment after experiment. Most students of elementary psychology are familiar with a series of pictures posed by Feleky; she attempted to portray various emotions in her facial expression, and observers were asked to guess what typical emotions were represented.[13] She found that the expressions of disgust, sneering, and breathless interest were the only emotions which tended to be judged correctly. Suspicion, religious feeling, anger, fear, hate, and rage were judged very poorly. In an experiment conducted by Langfeld, judgments were made of an artist's sketches of posed emotional expressions.[14] Altogether 525 judgments were secured from a small group of subjects. In general, Langfeld found that laughter could ordinarily be judged correctly; fear and anger were often confused, as were surprise and suspicion; and, on the basis of *posed* pictures, very few reliable judgments could be made. In both of these studies, an obvious difficulty is the question of whether the various descriptive terms used by different observers are synonymous.

Landis has undertaken a number of experiments pertaining to these questions. One of these involved a series of emotional situations for twenty-five different subjects.[15] Instead of having someone act out what he *thought* represented an emotion, emotions were actually produced in the individual subjects. Of seventeen different stimulating situations, examples were: popular phonograph music was played; technical phonograph music was played; the subject read aloud Luke 6: 18-49; the subject was told to write out the meanest and most contemptible thing that he had ever done, whereupon the experimenter read this aloud; the subject looked at pictures of skin diseases; he looked at nude art studies; and he placed his hand in a bucket of live frogs, whereupon he received an electric shock—a case of adding "injury" to insult. During this entire series of situations, systolic-blood-pressure readings were taken for each subject. Yet with the exception of sudden stimuli of the type called "surprising," there was no situation which resulted in any particular form or kind of blood pressure change.

Landis also secured photographs of subjects in emotional situations, together with a verbal report as to what each subject felt at the time the picture was taken.[16] Analysis of these data by Davis has shown that facial expressions in different circumstances have some common features, and some unique to the particular situation.[17] When the pictures were presented to other persons for judging what emotions were depicted, the names given to the expressions were not very much better than chance.[18] Other studies have also shown that our ability to judge emotions correctly on the basis of photographic records is not of very high order.

Although the results of such experiments seem inconclusive, nevertheless it should be pointed out that there were great individual differences among judges. Some persons did much better than others. Floyd H. Allport was impressed by this fact, and gave a group of subjects a list of fourteen names of emotions and fourteen pictures posed by an actor, and asked them to match the two.[19] Most of the subjects were able to attain close to 50 per cent accuracy, several times better than chance. Allport also had a group of college women judge photographs. Following this he gave them fifteen minutes of training on such principles as "open mouth and wide eyes indicate amazement"; and then he had them judge the pictures once more. Most of the subjects improved in rating ability after receiving such instructions. The judges who were poorest at the beginning gained most from the fifteen-minute study; apparently, owing to training, there are differences in perception of facial expression. On the other hand, the study period was probably confusing to some, for one or two of the best judges actually became poorer. In a better controlled experiment, Jenness showed that Allport's test of recognition was not too reliable; but he confirmed Allport's general results by demonstrating that an average increase in scores on a facial-expression test could be obtained by training subjects in the analysis of facial expressions.[20] Everyday observation also demonstrates that ability to judge emotional behavior depends upon the individual observer and his experience.

Knight Dunlap succeeded in arousing actual emotions in his subjects by such stimuli as jokes to produce amusement, firing a pistol to produce startle, bending the subject's finger joint to produce pain, presentation of dissected tissues which had a strong odor to produce disgust.[21] The faces of the subjects were photographed just after these various stimuli had been presented, and these photographs were later cut horizontally through the bridge of the nose. Judgments of emotion were then required from these persons who were presented with pictures of the upper half of the face, the lower half, and the entire face. The experimenter found that the mouth muscles played a much greater part in enabling the observer to discriminate between emotions than did the eye muscles. Certain emotions could even be correctly identified.

Wolff has conducted some ingenious studies, involving the splitting of a full-faced picture down the middle, then reversing one half and matching it with the same half by montage so that the picture of the face is now composed of two left sides, or two right.[22] He believes that the right side of the face gives it its most characteristic expression.

One of the most ingenious experiments in this whole field is reported by Munn.[23]

Candid camera photographs selected from back issues of *Life* and *Look* were made into lantern slides. The slides of one set pictured the whole situation. Those of the other contained only an enlargement of the subject's head. The latter slides were shown to 90 psychology students instructed to judge the subjects' emotional reactions. A week later these students judged the emotions expressed by the same faces while reviewing them in their original setting. No terminology was suggested in either of these experiments. From the most frequent terms used by this group, a vocabulary for a further experiment was arranged. Sixty-five psychology students on another campus were given the same test, but this time with a suggested vocabulary to which their own terms might be added.

The predominant judgments of both groups were quite similar. Seven of the expressions were judged with an accuracy (agreement) of from 65 to 99 per cent by both groups and there was no significant change upon perceiving the situation. Two of these expressions were designated *joy*. The others were *terror, pain, anxiety, surprise,* and *disappointment*. In the case of several other expressions, judgment changed markedly with knowledge of the precipitating circumstances. For instance, a predominant report of *sorrow* changed to *determination,* one of *anxiety* to *horror,* and one of *terror* to *surprise*. Some expressions aroused widely varying interpretations under both conditions.

Even when there was lack of agreement concerning the precise emotion being experienced, observers evidenced a marked ability to judge the affective term of the expression.[24]

W. A. Hunt has raised the question, however, whether there was truly a random selection of the pictures.[25] It is possible that Munn, without meaning to, selected facial expressions which his subjects would find easy to recognize.

SUMMARY OF EXPERIMENTAL CONCLUSIONS

To summarize the conclusions from these and similar experiments:

1. With the exception of one or two studies, there seems to be considerable disagreement among judges as to the emotions portrayed when judgments are made on the basis of facial expression alone.

2. Not only are the judgments not particularly accurate, but they do not seem to improve with knowledge of human behavior, although they may improve with specific training.

3. There is a great deal of agreement among judges as a whole as to certain expressions, even though their pooled judgments may not be absolutely accurate. People concur more frequently than not in their judgments of facial expression. In other words, even though we may not make accurate judgments of emotional expression, we may agree remarkably well among ourselves in our stereotyped conceptions of various emotions.

4. Wide individual differences exist in any group of judges as to their ability to make accurate judgments. Some people are better able to perceive the situation than others.

5. Apparently ability to judge emotions is increased considerably by letting the judge observe or know what the stimulus situation is, instead of limiting him to an observation of the facial expression. We may judge emotions incorrectly on the basis of facial expression alone, whereas if we know what the stimulating conditions were which produced that expression, we may judge with a fair degree of accuracy.

6. Finally, our judgments tend to depend upon the *total situation*. When the entire configuration of the whole organism in the total environmental situation is taken into account, we may make judgments which, although not absolutely accurate, have enough agreement with the judgments of other observers so that we rely upon them in many social situations. Thus in daily life we can usually interpret another person's facial expression correctly, *provided* we can also perceive accompanying stimuli. Try guessing what emotions are portrayed in Figure 15. The chances are that you will do better on the last four than the first four. However, in social situations we should not rely upon our subjective impressions; we usually need additional information before these data are truly meaningful.

1. ____________ 2. ____________

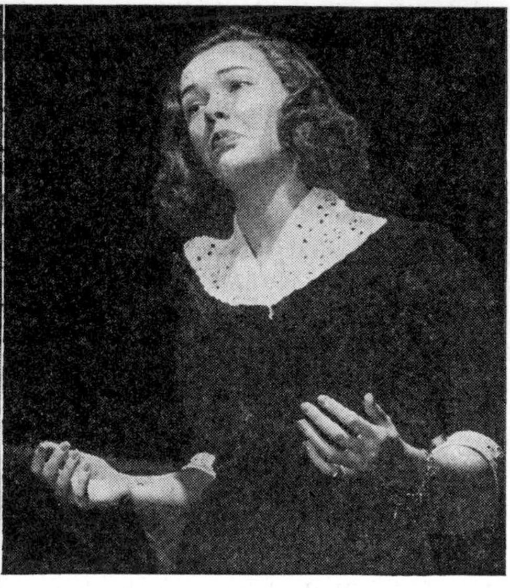

3. ____________ 4. ____________

FIG. 15. A PROBLEM IN JUDGING EMOTIONS[26]

Fill in the blanks with the names of the emotions portrayed. (Answers are given at the end of the chapter.)

5. 6. ____________

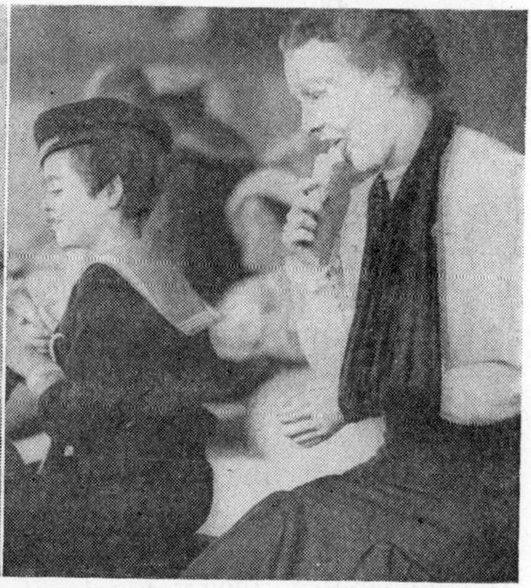

7. 8. ____________

FIG. 15 (*continued*)

▶ SUBLIMINAL STIMULATION

"SIZING UP" PEOPLE

On meeting someone for the first time, we sometimes have the unexpressed feeling, "I don't like you." Yet we cannot explain why. We sometimes have a "hunch"—the word is "intuition" when women use it—that some person cannot be trusted, or that he has a mean disposition. Asked to explain, we cannot. In such cases our judgments may be partially explained in terms of *subliminal stimulation.*

DEFINITION OF SUBLIMINAL STIMULATION

What does "subliminal stimulation" mean? The phase refers to all those stimuli which actually affect our behavior but of which we may never be aware. You are sometimes bombarded by sensory stimuli of which you are not conscious but which nevertheless affect your attitudes and behavior. There are visual, auditory, taste, smell, touch, kinesthetic, and other types of stimuli which affect you many times a day of which you may not be at all aware. These are subliminal, that is, below (sub) the threshold (limen) of consciousness. There are always a host of stimuli which may be so faint in intensity that you could not attend to them if you wished but which may affect your behavior and attitudes. Perhaps in some instances you might respond to a total pattern of several subliminal stimuli together, although one or two alone might be ineffectual for you. Leibniz wrote of "petit perception," which might be compared to grains of sand along the seashore, not having much influence singly, but having a cumulative effect taken together.

SOME EXPERIMENTAL STUDIES

A résumé of several experimental studies dealing with *subliminal perception* should make the concept clear. In these experiments individuals were subjected to stimuli without knowing that they were being stimulated, and yet their behavior was affected. The classic experiment is the one conducted by Sidis in 1898.[27] A series of cards with printed numbers or letters were held in view of the subject at a distance far enough away so that he was just unable to read them. However, upon requiring the subject to guess, Sidis found a smaller percentage of error than could be explained on the basis of chance. Apparently the subjects were responding to subliminal stimuli.

A student of Hollingworth's used a Müller-Lyer figure (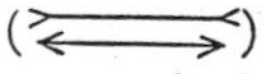) but with the two segments on different cards.[28] This is the famous optical illusion that one of two lines, actually of the same length, is longer than the other. Although the horizontal lines were perfectly visible to the subject, the arrows were drawn in so faintly and the subjects were placed at such a distance from the cards that the arrows were imperceptible. With fifty trials apiece, each of twenty subjects was then instructed to indicate which of the two lines appeared longer. The responses of seventeen of the twenty indicated that the imperceptible arrows were effective in creating the Müller-Lyer illusion.

Lynn E. Baker has reported an ingenious experiment dealing with the influence of subliminal stimuli.[29] He presented each subject with a card on which was a pair of crossed lines and required the subject to judge the position of the crossed lines and also to make an estimate of his confidence in the correctness of his judgment. By varying the intensity of the illumination from trial to trial in such a way that on many occasions the subjects were unable actually to see the lines at all, Baker forced his subjects to guess in every situation. The percentages of error in judgment when the stimuli were subliminal were found to be less than chance expectation. On the basis of these results and similar ones with subliminal sounds, Baker concludes that conscious *verbal* behavior is influenced by stimuli below the conscious judgment threshold.

Another experimenter had an apparatus consisting of a ground glass screen upon which three figures could be projected from the rear—a circle, a triangle, and a square.[30] By varying the brightness of the figures, the stimuli could be projected at a subliminal level. Eleven subjects of both sexes twenty-two to fifty years old were used. Three types of evidence indicated that the stimuli were definitely subliminal: (1) Many of the figures were named incorrectly, indicating that the subjects could not see them. (2) During part of the study, the subjects "protested about the fact that they couldn't see any figures and that it was just pure guess work on their part, and that it was foolish to continue."[31] (3) "From time to time blanks were introduced unknown to the subject. These seemed in no way to affect the subject. They did not change the speed of his reaction or the tone of his voice, and, as far as the experimenter could tell, passed unnoticed."[32] The subliminal stimuli elicited correct responses more frequently than would have been possible on a chance basis; but, when no subliminal stimuli were present, the frequency of correct responses was just what would be expected according to chance.

Discrimination and learning without awareness have also been demonstrated by other experimenters.[33] For example, Landis, Zubin, and their colleagues have demonstrated experimentally that auditory stimuli considerably below the determined minimal threshold can be recognized more often than chance would allow.[34] They have also shown that subjects can guess correctly more often than would be expected by chance which of three forms is being projected upon a ground glass screen when visibility is obscured by a flood of higher illumination.[35] Another investigator has used color as well as form stimuli below the thresholds, and has found that judgments concerning them were more accurate than chance.[36]

Subliminal stimuli also occur in sense departments other than vision and hearing. For example, there are many subliminal stimuli in the spheres of smell and touch. Of four identical new pairs of women's silk hose, housewives chose that pair to be of better quality which had been treated to overcome the mildly rancid scent left in the hose at the factory, even though the odor as such was not noticeable.[37]

In another experiment:

> . . . The subject was asked to lift his hand from the telegraph key the moment that a light was shown. With practice he reduced his reaction time to 200 one-thousandths of a second. But the experimenter inserted in the external ear a tiny cylinder containing a wire which could be made to hum as soon as a switch was thrown. The experimenter made sure in all cases that the humming was truly subliminal. No subject could tell when it started or stopped. In the next series of reaction-time experiments the switch was thrown a small fraction of a second before the stimulus light was flashed. The result, after practice with the method, was a reduction of the apparent reaction time in some cases to less than 100 one-thousandths of a second. The subject had been conditioned to the subliminal sound of the humming of the cylinder.[38]

SIGNIFICANCE OF SUBLIMINAL STIMULATION

The significance of this type of work is very well explained by Murphy, Murphy, and Newcomb:

> It is likely that a large part of our intuitive valuation of the social situation, our "instinctive" hesitancy to join in a game, our "instinctive" trust in a man with a bold proposal, is based in large measure upon subliminal conditioning. We learn day by day the meaning of gestures, facial expression, tone of voice; but a great deal that we learn functions beneath the level of consciousness, or may be above the threshold of consciousness today and function just as well when below it tomorrow. . . . It is quite likely that training in interpreting facial expression may bring some of these subliminal cues above the threshold, and that the result may sometimes be confusion, an improper attention to other cues which have been keeping their just place in the total situation until that moment. This seems to be exactly what is meant by F. H. Allport's . . . experiments in training subjects to interpret facial expression. . . . It is quite probable that some of the best judges of personality work in terms of subliminal cues. Under these circumstances a dog or a child may evaluate a stranger better than an adult. In confronting new or difficult personal situations, beginner's luck or the providence which watches over fools may be due to the more effective response to elements which are not consciously analyzed and which therefore do not over-dominate.

Woman's "intuition" may be in considerable measure the result of specific training in utilizing total impressions where a man would be more likely to give clear emphasis and hence over-simplification in response to some features of a complex.[39]

In other words, social behavior is undoubtedly affected by subliminal or at least unnoticed stimuli. Thus we may influence each other without anyone necessarily being aware of the mutual modifications in our behavior. We probably begin to be conditioned at an early age to these subliminal and unnoticed changes; and some of us become increasingly more responsive than others to reduced signs and cues from others.[40]

INTEGRATION OF SUBLIMINAL STIMULI

In reacting to subliminal stimuli, we cannot break down the stimuli and analyze them. If they are truly subliminal, they cannot be recognized. Instead, a great many of our feelings and emotions may depend upon a total configuration of *subliminal* cues. Although we are not at all aware (conscious) of these stimuli, the term "subliminal stimulation" is not offered as a substitute for the term "unconscious." Objections to that concept were given in Chapter 6. Neither is the term "subliminal stimulation" a substitute for the word "instinct." It is not even offered as a complete explanation of behavior. However, the concept of subliminal stimulation, coupled with an interpretation of feelings and emotions and an understanding of unconscious factors of motivation, may be very helpful in interpreting group situations. In other words, no single concept thus far discussed represents by itself a complete explanation for our behavior. But these various descriptions and explanations, taken together, may explain a great deal. A well-known rhyme may be used for illustration:

> I do not love thee, Dr. Fell,
> The reason why I cannot tell;
> But this I know and know full well,
> I do not love thee, Dr. Fell.

Why did not the speaker love Dr. Fell? If she had been asked for deliberate, conscious, rational reasons, she might have been "stumped." However, if she had made an analysis in terms of the factors thus far discussed, she might have appreciated why she did not love Dr. Fell and eliminated the second line, "The reason why I cannot tell." Slight unnoticed changes in facial expression and bodily posture may easily influence the attitudes of other persons.

The conditioned response, unanalyzed feelings and emotions, unconscious factors of motivation, and subliminal stimulation must all be considered if we are truly to understand any particular social situation. This is not, however, an attempt to limit the answer to these factors; in fact, as the discussion of various problems of social interaction continues, additional concepts emerge.

▶ THE STEREOTYPING PROCESS

THE WORD "STEREOTYPE"

A congressman spoke in the House of Representatives :

> As far as I am concerned, if a black man does the same work as a white man, he ought to receive the same pay.
>
> I do not see anything terrible about this. I think Negroes should have economic justice. If a Negro makes good pay, he spends it—just like a white man. Purchasing power builds business, prosperity, and the nation. If a Negro gets fair wages, he will spend, pay taxes, hire a doctor for his health, send his kids to school, be a better citizen, and contribute his part rather than being a burden.[41]

From what section of the country did this congressman come? About 90 percent of persons reply, "The North." Apparently no one but a "Yankee" could be expected to talk like this. As a matter of fact, this statement was made by a former congressman who belongs to one of the oldest families in the South. But people give the response, "The North," because of the "stereotyping" process. As Walter Lippmann has pointed out, the term *stereotype* is a useful one in the field of ideas and opinions because most of us—like the metal plate forms used by newspapers in printing—have become rigid in our ways.[42] Our thinking is apt to be highly stereotyped after a lifetime spent in forming individual habit patterns and in complying with cultural patterns.

INDIVIDUAL DIFFERENCES

Now, in spite of this stereotyping process there are tremendous individual differences, especially in the field of social behavior. Studies of personality characteristics indicate that we differ from each other in a remarkable number of ways. We cannot find some simple explanation for human behavior which will fit all people. Instead, we find extreme differences in intelligence, mental imagery, emotional reactions, and other aspects of life.

THE TYPE FALLACY

Figure 16 shows different curves of normal distribution, one of which usually emerges when we plot the incidence of various characteristics. The majority of people, so far as a given characteristic is concerned, tend to fall around the center of the curve, and there are relatively few people at either extreme. Most of us are between 5 and 6 feet tall, and very few are dwarfs or giants. However, extreme cases are sometimes so outstanding that they lead us to believe that there are separate "types." This may be referred to as the "type fallacy."

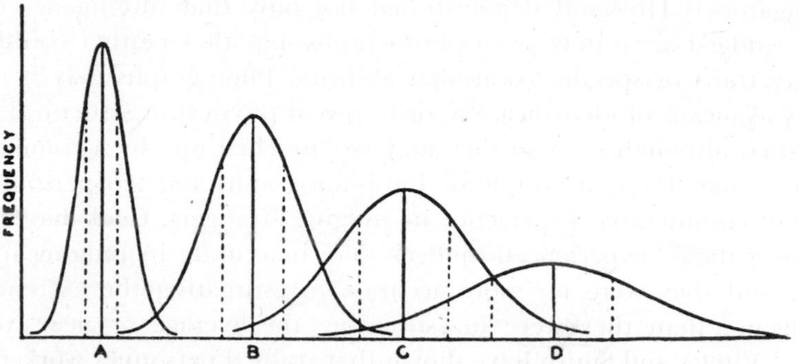

FIG. 16. VARIOUS TYPES OF DISTRIBUTION CURVES SHOWING NORMAL DISTRIBUTION BUT WITH A NARROW SPREAD, MEDIUM SPREAD, AND A WIDE SPREAD (From C. E. Skinner)[43]

Judging Intelligence, as an Example of the Type Fallacy. As one example of this type fallacy, most people believe that they can look at an individual's face and tell something about his intelligence. Wouldn't it be nice if we could know, because of a bright, eager look, that a person is brilliant? The world would be much simpler if our stereotyped ideas were always true. Numerous studies, however, indicate that intelligence cannot be judged accurately from facial characteristics alone. Pintner found that psychologists were only slightly better than physicians, businessmen, and teachers—who weren't good at all—in judging intelligence of children from photographs.[44]

> [The results would not] have been very different . . . if the actual children could have been used instead of the photographs. They would have been somewhat [better] if an interview of five minutes had been allowed with each child. They would only become very [good] when each observer makes use of some objective criterion or test.[45]

Laird and Remmers, after having 376 men and women judges sort uniformly sized pictures of ten college students—five men and five women—who were photographed in academic costume, found that the ability to estimate intelligence from photographs was practically zero.[46] Sex or age differences did not contribute to successful judgment. College students were neither more nor less successful than older persons. There was a tendency for the judges—both men and women—to overestimate the relative intelligence of the women on the basis of their pictures. No significant relationship was found between the possession of intelligence and the ability to estimate intelligence from photographs.

These conclusions, in general, have been confirmed by many other investigators.[47] Husband demonstrated not only that intelligence could not be judged accurately from photographs, but that neither could personality traits or specific vocational abilities. Photographs may be satisfactory as means of identification, or to reveal physical or structural characteristics, although even so they may be "touched up" by a commercial photographer. Using a sample of 150 photographs and ten persons who had had considerable experience in judging strangers, Cook has shown that even these "experienced" judges were inaccurate in judging intelligence; and they were no more accurate in estimating the extremes of intelligence than they were in estimating the average or near-average levels.[48] Viteles and Smith have shown that trained personnel workers can judge with no better than chance accuracy the "successfulness" of individuals on the basis of their photographs.[49] The experiments all show that when people make judgments of intelligence on the basis of facial expressions alone, they do only about as well as by flipping a coin, or throwing a pair of dice. But this does not prevent us from stereotyping people in our daily life and saying, "He is a bright-looking fellow" or "She is a dumb-looking gal." These descriptions may be justified upon the basis of other characteristics, but when they are made simply upon a stereotype basis of appearance or facial expressions alone, they may be completely fallacious.

Other Instances of the Typing Fallacy. Many an observer of human nature has tried to classify people into "scientific" psychological categories. Pavlov went so far as to classify dogs as belonging to three types—the choleric type, the phlegmatic, and the melancholic. An English artist has said that all people can be put into four categories—promoters, producers, developers, and distributors.[50] In your own observations of other people you constantly make judgments in terms of their backgrounds. Thus, when you meet a man who has been in the Army or Navy, you expect him to be different from someone who has not been in the service. We brand people as "intellectuals" or "athletes" or "foreigners," and then think that we know a good deal about them *because* we have labeled them. Thus we may have the common, although untrue, belief that all athletes are dumb. Many people think of an Englishman as being humorless, a Bohemian as carefree, a Jew as greedy, a Negro as lazy.

One of the most fallacious ideas is that there is a "criminal look." In Figure 17 are shown pictures of twenty-four people, half of whom are criminals. They have been convicted of crimes ranging from kidnaping

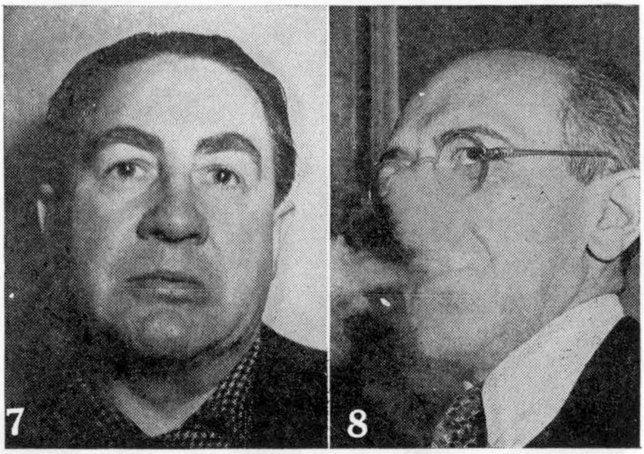

FIG. 17
A PROBLEM IN
PICKING CRIMINALS[51]

Half of these 24 photographs represent criminals; half, honest citizens. Which is which? See if you can tell—write down your answers, keyed by numbers, and then look at the correct answers given at the end of the chapter.

FIG. 17 (*continued*)

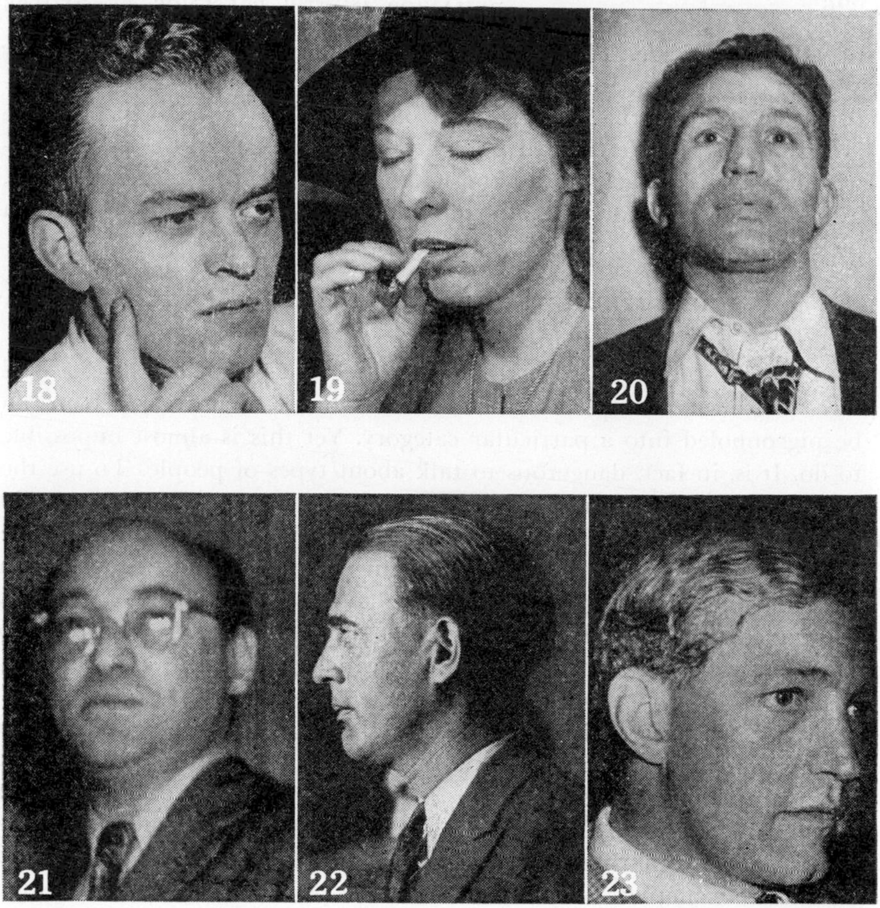

FIG. 17. A PROBLEM IN PICKING CRIMINALS (*continued*)

to willful homicide. The other twelve faces are of members of Mystery Writers of America, Inc., who have never been publicly accused of anything more serious than minor traffic offenses. Can you tell which people are criminals? Notice that all photographs were made in the same way—with bare walls as background and without special props to furnish clews. Yet our stereotypes of what a criminal looks like do not help much in picking the twelve criminals in the group.

INCONSISTENCIES IN THE STEREOTYPING PROCESS

There are two principal inconsistencies in this stereotyping process:

1. Stereotyping is based on the false belief that people can be classified into a number of simple, distinctive types, that is, that every person can be pigeonholed into a particular category. Yet this is almost impossible to do. It is, in fact, dangerous to talk about types of people. To use the word "type" suggests some sort of absolute distinction between certain kinds of persons and others. It has been facetiously suggested that people may be divided into three types according to which kind of toothbrush they use—the convex brush, the concave, and the straight, plus, of course, the mixed type who use different kinds (or none at all).[52] This is no more absurd than some classifications which have been seriously suggested.

When we get a sufficiently large number of cases and examine them for a given characteristic, we usually find that what appeared to be two types are simply the extreme ends of a normal curve of distribution (Figure 16) and that there are other people who are distributed all along the scale between these two originally selected extremes. Weight and height are examples. But when it comes to psychological characteristics, we are likely to forget that there are no types here either. You may notice that an individual has long, tapering, "sensitive" fingers and come to the conclusion that he must have great artistic ability. Are you selecting those instances where you find artistic ability in persons with slender fingers, at the same time forgetting about the great number of instances where the characteristic under observation turns out the other way? President Lowell of Harvard once called attention to this problem:

> When the writer compiled, a score of years ago, statistics about the relation of Harvard University between the ranks attained by students while in college and subsequently in the professional schools, a colleague remarked that while the statements were all very well he had known so many cases of men who had ranked low in college and high in the Law School that he could not accept the results. The writer asked him to mention any case of the kind in addition to the one instance he had found in a period of twenty years. The answer was, "That is the man I was thinking of." "Name any other." Another name was mentioned, but on reference to the statistics it appeared that, although this man

had doubtless done better than his college record would have given reason to expect, he had not graduated from the Law School with honors. Asked for more examples the colleague was and has ever since remained silent. Now the striking thing about this occurrence was that the attention of the colleague had been attracted to the single case he had observed rightly, and to a second case where he had not been quite accurate, not because these instances were typical, but because the careers of these students were unexpected, or, in other words, because they were exceptional.[53]

2. The second fallacious assumption is that a person remains consistently within his "type." If you will recall the material already presented in Chapter 7, you will remember that traits and attitudes vary from one time and place to another. Even if it were possible to pigeonhole people into "types," it still would be highly questionable whether they would remain within these classifications twenty-four hours a day. Your own behavior in a classroom is certainly very, very different from your behavior at a football game. A college student is not necessarily a "rah-rah boy" on the one hand or a "greasy grind" on the other.

THE KRETSCHMER HYPOTHESIS

Perhaps the best example of the stereotyping fallacy is contained in the conclusions drawn from the work of Kretschmer, a German psychiatrist, on body build and personality types.[54] On the basis of his studies of middle-aged males in a German mental institution, the unique idea has developed that perhaps normal individuals can be pigeonholed into certain personality types on the basis of their body build. Thus, it has been suggested that people who are "asthenic" (tall and thin, with long narrow heads), and people who are "athletic" in build, both tend to be "schizoid" in personality make-up, that is, supposedly more introverted and with more of the make-up of the schizophrenic mental patient than other individuals. Further, it has been suggested that "pyknic" individuals (rotund, with round faces) might be "cycloid" in personality, that is, presumably tending more toward manic-depressive behavior—ups and downs—from extremes of happiness down into "the dumps," and up again.

A number of difficulties present themselves, however, in such a classification. First of all, it completely overlooks the fact that most personality characteristics fall on a curve of normal distribution. In the second place, it is not applicable to all groups. It is evident, for example, that findings based on middle-aged psychopathic men will not enable young, normal coeds to make judgments of each other's personality on the basis of tallness and thinness. Finally, various studies in this country have disproved the Kretschmer hypothesis. Thus, in one experiment diagnoses were made by staffs of hospital psychiatrists of patients falling into the two psychotic groups discussed by Kretschmer—dementia praecox and manic-depressive psychosis—and these individuals were closely matched in age.[55] The two groups of patients were carefully measured as to their height, weight, cephalic index (head shape), chest expansion, and similar measures. No substantiation of the Kretschmer hypothesis was found, nor have other studies revealed much evidence in its favor.[56] Another investigator has pointed out two serious fallacies in Kretschmer's methods.[57] First, he failed to control the age factor in his subjects. Manic-depressive psychosis usually occurs later in life than schizophrenia, and since there is a general tendency for all individuals to become more "pyknic" with increasing age, the coincidence of manic-depressive psychosis with pyknic constitutions may very largely be a result of the age factor. Second, there is a much greater tendency toward bodily deterioration among schizophrenic patients than among manic-depressives. This means that you would naturally expect people of "asthenic" build to be in the category of schizophrenic patients. In spite of these obvious criticisms, the Kretschmer hypothesis has crept into numerous books in psychology and sociology as if substantiated. The hypothesis is an outstanding example of the type fallacy, although refinements have since been attempted; thus, the work of W. H. Sheldon and his collaborators represents a precise, scientific attempt to classify the varieties of human physique and to correlate these with differences in temperament.[58]

SOME EMPIRICAL STUDIES OF STEREOTYPING

We cling desperately to those stereotypes which we believe. In fact, any disturbance of our own stereotyped ideas seems like a personal attack upon ourselves. Most of us have built up over our lifetimes what we think is an adequate picture of the world around us. It *is* adequate in that it is true for us. We have adapted ourselves to our environment in terms of what we believe to be true. We know what to expect of certain people and certain places. Our mental pictures may not always correspond with reality, but at least they enable us to feel at ease.[59]

The extent of the stereotyping process may be illustrated by several empirical studies. Rice presented to college students photographs of nine unnamed men and asked the students to assign to each picture one of nine labels which represented these nine men.[60] Among the pictures was one of a man with a wing collar, Vandyke beard, and mustache, who was actually the Soviet ambassador to France. He was rarely identified as a Bolshevik; instead, he was labeled by most persons as a United States senator; second, as a premier; third, as a manufacturer. Senator Pepper of Florida was most often called a manufacturer and, second, a labor leader. The subjects in this experiment were simply responding to the stereotyped notions of what a Bolshevik or a United States senator is supposed to look like. Many people still picture Bolsheviks as men with long beards and smoking bombs clutched in their fingers. A great many people visiting Washington, D.C., each year are surprised to find that most senators do not have wing collars, black-ribbon ties, and long coattails as in cartoons and the movies. Rice's method and results have been closely paralleled in another investigation.[61]

In a study by Katz and Braly, college students were asked to list those characteristics which they felt best fitted certain nationality groups.[62] Although many of the students had had very little experience with some of the nationality groups represented, there was general agreement that Germans were scientifically minded, industrious, and stolid; that Italians were artistic, impulsive, quick-tempered, and passionate; that Negroes were highly superstitious, lazy, happy-go-lucky, ignorant, musical, and ostentatious. Most of the students had never even seen a Turk; yet they apparently had little hesitation in branding Turks as cruel, very religious, treacherous, and sensual—probably because of stories of harems, massacres of Armenians, and the like. Meenes found that Negro college students in 1935 considered the Chinese as sly, treacherous, and revengeful; but in 1942 (after Pearl Harbor) these terms were used by Negro college students to characterize the Japanese.[63]

Fink and Cantril asked college men at Dartmouth, Harvard, Princeton, and Yale, and also college women at Smith, to select certain terms which they felt were most representative of the four men's colleges.[64] Interesting stereotyped results appeared. Thus, the students of the "big four" of the Eastern colleges were stereotyped by the members of their own and of other college groups as follows: *Dartmouth—outdoor men, college-loyal,* hard drinkers, athletic, the rah-rah type. *Harvard—blasé, indifferent, snobbish,* conceited, intellectual, socialites. *Princeton—style-setting, gentlemanly, smooth,* college-loyal, socialites. *Yale—college-loyal, athletic,* typical college type, hard drinkers, socialites.

REALITY OF STEREOTYPES

There must be some basis for stereotypes; otherwise they would not exist. However, we are often led to overlook the tremendous number of individual differences within a group and simply pay attention to those exceptional cases where the characteristic is outstanding. In the world of tangibles, it makes a lot of difference whether something is actually true or not. In social psychology, however, the primary consideration is not whether something is true which people believe to be true. The important thing is that *whatever people believe to be true is true for them.* It may make little difference psychologically whether myths or stereotyped beliefs have any real foundation. If the "pictures in our heads" are believed by us to represent the world around us, then they are of the utmost psychological significance in determining the things we will do.

PREDICTIONS FROM STEREOTYPES

We are often able to make fairly good predictions about the covert attitudes and overt behavior of another person from "the company he keeps." This indicates that there is some valid basis for the stereotyping process. If you know that a man is a Harvard man and a Republican, you may be justified in stereotyping and predicting what his attitudes will be toward the New Deal or the C.I.O. If, on the other hand, you know that another man comes from a long line of Southern ancestors and graduated from the University of Mississippi, you may be justified in guessing his attitudes toward "Yankees" and toward the Catholic Church. Similarly, if you know that an individual has graduated from your college, you may be able to guess certain of his attitudes accurately.

Cantril has reported the following experiment:

The [interviewers] stood near two localities that were being picketed, one on 33rd at Broadway, and the other at 59th at Madison, the latter being in a more fashionable shopping district. At each location they asked one hundred people who passed by the following questions:

1. When you see a picket, are you sympathetic with the employer or the worker?
2. What is your occupation?
3. For whom did you vote, or would you have voted in the presidential election of 1936?

The sex of the respondent was also tabulated.

Results were as follows: Sympathy for workers, 60 per cent; sympathy for employer, 28 per cent; neutral, 12 per cent.

Sex differences were noticeable probably because of the pro-labor efforts of the League of Women Shoppers. Whereas 55 per cent of the men favored the workers, 93 per cent of the women did so.

Significant *differences* were obtained *between the two localities.*

In the *more fashionable* districts: 50 per cent favored the worker; 34 per cent favored the employer; 16 per cent were neutral.

In the *poorer* districts: 70 per cent were for the worker; 22 per cent were for the employer; 8 per cent were neutral.

If, on the basis of *occupation,* the probable incomes of the respondents are roughly bracketed, the following figures are available:

	Sympathetic with worker	*Sympathetic with employer*	*Neutral*
High income group (over $3,000)	22%	74%	4%
Low income group	70%	17%	13%
Unemployed	80%	0	20%

The relations between the sympathies aroused by the picketing and *party affiliation* are clear cut. Those who expressed sympathy for the *Democratic party* showed: 71 per cent pro-worker; 19 per cent pro-employer; and 10 per cent neutral. *Republican party* showed: 23 per cent pro-worker; 68 per cent pro-employer; and 9 per cent neutral.[65]

This same sort of problem was investigated experimentally by Vetter, who secured the reactions of students toward various social problems.[66] Their views were studied on the following subjects: birth control, miscegenation, powers of labor organizations, socialized medicine, academic freedom, divorce, the protective tariff, our Latin-American policy, and social limitations on mating. Vetter found that individuals who tended to be "radical" on one issue usually had "radical" attitudes on other issues. Likewise, those individuals who tended to be "conservative" on one issue were also "conservative" on other social issues represented. Kornhauser has found that only 17 per cent of those persons satisfied as to their children's opportunities favored government ownership of big industries, whereas of those dissatisfied 44 per cent favored it.[67] Such studies demonstrate the psychological advantages of stereotyping. To know an individual's attitudes in certain situations may tell you a great deal about what attitudes to expect from him in other situations.

THE INDIVIDUAL BASIS OF STEREOTYPING

Stereotyping depends not only upon objective facts but upon your ability as an observing individual. Every time you pigeonhole another person as having certain characteristics, you do this partly upon the basis of your own background and experience. Depending upon your entire lifetime of activities and experiences, you will interpret the world around you differently from other people. Take such a simple thing as stating what this represents: **T**. You say, "It is a letter **T**." But why should you say that it is a **T** except that you have learned not once but millions of times to call this combination of lines a **T**? You actually see nothing more nor less than two lines, and even the fact that you may say "two" represents a judgment based on past experience. Now, when you make judgments of another individual, you likewise bring into play the attitudes based on your own past training and experience. As we have seen, these attitudes may be largely dependent upon the particular conditioning processes which you have gone through and the later generalization and differentiation of these conditioned responses. As a college man or college woman, for example, your judgments of other individuals reflect the fact that you are a college man or woman.

Therefore, it is of the utmost importance to know all those combinations of factors from the past experience of an individual which might color his present perception of his fellows. All of us interpret the experiences around us in different ways because of the individual differences among us. No two students in a classroom ever hear or see exactly the same things so far as the behavior of the instructor is concerned. Each one perceives slightly different things, not only because of his physical location in the classroom but also on the basis of his past experiences, plus his present subjective interpretation based upon his particular and unique background.

> But quite apart from conscious preference we notice and observe the things in which we are interested. Two men travel across the same region; one of them observes the progress of industry, the rotation of the crops and the standards of life of the people; the other is struck by the varieties of wild flowers, the forms of undulation of the landscape, the colors and the play of light and shade. A charity visitor going to see a patient in her last illness took with her a friend who, to her disappointment, was chiefly impressed by the beautiful old bedstead in which the poor woman was dying. Everyone knows that the man who collects wild flowers, or insects, or Indian arrowheads, can find them much more rapidly than his friend who does not care for them; and that when the friend becomes interested in the search he very soon discovers that, although he knows little about them, he finds them much more rapidly than he did before.[68]

Because of our psychological "set," because of our present attitudes based on our past experiences, we perceive the world around us and interpret it in those ways which are most satisfying to *us.* We do not want interference with our interpretations. We do not want to change our stereotypes. We hear and see largely what we want to hear and see, and as we grow older we associate for the most part with people who perceive things as we perceive them, and not with the "awful" people who see things differently. We read those newspapers which mirror our own thoughts, and listen to radio programs which reinforce our own attitudes. We simply do those things which are the easiest for us to do.

What engages our attention affects not only what we perceive, but also what we consider "good" or "bad." The people who think differently may be considered either idiots or fools. It is not surprising that in our daily lives we are influenced by such stereotyped words as "bum," "old maid," "nigger," "dago," or "communist." The world with which we are dealing *psychologically* is largely intangible, covert, unobservable. In other words, those things which people believe to be so *are* true for them, as we saw in Chapter 9.

> It is often very illuminating, therefore, to ask yourself how you got at the facts on which you base your opinion. Who actually saw, heard, felt, counted, named the thing, about which you have an opinion? Was it the man who told you, or the man who told him, or someone still further removed? And how

much was he permitted to see? When he informs you that France thinks this and that, what part of France did he watch? How was he able to watch it? Where was he when he watched it? What Frenchmen was he permitted to talk to, what newspapers did he read, and where did they learn what they say? You can ask yourself these questions, but you can rarely answer them.[69]

THE PRACTICAL USE OF STEREOTYPES

We should conclude this section by indicating the practical use of stereotypes. By the skillful manipulation of stereotypes, the conduct of other persons can be controlled. The danger is that stereotypes are too often used in malicious propaganda. Your job, therefore, is to learn to recognize such propaganda so that you will not be misled by it.

If you are sure that someone had a happy childhood and was devoted to his mother, you can make use of the stereotyping process by appealing to him through the symbol of "motherhood." If you know that another person is extremely patriotic, you may appeal to him in terms of "100 per cent Americanism." If someone has certain attitudes toward Negroes or any other group, you can make use of this information in influencing his actions, his vote, for example. In a supposedly rational discussion, if anyone throws in a stereotyped word or phrase which is emotionally toned, a continued rational discussion immediately becomes impossible. Try to discuss the race problem, war, social security, the activities of the National Labor Relations Board, or any other important social issue, and let someone interject such a word as "nigger lover," "kike," "wop," "the dole," or "scab," and logical, realistic conversation is finished.

As Joseph Conrad said, "He who wants to persuade should put his trust not in the right argument, but in the right word. . . . Give me the right word and the right accent, and I will move the world."[70] Consider the following slogans in the history of the United States, and their effect on some great social movements: "No Taxation without Representation"; "United We Stand, Divided We Fall"; "Fifty-four Forty or Fight"; "Remember the Maine"; "Make the World Safe for Democracy."

If men were entirely logical animals, all that would be necessary to control human behavior would be to discover what the "facts" on any issue are, and people would behave in rational ways. However, the experiences of politicians, courtroom lawyers, reformers, advertisers, radio men, newspapermen, all indicate that it is not necessarily the correct argument which wins, but rather the emotionally toned stereotypes and the ways in which they are presented. Nearly every president of the United States has realized the advantage of stereotyped phrases. Theodore Roosevelt waged war on "big business," "the Yellow Peril," "race suicide," "standpatters," "mollycoddles," "pussyfooters," "hyphenated Americans," and "pacifists." Woodrow Wilson came along with attacks on "special privilege," "dollar diplomacy," "warmongers," and "lowbrows." Franklin D.

Roosevelt condemned "monopolists," "unscrupulous money changers," "rugged individualists," "manipulators," "unethical competitors," "prophets of evil," "the overprivileged," and "economic royalists."

Businessmen have long realized the advantages of stereotyped phrases and slogans, and they know that those slogans have the most far-reaching effects in the situation which is fairly indefinite or about which the minds of the people are not actually made up. Numerous experiments have indicated that if a stimulus field presented to a subject has no pattern of itself, the subject will perceive it as if it had pattern; and if a group of subjects in an unstable-stimulus situation are asked to report on it, they will experience the situation in terms of a common reference point.[71] Thus, many advertising slogans of a stereotyped nature have had tremendous appeal, perhaps even for you: "Keep That Schoolgirl Complexion" (Palmolive soap), "Time to Retire" (Fisk tires), "They Satisfy" (Chesterfield cigarettes), "Ask the Man Who Owns One" (Packard automobile). A university advertised once, "Summer School Where Summer's Cool."

One elderly lady still prefers "Jello" with its six delicious flavors to "Royal Gelatine," because she used to enjoy Jack Benny's radio program and consequently feels that the product he represented must be good. His "Jello Everybody" introduced a pleasant half hour, and she still remembers the phrase when she is ordering a special type of gelatine.

You cannot argue with stereotyped beliefs or with slogans. Proponents of a child-labor amendment to the Constitution have relied on such positive stereotyped ideas as "drawn up in America by American citizens" and on negative symbols such as "horde of sweated little slaves." Those against a child-labor amendment have used positive appeals like "sacredness of the American home" and negative ones such as "unadulterated Bolshevism."[72] Although the factors which make slogans and stereotyped phrases effective as means of influencing human behavior are too complex to discuss in detail, Lumley has listed fourteen of primary importance:[73]

1. Rhythm.
2. Alliteration.
3. Alliteration and antithesis.
4. Ringing repetition of sounds.
5. Brevity.
6. Appeal to curiosity.
7. Punning.
8. Sentiment of patriotism.
9. Entrance into the inner sanctuary of one's private life.
10. Appearance of meatiness, the unavoidable conclusion of profound thought.
11. Authoritative note.

12. Class appeals.
13. Apparent obviousness of meaning.
14. Obscurity of origin, combined with euphoniousness, timeliness, and other features.

Some of the terms appearing in two metropolitan daily newspapers, the *Chicago Tribune* and *The New York Times,* with reference to the same news stories, are set forth in Table 10. The twelve terms from the news columns of the *Chicago Tribune* have considerably more emotional stress than the twelve parallel terms from *The New York Times.* For example, where the *Times* speaks of "progressive action," the *Tribune* brands it as "radical" action. Emotional reactions of sixty college students were less favorable in all instances to the terms in the right-hand column.

TABLE 10

Comparison of Terms Used by "The New York Times" and Those Used in the Same Connection by the "Chicago Tribune" (After Sargent)[74]

New York Times	*Chicago Tribune*
Progressive	Radical
Senate investigation	Government witch hunting
Regulation	Regimentation
Maritime leader	Communist C.I.O. leader
Labor organizer	Labor agitator
Home relief	The dole
Crop control	Farm dictatorship
Nonstrikers	Loyal workers
Investigator	Inquisitor
C.I.O. Chieftain	C.I.O. Dictator
Foreign	Alien
Picketing	Mass picketing

As we shall see in Parts V and VI, stereotyping devices are used in all sorts of social institutions. Stereotypes are stimuli which arouse standardized preconceptions which are influential in determining one's behavior.[75] We find stereotypes employed in the family, school, church, fraternity, club, political party, professional and occupational groups. Their psychological effects are not to be dismissed lightly.

QUESTIONS AND PROBLEMS FOR DISCUSSION

1. *Is it true that prejudice arises only where we find rather intimate contact?*
2. *If prejudices are fairly permanent, is there any way at all that they can be slightly modified?*
3. *In what ways do you think that you make judgments of other persons?*

4. *Can you think of some behavior of your own which might be explained in part by subliminal stimulation?*
5. *"All men are created equal in capacity for achievement." Is this true? Why so, or why not?*
6. *Discuss: "The social psychologist must take into account the pictures or images in people's heads."*
7. *Find some examples of stereotyping in your local newspaper.*
8. *Make a list of advantages of stereotyping, and then one of disadvantages. Compare the two lists.*
9. *Write the copy for an advertisement using the stereotyping process.*

RECOMMENDED READINGS

Anastasi, A., *Differential Psychology.* New York: The Macmillan Company, 1937.

Collier, R. M., "An Experimental Study of the Effects of Subliminal Stimuli," *Psychological Monographs,* 1940, **52,** No. 236, pp. 59.

Freeman, F. N., *Individual Differences.* New York: Henry Holt and Company, Inc., 1934.

Landis, C., "Emotion: II. The Expressions of Emotion." In Murchison, C. (editor), *A Handbook of General Experimental Psychology,* Worcester: Clark University Press, 1934, Chap. 7.

Lippmann, W., *Public Opinion.* New York: The Macmillan Company, 1922.

Miller, J. G., *Unconsciousness.* New York: John Wiley & Sons, Inc., 1942.

Wolff, W., *The Expression of Personality; Experimental Depth Psychology.* New York: Harper & Brothers, 1943.

*Newcomb, T. M., Hartley, E. L., and others (editors), *Readings in Social Psychology.* New York: Henry Holt and Company, Inc., 1947. (The following selections are listed according to the sequence of related discussions in the chapter you have just read.)

Hayakawa, S. I., "Meaning, Symbols, and Levels of Abstraction," pp. 190–203.

Katz, D., and Braly, K. W., "Verbal Stereotypes and Racial Prejudice," pp. 204–210.

Sargent, S. S., "Stereotypes and the Newspapers," pp. 558–561.

The names of the emotions portrayed in Figure 15 are:

1. Contentment	5. Surprise
2. Horror	6. Shyness
3. Happiness	7. Grief
4. Anguish	8. Happiness

Brief descriptions of the people whose pictures appear in Figure 17 are given below. The pictures of all of the writers were posed, based on special instructions from a photographer.

1. George "Bugs" Moran—once *bossed a Chicago gang;* was among survivors of St. Valentine's Day Massacre engineered by Al Capone.
2. Alfred Cline—Colorado choir singer; made a good living by marrying ladies he met at church socials; they all "died" suddenly; *sentenced to 126 years.*
3. Lawrence Treat—former *Vice-President of Mystery Writers of America;* has written crime books such as "B as in Banshee," "D as in Dead," and "V as in Victim."
4. John Fiorenza—a New York City upholsterer; *raped and strangled an authoress;* was electrocuted.
5. Veronica Parker Johns—*writes mysteries* like "Shady Doings," and "The Singing Widow."
6. Lawrence G. Blochman—ex-reporter; his *mysteries* include "Bombay Mail" and a movie, "Quiet Please, Murder."
7. Kurt Severin—formerly a night-club master of ceremonies; now a *photographer and writer,* who specializes in writing up fact-crime material.
8. Clayton Rawson—former *crime-story editor* for Ziff-Davis Publishing Co.; among his books are "Footprints on the Ceiling," and "Death from a Top Hat."
9. Brett Halliday—his *well-known mystery plots* feature a detective named Michael Shayne; husband of Helen McCloy (see 19).
10. Winnie Ruth Judd—*murdered two women;* shipped their bodies to Los Angeles in a trunk; was declared insane and committed to a mental institution.
11. Johnny Torrio—a former big *racketeer* in Chicago; one of Capone's henchmen.
12. Arthur D. Payne—Texas attorney; *murdered his wife* with dynamite; while waiting for his trial, killed himself with another charge.
13. F. Orlin Tremaine—editor and writer; formerly associated with *Macfadden Publications;* writes mystery stories about a scientist named Professor E. Z. Bart.
14. Manfred B. Lee—is *one half of the partnership which produces all Ellery Queen mystery stories;* other half is Frederic Dannay (see 21).
15. Henry Klinger—an *assistant story editor* for 20th Century-Fox.

16. Basil "The Owl" Banghart—*machine gunner* for the old Chicago Touhy gang; got 99-year sentence for *kidnaping.*
17. Joseph R. "Yellow Kid" Weil—one of the Midwest's *most talented swindlers*—in and out of prison since 1909.
18. Robert Irwin—ran amuck, murdered his sweetheart's sister, her mother, and spiked a roomer with an ice pick; got a *270-year prison term.*
19. Helen McCloy—*created the fictional character Basil Willing,* who solves crimes through extensive knowledge of psychiatry; wife of Brett Halliday (see 9).
20. William Manners—*editor of Mystery Novel Classics,* a detective pulp magazine.
21. Frederic Dannay—the *other half of "Ellery Queen"* with collaborator Manfred B. Lee (see 14).
22. Jack "Legs" Diamond—wound up a long career of *robbery and homicide* when he was murdered by underworld colleagues in a hotel room.
23. Neville George Heath—*killed two of his women friends;* was hanged.
24. Kathryn Kelly—wife of gangster "Machine Gun" Kelly; was convicted as an *accomplice in a kidnaping,* and sentenced to life imprisonment.

CHAPTER ELEVEN

THE INFLUENCE OF OTHER PERSONS

SOME "UNCONSCIOUS" FACTORS. Compensation—Rationalization—Identification—Regression—Projection—"Unconscious" Factors / SUGGESTION. A Demonstration—Definition—Suggestibility Not a Trait—Factors of Suggestion—Types of Suggestion—Practical Studies in Suggestion—Suggestion in Everyday Life / IMITATION. Types of Imitation—(1) Imitation of Conditioned-Response Type—(2) Imitation after a Trial-and-Error Period—(3) Deliberate Imitation—Imitation as Description, Not Complete Explanation—Uniformity of Action / LAUGHTER. The Problem—The Difficulties—Limitations of Any Theory of Laughter—Theories of Laughter—(1) An Antidote to Sympathy—(2) A Physiological Theory—(3) Autistic Thinking—(4) Superiority and Incongruity—Some Empirical Studies—Summary / THE INFLUENCE OF A GROUP ON INDIVIDUAL PERFORMANCE. Effect of Passive Spectators or Auditors—Effect of Those Working Alongside—Effect of Contestants—Social Encouragement and Discouragement—Group Discussion—Size and Prestige of the Group.

▶ SOME "UNCONSCIOUS" FACTORS

Compensation
Rationalization
Identification
Regression
Projection

Look over this list of words. How many do you know? How many can you recognize as somewhat familiar, or at least not total strangers? As a student of sociology or psychology, you are probably somewhat acquainted with them all. Even if you are not primarily a student, but are a business executive, lawyer, carpenter, bricklayer, radio announcer, photographer, merchant, salesman, dentist, artist, chemist, or engaged in any of a thousand other occupations, you probably have a passing acquaintance with these terms. These words are borrowed from the much-discussed field of psychoanalysis. They have become such a part of our verbal culture patterns that everyone not only reads such terms in short stories and newspaper articles, but tosses them about himself. What do they actually mean? What is their value in social psychology? Let us examine them one by one.

COMPENSATION

The term "compensation" has been used in two different ways. Some have employed the word to refer to the mechanism by which an individual overcomes some deficiency in his behavioral make-up. According to this meaning, an individual with a speech defect might pay special attention to his speech behavior and "compensate" by learning to overcome his speech impediments; or one who is physically weak as a child, like Theodore Roosevelt, may give special attention to building up a strong body. This, however, is not the sense in which the word "compensation" is employed in social psychology. Instead, the term is used to refer to those instances in which an individual, because of some deficiency or inferiority, attempts to develop special abilities *in some other field of behavior*. The deficiency or inferiority may actually exist so that it is physically observable by other people; or it may be covert or imagined by the person.

Therefore, if you are particularly incompetent or deficient in some field of behavior or have any sort of physical defect, you may try to compensate for this by achieving recognition in other fields. Likewise, even though you do not have an actual deficiency or physical defect but think of yourself as having some inferiority, you may also attempt to compensate. You may have developed feelings of inferiority by contrasting yourself unfavorably with other people, perhaps because you have chosen to compare yourself with superior people in some line of activity.

If someone has a very pompous manner, or constantly interrupts and drowns other people out in conversation, or is a "flashy" dresser, it may be that he is pompous, or noisy, or loud in dress because he has a real or imagined inferiority and is trying to compensate for it. Those people whom we may believe to be very conceited may turn out not to be conceited at all, that is, not to have inner feelings of conceit. In a study of twenty-five persons asked to rate themselves on various traits of personality including "conceit," it was found that those individuals rated by their fellows as being most conceited showed the least tendency to overestimate themselves in their own good traits.[1] In other words, the person whom we call conceited may simply be a person who has adopted a superior air in order to compensate for what he believes to be his deficiencies.

The mechanism of compensation is an extremely important one in enabling us to understand people's attitudes toward each other, as well as toward their schools, churches, fraternities, and various other groups. Of course, the behavior of others cannot be interpreted simply on the basis of compensation. In the first place, compensation by itself is not a complete explanation of why people behave in certain outstanding ways. In the second place, more data are needed than can be obtained merely from observing an individual's present actions. Just because someone is a good athlete, for example, it does not follow that he is therefore compensating for intellectual inferiority. Nor can it be said that simply because a student is a good scholar, he is, therefore, compensating for physical inferiority on the athletic field. Only when sufficient information has been secured about the individual's background, his early conditioning, present activities, and ultimate goals, can valid conclusions be drawn. From this standpoint, data obtained in the psychological clinic are of the utmost importance.

RATIONALIZATION

The second concept, rationalization, probably does not require a lengthy description. Most of us are familiar with this mechanism—giving good, socially acceptable reasons for our conduct rather than the real or actual reasons. It has been said that you have two reasons for everything you do—the good reason you give other people, and the real reason. You may have been interrupted in your work by a suggestion that you go to the movies and have gone with a "perfectly clear conscience" by rationalizing, "After all, I've been working hard and I need some relaxation." You can rationalize the imbibing of alcohol by saying that you are fighting a cold. Many a man buys a new car when the old one is perfectly satisfactory, but rationalizes his conduct by saying that it is important in his business to make a good impression. If you are a male and another man insults you, you can take a poke at him if he is smaller, and then rationalize your conduct by saying that your honor demanded it; or you may turn aside if he is larger, and then rationalize by saying that honorable men should not stoop to the level of animals.

Here is a mechanism often described as "saving face." We rationalize our conduct to maintain our self-esteem. We are constantly motivated by pride, prestige values, and fear of what other people might say. We try to pass off anything that is unpleasant by seeming indifferent. Every school psychologist has known at least one mother whose young hopeful does not do well on intelligence tests, but who then rationalizes by saying, "Well, of course, the tests are silly and worthless, and they don't really mean anything." This is sometimes called the *sour-grapes* attitude. Did you ever want to go to a party to which you did not receive an invitation and *then* say, "But after all, I really didn't care very much about being asked"? Were you ever slighted or snubbed by someone whom you wanted to impress, and then adopted an air of nonchalance and claimed that you were really too busy with important matters to worry? The very fact that you bother to call someone else's attention to the slight is some evidence at least of a "sour-grapes" attitude.

Neither compensation nor rationalization is to be looked on as something sinister. As a matter of fact, because we can compensate in various ways and can rationalize our conduct, we are able to lead happier lives. Rationalization also has a considerable effect upon group ways of behaving. It is a means of social control. "Make the world safe for democracy," a powerful slogan during the first World War, was actually a rationalization for some of us for our anger against the "Huns" and our desire to go to war.

IDENTIFICATION

Another important psychological mechanism is identification. The very term suggests mentally putting oneself in the place of another. This means dependence upon covert types of responses such as imagining oneself as the heroine of a movie, or a person who is greatly admired. This tendency accounts in large measure for the appeal of *Superman*. See Figure 18. Who is there who wouldn't like to be able to become invisible, hurtle through space, and have superhuman strength? Superman can outrun a speeding automobile, outfly an airplane, punch his way through armor plate. It is not surprising that in the early days of World War II the Navy Department decided that Superman comic books were to be included among essential supplies for the Marines at Midway island. At that time three Superman comic books had an estimated readership of about 12 million; Superman strips in the newspapers added approximately another 25 million readers; Superman radio programs were carried on 85 stations; and Superman movies were shown in the majority of some 17 thousand movie houses.[2]

You can so well identify yourself, your aims, ideals, progress or lack of progress with someone else or some group of individuals that their successes and failures become yours. In the 1930's, when Joe Louis went down to a sudden defeat, Harlem was pervaded by dark gloom because of the psychological identification of many an individual Negro with his hero. The next year Joe Louis was once more victorious, and many a Negro lad marched proudly through the streets immediately after the radio broadcast of the fight, chanting and singing his exultation as if he had won the fight himself. It was good strategy for the Republicans to have Joe Louis campaign for Wendell Willkie in 1940.

Identification also depends very much upon covert attitudes of *sympathy* for other individuals. In fact, sympathetic appeals are often resorted to by those who wish to influence other people. A speaker makes a series of addresses for the benefit of children starving in other countries. To be effective, his speeches should arouse already developed covert attitudes of sympathy in his hearers by asking, "What if your own baby didn't have enough to eat and was so emaciated that you could count his ribs?" This appeal is to underlying sympathetic attitudes in other individuals, designed to make them identify themselves with another situation.

Instances of identification are many. On the basis of clinical data on one hundred men and one hundred women, a prominent psychiatrist concluded that men who marry women similar to their (men's) mothers are better satisfied with their marriages than other men.[3] This suggests that psychological identification with the mother may at a later time be transferred to the wife. Certainly many parents identify themselves so much with their children that they try to live their childhoods over again through their younger counterparts. As we shall see in Chapter 16, they may and often do force upon their unwilling offspring attitudes and ways of behaving which are satisfying to them as parents, because they can vicariously experience the things which their children are doing, but which are eminently unsatisfactory to the new generation.

An apt illustration is that of a mother who was completely wrapped up in an only son who died at the age of eighteen. Shortly after his funeral the mother developed a case of hysterical paralysis in one arm and leg, and devoted herself to continual mourning for her dead son. Years later she refused to go out socially, still identifying herself with someone who no longer existed, and spent her time writing poems to the nobleness of her son's life. Here is one product of her pen:

The blue is gone from the sky—dear one
   And the way is hard to see
For the sparkle of life is no more—my son
   Since you—went away—from me.

. . . .

The days are sad and the nights are dark
   And my heart hurts constantly,
But the world rolls on and the work goes on
   Since you—went away—from me.

I'm lonesome, dear, and the road is long
   And my courage fails—all to see
For the music of life no more can play
   Since you—went away—from me.

Oh, take me, dear, to that land of "where"
   Wherever you may be
So I'll be with you and understand
   Why—you went away—from me.

FIG. 18. IDENTIFICATION IN *Superman*[4]

Politicians and advertisers constantly make use of the mechanism of identification. The great political figure is someone with whom the voter can identify himself, as we shall see in some detail in Chapter 14 on leadership. Look at almost any magazine for examples of sex appeal, made in order to sell everything from soap to soup, from tooth paste to tobacco. A *Saturday Evening Post* advertisement reads:

> Go to a motion picture . . . and let yourself go. Before you know it you are living the story—laughing, loving, hating, struggling, winning! All the adventure, all the romance, all the excitement you lack in your daily life are in—pictures. They take you completely out of yourself into a wonderful new world. . . . Out of the cage of everyday existence! If only for an afternoon or an evening—escape![5]

And escape you can to a world of tinsel and gold, with brilliant diamonds, beautiful blondes, champagne baths, midnight revels, love-making in the purple dawn—what more can you ask for? After all, why should you engage in realistic, objective thinking when identification with the characters played by your favorite movie stars is so much more fun?

The women's magazines recognize the fact that being a homemaker is not a completely satisfying occupation for most women, and publish fiction that is largely of the romantic, glamorous, happy-ending variety. Typical of the comments obtained in a survey among women readers is the following:

> I read about women who have nothing to look forward to; and then something good happens! *And that makes me feel better.* The things that happen don't happen to me. The stories are about rich girls and things like that. *They make me feel good, make me forget.*

REGRESSION

Another interesting mechanism is regression. This means adopting ways of behaving, thinking, or both, which are essentially childish. Regressive activities are modes of reacting to our environment which are not adult but represent a lower and simpler level of existence. Many instances of this are found in clinical cases. An individual who develops hysteria is able to engage in more infantile whimpering and get a great deal more sympathy from his family and friends than he could if he were a normal healthy individual. Similarly, a "delicate" or "sensitive" individual may be forgiven for actual temper tantrums which would not be stood for in another person.

However, the mechanism of regression is by no means limited to abnormal behavior or to the clinic, for we find all about us and even in ourselves regressive ways of thinking and behaving. Regressive mechanisms are indulged in by most of us in our daily existence. They represent infantile or childish adjustment to one's circumstances, but sometimes that is very desirable socially. When you go to a football game, you are expected to behave in a childish way. When you go to the movies, you demand the right to rock back and forth in your chair with laughter at slapstick comedies, or to let the tears flow down your face, demonstrating that you are not emotionally an adult. But after all, is there anything wrong about this? Regressive behavior is not necessarily bad or wicked; in fact, it may be extremely valuable in certain institutional situations. The next time you go to a meeting of your club or fraternity, see if you can find any indications of infantile behavior in the use of weird, wonderful names for officers. Watch for the various ways of dressing up as Oriental potentates or naval admirals—a childlike device for assuming temporary importance. Even in religious attitudes and behavior there are many signs of regressive thinking. It is so easy to cast all your burdens on the Lord, so simple to think of wearing a crown of gold, perhaps strumming a golden harp, walking in the golden streets, and basking in the sunshine of never-ending glory, that you can be persuaded not to worry too much about the big bad world around you.

The problem of regression can be attacked experimentally by setting up norms of behavior which indicate psychological maturity. For example, Charlotte Bühler developed various norms for small infants.[6] When a child is given two sticks to play with, a psychologically immature infant may simply take one stick, wave it about and strike various objects with it. A slightly more mature child may either do nothing but look at the sticks, or may hit one stick against the other. A still more mature child may take both sticks and place them so that they form a straight line, or try to fit them together. Gesell, through the aid of his associates in the Yale Clinic of Child Development, has established other norms of activity for small children.[7] These can be of tremendous advantage to an experimenter if he wishes to determine whether a child has regressed in his behavior.

Norms of behavior were established by Barker, Dembo, and Lewin for thirty nursery-school children; then the environmental situation was changed in order to determine to what extent each of the children would regress or go back to an earlier type of behavior.[8] The norms were established with various play objects for children from 2½ to 5 years old. Among the play objects were boats, ducks, ironing boards, toy trains, toy telephones, and paper and pencils. A small child who was not psychologically mature would simply use a toy telephone as a rattle, banging it about. A slightly more advanced child would take the toy telephone and shout into or at it. The most advanced child would actually use the toy instrument as a telephone and carry on long imaginary conversations into it. Similarly, norms of behavior were determined for such acts as drawing. The least mature child would usually make a jumble of lines. A more mature child would draw a rudimentary type of house or other object. The advanced child would make rather good, understandable drawings.

After the child had become adjusted to the play situation, a partition within the room was raised so that there was twice as much space as there had previously been. The child now found that the play equipment consisted of large and beautiful toy trucks, new ironing boards with dresses to iron, a pond for the boats. After he had familiarized himself with these play objects and had become adjusted to his new play situation, he was taken back to the first half of the large playroom and a wire-mesh screen was let down in the middle of the room so that the child could *see* the just-experienced new and fascinating toys, but could not get to them. (This seems somewhat comparable to the situation of a man who has acquired great paper wealth by making money on the stock market and then suddenly finds his profits wiped out.) Now, the question for observation was the extent to which the children might regress in their behavior as a result of the changed situation. Of the thirty children, twenty-five actually showed very real signs of regression; that is, they returned to earlier levels of constructiveness. For example, a child who had previously carried on an imaginary conversation on a toy telephone now regressed to the point of simply banging the phone about as a rattle; a child who had drawn a house now reverted to the level of mere scribbling. On the average, the children regressed in their behavior to a level fourteen months younger than before. The regressive effect of frustration upon play is not limited to the single-child situation, but also appears in group-play situations, as has been demonstrated by M. E. Wright.[9] Experiments such as these suggest certain very important implications so far as childish behavior by *adults* is concerned.

PROJECTION

One more mechanism of considerable importance is that of projection. In answer to a question on a psychology examination, "How do you define projection?" a student once wrote, "A sticking out." This was partially correct, for after all projection is a psychological means by which we "stick out" or push off on someone else our own delinquencies or deficiencies. That is, in our own thinking we tend to blame someone else for those characteristics which are perhaps well ingrained in ourselves. After being happily separated from her fiancé during the summer vacation, a college girl accused the fiancé of wanting to break the engagement. This, like compensation and the other devices discussed above, is sometimes called a "defense mechanism."

You are probably familiar with this alibi device in your own behavior.

If you lost at bridge last night, it was because *your partner* trumped your ace in that second rubber. If you have ever been involved in an automobile accident, you know perfectly well that it was the *other* person's fault. Why didn't *he* put on his brake? If you have been particularly unkind to someone else, after all, he deserved it, didn't he? If you have ever done poorly in an examination, did you think that the instructor who made it up was unfair? All of us project our own weaknesses onto someone else; and it is psychologically valuable that we do this, provided, of course, that projection does not result in extreme self-pity. Some adults certainly carry this business of fault-finding, coupled with pity for themselves, to an extreme degree.

Projection has been studied empirically by Sears, who had ninety-seven college men, living in three different fraternity houses, rate themselves and every member of their particular fraternity on four personality characteristics: stinginess, obstinacy, disorderliness, and bashfulness.[10] By pooling the judgments of fraternity brothers on any individual member, it was fairly simple to determine whether or not a person had insight into his own characteristics. Thus, if an individual rated himself as low or high on one of the four characteristics, and his fraternity brothers gave him a similar rating, this indicated that he had good insight as to what sort of a person he was with reference to this particular trait. On the other hand, if a man rated himself as, say, low in stinginess and his fraternity brothers rated him high in stinginess, it indicated that he had little insight as to his own characteristics. Two interesting results were obtained. First, those persons who tended to lack insight as to their own bad characteristics tended to attribute these same characteristics to their fellows. In other words, if a man seemed to have one of these characteristics to a rather high degree and did not recognize it by giving himself a high rating, he tended to project this trait on his fellows by giving *them* a high rating. By way of example, a man who was recognized by his fellows as stingy, but who did not realize this himself, tended to rate *other* persons as being stingy. Second, and in line with the first conclusion, persons who possessed insight as to their own characteristics showed a slight tendency in the opposite direction; that is, they tended to undervalue their own objectional traits in other people.

In a follow-up study, Sears was interested in determining the relationship between ideas of reference (projection) and feelings of self-criticism.[11] In order to attack this problem empirically, the experimenter secured answers from approximately three hundred subjects on two different scales. The first scale was a measure of ideas of reference. Sample questions were: Do people find fault with you more than you deserve? Are you troubled with the idea that people are watching you on the street? Are you ever bothered by the feeling that people might be able to read your thoughts? Do you think your friends talk sarcastically behind your back? Do you think strangers sometimes whisper about you when you pass them in a corridor or street? The second scale was a measure of feelings of self-criticism. It included such questions as: Do you worry too long over humiliating experiences? Are you frequently burdened with a sense of remorse? Do you feel that you are living up to your own ideals? Do you waste too much time on frivolous activities?

Contrast the samples from the two scales and you will see that the first involved reference or projection of ideas into other people, whereas the second related to feelings of self-criticism. The majority of subjects actually obtained very similar scores on the two scales. Obviously, this could be interpreted to mean either of two things—either that the two scales were measuring the same thing, or that the two things measured were closely related in most of the experimental subjects. The first hypothesis was eliminated by Sears through an inspection of the items themselves. Instead, his findings are believed to support the second possibility, namely, that the feelings of self-criticism and ideas of reference are closely associated. Thus, the usual clinical observation of the high relation between these two variables was verified.

Bellak sharply criticized stories invented by students as descriptions of pictures shown to them.[12] His assumption was that they would resent his criticisms, and would project their aggression by introducing more aggression into their stories. Later analysis showed that they had put a greater number of verbs and nouns connoting *aggression* into their stories than had other subjects who received no criticisms.

From a group of male college students Finger obtained information on their sex *practices,* and also sex *beliefs.*[13] The psychological mechanism of projection is revealed by the fact that those who reported a particular type of sexual experience believed, to a greater extent than those who reported that they lacked this type of experience, that other men had engaged in the same type of behavior. For example, the nonvirgins thought that 73 per cent of unmarried males over eighteen years of age, and 70 per cent of their best friends, had had intercourse; whereas the corresponding estimates among the virgins were only 61 per cent, and 45 per cent, respectively.

"UNCONSCIOUS" FACTORS

All five of the psychological mechanisms described are largely "unconscious." We make use of any or all of them every day of our lives. We compensate for our weaknesses, real or imagined. We rationalize our behavior, covert or overt. We identify ourselves with those whom we admire. We regress in our conduct when things become "hard to take." We project our own weaknesses on others. These activities are perfectly normal for us. Yet we do these things without suddenly stopping ourselves in our mental "tracks" and saying, "Aha! I'll now regress!" or "I'll now compensate!" In fact, it is extremely difficult for many of us to discover instances in *our own* behavior of these mechanisms, even though we may be rather good at pointing them out in other individuals.

There are some instances, of course, when we purposely carry on these psychological activities. For instance, baby talk and crying are types of regressive behavior which many a young lady employs, consciously or unconsciously, as a means of accomplishing certain ends. When a wealthy coed visited the psychological clinic to discuss some problems of motivation, the question was presented to her, "What is the thing which you want most in life at the present time?" The instantaneous reply was, "A new Buick convertible." Asked what was the best way of accomplishing this goal, she replied without hesitation, "Well, tears have usually done the trick with my father."

See if you can discover examples of compensation, rationalization, identification, regression, and projection in the following "Dear Diary" material. A college girl's diary for the first ten days of January for 1934, 1935, and then 1937 reads as follows:

1934: Jan. 1. New Year's Day. Went calling with the bunch. Oh! what a time.
" 2. Started to school and believe me I hated to get up to go. Went and saw a movie tonight.
" 3. Another day of school gone. Played basketball. Stayed home this evening & wrote letters. Also studied. Some study!
" 4. Not much happened. Went to show but can't say much for the time I had.
" 5. To-day was one of the coldest days I can remember. Stayed home until evening, then went to show. Had a dandy time.
" 6. Oh such a day! Out with Margy. Went to Otto's, Lucy's and our house.
" 7. Same old school. Everyone busy cramming for exams. Still war on between M & H.
" 8. This was the dumbest day I ever lived through. Peace with the bunch.
" 9. Last day before the exams. How I wish it were this time tomorrow.
" 10. One whole morning & afternoon of exams. Both rather easy. Played bridge tonight.

1935: Jan. 1. Slept until four today. Went to party at Bob's and had a dandy time.
" 2. Carl asked me for a date but Dad won't let me go. Went out with Carl and had a dandy time. He is a *dear*.

1935: Jan. 3. Well of all dumb days this caps the cookies. Haven't done or seen anything exciting all day. Saw Carl pass in car & that is all.

" 4. I feel like the very devil after almost making myself believe that I didn't care for Rudy. I had to see him and now I am as crazy about him as ever.

" 5. Some dumb day. Let Rudy read this but I haven't heard him say anything. He is absolutely mad at me for good. Had a marvelous time tonight, went out to Sophie's and had a peach of a time. Was with Rudy. I am crazier than ever about him.

" 6. Nearly fell asleep in all of my classes. Saw Rudy and talked to him and that is all. Jimmie called up and asked for date for to-morrow night.

" 7. Went out with Jimmie to-night and had a lovely time (damn this pen). Went to show and then came home and talked. I certainly am crazy about him.

" 8. What a day. Went over to school and then to Dick ———'s. Had some time believe me. Oo-la-la.

" 9. Pretty dumb day awfully tired. Rudy is some *mad*. But I can't worry forever. Saw Jimmie but he hardly spoke. How I wish he liked me.

" 10. Very dumb day. Didn't see or hear of anything interesting. Went to Sophie's for a while and had a good time–

1937: Jan. 1. Could a day have been ushered in more beautifully! Dear Lord, how I love him–

" 2. Got up rather late. With Lee all afternoon and evening. He is such a wonderful dear. How I love him.

" 3. Left home and back to school.

" 4. Broke up with Dick for good. I really feel quite sorry. I used to like him.

" 5. Life fails to be exciting.

" 6. Had breakfast with Rudy and we had such a grand old talk.

" 7. Was going out but felt so rotten I broke my date.

" 8. Date with Bert tonight. We were with Bill and went to show. Had such a good time.

" 9. Sleepy day. Not much to do. Date with Jimmy.

" 10. Just an awfully dumb day.

After reading material of this sort, one can get a reasonable insight into some of the personality traits and fundamental attitudes of the individual concerned. "Just an awfully dumb day" over a period of four years tells a good deal about the young lady in question.

▶ SUGGESTION

A DEMONSTRATION

The following conversation and demonstration took place in a psychology lecture:

INSTRUCTOR (addressing student): Have you ever played bridge?

STUDENT: Yes.

INSTRUCTOR: Well, then, what are the four suits of cards?

STUDENT: Clubs, spades, hearts, and diamonds.

INSTRUCTOR: Of these four suits, please name any two.

STUDENT: Spades and hearts.

INSTRUCTOR: All right. Of spades and hearts, name one.

STUDENT: Hearts.

INSTRUCTOR: Fine. That leaves spades. Now, in spades, there are both face cards (the Ace, King, Queen, and Jack) and the spot cards (2, 3, 4, 5, 6, 7, 8, 9, and 10). Of these two groups—face cards or spot cards—mention either face cards or spot cards.

STUDENT: Face cards.

INSTRUCTOR: All right. Of the face cards, that is, the Ace, King, Queen, Jack of spades, name any two.

STUDENT: King and Queen.

INSTRUCTOR: All right. That leaves the Ace and Jack of spades. Of the Ace and Jack of spades, name either one.

STUDENT: Ace.

At this point, the instructor removed the Ace of spades from his coat pocket and then showed that it was the only card in this pocket and that all other pockets were empty.

This is not just an artificial situation. In everyday life we are often concerned with social suggestions such as this, in which there is organization and presentation by one person of carefully chosen stimuli which will induce a desired response in another individual. Thus, in the card-trick demonstration the response desired from the student was "Ace of spades," and because of the manipulation of certain factors that response was secured. Reread the demonstration, and find what these factors are.

DEFINITION

The term "suggestion" refers to a process in which uncritical, and sometimes immediate, responses to stimuli are produced in a given situation because the behavior mechanisms involved have already been prepared to react in that way.[14] It involves "the acceptance of a proposition for belief or action in the absence of complete self-determination."[15] We can thus note: (1) instances of suggestion in social situations where the stimulus factors are purposely introduced by *someone else,* (2) cases where the suggestion stimuli occur in the *environmental situation* in which we find ourselves, and (3) instances where suggestion comes from *one's self.* Of course, many situations involve two, or even three, of these sets of factors. Here are some examples of suggestion, based on the conditioned response:

(i) A trained dog begins to salivate when a bell is sounded. (ii) A person who is susceptible to seasickness feels nauseated on board a steamer which is still in dock. (iii) The blood pressure of a woman mounts to 160 when she enters the doctor's office. (iv) Children are easily frightened by being reminded of punishment. (v) A person with a conscience who has committed a misdemeanor may manifest emotion when a word pertaining to the crime is suddenly spoken. (vi) A class in psychology which met at 12 o'clock complained to the instructor that his frequent references to hunger and food-getting made concentration difficult at this time of day.[16]

SUGGESTIBILITY NOT A TRAIT

Is suggestibility, then, a personality trait of the individual? This is extremely doubtful, considering the multiplicity of possible situations in which the process of suggestion may occur. You may be extremely suggestible when you are with a friend whom you wish to please, and extremely nonsuggestible with someone toward whom you have different feelings. Suggestion factors are of one sort where one person is supposed to speak with more authority than others, and quite the reverse in other social situations. As a matter of fact, an examination of the experimental literature on the psychology of suggestion reveals that many of the experiments have simply involved picking out some rather interesting instance of human gullibility and then testing various individuals until the desired results are produced. In one experiment, for example, boys and girls were told, after some preliminary verbal statements: "You can't close your hand. You can't close it at all. Try!"[17] Approximately half the children were unable to close their hands. In another experiment, each subject was shown an electrical machine and allowed to get a slight shock from it.[18] He was then told to report when he could feel the electricity again, the current *presumably* being turned on; the quicker the report, the more suggestible the subject was supposed to be. But suggestibility to an electric shock is a very specific problem, and a subject's responses of this sort tell us almost nothing about his tendencies to be suggestible except in that particular situation.

The matter is even worse if problems of suggestion are confused with other similar human tendencies which are psychologically quite different.[19] For instance, the tendency to make the same response which has been made in a similar situation, such as a man taking out a key when he approaches a door which resembles the door in which he ordinarily uses the key, is *not* an instance of suggestion alone. Again, the tendency to continue doing what one has started doing (discussed in Chapter 6) is not a matter of suggestion alone but of constant reinforcement of the conditioning process.

FACTORS OF SUGGESTION

On the other hand, a number of the factors probably important in suggestion situations should be mentioned. The internal condition of the person, such as whether he is hungry, fatigued, or emotionally disturbed, is extremely important. Knowledge of the internal conditions alone, however, is not sufficient to predict what a given individual will do; a "drunk" may be highly suggestible, or he may be resistant to suggestion to the point of complete stubbornness. The external conditions, as already indicated, may happen to be in the environmental situation or may be cleverly manipulated by some individual who wishes to achieve a particular goal. These might involve such things as repetition, volume, duration, or rhythm of the stimuli, or the prestige factors of the manipulator.

TYPES OF SUGGESTION

There are various kinds of suggestion—*direct* and *indirect, positive* and *negative*. First, as for direct suggestion, we are often aware of the fact that people around us wish us to behave in certain ways. Every parent makes use of this mechanism of suggestion. So does every teacher, every businessman. So do you. At the same time, however, indirect suggestion often will achieve results. You seldom win an argument by asserting the correctness of your facts and opinions. Rather, you get your opponent to agree with you on certain underlying premises, and then let him discover for himself that they lead to different conclusions from those he holds. When the person being influenced does not perceive what the ultimate result will be from a given stimulus situation, he may be led to do things or develop attitudes which he would not otherwise have. In education, business, politics, and a variety of social situations, indirect suggestion is one of the most useful devices.

The second distinction is between positive and negative suggestion. Positive suggestion refers to a direction or orientation of the individual toward a given goal, whereas negative suggestion is designed to produce the opposite result. In commercial advertising, for example, positive suggestion is found in such slogans as "The pause that refreshes" and "Say it with flowers." Instances of negative suggestion are likewise found in advertising when it is suggested that you avoid halitosis, or that you should use deodorants. Magazines and newspapers are full of examples of all four types of suggestion.

PRACTICAL STUDIES IN SUGGESTION

Although many experiments dealing with suggestion have little value, a few are worth noting, because of their practical implications. As already indicated they are of three sorts: (1) those in which the influence of *other people* affects individual subjects; (2) those in which "unconscious factors" in the *environment* lead a subject to do certain things; and (3) those where the *subject's own "set"* is the important element.

Subjects were required to select the better of two statements from a large number of paired statements on the basis of linguistic merit, to select the more offensive of various pairs of traits, and the preferable one in each of several pairs of musical selections.[20] Two days later, they made another set of judgments. After a lapse of 2½ months, when the subjects had presumably forgotten their original sets of judgments, the experiment was repeated. Again, two days later they made another set of judgments, but first were told what had been the *majority* preference for each pair. There was a much greater tendency to reverse judgments to conform to the majority opinion when that opinion was known; and the results were statistically significant.

In another investigation, students were asked which of two *identical* phonograph records they preferred, although it was not known to them that the two musical selections were identical.[21] They were told before listening to each pair of records which one was supposedly preferred by music critics. The great majority not only "heard" these records as different, but also agreed that the one designated by the experimenter as preferable was actually preferable! Both studies indicate how far-reaching are the social factors of suggestion. We are constantly influenced in what we may think our own judgments by what is socially acceptable or by what our friends feel. We tend to see and hear those things which we want to see and hear.

When a group of students are asked to write down a number between 1 and 25, more odd than even numbers are listed. When the instructions are changed for another group, asking for a number between 2 and 26, there is likely to be a predominance of even numbers. Ask your friends to "think of a number from 1 to 10," and you can bet that they will tend to pick 7;[22] and within a range of 1 to 4, they will nearly always select 3. Goodfellow has found that when people guess the flips of a coin as to "heads" or "tails" five times, there is a well-recognized pattern of judgments which will be most frequently chosen, and at the opposite extreme there is a pattern of judgments which will almost never be chosen.[23] Of thirty-two possible combinations of five flips—any one of the thirty-two combinations being equally likely to occur—"heads-heads-tails-heads-tails" is the most favored pattern, "tails-tails-tails-tails-tails" the pattern least frequently selected. There are more factors involved in the social psychology of suggestion than simply the "suggestor"; that is, the situation and set of the "suggestee" are also significant.

As Cantril has pointed out, two major psychological conditions tend to make individuals suggestible.[24] The first is one where the person lacks an adequate mental context to interpret the given stimulus or event. He is puzzled or bewildered, and is likely to accept ideas from others quite readily. "Thus the curious child who asks, 'What causes the wind?' may believe whatever his parents tell him; the ignorant, perplexed and anxious citizen may accept uncritically the oversimplified schemes of a crackpot utopian."[25] When a radio broadcast at Hallowe'en time under the direction of Orson Welles described realistically an "invasion" of men from Mars, thousands of citizens accepted the broadcast as an actuality and did everything they could either to escape or to prepare themselves to deal with the monsters![26]

A second psychological condition favoring acceptance of suggestions is when an individual's mental context is so rigidly fixed that a stimulus or event is automatically judged in terms of this context. The person already has a "will to believe" certain kinds of things. Thus, the Communist accepts, without question, propositions that have the stamp of his party leaders; the fundamentalist, the statement of any scientist that the world is controlled by God; and the successful businessman, any evidence against the value of cooperatives.[27]

Probably those who are of higher intelligence are less suspectible to suggestion than others. One investigator matched in sex and age an experimental group of children of I.Q.'s of 130 to 200 with a control group with I.Q.'s of 72 to 101.[28] Both groups were then introduced to six situations in which suggestions were offered. The superior group was reliably less suggestible in each test than the low-intelligence group. However, it should be emphasized that there was considerable "overlapping" between the two.

It has also been thought that those who are well informed of the purpose of a given situation involving suggestibility are less likely to be influenced than others; but Collier has presented some evidence to the contrary.[29] He tested two groups of students in April, and again in May, 1941, for their attitudes toward the Nazis. Prior to the second test the experimental group was instructed in principles and practices of propaganda, and also exposed to pro-German material from the German Library of Information; whereas the control group received no such instruction or propaganda. At the time of the second test the control group showed a reliable shift toward an anti-Nazi point of view; but the experimental group became somewhat more tolerant of the Nazis. This suggests that attitudes of individuals who are clearly aware of the character and purpose of propaganda, and who even attempt to approach it critically and analytically, can actually be influenced by it.

SUGGESTION IN EVERYDAY LIFE

How is suggestion used as a practical matter in everyday life? Stereotyped phrases are related to the process of suggestion, and words such as "scab," "kike," "wop," are used in that order to suggest unpleasant feeling tones. Similarly, such glib general stereotypes as "progress" or "liberty" result in a favorable response, as was indicated in Chapter 8 on language. With these stereotyped words may be linked sentence structures which have considerable suggestion value. For example, by saying, "You wouldn't want to" do this thing or that, you have already prepared your hearers for a particular way of acting or thinking. "You wouldn't want your daughter (or sister) to marry a nigger (or Jew, or Catholic, or Protestant)." In fact, when such emotional stereotypes are resorted to, rational and objective thought become almost impossible.

All sorts of people find suggestion of tremendous value in their lines of work. Consider three samples in the practical psychology of suggestion —from a football coach, an advertiser, and a radio network.

Knute Rockne demonstrated remarkably well how the psychology of suggestion can work in a "pep talk." He was making a dinner speech to an assembled audience of five hundred athletic coaches. He remarked toward the close of the speech that people often asked him what he said to the Notre Dame players between halves of a close game. He proceeded to tell what the events in the dressing room were like.

He pictured the atmosphere of the dressing room with its fumes of liniment and sweat, its nervous tension and uncertainty. Slowly Rockne went on, gradually building up interest, and finally giving one of his famous dressing room pep talks. Rhythmically he dropped to the chanting lines: "We are going out there to fight, fight, FIGHT—and Win!" Suddenly he demanded of his audience with smashing abruptness: "Are you with me?" En masse the twenty tables of young coaches shouted as one man, "Yes!" Then they looked at each other sheepishly and slipped back in their chairs with confusion as they realized how they had been tricked, how they had lost themselves completely to a magnetic personality playing on audience psychology.

Here is a sample of suggestion from the field of commercial advertising, with the intended responses added in brackets. A form letter begins:

Dear Sir:

I am looking for some peculiar people. Perhaps you are one of them. [Maybe I am. Perhaps I should read further.]

Those I seek must, first of all, have deep down inside an unshakable belief in Democracy. [That's me all right.] That is a tougher qualification than it would seem.

Second, they must live in the fast-moving present. [Here I am again.] We don't want those who dream of the good old days or of some wild Utopia of the possible future.

Third, they must be alert, well-educated, articulate. [That's me all over.]

And, last, they must have one dollar to gamble with. . . . [Well, I'd like to take a chance.]

After presenting a brief discussion of a popular magazine, the letter ends abruptly with the two sentences:

I am not enclosing the usual envelope. If you haven't an envelope, you're not our kind anyway. [Let me find an envelope.]

A final example is from the field of radio publicity. A small booklet prepared by the Columbia Broadcasting System went across the desks of hundreds of business executives throughout the country some years ago with a bold title, YOU DO WHAT YOU'RE TOLD. This heading alone was probably so effective in a great many instances that a businessman did more than make the usual gesture of tossing certain advertising matter toward the ever-ready wastebasket. If he looked inside, he found the opening paragraph loaded with suggestion so strong that he was intrigued to read further:

Seven times . . . eight times . . . nine times out of ten. . . .

You do what you're *told.*

You're sure, of course, that isn't so. It flicks your pride. It's nonsense.

You, sir, are a company president. You push buttons. Other people jump to answer them. *They* do what they're told, but not *you.*

And you, young man, are a cub full of fight. Do what you're told! Why, you wouldn't 'yes' anybody! . . .

Suggestion, then, involves not only the obvious factors, but may also include all sorts of subtle flatteries and thus "build up" another person to such an extent that the behavior which is desired from him can *later* be produced. You can think of other instances of social interaction, aside from these laboratory and commercial situations, which involve the subtle manipulation of factors of suggestion. The social psychology of the audience and of the crowd, described in the next chapter, includes this same interesting phenomenon.

▶ IMITATION

TYPES OF IMITATION

Another important type of behavior in the presence of others is *imitation.* A great many cases of imitation are simply examples of conditioning. Imitation is not some magical explanation of behavior. Instead, it is simply a convenient word used to mean: (1) conditioned-response mechanisms, or (2) imitation after a trial-and-error period, or (3) deliberate imitation.[30] These three different kinds of imitation affect us in many of our activities.

1. *Imitation of Conditioned-Response Type.* The first type of imitation is a product of the conditioned response. In the conditioning situation the experimental subject is not "consciously" imitating the experimental phenomenon. Just as Pavlov's dogs were not consciously attempting to drip saliva, most of us in learning new things through the conditioning technique have not consciously tried to learn. We have often adopted certain ways of behaving automatically through the process of conditioning. In other words, in instances both of animal and human conditioning, the experimental subject does not "make up its mind" to adopt the response which is the one to be conditioned, but the process is apparently "unconscious" and somewhat automatic. The sight of another person yawning may result in our yawning, not because we are trying to imitate, but owing to previous conditioning.

An interesting empirical study was conducted by Starch, in which 106 subjects were asked to give samples of their handwriting, and then to copy the material of four different passages.[31] Of the four passages, one was typewritten, whereas each of the other three was written with different degrees of width and slant to the letters. Although no specific instruction was given concerning the way the material was to be copied, every one of the 103 who said that he had written in his usual manner actually had adapted his own style of handwriting somewhat to each of the three types of handwritten material either in terms of the slant or of the width of his letters, or both. Here was imitation of a conditioned sort, yet carried on without the subjects' realizing it.

2. *Imitation After a Trial-and-Error Period.* A second instance of imitation is the kind in which we engage only after a trial-and-error period. You may wish to be a pianist like Paderewski or a baseball player like "Babe" Ruth; but unless you have developed specific mechanical skills, you are not able to imitate them until you have gone through a long period of trial and error.

3. *Deliberate Imitation.* Often, of course, we indulge in deliberate

imitation of someone else. A college freshman sees a senior smoking a pipe, and decides that he can look like a senior by smoking a pipe. We may quite consciously adopt the attitudes expressed by our favorite newspaper columnists and say, "This is where I got my view—from Walter Lippmann (or Westbrook Pegler or Walter Winchell)." Most of us perceive other individuals or other groups behaving and thinking in particular ways and then adopt their "ways." The movies have had their effect on what people deliberately do. In *It Happened One Night* Clark Gable was seen removing his shirt, and he was not wearing an undershirt. The sale of athletic shirts dropped off to such an extent that certain manufacturers went to the motion-picture producers and demanded that the scene be deleted.[32] A nineteen-year-old coed found that imitation of movie stars is not always effective:

> I saw a picture in which the heroine very coyly, when conversing with a young man, would close her eyes, slightly nod her head, and smile. And when she closed her eyes, her eyelashes were shown off to their best advantage. And so I decided that this was very "cute," and . . . I adopted the trick. It so happened that within about a week I attended a formal dance. During the evening I used my charms, but to my dismay they weren't appreciated, but rather criticised! After several closings of the eyes and noddings of the head, my friend asked me if I was tired and wished to start home.[33]

IMITATION AS DESCRIPTION, NOT COMPLETE EXPLANATION

Like the term "instinct," or for that matter the conditioned response, imitation is not a complete explanation of behavior but only a description of how we sometimes act. If we see certain people behaving or thinking alike, we must ask *why* they are behaving or thinking alike. Nor is similarity of behavior a certain sign that the imitative process is at work. The mere fact that two young ladies are both wearing similarly styled hats does not prove that one is imitating the other. After all, each girl may have adopted this mode without any reference to imitation factors, but in terms of subliminal cues from the general style trends of the year. The fact that you observe whole groups of individuals doing the same thing does not mean that their behavior can be explained in terms of imitation. It may simply mean that they are all responding to a set of common stimuli. An analogy may help. Go to the zoo and instead of focusing your attention on the lower animals visit the primate house. You will probably hear comments such as, "Oh, look, how the monkeys are imitating us! They handle things, they use their hands just like human beings." Would it not be just as logical to say, "Oh, look, at the human beings, look how they are imitating the monkeys! They even use their hands like monkeys!" A more adequate explanation would be that the skeletal and muscular make-up of the arms, hands, and fingers of both men and monkeys is quite similar, that the stimuli for each are quite similar, and that, therefore, the two groups manipulate their hands in much the same fashion.

UNIFORMITY OF ACTION

More fundamental than the psychology of imitation is the searching question of why there is uniformity of action among human beings. There is no single answer but a complexity of interrelated conditions:

1. Practically identical innate structures, plus common stimuli, result in common behavior. The way men and monkeys use their hands is a case in point.
2. Uniformity of action is economical and time-saving. Most men wear raiment called "suits" cut very much alike, largely because of the economy and time-saving of mass production.
3. If you act differently from others, embarrassment may result, or even the disapproval of others. If you do not conform to the folkways, customs, and mores of your group, you may be scorned or perhaps become a complete outsider. This is motivation enough for uniformity.
4. Conversely, uniformity is rewarded by the approval or even friendship of others. You are a "jolly good fellow" or at least "O. K." if you conform.
5. The group may have the same mores and habit patterns. In other words, through a long period in the culture of a particular group, the same ways of thinking and acting may have evolved so that every member of the group takes these "ways" for granted.
6. There may be a common language and other symbols of thought and action. If individuals in a particular group speak and think by use of the same sorts of symbols, this in itself promotes uniformity.
7. The actions of others may call attention to certain things and conditions (for example, food or danger). You may see someone on a street corner with his neck tilted back and his eyes pointed up. You then tilt your neck back and your eyes up, not with any desire to imitate him but simply because of your attention to outward stimuli.
8. In groups, there is often stimulation by enthusiasts or specialists in certain lines. In religious ceremonies, fraternal rituals, activities of audiences, some one individual may stimulate the group to behave or think a certain way. In fact, we hear a great deal today about "rabble-rousers."
9. Conditioning is an important factor. That is, your early background and experiences may result in your behaving very much like the other members of your group.
10. Uniformity in certain manners and activities may result in self-elevation. That is to say, going with the group may mean not only approval of others, but a boosting of your own self-esteem.[34]

Now, then, how do these factors apply to various situations in which we observe uniformity of action? We note all about us similarities of dress, manners, language, and fashions, and are likely to explain these away by the magic term "imitation." However, such uniformities may also be explained in part by reference to the factors just mentioned. For example, uniformity in dress may be explained in part by the conditions of topics 2, 3, and 10 in the foregoing list: uniformity of dress is economical and time-saving; if one acts differently, embarrassment may result, even the disapproval of others; and uniformity may result in elevation of oneself. Similarly, uniformity in manners may be explained in part by reference to factors 3, 4, 5, 6, and 10. Language uniformity is due partially to factors 5, 6, and 10. Other possibilities are uniformity in ceremonies and much of religious behavior, due to factors 3, 4, 5, 6, 8, and 10. Uniformity of mob action is largely a result of 7 and 8. Uniformity in apparatus, implements, and machines, such as in methods of lighting, heating, and transportation, are explainable in part in terms of topics 2, 3, 4, 7, and 10.

▶ LAUGHTER

THE PROBLEM

The Boss is sitting at his desk when a visitor enters, closing the doors behind him. Through the glass partitions the stenographer sees them talking earnestly. Gradually the Boss's face undergoes peculiar changes—his mouth widens and the corners turn upward forming curious wrinkles in his cheeks and around his eyes, which have narrowed perceptibly. His mouth then opens and his upper teeth are displayed. Suddenly through the closed door come the muffled sounds of blows and shouts. The stenographer sees that the visitor has collapsed in a chair, slapping his own knees, his chest heaving as though every breath came with the greatest difficulty.

Are these two fighting? Is the visitor ill? Should she call for help? No—the Boss just told a funny story.

A roller coaster or scenic railway carries great groups of people screaming with laughter from one dip to another. Why do they laugh? Someone buttonholes you and says, "Have you heard the one about the traveling salesman and the farmer's daughter?" and you smirk knowingly. Why do you smirk? Someone else pulls off the old saw, "Who's that lady I seen you with last night?" "That was no lady, that was my wife." And you smile condescendingly. Why do you smile? As that astute student of human behavior Groucho Marx has said: "There are all kinds of humor. Some is derisive, some sympathetic, and some merely whimsical. That is just what makes comedy so much harder to create than serious drama; people laugh in many different ways and they cry in only one." Instances of humor are found in all sorts of social situations; that is why the psychology of laughter should be analyzed in some detail.

THE DIFFICULTIES

It is a difficult problem to present any one reason why people engage in a type of behavior which varies from a slight twitching of the corners of the mouth, to holding the belly and rocking back and forth while the teeth are displayed. Situations which provoke laughter in a road gang are not the type of thing which will necessarily produce laughter in someone's drawing room. In fact, they may lead to a hasty exit. Contrariwise, situations which might be considered hilarious at a dinner party might be considered a bit boring to members of a road gang.

Various people have theorized about this problem of humor. Stephen Leacock, a really great humorist, has attempted to explain humor, its theory, and technique.[35] But when Leacock takes some excellent "gags," sets them forth and attempts to dissect them, the humor seems to disappear. When the same author theorizes that early man could laugh and cry long before he could talk, and that his eventual language developed out of his whines, grunts, and chuckles, the social psychologist in his skeptical way is forced to ask, "But, Mr. Leacock, how do you know?" This question of "How do you know?" recurs again and again in social psychology. While we cannot solve certain historical problems concerning the origins of language or of laughter, we can conduct certain types of empirical studies with regard to humor.

Omwake became interested in the problem of what situations are really humorous and what makes people laugh.[36] She asked six hundred high-school and college students to rate themselves on various points with reference to their sense of humor, and also to rank different jokes from best too poorest. In the list of jokes, Omwake included one joke which she and others considered "pointless," one which was considered "shady," and ten believed to be of various degrees of humor. Interestingly enough, however, not a single joke was consistently marked either best or poorest; that is, there was no common agreement as to what was the most humorous situation. In fact, every one of the twelve jokes was marked pointless by at least one student, and every joke was ranked best or poorest by at least one student. So far as the "shady" joke was concerned, the marking of this seemed to depend very much upon the individual's attitude toward "shady" jokes, the younger boys rating it higher than did girls of their same age and higher than did older boys.

Perhaps most interesting of all is the fact that when the six hundred subjects were asked to rate themselves as to their degree of possession of a sense of humor, only 1 per cent rated themselves as below average. Apparently judging from this study, nearly every one of us considers himself to be quite a humorous person. This is significant because of the importance we attach to a sense of humor in our acquaintances. If you ask a friend for an opinion on someone else and he replies, "Oh, he has a swell sense of humor," this is almost equivalent to saying not only that he is a jolly good fellow, but that he is intelligent, has a winning personality, and is, in general, a very excellent person.

In a later study, Omwake had high-school pupils check which one of four possible completions would make most humorous each of fifty situational descriptions.[37] Only seven of the two hundred possible completions received the votes of three-fourths of the subjects. In making a factorial analysis of responses to the comic, based on the administration of a Sense-of-Humor Test to three hundred persons, Andrews found no general or universal factor to be involved.[38]

LIMITATIONS OF ANY THEORY OF LAUGHTER

You can see from the foregoing studies and from various humor situations how small the chances are of hitting upon any one theory which will explain *all* kinds of laughter. First of all, humor varies with the *time* when the incident happened; that is, something which was once funny may at a different time be no longer funny. Your roommate's antics may be quite amusing in the forenoon, but when you are sleepy the same behavior may be annoying. The "wisecrack" which the professor got off at which you laughed so hilariously doesn't seem so hilarious when you tell it to one of your friends.

In the second place, what is humorous varies considerably from one *situation* to another. The embarassing experience of another student in the classroom is pretty funny, but when the same thing happens during a serious fraternity ritual, it is not so humorous. So-called men's jokes, and the stories that women tell women, do not always "go over" in the same way in a mixed group of men and women.

Finally, any examination of psychological theories of laughter applies only to our own *culture*. Situations considered amusing by Americans are not necessarily funny to Englishmen or Frenchmen. If you know an Englishman, you many conduct an interesting experiment by exchanging a copy of *The New Yorker* for a copy of *Punch;* mark the cartoons in *Punch* which you think are funny, and let your English friend indicate the ones in *The New Yorker* which amuse him. The great differences which appear will be surprising. It does not follow from this, of course, as some people seem to believe, that Englishmen have no sense of humor; it simply indicates that humor is of a different order in a culture different from your own.

An anthropologist returned from studying a primitive African group and related how various legal difficulties are settled by these people. He described how the two opponents draw a line in the sand or dirt, and then each one lines up his friends and relatives on opposite sides. A member of one group makes what might be called a "wisecrack." Then a member of the other group makes one. This continues until someone says something which is considered simply hilarious, whereupon everyone laughs and goes home. The anthropologist was asked by some Americans to give examples of the wisecracks. He related one after another, but what was considered humorous in a primitive African society was not funny to a group of Americans. Therefore, in considering the various theories of laughter we are confronted with the difficulty of finding some hypothesis which will not only fit particular time and place situations, but also apply to our own culture.

THEORIES OF LAUGHTER

There are all sorts of theories of humor and laughter, of which four different ones may be noted here:

1. *An Antidote to Sympathy.* One well-known theory of laughter was advanced by McDougall.[39] In connection with his list of instincts, primary emotions, and secondary emotions (referred to in Chapter 6), he discussed laughter as an emotional state dependent in part upon these other drives. McDougall believed that laughter is an antidote to sympathy, in other words, that we frequently laugh or show amusement in order to avoid the unpleasant feelings which we would have if we sympathized with someone else. In fact, McDougall believed that laughter arises only in situations which are mildly unpleasant, except in so far as they are redeemed by laughter itself; or in the presence of things which would excite a feeble degree of sympathetic pain if we did not actually laugh at them. He considered that the ability to laugh had a great survival value for the human race, by virtue of relieving us of the necessity of suffering for all the trivial anxieties which beset us in our daily lives.

2. *A Physiological Theory.* A second theory of laughter is primarily physiological in character. When you laugh, blood is sent to your face, the metabolism of your brain is increased, you breathe more deeply, and there is a stimulation of digestive secretions involving your liver, pancreas, and duodenum. This has led some observers to speak of a sudden "spilling over" of excess nervous energy when some unexpected situation occurs. At the Paris Institute of Psychology, Dr. Pierre Vichet used to give a practical course in laughing. He simply got the members of his group to relax and then, with a phonograph record of laughs as

a stimulus, the people let loose and laughed, giggled, roared, snorted, and grunted.

3. *Autistic Thinking.* A third theory of humor involves autistic thinking (discussed in Chapter 9). Although it might be argued that this is really not a separate theory, autistic thinking should not be overlooked as an important element in laughing. It is even involved in the Freudian notion of pleasure derived from "compression," making something convey two different meanings as in the sexual joke.[40] In the next siuation which causes you to smile or laugh, just stop and think whether objective, realistic, "hard" thinking was involved, or whether laughter was a means of mental relaxation and perhaps even temporary escape from the world around you. This applies particularly to that interesting type of wit or humor that is both damned and praised—the pun.

4. *Superiority and Incongruity.* A great deal of the discussion of laughter has centered around the ideas of *superiority* and *incongruity.*[41] All of us derive glee from the secure position of being able to look down on someone else; another person's blunder is amusing. Incongruity refers to an unusual, illogical situation or event; a chimpanzee that smokes is comical. These theories have been advanced by various philosophers, psychologists, and other students of human behavior, and, as we shall see, there are a few empirical investigations which bear out these theories.

Suppose that you see a professor slip on the ice. Stop right now and think about it. The mere thought of such an occurrence is laughable. This involves not only feelings of superiority over someone who "can't even keep his feet"; it also involves incongruity—at least, professors are not ordinarily found slithering about on the ice. We find instances of superiority and incongruity in the newspaper cartoons featuring Caspar Milquetoast, in the movies featuring Donald Duck, and on the radio with Jack Benny or Fred Allen. Humor may even be a symbol of "race" conflict.[42] Thus, certain stories—about supposed chicken stealing by Negroes or their sexual exploits—are humorous to many white people but not to Negroes; and likewise Negroes tell stories that lampoon whites, which are never heard by most Caucasians or, if they are, are not considered very funny.

Thomas Hobbes, usually credited as the founder of the theory of superiority, said that we laugh "when we feel sudden glory," that is, superiority. In his *Human Nature* (1650) and again in the *Leviathan* (1651) Hobbes associated laughter with the general idea of derision. "There is a passion that hath no name; but the sign of it is that distortion of the countenance which we call laughter which is always joy; but what joy, what we think, and wherein we triumph when we laugh is not hitherto declared by any."[43] He then declared that men laugh at their own actions when they perform even a little beyond their own expectations, and that laughter comes from a sudden conception of some ability in themselves. Note the significance of the word "sudden," for the sudden change in a situation is very important in producing laughter. Hobbes also pointed out that men laugh at the infirmities of others which set off their own abilities by comparison, and that they laugh at jests in which the wit consists of discovering some absurdity in another. Both Spencer and Bergson discussed laughter in a somewhat similar vein.

Of the more recent discussions of laughter, Max Eastman seems to be the principal dissenter.[44] He takes direct issue with this theory of "sudden glory" and instead holds to an "instinctive" theory, somewhat like McDougall. However, Ludovici has revived the Hobbes superiority theory of laughter and even enlarged upon it by stressing the importance not only of "superior adaptation" but also of the "unconscious" factors in humor.[45] He believes that we laugh when we feel that our adaptation to life is superior, and that this may come about in three ways:

1. Laughter may be *subjective.* Ludovici explains this by saying that the consciousness of freedom from restraint, or of physical well-being, is synonymous with the feeling of superior adaptation. On a bright summer day the boy who is free to follow his impulses will laugh without observable stimulation, and a girl knowing herself to be well dressed may laugh at the slightest provocation.

2. We may experience a feeling of superiority through *comparison.* This is the principle underlying the derision theories of laughter.

3. The comparison may be a *bluff.* The comparison between ourselves and others in certain situations results in a feeling of superior adaptation, genuine or feigned. If a man loses his hat on a windy day and our own hats are still in place, we experience a feeling of superior adaptation; but the man who loses his hat will look anxiously around and then also laugh with those near him and continue to laugh while he is trying to recover his hat. Ludovici believes that he does this to show that, appearances to the contrary, he is still superiorly adapted to this irritating situation.

A *sudden* change in a situation will frequently produce laughter. To carry this one step further, it might be said that we laugh at a surprise or an expectation that comes to nothing. Thus, babies usually respond with laughter when the gesture of throwing them through the air is started but not completed.[46] The expectation that come to nothing is also the basis for many a "build-up" in sustaining suspense until the "point" is reached. Even when that point is not very funny of itself, sudden freedom from restraint or release from tension results in laughter. Children laugh as they troop out of school, and older people laugh at nonsense pictures, perhaps because of the release from restraint.

Why do we laugh when we are tickled, or when we inhale nitrous oxide (laughing gas), or at the obscene? Ludovici has a ready answer. We laugh, says he, when tickled, because ticklish places are in highly vulnerable and defenseless regions of the body. The tensions caused by tickling are so serious that relief from them, when it is realized that the threat is not serious, causes a feeling of superior adaptation. He argues that we laugh when breathing "laughing gas" or when listening to anything obscene for much the same reason—joy brought about by a release from constraint or inhibitions. His theories may be compared with the analysis made by Willmann of various kinds of jokes.[47] He postulates that laughter is due to a situation that causes surprise, shock, or alarm, and simultaneously induces an attitude of playfulness or indifference.

SOME EMPIRICAL STUDIES

A few pages back some empirical studies that have dealt with the problem of laughter were mentioned. Another such investigation was conducted at Vassar College in which over one hundred students were asked to record for a period of a week every situation which produced a laugh.[48] The diaries produced 4,217 different laugh situations, and these were classified as shown below:

Instances of laughter with no apparent cause		54
Inferiority of persons	2,257	
Directed attempts at making people feel *inferior*	493	
		2,750
Incongruous situations	1,196	
Incongruous ideas	217	
		1,413
Total		4,217

Feelings of superiority and incongruity produced practically all the laughter recorded in this particular group of college women.

In another investigation people of different age levels were asked what instances produced their laughter.[49] Ten kindergarten children were asked to tell the funniest thing they knew; an analysis of the things and events reported showed that superiority and surprise were extremely important. Twenty girls, seven to ten years old, also gave information which supported the superiority and surprise theory, but in addition included items which were classed under the headings of incongruity and debasement of dignity. When eighty-two college women were asked the same question, all of these same categories were included, but the following were also added: play on words, vulgarity, sex. This study, in addition to showing the importance of superiority, is one more indication that there are tremendous individual differences in sense of humor not only from one time or place to another but from one age level to another.

In the Harvard laboratory, investigators presented to Jewish and Gentile subjects sixteen jokes, half of which were disparaging to Jews.[50] The materials were presented on a moving screen in typewritten form, one word at a time. The responses of the subjects were recorded by moving pictures of their facial expressions, and by appraisal of the subjects by other people who served as observers. The subjects themselves also rated the jokes as to "funniness." The following joke, for example, was put on the screen:

> PAT: "Will you help me by cashing this check?"
> IKIE: "I wouldn't cash a check, even for my own brother."
> PAT: "Well, you know your family better than I do."

When the name "Ikie" was replaced by a typically Scottish name, the Jewish subjects thought the joke was funnier. Similarly, jokes were considered funnier by the Gentiles when the person who was the object of he joke was a Jew. Similar comparisons were made with jokes in w ch names of men and women were substituted for each other. In these instances, women were more amused by jokes which were at the expense of men than by the same jokes which were at the expense of women. These data lend additional confirmation to the theory of superiority or superior adaptation. Those things which affect someone else unfavorably are much more amusing than the things that affect oneself or the members of one's own group unfavorably.

Omwake has reported another study in which she attempted to discover whether the response to jokes is determined by their inherent humor, or by the eye-ear factor of presentation.[51] She was also concerned with finding some relation between intelligence and sense of humor. With regard to the first question, one group of subjects was given visual presentation of the jokes, whereas the other heard the jokes on a phonograph record. With one striking exception, there was a surprising agreement in rank order of preference in the visual and auditory situation. However, it is interesting to note that visual presentation facilitated the comprehension of the joke to a great extent. As to the second problem, there was no indication that intelligence was a determining factor in the comprehension of the jokes used in the study. Certainly this lends additional confirmation to the belief that intelligence and sense of humor are not necessarily identified, even though many people do talk as if a "marvelous sense of humor" is closely related to superior intelligence.

SUMMARY

By way of summary, it may be said that it is impossible to set forth any one psychological factor which will explain every humorous reaction of every kind of person. However, there is a great deal of experimental material to suggest that the superiority and incongruity factors are more important than others, in a large number of humorous situations.[52] If we couple these factors of *superiority* and *incongruity* with *suddenness of perception* of the humor stimuli, we can say that humor may be explained as *the sudden perception of a contrast between things as they are, and things as they ought to be or are thought to be or are expected to be.* See if this applies to the cartoons shown in Figure 19.

We should also differentiate between *humor* and *laughter.* After all, many situations which may seem humorous do not evoke the overt response of laughter; and many instances in which a person laughs do not mean that he feels covertly that something is funny or humorous. As indicated at the beginning of this section, the overt responses of laughter may vary at one extreme from the tiniest hint of a smile to the other extreme of uproarious and violent guffaws. Here are some of the reasons for various kinds of laughter:

1. Humor. As stated above, a situation may be actually *humorous* because of the factors of superiority, incongruity, and suddenness of perception.

2. The *"correct"* thing to do. A student may think that the professor's attempt at humor is only mildly amusing, but he laughs out loud. A host and hostess smile and laugh as they greet their guests; and the guests reply in kind.

3. A bluff. Laughter may be a *"bluff."* That is, the person laughing may not even feel covertly that there is anything to laugh about; but he pretends that he does.

4. Good will. In giving orders to a domestic or other servant, it can be observed how frequently the person giving the instructions smiles, apparently as a gesture of *good will* in our democratic culture. Two people who do not speak the same language very well can be seen smiling at each other a great deal as they attempt to communicate, each one almost saying by this that his words and gestures are meant to be of the friendliest kind.

5. Laughter at self. Most of us *laugh at ourselves* occasionally. We usually do this when with others, but may do it when alone. In either case, it may be a mechanism involving actual humor (see above) with its attendant circumstances of superiority, incongruity, and suddenness of perception. It may also be a means of winning sympathy from others, or of self-tolerance.

6. Attention-getting device. A person may suddenly laugh out loud, simply as a means of *getting the attention* of other people present. A

"We've intended to ask you about it for some time, Doctor, but never got around to it."

By Permission. Copyright 1940 The New Yorker Magazine, Inc.

By Permission. Copyright 1940 The New Yorker Magazine, Inc.

By Permission. Copyright 1940 The New Yorker Magazine, Inc.

FIG. 19. EXAMPLES OF HUMOR[53]

Which of these cartoons is funniest? Analyze the basis of humor in each.

"... and, forsaking all others, keep thee only unto him, so long as ye both shall live? ... True or false?"

FIG. 19 *(continued)*

snort or guffaw is a pretty effective way of getting others temporarily to shift their conversation or thinking and ask, "What's so funny?"

7. *Imitation.* Sometimes people laugh because they see or hear others laughing. Uniformity of action is often socially acceptable.

8. Scorn or derision. There is the laugh of *scorn,* which is one type of language behavior that symbolizes that you feel superior to somebody else.

9. Release from tension. Almost everyone can recall some instance in which he laughed when the social situation actually called for a different type of overt behavior. After a funeral, for example, as a *release from tension* many people have been known to laugh to "keep up their spirits." There are also the many instances of hysterical laughing.

10. Physical enjoyment. Then, there is the *physical* act of *laughter for its own sake.* Thus, a person may actually smile or laugh out loud just for the joy of this type of behavior.

11. Habit mechanism. Some people have developed a *habit* of smiling or laughing a good deal of the time, just as certain other people frown or look serious most of the time. There is even the "nervous laugh" which may be an autistic type of gesture.

12. Daydreams. One's own *daydreams* or phantasies may cause him to smile or laugh. The extreme of this is found in the hebephrenic patient in the mental hospital whose behavior is characterized in part by silly, inappropriate smiling.

This is by no means an exhaustive explanation of laughter. The above factors should be considered individually, however, in understanding the many different types of laughter and laughter situations. These factors should also be analyzed in combination with each other, in various patterns, to explain the wide varieties of laughter in different individuals at different times.

▶ THE INFLUENCE OF A GROUP ON INDIVIDUAL PERFORMANCE

The present section deals with the achievement of the individual when others are physically present as compared with the same individual's achievements when he is alone.[54] The range of experimentation in this field is unlimited, for variations may be made in the type of material, size of group, motor skill, sensory activities, emotional components, age, sex, personality factors, and so on almost without limit. However, the studies may be conveniently grouped in terms of the effects (upon the individual's behavior) of: (1) *passive spectators or auditors;* (2) *those working alongside;* (3) *contestants;* (4) *social encourage-*

ment and discouragement; (5) the interchange of ideas, or *group discussion;* (6) *the size and prestige of the group.* Rumors and hearsay have already been discussed in Chapter 9 in the section on Myths and Legends.

EFFECT OF PASSIVE SPECTATORS OR AUDITORS

Stage fright is a well-known phenomenon which may involve quaking knees, hands, and voice. Yet Travis found no statistically significant differences between the averages of a group of subjects on a hand-steadiness test when working only in the presence of the experimenter as compared with working before a group of student spectators.[55] However, eighteen of the twenty-two subjects made better scores before the group, and sixteen of them made their highest scores before the group, as compared with work in the presence of the experimenter alone. Another study revealed insignificant differences in either individual or group scores on coordination, color naming, analogies, and word naming in the "alone" as compared with various-sized "audience" situations.[56] From similar experiments, one generalization that has been offered is that the mere presence of others probably tends to speed up the individual's work but to make it less accurate.[56a]

Hanawalt and Ruttiger have investigated the effect of an audience on remembering by having subjects read a story, and then retell it twice.[57] Half the subjects retold it once to the experimenter, and once to an audience of ten or twelve students; whereas the other half reversed this procedure. In the audience situation more words were used, more ideas were recalled, and apparently more pains were taken to make the story interesting and smooth, than in retelling the story to one person.

EFFECT OF THOSE WORKING ALONGSIDE

The classical experiments on this problem were done by Floyd H. Allport, who had subjects work at a variety of different problems, in one instance as solitary individuals in separate rooms with time signals given by buzzers, in another working together in a group.[58] He found that the presence of co-workers favored speed, although this varied with the type of work, and that the slower individuals were more affected than the fast. However, Dashiell, comparing subjects working (1) *alone,* (2) together *noncompetitively,* (3) with others as *rivals,* and (4) under the observation of *spectators,* did not find that speed was increased in the second situation as compared with the first, and obtained no appreciable change in accuracy.[59] This is partially explained in the results of a further experiment, where subjects working in different rooms but simultaneously with time signals operated from one common center were compared with a true "alone" situation where each subject worked in isolation with signals given by an automatic clock. Higher speed but lower accuracy was obtained in the first situation, indicating that an individual apparently in isolation may actually be under social influence of an imaginative character. In two different experiments with scores on intelligence tests taken in a group as compared with the "alone" situation, the results have been contradictory to each other.[60]

The development of a considerable *esprit de corps* among industrial workers has been well demonstrated in experimental surveys in the Hawthorne plant of the Western Electric Company, where a small group which was studied over a four-and-a-half-year period gradually but regularly increased their productivity.[61]

EFFECT OF CONTESTANTS

From the cradle we have been trained to compete against others, in school, in games, and in jobs. The favorable effects of competition on performance can, in general, be taken for granted. In fact, the Shah of Persia is supposed to have manifested boredom at the English Derby by commenting, "Everybody knows that one horse can run faster than another horse: what does it matter which one?"[62] Two sorts of competitive situations, however, may be noted—(1) interindividual rivalry, and (2) intergroup competition.

1. In experiments with college students who were asked voluntarily to assume competitive or noncompetitive attitudes, the results were consistent in showing that the amount of work turned out was greater, although it was poorer in quality, in the competing situation. The slower workers speeded up the most in the rivalry situation.[63] Dashiell found speed of work increased in the competing situation, although the results were not clear-cut so far as accuracy was concerned.[64] Contrasting results have been obtained by Whiting and English.[65] But this is not surprising since different sorts of conditions were used with varied types of groups. Competition may or may not lower accuracy, and the exact answer to any specific problem will depend upon a study of that particular situation. In general, however, competition tends to speed up most individuals in their output.[66] The initially inferior workers also seem to profit the most.

2. In addition to interindividual rivalry, there is rivalry between groups. The competing groups may be physically near each other or only psychologically so. Rivalry may be between groups of the same or different kinds, such as between relay teams, or between businessmen and politicians. In either case group rivalry produces both covert and overt changes in the individuals who constitute the groups. However, there are indications that *self*-motivated groups accomplish more than *group*-motivated groups.[67]

SOCIAL ENCOURAGEMENT AND DISCOURAGEMENT

Hurlock has demonstrated the advantages of reward over punishment as a motivator for school children on arithmetic problems.[68] This general superiority of encouragement seems to hold also for adult groups, as has been demonstrated in several investigations.[69]

GROUP DISCUSSION

Any number of studies have demonstrated that individual judgments are improved by conference with others. Among the best of these is one by Jenness, who used a simple situation of having students guess the number of beans in a large glass bottle.[70] When the subjects discussed the number, knowing the great diversity of others' opinions, approximately three times as many improved their estimates as compared with those who did not. Those without such knowledge did not improve their own estimates any more than if they had not entered group discussion at all. Also, knowledge of great diversity of opinions reduced the extent of differences within the group, that is, increased the typicality of opinion. Gurnee has also demonstrated the superiority of group learning over individual learning of a maze, of judgments of fact, and of numbers.[71]

Some of the studies of this problem have been fruitful for the legal question of jury verdicts. One investigator found that large committee groups are desirable when many hypotheses are needed, small groups when prompt formulation of opinion is desired.[72] This seems to be borne out in the fields of practical politics and administration. Dashiell has demonstrated that a jury tends to give a more complete and more accurate account of a definite number of details than an average individual juryman.[73] This has been substantiated by R. L. Thorndike, who has also found that individuals who are right hold to their position more often than those who are wrong, even if they are unable to win over an opposing majority.[74] When group thinking is found to be superior to individual thinking, it is because of the larger number of approaches to the problem, the suggested solutions, and the effective criticisms of each proposal, plus the necessity of accepting social criticism and not being "bullheaded."[75]

SIZE AND PRESTIGE OF THE GROUP

"A group of two people, one of ten, one of a hundred, and one of a thousand, are notoriously different factors to be reckoned with, whether they be spectators, coworkers, competitors, or what-not."[76] Various experiments have demonstrated the tendency for persons to shift their opinion in the direction of the opinion held by the majority (compare the section dealing with Suggestion).[77]

The tendency of persons to agree to a greater extent with the views of someone they like than dislike has been discussed in Chapter 7 (pages 123-124).[78] One study has indicated that the influence upon an individual of how his fellows or how experts are judging declines somewhat with increasing age.[79]

The studies mentioned in the last few pages indicate to some extent the ways in which the social situation differs from the solitary situation. In the presence of groups, whether spectators, people working alongside, or contestants, there are measurable social effects on individual performance and attitudes, especially if there is group discussion.

QUESTIONS AND PROBLEMS FOR DISCUSSION

1. *In what ways are the mechanisms of* projection *and of* identification *important in the personality development of the child in the family situation?*
2. *Think of an example in your own life to illustrate: (a) compensation; (b) rationalization; (c) identification; (d) regression; (e) projection.*
3. *List in two columns the advantages and disadvantages of rationalization.*
4. *To what extent do animals show evidence of learning by imitation? Do not rely on armchair philosophizing to answer, but go to the psychological literature.*
5. *Analyze some political speech designed to produce uniformity of action. What factors were employed?*
6. *Listen to a radio skit or look at some cartoons, and make up what you think is an adequate explanation of the humor involved.*
7. *Explain the difference between humor and laughter.*
8. *In your own life what are* all *the reasons why you laugh?*
9. *Plan an experiment to test the effect of the size of the group on individual performance. Give details as to number of subjects, apparatus, experimental procedure, etc.*

RECOMMENDED READINGS

Barker, R., Dembo, T., and Lewin K., *Frustration and Regression: An Experiment with Young Children.* Iowa City, Iowa: University of Iowa Press, 1941.

Cantril, H., *The Psychology of Social Movements,* New York: John Wiley & Sons, Inc., 1941.

Dashiell, J. F., "Experimental Studies of the Influence of Social Situations on the Behavior of Individual Human Adults." In Murchison, C. (editor), *A Handbook of Social Psychology.* Worcester: Clark University Press, 1935, Chap. 23.

Freud, S., *Wit and Its Relation to the Unconscious.* New York: Moffat Yard & Co., 1916.

Hull, C. L., *Hypnosis and Suggestibility: An Experimental Approach.* New York: D. Appleton-Century Company, 1933.

Ludovici, A. M., *The Secret of Laughter.* London: Constable & Company, Ltd., 1932.

Sears, R. R., *Survey of Objective Studies of Psychoanalytic Concepts.* New York: Social Science Research Council, Bulletin 51, 1943.

Tarde, G., *The Laws of Imitation.* New York: Henry Holt and Company, Inc., 1903.

White, W., *The Psychology of Dealing with People: Appealing to the Want for a Feeling of Personal Worth.* New York: The Macmillan Company, 1937.

*Newcomb, T. M., Hartley, E. L., and others (editors), *Readings in Social Psychology.* New York: Henry Holt and Company, Inc., 1947. (The following selections are listed according to the sequence of related discussions in the chapter you have just read.)

Barker, R. G., Dembo, T., Lewin, K., and Wright, M. E., "Experimental Studies of Frustration in Young Children," pp. 283-290.

Chapman, D. W., and Volkmann, J., "A Social Determinant of the Level of Aspiration," pp. 90-99.

Coffin, T. E., "Suggestibility and Levels of Difficulty," pp. 225-232.

Lewis, H. B., "An Experiment on the Operation of Prestige Suggestion," pp. 232-243.

Miller, N. E., and Dollard, J., "Imitation and Independent Learning," pp. 243-246.

Murphy, L. B., "Variations in Sympathetic Behavior on the Playground," pp. 246-256.

Dashiell, J. F., "An Experimental Analysis of Some Group Effects," pp. 297-303.

Shaw, M. E., "A Comparison of Individuals and Small Groups in the Rational Solution of Complex Problems," pp. 304-315.

Lewin, K., "Group Decision and Social Change," pp. 330-334.

CHAPTER TWELVE

GROUP BEHAVIOR

THE CROWD. What is a Psychological Crowd?—Le Bon and the "Group Mind"—McDougall's Views—Allport's Criticism—No Group Mind—The Psychology of the Crowd / THE AUDIENCE. A Special Crowd—Individual Psychology of the Audience—Types of Audiences—Audience Techniques—An Example—Preparation of a Speech—Devices within the Audience—Presentation of a Speech—Psychological, Not Logical, Values / BOOMS, CRAZES, FADS AND FASHIONS. Irrational Ways of Behavior—Booms—Crazes—Fads and Fashions—Definition of Fashion—Examples of Fads and Fashions—Rational Fads May Survive—The Psychology of Clothes—Women's Styles—The Spread of Fashions—Clothing and Morality—Reasons for Ready Acceptance of Irrational Ways.

▶ THE CROWD

WHAT IS A PSYCHOLOGICAL CROWD?

The word "crowd" has been used by some writers to refer to "a relatively non-interacting aggregate of people, certain types of audiences, panic situations, unco-ordinated and co-ordinated riots, and even the pattern of revolution."[1] As used here, however, the term "crowd" means a fairly large group of people who are in both *physical* and *psychological* continuity with each other.[2] In other words, a group of people milling about on a downtown street at noontime does not form a crowd from the psychologist's point of view. If, however, a fire engine races down the street and people focus their attention in its direction, they are temporarily transformed into a crowd. That is, there is a common *polarization* toward some object of attention. Crowd behavior, then, involves three aspects: (1) psychological continuity; (2) polarization of interest and attention; and (3) transitoriness or temporary character.

LE BON AND THE "GROUP MIND"

An interesting psychological controversy has centered around the question of whether a "group mind" can exist in a crowd. Obviously, people do not behave the same in crowd situations as they do as individuals. Can this be accounted for by assigning to the crowd a group mind, folk mind, mob mind, or collective consciousness? The name of Le Bon, French sociologist, stands out as one of the most important individuals in the group-mind controversy.[3] He wrote as though a "group mind" existed. He emphasized that not just any group of individuals is a crowd, but that there must be something of central importance to the group as a whole. As the various characteristics of crowd behavior he gave increased suggestibility, extremely emotional behavior, irrationality, and the loss of "personal will" in the will of the crowd. Finally, he characterized crowd behavior as being extremely low-grade behavior. A group is impulsive, changeable, and irritable, behaving in an unpremeditated way, and with a "sense of omnipotence."[4]

The writings of Le Bon had a marked influence on American sociologists and psychologists. Even though they may not always have used the specific terminology of "crowd mind," several have used similar concepts, which describe the emotional side of crowd behavior.

McDOUGALL'S VIEWS

McDougall advanced the idea that certain types of *group* behavior were extremely high-grade, because certain outstanding characteristics were present. These included: (1) some degree of continuity of existence of the group; (2) self-consciousness of the group—as to its nature, composition, functions, capacities, and relations of the individuals to the group; (3) interaction (in conflicts and rivalry) with similar groups, but with different ideals, purposes, traditions, and customs; (4) existence of traditions and customs and habits; (5) organization of the group: differentiation and specialization of functions.[5]

McDougall's main example of the effect of these characteristics was the army, which he contrasted with the ordinary crowd. In either case, however, he pointed out that there must be mental homogeneity, leadership, and communication, and that without these group action was impossible. McDougall's views tend to modify those of Le Bon, but both wrote as though there actually were a "group mind." In some places McDougall wrote as though the group mind were consciousness of an individual member of a group of membership in that group, but in other places as though the group-mind concept implied actual consciousness or "mind" on the part of the group as a whole.

ALLPORT'S CRITICISM

Such views have been widely criticized, especially by Floyd H. Allport.[6] He has pointed out the fallacies both of Le Bon and McDougall. He takes Le Bon to task for his emphasis on crowd behavior as something so essentially different from individual behavior. Allport argues that, even though people in a crowd did act in a certain way, it was not the *crowd* which caused the actions; the actions were, after all, those of individuals. Consider, for example, the French Revolution. Trouble had been brewing with many individuals for years. Antagonism against the existing order had grown up. All that had happened in the crowd behavior was that the feelings were intensified and resulted in overt actions for which the earlier attitudes and beliefs had been preparatory —overt actions not of a crowd but of *individuals*. Also, "mind" usually implies the existence of a nervous system—something which is found only in the individual.

NO GROUP MIND

It is utterly fallacious, of course, to talk as though there actually were a mind which integrates a crowd—some sort of superior mind of which individual minds are parts. This is about as accurate as to say that frosted windows are due to Jack Frost. Yet many writers use such phrases as "the German nation thinks that . . . ," "the French mind is such that . . . ," or "there is a strong consciousness in London that . . ." —as though these were entities, rather than being verbal symbols of attitudes of thousands or even millions of different individuals. The next time someone refers to the English mind or tells you what the German spirit is, you might ask where this English mind and German spirit actually exist. There is no such entity as a group mind.

We might note, however, that if people talk as if there were a group mind, then in one sense a group mind does actually have existence—for those persons who hold this concept. The materials of social psychology are not always observable and tangible, but consist of intangible attitudes and beliefs both true and untrue.

THE PSYCHOLOGY OF THE CROWD

Even though a crowd of persons does not have a collective nervous system, it is psychologically different from the same persons when they are by themselves. Their interaction in a crowd produces unique behavior patterns. These shoulder-to-shoulder patterns are transitory; the interrelations of the crowd are constantly shifting and always temporary in nature. Under the spell of an emotional situation, or owing to skillful manipulation by a leader, a typical crowd tends to accept irrational ideas as though they were rational. Many a belief which would be derided by a person as a separate individual will receive his hearty applause in a crowd situation. This applies to the most absurd sorts of statements. The simple manipulation of verbal symbols, such as "progress," "liberty," "Fascism," "Communism," are sufficient to evoke everything from cheers to hisses from individuals who do not have any common understanding of the exact meaning of such words. As individuals we may lose ourselves so completely in the crowd that we not only give up our rational ideas but actually increase our prestige and ego feelings by being one of the crowd and "joining in." People in a crowd like to be told what to do, or at least told that they *may* do what they already *want* to do. This is particularly true in mob and riot situations where the mechanisms of *identification* and *projection* are found. We may identify ourselves with the leader in a mob situation. We also may project upon some unfortunate victim various private attitudes which as individuals we have repressed; our inhibitions are released because we feel we can escape blame for cruel or primitive behavior in the anonymity of the crowd.

The leader of a crowd may play upon the unique attitudes of his followers in order to achieve his own ends. This will be illustrated in the next section dealing with the audience—one kind of crowd. The crowd leader has high dominance status (discussed in Chapter 13) and many of the characteristics of leadership (described in Chapter 14). As will be seen there, he must be both *above* the group and *of* the group—respected or revered, but also a "good fellow." He can effectively use *suggestion* and *imitation,* as described in the preceding chapter.

No one has ever subjected crowd behavior to experimentation. However, in an interesting study by Meier and others, use was made of experimental procedures closely approximating mob incitation—assemblage, dramatic episode describing the supposed formation of a mob for a lynching, and use of a leader.[7] At the height of excitement the reactions of the group were recorded. Only 35 per cent, predominantly women, would have chosen to remain away from the mob situation entirely, although the motives for the others varied from active participation to attempts at deterring the mob.

People behave differently in crowds and as individuals. Every fall thousands of people of various cities suddenly sally forth for a major demonstration—with yelling, horn-blowing, dishpan-beating, and general bedlam—because the local ball team has won the pennant. Under the stress of sudden fear, a crowd may suddenly behave in even more irrational ways. During the invasion of France in 1940, civilians were so panicked that they completely blocked the roads, and troops could not be used effectively. In a fire in 1942 that lasted only twenty minutes in a Boston night club, 488 men and women died, mostly from suffocation after blocking the exits. During a German air raid on London in 1943, a woman carrying a baby tripped near the bottom of a "subway" stairway; and 178 persons lost their lives in the panic that followed.

As a practical exercise, you might look for a crowd and observe how its members behave in the crowd as compared with their behavior in individual situations. You may have had an opportunity to observe members of some fraternal organization that is holding a national convention in your community. If so, perhaps you have seen a group of individually intelligent and responsible persons engaging in *regressive* behavior on a wholesale scale. Here is a brief description of the playful antics of the members of one national organization at their annual meeting:

> [The visiting members] engulfed Boston, held up traffic, misdirected traffic, stopped traffic. They drank, sang, played practical jokes dear to middle-aged men on a tear. They squirted water pistols on girls' dresses, stockings. . . . They used electric shockers (disguised as brief cases, as canes) . . . (some fiends used rubber bands, which stung).[8]

If a crowd continues any length of time, you may observe a compact core of people, and then a fringe or outer rim. The former may be packed closer together, and there may even be a distinct space between them and the fringe of people who are scattered about as an outer group. In order to be quite objective, you might imagine yourself as a Melanesian anthropologist from the Trobriand Islands, visiting an American city for the first time. Here is the way a Trobriand Islander might describe a crowd of persons in the lobby of a movie house:

> We may term this species of crowd as the "Theatrical Crowd." Unlike the Arapesh described by Mead, the members of this crowd are continually competing with one another, for they all strive to be those appointed to enter the "auditorium" whenever the game calls for this move. Most of the people have a token consisting of a small piece of paper printed with native formulae, and for which a price is exacted in the native coin. Nevertheless, despite the costliness of this token, everybody seems anxious to give it up to a uniformed individual called "usher," who proceeds very unceremoniously to tear it up.
>
> The *locus operandi* of this crowd is called a "lobby," although when I hazarded to call those pressing about me "lobbyists," I elicited spasms of laughter—the reason for which I am as yet unable to discover. The process of being bunched together in this so-called "lobby" is known as "waiting." It is quite laudable to see these hundreds of usually restless people remain almost quiescent despite the fact that no iron bars keep them from pushing forward. They are restrained by another "usher" whose only exertion is to move his jaws as in chewing, while between his teeth may be seen a sticky and gum-like substance.
>
> Conversation in this crowd is casual and is interspersed with considerable laughter. It seems strange that a people so capable of producing laughter among themselves should submit to such unnecessary "waiting" in order to be entertained.[9]

A realistic picture of an actual crowd is the following description of the thousands outside and then those inside a hall in Germany in the 1930's where a meeting of the National Socialist German Workers' Party was to take place.[10] Note the many techniques used to develop psychological continuity in the crowd, and then to polarize the attention of its members as it becomes a compact audience:

> . . . The spectacle is better than High Mass, Greek tragedy, and Wagnerian opera combined. Simple men, moreover, may here rub shoulders with generals, aristocrats, and millionaires and address them familiarly as "comrade." . . . The outside of the hall is gay with flags and banners. S. A. men sell papers, pamphlets, and song-books to the waiting throngs: heartening military songs full of hate for Frenchmen and Poles and most interesting pamphlets against the Jews, against the bankers, against Bolshevism. A company of S. A. men drill and sing in the street and perhaps stage a dramatic torch-light parade with bands and flags.
>
> . . . .
>
> Finally there is a stir among the packed thousands. Drums and trumpets crash at the door. A disciplined regiment of storm troopers marches in—slowly, solemnly, carrying bright standards and swastika flags with poles tipped with spear-points or bayonets. Scores of flags pass by in majestic procession to stirring martial music, or perhaps to the slow rhythm of "The Entry of the Gods into Valhalla." Then at the end a special body-guard—either in natty brown uniforms or in the striking black and silver of the *Schutzstaffel.* Within a hollow square of marching men are the party leaders, also uniformed. Then the centre of all eyes, Der Führer—in his tan raincoat, hatless, smiling, and affably greeting those to right and left. A man of the people! Germany's Saviour! Trained party members in the audience raise their arms in salute and shout: *"Heil!"* Again *"Heil!"* Many join. Other arms shoot up. The third *"Heil!"* swells into a great ovation, rushing upward like a mighty benediction from the sea of arms.

A *crowd,* then, involves a temporary *physical* gathering of people, experiencing much the same reactions from the same stimuli. Another type of social interaction is that of people who are separated in space —as the radio "audience" or the newspaper "audience"—but who respond in various ways to common stimuli. Strictly speaking, such people are not an audience at all, but should be refered to as a *public.* The true *audience* situation is the subject of the following section.

▶ THE AUDIENCE

A SPECIAL CROWD

An audience is a specific type of crowd. In the audience situation people ordinarily come together for a specific purpose—to be instructed or to be entertained, but more commonly the latter. Even information-seeking audiences do not like to receive too much information, preferring rather to be entertained. The audience situation consists of a common polarization or focusing of attention toward a speaker ordinarily seated on a platform or in such a position that he can readily be seen. The importance of the seating arrangement is illustrated in the classroom, where members of the student "audience" who sit in the front and center of the class tend, in general, to receive the best grades.[11] This is due at least in part to the tendency of lecturers to speak most directly to those in the front center.

INDIVIDUAL PSYCHOLOGY OF THE AUDIENCE

The psychology of the audience itself is in the last analysis the psychology of individuals. Persons who make up an audience are, of course, motivated by the desires for *recognition, response, new experience,* and *security.* Through shoulder-to-shoulder relations with their fellows a sense of unity is achieved by the individual members of the audience. If the speaker is able to secure psychological identification of his hearers with himself, or with a cause, or with a person about whom he is speaking, he can win over most of the individuals. If he can secure a reasonable acceptance of his ideas among those through the center portion of his audience, he can note the irradiating effects of this acceptance, as seen in the overt expressions of his hearers, extending to those individuals in the periphery. The members of the audience respond not only to the speaker but to the stimuli which they receive from each other; these may be overt and obvious, or they may be subliminal stimuli.

An information-seeking audience, feeling intellectual, logical, and rational, finds it difficult to sustain attention over very many minutes unless entertainment and recreation are introduced. In fact, many a college classroom—consisting of students supposedly hungry for knowledge—is filled with individuals who are delighted if the professor misses a lecture (since that means freedom from the drudgery of information) and who at the ritualistic sound of a bell refuse to absorb any more information. Even when members of professional groups get together for a lecture, the talk "goes over" better if certain jokes and well-understood conditioned stimuli are thrown in by the speaker.

TYPES OF AUDIENCES

Audiences may be divided into five main types—(1) pedestrian, (2) passive, (3) selected, (4) concerted, and (5) organized.[12] (1) The *pedestrian* audience—for example, a street audience listening to an orator or salesman—is the lowest in degree of orientation to the speaker. (2) The *passive* audience is found at a concert, theater, or lecture. (3) The *selected* audience is illustrated by a conference, jury, or committee.

(4) The *concerted* audience is exemplified by a college class or graduate seminar. (5) The *organized* audience may be illustrated by a gymnasium class or a military unit.

AUDIENCE TECHNIQUES

The main techniques used in influencing audiences are: (1) getting *attention;* (2) arousing *interest;* (3) developing *impressions;* (4) producing *conviction;* (5) *directing* the members of an audience.[13] The use of these techniques varies according to the type of audience, as illustrated in Table 11. Thus, in the pedestrian audience all five techniques must be employed, in the organized type only one.

TABLE 11

Types of Audience and Techniques (From H. L. Hollingworth)

	Types of Audience				
	(1) *Pedestrian*	(2) *Passive*	(3) *Selected*	(4) *Concerted*	(5) *Organized*
Techniques	1. Attention				
	2. Interest	2. Interest			
	3. Impression	3. Impression	3. Impression		
	4. Conviction	4. Conviction	4. Conviction	4. Conviction	
	5. Direction	5. Direction	5. Direction	5. Direction	5. Direction

1. The first technique is that of obtaining the audience's *attention.* This is principally true of the *pedestrian* audience; in other cases the audience members are present because they *want* to give attention. The best method of arousing interest is through a sensory channel, not being used by the potential audience at the moment. Mechanical devices are bad on the whole, although they work well with the young or the dull audience. The performer usually tries first to get the attention of the most susceptible and through them to attract others in the group.

2. The second step is to hold the audience's *interest.* This is where the performer must begin in the case of the *passive* audience. The intrinsic interest of the subject matter is the main thing. Making humorous or complimentary remarks and mentioning topics of common concern are well-known methods of holding interest. Ritual and ceremony play an important role here, and things such as community singing are of great value—as in religious revivals and political rallies. There should be no distracting stimuli. The performer should not consult notes too frequently and should not use long sentences. Where there is a platform, it should be entirely within the range of the audience's attention.

3. The third step is to *impress* the audience. With a *selected* audience, this is the technique with which to begin. The audience is impressed by

both what it sees and what it hears. If diagrams are used, they should precede the oral exposition for the sake of clarity. Most people are sufficiently visual-minded to grasp things more easily when they are presented graphically or with gestures. Often more can be got across by several lines drawn on a blackboard or by a single gesture of the hand than by several minutes of vocal expression. The voice is of most value when variations in pitch, loudness, and timbre are utilized.

4. The fourth step is to *convince* the audience. Frequently this can be done most easily by emotional appeal. Then more intellectual appeals may be added. Whether members of the audience believe the speaker, is determined by their individual hopes and desires. If these are appealed to properly, the performer has little to worry about. The desires for *new experience, security, response,* and *recognition* are important variables.

5. The fifth step is that of *directing* the audience to some attitude or act. This task is the main one for the speaker. The strength of the speaker's suggestions depends upon spontaneity, vividness, and the prestige with which they are presented. Repetition is a potent factor. A slogan or catchword is effective as a formula for action. The audience is more easily aroused to laughter, anger, hate, and fear than to love and sympathy, partly because the former types of reactions are more easily recognized than others and thus are apt to be picked up more quickly by other people.

AN EXAMPLE

Mastery of an audience situation is illustrated by an account of how the great orator William Jennings Bryan delivered a speech to the people of a small university town in the South:

> He was not very popular with most of the two thousand people who gathered to hear him, but in the hour and thirty minutes in which he spoke he won them over completely. The first fifteen minutes of his address he spent in compliments regarding their "beautiful little city," reviewing its show places, and in praise of the "splendid mothers and fathers" of that city, with their high ideals and their sacrifices for their children and community. Interest was intense and I saw a man in front of me nudge his companion and remark, "Pretty good!" With this preparation, aided by his melodious voice, the orator spent thirty minutes telling jokes on himself and his opponents. He spared neither himself nor his political enemies. All he said was in good humor, but with the grateful attitude of his hearers, aroused by the previous fifteen minutes of compliments, the political jokes on himself were turned into material for sympathy, and those on his rivals into mild ridicule, by the method of negative suggestion. The man in front of me said, "He certainly bears no grudge!" And seemingly that was the way all of the audience felt. His apparent objectivity won their hearty approval. The next thirty minutes were spent in trite

and fulsome praise of American institutions, very melodiously spoken. He could make the most banal statement appear to be of the utmost importance by the way in which he said it. There were the usual remarks about the greatness of the founders of the republic, the wonderful document, our Constitution, which came inspired from their brains, the glorious devotion to democracy of the hero of the southern people, Jefferson, a hint at the sorrows for the "lost cause" now turned into an effort for achievement for the future, well chosen references to the blood shed on many battlefields in defense of the liberties of the American people, in which they had always done at least their share. Some of the women with memories were crying. The men looked self-conscious, stoical and proud of themselves. He had only been manipulating a common stock of suggestion stimuli, but he knew with the unerring skill of the practiced orator what responses were conditioned to these stimuli. He held the audience in the hollow of his hand and their beliefs on the tip of his tongue. And here, with his compliment to their martial defense of their liberties scarcely spoken, he turned to the fourth part of his oration and said, in the last fifteen minutes of his harangue, what he had come there to say. The hour and a quarter of flattery and sentimental truism had been only preparation. He assured them that a more insidious enemy than armies was invading their land and liberties, called upon them to protect the republic for their children against unscrupulous greed and conscienceless exploitation, and to choose Woodrow Wilson as the leader of their civic army to do battle with this modern monster. . . . He left the audience enthusiastic for the very principles which most of them had previously opposed, because he knew how to assimilate or condition his liberal program to their preconceived beliefs and emotions.[14]

PREPARATION OF A SPEECH

There are a number of well-known devices for preparing and presenting oral material effectively. One of the fundamentals is to study the vocabulary and beliefs of the audience to which you plan to speak. For example, if you are giving a speech on the psychology of hearing, it will not do to talk to an audience of laymen about an audio-oscillator with a frequency variable from zero to ten thousand double vibrations per second and an attenuation of ninety decibels; but you can discuss an instrument which gives out tones, both low and high, both loud and soft. There is all the difference in the world between presenting material to high-school girls and to a labor union. If you are delivering a speech to automobile salesmen, you will probably find them bored with a discussion of Aristotle, but tremendously interested in problems of advertising. If you are speaking to a parent-teacher association, do not talk to them about the mechanics of automobiles, but about problems of child psychology.

Consider, too, the ways in which words can be put together. Alliterative phrases are often effective—the consecration of a cathedral, the might of a machine, the purity of pearls, the power of poetry. Regardless of the precise meaning of these words, the phraseology is such as to produce favorable responses in your hearers.

DEVICES WITHIN THE AUDIENCE

Certain devices within the audience itself help to achieve psychological unity.[15] First of all, the people in an audience should be induced to sit close together. Where there are not only psychological but also physiological shoulder-to-shoulder relationships, a greater sense of unity and coordination is developed. Actual touching of elbows adds to this. A type of hall is selected where the great majority of seats will be filled. It is much better psychologically to seat fifty people in a room which will hold only fifty or sixty than it is to bring the same fifty people together in a hall which could seat two hundred. If there is an overflow and some have to stand, the meeting is apt to be a success. To say "it was hard to get in" is practically the same as saying "the meeting was a success."

The mechanisms of ritual are often used effectively. The use of a joke at the beginning of a speech is notorious. If people can be induced to stand in respect for some cause or individual at the very outset of a talk, or to applaud as a group, or to sing in unison, or in some other way to be made to feel that they are commonly knit together in one organization, they will be won over more than halfway. And audiences respond rather well to terms and ideas to which they have been conditioned even though they do not know the precise meaning of the terms.

PRESENTATION OF A SPEECH

Various "tips" or rules can be laid down for the presentation of a speech:

1. Advance to the speaker's platform with a firm step. Do not mince.
2. Place the weight mainly on one foot rather than on both.
3. Never begin a speech at once. Wait until your hearers have become attentive.
4. At the outset, glance around and catch the eyes of the majority of your hearers to be sure that they are interested in you.
5. Speak in a clear, but not necessarily loud, voice.
6. Watch your audience all the time. Look directly at your hearers, not at some mythical object on the floor or ceiling.
7. When you move to one side of the room, speak to the people on that side.
8. Do not apologize for your speech, either for its content or for its delivery.
9. Likewise, speak with authority. Hearers listen to the person who speaks as if he means it, but do not pay much attention to an uncertain, timid speaker.

10. Secure the confidence of your hearers at the outset by demonstrating that you are one of the group. Do not "talk down" to your hearers as if you were a rank outsider.

11. Use figures of speech, clever alliterative devices, and examples frequently.

12. Change tones when the meaning demands it.

13. Realize that your hearers do not know ahead of time about the outline which you have in mind. Therefore, make it perfectly clear to them where the introductory portion lies; and at the end, give a conclusion. Similarly, make it perfectly apparent when you have left one point and gone on to the next.

14. Be natural. Rather than using stilted gestures, do things which are natural to you as an individual. If it comes easy to put one hand in your pocket, put one hand in your pocket.

15. Perhaps the most vital rule of all is: Tell your hearers what you are going to tell them—then tell them—and then tell them what you have told them.

PSYCHOLOGICAL, NOT LOGICAL, VALUES

Many an audience—or public—is swayed more by emotional than intellectual appeals. Logic is important, but psychology is more so. This is largely the psychology of close identification of the speaker with his audience or public, and of them with him. Every topnotcher on the radio knows this. The person represented by the radio voice may become very real. When Mrs. Emily Post was broadcasting, one woman would not listen to this arbiter of good manners without taking her apron off. Another always had tea during Mrs. Post's talk, one cup for herself and "one cup always, dear Mrs. Post, for you."[16] An excellent example of identification is Ted Malone's daily noon broadcast of some years ago, *Between the Bookends*—largely for a female radio audience. A typical program opens with soft music and slow soothing speech:

> Hello there
>
> Thank you
> I heard you answer me *that* time
> I know you have before
> sometimes aloud
> sometimes silently
> It's sort of a little game, isn't it?
> You see, I play it, too.
>
> Oh, yes—I do.
> I really feel I talk with you.

. . . . .

You really know more about me—
whether you realize it or not—
than any biography will ever tell.
And I know more about you
than you dream.
I know your height
I know your age
I know many of your likes and dislikes—
I know you.

No, I mean *you*—
you, who just now wondered if *I were*
really talking to some *one—today*—
someone *else*
I am—
but not someone *else*.

How shall I identify you to make you
know—now and always—that I really *know* you and
that these very little visits are very, very real to me?[17]

In the great game of politics, two fundamental principles are found.[18] *Rule 1.* Give them a good show. As a political asset, the ability to dramatize your issue or yourself is hard to beat. It is worth any amount of argument, statistics, facts. *Rule 2.* Probably the most important single accomplishment for the politically ambitious, the most effective asset they can acquire, is the fine art of seeming to say something without doing so.

As an example, an analysis of Hitler's speeches published in book form as *My New Order* reveals that over 80 per cent were merely elaborations of the basic themes, "they are weak"—"we are strong"; and "they are evil"—"we are good."[19] The pronoun "they" had a varying content—the Jews, the Marxists, the bourgeoisie, the English, etc.—and so did the evilness attributed to them—they kill, they rob, they enslave, they lie, they are cowards, they poison our blood, they are different from us, etc.

The rules above are presented, not necessarily for you to employ, but so that you may recognize them when they are employed on you. Their use is by no means limited to the political scene. They are used both with intelligent and unintelligent groups, with audiences of one sex and in mixed groups, with the economically secure and insecure. Following are examples from meetings of a national women's patriotic society—composed of intelligent women—and of Father Divine. The first quotation is from the address of the president of the patriotic society at an annual meeting. The second is a description of a meeting in the "kingdom" of a Negro who calls himself God, Father Divine. Here are two entirely different social groups, but the members of each are responding to a similar flow of words in their particular leader. The president of the women's organization began her address as follows:

> . . . *Bearers of Freedom's torch! Voices proclaiming liberty and opportunity for all, I salute you!*
>
> I rejoice in the work you are doing, and as I pass from state to state and see the fruits of your labors, I am filled with admiration and with wonder. Where inspiring spirits are at work, there is progress, there is hope!
>
> This memorable week . . . finds you on your annual pilgrimage, . . . bearing your gifts of service, prepared to render account of your stewardship, and to formulate plans for the future. . . .
>
> So onward and upward let us move, preserving the ideals entrusted to our care, and the country of our heritage, with feet well established in the past, with hands devoted to the problems of the present and with hearts set toward the realization of America's dream.[20]

Compare this with the following speech of Father Divine to his "children" (followers):

> Father rises to speak. His opening words sustain the identity in the minds of the children. "Peace, everyone." "Peace, Father," shout the children. "Here you are and there I am, there I sit and here you stand, and yet I sit and stand as well as sit in the midst of the children of men. As you are so am I and as you may be, so am I that you might be partakers of the Nature and the Characteristics of Christ." Or "Here we all are again, just the way we should be, just as I am. When I say, 'Here we all are again,' it means nothing less than the consciousness of the Allness of God in the likeness of man, and the nothingness of man, where such a recognition stands. Now isn't that wonderful? A place wherein you can stand, where all the Allness of God and the nothingness of matter will be a reality to you."[21]

This is *not* an attempt to discredit either the members of the women's organization or the followers of Father Divine. These samples are given to show that similar techniques are used effectively with both men and women, old and young, intelligent and unintelligent, dark-skinned and light-skinned. In neither instance is there much factual content to what the leader says, but there is great emotional appeal.

FIG. 20. GIRL CHASES BOY ON "SADIE HAWKINS DAY"[22]

The adoption of Sadie Hawkins Day as an unofficial U. S. collegiate holiday is a phenomenon due largely to modern syndicated journalism, since *Li'l Abner* is followed by millions of readers in hundreds of newspapers from coast to coast.

▶ BOOMS, CRAZES, FADS AND FASHIONS

IRRATIONAL WAYS OF BEHAVIOR

Many types of social behavior are not rational and can be dismissed on logical grounds. Yet they are perfectly normal phenomena of intelligent, civilized people; that is, they are normal in the sense that they exist for large numbers of people, as was indicated in the last section of Chapter 9. Changes in our "ways" are not always orderly or systematic but may grow up without rhyme or reason and continue on an illogical level.

Thus, on "Sadie Hawkins Day" every year, girls chase boys in colleges and schools all over the United States—an overt violation of our usual "ways." See Figure 20. Every fall, college freshmen and sophomores manage to get themselves as dirty as possible on a chosen afternoon in some kind of a unique contest, in order to settle a question such as whether the freshmen must wear a certain kind of headgear. For an example, see Figure 21.

Some irrational ways of behavior become a fairly permanent part of our culture if they have social significance, or if they provide sufficient means of diversion and relaxation to be carried over from one period or from one region to another. Certain unique patterns of behavior—temporary folkways, found in limited groups—have been designated as (1) booms, (2) crazes, and (3) fads and fashions.

BOOMS

The word "boom" refers to a rather long-time deviation from usual social behavior, as contrasted with fads and fashions which are more temporary in nature. That is, booms ordinarily build up rather slowly, gradually increase in scope until large numbers of people are affected, and then collapse rather suddenly. Many writers on social psychology point out instances of booms in history, but most of these have their counterparts today. For example, some write about the famous tulip mania in Holland in 1634 when tulip bulbs went sky-high in price; but have you ever contemplated the stock-market boom of the 1920's or the Florida land boom of the same period?

CRAZES

The word "craze" refers to a deviation in social behavior which grows up in an irrational way much faster than a boom, but collapses just as suddenly. Crazes are usually even less rational than fads or fashions, although they may grow out of fads and fashions. The "great fear" in France in 1789 illustrates the craze:

FIG. 21. GREASY POLE FIGHT BETWEEN FRESHMEN AND SOPHOMORES[23]

In this college, if the freshmen can fight through the defending sophomores, wade through a ditch of crankcase oil, climb up a 15-foot greased steel pole, and pull down a green flag at its top, then the entire first-year class may discard its traditional headgear—green "dinks." If not, they must wear the dinks until the homecoming football game in November.

> The months of July and August may be called the months of the "great fear." Men were afraid, both in town and country, of they knew not what. How this universal feeling of terror arose cannot be proved, but it was actually deemed necessary in some districts for a distinct denial to be published to the report that the king had paid brigands to rob the people. . . . This "great fear" was generally expressed in the words "The brigands are coming." Who the brigands were, whence they came, or whither they were going, nobody knew; but that the brigands were coming, nobody doubted.[24]

This had a modern counterpart in the late 1930's. Nearly everyone who expressed a liberal idea with regard to labor problems, academic freedom, racial or religious prejudice, wage-and-hours legislation, child labor, freedom of speech, the rights of women, or any question of social significance was accused either of being a Communist or a "dupe" of Moscow.

Some years back the popular crazes were the ouija board, flag-pole sitting, dance marathons, and walkathons, miniature golf, and the send-a-dime chain-letter craze. In 1939 college boys were having contests to see who could eat the most goldfish, *alive*. See Figure 22.

FADS AND FASHIONS

The words "fashion" and "fad" refer to trivial deviations from usual behavior which are noninstitutionalized and unstable, but which occasionally become a fairly permanent part of our culture. Fads and fashions may consist of either overt or covert forms of behavior, involving action or thought patterns. They are practically synonymous, although a rough distinction is that fads are likely to be more unstable and ephemeral than fashions. That is, temporary fads may grow into fashions in terms of greater intensity, duration, and adoption.

Definition of Fashion. The term "fashion" as used here is *not* limited to the conventional usages of "people of polite society." Fashions exist not only among the socially elite but also among sharecroppers, clerks, children, and members of all strata of society. Fashion may be defined as "impermanent convention or socially-accepted habit marked by fluctuation and change."[25] Clothes represent an outstanding example of fashion, but not the only one. The prevailing modes in manners, morals, ornamentation, architecture, vehicles, conversation, vocabulary, music, literature, art, diet, religion, and philosophy are also among the fashions of our times.

Examples of Fads and Fashions. Have you ever heard of any of the following fads—making whoopee, flea-hop dancing, the Varsity drag, Black Bottom, King Tut crickets? Did you ever use any of the following expressions—"And how!," "Oh, ye-a-h?," "Knock, knock, who's there?" "Don't hand me any of that jive," or "Kilroy was here"? Have you ever

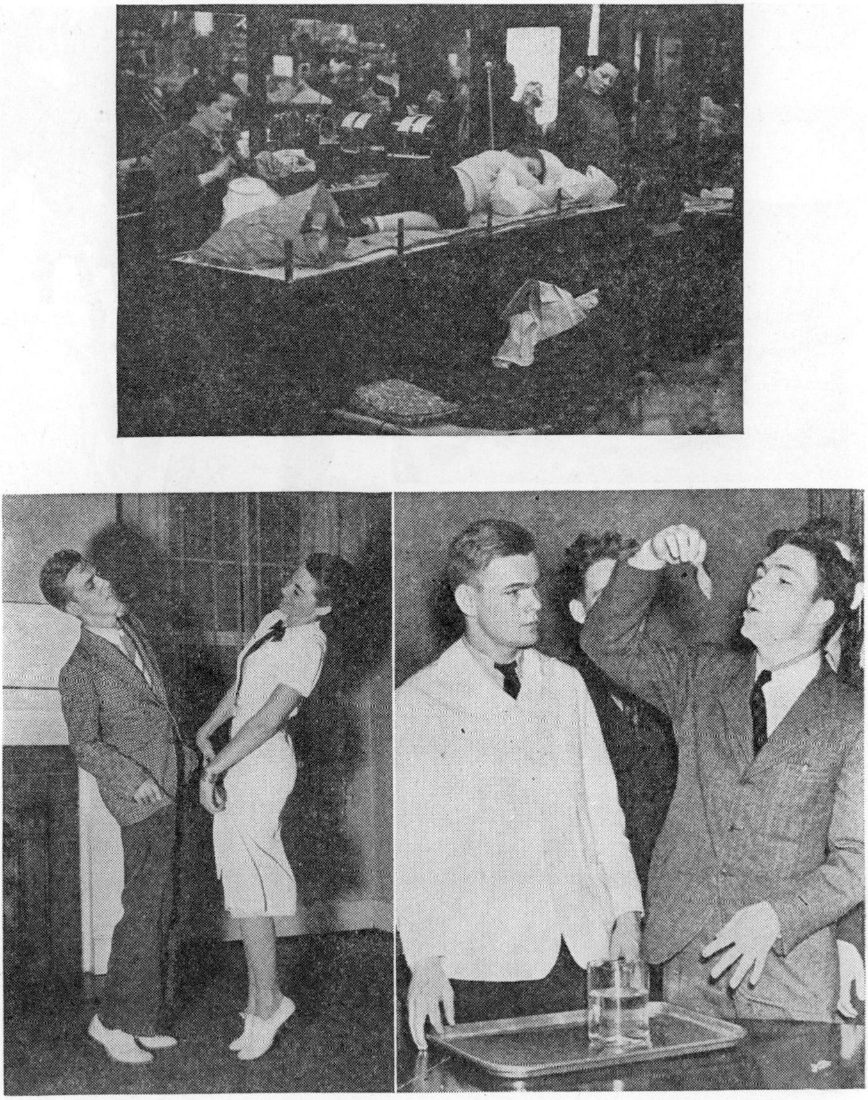

Fig. 22. SOME EXAMPLES OF IRRATIONAL BEHAVIOR OF THE 1930's[26]

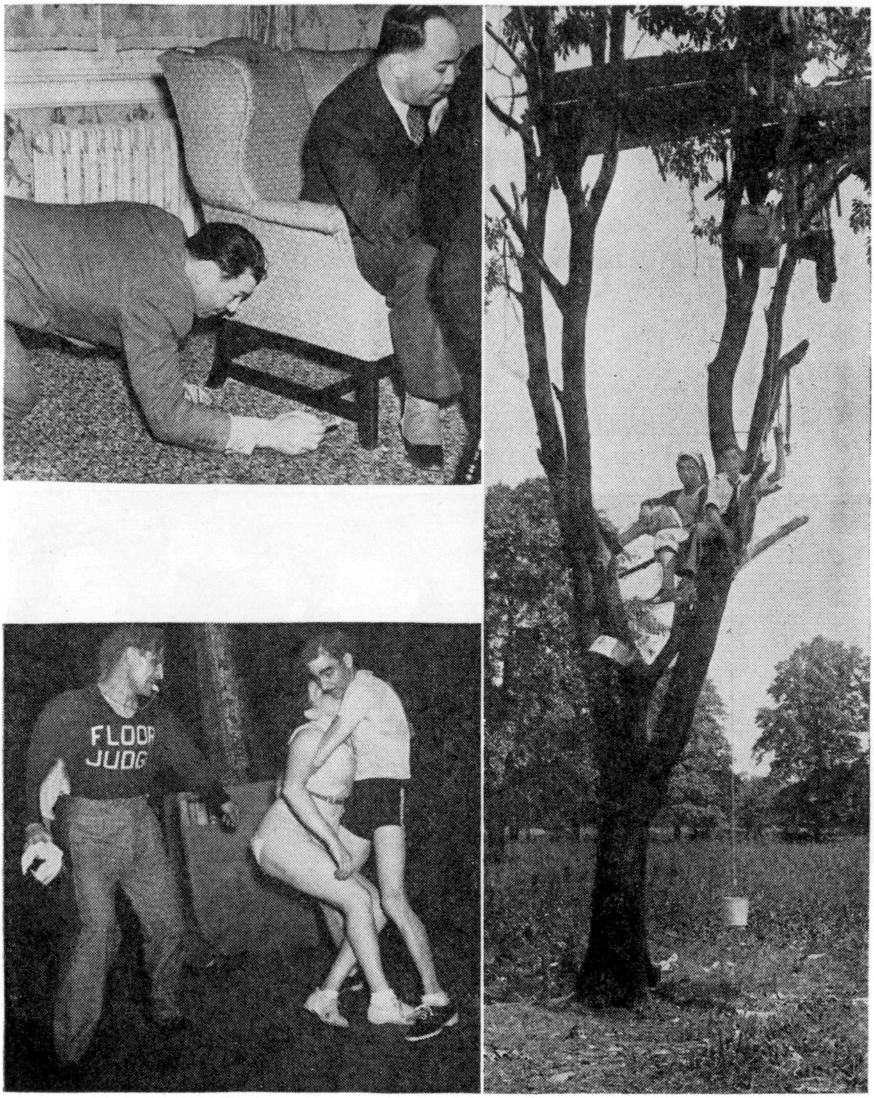

FIG. 22 (*continued*)

referred to other people as "droops," "drips," or "meatballs"? Skilled language performance of this sort is supposed to prove that you are "hep" or "in the know." At one time you were socially acceptable by glibly replying to any remark, "Oh, ye-a-h?" with rising inflection.

Many fads and fashions are not recognized by us as fads and fashions if we are caught up in them. It is only by looking back on them that we can recognize them for what they are or were. Here, for example, are some health fads listed by one writer:

> I can recall, for instance, the national sweep of Fletcherism—a medical principle which involved the chewing of food to impalpability and the subsequent permitting of it to trickle down the throat. . . . Some while later experiment proved that the amount of chewing applied upon beef, at least, had little to do with the speed of its digestion and, indeed, retarded it. People were urged to bolt down their beef in gobbets. The fresh-air school had everybody down with pneumonia. . . . There was a fad for cutting out tonsils, one for taking out wombs, and at least one each for removing breasts, adenoids, glands, and other vital objects. There was a bran and salad fad that must have given colitis to a tenth of the populace. . . . There was a fruit juice fad. . . . People were thrust into the sunshine for incredible periods; then it was discovered that too much sunshine is as onerous to the body as too little. . . . There are at least fifteen different fads that stem from the sinuses.[27]

Crossword puzzles, jig-saw puzzles, mah jong, riddles, and anagrams have come and in most cases gone. The radio has been jammed full of "quiz" programs—"Information, Please," "Professor Quiz," "Askit-Basket," and countless others. Grinning at us from our drinking-glasses, dishes, and paper weights have been Snow White and the Seven Dwarfs, Mickey Mouse, and Donald Duck. "Let's make whoopee" of a few years ago has died out and more recently "Confidentially, it stinks" was the pet phrase. Maybe both are "in the groove." The "upper classes" feel democratic when they use slang, and commoners are ultrasmart when they say, "But definitely" and "How amusing."

Fads and fashions may be a means of entree into certain social groups. Consider, for instance, the matter of pale or tanned skin. During the period when we were primarily an agricultural nation it was fashionable for women to be fair because a tanned skin indicated that a woman worked in the fields.[28] Sunbonnets were popular. It is fashionable today to show that you are a person of leisure by having a good sun tan; sun lamps are therefore used for purposes other than health.

Mrs. Emily Post is an arbiter of fashions concerned not with what to wear, but what to do and how to do it. She tells you how to go to bed on a Pullman, what clothes to wear when traveling in Europe, how to dine in a restaurant, how much to tip, and how to order breakfast in your room.

Souvenir collecting is an example on a wholesale scale of fadlike behavior. It has been estimated that Americans spend for souvenirs from $10,000,000 to $20,000,000 per year. The New York World's Fair of 1939 inspired 12,000 different designs of the trylon and perisphere which 900 dealers built into 26,000 different articles.[29]

> One chain store . . . reported disposing of 4,000 dozen souvenir scarves weekly at 25 cents each. Seventy companies alone [were] turning out trylon-and-perisphere ash trays, no two makes alike. The complete list [ran] from automobile emblems to wrappers, and [included] balloons, bar accessories, carpet sweepers, compasses, diaries, footballs, gum, lipstick, needles, pajamas, rattles, shoes and turtles. . . .
>
> The right to sell Fair novelties on the grounds was acquired by the Exposition Souvenir Corporation of Corona. This company [had] eighty stands and 325 employes, and I. B. Ury, its head, says the take [was] about $7,000 a day. If that sounds good, Mr. Ury remembers doing $35,000 worth of business one day at the Chicago Fair in 1933.[30]

Look about you at the automobiles loaded down with gimcracks. Automobile-accessory stores list over one thousand different items which can be added to an automobile. The total weight of all of them would come to approximately three hundred pounds and would cost at prewar prices, depending on the grade, from $200 to $400.[31] Some automobiles seem to be well on their way to attainment of all. Look at cars with coon tails streaming from the radiator cap; red, green, and amber jewels on the license plates; clearance lights on the running board; flopping mud guards; fog lamps; musical horns; fancy mirrors; gear-shift knobs; steering-column note pads; assist cords; monkeys, and "nudies" hung up in the rear window to shimmer and shake.

Rational Fads May Survive. Some of these apparently superficial fads and fashions survive over a period of many years. As examples, eyelash curlers could be originally classed as a fad or fashion, yet have apparently survived because of value. Men's wrist watches were looked upon at first as "effeminate" until taken up by various military men, engineers, and other outdoor men. Stop signs on automobiles were simply fads in the 1920's but have since become a stable part of our culture. Bobbed hair is another example. Where fads and fashions have certain rational and logical aspects, they often survive.

Actually most fads survive less than a year.[32] In Bogardus's list of fads, 63 per cent have to do with women's dress and decoration (57 per cent) and men's clothes (16 per cent).

The Psychology of Clothes. What, then, about the psychology of clothes? Most of us, especially men, burden ourselves with all sorts of odd-fitting and uncomfortable materials which do not keep us too cool in summer or warm in winter. What are the motivating factors? The wearing of clothing is not motivated by the desire for modesty and protection alone.

Consider the discussion of *imitation* and *uniformity of action* in the last chapter. We tend to dress alike because uniformity of action is economical and time-saving, in order to *avoid the dissapproval of others,* and for purposes of *self-elevation.* "The high gloss of a gentleman's hat or a patent-leather shoe has no more of intrinsic beauty than a similarly high gloss on a threadbare sleeve; and yet . . . all wellbred people (in the Occidental civilised communities) . . . cleave to the one as a phenomenon of great beauty, and eschew the other as offensive."[33] Also the processes of *compensation, identification, projection, rationalization,* and *regression* are at work. By wearing a garb like a movie star's, we can identify ourselves with our hero or heroine. We can wear ankle socks or put on our sweaters backward, thus regressing to a more infantile level.

By means of our clothing we can call attention to ourselves and compensate for defects in other fields. Some data indicate that a large percentage of people choose their clothes with the idea of covering up certain defects.[34] The desires for *new experience, security, response,* and *recognition* are other important motivating forces in spending money for clothing.[35] The desire to remain secure or protect ourselves from warmth or cold are apparently not so important as our wish to appear pleasant in the eyes of other people. E. L. Thorndike found that only 41 per cent of the amount expended for clothing is for a shield against cold, heat, and wet.[36] The balance was attributed to the desire for approval of others, self-approval, pleasure in courtship and sex activities, pleasures of vision, mastery over others, to win affection, and for protection against animals and disease.

Women's Styles. There are differences, of course, in the motivating factors for men and women in their dress. In his *Theory of the Leisure Class* Veblen pointed out that woman, in addition to being a sex object for man, has also served as a means for his social recognition.[37] She may serve as a means of his vicarious indulgence in conspicuous waste, and the more she indulges, the greater may be his prestige. Thus, the male may buy his mate a fur coat not merely out of generosity but because it demonstrates his high financial status. This is an example of what Veblen calls "conspicuous consumption."

Women's styles also change with different sex *motifs.* The "boyish" flat-chested women of the 1920's attained full-blown maturity in the 1930's, and in the 1940's went in for the "uplift" brassiere. The pictures

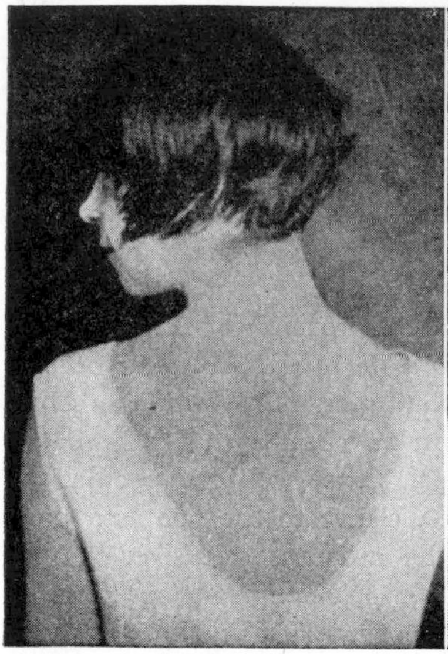

"Windblown" bob

Beach pajamas

Knitted cardigan suit

Evening dress

FIG. 23. WOMEN'S STYLES OF THE 1930's[38]

in Figure 23 give some indication of what was "stylish" over a period of ten years in the 1930's, and of how great the changes were.

Many women copy men's clothes—men's slacks, man-tailored suits, and mannish hats—but the reverse occurs infrequently. In what is primarily a "man's world," it is not surprising to find some of the aspects of men's behavior being copied by members of the sex which has the less dominant role. One survey shows that a fairly high percentage of girls have at some time wished to be of the opposite sex, whereas comparatively few boys have ever wanted to be girls.[39] Adoption of men's clothing styles, haircuts, and even language behavior may be used by women, who have occupied a relatively inferior role until quite recently, as a means of attaining greater dominance.

As for the general uniformity and slowness of change in men's styles, a prevalent male attitude in our culture is not to waste too much time on such trivia as clothing, for other matters such as business are more important. There is only one men's magazine which regularly shows men's clothing fashions, as contrasted with the large number of women's publications which deal with clothes and dress design. Actually styles in men's clothing do change over the years, as shown in Figure 24, but the process is much slower than in the case of women's styles.

The Spread of Fashions. How do clothing fashions spread? First of all, they are handed down from one generation to another. Second, they spread from one group to another, either from community to community or within a community.[40] Historically, most clothing fashions have spread downward, that is, from the socially elite to the lower classes. In fact, most styles go out when they "become common." More recently, however, opposite trends have occasionally been observed; in the late 1930's not only did many women copy their clothes after the Duchess of Windsor and many men buy black Homburg hats because worn by Sir Anthony Eden, but some styles spread from the working groups upward to the leisure classes. Examples are the peasant costumes worn by women in 1938, their coveralls in 1939, and the slacks which began to be worn by men in 1939 and 1940.

In an empirical study of the spread of fads and fashions among undergraduates on one college campus, Janney found that a very small number of girls, who were members of prestige-bearing cliques and who were leaders in choreography, design, and similar activities, originated most of the fads.[41]

The spread of fashions can also be attributed to designers and manufacturers who deliberately change or alter styles to make money.[42] Kroeber has shown the increased speed of change in women's styles from 1844 to 1919.[43] People do not want to wear exactly what everybody else is wearing; one can attain a maximum of prestige by being somewhat different, if he is not too much so. It is partly due to this fact that labels have social value.

FIG. 24. CHANGES IN MEN'S STYLES[44]

"Made in France" boosts the price of a garment as contrasted with "Made in Brooklyn." The stamp "Imported" boosts the price as compared with home products exactly comparable in every detail. The labels of fashionable shops are so important that many a woman carefully hangs her coat or wrap over the back of her chair so that the label will show; and some clever manufacturers put the tags in upside down so that they can be read by those sitting behind the wearer's chair. War always has its effect on styles. In the fall of 1939 curls were shorn off, women's slacks and rough sweaters appeared more frequently; and clothes of this sort were prevalent in many cities during the war years.

Clothing and Morality. How people dress is also related to the problem of morality. By dressing in striking ways greater prestige is attained, as well as more success in the competition for affectionate response. Fashions in dress, particularly among women, permit a rather wide range of stimuli for the exhibition of the sex drive. Therefore, it is not surprising to find that certain styles of dress are considered taboo, although these vary with time and place. The portion of the body which must not be revealed has varied from the ankle to the "midriff." It also depends on the culture and the times, there being no universal pattern of modesty or immodesty. In the Philippines it is the navel, among Chinese women the feet, among Arab women in Egypt the top and back of the head which must be concealed.

In the United States women are arrested sometimes for wearing on a city street a costume which is accepted on the beach. Certain groups become concerned if dresses are too far above the floor or if necklines are too low. It has even been suggested that the number of sex crimes might increase during those periods when greater portions of female anatomy are revealed.

One analysis, for the years 1914 to 1940, shows a rather close relationship between length of skirt and business conditions, the years when skirts were a greater distance from the floor also being the years of greatest industrial production.[45]

Parents and older persons of each succeeding generation are shocked at the clothing of the younger people. But a style war arose in one town when the parent-teacher association took active steps to force girls to give up short skirts, bobbed hair, and other signs of "flapperism." The young girls stormed the meeting, chanting as they marched:

I can show my shoulders,
I can show my knees.
I'm a free-born American
And can show what I please.

REASONS FOR READY ACCEPTANCE OF IRRATIONAL WAYS

The psychology of booms, crazes, fads and fashions indicates that people easily fall into irrational ways of behavior. Why do they? One reason is that we want new experiences, adventures, and thrills. We tire of doing the same old things day in and day out. We crave new experience. Adherence to fads and other irrational ways of behavior is a means of releasing tensions and escaping from inhibitions.

Then, too, we gain prestige, superiority, and even dominant social status by accepting the fashions of our day. From infancy on we strive to be noticed, and in adult life we still want to get attention. We do this in ways that are conspicuous, but not too conspicuous. We have *ambivalent* tendencies in that we want to be very individualistic and yet, at one and the same time, follow the herd. We can attain our desires for individuality by introducing the current fad to our intimate group, while we are still doing what "everyone" else does.

Imitation, suggestion and the *desire for social approval* also make us accept fads. One girl wears a bow or flower in her hair, and the next day ten girls are displaying ribbons or flowers. Finally, fads are commercialized as a means for making money and are practically forced upon us through high-powered advertising.

QUESTIONS AND PROBLEMS FOR DISCUSSION

1. *What is the significance of the "group-mind" controversy?*
2. *Make a scientific analysis of some crowd in action. How was it formed? What attracted it? How was it dispersed? Why? Be objective.*
3. *"The crowd does not change the fundamental attitudes of its members very much, but does change the overt behavior in which their attitudes are expressed." Do you agree or disagree? Why?*
4. *Show the psychological effects on an individual of becoming part of an audience.*
5. *What have you learned in this and the preceding chapters that will be of use to you in making an effective speech in public?*
6. *Suppose you were setting up a radio program concerned with educational broadcasting. What principles of learning and remembering would you apply?*
7. *"He who wants to persuade should put his trust not in the right argument, but in the right word. . . . Give me the right word and the right accent, and I will move the world." Find an example of this (1) in your daily newspaper; (2) in a radio broadcast.*
8. *Why do men seldom, if ever, adopt women's styles?*

RECOMMENDED READINGS

Hollingworth, H. L., *The Psychology of the Audience.* New York: American Book Company, 1935.

Hurlock, E. B., *The Psychology of Dress: An Analysis of Fashion and Its Motive*. New York: The Ronald Press Company, 1929.

Kent, F., *Political Behavior: The Heretofore Unwritten Laws, Customs, and Principles of Politics as Practiced in the United States*. New York: William Morrow & Company, 1928.

Le Bon, G., *The Crowd: A Study of the Popular Mind*. New York: The Macmillan Company, 1925.

Lee, A. M., and Lee, E. B., *The Fine Art of Propaganda: A Study of Father Coughlin's Speeches*. New York: Harcourt, Brace and Company, 1939.

Martin, E. D., *The Behavior of Crowds: A Psychological Study*. New York: Harper & Brothers, 1920.

Murphy, L. B., and Murphy, G., "The Influence of Social Situations upon the Behavior of Children." In Murchison, C. (editor), *A Handbook of Social Psychology*. Worcester: Clark University Press, 1935, Chap. 22.

Nystrom, P. H., *Economics of Fashion*. New York: The Ronald Press Company, 1928.

Scott, W. D., *The Psychology of Public Speaking*. New York: Noble and Noble, 1926.

Veblen, T., *The Theory of the Leisure Class*. New York: Modern Library, Inc., 1934.

Yeager, W. H., *Effective Speaking for Every Occasion*. New York: Prentice-Hall, Inc., 1940.

Yeager, W. H., and Sandford, W. P., *Principles of Effective Speaking: A Textbook for Colleges and Universities*. New York: Thomas Nelson and Sons, 1934.

*Newcomb, T. M., Hartley, E. L., and others (editors), *Readings in Social Psychology*. New York: Henry Holt and Company, Inc., 1947. (The following selections are listed according to the sequence of related discussions in the chapter you have just read.)

Johnson, D. M., The 'Phantom Anesthetist' of Mattoon: A Field Study of Mass Hysteria," pp. 639-650.

Douglass, J. H., "The Funeral of 'Sister President,'" pp. 650-654.

CHAPTER THIRTEEN

SEX, DOMINANCE, AND PRESTIGE

MASCULINITY AND FEMININITY. Significance of Sex—Use of Terms—Sex Differences—(1) Biological Differences—(2) Influence of Culture Patterns—(3) Differences in Training—The Kinsey Report—Sex Behavior of American Males / DOMINANCE IN SEXUAL AND SOCIAL BEHAVIOR. Dominance and Subordination in Other Species—Maslow's First Investigation—"Prostitution" Behavior—Maslow's Second Study—A Follow-up Investigation—Interpretations of These Data—(1) Tissue Needs—(2) Repression—(3) "Masking" of Sex Drive—(4) "Dating" Behavior—(5) Hierarchy Changes with Different Numbers / DOMINANCE FEELING, DOMINANCE BEHAVIOR, AND DOMINANCE STATUS. The Distinctions—Domination—Adoption of Dominant and Subordinate Ways—Competitive Behavior in Children—Variations in Dominance Behavior—Difficulties of Predicting Dominance Status—Intimacy as a Factor in Dominance Behavior.

▶ MASCULINITY AND FEMININITY

SIGNIFICANCE OF SEX

Sex is important. Although this was often denied in your great-grandmother's time, most people admit it today. The influence of sex is seen in art, literature, the theater, movies, recreation, religion, and economic and political life. However, many of those who will admit that sexual aspects of behavior are significant still avoid objective discussions of sexual behavior and attitudes. The "hush-hush" idea still tends to persist.

To say that sex is important does *not* imply that sex is the only key to human behavior. The sex life of an individual is only one aspect of his total personality. We have already seen that *conditioning, suggestion, imitation,* and other psychological mechanisms do not necessarily cut across sexual factors. Sexual behavior and attitudes are simply parts of man's total behavior which cannot be neglected if we are to understand his dominance behavior, his leadership in certain situations, and various types of social interaction.

USE OF TERMS

The words "sex" or "sex activity," as used in the present discussion, do not always imply sexual intercourse. This may be included, but the term is not to be limited in that way. After all, having a date, going to the movies with a friend of the opposite sex, attending a dance, romantic courtship, "necking or petting," the use of affectionate words—all these come under the general category of sex activity, *psychologically* speaking. In other words, the term "sex behavior" may refer to dating, or romantic and affectionate love, physiological sex activities, or any combination of these.

SEX DIFFERENCES

The actual sex activities carried on by any given individual depend upon the interrelation between (1) his biological make-up, including not only "maleness" or "femaleness," but general physique and health; (2) the folkways, customs, and mores of the culture in which he lives; and (3) the particular set of conditioning experiences which he as an individual has undergone.

Over two thousand years ago, Aristotle summed up his ideas as to sex difference in this way:

> Woman is more compassionate than man, and has a greater propensity to tears. She is, also, more envious, more querulous, more slanderous and more contentious. Farther still, the female is more dispirited, more despondent, more imprudent and more given to falsehood than the male. She is, likewise, more easily deceived, and more apt to remember, and again, the female is more vigilant, less active and in short, less disposed to motion, and receptive of less nutriment than the male. But the male . . . is more disposed to give assistance in danger, and is more courageous than the female. . . .[1]

Most people today still think of men and women in much the same way that Aristotle did. All we need to do is to examine the place of woman in the realms of business, science, art, and religion, in order to realize how far-reaching the implications of these beliefs are. The "man in the street" still holds to the belief that men and women are two utterly different species of mankind. Not only are they physiologically different, says he, but they are different in terms of their thinking—"Women don't think through a problem the same way that men do"—and in terms of their emotional behavior—"Women are more emotional than men; they break down and resort to tears." What are the actual facts of the case?

1. *Biological Differences.* First of all, there are obvious sex differences of a physiological sort. Not only are there differences in physical structure, sexual equipment, and secondary sex characteristics, but also in activities. Thus, in general, men have greater muscular strength than women, a more constant body temperature, a higher basal metabolism, and a higher muscular tension while at rest; and they are, of course, free from such physiological processes as menstruation and childbearing.

Naturally, then, we should expect some differences between the two sexes as a counterpart to these differences in physiological background. Yet, strangely enough, there are fewer *psychological* sex differences than might be expected. The psychological behavior of boys and girls is often quite similar so far as test scores are concerned, although some differences do show up. A slight superiority of boys over girls has been found in studies of mechanical ability, while girls seems to be better in language facility, beginning to talk earlier than boys and surpassing them later on in most verbal activities. (Some men insist that even after little girls grow up they continue to talk indefinitely.) Data on sex differences may be summarized as follows:[2]

1. General intelligence does not favor one sex over the other.
2. There are *slight* differences in:
   a. Psychophysical tasks.
   b. The performance of specific mental tasks.
3. There are *fairly large* differences in:
   a. Tasks involving intellectual and physical elements, that is, skill plus bodily strength.
   b. Tasks involving intellectual plus social elements.
4. There are *great* differences in complex activities involving intellectual element plus:
   a. Large strength element, or
   b. Large social element, or
   c. Close relationship to biological function, or
   d. Any combination of these.

To account for these differences simply on the basis of original nature would be to tell only half of the truth or less. As already indicated, such psychological sex differences as are found can be accounted for on the basis of biological differences, *plus* the influence of the culture patterns, *plus* differences in training. The interplay of these three sets of factors is evident in differences in social attitudes:

> The more marked social orientation of girls, present in early childhood, is fostered by the cultural pressures directed toward marriage and motherhood. At the same time, the free expression of social impulses is hindered both by certain cultural inhibitions and by subjective inferiorities which are more prevalent in females. The result is that despite their stronger social interests, women appear more introverted than men when the measure of introversion is based on behavior or on reports of behavior.[3]

2. *Influence of Culture Patterns.* In social psychology we are concerned not only with the physiology of sex differences, but also with

differences between the two sexes in attitudes and ways of thinking that are dictated by the culture into which we are born. The problem of *maleness* or *femaleness* is a biological problem, but in social psychology we are more interested in those aspects of personality called *masculinity* and *femininity*. The mere fact that one is physiologically a male is no guarantee that he either feels or behaves like a male, that is, in terms of our particular culture. Similarly, the fact that one is a female physiologically is no guarantee that she is "feminine" in terms of the characteristics of our culture. Earlier we described some types of sexual behavior in cultures other than our own. Malinowski noted in the Trobriand Islands that very active sex behavior starts at an extremely early age, actual sexual intercourse occurring as early as six or eight years for girls and as early as ten or twelve years of age for boys. The parents are indifferent to these activities. In Samoa, Mead found almost no taboos on free indulgence in heterosexual relations, and noted the natural and unrepressed attitudes of girls toward sex life. On the other hand, there seems to be no one-to-one relationship between "civilization" and taboos on sexual behavior; in fact, the taboos which exist with regard to sexual conduct are in many instances very far-reaching in primitive groups, with even greater regulation than in highly civilized cultures.

Also, it is difficult to say what is the best type of behavior for the two sexes, except in terms of cultural standards. We have previously noted (Chapter 4) from the work of Mead that sex—that is, being a male or female—is not necessarily linked with being either aggressive or passive.[4] In our own culture, we seem to take it for granted that a male must necessarily think and act aggressively and that a female must or should think and act passively. We are apt to take it for granted that "it's a man's world," and that men—simply because of being males—are, therefore, entitled to be dominant. You will recall that in the Arapesh studied by Mead both the men and the women were extremely passive, gentle, quiet individuals. In fact, Mead was unable to discover any distinction between the two sexes in terms of aggressive characteristics. Among the Mundugumor, on the other hand, she found that both the men and the women were aggressive. In fact, the women had as many fights over sexual matters as the men, and engaged in just as many conquests. Among the Tchambuli, however, Mead found that the traditional roles played by the sexes in our own culture are actually reversed. The women among the Tchambuli were the aggressive, dominating individuals, whereas the males were quite passive and were primarily interested in dancing, artistic pursuits, and what we call "feminine" activities.

In other words, our criteria for masculine and feminine traits are quite unsatisfactory.[5] In our culture most people have decided that certain traits are masculine or feminine, and they govern themselves accordingly. Men are expected to display masculinity, women femininity. Since aggressiveness is considered a masculine trait, a man has to affect this quality, whether he is inclined that way or not, in order to conform to our cultural standards. An individual male may feel masculine and be interested in "men's affairs," or he may simply force himself to conform because it is expected of him. Women are expected to assume a passive role not only in business activities but often even in the home, and figuratively "take a back seat." They must suppress their tendencies to dominance. Their only solution in our culture is to "mask" their aggressive characteristics in ways which are well understood by many women, but apparently not by many men.

An interesting study of this problem of sex differences is by Terman and Miles who made a ten-year investigation of interests, attitudes, and thought trends.[6] These investigators developed a masculinity-femininity scale which is not only highly reliable, but seems to be fairly valid for the personality characteristics of masculinity and femininity. The M-F test in its present form is entirely a pencil-and-paper test of the questionnaire variety, composed of over nine hundred items. All the items are responded to by checking one of two, three, or four alternatives. The test is administered without a time limit, a single form requiring forty to fifty minutes for the majority of subjects. The scoring is entirely objective. Each response is scored either +1 or —1, that is, masculine or feminine.

On the basis of this and similar investigations, students of human behavior are coming to realize that a knowledge of an individual's sex gives only a partial clew to his personality and his relations to his fellows. On the scale of masculinity-femininity some females turn out to be more masculine than the norm for men. Likewise, individual males—for example, some passive homosexuals—occupy an extremely feminine position on the scale. In a study of 326 subjects, Ferguson found only slight differences in the responses of the twenty-five most feminine-scoring men and the twenty-five most masculine-scoring women.[7]

3. *Differences in Training*. A great many sex differences are due not to biology but to differences in the training of children from the cradle upward. A little boy is treated as a man-to-be. It is permissible for him to get his fingers soiled, to get dirt on his clothes, to engage in scuffles and fights ("he's a real *boy!*"), and even to say some "nasty" words. A little girl, on the other hand, is trained from the cradle to be a "little lady," to sit just so, to tuck her dress over her knees, not to engage in rough-and-tumble activities, and even in early years to prepare to become a desirable wife for some man.

In our culture we even give lip service to a difference in sex attitudes for the two sexes. Overt sex activity is theoretically taboo for both groups. However, for a young man to engage in promiscuous sex activity, and for it to be known, may not only be excused on the basis that "every young man should sow his wild oats," but may actually be praised as an indication that he has come into manhood, that he is now truly "masculine." Indications of "grown-up" behavior are seen even among young boys; they learn to take on the outward, observable aspects of "manly" behavior by spitting, swearing, swaggering, and smoking. On the other hand, a young lady in her adolescent years is expected to be much more restrained. Although she may engage in a certain amount of sex experimentation, it is not permissible for her to admit this even to another girl, for people would say that she is not behaving as a "lady." In other words, a double standard is well recognized and adhered to in our society, even though our polite verbal culture may deny it.

Studies of delinquency illustrate this point well. Among juvenile delinquents one of the most common types of offenses for girls is sexual misconduct, whereas this accounts for very few cases of boys in reform schools. Does this indicate that the sex drive is stronger in young girls than in young boys? No; it simply suggests that sexual activities of boys and girls are differently judged.

Not only do these differences exist in our attitudes toward men and women, but within each sex there are considerable differences in attitudes toward sexual matters. This is partially due to the extent to which cultural values have or have not taken hold of given individuals. All persons look on eating as "good," a pleasant, desirable pastime; but as to sex activity, some look on it as "good," others as "bad," and many have mixed or *ambivalent* attitudes about the matter.

> We are hungry and we eat. On the other hand, few people eat merely to satisfy the needs of the body, although a few who are overweight may carefully . . . avoid eating as much as they would like. Generally, however, society concedes that it is proper and healthy to make a pleasant ceremonial out of eating. We do not want an individual to be a glutton, but a healthy appetite and enjoyment of one's food are regarded as signs of a healthy, normal individual.
>
> Toward . . . sex—we have developed an entirely different attitude. We have brought children up with the attitude that any appearance of sex is indecent and is to be punished—in fact, that they must not even talk about the subject of sex.[8]

Finally, with reference to all kinds of sexual behavior, we should note that the mere outward manifestation of sexual activity does not necessarily indicate a strong "sex drive." In other words, one's overt, observable behavior does not necessarily square with his covert, unobservable attitudes and ways of thinking. Thus, an unmarried person who actually has a strong sex drive may lead a life almost free of sex contacts with others; and, on the contrary, another individual who actually has less sex drive may lead a sexually promiscuous life. The explanation for these two different types of behavior is not found in the biology of sex, but in the covert ways of thinking. One person may, because of religious attitudes, early childhood conditioning, or a variety of emotions, restrain his overt manifestations of sex. Another individual may engage in a great many "sexual conquests," not so much because of an unusually strong sex drive but because licentiousness may be looked upon by others as an indication of dominance and superiority. A Don Juan may be compensating for some inferiority, real or imagined.

Psychiatrists and clinical psychologists know of many instances of sex activity among girls and women who are sexually frigid. In fact, in many instances of sexual promiscuity among women, the woman in question actually achieves little sex satisfaction but uses sex activity in order to achieve friendship, companionship, perhaps money. Therefore, in order to examine the psychology of sex activities in our own human culture, we are faced with the very difficult problem of distinguishing between sex behavior which is carried on because of a sex drive, and the many types of sex activity which are carried on in order to achieve something else—prestige, dominance, companionship, food, shelter, or perhaps simply money.

THE KINSEY REPORT

The material thus far in this chapter illustrates the complexity of the social psychology of sex in human beings. You might suggest, as with many psychological problems, that the best way to study sexual phenomena is to ask people what they think and what they do. The difficulty is that people usually regard their sexual attitudes and behavior as their own private business, not to be investigated even by a social scientist concerned with the *scientific* study of sex. The result has been that until 1948 there was very little factual evidence available on actual patterns of sex behavior except for data based on a few dozen or a few hundred case histories; and most of these studies were of selected segments of the population.[9]

In that year—after nine years of collecting data from *confidential* interviews with a cross section of thousands of people, involving the answering of several hundred questions each—Kinsey, Pomeroy, and Martin published their book, *Sexual Behavior in the Human Male.*[10] The "Kinsey Report," as it became known, went to the top of the best-seller lists, and immediately became a center of controversy. The adequacy and representativeness of the sample of people interviewed was questioned by a number of social scientists; and the Kinsey findings upset the traditional views of people in the twentieth century, probably even more than Darwin's *Origin of Species* had affected people in the nineteenth century. The entire Kinsey research program—sponsored by the Committee for Research on Problems of Sex of the National Research Council, and financed primarily by the Rockefeller Foundation—involves the publication eventually of volumes on such topics as sexual patterns in women, marriage, and prostitution. The purpose throughout is to obtain scientific facts about sex, *completely divorced from moral interpretations.*

SEX BEHAVIOR OF AMERICAN MALES

In the study of American males, Kinsey defines "sexual outlet" as any sexual activity resulting in orgasm; and he classifies the *sources* of outlet as masturbation, nocturnal emissions, heterosexual petting (to climax), heterosexual intercourse (premarital, marital, extramarital), homosexual outlet, and animal contacts. He finds that there are at least eleven factors of primary importance in determining both the *frequency* and the *sources* of sexual outlet: sex, race, age, age at onset of adolescence, marital status, educational level, occupational class, parental occupational class, rural or urban background, religious affiliation, and extent of devotion to religious affairs.[11]

His analysis shows that there is no one American pattern of sexual behavior, but rather scores of different patterns. These vary according to the eleven factors just mentioned, and with various combinations of them. A division of the data from those who did not go beyond grade school, those who did not go beyond high school, and those who went to college, reveals significant differences in *frequencies* of total sexual outlet. "Among single males, at all ages . . . the highest total outlets are found among those boys who go into high school but never beyond. This is true while they are still in grade school, while they are in high school, and after they have left high school."[12]

There are many striking differences between the sex behavior of men of the "upper" and "lower" economic and social brackets. Premarital intercourse is much less frequent in the former group, but the amount of masturbation and petting is greater. As another example:

> Many persons in the upper levels consider a certain amount of oral eroticism as natural, desirable, and a fundamental part of lovemaking. Simple lip kissing is so commonly accepted that it has a minimum of erotic significance at this level. . . . Many a college male will have kissed dozens of girls, although he has had intercourse with none of them. On the other hand, the lower level male is likely to have had intercourse with hundreds of girls, but he may have kissed few of them. What kissing he has done has involved simple lip contacts, for he is likely to have a considerable distaste for the deep kiss which is fairly common in upper level histories.[13]

Kinsey reports that the "deep kiss" is regularly experienced by nine out of ten males of the upper level, whereas with lower level males it is usually thought to be "dirty, filthy, and a source of disease."[14] Yet the former group disdains for hygienic reasons the use of a common drinking glass, often wholly acceptable to the latter group. As we saw in Chapters 4 and 5, *cultural* factors are of tremendous importance in determining sex behavior.

Kinsey's materials indicate that erotic urges begin in very early childhood. The peak of sexual energy occurs in adolescence and the early twenties; but sexual outlets continue longer than has been believed, in diminishing amounts even into the seventh and eighth decades of life. By age fifteen, over 95 per cent of American boys are experiencing sexual outlet.[15] By age twenty-one, approximately three-fourths of all unmarried males—but only about half of those with college education—have had premarital intercourse.[16] Of all men who marry, approximately nine out of ten apparently have had sexual relations with women before marriage.[17]

For our purposes, probably the most significant aspects of the survey are the discrepancies between what males *say that they believe* is ethical in sex conduct, and what they *actually do*. American moral codes and sex laws accept no form of sexual outlet outside of the marital state; and even marital intercourse is supposed to be limited to particular times, places, and techniques.[18] *All other kinds of outlet are illicit.* Yet, according to Kinsey, "at least 85 per cent of the younger male population could be convicted as sex offenders if law enforcement officials were as efficient as most people expect them to be";[19] and the persons involved in *"illicit"* sex activities "constitute more than 95 per cent of the total male population."[20]

It should be noted, however, that these generalizations are based on an analysis of replies from a *selected* portion of the male population regarding taboo types of conduct. Most social scientists agree that the men interviewed did not represent a true or adequate cross section of the population; and, therefore, it may be questioned whether the percentages given are exact or "representative" of the entire population of United States males.

▶ DOMINANCE IN SEXUAL AND SOCIAL BEHAVIOR

DOMINANCE AND SUBORDINATION IN OTHER SPECIES

Prior to the publication of the first Kinsey volume, many students of human behavior had made studies of lower animal forms in order to obtain factual information about sexual behavior. Attention has been especially focused on the infrahuman primates. Our own cultural standards, taboos, and attitudes of repression make it extremely difficult to understand the social psychology of sex behavior in ourselves; but if we take the trouble to investigate the lives of monkeys and apes, who are closely identified biologically with men, we may discover some data which will be of aid in interpreting *human* sexual behavior.

Here is a case in point: A family physician—not a psychiatrist—relates that during some fifteen years of active practice, one assignment in his undergraduate work has been of untold value to him in interpreting certain problems of health, particularly those of family adjustment. He tells how his psychology professor told him and the other members of his class to take off a week from class recitations, go to the zoo, and simply observe the monkeys and apes, taking down notes on their behavior. He admits that this was to him, at the time, a ridiculous assignment, but believes that the interest which he developed in infrahuman primates, leading to more extensive observations of their sexual, social, feeding, and aggressive behavior, has been of untold benefit to him in his medical practice with normal adult human beings.

A number of observers have been concerned with questions of sex development and sexual behavior in lower animal forms, particularly the primates. For example, in one extensive study of apes, sex behavior was found to be in no sense limited simply to copulatory activity, but was closely associated with acts of aggression and with social activities such as play.[21] The investigator also noted the tendency of the apes to show off sexually in the presence of interested observers. In many animal forms, there is a tendency to show off sexually, particularly in the presence of members of the opposite sex. This same phenomenon, incidentally, has been observed by child psychologists; in fact, it is quite natural in early-childhood behavior.

Zuckerman made an analysis of the behavior of Hamadryas baboons in the London Zoological Gardens.[22] Studying a large colony of these animals, he noted some very interesting relations between their sexual and social behavior, and those types of activity were closely identified with feeding behavior and with various aggressive acts. Although he did not work out an exact hierarchy of aggression in these animals, he did observe many instances of male baboons who occupied the position of overlords or who initiated a great deal of the fighting and engaged in most of the sex activity, as contrasted with male "bachelors" who were frequently bullied by the other males.

This problem of dominance-subordination behavior has also been studied by animal investigators without relation to the sex factor at all. The term "subordination" is used rather than the term "submission," since the less dominant animal does not always occupy his secondary position with any indications of willingness or *submission,* but rather is forced to assume this role by the dominance of his superiors.[23] One investigator has carried on extensive research as to despotism among birds.[24] He finds that in numerous species of bird life there is actually a hierarchy of rank, called a "pecking order," so that, for example, one bird *A* may peck *B, C, D,* and *E; B* will be pecked by *A* but will be sufficiently dominant to peck *C, D,* and *E;* and so forth. The dominant bird may be either a male or female. *E* (either male or female) is subordinate or stands at the bottom of this pecking order. There are occasional exceptions where a bird pecks out of order; for example, although *C* is in the middle of the pecking order, it might actually peck *B* as well as *D* and *E,* although it would not peck *A*.

Murchison has conducted a series of experiments on "social hierarchies" among chickens.[25] A "pecking order" can be established; thus, one chicken is dominant in terms of pecking all the others; while at the opposite end of the scale is one which is pecked by all the others. In the pecking order, size and strength are somewhat important, but even more so is the *first* combat in which each of a pair is conditioned to its role with respect to the other. This is also an important factor among human beings.

Dominance-subordination is a well-defined rank order in many animal groups. It has been experimentally tested in mice;[26] and a social hierarchy has even been reported among fishes.[27] The importance of the period of resistance in relation to dominance in various species has been noted by a number of investigators. When a new animal is introduced into the group his dominance position with respect to the rest of the animals is very quickly established, and he continues to hold this position within the dominance hierarchy thereafter, with the exceptions of illness, or in the case of the female estrous cycle. If you have ever been interested in dogs, particularly packs of hounds, you may have noted that a dominance hierarchy exists in these animals as well. One dog in a pack will usually be the dominant one, initiate most of the fights, and secure more than his share of the food. At the opposite end of the hierarchy will be an animal who initiates few or no fights and gets very little of the food except what is finally left over by the more dominant ones. In some conditioned-response work with rabbits, R. H. Brown found that the more dominant an animal, the greater the consistency and the magnitude of the conditioned response from day to day.[28]

MASLOW'S FIRST INVESTIGATION

A series of important studies on dominance has been carried on by Maslow. His work was both observational and experimental. We have already noted that there may be a "pecking order" or order of dominance among birds, roosters, fishes, and dogs. Sexual factors may or may not be involved, although there is some indication of a relationship between sex factors and dominance. Maslow was actually interested in the relationship between sexual and dominant behavior in humans, but he turned to a study of primates in order to get reliable, objective information. In two of his studies, which will be considered here, he was interested in finding the relations between sexual, feeding, aggressive, and social types of behavior.

The *dominant* animal was defined as "one whose behavior patterns (sexual, feeding, aggressive, and social) are carried out without deference to the behavior patterns of his associates. The *subordinate* animal is one whose behavior patterns (sexual, feeding, aggressive, and social) are suggested, modified, limited, or inhibited by the behavior patterns of its more dominant associates."[29] In other words, the animal that is dominant does not have its behavior patterns influenced very much by the behavior patterns of its associates, whereas the subordinate animal does.

The first portion of Maslow's work was carried on by making observations in the zoo over a total period of fifteen months for three days a week, two hours a day. He studied thirty-five infrahuman primates, both monkeys and apes. Aside from simply observing and taking careful notes on the behavior of the animals in the cages, the investigator dropped food into the cage of two or more animals in order to find out which one would get the food. The behavior typical of dominance and of subordination was very striking:

> The sexual behavior of the dominant animal will almost always be masculine . . . *and this masculinity of behavior is independent of the sex* (gender) *of the dominant animal.* A dominant female will mount in masculine fashion other animals in her cage, both male and female. The (typical) sexual behavior of the subordinate animal is female sexual behavior, *again regardless of gender.* Subordinate males will assume the female sexual position as often as subordinate females under similar circumstances. The dominant animal, on the other hand, whether male or female, will rarely assume the female sexual position, except if the dominant animal be a female in heat.[30]

The dominant animal was also the one who had the run of the cage, who would get most of the food, and who would initiate most of the play activities, attacks, and fights. The dominance role was established very shortly after animals were put in the same cage; and the dominance hierarchy, once established, did not change. The only three exceptions were illness, accident, or a female coming in heat; then the dominance hierarchy might shift so that the sick animal or the one in heat might occupy a more subordinate position with relation to the others. Although size had something to do with the establishment of dominance, there were instances where a slightly smaller animal would actually dominate a larger animal. This was true for both males and females. Apparently the *early* establishment of the dominance-subordination relations of two animals resulted in a fairly permanent relationship.

"PROSTITUTION" BEHAVIOR

One further element of this study concerns what various investigators have called "prostitution" behavior. This concept has been used to describe sexual behavior which takes place in inherently nonsexual situations, apparently in order to obtain some "economic" advantages such as food, protection, or immunity from attack. So far as actual prostitution in human society is concerned, the word is used in exactly the same way. A professional prostitute is one who receives gratification for the sex act *indirectly* by attaining money, food, clothing, or entertainment. In other words, "prostitution" refers to what is *overtly* sexual behavior but which is carried on psychologically in order to achieve some nonsexual satisfaction. As indicated previously, the mere fact that an individual engages in sexual activities is no indication that there is a "sex drive" involved. Sexual behavior may be engaged in for nonsexual reasons, and this applies both to animal and human society.

In Maslow's study, prostitution behavior usually consisted in the assumption of the female sexual position by an animal that was being attacked, or that was being prevented from obtaining food. The animal, either male or female, would assume the female position and thus ward off an attack or be allowed to partake of the food.

> A pan of food is thrown to the cage floor, enough for all. In many cases, the dominant overlord will threaten all the other animals as he gathers the food into his mouth and cheek pouches with both hands and both feet. The other animals will approach hesitantly, half presenting all the time [that is, in the female sexual way], and in this way will reach the food and be allowed to partake. Any direct attack on the food by the subordinate animals would be likely to call forth the resentment of the overlord.[31]

MASLOW'S SECOND STUDY

In a second study, Maslow experimented in the laboratory with twenty monkeys, who were put together in various pairings and whose behavior was studied and recorded on time charts.[32] Two animals would be introduced into the same cage at the same time. Types of behavior similar to those observed in the zoo were found. The dominant animal pre-empted all, or almost all, of a limited food supply; assumed the masculine position in copulatory behavior, regardless of the sex of either animal; assumed the bullying role; started most of the fights; initiated approximately twice as much play as the subordinate animal; and showed tendencies to greater activity and freer exploration. The subordinate animal, on the other hand, cringed; was passive under aggression and sexual attempts; and fled from danger of aggression.

A FOLLOW-UP INVESTIGATION

However, in a follow-up study using monkeys, the dominance pairings held true for two individual primates only so long as that particular pairing was kept.[33] That is to say, two animals put together, where the dominance of one and the subordination of the other was clearly established, did not necessarily retain that same relation to each other when a third or fourth animal was introduced into the group.

It was found that new behavior emerged in these groups that was unpredictable from the data on pairings, since certain behavior is definitely a function of the size of the group. A group of three animals is a different *kind* of a group (in a qualitative sense) from a group of two animals. Animals that had been dominant in the pairings were, in the group, beset by alliances of their subordinates and beaten severely. The animal that had been at the bottom of the dominance hierarchy in the pairings turned out to be the most vicious and aggressive of the animals in the groups of four animals. This same animal, when paired separately soon after with one animal that she had almost killed while in the group, turned out to be as subordinate to him as she had been in the original pairing.[34]

INTERPRETATIONS OF THESE DATA

Maslow's data suggest a very close interrelation between sexual, feeding, aggressive, and social behavior. In other words, there is a close relation betweeen dominance-subordination and certain other primary activities, such as feeding, fighting, playing, and sexual activities, a leader in one tends to be the leader in another within the same group. As Yerkes says, "When two or more chimpanzees are associated, dominance appears as a principle of social relation and a hierarchy is constituted by the dominance order, for every individual tends to be more or less dominant or subordinate to every other."[35]

The fact of male or female sex does *not* determine the dominance-subordination relations; the female may take the dominant role as often as a male, and, when she does, behaves exactly like a male. The dominance-subordination relations seldom change, except when the group composition changes, or when an animal changes, or when an animal becomes ill or in heat. "Prostitution" behavior in the sexual field is often used as a means of securing satisfactions in other activities. Crawford, in a study of fifty-four pairs of female chimpanzees introduced into the same living cage after periods of separation varying from five weeks to three years, found that dominance relationships were established within the first ten to thirty minutes; the dominant animal was more likely to enter the other's cage, to be groomed first by the other animal, and to attack or bluff the other animal.[36]

These studies are not only of considerable significance for an understanding of lower animal forms, but they have a very real bearing on the social psychology of human beings in everyday life. Some of these relations will be discussed next.

1. *Tissue Needs.* You will recall that in Chapter 3 some emphasis was placed upon tissue needs as related to the cycle of activity of the organism. In examining animal behavior, we can observe the types of sexual activity with no intellectual or cultural patterns superimposed on them. Just as Mead and other anthropologists have found that the supposed "masculine" and "feminine" characteristics are very lightly linked with the biology of sex, so Maslow observed that "masculine" behavior occurs in both males and females.

When we examine instances of very masculine behavior in women or very feminine behavior in men, there are many indications that these types of behavior are not in most cases caused by differences in sex hormones or chemicals alone, but that they are also caused by environmental factors, particularly in the early years of the family. The emphasis placed by many anthropologists upon the cultural causation of sexual differences seems to be borne out again and again in our own society. Certain data on the sexual behavior of adult men and women reveal that some females may behave in what is regarded as "masculine" fashion, and some males in what is ordinarily thought of as "feminine" fashion.

2. *Repression.* In the second place, the data of Maslow and others have a direct bearing upon the question of repression. The term "repression" comes from the psychoanalysts, who have called attention to the tendency in our culture to repress or avoid giving direct satisfaction to sex drives. Many clinicians, following the lead of Freud, have even suggested that most neuroses involve a deep-rooted sex problem, owing to repression or suppression of unconscious sex urges. In investigations of apes and monkeys, we find no mechanisms of repression involved. They apparently have freedom of sex behavior, and no cultural taboos are imposed on animal behavior. In other words, we are in a position to observe sexual behavior with no limitations of repression. Both heterosexual and homosexual behavior are observable.

> The sexual behavior of monkeys seems to the casual observer to proceed on no fixed principles and to have no discernible order whatsoever. Every conceivable kind of sexual behavior may be observed, and even the biological sex differences seem at times to have no meaning, for males act like females and females like males. Even this behavior is not consistent, for the same monkey may act like a male with one animal and like a female with another, a few moments later. Aside from these considerations, their sexual behavior is astonishing for its frequency alone.[37]

3. *"Masking" of Sex Drive.* In thc third place, these studies suggest that various types of motivation might be masking as sexual activity in human beings. If we can generalize from the behavior of infrahuman primates, there are implications that a great deal of overt sex activity may take place in humans when the sexual drive is not actually the motivating force. In the apes and monkeys, sexual behavior may be exhibited both in sexual and in nonsexual situations, apparently because of the sexual drive but also because of dominance factors. For example, Maslow reports that "dominance sexual behavior" occurs when a dominant animal does not get what he wants; to end a situation apparently not liked by the dominant animal; when a situation, desirable to the dominant animal, ends; when there is any challenge to the dominance of the overlord; in any situation in which bullying or attack or fighting might have occurred.[38] It seems possible, then, that in the behavior of human beings, sexual behavior might occur as a means of maintaining a position of dominance. Human beings may often engage in dating, other mild sex activities, or even in sexual conquests, not as a means of satisfying the sex drive directly, but as a way of establishing dominance and gaining prestige.

4. *"Dating" Behavior.* In the fourth place, the animal studies cast some light on "dating" and courting activities. The label "prostitution behavior"—as indicated above—has been applied to behavior which *overtly* seems sexual in nature, but which takes place apparently in order to achieve something other than sexual satisfaction, such as food or protection from attack. Now, a great deal of dating and courting behavior is of this sort, actually involving physical manifestations of affection and love which are used to achieve certain ends other than sexual satisfaction. Obviously this is not prostitution behavior as thought of by the layman, but *as employed here* the term "prostitution behavior" is *not* limited to the meaning of the layman. Neither is the term used in any moral sense—this is important because of the emotional character of the phrase (see Chapter 8 on language).

This sort of behavior is most frequent among girls because our culture patterns dictate that males pay for food and entertainment; but it is also found among boys, who sometimes make "dates" in order to get a meal or to gain prestige. Consider the matter of dating among college students. A man from Mars might assume naïvely that two young people go out together simply because of a sex drive. Yet the behavior of college students demonstrates that this is only one element in this unique type of behavior. The so-called "line" of the male and female—a combination of verbal flattery, wit, and sweet nothings—is designed to enhance the ego feelings of both. Each acts out a game of skill, often without deep emotional involvement.

Other factors in dating are: prestige of the one who is being dated; "smoothness," which is a compound of clothes, car, and "line"; membership in a "top" fraternity or sorority; economic status; general prestige on the campus. In fact, many a coed is able to achieve position and prestige, not in terms of the actual number of dates, but in terms of *who* these dates are. Likewise, the behavior of the college man is interesting when he realizes himself, or is told by members of his group, that his own prestige on the campus will be greater if he is seen with certain females who are recognized as "campus queens" or who are physically beautiful.

As Waller pointed out, dating is not necessarily true courtship, with marriage the objective.[39] It is more of a dalliance relationship, regarded as one form of amusement or recreation. The psychological motivation of sex behavior can, in fact, be broken down in terms of Thomas's four wishes, discussed in Chapter 6. The desires for *new experience,* for *security,* for *response,* and for *recognition* are ever important in love-making behavior. In making love we can get a new thrill, gain a partner "for keeps," have intimate responses, and secure prestige among our friends.

5. *Hierarchy Changes with Different Numbers.* In the fifth place, note that the dominance-subordination relationships for a pair of animals were likely to change when a third or a fourth animal was brought into the social situation. You can probably observe instances of this same sort in your own social groups. Try to think of an instance where you and some individual friend understand perfectly well—without ever discussing it—who is dominant and who is subordinate in most situations. Now, think of a situation in which the two of you are grouped with a third person, or perhaps two other persons, and how the dominance situation may change. You may find, as the dominant person of the two, that in a group of three or four you become more subordinate and your friend comes to occupy a more dominant role with regard to the entire group.

▶ DOMINANCE FEELING, DOMINANCE BEHAVIOR, AND DOMINANCE STATUS

THE DISTINCTIONS

We have already analyzed some of the differences between overt and covert behavior, especially with respect to external conduct as contrasted with internal attitudes. To carry this further, we should distinguish here between (1) *dominance feeling,* (2) *dominance behavior,* and (3) *dominance status.*[40] An individual may feel or think of himself as dominant; he may act in a dominant way; or he may occupy a dominant status or position within a certain group. However, there is no necessary agreement among the three. A man may have a dominant status within his business organization and yet not feel very dominant. Another man may have a dominant status in the field of politics, and one reason may be that his overt behavior is of a *non*dominant sort, that is, he avoids bossing or domineering his fellows. Or again, another person may feel quite dominant and behave in a dominant way, and yet not have dominance status. Or, an individual who does not feel dominant may behave in a dominant way in an attempt to achieve dominance status.

DOMINATION

We should also distinguish between dominance and domination. Some ways of behaving may represent means of maintaining dominance position, although they may not look, on their face, like dominance behavior. That is to say, one may be *dominant* without being dominating. "Domination is the behavior of a person who is inflexible, rigid, deterministic, who disregards the desires or judgment of others, who himself in the conflict of differences has the answers. Examples are the use of force, commands, threats, shame, blame, attacks against the personal status of another. Domination is the technique of autocracy or dictatorship; it obstructs the growth processes in others."[41]

ADOPTION OF DOMINANT AND SUBORDINATE WAYS

A woman may feel extremely dominant, yet not be allowed to achieve dominance status because of living in a "man's world." In fact, because of the impact of our culture patterns, she may be forced to compensate for her feelings of dominance by adopting "ladylike" ways. However, ladylike ways may be used in our culture to achieve dominance status. Tears—usually thought of as "feminine"—may be used in order to achieve the role of "boss." Similarly, our intricate ritual of manners of greeting or speaking to each other, of sitting or standing in a room, or of correct places at a dinner party are also examples of the careful maintenance of dominance status, even though we might assume naïvely that no dominance behavior is represented.

Throughout our society, in fact, we have learned to adopt ways of behaving which will achieve certain ends with a minimum of conflict. A great many of these things relate very closely to matters of dominant or subordinate position. Thus we use various symbols and rituals and attitudes of both dominance and submission in order to demonstrate our position in relation to that of others. Doffing of the hat, salutes, bows, tones of command, the use of "Sir" and "Ma'am" are subtle indications of dominance.

Some persons find that submissive attitudes will achieve certain ends such as keeping one's job, or getting along well with other persons, perhaps even "winning friends and influencing people." There are all sorts of daily activities which have no connection with sex but which do demonstrate intricate dominance-subordination hierarchies, quite subtle but perfectly understood by all.

> The code of salutation ultimately becomes complicated with social conventions which on the surface are very far removed from personal greetings. Note the different ways in which we greet people, even in a highly democratic society like that of the United States, persons of different appearance. One speaks to a man dressed in working clothes with a degree of freedom and informality which would not be regarded as permissible in the presence of a man dressed for an afternoon reception. One speaks to a child when one would not venture to speak to the parents. The position of woman is very different from that of man in the matter of priority in salutation and all that it implies. In each of these cases we see that salutation is not a separate convention; it is part of the general social scheme.[42]

COMPETITIVE BEHAVIOR IN CHILDREN

Thus far, dominance behavior in adults, among primitives, and in the infrahuman primates, has been emphasized. Is it possible to observe types of dominance behavior in infants and very small children which will suggest who will be dominant—who will occupy roles of leadership—at a later time in life? Most of the studies in this field involve a pairing of two children—exactly the same sort of technique Maslow used with infrahuman primates—and a series of observations of who occupies the dominant and who the subordinate role. Thus Goodenough and Anderson have used the technique of putting two babies of the same age in a playroom; a toy is dangled before them, and then dropped on the floor between them for a period of two minutes.[43] During this time the observer notes the number of times that each baby reaches for the toy, reaches for the other child, secures the toy, offers the toy to the other child, tries to pull the toy away, resists, yields without perceptive resistance, cries, vocalizes, watches the other child, watches the toy. In such a simple situation, it is relatively easy to determine every time which child gets the toy, and *how* he achieves it—through overcoming the other child or by crying and whining behavior.

One investigator has paired children, using a toy, and has observed whether pleading or commanding was used by a child in order to attain the toy.[44] One child pleaded two hundred times, no matter with which other child he was paired. Another, however, commanded two hundred times and pleaded only ten.

Hanfmann has paired children, giving them colored blocks for periods of fifteen to thirty minutes, and having two observers record their actions and remarks.[45] Each of nine five-year-olds was paired with every other child, and at each session the dominant number of the pair was determined by a criterion of control of the play, control of the partner, or both. Of the subjects, *A* dominated six others; *B* dominated seven; *C*, seven; *D*, six; *E*, four; *F*, three; *G*, two; *H*, one; *I*, none. In other words, this is the same sort of "pecking order" which we have already noted in lower animal forms. Each of the last five subjects dominated the ones below him; but in the first four, regarded as most dominant, the relationships were more complex; *A* dominated *B*, *B* dominated *C* and *D*, *but* both *C* and *D* dominated *A*.

In a study of twenty-four subjects six to twenty-five months of age, it was noted that children younger than nine months responded to their surroundings, but indulged in practically no social activity, and any games or fights between them were of an "impersonal" sort.[46] Even to age fourteen months, social behavior is largely negative, and interest is mainly in play materials. From fourteen to eighteen months of age, however, there is a gradual transition in which social and play interests are integrated, so that socially positive behavior actually predominates. If you will visit a fairly large nursery school, you can see for yourself these differences in social and dominance behavior from one age level to another, the very young children three years old engaging in relatively little social and competitive behavior, but the older children aged four and five devoting much of their time to competitive and social behavior.

In another series of experiments, children were allowed to build with blocks; then they were asked, "Which is prettier?"[47] Again, they were told to see who could make the prettier building, and in another period who could make the bigger building. Remarks of a competitive nature were recorded. For the three-year-olds, only 10 per cent of their remarks were competitive; but for the four-year-olds, 26 per cent; for the five-year-olds, 43 per cent; and for the six-year-olds, 70 per cent. In addition, reactions of a competitive sort were noted, such as stealing blocks, hiding blocks, nagging, triumphal singing, and fighting. The data indicate that competition develops progressively from ages three to seven.

In her studies of play activities, Parten mentions one child who never talked at all, as contrasted with another who spent 90 per cent of the total experimental period in talking.[48] She also reports that one child acted as leader in the experimental situation only 5 per cent of the time, whereas another served in the role of leader 95 per cent of the time. Another investigation by Parten reveals two different "types" of leader among nursery-school children, the "diplomat" and the "bully"—"The former, by artful and indirect suggestions, controls a large number of children; the latter employs brute force in 'bossing' the small group he has chosen for his 'gang.' "[49]

A number of studies have dealt with the problem of competition in a group situation. Many an investigator has produced interesting quantitative results of the superiority of children when they knew they were actively competing with other children, as compared with the results in individual situations. As an example, one experimenter studied the ability of boys to withstand so-called "intolerable" pain; he found much greater ability to withstand pain when the subjects were competing with other boys than when they were trying separately to withstand the pain.[50] Maller has demonstrated that competitive efforts are much greater when children choose their own competitors than when their competitors are selected for them by other individuals.[51]

VARIATIONS IN DOMINANCE BEHAVIOR

Situations of this sort demonstrate the difficulty of finding a general trait of dominance or of leadership in any given individual which will be manifested in all situations. Dominance varies from one situation to another. The college student who is dominant in a classroom situation may take a "back seat" when it comes to the athletic field, or the student who is dominant in organizing a party may or may not be dominant in other group situations. Also, as we have previously noted, one's dominant or subordinate position may shift considerably according to the number of people in the group and their prestige.

However, Maslow has reported data on 130 women college graduates, indicating that those high in dominance feeling tended to be leaders, self-confident, and poised.[52] On the other hand, those women extremely low in dominance feeling tended to be self-conscious, easily embarrassed, conventional, modest, envious, jealous, distrustful, quiet, and neat. Maslow has also reported some clinical-experimental data which indicate that the sexual behavior and attitudes of another group of women subjects "were much more closely related to dominance-feeling than to mere sexual drive."[53]

DIFFICULTIES OF PREDICTING DOMINANCE STATUS

We can analyze a given person's behavior in a certain kind of situation and then look to see if he is always dominant or subordinate in that *kind* of situation, with the same *kind* of persons. But we cannot predict that a fairly dominant child will continue, as he grows older, to be dominant in most situations; nor, on the contrary, are we justified in saying that a child who is subordinate in some special situation will necessarily be subordinate a few years later in most social situations. Although a boy or girl who excels in athletics or in scholarship in grade school may be expected to be a leader in the same type of activity in high school and sometimes in college, the dominance or leadership hierarchy may be upset by new situations or new persons, or both.

There is one study which indicated what some of the actual factors may be among women which produce dominance as contrasted with subordination.[54] The data from two extreme groups—college women known to be very dominant and others known to be the opposite—suggest that the dominant group tended to come from families of higher socioeconomic status and with greater prestige. The dominant college women also seemed to have received a different type of training from that of the nondominant ones; they had been given more freedom during childhood and adolescence and had been allowed to arrange their activities without consulting their parents. Finally, and of considerable interest psychologically, is the fact that the dominant women apparently had a much greater attachment and psychological identification with their fathers, and less emotional dependence on their mothers, than the nondominant women.

INTIMACY AS A FACTOR IN DOMINANCE BEHAVIOR

Adult relationships are so complex that it is extremely difficult to predict dominance behavior or dominance status except for known circumstances. A person will behave in dominant ways in one group, and not with another, often depending on little less than how well the individual members of the group are known to the person. The degree of intimacy between competitors may determine to a considerable degree how far one carries his competitive behavior. A businessman may be very hesitant about jeopardizing a friend financially in business competition, but may not hesitate to imperil the fortunes of other men whom he has never seen or does not know at all. To take another example, most men in such sports as boxing or wrestling carry on these activities in terms of play, with no desire actually to injure the friend with whom they are boxing or wrestling; on the other hand, when it comes to a matter of warfare, many men —individual Americans, Frenchmen, Germans, Englishmen, Russians, and others—will not hesitate to maim or destroy completely whole groups of men whom they have never seen. Dominance, then, not only varies with the actual group situation, but it may be colored very much by intimacy of contact.

QUESTIONS AND PROBLEMS FOR DISCUSSION

1. *Give a psychological explanation of why most persons think of sex mainly in its biological features and overlook the importance of the cultural factors.*
2. *What is the relation between the curve of normal distribution and the concepts of masculinity and femininity?*
3. *What bases are there for the view that men are inherently superior to women? That women are inherently superior to men?*
4. *What is the* significance *of the studies of sexual behavior of infrahuman primates?*

5. *Why is it so difficult to predict the later dominance status of a child?*
6. *Explain what is meant by a dominance hierarchy. Give an example among people you know.*

RECOMMENDED READINGS

Beard, M. R., *On Understanding Women.* New York: Longmans, Green & Co., 1931.

Beard, M. R., *Woman as a Force in History: A Study in Traditions and Realities.* New York: The Macmillan Company, 1946.

Calverton, V. F., and Schmalhausen, S. D. (editors), *Sex in Civilization.* New York: Macaulay Company, 1929.

Calverton, V. F., and Schmalhausen, S. D. (editors), *Woman's Coming of Age.* New York: Liveright Publishing Corporation, 1931.

Deutsch, A. (editor), *Sex Habits of American Men.* New York: Prentice-Hall, Inc., 1948.

Ellis, H., *Studies in the Psychology of Sex* (3rd ed., revised; 7 volumes). Philadelphia: F. A. Davis Company, 1920.

Groves, E. R., *The American Woman: The Feminine Side of a Masculine Civilization.* New York: Emerson Books, 1944.

Lundberg, F., and Farnham, M. F., *Modern Woman: The Lost Sex.* New York: Harper & Brothers, 1947.

Miles, C. C., "Sex in Social Psychology." In Murchison, C. (editor), *A Handbook of Social Psychology.* Worcester: Clark University Press, 1935, Chap. 16.

Scheinfeld, A., *Women and Men.* New York: Harcourt, Brace and Company, 1944.

Terman, L. M., and Miles, C. C., *Sex and Personality.* New York: McGraw-Hill Book Company, Inc., 1936.

*Newcomb, T. M., Hartley, E. L., and others (editors), *Readings in Social Psychology.* New York: Henry Holt and Company, Inc., 1947. (The following selections are listed according to the sequence of related discussions in the chapter you have just read.)

Young, K., "Sex Roles in Polygynous Mormon Families," pp. 373-383.

Waller, W., "The Rating and Dating Complex," pp. 388-394.

Linton, R., "Concepts of Role and Status," pp. 367-370.

Cottrell, L. S., "The Adjustment of the Individual to His Age and Sex Roles," pp. 370-373.

Moreno, J. L., "Changes in Sex Groupings of School Children," pp. 383-387.

CHAPTER FOURTEEN

THE PSYCHOLOGY OF LEADERSHIP AND INVENTION

THE PSYCHOLOGY OF LEADERS AND "LED." Competition Plus Cooperation—The Problem of Leadership—Qualities of Leaders—Specificity of Leadership Traits—A Study of Philanthropists—The Stereotyping of Leaders—How Do Leaders Influence Other People?—Two Mechanisms of Leadership—(1) Membership in the Group—(2) Position Above the Group—Why Do the "Led" Follow the Leaders?—Temporary Leadership—Institutional Conformity / LEADERSHIP FOR SOCIAL CHANGES. The Problem of Social Reform—Who Are the Leaders and "Experts"?—Age of Leaders in Reform—Family Background—Intelligence of Liberals—Liberalism and Amount of Information—Resistance to Changes in the *Material* Culture Patterns —Resistance to Changes in the *Nonmaterial* Culture Patterns—How Social Reforms Occur / THE PSYCHOLOGY OF INVENTION AND CREATIVE PRODUCTION. Types of Invention—(1) Psychologica Factors of Inventior—(2) Social Factors of Invention—"Lag" in Inventions—The Influence of Inventions—The Inventors—The Creative Years—Concluding Remarks.

▶ THE PSYCHOLOGY OF LEADERS AND "LED"

COMPETITION PLUS COOPERATION

Place two persons in complete isolation from the remainder of society and, regardless of the simplicity of their existence, one of the two will assert himself as the more dominant individual or leader in most situations. Yet dominance is not the whole story of human behavior, and we should not overlook the extent of *cooperative* behavior among human beings. Competition for positions of dominance is extremely frequent in all sorts of social situations, but so is cooperation in its various aspects. In fact, most of us engage in a tremendous number of cooperative enterprises. "Teamwork" has become an American slogan not only in athletics but elsewhere. No educational enterprise, no religious organization, no business house, no governmental bureau can possibly carry on its functions without a great deal of active cooperation between the members of the group.

. . . The picture of the competitive society ordinarily drawn forgets the daily round of friendly conversation, "joshing," amusement, listening to the radio, taking the family for a drive, going fishing, dancing, loafing. Business itself, for many people, is a quiet routine affair in which one keeps going, scarcely competes. The frantic picture of the poor youth struggling up, the Alger-book model, has been taken so seriously by sober thinkers that we suspect them of forgetting the garage man's son who is quite content to be baggage man at the village station; the carpenter's son who decides he would rather be an embalmer; the barber's boy who has a "fine job" as stock clerk in a warehouse; and the enormous masses of research data which show that *most* young Americans (before, during and since the depression) have asked chiefly for a job, for security, for a chance to live. They hope for a pleasant life, enjoy their friends, the car, a radio, "want to get married pretty soon."[1]

Such are the activities of many human beings. Ours is both a cooperative and a competitive society, both within groups and between groups. We may even be *ambivalent* in this respect. Note "the oppositional character of identification, sympathy, and cooperation, on the one hand, and of antagonism, aggression, and competition or conflict, on the other."[2] Whether individuals are more competitive or more cooperative depends in part at least on the *cultural* patterns of the particular group.

The Arapesh eat little flesh;
They live secure, but futile.
They're not competitive or harsh,
As are the Kwakiutl.

. . . . .

Bachiga think that food and drink
Should come from lone endeavor.
The Zuñi, herding sheep in peace,
Cooperate forever.

Samoans feel the great ideal
Is helping one another.
Ojibwas try to stand alone,
And no one loves his brother.

The Maori loaned whate'er they owned
From Kingdom Come till now;
But interest rates are very high
Among the Ifugao.[3]

THE PROBLEM OF LEADERSHIP

Within the intricate network of competing and cooperating, we resort to such social factors as imitation and suggestion, but these in turn are dependent on leadership. Certain individuals stand out in any group as leaders.

What is leadership? Who are these leaders? What characteristics do they have? What are the techniques which they use to influence others? Particularly, how do they bring about social changes?

QUALITIES OF LEADERS

One controversy has centered around the question of whether leaders come forward because of their innate and acquired talents or because of the circumstances of their times. For example, did the stress of the times produce George Washington, or did he come forward because he was a natural leader? This sounds suspiciously like the old problem of which is more important, heredity or environment. It is probable, however, that a combination of complex circumstances must arise before there is any demand upon potentially great leaders to come to the front. As Pigors has pointed out, the essentials of leadership are: (1) a common cause, (2) a leader, (3) followers, and (4) the present situation.[4]

Various investigations have been concerned with the size and weight of leaders. You will recall that Maslow noted a general tendency for larger primates to be dominant, but also found instances in which a slightly smaller animal would dominate larger ones. Most humans have had experiences in childhood which have conditioned them to respect persons of some size and strength. In addition, other factors than size —manner of speaking, ways of dressing, various types of ritualism—are used by leaders to maintain their positions. Accordingly, we should not expect size to be as closely related to dominance among humans as among other primates. However, one study of 221,819 applicants for life insurance and of 6,037 male "leaders" showed that the latter averaged about three inches taller and over twelve pounds heavier than the average men.[5] Again, in a study of leadership among adolescent boys, Partridge found that the most popular leaders scored higher in Army Alpha intelligence tests, were taller, weighed more, impressed their fellows as being more independent, were better looking, and were better athletes.[6]

In a study by Terman, leaders in problem-solving situations were later rated by their fellows on various characteristics.[7] The leaders were most likely to be rated as *either first or last* in dress, health, social status, quality of schoolwork, boldness in behavior, fluency of speech. In other words, they stood at one extreme or the other on all of these characteristics; they apparently were not average or "colorless" individuals.

Simpson has presented controversial questions to groups of people in supervised discussions, and has then made determinations of which individuals influenced the discussion the most (so that a change of opinion was brought about in the group) and which influenced it the least.[8] A very high relationship was found between ability to influence the group and high grades in college; and likewise, a high relationship was found between ability to influence the group and the attainment of high grades on a *verbal* scholastic-aptitude test.

One study was made of "leaders" and "followers" among three groups—criminals, students, and Army men.[9] Twenty criminal leaders were compared with twenty followers, twenty student leaders with twenty followers, and twenty noncomissioned Army officers with twenty privates. The leaders in each case excelled in three respects—they believed in themselves, arrived at their decisions quickly, and stuck to their decisions. However, the leaders in the three different situations had many dissimilar traits. An analysis of the opinions of newspaper correspondents concerning the "ablest" congressmen has revealed three important factors—industry or "push," intellectual fortitude, and popularity.[10]

Hunter and Jordan have conducted one of the most far-reaching investigations ever made of leadership among college students.[11] Their eighty-two leaders were selected from a large college population by a combination of student ratings, faculty ratings, and leadership records. Twenty-five who rated the highest of all were labeled "outstanding leaders." The nonleaders comprised 103 students. Statistically significant differences were found between the leaders and the nonleaders, and between the outstanding leaders and the nonleaders, with respect to a great many factors. The leaders, as compared with the nonleaders, were significantly younger, were lighter in weight (possibly because of being younger), had parents who were college trained, had parents belonging to the professional classes, had law or journalism as vocational preferences, were superior in tests of intelligence and of vocabulary, and were higher in scholarship.

The qualities necessary in a leader have been listed by many students of behavior. Although the lists do not coincide exactly, they have many qualities in common, and taken together they constitute a fair representation of the principal attributes of leadership.

F. H. Allport:[12]

1. Trait of ascendance
2. Physical power
3. High motility
4. Tonus
5. Erect, aggressive carriage
6. Tenacity
7. Face-to-face mode of address
8. Reinforcement of energy
9. Restraint
10. Inscrutability
11. Expansiveness in field of action
12. High intelligence
13. Understanding
14. Keenly susceptible to social stimulation
15. Tact
16. Zeal
17. Social participation
18. Character
19. Drive

L. L. Bernard:[13]

1. Striking physical personality
2. Size
3. Good looks
4. Appearance of strength of body
5. Appearance of strength of character
6. Ready speech
7. Oratorical gift of emotional appeal
8. Readiness in repartee
9. Sympathy
10. Sense of justice
11. Humanitarianism
12. Honesty
13. Good faith
14. Insight
15. Courage
16. Persistence
17. Good natural ability
18. Originality
19. Initiative
20. Good intellectual training
21. Soundness of judgment
22. Mental flexibility
23. Forethought
24. Intellectual vision
25. Moral vision
26. Positive idealism
27. Cheerful, even temper
28. Poise
29. Self-confidence
30. Organizing and executive ability
31. Knowledge of human nature and of society

O. Tead:[14]

1. Physical and nervous energy
2. A sense of purpose and direction
3. Enthusiasm
4. Friendliness and affection
5. Integrity
6. Technical mastery
7. Decisiveness
8. Intelligence
9. Teaching skill
10. Faith

The difficulty with such lists is the duplication of the same or similar trait names; and the circularity of definition, for example, "good natural ability." The problem is as difficult as that of making up lists of instincts (compare Chapter 6). Accordingly, Coffin has suggested that *leadership traits* may fall into a few general groups or clusters:

1. *Intelligence:*
   High intelligence, insight, intellectual vision, brilliant, clever, well informed.
2. *Moral sensitivity:*
   Fairness, justice, sound judgment, open-mindedness, devotion to truth, moral vision, altruism, idealism.
3. *Imagination:*
   Originality, imagination, forethought, inquisitiveness, mental flexibility, wide interests.
4. *Restraint:*
   Restraint, inscrutability, self-control.
5. *Drive and determination:*
   Zeal, drive, enthusiasm, dynamic personality, face-to-face mode

of address, aggressive, ambitious, ascendant, desire for eminence, brave, persistent, tenacious, perseverance, singleness of purpose.

6. *Responsibility:*
   Mature, dignified, frank, appearance of character, stable, reliable, neat, integrity, devoted to duty, industrious, love of work, concentration.
7. *Self-reliance:*
   Sense of purpose and direction, self-reliance, self-confidence, self-trust, decisiveness, initiative, finality of judgment.
8. *Dynamic physical characteristics:*
   Physical power, size, strength, tonus, erect carriage.
9. *Imperturbability:*
   Poise, serenity, self-composed, even-tempered, cheerful, optimistic, patient, tolerant.
10. *Social responsiveness:*
    Susceptibility to social stimulation, social participation, friendliness, affection, sociable, extroverted, expansive.
11. *Easy maintenance of good relations with others:*
    Tact, diplomacy, kindness, sympathetic, cooperative, humanness, knowledge of human nature.[15]

Coffin also points out that *leadership functions* probably include three general categories—*planning, organization,* and *persuasion.* In executive management, these three functions could be grouped as follows:

I. *Planning:*
   1. Determination of problems (of supply, production, etc.).
   2. Planning the solution to these problems.

II. *Organization:*
   3. Organization of personnel and physical equipment to carry plans into operation.
   4. Coordination of organization into a balanced unit.
   5. Testing, checking, and modifying organization to compensate for inevitable changes.

III. *Persuasion:*
   6. Delegation of responsibility for execution of plans.
   7. Supervising agencies operating to carry out plans.
   8. Maintaining control of organization, applying techniques of control.[16]

Of the eleven clusters of traits above, the first four—intelligence, moral sensitivity, imagination, and restraint—are probably most clearly relevant and valuable to the *planning* function. The characteristics related especially to the *organization* function are probably the next three—drive and determination, responsibility, and self-reliance—and perhaps dynamic physical characteristics. The third function, of *persuasion,* seems most closely related to imperturbability, social responsiveness, and easy maintenance of good relations with others.

An analysis has been made by Stogdill of practically all reported studies bearing on the problem of traits and personal factors associated with leadership.[17] His conclusions are well worth quoting verbatim:

1. The following conclusions are supported by uniformly positive evidence from fifteen or more of the studies surveyed:

a. The average person who occupies a position of leadership exceeds the average member of his group in the following respects: (1) intelligence, (2) scholarship, (3) dependability in exercising responsibilities, (4) activity and social participation, and (5) socio-economic status.

b. The qualities, characteristics, and skill required in a leader are determined to a large extent by the demands of the situation in which he is to function as a leader.

2. The following conclusions are supported by uniformly positive evidence from ten or more of the studies surveyed:

a. The average person who occupies a position of leadership exceeds the average member of his group to some degree in the following respects: (1) sociability, (2) initiative, (3) persistence, (4) knowing how to get things done, (5) self-confidence, (6) alertness to, and insight into, situations, (7) cooperativeness, (8) popularity, (9) adaptability, (10) verbal facility.

3. In addition to the above, a number of factors have been found which are specific to well-defined groups. For example, athletic ability and physical prowess have been found to be characteristics of leaders in boys' gangs and play groups. Intellectual fortitude and integrity are traits found to be associated with eminent leadership in maturity.

4. The items with the highest over-all correlation with leadership are originality, popularity, sociability, judgment, aggressiveness, desire to excel, humor, cooperativeness, liveliness, and athletic ability, in approximate order of magnitude of average correlation coefficient.

5. In spite of considerable negative evidence, the general trend of results suggests a low positive correlation between leadership and such variables as chronological age, height, weight, physique, energy, appearance, dominance, and mood control. The evidence is about evenly divided concerning the relation to leadership of such traits as introversion-extroversion, self sufficiency, and emotional control.[18]

SPECIFICITY OF LEADERSHIP TRAITS

After perusing the foregoing lists, you may ask, "How can *I* get that way? How can I, too, win friends and influence people?" It is questionable whether such generalized lists can aid you to achieve a position of leadership. We have emphasized again and again that all sorts of supposed traits—honesty, kindness, masculinity, and now leadership—appear only in particular situations. There seems to be a definite *specificity* in qualifications for leadership.[19] The traits that suit a leader for one purpose do not necessarily suit him for leadership in all activities. To say that a leader is one who has size and good looks may apply in the world of a candidate for a political office, but does not necessarily apply to a leader in the world of science working with test tubes and other physical apparatus. Similarly, honesty and good looks do not typify all leaders.

Leadership in any one activity requires a certain amount of skill in *that* activity as well as evidence of other skills. A person cannot lead in all spheres; he must at times be a follower. In other words, if you wish to analyze the social psychology of leadership so that the materials will be useful to you personally, you should choose some *particular* situation and then, by observational or experimental methods, make a careful study of leadership in that particular kind of situation.

For example, Starch has analyzed certain differences in executive ability on the basis of interviews with fifty executives with annual salaries of over $50,000, fifty with salaries between $7,000 and $50,000, and fifty with salaries below $5,000.[20] Three characteristics of executives were considered especially important by the first two groups—ability to think, inner drive, and capacity to assume responsibility—and ability to handle people was rated high by all three groups. Some additional differences indicated were the following:

	Top Salary Group (%)	*Middle Salary Group (%)*	*Lowest Salary Group (%)*
College graduate	72	74	20
School level (upper third)	68	66	32
Work hard and long	78	62	20
Liking for their work	84	76	44
Sought new responsibilities	90	68	16

Another example of specific leadership situations is the military; and several investigations during World War II had as their objective the prediction of military leadership. Williams and Leavitt administered a variety of tests to men in the Marine Corps Officer Candidate School, most of whom became combat platoon leaders.[21] Follow-up data indicated that the best predictors both of success in OCS and of combat performance consisted of recorded opinions of the members of training platoons. Group opinion was calculated from the responses of platoon members, after they had been associated for about five weeks, on traits such as desirability as a roommate, fairness in making military court decisions, leadership in an emergency, sense of humor, and all-round ability as a combat officer.

One of the most important group experiments ever conducted on the selection of leaders involved the psychological analysis of the aptitudes and abilities of recruits for OSS (the Office of Strategic Services).[22] Groups of psychologists cooperated in devising, developing, and utilizing unique psychological tests and stress situations for groups of OSS candidates, who lived with the psychologists at secret locations for three-day analysis periods while they were subjected to almost constant scrutiny and observation.

All candidates wore Army fatigues, so that there could be no indication of branch of service or rank or civilian status; and all used assumed names and "cover" stories about themselves, so that their actual identity was completely unknown to each other. Because of the unusual nature of their proposed assignments and necessity for complete teamwork, the job of the psychologists was not just to weed out the less intelligent; but to identify those men who in the field might become sloths, free talkers, bad actors, or irritants to others, and thus do irreparable harm to the program or endanger the lives of themselves or others.

Will this man favorably impress the resistance group into whose territory he will parachute? Will he find long periods of isolation intolerable? Will he be able to keep security? Will he rant and boast too much? Will he lower the morale of his co-workers? To answer questions of this sort, over five thousand persons were "assessed" either in the three-day program or in a special one-day psychological testing situation. Several hundred cases were followed up to determine the general validity of the tests.

These tests and stress situations for assessing motivation, emotional stability, leadership, effective intelligence, and other important personality characteristics varied all the way from paper-and-pencil tests to out-of-doors problems with obstacle courses and other kinds of physical competition. Candidates were put in ridiculously frustrating situations, subjected to almost third-degree type interviews, prodded in ingenious ways to break their "cover" stories, and some were plied with liquor—at all times being carefully observed. Information was thus obtained on who could "take it," who emerged as leaders, who were emotionally stable, who were physically well coordinated, and a wealth of other personality data.

At the end of each assessment period the psychologists met for an interchange of their observations and test scores. The end result was a carefully documented personality analysis of each candidate, including judgments of his potential usefulness or lack of it for particular kinds of OSS assignments.

A STUDY OF PHILANTHROPISTS

The *specificity* of leadership characteristics may be further illustrated by a study, by Beckwith, of notable American philanthropists—one type of leader—listed in the *World Almanac.*[23] Philanthropists are leaders in that they bring about increased activity in the arts, sciences, and social services by giving their wealth to society. Another study has revealed the tendency of people of means to write their wills so that their money and property is distributed among a small circle of relatives and friends.[24] The tendency is to preserve the family as a significant social unit rather than to cultivate philanthropy. Beckwith secured biographical data on 508 individuals, who, while alive, made a total of 954 gifts outside of their families, totaling over $588,000,000. The greater percentage of these gifts was made by men whose parents were classified as rich or very rich. It was found "that donors of rich parentage were notably more generous to universities than were donors of very rich, modest, or poor parentage . . ."[25] On the other hand, donors of poor parentage were notable pre-eminently in their gifts to religion.

The majority of these philanthropists were born in New York, New Jersey, and Pennsylvania, these three states alone accounting for over two-fifths of the total gifts. Although the South had a population representing 25 per cent of the nation's total wealth in 1870, an almost negligible percentage of gifts came from donors born in the South—probably not because Southerners were less generous, but because there were few great fortunes in the South. People of New England birth were responsible for a relatively larger total number of gifts to science and welfare than any other group.

One of the most interesting sets of findings concerns the amount of education of the donor:

> . . . Both number and value of gifts increase considerably with every increase in amount of education. Men with a record of graduate university work (0.2 percent of their generation) gave 21.2 percent in number and 18.7 percent in value of all gifts. Men with a college degree but with no record of graduate work (1 percent of their generation) gave 22.2 percent in number, and 19.2 percent in value of all gifts. Men who attended college but did not graduate (1 percent of their generation) gave 13.9 percent in number and 12.4 percent in value of all gifts. Men with a record of high school work or with no evidence to the contrary, and no further education (5 percent of their generation) gave 30.3 percent in number and 40.1 percent in value of all gifts. Men with a record of a grammar school education only or less (90 percent of their generation) gave only 12.3 percent in number and 9.5 percent in value of all gifts.
>
> *Education.* The relative number of gifts to education varies directly with the amount of education of the donor, with one exception. . . .

Science and Public Welfare. In relative number of gifts to total science and public welfare, donors with a college plus education are notably preeminent. . . .

Charity. [In the field of charity, on the other hand] there is a very marked tendency for the relative number of gifts to total charity to vary inversely with the education of the donor . . .[26]

Although Beckwith's data are incomplete as to church membership, since he could include data on religion only for those individuals for whom church membership was specifically mentioned in biographical reports, he found that the relative number of gifts to universities varied inversely with the religious interests of the donor. That is, those donors listed as church members gave less to universities than those not listed as church members. This same trend was apparent in contributions to science and public welfare, church members giving less than non-church members. Philanthropists of known sympathies for the Republican party made almost four times as many and over four and one-half times as valuable gifts as did donors sympathetic to the Democratic party.

THE STEREOTYPING OF LEADERS

Analyses of this sort are extremely valuable in social psychology. Referring once more to our earlier discussion (in Chapter 10) of stereotyping and prediction of attitudes, we noted some of the fallacies involved in stereotyping. However, we were also concerned with the ways in which stereotypes grow up because of statistical modes; and we were also interested in the fact that if one or two characteristics of an individual are known, we may be justified in stereotyping to the point of predicting his attitudes and behavior. If we know nothing about two wealthy men except that one is a Republican and has done graduate work in a university, whereas the other is a Democrat with a grammar-school education, we can predict that the former will *probably* give a great deal more money away, and that more of it will go to education, science, and public welfare than to charity and religion. Roughly, we can note the difference between men who are leaders in such fields as business and politics, as contrasted with those who are leaders in science, art, and religious thought. The characteristics which would make up a leader in one field would not be likely to hold true for a leader in the other.[27]

HOW DO LEADERS INFLUENCE OTHER PEOPLE?

What do the leaders do to influence other people? Leadership may be defined as "the activity of influencing people to cooperate toward some goal which they come to find desirable."[28] In other words, a leader produces changes in attitudes and in external behavior of the "led" in such a way that the people who are led come to find the views and activities of the leader desirable. The leader is one to whom sufficient prestige attaches because of dominant behavior or dominant status—such as general social or economic position—that greater feelings of loyalty are developed in the people who are led if they follow a common cause and common ideas. The leader, in turn, acquires more and more prestige as his leadership increases and continues. "Leadership is the process of mutual stimulation [or reciprocal reinforcement] which by the successful interplay of relevant individual differences, controls human energy in the pursuit of a common cause."[29]

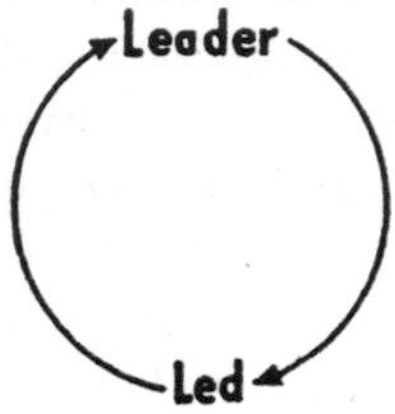

FIG. 25. CIRCULAR PROCESS OF LEADERSHIP

This, then, is a circular process, as indicated in Figure 25. The leader gradually influences those who are led, but they in turn influence his views. History has amply demonstrated that, in the majority of instances where a leader has attempted to lead people to views or ways which are far removed from their own ways, he has not been successful and often has been ridiculed by them as a visionary, and by later generations as "ahead of his time." Leaders must conform to the judgment of the people. Franklin D. Roosevelt gained popularity in the early 1930's partly because he represented the desire of Americans to end the maladjustments which led to the economic crash of 1929. It is important for the leader to realize that he can produce changes, as a rule, only by *slowly* manipulating the attitudes of the people who are led, somewhat in accordance with their preconceived attitudes. These gradual changes in their attitudes prepare the way for further changes.

Successful leaders usually understand perfectly well that they are not suddenly changing all the attitudes of multitudes of people. They may talk as if they think so—witness political speeches—and in some instances, of course, they may convince themselves. Ordinarily, however, a leader simply vocalizes those ways of thinking which are typical of the mass of his hearers and helps the group to translate their already formed attitudes into action. First of all, he identifies himself with their attitudes and ways of thinking. He may restort to the "plain-folks" device and tell how "I grew up as a country boy"; only by degrees does he attempt to shift the views of his hearers. He realizes that any sudden or extreme break with the common attitudes of the people will be disastrous to his leadership. Therefore, he makes use of the psychology of *suggestion* and *imitation* in order to achieve uniform ways of acting and thinking. Stereotyped words and phrases help him to do this. The words "home" and "mother" flood the individual with emotion, and "Old Glory" calls up the beloved flag and country. Once more—"He who wants to persuade should put his trust not in the right argument, but in the right word. . . . Give me the right word and the right accent, and I will move the world."[30] In opposing the entrance of the United States into the World Court in 1926, a senator from South Carolina simply relied on the word "nigger":

> I call attention of Senators from the South . . . to the fact that they are voting for a court where we are to sit side by side with a full-blooded "nigger," who has as much right as we have in the election of the judges of this court. I ask them if they realize the fact that there may be and very probably will be a representative of Haiti as a judge on this court, so that the southern Senators are voting to throw the destinies of southern women and southern men into the lap of a black man.[31]

TWO MECHANISMS OF LEADERSHIP

A psychologically effective leader should be dominant, without being too dominating. J. F. Brown has pointed out that a successful leader must do at least two things:

1. *Membership in the Group. "The successful leader must have membership-character in the group he is attempting to lead."*[32] That is, he must be recognized by the "led" as sufficiently one of them that they will not look on him as an outsider. He must demonstrate ways of acting and ways of thinking—both overt and covert behavior—which are a good deal like the "ways" of those whom he leads. The emphasis is frequently on simplicity. He is a "regular fellow." "He doesn't put on the dog." "He seems just like one of us."

2. *Position above the Group. "The leader must represent a region of high potential in the social field."*[33] That is, he must demonstrate that, in certain ways, he is not just one of the herd, but that he possesses unique characteristics which set him apart from his fellows. He maintains his position owing to the use of psychological symbols which set him apart from others. He may use titles—President, Director, Doctor, Professor, Judge. He may use uniforms—long black robes, brass buttons, badges. He may have very impressive quarters or offices where the common person cannot get at him without making an appointment or "seeing my secretary." He may make himself inaccessible for the most part, but occasionally make rather sudden, dramatic appearances. Hitler's refuge

at Berchtesgaden and his occasional dramatic speeches to enthusiastic crowds was an example of this device.

Study the characteristics of any of the great leaders in the world and you find them making use of these two mechanisms. A nice balance between the two is necessary. Excellent examples are various presidents of the United States—Jefferson, Lincoln, both Roosevelts.

WHY DO THE "LED" FOLLOW THE LEADERS?

Owing to these two beliefs—(1) that our leader is one of us, but also (2) that he is something apart—we are able to identify ourselves with him, to experience a vicarious or substitute thrill from his experiences. In what he does we may have some of our basic wishes satisfied. In other words, the desires for *new experience,* for *security,* for *response,* and for *recognition* may be achieved without budging from our own daily routine. We can achieve some of our wishes by looking to our leaders for security and thinking of ourselves in their unique or adventurous roles. We can even achieve some feeling of superiority by copying some of the external trappings of leaders—by wearing certain clothes, by owning the "right" automobile, by belonging to an "exclusive" club.

We may secure vicarious thrills and satisfy our desires for new experience by identifying ourselves with, or admiring, leaders who actually hold antisocial roles in our society. It may be fun to be a G-man, but it may also be very satisfying to admire an Al Capone. Our admiration of leaders is not due solely to the purposes or ideals for which they stand, but may be a means of achieving ways of behaving and thinking which we fear to engage in ourselves because of the taboos of our culture. The "headman" in our tribe can "get by" whereas the other people may have to look out for what their gossiping neighbors may say across the back fence.

There are many indications, both from clinical data and from observations of the political and business scene, that those people who are led expect the leader to play the *father* role for them. This does not imply an extreme psychoanalytic view. It is simply an indication of the continuance of a trend which most of us had as children, to look to someone else as an authority, a true guide, an all-powerful person. For a great many in our culture, it has been the father who has been the leader in childhood years, the omniscient, omnipotent person. It is not surprising that as adults we expect someone in authority to tell us what to do in many political and business situations. We are uncertain or afraid, and this is terrifying. We want certainty and security, and so we accept the judgment of some authority.

We may also follow a leader because of the "office" he holds. We follow him, not because we think he is an ideal character, but because his office is "sacred" or honored. Many a person walks into the United States

Supreme Court with a very reverent attitude because of the impressive marble entrance, the dramatic appearance of the Justices on the stroke of 12 o'clock, the black robes, and the hushed atmosphere—yet is very critical of the work of the Court. Often we accord tremendous respect to the office of "Mayor," although we may not like the Mayor's behavior. Try taking notes of crowd behavior when a man called the President of the United States appears in public; then make observations some years later of another crowd's behavior when exactly the same man appears in public, as an ex-President. He is greeted with wild cheers and acclaim so long as he is President; later he finds only a handful of people to greet him wherever he goes.

TEMPORARY LEADERSHIP

Finally, one dubbed a "leader" even in a specific situation may be a leader only temporarily and does not necessarily continue to occupy that position. For example, a person who is looked upon as a leader in politics, art, literature, or almost any field may later pass out of favor. Or we may accept as a leader a person who is simply a "Babbitt," one who is able to give lip service to the common beliefs of the group and to behave in socially acceptable ways, but who does not actually lead.

INSTITUTIONAL CONFORMITY

Katz and Schanck have presented five reasons for conformity behavior.[34] These reasons also serve as an excellent summary of why the "led" follow the leaders:

1. "It is much easier to follow the suggestion of the leader or the action of one's fellows than to work out one's own solutions." Conformity saves time, energy, and thought. Witness Army and Navy life, which in spite of many drawbacks is comfortable for many.

2. "In actual experience with individual solutions people frequently find that it is more economical and efficient to follow leaders." If each of us tries to do things his own way, confusion results. Leadership means greater productivity than can be achieved by uncoordinated efforts.

3. "In most institutions nonconformity is punished." Leaders themselves enforce sanctions. We do not want to be too much unlike our fellows; we are afraid of public opinion.

4. "Through identification with a larger group we enhance our egos." By conforming, we become part of a large organization, a religious group, a fraternal organization, a political party. We can then point to the accomplishments of our fellow members and our leaders, and take partial credit for them.

5. "In our society, institutional conformity is also a matter of conditioning. From early childhood we have been raised in groups and have

done things in unison." Through play groups, kindergarten, grade school, assemblies, public ceremonies, we have learned to applaud at the proper time, to follow the suggestions of leaders without too much questioning.

▶ LEADERSHIP FOR SOCIAL CHANGES

THE PROBLEM OF SOCIAL REFORM

Is ours to be a static society or a dynamic one? Are we content with things as they are, or should we seek improvements and "progress"? If the latter, where are we to get our leadership in tackling problems of social significance?

WHO ARE THE LEADERS AND "EXPERTS"?

There are leaders among politicians, businessmen, organized laborers, newspaper publishers, and all sorts of groups. A leader in one field is not necessarily capable of leadership in other fields, however.

One of the greatest temptations of every politician, businessman, engineer, lawyer, physician, scientist, and college professor, is to express supposedly "expert" opinions on matters which are completely outside his own field of specialization. Equally strong are the demands of other persons for this "expert" advice. The town banker, the family physician, the lawyer who draws up your will, the teacher in physics, may be sought after to give advice on everything from the psychology of personal adjustment to the economics of the international situation; and the temptation is very great to give advice when people seek it. Movements for social change are sometimes brought about by people who have made no study at all of social problems. Every man seems to regard himself as a combination psychologist, sociologist, political scientist, economist, and historian—all rolled into one. He does not regard himself as a physicist or chemist because these people are "men of mystery." But the conversation in your barbershop or at the soda fountain demonstrates that many people think that they are capable of solving the social and economic problems of the country.

AGE OF LEADERS IN REFORM

Several investigators have been concerned with the age of leaders in social reform and the types of families from which they come. Gowin compared periods of reform and periods of quiet in modern history with respect to the age of their leaders.[35] The average age of the dozen leading men in ten historical periods of reform varied from thirty-two to forty-six years. On the other hand, the average age of the leaders in more conservative periods varied from fifty-four to sixty-six years. The champions of change have been from fifteen to twenty years younger than the upholders of the *status quo,* and this finding is of great practical importance.

This is interesting in connection with a study by Lehman, which shows that certain types of present-day leaders—legislative, judicial, diplomatic, military, naval, religious, and educational—are significantly older than were their predecessors who held the same nominal positions.[36] Other data of Lehman's indicate that leadership optimum ages, in such fields as these, are a function not so much of the physiological factors associated with chronological age as of social conditions and expectations.[37]

FAMILY BACKGROUND

From what sorts of families do leaders come? Sorokin became interested in the origins of labor leaders.[38] He selected for his study *The American Labor Who's Who for 1925,* the individuals listed representing labor leaders as contrasted with an unselected group in the field of labor. Interestingly enough, the greater percentage of labor leaders were found to come, *not* from the families of laborers, but from families in the professional, business, and managerial occupations. "These classes have produced a share of the leaders far above their percentage in the population, and several times greater than the quota of leaders produced by semiskilled or unskilled labor."[39]

A study closely related to this is that by Taussig and Joslyn, who found that business leaders also tended to come largely from the sons of successful businessmen.[40] According to their figures, over 50 per cent of the business leaders had businessmen fathers; and 10 per cent of the American population produces 70 per cent of the business leaders. On the other hand, American men of science have come primarily from the families of professional people, and not so much from families engaged in agriculture or in trade, transportation, manufacturing, and mechanical pursuits.[41] One investigation has disclosed a fairly high relationship between extreme radicalism, and antagonism toward the fathers of the persons in question.[42]

INTELLIGENCE OF LIBERALS

Another group of studies centers around the relationship of radicalism to intelligence. In the 1924 presidential campaign, subjects who were supporters of La Follette, the Progressive candidate, were characterized by decidedly higher average intelligence-test scores than the supporters of either Calvin Coolidge or John W. Davis, the conservative candidates.[43]

Howells made a comparative study of those who accept as compared with those who reject religious authority, and found statistically significant differences in favor of greater intelligence among religious radicals than among religious conservatives.[44]

> Few such decided relationships have since been shown, but the trend of the evidence is fairly consistent. Measures purporting to measure liberalism-in-general have almost invariably been reported to show [small] but positive [relationships] with intelligence test scores, and "international-mindedness" scores have often shown about the same degree and direction of relationship to intelligence. Zero or near-zero [relationships] with intelligence have repeatedly been reported for such diverse attitudes as those toward prohibition, pacifism, the Negro, and superstition. Totally unreliable [relations] have also been noted between intelligence and susceptibility to propaganda.[45]

One of the most significant sets of findings on this general problem comes from the study of college leaders by Hunter and Jordan, already mentioned above.[46] The leaders, you will recall, were above average in intelligence, vocabulary, and scholarship. These people of superior intelligence were also more liberal in their attitudes than were the nonleaders:

> The typical leader . . . showed more "liberal" attitudes than his fellows toward the Negro, toward war, toward labor and economic issues, toward social convention, and toward governmental questions. He was more disposed than his fellows to regard as desirable definite changes in social institutions purporting to advance social welfare. He was more strongly opposed to the *status quo* and to the doctrine of class or vested interests than were his classmates. He was sympathetic with the interests of labor. His attitude was more strongly pacifistic than that of his fellows. He was more accurately informed, read more carefully, offered more resistance to suggestion, used more caution in response to extreme statements, and exercised more discriminating judgment than was true of his classmates and fellow students.[47]

LIBERALISM AND AMOUNT OF INFORMATION

In a survey made by Odegard of three thousand college students, he came to the conclusion "that invariably the radical student actually knew more about the subject under consideration than the conservative."[48] This idea has been borne out by a number of other investigations which tend to show that those people who are more liberal or radical on some particular issue actually are better informed than those who would maintain the *status quo.* This is not surprising when you stop to consider that an individual who is radical is one who is not pleased with the *status quo* and has, therefore, probably taken the trouble to inform himself on the issue involved, whereas the conservative is ordinarily content with things as they are and has, therefore, not bothered to make extensive investigations.

This general relationship between liberalism and amount of information has been borne out in at least two other investigations of college students. Moore and Garrison found a general trend among undergraduates from the freshman to the senior years toward greater liberalism and radicalism on questions relating to politics, sex, individual freedom, economics, tradition, international affairs, and race.[49] Also, high liberal scores tended to be associated with high scholarship. In their study of over four thousand students in Syracuse University, Katz and Allport reported a greater number of radical beliefs among graduate students than among undergraduate students.[50] One study, however, suggests that while in some situations liberals may actually know more than conservatives, there are other situations where conservatives know more than liberals.[51] These various studies can be summarized by saying that there is a positive relationship between liberalism and information, although, as suggested in other connections, it is necessary to talk about liberalism not simply in a general sense but in a specific type of situation.

There are also indications that those individuals who hold atypical opinions are usually much more convinced of the "rightness" of their views than those who have typical views. This seems to hold both for extreme radicals and for extreme reactionaries, according to the data of F. H. Allport and D. A. Hartmann.[52] It fits in with the study reported in Chapter 7 on the prediction of social events, in which Cantril found that Communists at one extreme and bankers at the other were more sure of the correctness of their predictions than were a group of social psychologists and sociologists who were not so emotionally convinced of the correctness or incorrectness of their views.[53]

RESISTANCE TO CHANGES IN THE *MATERIAL* CULTURE PATTERNS

We are usually faced with greater difficulty in changing our *nonmaterial* than our *material* culture patterns, as was pointed out in Chapter 5. New types of machine efficiency may be difficult to bring about, but never so much so as the nonmaterial ways, such as new systems of education, new devices in the law, new ways of slum clearance. Historically, there has always been tremendous opposition to change. As to the material culture patterns, for example, a wealthy citizen of *Middletown* was forbidden by the City Council in 1890 to lay a "new-fashioned concrete walk" in front of his home; he was ordered to make it of brick.[54] New ways are "suspect" ways. An individual who suggests a drastic way of doing things is apt to be scorned.

Up to recent years in white society no important or trivial noticeable cultural trait or divergent view was introduced without strong and often violent resistance. This was true in the case of medicine (anesthetics, vaccination), railroads, new varieties of foods, illuminating gas, stoves in churches, chimneys, sawmills, iron plows, silk hats, umbrellas. . . .

There was a bitter fight in Europe against the introduction of potatoes on the ground that they were "injurious to society," and against tomatoes as injurious to health. The first bananas sent to London could not be given away even in the slums. Sir Walter Scott called coal gas "a pestilential innovation," Napoleon called it "une grande folie" and Byron satirized it. In Berlin street lighting was opposed on a number of counts:

> "on theological grounds as being a presumptuous thwarting of Providence, which had appointed darkness for the hours of night; on the ground of objections to taxation in any form; on medical grounds, gas and oil being unwholesome and it being a bad thing to encourage people to wander after dark and catch cold; on moral grounds, people's ethical standard of conduct being lowered by gas lighting in the streets, for the drunkard would feel there was no hurry to go home, and late sweethearting would be encouraged, whereas black darkness sent people home early and thus preserved them from a multitude of sins; on police grounds, as the lighting would make horses shy and thieves alert; on political grounds, having in view the money which would have to go out of the country for coal and oil; and on the patriotic ground that national illuminations would lose their stimulating effect if there was a quasi-illumination every night of the year, year in and year out."[55]

RESISTANCE TO CHANGES IN THE *NONMATERIAL* CULTURE PATTERNS

Yet resistance to change in the material culture pattern is no problem at all as compared with resistance to the introduction of new ways into the nonmaterial culture pattern. We find that the attitudes of people in "civilized" society are quite comparable to those of primitives who resist change. The "cake of custom" does not differ noticeably in primitive groups from that in civilized groups. There is nearly always resistance to change in our habits, and only after a period of gradual adaptation, sometimes lasting years, are the new ways truly accepted.

More than one ambitious man has been destroyed by hurling himself against the wall of conventional morality. In our own day, in some particulars at least, *change* is in the folkways. The masses expect alterations in our material culture —newer models of automobiles, better radios, faster mail service, improvements in culture and luxury. . . . It is not so evident, however, that the masses feel any need for changes in the basic economic and social formulations which underlie our material culture. In the mores of sex, of private property, of religion and of political organization, their conservatism restrains the inventiveness of men anxious to be leaders.[56]

As examples of the nonmaterial culture patterns which have changed during the present century but only after long, long years of struggle, consider various types of social legislation. Today you take most of them for granted—the direct election of senators, the federal income tax, woman suffrage, child-labor laws, workmen's compensation for accidents, to say nothing of the conservation of natural resources and the beginnings of slum clearance. You are apt to think it "natural" that senators should be elected by the direct vote of the people; that there should be a federal income tax, and that women should be allowed to vote. Now, suppose that someone should suggest going back to the old order of things. Ponder this, and you will see how great the problem of changing the current nonmaterial culture patterns actually is.

But if you will go back and examine historically the ways in which these developments have come about, you will find that anyone who favored them was frequently accused of being a radical and a "Socialist." The growth of labor unions has been a process particularly beset by antagonisms, pressures, and hindrances. Many people will still say that although labor unions may be all right, we do not want too many of them and we do not want them to behave badly. A person who suggests that the only way labor can be effective is to be well organized may bring down upon himself the label "Communist."

In the 1930's we saw changes in attitudes concerning our national resources. For generations farmers, miners, ranchers, foresters, and fishermen had wasted our natural resources, and not many bothered to care. In a democratic society, the argument ran, "Who has the right to tell me what I can or cannot do?" Today we find active cooperation on the part of thousands of people, particularly throughout the Middle West, in preventing future dust storms and in keeping the soil of the Mississippi Valley from eroding and slowly washing into the Gulf of Mexico. But it has taken two full generations for this obviously necessary reform to be brought about.

HOW SOCIAL REFORMS OCCUR

How are such changes in attitudes brought about? A few of the many causes of change in our nonmaterial patterns may be mentioned:[57] (1) First of all, if our material culture does not agree with pre-existing general attitudes, the latter may shift. As an example, no one in the 1920's—aside from people called "visionaries"—could talk seriously about a planned society. Yet, in 1932 we had the amazing spectacle of millions of people actively supporting Roosevelt in his first campaign for election because they had become convinced that a "business" government was desirable. (2) Nonmaterial traits are often accepted by the discontented members of a group if the prevailing cultural values are believed to be the cause of the unrest. For example, many persons push for various social changes because of discontent with the *status quo*. (3) New ideas may be accepted if they look toward an "easier" way of life. Getting an education comes to be perfectly acceptable if it also means getting a bettter job and leading a life of greater ease and luxury. (4) Education and propaganda may eventually result in changes in our "ways."

As was pointed out earlier, the leaders of social reform are *usually* influential only in so far as they try *gradually* to change the existing attitudes and ways of thinking of those who are led. Ordinarily, if a man who wishes to occupy the role of leader behaves or thinks in too radical a fashion, he is regarded as such an extremist that he is ineffective. Some people even tend to keep their ideas to themselves, for fear of being considered radical or "different." This whole problem is well summarized by Folsom:

> The question for you to decide as an individual is what *role* you want to play in cultural change. For what part are you best fitted? In what capacity will you be happiest, best able to mobilize your energies? You cannot play a double role. If you want to elevate the Negro you can raise perhaps a hundred thousand dollars in some Southern city to build Negro schools, or you can entertain some Negro leaders at dinner. But you cannot do both.
>
> There will always be daring radicals who are so far ahead of the common herd that they cannot be sure the herd will ever follow in their particular direction. But they play a necessary role. They are the outposts of progress, the experimenters, the stimulators of thought. But they are not the leaders of action. Again, there are many more who are just a little ahead of the herd. They never get too far ahead, and they are quick to see when a change of direction is necessary. They are the "practical" leaders. Their eyes may sometimes look impatiently toward the brave men of principle who are marching far ahead, or off to one side, scoffed at by the herd. But they hold their place and carry on.[58]

Although this is not an exhaustive treatment of the dynamics of social change, several important points have been brought out. Social reforms are being made, but not always by those best qualified to make them. Resistance to change is usual, especially with nonmaterial ways of doing things, but this resistance breaks down and reform occurs under certain circumstances of adjustment between leaders, "led," and culture patterns. The *leaders in social change* tend to be younger, more intelligent, and better informed than the opponents of change.

▶THE PSYCHOLOGY OF INVENTION AND CREATIVE PRODUCTION

TYPES OF INVENTION

A special type of leadership is that of the inventor. Here we are concerned not so much with the interaction of the leader and the "led" as with the leader (inventor) and his eventual influence on society as a whole.

Inventions do not consist simply of gadgets and mechanical things. Invention and creative production occur in a number of nontangible as well as tangible fields. In fact, inventions are of four different kinds—*physical* inventions, such as the printing press, electric lights, elevators, carburetors, the Diesel engine; *social* inventions, such as fraternity rituals, systems of education, economic and political reforms; *method* inventions, that is, the development of principles, laws, scientific formulas and concepts;[59] and *artistic* inventions, including creative work in such fields as poetry, prose, literature, sculpture, and painting. There are a number of (1) psychological and (2) social factors involved in the process of invention.

1. PSYCHOLOGICAL FACTORS OF INVENTION

An analysis of invention and creative production reveals certain fairly universal psychological characteristics. The problem of creative thought has been attacked empirically by Patrick in a series of studies.[60] She has investigated the development of creative thought in poetry, art, scientific thinking, and creative writing and drawing. Four stages in creative thought have been found: (*a*) *preparation,* the assembling of ideas; (*b*) *incubation,* including repetition, modification, and selection from the associations; (*c*) *illumination,* the crystallization of the final idea; and (*d*) *verification* or *revision.* These four stages are, of course, not sharply separated from each other; rather there is a gradation from one stage into the next.

Typical of Patrick's investigations is her study of artists. She secured as subjects for her experimental group fifty artists whose work had been shown in important exhibits. Her control group consisted of fifty non-artists. She was able to get each of these individuals to paint a picture in her presence, and to give introspective judgments and make various analyses of the painting while it was in progress. In a detailed analysis of her results, she found (*a*) the period of *preparation,* when associations were shifting rapidly and the subject was receiving new ideas. This is somewhat comparable to the "warming-up" period when you are searching about for what to do and how to do it. (*b*) She found next a period of *incubation,* that is, the spontaneous recurrence from time to time of

By permission. Copyright 1940 *The New Yorker Magazine Inc.*

By permission. Copyright 1947 *The New Yorker Magazine Inc.*

Reprinted by permission from *The Saturday Evening Post*, copyright 1948 by the Curtis Publishing Company.

FIG. 26. CARTOONS WITH THE SAME THEME BY DIFFERENT ARTISTS[61]

The cartoon by Ned Hilton (compare Fig. 19) appeared in *The New Yorker* February 10, 1940; the one by O. Soglow in *The New Yorker* November 1, 1947; and the one by Lester Colin in *The Saturday Evening Post* June 5, 1948.

a mood or idea with some modification, even while the person was thinking about other topics. Actually this incubation period may last from a few minutes to as long as several years. Popularly we speak of this as "turning over" an idea in our minds.

> I often carry an idea around for several weeks before I make a picture though sometimes longer. I got ideas in Santa Fe last summer to do now. The ideas recur from time to time while I am occupied with other things.[62]

(*c*) *Illumination* occurred when the mood or idea which had been incubating was sketched out for the first time. Perhaps this is comparable to "insight"—a sort of "Aha!" experience. (*d*) Last was the period of *verification* or *revision*. This may also involve considerable elaboration.

In reply to the question, "Have you ever received assistance from the scientific revelation or 'hunch' in the solution of an important problem?" Hutchinson has reported an affirmative answer by 83 per cent of 232 directors of research laboratories and other scientists listed in *American Men of Science*.[63] The following quotation from Bertrand Russell is paralleled by statements of a great many other scientists: "In all the creative work that I have done, what has come first is a problem, a puzzle, involving discomfort. Then comes concentrated voluntary application involving great effort. After this, a period without conscious thought; and finally a solution. This last stage is usually sudden."[64]

2. SOCIAL FACTORS OF INVENTION

In addition to the psychological factors of the individual, there are important social or cultural elements in invention. In fact, Kroeber has even argued that the individual inventors are relatively unimportant and that inventions are the result of the culture in which inventors live.[65] The following cases of dual inventions bear this out. The nebular hypothesis was apparently invented by both Kant and Laplace. The calculus was invented by both Newton and Leibniz. Oxygen was discovered by two different investigators independently. The invention of the steamboat has been attributed to three other individuals in addition to Robert Fulton. Three different persons discovered the telegraph independently in 1837. Photography was invented twice in 1839, the telephone twice in 1876, and the phonograph twice in 1877. In fact, Ogburn has made a list of approximately 150 inventions made by two or more individuals working independently.[66] In practically all of these instances, it is to be noted that the persons who discovered the same thing were living in the same period of time, in the same cultural area, and under the influence of the same need.

This tendency of different people to invent somewhat the same idea at approximately the same time may be illustrated by ideas for cartoons.

EASTER 1941

EASTER PARADE

FIG. 27. SIMILAR CARTOONS BY DIFFERENT ARTISTS PUBLISHED ON THE SAME DAY[67]

"Easter 1941" is by Gene Elderman in *The Washington Post,* "Easter Parade" by Edwin Marcus in *The New York Times. Both cartoons appeared on the same day*—April 13, 1941 (Easter Sunday).

"Darling, you must have two stations on at the same time!"

By Permission. Copyright 1946 *The Saturday Review of Literature*

"Do you suppose you could have two stations?"

By Permission. Copyright 1946 *The New Yorker Magazine, Inc.*

FIG. 27 *(continued)*

The upper cartoon is by Ben Roth in *The Saturday Review of Literature,* the lower one by Richard Decker in *The New Yorker. Both appeared on the same day*—August 24, 1946.

The cartoons in Figure 26 have much the same theme. Yet the first is by Ned Hilton in 1940, the second by O. Soglow in 1947, and the third by Lester Colin in 1948.

You are mistaken if you think that either of the later cartoons was consciously adapted from the first. This is *not* plagarism, but rather an illustration of how creative people in the same field of endeavor may tend to have similar ideas.

This point may be demonstrated by comparing the two pairs of cartoons in Figure 27. The two showing the Nazi boot crushing out the French lilies appeared on the *same day* (Easter Sunday, 1941) by two different artists in *The New York Times* and the *Washington Post*. The two cartoons by different cartoonists about two television stations were published on the *same day* (August 24, 1946) in *The Saturday Review of Literature* and *The New Yorker*. In other words, two different men—living at the same time in the same culture and with similar motivation—had essentially the same idea.

A final example is found in the work of two artists whose illustrations of the same general theme appeared on the front covers of two different national magazines *during the same week*. See Figure 28. Both Alajálov for *The Saturday Evening Post* and Shermund for *Esquire* show groups of women sightseers far more interested in a handsome young guide than in the local sightseeing attraction. Yet each illustration was developed independently, and with no knowledge by either artist that someone else had a similar idea. This is simply one more instance of two highly imaginative and creative people inventing or developing similar ideas at the same time.

Apparently invention, no matter what the end result, requires at least three factors: (*a*) a felt need; (*b*) a person or persons of requisite ability; (*c*) the proper cultural base.[68]

a. A Felt Need. Most popular theories have attributed inventions simply to a need—"necessity is the mother of invention"—or to a brilliant inventor. As to the first factor, however, "necessity," that is a relative matter. Certainly with the rapidly diminishing supply of gasoline we now need a less expensive substitute for it; but the necessity has not yet produced a substitute in general use. Certainly men needed railroads and automobiles long before the present time. The need or necessity was there, yet the inventions did not come until the cultural period had involved considerable preparation.

b. A Man or Men of Requisite Ability. As to the second factor, the inventor, although he is ordinarily of superior intelligence, an examination of inventions indicates that many an inventor simply created or discovered some idea which would have been discovered by somebody else if he had not done it. In other words, if you have a certain interaction of social forces, they will result in an invention by one person or another.

The fact that so many inventions have been made by two or more people is an indication of this.

c. The Proper Cultural Base. The third factor is of the utmost importance. No invention is ever made until its elements are present in the existing culture. Every invention is made on the basis of previous inventions. For example, the automobile could never have been invented (1895) unless there had been a number of other inventions before it, namely, the water jacket (1833), the differential gear (1840), pneumatic rubber tires (1845 and 1883), the electric gap and spark (1860), the compression engine (1876), the clutch and gear (1887), the gas engine (1888), the friction clutch and drive (1891).[69] Without these other inventions, the automobile never would have been possible. The need for it was great long before it was invented, but the cultural basis had not been prepared. The same applies to electricity, and to radio and television.

Actually the cultural base for most inventions has existed only very recently in man's cosmic history.

Let us imagine the whole history of mankind crowded into twelve hours, and that we are living at noon of the long human day. Let us, in the interest of moderation and convenient reckoning, assume that man has been upright and engaged in seeking out inventions for only two hundred and forty thousand years. Each hour of our clock will represent twenty thousand years, each minute three hundred and thirty-three and a third years. For over eleven and a half hours nothing was recorded. We know of no persons or events; we only infer that man was living on earth, for we find his stone tools, bits of his pottery, and some of his pictures of mammoths and bison. Not until twenty minutes before twelve do the earliest vestiges of Egyptian and Babylonian civilization begin to appear. The Greek literature, philosophy, and science, of which we have been accustomed to speak as 'ancient,' are not seven minutes old. At one minute before twelve, Lord Bacon wrote his *Advancement of Learning,* and not half a minute has elapsed since man first began to make the steam engine do his work for him.[70]

"LAG" IN INVENTIONS

There is often a tremendous "lag" between the time that someone first thinks about an invention and the time of its ultimate success and widespread use. Our modern television, for example, actually began to be invented in 1877—a lag of approximately sixty years. There was a lag from the time of first invention to the time of practical use of approximately seventy years in the case of the wireless, twenty-three years for radiotelephony, over seventy years for the airplane, and forty years for the "talking" picture.[71] Taking nineteen inventions introduced between 1888 and 1913 which have been voted the most useful, the length of time elapsing from the year the invention was first thought about until its first working model was an average of 176 years. The time from the perfecting

FIG. 28. MAGAZINE COVERS WITH THE SAME THEME BY DIFFERENT ARTISTS PUBLISHED DURING THE SAME WEEK[72]

The two magazines with these front covers were both published during the first week of August, 1948. *The Saturday Evening Post* cover is by Alajálov, the *Esquire* cover by Shermund.

FIG. 28 *(continued)*

of this first working model or patent to the time of widespread use was approximately fifty years more, on the average. This average fifty-year period was broken down as follows: from the time of the first model until the first practical use, twenty-four years; from then until the first commercial success, fourteen years; from then until important use, twelve years.

THE INFLUENCE OF INVENTIONS

Individuals responsible for new inventions have tremendous influence upon our culture. This is recognized by society, provided the invention is considered "useful"; but the influence of inventors in the field of "pure" research, those who have prepared the way for later inventions, is often overlooked. Consider the example just given concerning the automobile. The average American associates its invention with Henry Ford's name, but knows little or nothing about the inventors of the gas engine, the differential gear, or pneumatic rubber tires. Similarly, people think of the Wright brothers in connection with aviation, yet know little about the inventions which prepared the way for their famous flight. Many a person thinks of Marconi, "inventor" of wireless or radio, as one of the world's greatest scientists. Yet Marconi's share in developing radio was almost negligible.

> Marconi was inevitable. The real credit for everything that has been done in the field of wireless belongs, as far as such fundamental credit can be definitely assigned to anyone, to Professor Clerk Maxwell, who in 1865 carried out certain abstruse and remote calculations in the field of magnetism and electricity. Maxwell reproduced his abstract equations in a treatise published in 1873. At the next meeting of the British Association Professor H. J. S. Smith of Oxford declared that 'no mathematician can turn over the pages of these volumes without realizing that they contain a theory which has already added largely to the methods and resources of pure mathematics.' Other discoveries supplemented Maxwell's theoretical work during the next fifteen years. Finally in 1887 and 1888 the scientific problem still remaining—the detection and demonstration of the electromagnetic waves which are the carriers of wireless signals—was solved by Heinrich Hertz, a worker in Helmholtz's laboratory in Berlin. Neither Maxwell nor Hertz had any concern about the utility of their work; no such thought ever entered their minds. They had no practical objective. The inventor in the legal sense was of course Marconi, but what did Marconi invent? Merely the last technical detail, mainly the now obsolete receiving device called coherer, almost universally discarded.[73]

Certain inventions have revolutionized our pattern of living. Until your great-grandmother's time, the number of material inventions was relatively few, but the latter part of the industrial revolution brought great changes in our social and economic structure. Today, as contrasted with the time of your great-grandmother's childhood, you are living in a world where economic organization, the community in which you live, the social structure of the state, the educational system, recreational activities, and even family life have been greatly changed by inventions of a material sort.[74] Consider how the patterns of our nationalistic society have been influenced by the invention of gunpowder, the printing press, hard-surfaced roadways, vehicles using these roadways, and mechanisms such as the phonograph, radio, and "talking" movies. Your community life has been influenced by inventions in the field of transportation and stationary machines which use nonanimal sources of power.

Two types of inventions alone have changed the social patterns of family life tremendously. The first consists of mechanical inventions such as those using steam, electricity, and the internal-combustion engine. Rapid means of transportation, for example, have tended to break down the close integration of community and family life, while electrical gadgets such as vacuum cleaners and washing machines have reduced the amount of labor and time devoted to duties in the home almost to a minimum. The second type of invention is the contraceptive, which has had a great influence on family and social life, as evidenced by the reduced birth rate, especially among people in the higher economic brackets.

THE INVENTORS

What sort of people are inventors? The popular superstition is that they are geniuses, and, in turn, that all geniuses are really "insane." We may immediately scotch the first notion that inventors are all geniuses. The evidence is that they are of above average intelligence, although some few are, of course, in the very top brackets of the intelligence scale.

The second notion, that inventors are "insane," or that they differ considerably from other people, is not so easily dismissed. Certainly there is some evidence to show that artists and writers tend a bit more toward instability and perhaps toward nervous disorders than do scientists and statesmen.[75] This might be expected, since they are often frustrated by popular opposition to innovation. However, the popular notion that inventors are eccentric attaches even to scientific inventors. This can be accounted for in at least two ways.[76] First of all, an inventor, particularly if he invents something which becomes popular, gets a good deal of publicity. Any deviations in personality traits are likely to be described in exaggerated terms by other people, thus bolstering the popular stereotype. Second, legends are likely to be created about an inventor because he is atypical of the population.

The atypical characteristics of inventors are illustrated in the desires that motivate them. The motivation for invention and creative work seems to be based more upon curiosity and the joy of manipulation than upon desire for monetary reward or other factors. This in itself is an unusual characteristic. Many research investigators report that they have made various discoveries simply because of an "itch" to find out things. In reporting his important research in 1905 on the development of incandescent electric lamps, Nobel prize winner Dr. Irving Langmuir of the General Electric Company said in 1945:

> *Purely out of scientific curiosity and without any thought of applying the results to an improvement of the lamp* I started to put various kinds of gas into the lamp—gases such as oxygen, nitrogen, etc. *just to see what happened.* (Italics ours). . . . You now have the advantage of an electric lamp which is vastly superior to that which existed some forty years ago. It was only by combining several types of new knowledge that the improved lamp became possible. It is highly improbable that this necessary new knowledge would have resulted from any planned research program aimed directly at improving the efficiency of tungsten lamps.[77]

In many of the most important scientific discoveries, the inventor has simply been curious to find the answer to a particular problem, with little or no concern as to whether the answer involved anything of "practical" value. Again and again those discoveries of a "pure" sort as contrasted with those of an applied nature have had tremendous effect upon our culture. Yet the inventors have frequently not been concerned with the results of their inventions, but simply with inventing. One analysis, involving the lives of 171 inventors, revealed as leading motives in invention, first, joy in manipulation, and, second, a feeling of a need.[78]

THE CREATIVE YEARS

At what periods of their lives do the great poets, scientists, inventors, artists, and other creative people make the greatest number of contributions? And at what age do they make their *best* contributions?

> In the writings of those who have attempted to answer these questions four principal fallacies, or weaknesses, are to be found . . . (1) Mere assertions, or assumptions, unsupported by quantitative evidence, that men do their best work at this or that particular age level, (2) quotations from earlier writers whose names may have great prestige value but whose quoted statements are likewise unsupported by quantitative evidence, (3) conclusions which are bolstered by the citation of one or a very few exceptional cases, and (4) claims which are sustained by a procedure which the propaganda analysts have called 'card-stacking.'[79]

Instead of relying on statements and claims of this sort, Lehman has made a series of studies that give factual answers to the question of what are man's best creative years.[80] It seems that from age thirty-five to forty represents the peak of productivity in general, although a high level of output is often maintained into the sixties. However, the quality of work seems to be at its height at about thirty-five to forty, and then to drop off somewhat until age fifty, with a considerable decrease from then on. There are individual differences in these curves of productivity, of course, according to the type of work represented. Table 12 shows some age differences with reference to various types of literature.

TABLE 12

Age Intervals During Which Various Types of Literature Are Most Frequently *First* Published (From Heidler and Lehman)[81]

Ages 20 to 29
Nonepic narrative poetry
Tragedies
Pastoral poetry
Elegies
Odes
Travel prose
Lyrics and ballads (dates of composition)

Ages 30 to 39
Narrative prose
The novel
Comedies
Satiric poetry
Religious prose
Miscellaneous prose
Political poetry
The short story

Ages 40 to 49
Satiric prose
Educational prose
Epic poetry
Scientific prose
Political prose

Ages 50 to 59
Philosophical prose
Historical prose (not including novel)
Critical prose

Ages 60 to 69
Biographical prose

Data for renowned men of science and in the humanities show that they tend to have contributed their first important creative work before age twenty-five. These earlier starters also have produced, on the average, "both more and better creative work" than those who start to contribute later in life.[82]

As to *best* contributions, Lehman had several types of work rated by competent men in the various fields of endeavor represented. He then determined the ages at which the *best* work was done. Although the best contributions may come anywhere from age twenty to eighty, there are certain periods when the best quality of work is most frequently done—roughly from about twenty-six to forty-seven. The ages of best work differ from one field to another, as Table 13 illustrates. In general, literary masterpieces of the first rank have been published most frequently by men who were not over forty-five years of age.[83]

TABLE 13

Age Intervals During Which the Largest Number of *Best* Contributions are Made In Science, Invention, and Literature (From Lehman)

Field	*Best Years*
Poetry	26-30
Chemistry	28-32
Physics	30-34
Etchings	30-34
Inventions	31-35
Short stories	31-37
Oil paintings	32-36
Mathematics	34-38
Medicine and Surgery	35-39
Philosophy	35-39
Literature	38-42
Architecture	40-44
Astronomy	43-47

Other students of the problem have arrived at similar conclusions. One investigation, limited to 331 great names, puts the age of the masterpiece at about forty-seven.[84] Another study of 243 men of science and letters shows the age of highest attainment to be about thirty-five.[85] According to results of this sort, it would seem possible to construct for each specific type of measurable behavior standards of excellence for various ages, somewhat comparable to the mortality tables of insurance companies.[86]

These figures do not mean that older individuals create no important new works and discoveries. Many do continue producing, although the quality of the work is often not so great. "Within any given field of endeavor, . . . age-curves can be constructed which show the rise and fall of creative output at successive age levels. The shape of any one of these curves is in part a function of quality of performance."[87] Compared to *quantity* of performance, the peak representing *quality* is likely to be more narrow or pointed. Within any given field of endeavor, quantity and quality of output are not necessarily correlated; in fact, output of highest merit tends to fall off at an earlier age than output of lesser merit.

There are notable instances, however, of outstanding achievements in very late years, although in these instances the worker had already produced outstanding achievements in earlier life. For example, Galileo discovered important facts about the moon at seventy-five; Goethe finished *Faust* in his eighties; Tennyson wrote *Crossing the Bar* at eighty-three; Titian painted a masterpiece at ninety-eight.

Lehman's analyses of the ages of *peak* performances of intellectual workers, and of golfers, bowlers, and the like, show considerable agree-

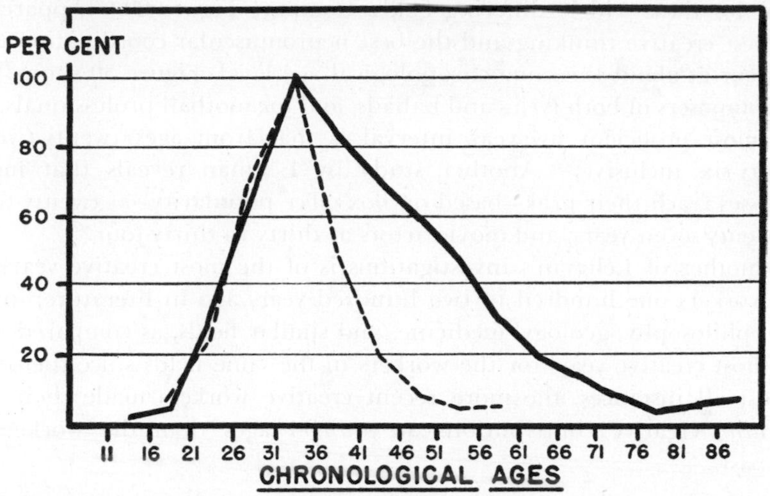

FIG. 29. AGE VERSUS OUTPUT IN SCIENCE, MATHEMATICS, AND INVENTION; AND IN CERTAIN NEUROMUSCULAR SKILLS (From Lehman)

The solid line (——) represents 1,059 superior contributions by 933 scientists, mathematicians, and inventors. The broken line (– – –) represents 577 championships at golf, billiards, rifle shooting, pistol shooting, bowling, and duck-pin bowling.

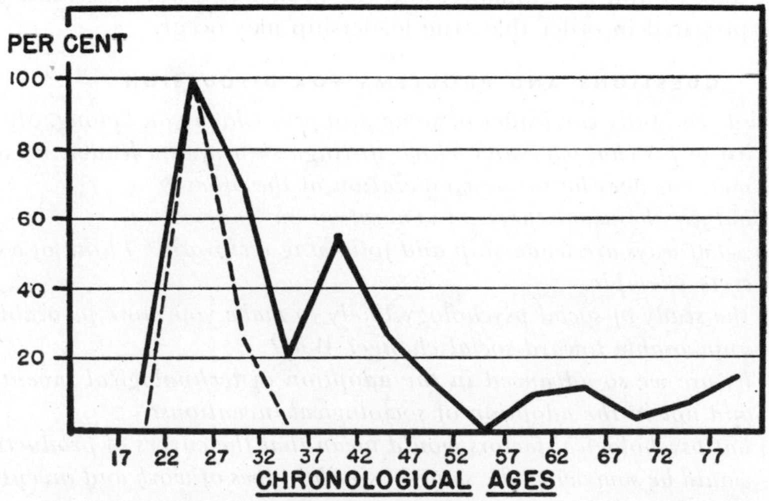

FIG. 30. AGE VERSUS LYRIC WRITING AND FOOTBALL PROFESSIONALISM (From Lehman)

The solid line (——) represents 148 lyrics and ballads by 36 poets. The broken line (– – –) represents 485 top professional football players.

ment for these widely differing fields. Compare Figure 29.[88] Apparently the best creative thinking and the best neuromuscular coordination tend to occur at about the same chronological age level. Figure 30 shows that for composers of both lyrics and ballads, and for football professionals, the one most proficient five-year interval is that from ages twenty-two to twenty-six inclusive.[89] Another study by Lehman reveals that movie actresses reach their peak—based on box-office popularity—at twenty-three to twenty-seven years, and movie actors at thirty to thirty-four.[90]

Another of Lehman's investigations is of the most creative years for the workers one hundred to two hundred years ago in literature, invention, philosophy, geology, medicine, and similar fields, as compared with the most creative years for the workers in the same fields since then.[91] In almost all instances, the more recent creative workers made their *outstanding* creative contributions at *younger* ages than the workers of the past.

CONCLUDING REMARKS

Leadership and invention, then, is something that involves both psychological and sociological considerations. The individual leader or inventor is influential because of his individual background and characteristics, but only in relation to other persons and to the culture patterns of the society in which he happens to live. Leadership must be needed in specific situations, the leader must have some ability in these situations, others must look to him for guidance, and the proper cultural base must have been prepared in order that true leadership may occur.

QUESTIONS AND PROBLEMS FOR DISCUSSION

1. *Study carefully the leader of some group to which you belong. Make a list of his characteristics which distinguish him as a leader. By what methods does he secure cooperation of the others?*
2. *What are the usual effects of veneration on leaders?*
3. *In what ways are leadership and following reciprocal? Think of a concrete example.*
4. *Is the study of social psychology likely to make you more favorable or unfavorable toward social change? Why?*
5. *Why are we so advanced in the adoption of technological inventions and not in the adoption of sociological inventions?*
6. *What psychological factors would mean that the curves of productivity would be somewhat the same in similar types of work and invention?*
7. *How do social reforms usually occur?*
8. *Why are persons who are leaders in one field not necessarily leaders in other fields?*
9. *What would be some practical rules for development of leadership? For development of creative ideas?*

RECOMMENDED READINGS

Bogardus, E. S., *Leaders and Leadership*. New York: D. Appleton-Century Company, 1934.

Bureau of Naval Personnel, *Manual for Practical Development of Leadership Qualities*. Washington, D. C.: U. S. Government Printing Office (Nav Pers 16154), 1944.

Burlingame, R., *Engines of Democracy*. New York: Charles Scribner's Sons, 1940.

Chapin, F. S., *Cultural Change*. New York: Century Company, 1928.

Gowin, E. B., *The Executive and His Control of Men*. New York: The Macmillan Company, 1915.

Hadamard, J., *An Essay of the Psychology of Invention in the Mathematical Field*. Princeton: Princeton University Press, 1945.

Herring, P., *Presidential Leadership*. New York: Farrar & Rinehart, Inc., 1940.

Mead, M., *Cooperation and Competition among Primitive Peoples*. New York: McGraw-Hill Book Company, Inc., 1937.

Minton, B., and Stuart, J., *Men Who Lead Labor*. New York: Modern Age Books, Inc., 1937.

Ogburn, W. F., *Social Change with Respect to Culture and Original Nature*. New York: B. W. Huebsch, 1922.

Pigors, P. J. W., *Leadership or Domination*. Boston: Houghton Mifflin Company, 1935.

Taussig, F. W., and Joslyn, C. S., *American Business Leaders*. New York: The Macmillan Company, 1932.

Tead, O., *The Art of Leadership*. New York: McGraw-Hill Book Company, Inc., 1935.

Webb, E. T., and Morgan, J. J. B., *Strategy in Handling People*. New York: Garden City Publishing Company, Inc., 1932.

Young, J. W., *A Technique for Producing Ideas*. Chicago: Advertising Publications, Inc., 1940.

*Newcomb, T. M., Hartley, E. L., and others (editors), *Readings in Social Psychology*. New York: Henry Holt and Company, Inc., 1947. (The following selections are listed according to the sequence of related discussions in the chapter you have just read.)

Whyte, W. F., "Leader-Follower Relations in Street Corner Society," pp. 403-407.

Jennings, H. H., "Leadership and Sociometric Choice," pp. 407-413.

PART FIVE

THE SOCIAL PSYCHOLOGY OF INSTITUTIONS

▶ THIS PART is a social-psychological discussion of some representative primary and secondary groups and of how they affect our attitudes.

After a brief explanation of kinds of groups, the first chapter in the section deals with institutional patterns of belief and action, especially conformity behavior.

The psychology of the *family* is discussed in three ways—the personality development of the child, the problems of parenthood, and the factors of marital adjustment and maladjustment.

American *education* is next described both as to its aims and as to its problems. The question of character education is dealt with at some length. A psychological analysis of the teaching profession is also given.

The social psychology of *religion* is presented in terms of its psychological bases, motivation, and ritual. Representative beliefs and conflicts are considered, and finally an analysis of the ministry is tentatively offered.

Next, the psychology of the *fraternity* and *club* is analyzed, including a study of their ideologies and psychological values. This leads to a consideration of the *political party* and voters' prejudices, with an explanation of several different kinds of voting behavior.

The last chapter in this section deals with *occupational groups.* First, professional groups are briefly described. Then, horizontal and vertical differences between all sorts of occupational groups are explained, especially with reference to attitudes of the "business class" and the "working class."

CHAPTER FIFTEEN

GROUPS AND INSTITUTIONS

TYPES OF GROUPS. (1) In-groups Versus Out-groups—(2) Primary and Secondary Groups / INSTITUTIONAL BEHAVIOR. Institutions—Studies of Institutions—Institutional Ideology—Conformity Behavior—Effect of Group Standards.

▶ TYPES OF GROUPS

Two different types of groups should be distinguished: (1) the *In-group* as compared with the *Out*-group, and (2) the *primary* group as compared with the *secondary* group.

1. IN-GROUPS VERSUS OUT-GROUPS

The *In-group* or "We-group" is characterized primarily by *belongingness* —those who are in your group or organization are people whom you recognize as "belonging." If you are a member of Alpha Alpha Alpha, the Methodist Church, and the Democratic party, all men over the country who have also gone through the ritual of Alpha Alpha, all the individuals who make up the Methodist Church, and to a certain extent fellow voters in the Democratic party make up your In-group. On the other hand, those awful people, the Omega Omega Omegas, the Baptists, and the Republicans, constitute for you an *Out-group* or "Others-group." Members of the In-group ordinarily feel a certain amount of loyalty and cooperation for each other, are generally concerned with the social welfare of other members, and often give mutual aid to each other. Certainly, belongingness implies a sense of social solidarity and oneness among the members of the group.

Remember, however, that for every In-group to which you belong, the members of the Out-groups are for themselves also members of In-groups; your particular groups may be looked on by them as Out-groups. Thus, the Omegas, Baptists, and Republicans look on you and your fellows as members of Out-groups. The Out-group is usually looked upon with mild dislike and prejudice, or, in some instances, with disgust or fear. Your family is, of course, excellent in every respect as compared with those Joneses down the street. Your fraternity undoubtedly has the most illustrious of alumni—what fraternity does not?—but that other group next door has produced a pretty ordinary lot of people.

These characteristics of the In-group and the Out-group may in certain instances present the problem of *ambivalent* attitudes, mentioned at the close of Chapter 7. That is, you may have feelings of loyalty and cooperation for a group to which you belong, but at one and the same time feel suspicious of many of its members, and even dislike particular individuals. In other words, you may have a "yes-and-no" attitude toward the group at one and the same time. For many a college student, it seems that this is a very real problem. "Belongingness" and loyalty to the family are esteemed, but at the same time attitudes arise of wanting to be superior to the old folks and of wishing to discard their mores and folkways.

2. PRIMARY AND SECONDARY GROUPS

In the second place, we may contrast the *primary* groups, such as the family, the neighborhood, the play group, and the gang, with the *secondary* groups, such as the school, the church, the fraternity, the political party, and the occupational group. Cooley pointed out that primary groups are "characterized by intimate face-to-face association and cooperation."[1] Thus, your family, play group, neighborhood, village community, and in many instances the gangs or clubs in which you found yourself as a child were for you primary groups. They involved face-to-face contacts—gestures, touch, smell, vocalization, visual stimuli, auditory stimuli, in a very intimate way. These psychological factors are a bit different from those in the secondary group which is distinguished from the primary group in that, first, it is consciously organized, and second, it does not depend altogether on face-to-face contacts. In general, the motivation and attitudes of the members of a primary group are more intimate than those of a secondary group.

You have been a member of every primary group to which you have ever belonged through no choice of your own. That is, you did not select your parents, or determine for yourself on which side of the railroad tracks you would grow up. You were a member of these primary groups of family and neighborhood without any conscious direction on your part. In your secondary groups, however, you have usually *chosen* to become a member; and your contacts, although sometimes face-to-face, depend upon other types of association as well. Thus, we have secondary groups such as fraternal orders—the Odd Fellows, Modern Woodmen of the World, the Moose, the Elks, the Eagles; religious sects—Episcopalians, Presbyterians, Rosicrucians; political groups—the Republicans, Democrats, Farmer-Laborites; scientific societies—the American Association for the Advancement of Science. Every one of these is consciously organized and depends not only on face-to-face relations but upon ideas transmitted through intricate systems of communication—mail, telegraph, telephone, radio, the printed word.

Of course, you can belong to these two types of groups at the same time. An In-group or Out-group may be either primary or secondary in nature, and similarly a primary or secondary group may be either an In-group or Out-group. For example, your family is for you an In-group and at the same time a primary group, whereas the Joneses down the street are for you an Out-group but also a primary group. Likewise, a particular club or fraternity is an In-group or Out-group, depending upon whether you are a member or not, and is at the same time a secondary group consciously organized and depending upon something more than intimate face-to-face relations. Perhaps a word of caution from Kimball Young is appropriate here:

> We do not assume that for every group to which one belongs there is a corresponding out-group. Moreover, not every group in which one does not participate as a member is necessarily to him an out-group. There are outside associations toward which we are totally indifferent. The attitude of the we-group toward an others-group depend upon the functional relationship of the two groups to each other, fostered by competition and conflict. Any primary or secondary group can on occasion develop an in-group-out-group relationship, but there are many associations of people which do not.[2]

All of the primary and secondary groups are extremely important so far as the personality integration of the growing human is concerned. They are agents which mold and control the behavior of both young and old, and transmit culture patterns from one group to another and from one generation to another.

▶ INSTITUTIONAL BEHAVIOR

INSTITUTIONS

Most of these various groups, either primary or secondary, can also be talked about as *institutions.* They have unique patterns of behavior; in fact, many a social scientist discusses the institutions of the family, fraternity, and political party in the sense of closely fitting organizations of common attitudes and ways of thinking. The word "institution" should not convey to you the restricted meaning which it has to the "man in the street"; an institution is not simply a bank or prison or reform school or, necessarily, anything very tangible and visible. The term means much more than this, for it implies a certain permanence of structure in closely knit organizations, whether these groups have tangibility or not. Institutions consist of cooperative and collective endeavors within the framework of various social organizations. They involve sets of habits, attitudes, and ideas which center around certain well-understood needs of individuals. Actually the word "institution" is interpreted in a good many different ways, as has been demonstrated by Hertzler.[3] One useful definition is: "Culturalized, more or less standardized, set of habits and associated attitudes and ideas centering around some primary or derived want or need of individuals, such as sustenance, sex, transmission of culture, etc."[4]

We can speak not only of the institution called the family, but we can talk equally well of the institutions of religion, education, law, science, art, politics. We are not limited to studying the tangible evidence of these institutions, such as buildings, but are also concerned with common ways of thinking within each of these institutions. An analysis of an institution should take into account: (1) its members, (2) its leaders, (3) its physical aspects, and (4) the social context in which these are found.[5] For this reason we are interested not only in the institution of the family, but are also concerned with education (the school), religion (the church), fraternalism (the lodge), politics (the political party), economic attitudes (the professions and types of work). In every instance, our problem is a bit different from that of the "straight" sociologist or psychologist who may limit himself either to group or to individual behavior. A psychologist might simply examine representative individuals in particular family situations, whereas a sociologist might give a historical description of family life in our culture. The social psychologist, on the other hand, raises questions as to the attitudes which grow up and exist in these various groups and institutions (such as the family), and the effects which these attitudes have upon the personalities of various individuals in these groups.

STUDIES OF INSTITUTIONS

The study of institutions is not limited to the field of social psychology alone. In fact, the investigation of any particular institution necessarily involves some background in other fields such as economics, political science, history, law, philosophy, anthropology. Actually the materials for the study of any particular institution are often found in fields such as these, so that the social psychologist must first master the pertinent material of such fields and then apply his psychological training and techniques. Regardless of the particular institution studied, however, it must be examined objectively.

As typical of an institutional study, we have Jerome Frank's *Law and the Modern Mind.*[6] This author deals with the concept of *law,* his central thesis being that the law is not rigid and certain, but is necessarily subject to fluctuation and change. Starbuck, James, and Ligon have examined various phases of the institution of religion.[7] Rice has studied various political problems, such as free trade, and used the institutional approach in *Quantitative Methods in Politics.*[8] In one sense Adam Smith's *Wealth of Nations* was an institutional study.[9] Similarly, an examination has been made of the institutional characteristics of *property.*[10]

INSTITUTIONAL IDEOLOGY

Every institution renders some type of service to its members. This may be of a tangible or a completely intangible sort, but in either instance it is of psychological value. The existence of the institution means that its members cannot satisfy their needs as well individually as through common routine actions with others. Although coercion by the leaders accounts for the continued existence of many social institutions, this is only part of the story, for the "led"—members or followers of the institutional organization—are sufficiently alike to have many motives and problems in common.[11] When these motives and problems are met or satisfied by particular institutions, these institutions flourish. There may be modifications of institutions as time goes on, but ordinarily there are few sudden changes.

The family, built around sex and economic needs, has been historically a basic institution. However, with social changes in man's needs and fears, conflict has gradually resulted. Today the family as an economic unit has lost a good deal of its earlier significance, and its satisfaction of various motives has been questioned, as we shall see in the next chapter. If the family is to maintain its strong position in our society, some basic changes may take place. Another example of an institution undergoing change and experiencing difficulties is organized religion. The church developed to a great extent around the fear of the unknown and the desire to appease and control it. Today, however, these needs and fears are not present to nearly so great an extent as in the past. Unless adjustments are made, the church may have less significance as a social institution than formerly.

So long as a given institution is strong, at least four characteristic beliefs are found among many of its members. They believe: (1) that their particular institution is some sort of an *entity* or reality which transcends the individual members; (2) that it is *superior* to other institutions organized to meet the same needs; (3) that their institution is absolutely *right* in its aims and ideals; (4) that it is *bound to succeed.*[12] These beliefs are adhered to, provided not only that the members are loyal but that the institution itself is recognized as significant by members of Out-groups in other institutions of the same sort. Take a college fraternity as an example. Most of its members believe all these things about their own fraternity, especially if it has considerable prestige among other fraternities. Katz and Allport found that two-thirds of the students at Syracuse University were "institutionalists" who believed that their fraternities were sort of superindividual beings.[13] The second belief, the superiority of one's own group, is illustrated by the superiority of Alpha Alpha Alpha to Omega Omega Omega, and vice versa. The third belief, the absolutistic rightness of one's own fraternity, is ordinarily impressed on the neophyte by a long period of pledgeship and then reinforced by an impressive ritual. Finally, competition with other groups and the encouragement of ever-present alumni, keep before the members the notion that their fraternity is "bound to win."

CONFORMITY BEHAVIOR

The degree to which we are conformists or nonconformists is affected very much by our institutional ideologies. Largely owing to the work of Floyd H. Allport we have quantified some of the differences of behavior in institutional as compared with noninstitutional situations. You already know that a great many psychological characteristics tend to distribute themselves along a curve of normal distribution. However, as Allport and others have pointed out, the curve of behavior will be entirely different in most institutional situations. We will get a "J-curve"—called that because it is shaped somewhat like a reversed letter J in which steps plotted along a continuum have the mode or topmost position falling on step 1 and then progressively smaller steps in the scale from left to right.[14] See Figure 31.

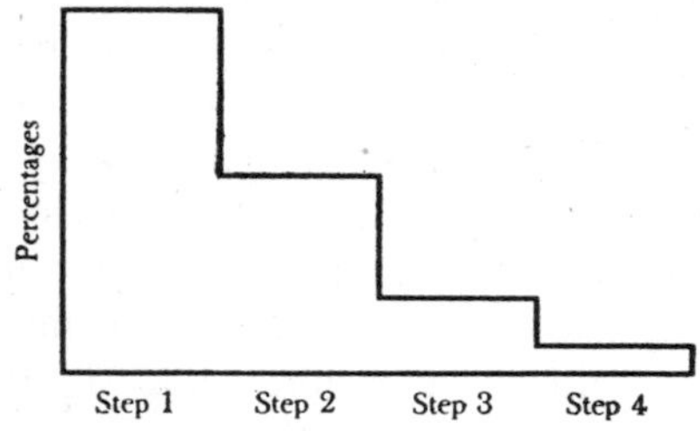

FIG. 31. A SCHEMATIC J-CURVE

This type of curve has been discovered again and again in most—although not all—situations where institutional behavior has been studied. Where noninstitutional situations are involved, we continue to find the curve of normal probability or something approaching it—see Figure 16, page 221. In the J-curve, on the other hand:

a. More instances will fall upon the step at the extreme left than upon any other.

b. The successive steps from left to right will have a respectively diminishing number of instances.

c. The decline in the number of instances will decrease as we proceed by successive steps from left to right.[15]

In other words, institutional uniform ways of behavior arise among the members of various groups—in the church, the community, the school, the family, the fraternity. For example, studies of the patterns of behavior of crossing oneself in a Catholic church, of the time of arrival of employees at work, and of automobile drivers to a red light show conformity approaching that of the J-curve.[16] One investigation has shown that when sex behavior is left relatively free and unregulated, the individual differences are distributed normally, but when sex behavior is highly institutionalized, a mode appears (as in Figure 31) at one end of the distribution.[17]

Another investigation concerned the behavior of pedestrians who were supposed to walk across traffic intersections only when the traffic light showed green (or "walk") and to wait on the curb while the light showed red—conformity to a legal institution.[18]

Four different degrees of fulfillment of the purpose of the prescribed act—steps or positions of Allport's "telic continuum"—were chosen for tabulation. (1) *Waiting on the intersection curb while the light shows RED* represents the maximum degree of fulfillment of the regulation. (2) *Waiting just off the intersection curb* is the next readily distinguishable degree of the purpose of the law. (3) *Proceeding to the middle of the intersection and waiting* is the third position, representing still less satisfaction of the purpose. (4) *Walking across the street disregarding the light,* represents no fulfillment whatsoever of the purpose of the law.[19]

The data on downtown areas as contrasted with residential sections, and on the earlier as contrasted with the later days of operation of the

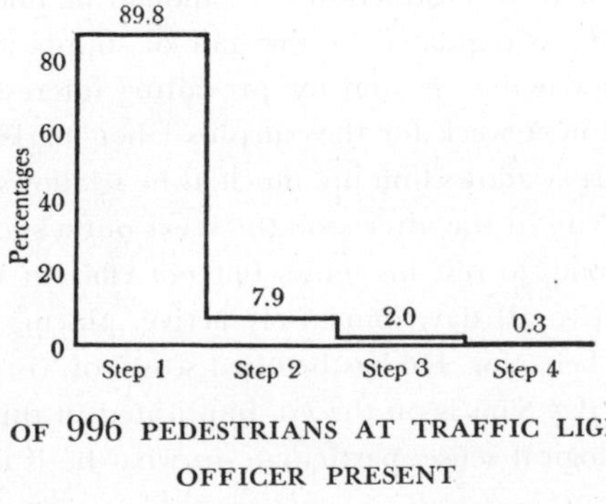

FIG. 32. J-CURVE OF 996 PEDESTRIANS AT TRAFFIC LIGHT WITH A TRAFFIC OFFICER PRESENT

pedestrian-traffic law gave approaches to J-curves. Observations of 996 pedestrians for a 45-minute period during the afternoon "rush" hour at a downtown intersection *with a traffic officer present* forty-eight days after the law went into effect resulted in a typical J-curve. This is shown here in Figure 32, with 89.8 per cent of the persons on step 1 (complete conformity), 7.9 per cent on position 2, 2.0 per cent on position 3, and only 0.3 per cent on step 4 (complete nonconformity).

EFFECT OF GROUP STANDARDS

The instances of J-curve studies might be multiplied.[20] The point is that, in an examination of various institutional situations, we are concerned not only with the development of attitudes for given individuals within the group, but also with the question of how their attitudes influence other members of the group toward conformity. We now have sufficient data on institutional behavior that we can reasonably expect in most of the groups and institutions under discussion to predict J-curves for a good many attitudes. For example, in a family situation, the conformity-producing agents will probably be sufficient to give us J-curves for most attitudes characteristic of some particular family.

Gordon W. Allport has given an apt illustration of the impact of institutions and group standards on the life of the individual:

> Take, for example, Citizen Sam who moves and has his being in the great activity wheel of New York City. Let us say that he spends his hours of unconsciousness somewhere in the Bronx. He wakens to grab the morning's milk left at the door by an agent of a vast Dairy and Distributing system whose corporate manoeuvers, so vital to his health, never consciously concern him. After paying hasty respects to his landlady, he dashes into the transportation system whose mechanical and civic mysteries he does not comprehend. At the factory he becomes a cog for the day in a set of systems far beyond his ken. To him . . . the company he works for is an abstraction; . . . though he doesn't know it his . . . activity at his machine is regulated by the 'law of supply and demand,' and by 'the availability of raw materials' and by 'prevailing interest rates.' Unknown to himself he is headed next week for the 'surplus labor market.' . . . At noontime . . . Horn and Hardart swallows him up, much as he swallows one of its automatic pies. After more activity in the afternoon, he seeks out a standardized day-dream produced in Hollywood, to rest his tense, but *not* efficient mind. . . .
>
> Sam has been active all day, immensely active, playing a part in dozens of impersonal cycles of behavior. He has brushed scores of 'corporate personalities.' . . . Throughout the day Sam is on the go, implicated in this task and that,—but does he, in a psychological sense, participate in what he is doing?[21]

Conformity to the standards of the group is very important. Every group or institution has its own unique norms of behavior which affect the behavior and personalities of those who come in contact with them.

In succeeding chapters we shall see some of the effects of the family, the school, the church, the fraternity, the political party, and occupational groups. These institutions will be taken up in the order named, because that is the order, in general, in which they affect the growing child. He is born into a family, after a few years goes to school, joins a church, a bit later is taken into a fraternity, then grows old enough to vote, and finally becomes a member of an occupational group. In the present section we are not so much concerned with group behavior itself as with the effects of each of these institutions on the socialization of the growing individual.

QUESTIONS AND PROBLEMS FOR DISCUSSION

1. *Think of an example of an* (a) *In-group,* (b) *Out-group,* (c) *primary group, and* (d) *secondary group to which you belong. To what extent do the interests represented by these different groups conflict?*
2. *What is an institution? Give examples.*
3. *What is the significance of the J-curve hypothesis of conformity behavior?*
4. *How do you account for the growth of the various institutional ideologies?*
5. *Why do most people believe what they do regarding their* own *institutions?*

RECOMMENDED READINGS

Albig, W., *Public Opinion.* New York: McGraw-Hill Book Company, Inc., 1939.

Allport, F. H., *Institutional Behavior: Essays Toward A Re-Interpreting of Contemporary Social Organization.* Chapel Hill, North Carolina: University of North Carolina Press, 1933.

Arnold, T. W., *The Folklore of Capitalism.* New Haven: Yale University Press, 1937.

Beaglehole, E., *Property: A Study in Social Psychology.* London: George Allen & Unwin, Ltd., 1931.

Hertzler, J. O., *Social Institutions.* New York: McGraw-Hill Book Company, Inc., 1929.

Judd, C. H., *The Psychology of Social Institutions.* New York: The Macmillan Company, 1926.

LaPiere, R. T., *Collective Behavior.* New York: McGraw-Hill Book Company, Inc., 1938.

Robinson, E. S., *Law and the Lawyers.* New York: The Macmillan Company, 1935.

*Newcomb, T. M., Hartley, E. L., and others (editors), *Readings in Social Psychology*. New York: Henry Holt and Company, Inc., 1947: —Allport, F. H., "The J-Curve Hypothesis of Conforming Behavior," pp. 55-67.

CHAPTER SIXTEEN

THE FAMILY

THE CHILD. Early Development of the Personality—Later Personality Development—Illustrative Case Histories—The First Few Years—Habit Formation—Eating—Elimination—Sleep—Fears—"Breaking" of Habits / THE PARENT. Substitution of Constructive Responses—Conditioning—Reward and Punishment—Personality Models—Phantasies—"Problem Parents"—Identification and Projection—Overprotection—Position in the Family—Relationships between Parents—Adolescence / MARRIAGE AND DIVORCE. Choosing a Marriage Partner—The Problem of Adjustment—Utilities of the Marriage Relationship—(1) Satisfaction of the Sexual Urge—(2) Affection and Love—(3) Procreation and Care of Children—The Problem of Divorce—Causes of Maladjustment—Predicting Success in Marriage—Companionate Marriage—The Future of Marriage.

The material presented here on the family is divided for purposes of analysis into three sections: (1) The Child, (2) The Parent, and (3) Marriage and Divorce. Obviously these are arbitrary and even artificial distinctions. The family is, of course, an organization of individuals, the members of which are in constant interaction with each other, whether they are infants, children, adolescents, or adults; and any family is influenced in its attitudes not only by its own In-group characteristics but by the impact of various Out-groups. However, it seems useful to make the threefold division and to examine separately the psychological situation of the child, the parent, and the spouse in the family.

In the first two sections of this chapter, we are concerned primarily with the personality development of the child and the growth of his attitudes.

▶ THE CHILD

EARLY DEVELOPMENT OF THE PERSONALITY

About one-third of a group of college students have said that they would choose total annihilation to the alternative of living their lives over again exactly as they had been lived up to that moment. This has consistently been the result of *anonymous* polls, with the following question presented:

Assume that you are offered your immediate choice of the following:

(*A*) To be totally annihilated.

(*B*) To begin your life over again, and live it up to the present moment *exactly as you have lived it, not profiting by any experience of your former life,* and be given the same choice of repeating your life, or annihilation.

Put a check mark before whichever alternative you would prefer.[1]

This has been read aloud and reread until all the students understood it. The fact that a fairly large percentage preferred annihilation, as compared with the possibility of going through infancy, childhood, and adolescence *in exactly the same way as before,* raises serious questions concerning the kind of training which some children get in their families, and gives some indication of the storm and stress of emotional development.

All authorities seem to be agreed upon one point, that the family group is largely responsible for the child's future social adjustment. This is no longer a matter of armchair philosophizing. There are a vast number of empirical studies which show the significance of the very early family situation in determining what sorts of personalities children will later develop. Reading this now, you may be inclined to take the position that this is something that people have always known. You will probably say that this is "old stuff," since a recognition of the importance of family relationships is fairly universal. Strangely enough, however, this recognition is only beginning to be appreciated by many parents, teachers, religious workers, social workers, and college students. It is a way of thinking which is just beginning to be understood by most people.

An examination of the *Readers' Guide to Periodical Literature* beginning in 1900 indicates that the number of articles of a popular nature dealing with questions of health, parents, and parent education has taken a rapid turn upward during the last decade or so. Relatively few articles were devoted to these questions forty and fifty years ago, but newspapers and magazines today contain an abundance of such materials. Exactly the same trend is found so far as scientific journals are concerned. More and more research studies are being done in this field—studies concerned not merely with whether there is a relationship between the child's developing personality and his family situation, but devoted to specific questions of *what sort* of relations exist.

LATER PERSONALITY DEVELOPMENT

In the discussion of the conditioned response in Chapter 6, we saw that conditioning during childhood is of the utmost importance to *later* personality development. Child psychologists and pediatricians now agree that many of our principal characteristics are acquired before we are five years old. By that time we have become creatures of habits, conventions, and attitudes from which we never completely escape. Many would even put the age earlier and say that by age three our personalities are fairly well developed. At a later time, of course, environmental factors may change the personality; but generally the type of treatment which an infant receives during his first two or three years will determine to a great extent what his later attitudes and behavior will be.

In a family with two or more children, we recognize that the heredity of the brothers and sisters is not the same, even though they have the same father and mother; that is, the mechanisms of inheritance are such that having the same father and mother does not mean that children have the same biological background. Equally important is a recognition of the fact that no two brothers and sisters have the same environment. Even if two brothers grow up in the same family, one receives different treatment from the other. The younger child may even grow up in a different social and financial environment from the older child, if the family's fortunes change. These factors may modify tremendously initial personality trends.

ILLUSTRATIVE CASE HISTORIES

In one family, the parents were very much concerned with their little girl, aged nine. She showed up poorly in contrast with her older sister, who was twelve. Both the father and the mother argued to the clinical psychologist that the little girls had the same splendid heredity, that both had an excellent environment, and that there was no reason why the younger girl, Joanna, should not be the model child which her older sister Jean was. But the parents had failed to take into account the differences in family attitudes toward Jean and Joanna. Careful investigation of the life histories of both little girls revealed that Jean had constantly been dealt with by both parents as a "model child" and had always been rewarded for good deportment, keeping a neat room, and bringing home an excellent report card. Little Joanna, on the other hand, from the time that she was able to talk, had been told that her older sister was an ideal and that she should model her behavior after her older sister. Constant repetition of such statements convinced Joanna that she needed other ways of calling attention to herself. Since she was three years younger, she could not possibly compete with her older sister, who was already a model child, able to do everything to the satisfaction of her parents and teachers. Joanna discovered that by untidy habits, disorderliness, throwing her clothes about the room, constant whispering in school, and getting very poor grades on her report card, she became an important person! The problem psychologically in this family situation did not concern the attitudes of the children. It concerned the attitudes of the parents. When they stopped giving the younger child an inferior role to play, the problem behavior gradually ceased.

In another case history, a college senior complained of insomnia. Through military school and college he had noted his increasing inability to go to sleep at night. A brief investigation revealed that he took a nap every afternoon, and, having sufficient sleep in the afternoon, he was not fatigued at bedtime. Then because of lack of sleep at night, he was so fatigued the next day that he required another afternoon nap. Obviously, the first solution to the problem was to eliminate the afternoon nap. This man's experience in early infancy and childhood also related to his problem, however. He had been extremely devoted to his mother, who had died when he was eight years old, and he could recall that every night after he had been tucked into bed his mother sat by his bedside and held his hand until he went to sleep. This process of conditioning had been repeated 365 days of the year for several years, and was sufficient to build up faulty sleep habits in the individual, so that even as a man he was having difficulty in going to sleep without the presence of the conditioned stimulus. A rather long program of training and reconditioning was undertaken in order to develop sleeping habits which were psychologically sound.

Many of the problems of the people who come to the psychologist for advice are traceable to early-childhood situations. One of the most difficult cases confronting one psychologist involved a freshman in a large metropolitan university. The boy had previously lived in a very small town and had been the high-school hero. From being a big frog in a little pond, he suddenly found himself in the awkward situation of being a very small frog, or practically no frog at all, in a big pond. The difficulty, however, was not simply that he had been president of his high-school graduating class of twelve and had played the "lead" in the senior play; it also derived from the type of treatment which he had received from early babyhood on. He was the "fair-haired" boy of his family. He had strong emotional ties to both his mother and father, who praised him at every opportunity and were lenient with him for all mistakes. The product of this treatment was a very pampered, spoiled young man who was not able to "take it" when it came to rough-and-tumble activities of sports and freshman hazing.

THE FIRST FEW YEARS

In our analysis of dominance and leadership, we noted that leadership characteristics in one situation will not always carry over to another situation. However, we do find indications of some personality characteristics carrying over from one period of life to another. Thus, in Shirley's study of the first two years of life, in which she kept careful records on twenty-two babies, starting one day after birth and lasting for a period of two years, she found that in many instances personality characteristics had remained fairly constant over the two-year period.[2] The great majority of parents will claim that nothing which happens around the child during the first year or two of life really matters because he is "too young to understand." But in well-controlled studies of general development, motor development, vocalization, and social traits of infants, Shirley was able to trace for two years the actual significance of events which had occurred during the very first few weeks of their lives.

Gordon W. Allport reports a careful day-by-day record on one infant kept by two psychologically minded parents.[3] Based on the boy's characteristics at four months, the following prophecy of *future* behavior was recorded: "Ready laughter, well adjusted, *i.e.,* 'normal' and 'extroverted,' capable of considerable temper, active, sensitive to rhythm, adaptable, wiry and muscular, tall, mischievous, with linguistic superiority."[4] After the age of four years, various teachers gave ratings of the boy's personality with no knowledge of the earlier entries of the parents or of the entries of other teachers. By age nine, "temper" seemed to have given way to excitability, and "mischievousness" to imaginativeness. As a result of later experiences, a certain reserve had developed, making the boy more reticent and less dominant socially. But in general the predictions made at the age of four months were correct, in that the boy at age nine was "a bright, not rugged, excitable child with marked masculine interests, adaptable to groups and friendly."[5]

From this record two important hypotheses concerning personality in early life are suggested. In the first place, it appears that *vague and variable indications of distinctive traits are evident at an early age,* in this case at four months. The second hypothesis is of special and far-reaching significance: *from early infancy there is consistency in the development of personality.*[6]

Probably the most significant study of the effects of the first few months and years is an investigation by Burtt.[7] This was an empirical study of early-childhood memory. Beginning at the age of fifteen months, when the average child knows only three or four words, Burtt read to his son every day for three months approximately 60 lines or 720 syllables of iambic hexameter taken from Sophocles' *Oedipus Tyrannus* in the original Greek. This was probably just the same as reading "nonsense material." At the age of eighteen months these lines were discontinued and 60 other lines of the same length were read daily for another three months, and this process was continued for each three months until the boy was three years old.

Nothing was said about this material until the boy was 8½ years old. At this age he learned by a modified prompting method various portions from *Oedipus Tyrannus* which had never been read to him, and others which had. The "relearning" required approximately 30 per cent fewer repetitions of the material which he had heard as a baby than did the learning of new material which was exactly comparable in every respect! From this study we can theorize that when it comes to attitude development or personality characteristics, the sorts of behavior which surround the child in his first few months and years may have far-reaching effects. If the reading of Greek to an infant has a measurable effect, what might be the influence on his later emotional life of the myriad of events which occur in his presence as a small child?

HABIT FORMATION

The material presented thus far is designed to give some general indications of the development of personality in the child. Recall the four main aspects of conditioning and attitude development: (1) the *generalization* of conditioned responses, (2) the *differentiation* of responses, (3) the occurrence of *traumatic experiences,* and (4) the adoption of *ready-made attitudes* from other persons. Many of the habits of the child come about through the mechanisms of generalization and differentiation of conditioned responses, while particular experiences may be sufficiently dramatic or traumatic to influence or alter these habits, and all may be overlaid with ready-made attitudes accepted almost unquestioningly from parents, teachers, and older children.

Eating. The various organic habits have a very close relationship to the child's personality development. In the psychological clinic we have a great deal of evidence showing the effect of early feeding habits on later personality development. Some psychiatrists and clinical psychologists have noted very definite relationships not only between interruptions during feeding in infancy and later food habits, but also between feeding interruptions and general personality characteristics. Not only are the types of food the child receives important, but also the conditions under which he eats are of the utmost significance for his development as a wholesome personality. We find many instances of children only two or three years old developing well-marked food preferences; and these, in most instances, are not traced simply to the pleasurable gustatory aspects of the particular food but rather to the conditioning factors which surround eating. Refusal to eat either a specific food or to eat at all at mealtimes is a very real problem for many parents. It often suggests that the child is not well, that the family physician should be consulted. Yet an examination frequently points to psychological factors of which the parents were unaware. For example, one child suddenly developed a refusal habit for his morning cereal, and because the advertisements insisted that this particular brand was desirable for little "tummies," his family considered this a major catastrophe. Yet the refusal of the breakfast food was due to a growing understanding by the child that his parents had food preferences, things which they liked, and which they disliked, and that he was also entitled to his foibles.

The conditions surrounding eating are of the utmost importance. Consider the amount of wheedling, coaxing, fretting, and nagging which may surround a child while he eats his oatmeal or spinach.

> The child thrives on its achievements and soon holds the center of the stage in the domestic performance; especially at meals the child may stage a little drama with himself as the star actor, while mother, fond aunts, and the older children tempt him to eat this and to eat that and perhaps with snatches of song and rhyme urge a few more bites to make up the necessary vitamins and calories.[8]

Psychiatrists and clinical psychologists agree that attention to vitamins and calories is important, but should not be the whole story. Many an adult who comes into the clinic with emotional problems is found to suffer from digestive disturbances traceable, not to a present-day emotional upset, but to a lifetime of faulty eating habits going back to his very early years. Jersild tells of a two-year-old child who consistently refused to eat at home, and who was suffering from partial starvation, simply because of feeding conditions in the home environment.[9] Physicians found no organic cause, and "medicine" did no good. But when the child was taken away from the frantic coaxing, forcing, fretting, and wheedling which persistently occurred in the home at mealtime and was put under the care of a nursery-school teacher, he began to eat normally.

The dental profession is beginning to recognize the importance of personal adjustment on normal living. Dentists are now calling attention to the fact that the treatment of carious teeth, spongy gums, malformed arches, and constricted sinuses cannot be limited simply to prophylactic measures or othodonture, but that the family situation must be taken into account. Many dentists comment on the fact that children with spongy gums and decayed teeth often present very definite personality problems, and that one method of treatment is a clearing up of family tensions and maladjustments. After all, nervous upsets are known to interfere with thyroid functioning, which in turn has a great deal to do with calcium metabolism. Children who have been treated harshly by their parents have been known to develop habits of tenseness and nervousness, to clench their jaws, and grind their teeth. These manifestations may take place alone or in connection with temper tantrums, and it is not surprising to find that these have their effects on the personality.

Elimination. One of the most difficult problems for the parent is to train the child in proper habits of elimination. This is something, too, which markedly affects personality development. Bowel control is learned ordinarily at least six or seven months prior to bladder control, but in some instances neither is effectively established until the child has reached the age of three or four years, or even later. This tardy learning of elimination habits is not due to faulty muscular control alone but may also be a psychological problem. In cases of enuresis—involuntary discharge of urine during sleep—pediatricians first look to possible organic causes, but, if they do not find any, they turn to a consideration of the family situation. This means an examination of the child's relations to his father, mother, brothers, and sisters. Enuresis may be to the child a type of activity which calls attention to him and gains for him the sympathy and affection which he definitely desires.

Much of the training for control of digestive activities centers around the conditioning process. That is, a whole series of stimuli—such as the same place and time of day—must be associated with acts of elimination so that the desired effect will be produced. Many parents here fall into the error of coaxing, wheedling, and scolding, as in dealing with the eating problem, and this many have disastrous effects.

Mrs. V. is a highly efficient, executive type of woman. She is large in stature, aggressive in manner, with a fine, stately carriage. She is well read in the physiology of child training and is over-anxious for the health of her family, which has in spite of her concern been given to ill-health. The second child, a boy of three and a half, was bothered by constipation at the time the observation was made. He was also developing a good deal of fussiness about his meals. At mealtime his mother stood over him literally morning after morning until he ate his cereal. Then promptly at 8:30 every morning he was taken to the toilet to stool. "And I make him do it," she remarked proudly to a friend. "Why just yesterday I made him sit there until 9:30 but I'll tell you I did not let him get up until he had finished."

The boy is intelligent, alert to the world around him, but developing a whole set of escapes from the mother's severity and one negativism piled on another. He is still too weak and young to use physical force in resistance, but one wonders what lies ahead of him. As he grows older the mother's domination, in which both the grandmother who lives there and the father, often conspire with the mother, will probably spread from one activity to another.[10]

Sleep. Many parents are worried because their young hopefuls do not go off to sleep instantly when they are put to bed, either for the afternoon nap or at night. Yet records show that the "normal" or average time required for going to sleep is about one half hour. Owing to a lack of recognition of what is normal, many parents become concerned over the sleeping habits of their children, and exercise a type of control over these habits which may affect the children's personality development. Children who have learned to require rocking, singing, patting, storytelling, and similar diversions before falling asleep often develop poor sleep habits.

Fears. Also of interest is the age-old question of fear of the dark. As we have indicated in Chapter 6, fear of the dark is not something which is inherent or "instinctive," but is in all cases learned, often through traumatic experiences or by the acceptance of ready-made attitudes (learning that other persons are a bit afraid, and thereby learning to be afraid of the dark). These reactions to the dark or to other fear stimuli may be produced by story-telling which involves ogres or wicked people, or may be picked up by the child because of such stupid statements as, "Don't be afraid of the dark! Nothing is going to hurt you."

Jersild reports many other fears besides fear of the dark.[11] Among four hundred children from five to twelve years of age, 21.1 per cent reported fears of the occult, supernatural, mystery, skeletons, corpses, and death; 17.8 per cent had fears of animals; 14.1 per cent had fears of strange happenings and places, of being alone or in the dark; 8.8 per cent were afraid of nightmares and apparitions; and 7.3 per cent feared bad people, such as robbers and kidnapers. How do such fears grow up? All cannot be traced to traumatic experiences. Many apparently develop from acceptance of attitudes which older persons demonstrate in the presence of children; many others come from threats of "bogeymen," kidnapers, and other fearsome persons described by parents to "scare" their children into good behavior—a psychologically unsound practice, if there ever was one.

"BREAKING" OF HABITS

Suppose that faulty habits have been established. What can be done to "break" them? If a child has been faultily trained as to feeding, eliminating, sleeping, or other activities, can he be retrained? The answer is "Yes." If the habits are explored very shortly after they have developed, there are especially good chances of changing them. If, however, a child is allowed to develop faulty habits over a period of years, no psychologist or pediatrician can be expected to wave a magic wand and remake the child's personality overnight, or even in a few weeks of treatment.

Breaking a habit can be accomplished only (1) by the substitution of some new reaction pattern for the old one, and (2) by letting the child learn that the new pattern will be *more* satisfactory to him than the old one. That is, the new habit must not be forced on him, but he must be allowed to practice it over a period of time until it comes to be more satisfying than the previous habit. Conditions should be arranged so as to lead naturally away from the old toward the new way. This may be illustrated by the following change in reading habits of a ten-year-old boy:

> The mother worried because her son was spending almost all his spare time reading what she regarded as "trashy" literature, that is, books and magazines that were poor in grammar and style, and "vulgar." She wished to censor his reading completely and had already put a taboo on all such materials.
>
> It was pointed out to her that, even if she should try to put a stop to this type of reading, her censorship would not actually be effective but that the

boy would get hold of the same sort of reading, only without letting his mother know about it. It was further pointed out that a *sudden* switch-over to more desirable reading materials would be ineffective, because the boy did not have the background either in vocabulary or in general information to appreciate the type of books and magazines which his mother called "good" reading.

Therefore, the suggestion was made that the mother *do nothing* so far as any attempt to prohibit reading of "trashy" materials was concerned, that this reading should be neither encouraged nor discouraged. In other words, it should be ignored.

However, a *gradual* substitution of more desirable reading materials should be made. This was to be done by a judicious selection of magazines and books appropriate for this boy's age and background (materials that were not "over his head"), and by the gradual development, over a period of months, of interest in more advanced works. These objectives were to be accomplished by leaving the desired reading materials carelessly about in convenient places—in the living room and in the boy's bedroom—where (with his general liking of reading) he could browse, and by trips to the public library where the boy was to be free to select his own books without any interference from his mother—a "big" event for him in which permission was secured for him to wander about in the stacks and look at all the books and then select his own.

A report from the mother two years later—the boy now aged 12—indicates that her son is engrossed in Dickens and Scott![12]

If pleasant results are obtained from "proper"—that is, desired—actions and if the improper acts are ignored or punished, in most cases the child will learn to prefer the habit which gives the pleasant results. In order to accomplish these things, the entire social situation must be considered. The treatment sometimes concerns the parents even more than the child. For this reason many pediatricians and child psychologists have great difficulties, even when they understand perfectly well what mechanisms should be changed. It is sometimes very ticklish business to convince a parent that Father and Mother need to change their habit patterns if the child is to be changed in his.

▶ THE PARENT

Parents in our culture are primarily concerned with converting healthy young animals into civilized human beings. "Civilizing" them means getting them to adopt those ways of thinking and acting which are typical of our particular culture.

SUBSTITUTION OF CONSTRUCTIVE RESPONSES

Thus, adults demand from a child an increase in cooperative behavior and a decrease in competitive and dominating behavior. "Constructive" responses must be substituted for "emotional" ways of acting, and verbal habit patterns must be substituted in part for physically active ways of behaving. These are difficult ways of behaving for the child to learn. Being physically active, emotional, and often dominating the situation with his egocentric desires, it is hard for him to learn that adult society demands cooperation among its members, relatively quiet behavior, and constructive activities.

> To the child the adult represents society in its protective and prohibitive aspects, and the main problem of the child is to accept its protection without becoming too dependent upon it, and to accept the prohibitions without being too cramped or limited by them. The direction of contemporary research indicates that adults themselves are most concerned by undue "dependence" on the one hand and undue "resistance" on the other; relations with adults are considered adequate when the child is independent in relation to the activities in which the adult approves his independence, and cooperative or obedient in those activities which the adult still chooses to dominate.[13]

In dominating the child's behavior, the parents can either be patient and gradually substitute new habits for old ones, or suddenly demand a change. In the latter case serious emotional upsets may result. One little girl three years old suddenly became mute because in teaching her the strange business of table manners, her father had screamed angrily in her ear, "Say 'Please!' " and the other members of the family had joined in his demands.[14] The little girl became excited, and for eleven months afterward did not speak. This type of conduct is not unique; there are similar instances of emotional upsets and accompanying physical changes which have occurred because some adult had no understanding of habit formation. Many parents consult psychologists about the management of their children when they could solve the problem themselves if they would only examine their own behavior more closely.

CONDITIONING

In conditioning a dog to drip saliva, we use the method of constant repetition of the original and conditioned stimulus, presented together until the response to either stimulus is practically automatic. In training horses, every farmer or equestrian knows that they will respond to the wishes of people only if a very careful training period has been instituted, during which no exceptions are allowed to occur in the development of habit. Owners of every kind of dog from the Pekingese to the great Dane know the same thing. They also know that undue spoiling of the dog, on the one hand, or beating him, on the other, may make him "neurotic" or break his spirit. Yet when it comes to rearing their own children, many parents lose sight of these basic facts. They give dozens, sometimes hundreds of commands per day, without seeing that more than a few of them are carried out. They do not use rewards or punishments consistently. How can a child who is attempting to adjust to the world about him be expected to develop well-integrated habits when only 5 or 10 per cent of the commands he receives "mean business"? Alternating harshness and laxity result in the child being at a loss as to what is expected of him. One of William James's maxims of habit formation was:

> *Never suffer an exception to occur till the new habit is securely rooted in your life.* Each lapse is like the letting fall of a ball of string which one is carefully winding up: a single slip undoes more than a great many turns will wind again.[15]

REWARD AND PUNISHMENT

Finally, praise is more often effective than blame in habit formation. Reward is usually better than punishment. This generalization is made on the basis of many observational studies, and particularly from a number of experiments on learning. A study by Hurlock, for example, of the effects of praise and blame on school children in solving problems indicated that the ones who were praised for their behavior surpassed those who were reproved.[16] Other investigators have demonstrated that encouragement is superior to discouragement in getting students to excel a previous performance.[17] Some studies with different conditions, however, have shown the desirability of blame as compared with praise.[18] Obviously neither praise nor blame should be used indiscriminately, although in general praise is superior.

PERSONALITY MODELS

Of course, no simple set of rules can be devised for breaking bad habits. We have emphasized the complexity of interrelations which exist in the family situation. In this connection the personality "models" or examples that the child finds about him are of the utmost significance. He may develop habits because they are forced upon him, or because of traumatic experiences; but he also tends to accept unquestioningly attitudes and ways of behaving which are engaged in by those persons whom he admires. Who hasn't seen and heard children playing at being Superman, Dick Tracy, Roy Rogers, Babe Ruth, or some other popular personality, real or imagined?

The person whom the child respects and whose wishes he follows may also be a parent, an older child, a teacher, a favorite aunt. The "sociological mother," that is, the older person who plays the mother role—a nursemaid, a grandmother, older brother or sister—is often as important as the biological mother. The psychological clinic furnishes evidence again and again of the extent to which small infants have been old enough to understand and be impressed with ways of acting and thinking of older persons. But these persons are not always alert to the fact that they themselves are personality models for the growing child, that they represent tangible ideals.

Other sorts of personality models are also thrust upon the child. They consist of characters ranging from Peter Rabbit to Donald Duck, from Santa Claus to a conception of God as a great, good fairy. It is small wonder that little children become confused in trying to comprehend the world about them. They have difficulty in differentiating between those things which are real and those which are make-believe. Serious behavior problems occasionally develop because of this confusion. Parents worry because little Johnny comes home to tell of the hundred wolves or bears from which he just escaped. They should hardly worry, considering how many phantasies they themselves instill into their children. Try to imagine yourself back at the five-year-old level, not having had any experience except the very restricted activities of your environment, and you can readily understand the confusion between reality and unreality that is so typical of children at this age. Peter Rabbit and Donald Duck are as real as the characters in the adventure stories about the G-men or "Red Injuns."

Watch the newspapers next Christmas, and you are sure to find the pros and cons argued as to whether or not it is desirable to continue the Santa Claus myth. Fond mothers will say, "It's the worst thing I ever heard of, to tell children there isn't any Santa," and, "To take away the sweetest and loveliest thoughts a little child can have at Christmas is certainly an unkind thing." What does this actually mean? Adults do not want to abolish myths and legends, with which they themselves have a strong identification, and they use the child as an excuse for retaining them. The result is that children who are taught to believe in Santa Claus may experience a severe shock when they are disillusioned; and if they are told that Santa Claus is a myth, they are apt to be criticized by the parents of their playmates as "naughty." It is psychologically much sounder to tell stories which concern real characters in real situations, so that life-and-blood personality models may come to be substituted. After all, American culture is full of "success" stories—of Daniel Boone, young Tom Edison, Theodore and Franklin Roosevelt—and these may serve as useful personality models. Certain older children or adults in the community may also serve as desirable models whose habit patterns may be consciously imitated.

PHANTASIES

Parents are apt to overlook the importance of overcoming the phantasy difficulties of the small child. Many a child is so afraid of being laughed at for the autistic-thought world in which he lives that his parents are the last persons in whom he would confide. He may withdraw from overt activities to covert phantasy and make-believe to so great an extent that the "switch-over" to reality becomes extremely difficult. Conklin has found that the phantasy or secret belief of being a foster child is fairly prevalent among children in our culture, probably about one-fourth having this belief.[19] Recall your own early childhood days, and you many remember that you were "worried" for fear your parents were not your own, that you had been adopted. Again, you may be among those persons who in childhood had a well-developed phantasy of an imaginary companion. One investigation of a group of unselected children over four years of age showed that 13 per cent had very vivid and imaginary phantasies concerning an imaginary playmate; this day-dream tends to disappear when the child is about seven to nine years of age.[20] Another study "suggests that the appearance of imaginary companions and related phenomena occurs in many, though not in all, children, as a natural developmental phenomenon, characteristic of the age period from 2½ to 4½ years, and perhaps persisting secretly considerably past that age."[21]

If you can retrospect still further, you may recall the surprise you felt when you found out that certain things told you by your parents were not true. This has been a serious traumatic experience for many a child. He grows up in an environment in which his father and mother have been all-powerful and all-knowing. Suddenly he discovers that they have been pretending with him much of the time, and his world temporarily drops away from him. This has been particularly true so far as religious values are concerned.

"PROBLEM PARENTS"

A number of childhood problems have been presented thus far, and most of them can be summed up in one word—*parents.* A psychologist attended a small dinner party where during the evening the family's five-year-old was allowed to run rampant over the floor and to climb over the laps of the guests. After enduring this treatment for some hours most of the guests, as they climbed into their respective automobiles out of earshot of the host and hostess, confided in no uncertain tones to each other, "What a horrible child!" The psychologist, however, said, "Not at all—a very healthy, normal, interesting child. But what horrible parents!" Much has been written about the so-called problem child, but not enough about the "problem parents."

IDENTIFICATION AND PROJECTION

In Chapter 11 we examined the psychological mechanisms of identification and projection. Both of these are found in the parent-child relations. *Projection* is manifested when a parent criticizes and nags his child for those very characteristics which he may recognize as being "bad" traits in himself. *Identification* is exemplified when parents try to live over another childhood in terms of what their children are doing. This often takes the form of trying to give the child—even trying to force upon him—those things which the parent desired but was deprived of at the same age. Two different businessmen report entirely opposite views concerning the college education of their sons. One tells of his son away at college who is not getting very good marks, but the father says that this does not really matter if the son can instead do some "socializing" of the sort that the father himself missed because he had to work his way through college. The other man reports that his son also is bringing home inferior marks from his college courses but says in no uncertain tones, "That boy's going to toe the mark, or I'll know why!" This father feels that he himself frittered away most of his time when in college, and that study is the thing that really counts.

It is important for parents to recognize these two psychological mechanisms. Parents should ask themselves: Are they interested primarily in enjoying their children for a few short years in the same way that they might secure pleasurable sensations from stroking a lap dog, or are they interested more in what sort of adults their children will turn out to be?

> The child has to take what is meted out to him and if the parent does the unwise thing for his own gratification, he can cover up his motives by insisting that he is doing it for the good of the child. . . . Many parents wish the happiness of their children only as long as that happiness is in agreement with their own purposes. The child represents an outlet for their emotional immaturity, which they by no means wish to lose.[22]

The following is a case history, involving thwarted ambition and an unhappy marriage of the mother of a college girl:

> The mother of Louise M. married when she was very young. This had meant for her the foregoing of three desires: (1) a college education; (2) the study of music in which she had a great interest; and (3) experience as a teacher. The marriage proved an unhappy one with considerable conflict between parents. Two children were born, one a son "much like his father" whom the mother "could influence very little," the other a daughter who became the "pride" of the mother's life. For Louise the mother wished all the things which her own inhibited life had lacked. The girl was forced to take music lessons, although she was not musically inclined. She was also sent to college quite as much because the mother had failed to secure this privilege as for any other reason. Moreover, the mother decided the daughter should be a school teacher as she had once wished to be.
>
> In college Louise fell in love much as co-eds are likely to do. She wished

to discontinue her education and marry. Although the mother now admits that she had nothing against the young man who courted her daughter, in fact she now says she rather liked him, she refused to permit the marriage. Louise was, to her mind, too young. She herself had married too early which had spoiled her own life and she simply would not allow her daughter to duplicate her own sad experience. The marriage must be indefinitely postponed and Louise continue her education until she might teach. The young man was unwilling to defer matrimony in this indeterminate manner, while the daughter, obedient to the mother's wishes, began teaching school not long after, only to make a rather miserable failure of it all. Louise has been entirely unhappy. She is now at home doing nothing in particular, broken in spirit and unable to organize herself for any kind of valuable activity.[23]

A motto which might well be adopted for the training of children is—*Live with them but not for them.*[24] And another might be added—*Let your child grow up!*[25] In other words, a parent should do everything possible to make a child self-sufficient, able to eat, eliminate, dress, and sleep without adult direction or interference. To train a child to remain dependent upon older people is certainly no kindness to him; if he develops habits of dependence in early years, it means that these habits will continue into maturity. Planning in industry has long been accepted as essential if waste and inefficiency are to be kept at a minimum; but planning a family life is too infrequent a phenomenon.

OVERPROTECTION

In their desires to aid their children, or perhaps to satisfy their own emotions, many parents go to one of two extremes. One extreme consists of authoritarianism, nagging, holding up of other children as ideals, and constant insistence that the child "behave." The other is pampering, spoiling, oversolicitude, and overprotection which many parents engage in, reputedly as a means of protecting their children, but oftentimes because of their own desire for someone to love and from whom to receive affection.

Because of the importance of the mother role in our society, tendencies toward maternal overprotection are frequently prevalent; and where there is too great overprotection, conflicts may easily result for children in their own age groups, as has been shown by Levy.[26] He has described four symptoms shown by overprotective mothers.[27] *Excessive physical contact* between mother and child is manifested by fondling and hovering care, prolonged nursing during illness, and sleeping with the child long past infancy. *Infantilization* refers to breast feeding over an extended period; and Levy presents data that indicate that overprotective mothers nurse their babies longer than rejecting or emotionally wholesome mothers. *Prevention of independent behavior* results from maternal interference, illustrated by restriction of play with other children, refusal to allow the child to take the ordinary risks at play, helping the child with schoolwork, and taking hostile attitudes toward teachers. *Maternal control* may take the form of overindulgence, or of overdiscipline. Levy describes cases in which a mother helps her thirteen-year-old son to dress, where she runs errands for her twelve-year-old boy, and where she puts her adolescent son to bed in the middle of the afternoon as a means of punishment.

The "pet" names which parents use for their children are revealing. In one collection of names by which children were known in their families there were included Pet, Darling, Baby, Sweetheart, Sweetness, Bub, Sissy, Angel, Precious, Girlie, Midget, Bunnie.[28]

In the clinic, psychologists are impressed with the number of parents who turn to their children as an outlet for their own affections when their own marriage relations have proved unhappy. This has held not only for mothers but for fathers as well; when the psychological factors of general love and affection in the marriage relation have not proved satisfactory, it is easy—too easy—for the parent to force his or her affections upon the child and thus to do the latter great harm. Nagging and perfectionism on the one hand, or oversolicitude on the other, usually result in the child's being too dependent upon his parents. Among the worst things you can do is to feed a child already capable of feeding himself, or to make him too keenly aware of dangers, or to give him too much physical affection.[29]

POSITION IN THE FAMILY

In aiding the child to grow up, the child's position or birth order in the family is probably not so nearly important as some would insist. The psychoanalyst Adler developed an interesting theory concerning craving for superiority which he applied to younger children in a family who he claimed felt a desire to prove that they were not inferior to the older ones in the family.[30] Also, various parents and laymen insist that the only child is a problem child. Yet a careful examination of over fifty different studies on birth order reveals inconclusive and contradictory data.[31] No series of studies yet made indicates that being the oldest, middle, youngest, or only child is *in itself* a benefit or a handicap. In other words, birth order in the family is not so important as are the psychological factors which go to make up an individual's relationship to the other members of his family. Whether a child is well loved and seems to be accepted by his family, whether he is relatively free to develop, or whether he is spoiled or pampered, these are the psychological factors which are much more important than mere position within the family.

RELATIONSHIPS BETWEEN PARENTS

The physical care of infants and children is important, but the psychological interactions between parents as a factor in child development have been overlooked until recently. Many a person would resent the statement that the unhappiness or emotional maladjustment of his child or children is due largely to the marital maladjustment of the parents; yet that is exactly the conclusion to which many child psychologists are coming. This is borne out by results of many years of investigations in the Institute of Child Welfare at the University of California.

We have found in our guidance study group that the relationship between the parents in a home—whether it be a straining or a supporting one—looms much larger in its bearing upon the children's behavior than do such things as the education or the economic advantages or handicaps which the parents have had. In fact, *the marital relationship appears to be more important than any other factor in the homes thus far studied.* [Italics ours.] Food-finickiness, over-dependence, attention-demanding, negativism, temper tantrums, and urinary incontinence in the day-time are recruited more largely and consistently from homes where a straining and inharmonious parental relationship exists.[32]

Harmonious or inharmonious parental relations imply much more than sexual relations. They include the general bonds of affection, respect, and love which exist between two married persons. If the child senses friction in these relationships, he may develop definite conflicts in his own personality make-up. Many a person reports to the clinical psychologist of his early conflicts as a small child, when, out of loyalty to both father and mother, he tried within his own thinking to carry the burdens of each. Maladjustment in the adolescent is sometimes traced directly to an attempt on the part of the child himself to solve the quarrels or inharmonious relations which he finds in his father and mother. Of course, the importance of the actual sex relations of the parents should not be minimized.

A mutually satisfying sex adjustment brings enough support, when it involves affection, to make the adjustments . . . seem relatively minor; but if either of the pair is thwarted or feels inadequate to meet the drives of the other, then all sorts of minor items are saturated with the strains projected from erotic tensions.[33]

ADOLESCENCE

We have noted the dangers attached to inharmonious relations, and the importance or organic habits in relation to personality development. As a child grows older and reaches the period of adolescence, his problems often increase. Parents are not consistent in what they demand of him at this time. One day they will be in a mood for treating the adolescent as a baby who is still dependent on them, and the next day they will demand that he develop attitudes of independence and individual initiative. They exhibit an *ambivalent* attitude; they want the child to be cooperative and considerate, but at the same time demand that he learn what is meant by initiative and individuality. How can young people expect to have their parents decide things for them, and at the same time "learn to think things through for themselves"?

In adolescence there are four important problems to face: *emancipation* from the home, together with the ability to make decisions independently; *feelings of personal responsibility* for conduct; development of greater *self-control* than in childhood; and adjustment of *sexual attitudes and behavior.*[34] It is no wonder that adolescence has often been referred to as "the period of stress and strain." Although that may be an exaggeration, there is no question that there are many psychological conflicts in the family relationship which come to a head during late adolescence, as in college years. The Lynds found as leading sources of disagreement between boys and girls and their parents: the use of the family automobile, the boys or girls the youth chose as their friends, the number of times they went out on school nights during the week, the hour they got in at night, grades at school, and spending money.[35]

> Much maladjustment among children and youth is due to restraints placed by their parents upon their going to the movies, having dates, and using the family car. If all children were denied these things there would be no frustration, for the wishes would not develop. But the more rigorously disciplined children see others more leniently handled, and there is no convincing argument to prove to them that they gain by the restraint.[36]

The college student is expected to work out a very nice balance between conformity to the demands of his family on the one hand, and assertion of his own individuality on the other. As you know, this is not always an easy problem. These are the years when remonstrance develops. A college person has practically reached physiological maturity and wishes to "try his wings" for himself. Yet his attempts meet with opposition. These are the years during which maturing individuals go through what older people call "preparation for life," and yet on many sides, in the home, the classroom, the church, the community, they find hindrances and restrictions. They are to be "protected" in order that they may be prepared.

The young man or woman is physiologically capable of sexual satisfaction, but comes in conflict with the mores of the community and with the well-defined attitudes of the family concerning premarital relations. As Kingsley Davis has said, "The young person is permitted to associate closely with the opposite sex but is put on his honor to remain virtuous, is supposed to choose his own mate independently but is in many ways still under the authority of the parents, and is forced to compete for love in a rating and dating system that interferes and gets entangled with his fortunes in that other competitive system, the occupational."[37] He finds himself in a world where most older people seem able to meet their life situations, and yet, when he tries to find a place for himself in the world, the odds against him often seem overwhelming. He has reached a point where he wants a "philosophy of life" for himself, and yet finds that this may conflict with the religion and mores of his family and other older persons with whom he comes in contact. Not only do serious religious doubts often arise, but many of the attitudes which he had accepted as true, because they were true in his family, cease to be real.

The problems of the adolescent can in turn often be traced to his early childhood ideals—to attitudes and ways of behaving which have been foisted on him by his parents. A social psychologist wonders whether a thorough overhauling of parental, school, and church attitudes might not be advisable if the problems of adolescence are to be dealt with intelligently.

MARRIAGE AND DIVORCE

CHOOSING A MARRIAGE PARTNER

Among the important events in life, three stand out—birth, marriage, and death. You have no control over who your parents will be, or in what environment you will be born. You are able to cope with death only to the extent of keeping yourself in fairly decent health so as to postpone it as long as possible. But as to marriage, you have some opportunity to decide this very important factor in your life in an intelligent, rational, logical manner, although here there are limitations and restrictions to free choice, depending on the existing factors of environment, financial and social status, personality, and so forth.

How are marriages decided upon? The answer is, largely by a process known as "falling in love," which may consist simply of physiological urges toward someone of the opposite sex with whom you have been thrown in contact. The oldsters in our culture still insist that "the right man will come along." The fond mother says to her dear son, "This girl isn't good enough for you. Wait awhile. You will know when the right one has come." How does one know? A mysterious glow of passion and loss of appetite are supposed to be signs that the great event has occurred.

But the determining factors are found in the type of individual and the community. Gaskill reports that, among seven thousand students, *health* and *intelligence* are considered the most important "traits" of personality in a prospective husband or wife.[38] E. L. Kelly has demonstrated a tendency toward "assortative mating," that is, selection of a mate who has similar psychological characteristics.[39] There is also a tendency for the butcher's boy to marry some girl a few blocks away or at least living in the same city; for the college student to marry someone with whom he has come in contact in his neighborhood or in the college community, after "falling in love." Tabulations of marriage licenses in New Haven and in Philadelphia reveal that nearness of residence, measured in blocks, is an extremely important variable in determining who will marry whom.[40] Abrams has shown that in Philadelphia more marriages were contracted between persons living within five blocks of each other in 1931 than in 1885, 1905, or 1915.[41] We try to plan what college we will attend, what vocation we will follow, how we will invest our money, what ticket we will vote, on a logical, rational basis; but *propinquity* or nearness is usually more important than planning in determining those whom we select as our mates.

THE PROBLEM OF ADJUSTMENT

In our culture, marriage is not ordinarily approached on a rational, logical basis; and yet people are still surprised when marriages do not turn out to be "made in heaven." We have some interesting patterns of romantic courtship,

> There is first of all the whole romantic love pattern itself, with emphasis upon thrill, lyrical expression of affection, high idealization of the prospective mate, and constantly reasserted loyalty and constancy. . . . Then, too, in the middle classes in this country, there is a good deal of lavish expenditure of money during courtship. The free spending gives the girl a certain idea of luxury which the young man, once married, may neither be able, nor even intend, to carry on. . . .
>
> But the most notable feature of courtship is that much of it goes on—using an old homely expression—in what may be called one's Sunday clothes. That is, young people tend to do their courting, at least in a wide range of social classes, as a leisure-time activity, often on holidays and Sundays, and through it all there runs a certain "dressed-up" attitude. Not only is this seen in matters of clothes, but the whole courtship tends to take place in a sort of Cinderella or daydream world which they and others build up. . . .
>
> . . . The honeymoon is often undertaken in the same romantic tenor as the traditional courtship. Expensive living in hotels and leisure-time activities sometimes give the couple . . . a false start as to the obligations and roles which will follow in ordinary daily life.[42]

Up to the age of marriage, a young woman has usually lived the life of a little girl with all the "niceness" and absence of rough conduct which this implies. Training in what people in our culture conceive to be "femininity" has probably convinced her that she thinks like a woman, that she is entitled to be emotional, and that she is justified in remaining relatively helpless. Add to this young woman one young man who all his life has been treated as a dominant male, with greater freedom, opportunity to "think like a man and act like a man," and some opportunity to break away from his family. Is it surprising that these two entirely different individuals, after a ritual has been performed, do not suddenly find themselves in perfect accord and understanding with each other? Each comes to the marriage with preconceived notions as to what the *other* should be like. This involves for the husband the notion, in general, that women are purer and more moral than men, but that they are "relatively impractical, emotional, unstable, given to prejudice, easily hurt, and largely incapable of facing facts or doing hard thinking."[43] It involves for the wife the notion that, in general, "men are nothing but big little boys who have never grown up and must be treated as such."[44] It also involves the belief that the other individual is somehow perfect in every respect, different from all others of his or her kind, and that "our marriage will be different." The process of adjustment in the first few weeks or months is inevitably hard. But it may to a large extent determine the success or failure of a given marriage. Once more, the four principal factors of the individual's past conditioning—*generalization, differentiation, traumatic experience, ready-made attitudes*—color and influence the marriage relationship. These are more powerful than all the fictionalized notions of the adolescent in determining whether barriers and differences will be overcome.

UTILITIES OF THE MARRIAGE RELATIONSHIP

What is it that people expect from the marriage relationship? Westermarck pointed out that there are at least three utilities in the marriage relation: (1) the satisfaction of the physiological sexual urge; (2) the provision of a wholesome environment for affection and love; and (3) the procreation and care of children.[45] How important are these three factors and to what extent do they work in our society?

1. *Satisfaction of the Sexual Urge.* As to the first item, many people believe that the marriage ceremony makes "the wrongest thing in the world the rightest thing in the world."[46] Data from one study of successful marriages among the parents of college students show that it took more time to work out adjustment in sex relations than in any other area of family life.[47] The husbands and wives agreed in listing the rest of the areas in the following order: spending the family income, social activities and recreation, in-law relationships, religion in the home, and associating with mutual friends.

Without adequate sex education in the family, the school, or the church, a person of marriageable age is suddenly supposed to engage in sexual relations with another individual, and these relations are expected to be harmonious and perfect from the beginning. Discussions in marriage clinics and courses in colleges on adequate preparation for marriage are helping to solve this problem for a small percentage of the population. Burgess and Cottrell have demonstrated that problems of sexual adjustment in marriage are not so much due to biological factors as to psychological characteristics and conditioned attitudes toward sex.[48] Here is a typical case history:

Mr. B. complained that his wife never wished to have sexual relations with him. She frequently refused on the ground of feeling ill or fatigued. . . . When sex relations occurred (as they did very rarely), she did not respond. The husband . . . was fairly well informed on sexual anatomy, physiology, and contraceptive methods. He tells of two premarital affairs in which he seemed to demonstrate competence in the art and technique of the sexual act. He takes considerable time in sexual foreplay in an effort to stimulate his wife, but says "her lack of any response to the situation cramps my style."

Mrs. B. thinks her lack of desire is due to her being easily fatigued. "I'm probably not as strong as other women, and do not have the physical energy to want sex." But she adds she can work hard all day and not be too tired to go out to parties or to the theatre. She says she has noticed her feelings of great fatigue will come suddenly just before her husband arrives home at night or just before her usual time for retiring. Her feeling ill or very tired is especially marked on Sundays. At one point in her narrative she told of her husband's being away for a week. She remembers this week particularly for her lack of fatigue, and the Sunday of that week as one of those rare week-ends when she "felt like going places and doing things." She admits that there may be some basis for the suggestion that her feeling of being ill or fatigued might be ways of avoiding sexual intercourse. She adds that the thought of sexual intercourse was sometimes enough to give her these feelings.

Mrs. B. was very closely identified with her strictly religious mother. . . . But it is found that her mother was herself an extremely frigid woman and frequently expressed to her daughter the idea that men are animalistic and women have to submit to the indignity of sexual relations because men could not remain healthy or content if denied such gratification. Mrs. B. says she was nearly twenty-one years of age before she realized (with considerable shock) that there are women who passionately desire sexual intercourse. She thought the woman depraved who expresses such desires.[49]

2. *Affection and Love.* General affection and love between the marriage partners is something more than satisfaction of the sex drive. The success of this second aspect of the marriage relation depends not only on physical attractiveness and health but on the subtle psychological factors of *suggestion, imitation, sympathy, identification,* as well as the satisfac-

tion of fundamental desires for *security, new experience, response,* and *recognition.* The importance of this part of the marriage relation cannot be overemphasized.

3. *Procreation and Care of Children.* Are procreation and care of children still principal goals in all American families? Apparently they are not, particularly in some of the higher socioeconomic groups. People in the professional groups are not producing enough children to replace themselves in the next generation. We have a greater percentage of old people and a smaller percentage of children in the United States than ever before.[50] From 1890 to 1930 the percentage of children under ten years of age dropped 4.7 per cent, while the percentage of people fifty-five and over increased 3.5 per cent.[51]

In a culture where it is considered desirable to keep up with the Joneses, children are often considered an economic liability. This is especially true in the city. In a culture where the number of married women outside the home has more than doubled within the last forty years, children may be considered by some to be a handicap. In a society which permits, legally or otherwise, the sale of contraceptives on a wholesale scale, and where even the Catholic Church has condoned a rhythm method of birth control, not so many children are produced. Birth-control information and devices are widely sold and easily accessible to all. A survey in the 1920's of one thousand married women showed that about 70 per cent used contraceptives, and the figure might actually have been larger if more accurate information had been obtainable.[52]

Apparently college students do not desire enough children to maintain their numbers in the next generation. In one study, about one-fourth of a group of college men and women expressed no desire to have children at all, and for those who did wish children the men wanted on the average only 2.4 children, the women only 2.7 children.[53] These figures are not much lower than those for a cross section of the "public." A Gallup poll in 1942 gave the following results for the ideal number of children: two, 31 per cent; three, 27 per cent; four, 27 per cent; other, 15 per cent.[54] Inquiries of expectant mothers attending prenatal clinics challenge the notion of procreation as an ideal of women. To the question, "Are you glad that you are going to have a baby?" sixty-five of eighty-seven women answered in the negative.[55] Of sixty-six women expecting their first-born child, forty-three said they had not planned to have the child.[56] The majority of the most outstanding women in this country are unmarried, and of those who are married, most have no children. And these are the people who might be expected to give a superior heredity and a superior cultural environment to children.

THE PROBLEM OF DIVORCE

"I now pronounce you man and wife." With some such words, over one million couples are married each year "for better or for worse," most with the confidence that their union will last "till death do us part." Yet about one marriage in every three today ends in divorce! Our newspapers and periodicals are filled with such terms as the drifting home, marriage in transition, the marriage crisis, family disorganization, family disintegration, trial marriage, companionate marriage, conservation of the family. Figures indicate that in a rapidly increasing number of cases marriage has failed to make "the twain one flesh." Thus, many young people develop the notion that marriage is almost bound to bring conflict, disillusionment, and eventually Reno. It has been predicted that the divorce rate may reach the ratio of one divorce per two marriages by 1970 or 1980.[57]

That divorce is taken for granted is revealed in the society pages of our newspapers. Consider the following intricate situation, gleaned from the society columns of *The New York Times:*

> Bridgeport, Conn., April 4.—Norman P. Gaynor . . . announced today the marriage . . . on Friday of his sister, Mrs. Marion Gaynor Jackson to Frank Carley Hunt.
>
> It was Mrs. Jackson's fourth marriage. Her previous marriages ended in divorces. Her former husbands are Colonel Ralph H. Isham, Carl Mengal and Congreve Jackson. . . .
>
> Friday's marriage is the third for Mr. Hunt. His first wife is now Mrs. Herbert Smith of New Canaan. His second, Mrs. Minnie Nichols Hunt, died two years ago.

The rapid increase in number of divorces does not necessarily mean that there has been an increase in marital maladjustment. Actually, termination of marriage in divorce might possibly mean a decrease in marital unhappiness. Divorce does not strike out of a clear sky, but is simply the final step in a series of incidents which mark the disintegration of a marriage. Certainly, however, the increasing number of divorces does represent a change in our mores.

The divorce rate varies considerably according to type of community. It is about twice as high in the cities as in the rural areas. In the country, primary-group control operates to make people obey the old mores regarding marriage, but in the city—at least in most sections of the city—this control tends to become weakened or to disappear altogether. City contacts and relations are much more casual, and an individual may to a much greater degree determine his own standards of behavior. Within a given city, there are differences from one section to another. For instance, a study made in the 1930's revealed that in some seventy-five communities in Chicago there was hardly a divorce from one year to the next, whereas in another community the divorce rate was over four times that for the United States as a whole.[58]

CAUSES OF MALADJUSTMENT

Lawyers should be psychologically trained, in order to deal intelligently with problems of family adjustment. Consider, for example, the so-called "grounds" for divorce in our various states. Adultery leads the list. Next in order are desertion, cruelty, imprisonment, drunkenness, impotence, insanity, and a host of other factors. These differ from one state to another. Does it make sense psychologically to find over forty-eight different sets of rules obtaining on such a delicate problem as family relations?

The supposed grounds by which people obtain divorces are not, of course, the true reasons for their family disorganization. In many states persons are forced to bring accusations against their marriage partners which are entirely unjust or untrue. In New York State, for example, where adultery is the only ground for absolute divorce, either the husband or the wife is forced to go through the rather sordid business of pretending to be caught in adultery, although the true causes of strife are in the majority of instances entirely different. In other states, newspaper stories of divorces mislead readers into thinking that John Jones, that outwardly nice man, is really a very terrible fellow because the newspaper says that his wife divorced him on grounds of mental and physical cruelty, and the legal documents say that he not only used harsh and blasphemous words but was even known to strike his wife in the face. What a cruel shock to John Jones's neighbors! It would be even more of a shock if they knew that no such things ever happened, but that instead the roots of the Jones family's disorganization lay in subtle psychological factors that had no legal counterpart. Some of the factors overlooked in our legal setup are differences in childhood attachments, family background, intelligence, standards of living, health, sex drive. Of these the law takes little or no account. The problem of divorce has not been treated realistically.

Suppose that a person went to a physician complaining of a pain in his right side and asked to have his appendix removed. No physician worthy of the name would immediately rush the person off to the hospital for an appendectomy without further investigation. Yet this is exactly the sort of thing that frequently occurs in our divorce courts. A woman, for example, may come to a lawyer and demand a divorce, complaining that she is not getting along well with her husband. The so-called divorce lawyer sometimes performs the role of a mechanic in looking up allowable grounds for divorce in his particular jurisdiction, and fails to take account of the family background in order to give some competent advice to the members of the family. Courts of Domestic Relations in many of our cities, however, are coming to perform this latter function.

At the very beginning of a marriage, many stumbling blocks to a satisfactory relationship are found. Most important is the lack of adequate training or preparation for marriage. A few colleges are beginning to offer courses in marriage; but no such type of training is available for the great majority, who do not go to college.

Legal reforms with reference to the process of getting married have often been opposed because of inertia or sheer selfishness. Only in the last few years have we begun to require premarital blood tests so as to help prevent the spread of syphilis which causes ill health and, in turn, family disharmony. These blood-test laws have met with decided opposition in every state into which they have been introduced. Similarly, "waiting periods" for persons who intend to marry have been introduced into our legal setup only very recently, and these constructive proposals, too, have met with opposition. A typical law of this kind provides that both parties must apply in person for the marriage license, and that one of them must then come back for it not less than three—sometimes five—days later.

> At first sight no law could appear more innocuous than this. If people are to spend the rest of a lifetime together, it would seem that three days more or less at the start would not be vital. It is interesting, therefore, to see the havoc that the law has wrought in every state in which it has been adopted. Frequently, it has committed the unpardonable sin—it has "hurt business," and has been repealed at the next session of the legislature under the onslaught of those whose pocketbooks were adversely affected: hotel proprietors, florists, jewelers, firms that take the first payment on furniture, and justices of the peace for whom every marriage that did not take place meant the loss of $5.[59]

Kirkpatrick finds some experimental confirmation for the belief that patriarchal attitudes in husbands tend to be associated with marital maladjustments.[60] He has also called attention to some of the problems of adjustments for the married woman.[61] She is expected to play three entirely different roles—that of wife-and-mother, companion, and partner. One form of conflict and tension for her results when she has difficulty in choosing between roles. Second, a wife may be expected to perform one of these roles only, while actually longing to perform a different one. Third, the husband may expect his wife to play one role, and she may prefer another. Finally, there may be an unfair distribution of obligations in her role as compared with her privileges.

PREDICTING SUCCESS IN MARRIAGE

Now, it is obvious that family disharmony does not always end in the divorce court, that in a great many instances husband and wife continue to live together and to support the institution of the family. What are the psychological factors which can be looked upon as indexes to probable marital happiness or marital unhappiness? Or, to put it differently, are there any variables which will enable you to predict the success or failure of given marriages before they occur? Terman and Buttenwieser found no significant relationships between marital happiness and any of the following factors which are commonly believed to be important: age at marriage; age differences between husband and wife; or number of offspring.[62] Similarly, Burgess and Cottrell who studied the premarital and postmarital backgrounds of 526 couples found no significant correlation between marriage adjustment and differences in religious preference of bride and groom, or in educational level, or economic status of their parents.[63] On the other hand, a number of factors did show a marked relation with success in marriage. The seven most important were:

1. The parents of both husband and wife are happily married.
2. Husband and wife are both agreed in desiring children.
3. Husband and wife are closely attached to their respective parents.
4. Superior cultural background of the families of both husband and wife determined by a number of factors such as their nationality, church activity, educational, economic and social status combined into an index.
5. Similarity of family backgrounds of husband and wife combined to bring out their likenesses and differences.
6. Positive religious attitudes and behavior as exemplified by length of attendance at Sunday school, regularity of church attendance, married by a minister and a church wedding.
7. Length of periods of acquaintance, keeping company, and engagement.[64]

Perhaps the most significant of the Burgess and Cottrell findings is that the background items of the husbands are much more important than the background items for the wives. In other words, contrary to the popular notion, *American wives make the major adjustment in marriage.* Also, the affectional relationships in childhood, especially of the son for his mother, and of the daughter for her father, tend to determine the choice of love object as an adult. This is borne out by a detailed analysis of 792 married couples, by Terman and his co-workers.[65] Two conclusions have both been arrived at independently in the two different investigations:

1. Happy marriages of parents are correlated with happiness in the marriage of their children. This relationship is the outstanding association noticed in the study of the relation between background items of both husbands and wives and their adjustment in marriage.
2. Close attachment in childhood to father and mother and absence of conflict with them is positively correlated with the person's adjustment in marriage.[66]

The Terman study also holds that only two of the many possible sex factors are probably important determiners of happiness in marriage, namely, the wife's orgasm adequacy, and the near equality of husband and wife in sex drive. Kinsey and his colleagues have reported that the sex factors which most frequently cause difficulties among "upper level" marriages are: failure of the husband to show skill in sexual approach and technique; and failure of the wife to participate "with the abandon which is necessary for the successful consummation of any sexual relations."[67]

In a comparison of marriages ending in divorce with marriages outsiders judged to be the happiest known to them, Locke finds considerable evidence to support the Burgess-Cottrell conclusions.[68] He comments especially on the high association between the ratings that subjects gave their parents' marriages and the degree of marital adjustment of the subjects; length of acquaintance prior to marriage; affiliation with a church; frequency of church attendance; and marriage by a minister in a church. "More than one out of four divorced men and women as compared with one in eight married men and women were married by a justice of the peace."[69]

If you are planning to choose a marriage partner soon, you will not necessarily attain a happy married life simply by selecting someone whose desire for children is equal to your own, or whose parents were happily married. No single factor can be used as the basis of prediction. Rather, there are a number of interrelated factors which, taken together, seem to be the important variables in determining which marriages will probably be successful. Even though factors have been and can be discovered which will make for satisfactory marriage relations, it is highly probable that people will continue to choose their spouses on the basis of "falling in love"—not on a logical basis of what social psychologists have demonstrated to be true.

COMPANIONATE MARRIAGE

A large number of couples are entering into "companionate marriage." This phrase should not be misunderstood. It does not imply a relatively permanent illicit union; neither does it involve the notion of Judge Ben B. Lindsey of right to divorce by mutual consent for childless couples, usually without payment of alimony.[70] The term "companionate marriage" was coined by Knight to describe lawful wedlock entered into solely for companionship, and not primarily for having children.[71] He had noted that the family of the historic sort, with procreation and care of children, still existed, but that a second type of family had grown up alongside it, based on the same sort of courtship and identical marriage rites, but not resulting in reproduction or care of the young. This second kind he called the companionate marriage.

This type of marriage exists on a fairly large scale today, particularly among the higher socioeconomic groups. It has grown up because of a new outlook on the role of sex and marriage. Historically, the church had taught that sex was a necessary evil and that the sexual act was to be tolerated only in so far as its motive was the production of offspring. Had this attitude continued to be accepted, the companionate marriage could never have arisen; instead, we would probably have had a sharp drop in the marriage rate. But traditional controls lost their force and in their place came a recognition that the pleasurable aspects of sex could be divorced from its reproductive aspects. This was coupled with the invention and widespread use of contraceptives. Flanagan has reported that in a group of four hundred married men those under forty years of age had a smaller percentage of "unplanned" or "accidental" children than those over forty.[72] This is probably due to differences in the mores of the two groups.

THE FUTURE OF MARRIAGE

With decreasing interest in procreation and care of children among some, there is also less emphasis on a wife's being an economic asset to her husband in our mechanized society. With the desires of many modern women for a "model home" and a suite of furniture, their demands that their husbands must have an automobile, and notions that they must not get "dishpan hands" in the sink or laundry tub, many questions arise as to what the future of the marriage relation may be. Many a modern wife has no children to care for, no house to clean, and few or no meals to cook.[73]

Is she to become merely an expensive ornament for the satisfaction of sexual needs? Probably not. Most couples still desire children and have them; there are indications that the fall in the birth rate among the higher economic classes has ceased. Motherhood has even taken on professional characteristics, requiring training and expertness. Even in the absence of children, many a wife is a companion and a social asset to her husband.

With the breakup of the economic, religious, and legal bonds which once made of the family a strong unit, the affectional bond has become the one by which many a family either lasts or disintegrates. It seems that the second of the three factors mentioned at the outset—the provision of a wholesome environment for affection and love—is of the utmost importance for the maintenance of any type of family. And this matter of affection and love is dependent on attitude development and on adequate sexual adjustment.

QUESTIONS AND PROBLEMS FOR DISCUSSION

1. *What relationships are there between early habit formation and the development of self-sufficiency?*

2. *Describe two or three methods that you might use to "break" a habit in a growing child—say, thumb sucking.*
3. *Explain Thomas's four wishes as related to the early social conditioning of the child.*
4. *Why should the "overprotected" and the "underprotected" child perhaps have many similar personality characteristics?*
5. *Does the fact that our parents taught us to do certain things in socially approved ways indicate that these ways are best?*
6. *In what ways do the occupations of fathers influence the personalities of their children?*
7. *List in two columns the psychological advantages and disadvantages of telling animal stories to children.*
8. *Make a list of* definite *problems which face most adolescents. Suggest at least one psychological solution for each problem.*
9. *In what ways are the so-called grounds of divorce frequently not the causes of divorce?*
10. *Is the family necessarily the basic social group in our society?*

RECOMMENDED READINGS

Arlitt, A. H., *The Adolescent.* New York: McGraw-Hill Book Company, Inc., 1938.

Baker, H. J., and Traphagen, V., *The Diagnosis and Treatment of Behavior-Problem Children.* New York: The Macmillan Company, 1935.

Bossard, J. H. S., *Marriage and the Child.* Philadelphia: University of Pennsylvania Press, 1940.

Bossard, J. H. S., *The Sociology of Child Development.* New York: Harper & Brothers, 1948.

Brooks, F. D., and Shaffer, L. F., *Child Psychology.* Boston: Houghton Mifflin Company, 1937.

Burgess, E. W., and Cottrell, L. S., Jr., *Predicting Success or Failure in Marriage.* New York: Prentice-Hall, Inc., 1939.

Burgess, E. W., and Locke, H. J., *The Family: From Institution to Companionship.* New York: American Book Co., 1945.

Cole, L., *Psychology of Adolescence.* New York: Farrar & Rinehart, Inc., 1936.

Folsom, J. K., *The Family: Its Sociology and Social Psychiatry.* New York: John Wiley & Sons, Inc., 1934.

Folsom, J. K., *Plan for Marriage: An Intelligent Approach to Marriage and Parenthood Proposed by Members of the Staff of Vassar College.* New York: Harper & Brothers, 1938.

Goldstein, S. F., *Marriage and Family Counseling.* New York: McGraw-Hill Book Company, Inc., 1945.

Goodenough, F. L., *Anger in Young Children.* Minneapolis: University of Minnesota Press, 1931.

Goodsell, W., *Problems of the Family* (revised edition). New York: D. Appleton-Century Company, 1936.

Groves, E. R., *The Drifting Home.* Boston: Houghton Mifflin Company, 1926.

Groves, E. R., *Marriage.* New York: Henry Holt and Company, Inc., 1933.

Groves, E. R., *The Family and Its Social Functions.* Philadelphia: J. B. Lippincott Company, 1940.

Groves, E. R., and Brooks, L. M., *Readings in the Family.* Philadelphia: J. B. Lippincott Company, 1934.

Groves, E. R., Groves, G. H., and Groves, C., *Sex Fulfillment in Marriage.* New York: Emerson Books, 1942.

Groves, E. R., and Ogburn, W. F., *American Marriage and Family Relationships.* New York: Henry Holt and Company, Inc., 1928.

Isaacs, S. S., *Social Development in Young Children: A Study of Beginnings.* London: George Routledge & Sons, Ltd., 1933.

Jersild, A. T., *Child Psychology.* New York: Prentice-Hall, Inc., 1933.

Levy, D. M., *Maternal Overprotection.* New York: Columbia University Press, 1943.

Lichtenberger, J. P., *Divorce, A Social Interpretation.* New York: McGraw-Hill Book Company, Inc., 1931.

Morgan, J. J. B., *Child Psychology* (third edition). New York: Rinehart & Company, Inc., 1943.

Mowrer, E. R., *Family Disorganization* (second edition). Chicago: University of Chicago Press, 1939.

Powdermaker, F., and Grimes, L. I., *Children in the Family: A Psychological Guide for Parents.* New York: Farrar & Rinehart, 1940.

Preston, G. H., *The Substance of Mental Health.* New York: Farrar & Rinehart, 1943.

Rogers, C., *The Clinical Treatment of the Problem Child.* Boston: Houghton Mifflin Company, 1939.

Stoddard, G. D., and Wellman, B. L., *Child Psychology.* New York: The Macmillan Company, 1934.

Symonds, P. M., *The Psychology of Parent-Child Relationships.* New York: D. Appleton-Century Company, 1939.

Teagarden, F., *Child Psychology for Professional Workers.* New York: Prentice-Hall, Inc., 1940.

Terman, L. M., Buttenwieser, P., Ferguson, L. W., Johnson, W. B., and Wilson, D. P., *Psychological Factors in Marital Happiness.* New York: McGraw-Hill Book Company, Inc., 1938.

Van de Velde, T. H., *Ideal Marriage: Its Physiology and Technique.* London: William Heinemann, Ltd., 1926.

Waller, W., *The Family: A Dynamic Interpretation.* New York: Dryden Press, 1938.

Westermarck, E., *The Future of Marriage in Western Civilisation.* New York: The Macmillan Company, 1936.

*Newcomb, T. M., Hartley, E. L., and others (editors), *Readings in Social Psychology.* New York: Henry Holt and Company, Inc., 1947. (The following selections are listed according to the sequence of related discussions in the chapter you have just read.)

Keister, M. E., and Updegraff, R., "A Study of Children's Reactions to Failure and an Experimental Attempt to Modify Them," pp. 291-296.

Ericson, M. C., "Social Status and Child-Rearing Practices," pp. 494-501.

Murphy, L. B., "Social Factors in Child Development," pp. 129-139.

Davis, A., "Socialization and Adolescent Personality," pp. 139-150.

Thomas, W. I., and Znaniecki, F., "The Definition of the Situation," pp. 76-77.

CHAPTER SEVENTEEN

EDUCATION–THE SCHOOL

WHAT IS EDUCATION? The Extent of Education—Confusion of Aims—Definition of Education—College Education—Facts and Attitudes—Freedom of Teaching—Transfer of Training—Attitude Development—Major Problems of Education / CHARACTER EDUCATION. Moral and Ethical Values—Socialization—The Activity Program—Specific Character Education—Practice in Specific Habits—Criticism of Specificity—Indirect Methods of Training—Avoidance of Two Fields of Character Education—(1) Sex Education—Taboos and Conflicts—(2) Religious Education—Limitations of Character Education in College—The Question of "Desirable" Character Traits—Teachers' Reactions to Behavior Problems / THE TEACHING PROFESSION. Lack of Prestige—Low Pay—Lack of Organization—Education as a Symbol—Teaching, Woman's Work—Serving Five Masters—(1) The Pupils—(2) The Parents—(3) The Board of Education—(4) The Administrator—(5) The Community.

▶ WHAT IS EDUCATION?

THE EXTENT OF EDUCATION

Education is the biggest business in the United States. Approximately one-third of the total population is engaged in education: as pupils, teachers, other instructional staff, custodial and other employees, administrators, and suppliers of goods and services to the schools. Approximately one-fourth of the total population is getting an education in full-time public day schools. By 1940 there were almost three and a half million persons twenty-five years old and over, with four or more years of college education.[1] Therefore, the institution of education deserves careful analysis.

All this may sound as if education were a well-organized and highly integrated business. In the United States, however, there are 127,000 separate public-school "systems"—some of which maintain no schools—within the forty-eight separate state school systems. There is no national "system" except for the military, naval, and coast-guard schools. There is one school board member to every two teachers. Beyond "elementary" and "secondary" public schooling, there are 1,709 institutions of "higher education" with their personnel and students that are part of the state school systems.[2]

CONFUSION OF AIMS

With this complicated mass of systems and schools, it is not strange that there is disagreement among American citizens concerning the aims of education. This is true from the nursery school on through the graduate school. It is not surprising that at the end of any given academic year some two million young people permanently leave the confines of the classroom with grave misgivings as to just what kind of learning they have acquired. The source of their misgivings lies in the confusingly wide variety of benefits which education is supposed to give them. The rough pattern of values of people in *Middletown* is as follows:

> That schools should teach the facts of past experience about which "sound, intelligent people agree."
>
> That it is dangerous to acquaint children with points of view that question "the fundamentals."
>
> That an education should be "practical," but at the same time, it is chiefly important as "broadening" one.
>
> That too much education and contact with books and big ideas unfits a person for practical life.
>
> That a college education is "a good thing."
>
> But that a college man is no better than a non-college man and is likely to be less practical, and that college men must learn "life" to counteract their concentration on theory.
>
> That girls who do not plan to be teachers do not ordinarily need as much education as boys.
>
> That "you forget most of the things you learn in school." . . .
>
> That schoolteachers are usually people who couldn't make good in business.
>
> That teaching school, particularly in the lower grades, is women's business.
>
> That schools nowadays go in for too many frills.[3]

A number of values other than intellectual ones color the picture of what is important in the school. Social prestige and clothes are considered important. One mother whose son dropped out of school said, "We couldn't dress him like we'd ought to and he felt out of it"; and another, "The two boys and the oldest girl all quit because they hated Central High School. They all loved the Junior High School down here, but up there they're so snobbish. If you don't dress right you haven't any friends."[4]

DEFINITION OF EDUCATION

It is as difficult to define "education" as it is to define "religion" or "democracy." Countless definitions have been offered. One useful one is the following: *An educated man is one who is master of himself, who is free from herd opinion, who has a capacity for self-criticism and suspended judgment, and who can place himself above, rather than remain within, the domain of his own beliefs and ideals.*[5] Certainly this is the ideal which is stressed by the word "objectivity." If one is truly objective about his fellows and about himself, he will be able to examine intelligently not only the world about him, but himself as well, and will be sufficiently removed from the existing culture patterns to develop his own thinking and acting accordingly. Sixty out of a hundred college presidents have said that the trend in education is to "educate for life."[6]

COLLEGE EDUCATION

There are apparently three principal reasons why young people go to college: (1) the "bread-and-butter" purpose, (2) the "superkindergarten" purpose, and (3) the "knowledge" purpose.[7]

1. The *bread-and-butter purpose* is stressed in the huge number of books, magazine articles, and speeches that are concerned with the money value of an education. Elaborate tables and charts have been prepared to show that it is the college men and women who earn the most money. Many young persons have been inveigled into becoming "students" because the acquisition of two capital letters—A.B. or B.S.—after their names has become a partial guarantee of a job and success in the "great game of life." It is questionable, however, whether a money value can be put on many of the facts and attitudes learned in college. No exact money value can be assigned to becoming familiar with the works of Shakespeare, Leonardo da Vinci, or any of the other great masters of pen or brush.

The prevalent belief in this country, that anyone who "went to college" is a more intelligent citizen than one who did not, is also beginning to be displaced. Being educated, as defined above, is not just a matter of having attended school and college. At least, young men and women now in college realize that merely attending a certain number of lectures is no guarantee of success, financial or otherwise. More and more people are rejecting the purely bread-and-butter purposes of the liberal arts college.

In a survey of the Harvard class of 1911, conducted twenty-five years later, half of the men admitted that they were disappointed in their lifework. "My business is rotten. I have never held public office. I have no money to travel. My chief occupation is trying to get a living for my family."[8] Again, "After twenty-five years, I am an utter failure, morally, mentally, and financially."[9] These Harvard men decried the fact that their average earned income was under $5,000 per year. They also questioned whether some of the standards of college really should be stressed. In answer to the question, "Were college courses of lasting value?" every third man said "No." "Which professor was of most influence?" "Not a one," replied 41 per cent.

2. The second purpose, the *superkindergarten* one, seems also to be dropping by the wayside. Some colleges have been bold enough to adopt the attitude of a foreman employing a man on a construction job—"You're lucky to be here. See that you learn what you can!" But pampering of college students in an attempt to get them through has typified certain colleges and universities. On top of all the other problems of higher education, it seems that some colleges have fulfilled their purpose if they house, feed, exercise, and amuse the young. These are exactly the things advertised by resort hotels.

3. As to the third purpose, the *acquisition of knowledge,* this aim has typified education from the times of the Greeks through the period of Scholasticism and even to date. This goal still exists. But all colleges and universities do not transmit knowledge to an equal extent. A survey carried out under the auspices of the Carnegie Foundation for the Advancement of Teaching showed an amazing variation among colleges in the amount of information they were able to impart.[10] On the basis of elaborate tests, the dullest boy in one superior college was actually ahead of the brightest boy in an inferior institution. In other words, the individual differences between institutions which called themselves colleges were so great that the earning of a degree meant entirely different things in various institutions. This investigation further revealed that standards for advancement from one class to another, freshman to sophomore, for example, were notoriously low. A high percentage of students ranking as freshmen and sophomores had a great deal more factual information than a great many students in the senior class.

FACTS AND ATTITUDES

Two different emphases have been found in supplying knowledge and education—the memorizing of facts, and the instilling of attitudes. While the former is important, it is not the whole story. Memorizing information is not in itself education. Many of the "facts" which are memorized in high school and college later cease to be facts—new principles are formulated and discoveries made which change our previous knowledge. If you will examine textbooks of only ten or fifteen years ago, you will find that "facts" in the physical sciences, the social sciences, and even in literature, have changed. As an example, the thinking of physicists during the last decade has been revolutionary. Knowledge is not static. The process of education is designed to present the "facts" as they are *now* understood; but these, too, may change. In the social sciences this is often stressed, sometimes to the alarm of the student. After all, he says, if what we are now learning may not be true, why should we bother to learn it?

> Because people are impressed by miscellaneous information, [many] teachers have devoted themselves to human taxidermy, stuffing the skins of their students

with enough miscellaneous information to convince other people, and even themselves, that they actually know what it's all about. Because it is popular to agree with one's neighbors and business associates, [many] schools have lent themselves to turning out innocuous young men and women who will never embarrass their relatives and friends.[11]

Students need to be trained to think through certain issues for themselves, and this means that they must constantly keep in mind that every "fact" they learn from a book is based ultimately on what some other person has said. "My history book says that Columbus discovered America." "My physics book says that energy cannot be created." "My teacher says that all men are equal." Did Columbus discover America? Can energy not be created? Are all men equal? The amount of truth contained in many statements of "fact" seems to vary with who said them, and students must determine what sources of information are the most reliable.

A great deal of American education has consisted of a process in which ideas get from the notebook of the teacher to the notebook of the student without going through the mind of either one. If people are really to be educated, they must be trained to dig out some things for themselves. Many of our college courses have consisted of reading one textbook, taking down some class notes, and then regurgitating onto examination papers a summarized account of the notes. Emphasis has not always been placed on getting away from textbooks and hunting out facts for oneself.

Any teacher who has had much experience in reading student examination papers can recall amusing instances of "boners" or "howlers." Thus a student is reported to have written, "The French Revolution wrote insulting letters to the American Revolution." She justified this, when questioned about it, as a paraphrase of the statement made by the instructor himself. Her notes, confirmed by the instructor, showed the statement to be: "The French Revolution corresponded in a rough way with the American Revolution." In a recent investigation by Newburn, one student wrote, "All conservatives are radicals and should be jailed." Scott and Myers report that some members of a class of rural teachers "were thinking of the United States foreign minister to Japan as a Presbyterian clergyman, some as a Methodist, some as a Catholic priest, and so on. . . ."[12]

Attitudes must also be stressed. We often hear the catch phrase, "Teach pupils how to think, not what to think." Certainly, the aim or teaching people how to think is desirable; but it is also necessary to teach people what to think in so far as existing knowledge permits. A social psychologist would insist that the emphasis should be placed upon the scarcity of knowledge in any field, and that attention should be called to how the supposed facts may change.

FREEDOM OF TEACHING

However, this necessitates the discussion of controversial issues, and sometimes pressure is exerted on the schools to prevent the teaching of more than one side of certain social issues. This applies particularly to the social sciences—history, economics, political science, sociology, anthropology, and social psychology.

> . . . Dominant minorities and would-be majorities in every community seek to use the schools as agencies for the perpetuation of their own cherished points of view and causes. Religious groups, favored economic classes, political parties, patriotic associations, workers' organizations—these and many other such pressure groups try constantly, and often successfully, to control the formal education of the young. Thus it happens that in every society the school's basic objectives, curricula, and methods grow out of and reflect the dominant mores of those groups which happen to have the strongest influence.[13]

Mr. Average Citizen knows that he isn't a skilled mathematician or an expert physicist, but Mr. Average Citizen is convinced that he knows history because he belongs to a patriotic society, that he is a political scientist because he reads the newspapers, and that he is most certainly a social psychologist because he sees people around him all the time and studies human behavior. Therefore, citizens' groups, special-interest groups, and innumerable patriotic organizations bring pressure on boards of education, administrators, and teachers themselves to teach only the "true facts," these consisting of the beliefs or aims of some particular organization. An Associated Press dispatch of some years ago reported that an officer of one such organization sought the ban of a well-known social-science text from the schools of Philadelphia because the book "tried to give the child an unbiased viewpoint instead of teaching him real Americanism." And yet if you will examine historically every instance of censorship, you will find that the censorship has never been effective for more than a short time. One of the surest ways in which an ideology becomes talked about and perhaps accepted is through efforts to suppress it.

> The teaching profession has chosen to include controversial issues in the school because of its conviction that the truth regarding each side of these controversies should be known. This decision makes it mandatory that there should be no withholding of essential information, no stifling of thought, and no wavering from the intellectualization of the issues. In short, there must be freedom of thought and teaching. How else can the basis for intelligent judg-

ment be formed? The vital condition for government "of the people, by the people, and for the people" is the free and unpolluted flow of knowledge and the unrestricted use of critical discussion.[14]

TRANSFER OF TRAINING

If education should teach people how to think, how is it to be done? The answer consists of *transfer of training*—that is, the utilization of past experiences in dealing with new situations. A student who has studied economics and political science should be able to "transfer" these studies to problems of international finance. A fundamental problem which confronts the school and the college is to present ideas and "ways" in the school environment in such a form that they will be transferred or carried over to other life situations. This is extremely difficult because a great deal of education has consisted of training people to memorize verbally and to engage in the art of putting one word after another. The fact that a student becomes symbolically proficient in moving his tongue and producing sounds, or in scratching written symbols on a paper, is no guarantee that he has become nonsymbolically proficient, that is, that he has developed any true understanding of the ideas concerned.

It is beside the point here to discuss the various hypotheses concerning transfer of training, such as the theory of "identical elements." Regardless of the exact explanation of transfer of training, it is clear that the more fully relationships between school and other situations are recognized, the greater is the likelihood of transfer. "If we want our in-school teaching to transfer in the greatest degree to out-of-school behavior, it behooves us to make the student acutely aware of the possibilities of transfer. We must bring him, as frequently as possible, to see the relationships between in-school and out-of-school situations."[15]

This is not always done. Rather than transfer of training in many school situations, we have the opposite, namely, a stress on the words which are used. You can perhaps recall instances where you received a higher grade for giving back the *exact* words of the book, or even of the instructor. The point may be illustrated by the following story told by William James:

> A friend of mine, visiting a school, was asked to examine a young class in geography. Glancing at the book she said: "Suppose you should dig a hole in the ground, hundreds of feet deep, how should you find it at the bottom,—warmer or colder than on top?" None of the class replying, the teacher said: "I'm sure they know, but I think you don't ask the question quite rightly. Let me try." So, taking the book, she asked: "In what condition is the interior of the globe?" and received the immediate answer from half the class at once: "The interior of the globe is in a condition of *igneous fusion*."[16]

Parroting and formalism are not limited to the grade schools but are found even in the college and university. Routine, drill, and meeting one's classes in a perfunctory way are very easy solutions for some college instructors. This mechanism may carry over to the types of examinations and to grading systems.

ATTITUDE DEVELOPMENT

The psychology of attitude development is a problem of transfer of training in the sense that attitudes are supposed to transfer or carry over to later situations. Ellis Freeman has called attention to the fact that a book on as impartial a subject as arithmetic may actually contain a good deal of unintentional manipulation of attitudes, stressing various concepts of capitalism.[17] In Italy, the state-issued textbooks used to be full of pro-Fascist materials:

> Primers, illustrated with colorful pictures of Fascist soldiers, taught the alphabet with such examples as "F as in *fascio*." One of the first reading lessons: "'Duce, Duce,' the voice of the children reaches up into the office where the Duce is working. The Duce hears it and smiles and works for them. Says the Duce: 'Be good children and obey. To obey is your first duty.'"
>
> Arithmetic books offered this typical problem: "In order to live Mussolini once had to work as a stone mason. He describes it in his diary. He worked eleven hours per day, received 32 centèsimi per hour, made 121 trips per day with his wheelbarrow full of stones. How many lire did he make per day, per week? How many trips with his wheelbarrow did he make per month?"[18]

Patriotic attitudes are desirable in our culture. Yet the development of patriotic attitudes often consists of mere drill, rather than a frank discussion of the problems of the United States and what is meant by democratic ideals. For example, a tempest in a teapot raged in New York some years ago when it was suggested that the pledge of allegiance to the American flag should be changed by having the pupil place the left hand over the heart and then extend the right hand straight forward palm upward. This looked too much like a Nazi salute. Prior to this, a bill had been introduced that would have required all New York school buses to be painted red, white, and blue. Few took the trouble to concern themselves with an examination of how patriotic attitudes could be realistically developed in the students.

It has even been suggested that respect for the flag can be taught by force. Three legislators argued before the California Assembly in 1939 that children should be taught to respect the flag "with whippings if necessary just as they are compelled to learn the three R's." "In these days of dictators we should use the iron fist to teach patriotism," said one of them.[19]

In a democracy not of theory but of fact, greater advances will be made toward truth where all sides of a question are discussed and where there is allowance for give and take, on the part of both students and teachers. Neither democracy nor patriotism can be taught by flag salutes *alone,* nor *only* by pledges of allegiance, which may become meaningless ceremonies involving the reciting of a string of beautiful syllables. These rituals may be popular, but *in themselves* they do not result in true love of our country.

MAJOR PROBLEMS OF EDUCATION

One serious problem in education is that it attempts to do everything for everybody. "We provide our young people with an intensive four-year training in football, fraternities and fun. On the side, we offer them a series of unrelated courses . . . to prepare them to make money in anything from beauty culture to bond selling."[20] One survey, involving the testing of seven thousand students in thirty-six colleges and universities in all sections of the country regarding their knowledge of United States history, revealed that 25 per cent did not know that Abraham Lincoln was President of the United States during the Civil War; that 30 per cent did not know that Woodrow Wilson was President during World War I; and that 81 per cent of the college freshmen could not name *two* contributions of Theodore Roosevelt to our political, economic, or social development.[21]

A second major problem of education relates to the tendency to teach as though there were a democracy of brains—on the theory that "all men are created equal." Many American parents believe that all children, whether dull or bright, should get equal benefits from their schooling. If they do not, there is not something wrong with the children, some parents will insist, but with the teachers, the school, or the educational system. If all contribute equal amounts of money to the school, in taxes and tuition, it follows that each pupil should derive equal benefit—thus speak many parents. As a result of this attitude, the tremendous individual differences between students in intelligence, attitudes, and personality traits are likely to be overlooked.

This leads to a third problem, that of mass production in education. Because conveyor belts have proved successful in factories, it does not follow that they can be used with equal success in the training of the young. A standardized program of instruction in which all individuals are treated alike frequently results in warped personalities. Age, ability, social training, intelligence, personality, achievement, of all kinds are found in varying degrees in a student, and many schools have failed to cope with these individual differences in order that each student may develop to his full extent.

A fourth difficulty concerns the students themselves. In every other enterprise besides education, Americans insist on getting their money's worth. In education alone do many do their best to get as little as possible for their money! A great many high-school and college students take valuable years of their lives, financed with the hard-earned dollars of their parents (or themselves), and then do their best to derive as *little* as possible from most of their courses. One thing they do demand, that at the end of the prescribed number of years of sitting in classrooms they shall get a sheepskin diploma.

▶ CHARACTER EDUCATION

MORAL AND ETHICAL VALUES

In all communities the job of the teacher is not only to teach facts and attitudes, but also to engage in moral training and, particularly in the earlier years, to look after the physical health and cleanliness of the pupils. Historically, the school has been concerned with the teaching of information and techniques. Recently, however, an emphasis has also been put on the social and moral sides of conduct. This has never reached the absurdity of any teacher saying to a group of youngsters, "Now children, we are going to devote the next half hour to character education." It has meant instead that moral, social, and ethical values have been introduced along with the teaching of the material culture patterns, and this has been brought about largely at the insistence of noneducators. Parents in particular insist that the correct ways of behaving be taught in the school system. In sending their children to school or college, they want their behavior to become "civilized," their morals to be elevated, their character developed, their family mores kept intact, to say nothing of learning what parents call the "fundamentals."

SOCIALIZATION

Parents even criticize the school for placing too much emphasis on individual accomplishments, because the students are led to look upon their classmates as competitors whom they must struggle to surpass. Competition has been utilized since it represents a fairly easy and effective method of motivation. School marks, honor rolls, and special awards promote a desire to get ahead of the other fellow. In the "newer-type" schools, however, there is a recognition that the student must learn to adjust the satisfaction of his own desires to the needs and rights of others. Socialization is the keynote of the school's program.

In follow-up studies of the effects of dominative and integrative contacts on children's behavior, H. H. Anderson and his co-workers have demonstrated that children's social behavior tends largely to change with different teachers.[22] In an experiment by G. G. Thompson, involving preschool children, teachers in one group were instructed to adopt an impersonal policy, and to give information and help only upon specific request from a child; whereas teachers in another group were to help the child in his relations with other children and in his use of play materials according to how the teachers thought each child's social and emotional needs might best be met.[23] The latter group showed superior development in ascendance, social participation, leadership, and constructiveness.

THE ACTIVITY PROGRAM

The "activity program" is a term used to connote a method of instruction which is an outgrowth of the school's efforts to provide opportunities for socialization as well as to develop other desirable qualities of pupil personality. Under the activity program a broad project, usually built around present-day problems and activities, is initiated by the teacher, or in some very progressive schools by the pupils themselves because of their interest in a particular subject. The project involves the integration of most of the subjects in the school curriculum, and is set up so as to include a great deal of experiencing as well as discussing. The class may be divided into groups, each of which is responsible for the development of certain parts of the program, or the pupils may all work together deciding on the best ways of finding out the information they need and of using it.

Work together on a common interest fosters cooperation. Differences of opinion have to be ironed out. Lessons in getting along with others are provided through actual experiencing of the resolution of conflicts. Working with teacher stimulation but without teacher domination provides an opportunity for the development of pupil initiative. In the standard-type schools special emphasis is placed upon memorization through assigned lessons and recitation of subject matter; in the more progressive schools pupils are encouraged to make voluntary reports of experiences and to suggest ways of solving problems. Pupils who are generally less able than most of their classmates are encouraged along some line in which the teacher has discovered they have ability.

The social activities of the pupils are the centers around which the activity program is built, which means that in the primary grades the projects deal with home and neighborhood activities, expanding to include larger areas as the child goes on into the more advanced grades. In so far as it gets away from the old formalized concepts of education, the school is attempting to provide real-life situations for the student—experiences more nearly approximating those which he will meet in life outside of school. This again involves the problem of *transfer* or carry-over of attitudes developed in the school situation.

SPECIFIC CHARACTER EDUCATION

With a background all his own, limited by hereditary factors and conditioned by the influences of his family and community, the student comes to school. And it becomes the job of the school and the teacher to modify his personality through education—to break up the fears, anxieties, and feelings of superiority or inferiority with which he is burdened, to instill in him the attitudes necessary to a successful social adjustment, to make for him a satisfying personal development, and to inculcate those principles which are the mores of his society. Truly this is a large order. Gradually the school has taken over many functions which in the nineteenth century were unquestionably limited to the home. Pupils in schools all over the country are concerned with items of behavior such as these:

1. We eat slowly and chew our food well.
2. We try to be happy and have pleasant conversation while we are eating.
3. We wash our hands before eating.
4. We try to sit and stand erect.
5. Each pupil has a clean handkerchief every day.
6. Each one puts his handkerchief before his mouth when coughing or sneezing.
7. We avoid spitting.
8. We remove our wraps when inside.
9. We do not put our fingers or pencils into our mouths.
10. We eat only fruit between meals.
11. We keep our nails trimmed and properly cleaned.
12. We keep our food covered and away from flies.
13. We put on our wraps and overshoes before going outside in cold or stormy weather.
14. We play outside during intermissions unless stormy weather prevents.[24]

This is a type of training, of course, which is highly desirable psychologically in that the situations are made very specific. A great deal of character education at the present time reduces itself to teaching specific ways of acting in order that these may transfer over to nonschool situations. Trying to teach character traits in the abstract accomplishes little or nothing. Any student might write one hundred times a day, "Honesty is the best policy," but this would be no guarantee that he would become an honest individual. He might become proficient in reciting the word symbols of the Ten Commandments and the Golden Rule, and still not apply these codes.

The classical studies by Hartshorne and May, for example, illustrated that the supposed character trait called "honesty" was highly specific to a given situation.[25] Children who cheated in a spelling test were not necessarily the same ones who cheated in a contest of muscular strength or in other situations. Honesty was found to be not some general "catch-all" characteristic, but was a composite of a great many specific ways of behaving in highly specific situations. A boy who is honest in playing ball may be the one who steals an eraser from the girl at the next desk when recess is over.

PRACTICE IN SPECIFIC HABITS

Most of us have "watertight compartments" in our thinking and acting. Therefore, if character education is to be meaningful, it has to involve very specific ways of behaving. Lip service to an ideal may have no relation to actual conduct. Generalizations often fail because actions must fit the needs of specific situations. General traits such as honesty, loyalty, helpfulness, courtesy, obedience, and thrift are generalized concepts of *specific* types of the trait, each of which needs to be practiced and discussed. Therefore, the type of moral and ethical training which is being introduced in many educational systems at the present time seems quite sound psychologically in that it involves specific healthful situations or specific habits of cleanliness such as, "We keep all papers picked up off the floor," or "We keep our desks neat and orderly."[26]

Many of the subjects in the Hartshorne and May studies were able to make higher scores on pencil-and-paper tests of honesty than other pupils; yet when it came to *specific* situations they made poorer scores. An "honest" student may be honest with reference to paying his debts, but may not hesitate to take an unfair advantage of another in a game. One boy, known to steal after school hours, wept when a classmate cheated; the code of the class against misconduct in school made no reference to stealing out of school.[27] An individual who has the reputation of being "courteous" may be so to his teachers and friends, but this may not carry over to his home relationships.

Furthermore, certain traits are not necessarily desirable under all circumstances. Thrift is excellent, but may become penuriousness and selfishness. Constant cheerfulness can be annoying. Obedience in some situations is a sign of weakness. Loyalty must be discriminating.

CRITICISM OF SPECIFICITY

Gordon W. Allport has criticized this notion of specificity in our moral behavior. He maintains that the children in the Hartshorne and May studies were not inconsistent; they were simply not consistent in the same ways.[28] Thus, children who steal do not necessarily lie; but the habit of stealing may be an integral part of *some* trait in each child's life, even though rarely related to the habit of lying. For example, child

A might steal pennies because of a consistent trait of *bravado,* child *B* because of a persistent *interest in tools and mechanics* for which he needs money, child *C* because of *feelings of social inferiority,* stealing pennies to purchase candy for his playmates to win their favor. Other children do not steal pennies, but do lie—child *D* because of a general trait of timidity and fear of consequences, child *E* because he wants to please his teacher, and child *F* because he is greedy for praise. "Each of these children behaved as he did toward these tests, not because he had specific habits, but because he had some deep-lying and characteristic trait."[29] To use an analogy, it would be absurd to think that a person would have a trait causing him to borrow books from the library which have only red, or blue, covers.[30] The organized traits of interest would be found in the subject matter of the chosen books, not in their bindings.

INDIRECT METHODS OF TRAINING

Shall we teach character and morals *directly* by calling the attention of students to certain moral principles that underlie conduct? Or shall we expect these moral principles to become important in their lives through *indirect* learning which involves experience and discussion rather than formal instruction? Results of experimental studies have shown the indirect method to be superior. One investigator set out to determine the effect of a series of three short lectures on dishonesty on college students in their examinations. Although it seemed as if the three lectures were effective when delivered, they did not result in a reduction in the amount of dishonesty of the group hearing them—33 per cent of the trained group cheated, as compared with 34.6 per cent of the control group.[31]

Even though the indirect method of character education does seem superior, Vernon Jones warns of the danger of not having a *planned* program of character education.[32] The training must be systematically presented by the teacher, without appearing to be too direct. Jones conducted an interesting experiment in the seventh and eighth grades of the New Haven public schools. In each of the two grades three classes were given special instruction in character and citizenship, and one was held as a control. In two of the six trained classes—one seventh and one eighth grade—the firsthand experiencing method was used, any instruction being of a very specific nature and directly related to the situation. In two other classes, instruction consisted exclusively of discussion, freqently opened by a concrete happening or by a story from biography; discussion, however, included a wide variety of related situations but no firsthand "experiencing." In the two other trained classes the experiencing-plus-discussion method was used, which consisted of relating specific activities to generalized principles and also the consideration of other situations which might have elements in common with those actually faced. Although improvement was small on the average for the various groups, the most successful teaching method was the experiencing-plus-discussion method; it was the one method which yielded results significantly superior to those of the control groups.

AVOIDANCE OF TWO FIELDS OF CHARACTER EDUCATION

Although there has been a gradual and continuous shift from the family and home situation to both the school and the church as institutions for character education, still suspicions attach to certain types of training within the school system itself. There are two fields of interest which parents usually insist must be avoided, although questions concerning them are among our most important social problems. The two fields are sex and religion. Although sexual knowledge and attitudes cut across many other social fields, most parents insist that educators remain silent on any point remotely associated with sex. Likewise, concerning one of our greatest social forces, namely, religion, parents also insist that the subject shall be taboo because of the danger of their children's coming into contact with religious ideas which are in opposition to the "true" ideas of their particular sect.

1. *Sex Education.* Children are taught manners, social behavior, habits of healthful living, what to eat and not to eat, how to cook, sew, manage a household, dress, and in some instances how to engage in various vocations such as carpentry or printing. Yet when it comes to one of the most vital problems of living, particularly for the adolescent, most schools and colleges will have none of it. A revised syllabus on general science prepared for the Board of Education of New York City in 1938 touched upon the reproduction of flowers, plants, and birds, but omitted mammals completely. The Board of Superintendents asserted that pupils of the seventh, eighth, and ninth grades were not mature enough to receive sex education above the level of bird life! Remember that these children are at the age of puberty.

A college student says of her high-school training:

> The hygiene classes at high school were a farce. We read about the work of Florence Nightingale and Louis Pasteur, and learned nothing about ourselves. When I revisited a class three weeks ago, I found the same phlegmatic, uninteresting and uninterested attitudes on the part of the students and instructor. The nearest approach they made to learning about the origin of life was to read a pamphlet which tells about the mother salmon and the father salmon; in the foreword of the pamphlet it is stated that it is intended for children of from 6 to 10 years of age!

A young man in an eastern university says:

I was born in a small town in the Middle West. Sex and sexual problems were and are taboo, and any teacher speaking of sex is immediately ostracized from the community. Like others, I received my education on the subject in the alley and in so-called "bull" sessions. I do not feel that my parents need be blamed for this, for they were brought up under the same conditions. Later I became enlightened by reading some books on the subject. This was done in the seclusion of my room and without the knowledge of my parents. I had always been very curious to know more about it and at the same time had a fear of being found out. It is this general background which has made me an advocate of sex education in the schools.

Taboos and Conflicts. Probably there is no phase of our mores where there is so much superstition and half knowledge as in the field of sex. This is largely because so many people see sex as something different from other normal aspects of life, and surround it either with a halo of sacredness or a hedge of taboos. In some schools sex education has been combined with lectures on venereal disease, a most unfortunate and socially harmful association of ideas. A great deal of our thinking is like that of the primitive who sees in different sexual manifestations the evidence of an unknown power which he does not understand.[33] Because of the cultural taboos on sex there is almost ceaseless conflict in young people in our culture between fear of society and the desire to know more about each each other.[34]

The problem is partly one of language behavior. As was pointed out in Chapter 8, words have great *reality* for most persons. Until we are able to talk intelligently in objective terms about sex and sexual activities, we cannot dispel the embarrassment which most people seem to experience when any discussion is given of the perpetuation of life in its higher forms, or of manifestations of love and affection. Children are not ashamed of the "facts of life" but only of giving them their proper names.

At an early age the child becomes sensitized to certain words. He has been admonished not to say them and he has heard the embarrassed laughter of children and adults whenever these words were spoken. It is not the thing itself which is dirty, sinful or gives rise to the feeling of shame, but its verbal symbol. [Certain things are] as much a fact as any other fact which the child has experienced, and he can report what he has seen without any feeling of embarrassment. It is the name or label that he finds great reluctance in divulging.[35]

Many people believe that ninth-grade or tenth-grade students are too young to receive any sex instruction. Yet Kinsey finds that the average *boy* of this age level already has had a wider variety and greater amount of sexual experience than many of his female teachers ever will have.[36]

2. *Religious Education.* The field of religion is an equally difficult one for the educational system to handle. An *ambivalent* attitude seems to exist in the minds of many parents. That is, they *want* religious ideals taught in the school system, but at the same time they feel strongly that *nothing* should be taught but *the* religion—namely, the parents' own religion. We have an interesting framework of legislation on the subject: Some states make it either mandatory or permissive that religious lessons be read, whereas others prohibit the reading of Scriptures in the schools.[37] Apparently parents feel the desirability of perpetuating the social and ethical ideals represented in various kinds of religions, but want to avoid frank discussion of the question.

> Jews lodge complaint in requiring to be read to their children passages from the New Testament which extols Christ as the Messiah and virtually infers that their religious teaching which they have endeavored to teach their children is untrue. Likewise, Catholics do not believe it right to have read to their children passages from the Bible without the interpretation given by the church. . . . Even Protestants quarrel among themselves as to the portions to be read, the emphasis to be placed upon passages read; as, for example, the Ten Commandments, baptism, the state of the dead, and many other questions, while the infidel condemns all.[38]

In 1948, the United States Supreme Court declared that religious instruction in public-school buildings was unconstitutional.[39]

LIMITATIONS OF CHARACTER EDUCATION IN COLLEGE

Suggestions that character education should be considered even at the advanced level of college work has brought the reply that this is "kid stuff." Some would say that the job of the colleges and universities is to promote thinking, but not necessarily to turn out mature citizens. When a social psychologist proposes that it would even be desirable to give some formal education concerning marriage and family relations, this is considered not only "newfangled" but highly dangerous in some communities, although in some few the idea has been well received. If he suggests that a course in religious values might be important for modern young Americans, that is considered highly questionable because of the dangers of indoctrination. Any suggestion as to changes in *nonmaterial* culture patterns, such as in the educational system, always meets with opposition, and the "cultural lag" usually extends for a number of years before any change is brought about.

THE QUESTION OF "DESIRABLE" CHARACTER TRAITS

One difficulty with character education is the disagreement as to what the best character education is. What are the desirable traits or ways of behaving which people should learn in the school system or college? The values obviously depend upon those who are responsible for instilling them; what is thought to be ethically desirable by one teacher or administrator may not be considered at all desirable by another.

Clinicians disagree with teachers as to what are "desirable" and what are "undesirable" ways of behaving. In a study by Wickman involving classes of children rated both by teachers and by mental hygienists, many of the characteristics rated by the teachers as most important behavior problems were considered the least important by the clinicians, and some of the problems considered serious by the clinicians were generally regarded as the least serious by the teachers.[40] Table 14 illustrates the differences in the two points of view.

TABLE 14

Behavior Problems Ranked by Teachers and by Clinicians

Teachers	*Clinicians*
Most Important Problems	
Stealing	Unsocialness
Heterosexual activity	Suspiciousness
Obscene notes	Unhappiness
Talkativeness	Depression
Untruthfulness	Resentfulness
Least Important Problems	
Shyness	Disorderliness
Inquisitiveness	Profanity
Sensitiveness	Interrupting
Unsocialness	Smoking
Fearfulness	Whispering

Unsocialness is regarded by the clinicians as the greatest problem of childhood, yet teachers rate it almost at the bottom of the scale. Obviously the unsocial child who may also be shy, sensitive, and fearful, may be a model pupil for a teacher concerned with "keeping order." On the other hand, clinical psychologists agree that unsocialness in children is a serious symptom. If you know a small child who is extremely unsociable, who shies away from his playmates and perhaps shows periods of depression, you can predict rather accurately that this child will grow into an adult who will have serious personality problems; this does not mean he will "break down" or develop a neurosis, but if the trend continues, he will not be well adjusted to his environmental situation. Similarly, talkativeness is considered a very serious problem in school situations. Yet interrupting is considered unimportant from the standpoint of the clinician; in fact, a child given to interrupting may be very intelligent.

TEACHERS' REACTIONS TO BEHAVIOR PROBLEMS

One investigation of the treatment of behavior problems by teachers in the elementary schools revealed a need for teachers with more training in making detailed analysis of the causes of behavior problems.[41] This study showed that teachers were inclined to apply direct measures such as rewards and punishments when treating classroom behavior of children, without studying the individual to determine the causes of the behavior. The conclusions are in line with those of Wickman, who found that teachers' reactions to the behavior problems of children are largely determined by the direct effect which the behavior produces on the teachers themselves; and that the usual treatment of behavior disorders is directed toward the undesirable behavior which may be the symptom of maladjustment, rather than toward the underlying causes that produce the maladjustment.[42] As for the members of the teaching profession, they are our next consideration.

▶ THE TEACHING PROFESSION

LACK OF PRESTIGE

Whatever schools can or cannot do in the development of personality is dependent largely upon the teachers. Their personalities and preparation for their jobs are factors of the utmost importance. It is the teachers who take the place of parents during the hours when the child is in school, and they are the ones who by precept and example will lead the child into desirable paths of conduct and satisfactory social relationships. Yet how important are teachers considered by other members of the community?

> . . . Few things about education . . . today are more noteworthy than the fact that the entire community treats its teachers casually. These . . . persons to whom this weighty responsibility of training the young is entrusted are not the wise, skilled, revered elders of the group. . . . Rarely does one run across a teacher at the weekly luncheons of the city's business men assembled in their civic clubs; nor are many of them likely to be present at the social functions over which the wives of these influential men preside. [The community] pays these people to whom it entrusts its children about what it pays a retail clerk . . . and rarely stumbles on the individual teacher thereafter save when a particu-

larly interested mother pays a visit to the school "to find out how Ted is getting along." The often bitter comments of the teachers themselves upon their lack of status and recognition in the ordinary give and take of local life are not needed to make an observer realize that in this commercial culture the "teacher" and "professor" do not occupy the position they did even a generation ago.[43]

Supplement this with your own observation of the social status of teachers, and you find that this same situation exists in most communities. Although the teacher is looked upon as someone to whom a certain amount of prestige *should* attach, at the same time it seems perfectly clear to most people that he or she is a mere theorist—not a practical man or woman—who has become a teacher simply because of inability to make a living at any other possible occupation. The old saying is, "Those who can, do. Those who cannot, teach."

However, the parent-teacher movement, begun in the 1890's and formalized in the National Congress of Parents and Teachers in 1924, has done much to bring schoolteachers and citizens in the community together regarding problems of children. This organization and its branches have fostered social contact between parent and teacher, discussion of school problems, and child-study and parent-education groups.

LOW PAY

The average annual salary of public-school teachers, supervisors, and principals—not including colleges—in the United States in 1940 was only $1,441.[44] The range was from $559 in Mississippi to $2,604 in New York. See Figure 33.

In 1930 the average salary was $1,420; and in 1920, only $871. However, half of the states paid lower average salaries in 1940 than in 1930; and in the other half increases were very much less than between 1920 and 1930.

In 1940 only four states—New York, California, New Jersey, and Massachusetts—paid an average salary of more than $2,000. Fourteen paid an average of less than $1,000—two New England states, nine Southern states; and three Midwestern states. All of them are largely rural, as contrasted with the states paying highest salaries to teachers, which have large urban and industrial areas. The differences in average salaries between the two groups are partly explained by differences in living costs; but are chiefly due to differences in *taxpaying ability.*

LACK OF ORGANIZATION

The teachers themselves, although frequently protesting the inadequacy of their salaries, are usually inclined to let well enough alone. For example, when the Merchants' Association in New York City demanded in 1939 that the teachers take a cut in salary in order to make up the

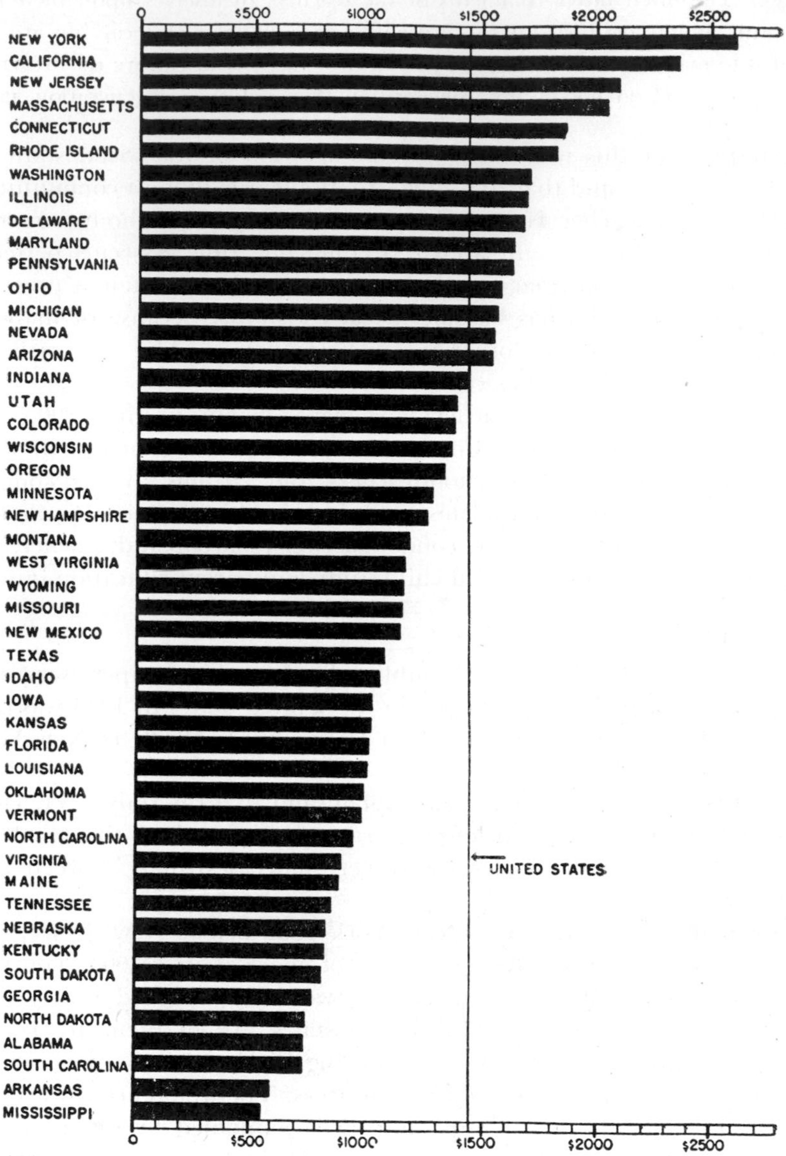

FIG. 33. AVERAGE SALARIES OF PUBLIC-SCHOOL TEACHERS, SUPERVISORS, AND PRINCIPALS, 1939-1940[45]

city's deficit, large numbers accepted the situation quite mildly. On the other hand, the school year 1946-1947 saw more than a dozen major walkouts or strikes for more pay by teachers in various sections of the United States.[46]

Teachers are one of the most poorly organized groups. They have not succeeded on the one hand in being powerful lobbying organizations, such as the American Medical Association and the American Bar Association, nor on the other hand of being strong union groups. Their organizations are usually ineffective in achieving either salary advances, or in fighting various types of pressure brought to bear on teachers from all elements of the community. Do these facts not help to explain why being a "teacher" is held in low esteem by some businessmen and politicians?

EDUCATION AS A SYMBOL

As we have indicated, most parents want their children to be made fairly literate and even to memorize supposed facts which are acceptable to the mores of the community; but most people want education simply because it is a symbol that one has "arrived," either economically or socially. In fact, education received in the schools does not have very much bearing on the kind of daily activities in which most people engage:

> Square root, algebra, French, the battles of the Civil War, the presidents of the United States before Grover Cleveland, the boundaries of the state of Arizona, whether Rangoon is on the Yangtze or Ganges or neither, the nature or location of the Japan Current, the ability to write compositions or to use semicolons, sonnets, free verse, and the Victorian novel—all these and many other things that constitute the core of education simply do not operate in life as Middletown adults live it. And yet, the world says education is important; and certainly educated men seem to have something that brings them to the top—just look at the way the college boys walked off with the commissions during the war.[47]

With this attitude of education as a sort of magic key which will be an open sesame to jobs and the society page of the newspapers, it is not surprising that most citizens are not too much concerned with teachers who in many instances are looked upon as temporary "keepers" of the young. Who the teachers are is not considered so important as some other things in life.

TEACHING, WOMAN'S WORK

Another reason for the low prestige attached to teaching is that it is "woman's work." Approximately 80 per cent of the teachers in the public schools of the country are women. In a culture which is predominantly "a man's world," any occupation made up primarily of women is considered feminine and, *ergo,* inferior. Add to this the fact that a great majority of the teachers are unmarried and, therefore, without the social prestige which marriage brings in our society, and we have an additional reason for their lack of influence in the community. In the great majority of communities, married women have not in normal times been allowed to teach. Data collected from nearly 1,500 city-school systems in the 1930's revealed that 77 per cent did not employ married women as new teachers, and that 63 per cent required women teachers to resign if they married.[48] This, of course, simply amounts in most instances to turning over the education of our children to extremely young girls or to spinisters.

A man from Mars or a Trobriand Islander would be inclined to raise questions about our schools. He might ask the typical American businessman why it is that he does not turn over the management of his business affairs to people who have had little or no experience in business, because after all that is the way he behaves with regard to his offspring. He turns over the training of his children during their formative years to people who for the most part have had little training in problems of child development and family relationships. Yet he expects these teachers to engage in real character education.

SERVING FIVE MASTERS

The teacher and professor must serve not two masters, but at least five: the pupils, the parents, the board of education or board of trustees, the administrator, and the community. Each of these expects and demands different things. To "rate" with one group may easily result in loss of prestige so far as the others are concerned.

1. *The Pupils.* The teacher satisfies the pupils if he is not too hard, is a "good egg," or gives good grades. Little concern is given by large numbers of students as to whether their teachers have made conscientious efforts to work and rework their materials in order that they may be of the greatest benefit. Lyrics sung by young children when adults are not around reveal some of the attitudes toward teachers:

Up the river,
Down the lake;
The teacher's got
The bellyache.

Hot roasted peanuts,
Tell the teacher she's nuts;
If she asks your name,
Tell the teacher she's a pain.

Objective studies of the gossip of college students reveal many of the same ideas, although not expressed in rhymes. For many college students, there is a very real hang-over of attitudes toward teachers from their grade- and high-school days. There the teacher was someone who made you behave, sit up straight, blow your nose, not whisper; the prevailing attitude at first toward many a college professor is that he is someone who is so different from other people that the student must be on his good behavior in order not to offend his sensibilities.

2. *The Parents.* Fathers and mothers demand that teachers be paragons of virtue, and that they do not make the students think about certain things—at least not too much or in an unorthodox manner. If a teacher has the audacity to suggest that there are two and sometimes more sides to most questions, this may cost him his job. The teacher must be one who abides by certain rules made for teachers and ministers alone. Parents themselves may smoke, and play cards, but for a teacher to do these things is considered "horrible" in many communities.

3. *The Board of Education.* The third master is the board of education for the grade- or high-school teacher, the board of trustees for the college professor. The typical county board of education is composed of six members: one housewife, three farmers, one merchant, and one physician, three of whom have had no education beyond the elementary grades, one having attended high school, and two having been to college. The typical city board of education consists of one woman and five men, a merchant, a lawyer, a physician, a businessman, and a salesman, clerk, or laborer; the majority have attended high school or college.[49] The education of the board of trustees at the college level is much greater, of course.

Boards of education demand certain loyalties and allegiance on the part of the teaching profession—adherence to the folkways of the community and strict observance of the mores. In addition, special codes are invented for the teachers. One analysis of four hundred public-school teachers' contracts in forty-two states and Hawaii showed that in two-thirds of them the teachers must promise to abide by whatever rules and regulations the local board may see fit to enforce.[50] Regulations exist in many cities that teachers shall not receive presents from pupils, shall not visit rooms of other teachers, and shall not use the telephone except for school purposes.[51] A board of education in Alabama forbids teachers to "have company or go automobile riding" on school nights, and one in Ohio forbids them to "go with other teachers."[52]

4. *The Administrator.* The administrator—the principal, superintendent, or president—is in the position of employer or at least "foreman" to the teacher. Many administrators respect the judgments of their teachers completely, but in some instances where they lay down definite rules that must be followed, a problem is created, especially for teachers in the social

sciences who are dealing to such a large extent with hypotheses. Here, where tolerance is especially needed, it is often lacking.

The problem of academic freedom is not simply one of what is said in the classroom. It is also a matter of adherence to the rules laid down concerning grades and hours. In one state university, although a special examination in English had been set up as a criterion for graduation, a large number in the senior class failed on it. Realistically and logically, it would seem that a large percentage of seniors should not graduate. The solution was quite simple, however. The professors in the English department were simply asked to give a re-examination, which they did. The ritual was satisfactorily performed, and the majority of the seniors graduated with their sheepskins, happy in their newly acquired knowledge.

> The public wants Johnny to get a degree, perhaps with honors, but certainly without effort. . . . Consequently you can teach that Pontius Pilate was an ideal colonial governor, [and] that Herod's ideas of discipline are to be emulated, . . . without endangering your position as much as you will by . . . fighting for foreign language requirements.[53]

TABLE 15

Opinions of 622 Teachers On Probable Community Reaction to Teacher Out-of-School Behavior (from Cook, Almack, and Greenhoe)[54]

	Percentage Reporting Reaction of				*Percentage*
Teacher Behavior	*Approve*	*Tolerate*	*Disapprove*	*Discharge*	*Not Reporting*
Dating a student	1.6	3.5	73.8	6.9	14.2
Dating a teacher	42.8	31.0	12.7	0.2	13.3
Dating a town person	60.0	23.0	5.1	0.2	11.7
Smoking in public	8.2	25.6	55.6	4.0	6.6
Playing cards	33.6	35.2	23.5	0.8	6.9
Playing pool or billiards	9.6	33.0	40.4	1.9	15.1
Drinking alcoholic liquors	2.4	7.9	63.6	19.3	6.8
Using rouge, lipstick, etc.	57.9	27.3	3.2	0.0	11.6
Leaving often week ends	41.5	39.2	9.5	0.0	9.8
Owning automobile	82.5	7.7	1.6	0.0	8.2
Not attending church	7.9	44.0	36.3	0.5	11.3
Woman teaching after marriage	51.5	21.2	8.0	8.7	10.6
Nonschool work for pay	30.9	28.1	20.2	1.0	19.8
Pay for coaching, speaking, etc.	35.2	32.6	15.8	0.0	16.4
Making political speech	10.6	19.6	52.1	0.3	17.4
Running for political office	13.9	25.2	41.8	1.0	18.1
Joining teacher union	50.0	18.6	9.2	0.5	21.7

5. *The Community.* The final master whom the teacher must serve is a composite of the individual citizens in the community. In many small towns and rural surroundings teachers must abstain completely from card playing, dancing, or almost any social activity outside of church affairs. Tennessee has even had a state law forbidding teachers to smoke, and, as we have noted, many communities forbid the employment of married women. If teachers do not conform to the notions of the community as to skirt length, amount of lipstick, and dates, they may soon find themselves without jobs. An examination of teacher and community relations reveals that certain "ways" must not be violated, even though nothing is written down about them.[55] Examples are dating a student, smoking in public, playing pool or billiards, drinking alcoholic liquors, making a political speech, running for political office. See Table 15.

The types of behavior listed in Table 15 have been submitted to people in the community—such as housewives, professional persons, and board members—and in the main these persons judge the teacher's out-of-school conduct more severely than do the teachers themselves. Incidentally, these problems are not limited to the teachers in the public-school systems. Professors in some colleges are also expected to conform in their personal lives in a great many ways that are not demanded of other people.

The total effect of teachers on our culture patterns is enormous. Far-reaching indeed from one generation to another are the ideas and attitudes learned in the school. In a truly rational society, education would be much better organized and less of a symbol than at present, the pay and prestige of teachers would be increased, and many of the restrictions surrounding them would be removed. Over the years this could not help but have a desirable effect on the children of today, who are the adult citizens of tomorrow.

QUESTIONS AND PROBLEMS FOR DISCUSSION

1. *Why do most high-school students in America object to being educated?*
2. *Show in what ways the subjects of educational psychology and social psychology overlap.*
3. *"It is much more important for Americans to understand public policies and to think alike than to be able to perform any particular acts of skill." How and why do you agree or disagree?*
4. *What are some of the problems involved in "transfer of training" with respect to the school?*
5. *Should sex education be taught in the public schools? Why or why not?*

6. *How can ethics be taught in the school?*
7. *Make a psychological analysis of why persons enter the teaching profession.*
8. *Why is the teaching profession not a more closely knit group?*
9. *What practical suggestions would you make for improving the educational system?*

RECOMMENDED READINGS

Babcock, F. L., *The U. S. College Graduate.* New York: The Macmillan Company, 1941.

Barzun, J., *Teacher in America.* Boston: Little, Brown & Company, 1945.

Bowden, A. O., and Melbo, I. R., *Social Psychology of Education: Applications of Social Psychology to Educational Problems.* New York: McGraw-Hill Book Company, Inc., 1937.

Cole, L., *The Background for College Teaching.* New York: Farrar & Rinehart, Inc., 1940.

Hartshorne, H., May, M. A., Maller, J. B., and Shuttleworth, F. K., *Studies in the Nature of Character* (3 volumes). New York: The Macmillan Company, 1928-1930.

Horn, E., *Methods of Instruction in the Social Studies.* Report of the Commission on the Social Studies, American Historical Association, Part XV. New York: Charles Scribner's Sons, 1937.

Hutchins, R. M., *The Higher Education in America.* New Haven: Yale University Press, 1936.

Jones, V., *Character and Citizenship Training in the Public School.* Chicago: University of Chicago Press, 1936.

Keezer, D. M., *The Light That Flickers.* New York: Harper & Brothers, 1947.

Kelly, R. L., *The American Colleges and the Social Order.* New York: The Macmillan Company, 1940.

Louttit, C. M., *Clinical Psychology of Children's Behavior Problems* (revised edition). New York: Harper & Brothers, 1947.

Lunden, W. A., *The Dynamics of Higher Education.* Pittsburgh: Pittsburgh Printing Co., 1940.

Pressey, S. L., *Psychology and the New Education.* New York: Harper & Brothers, 1933.

Tunis, J. R., *Was College Worth While?* New York: Harcourt, Brace and Company, 1936.

Wickman, E. K., *Children's Behavior and Teacher's Attitudes.* New York: Commonwealth Fund, 1928.

Wilson, L., *The Academic Man: A Study in the Sociology of a Profession.* New York: Oxford University Press, 1942.

*Newcomb, T. M., Hartley, E. L., and others (editors), *Readings in Social Psychology*. New York: Henry Holt and Company, Inc., 1947. (The following selections are listed according to the sequence of related discussions in the chapter you have just read.)

Piaget, J., "Social Factors in Moral Development," pp. 158-168.

Warner, W. L., Havighurst, R. J., and Loeb, M. B., "The Social Role of the Teacher," pp. 479-480.

CHAPTER EIGHTEEN

RELIGION—THE CHURCH

WHAT IS RELIGION? Difficulty of Objectivity—Social Psychology of Religion—Social and Personal Values of Religion—Religion and Science—History and Definition of Religion—Transmission of Religious Attitudes—Motivation of Religious Behavior—Some Ritualistic Aspects of Religion—The Problem of Transfer of Behavior Patterns / BELIEFS AND CONFLICTS. Religious Beliefs—(1) Sacrifice—(2) Magical Rites—(3) Group Ceremonies—(4) Prayer—(5) Right Conduct—Beliefs of Students and Scientists—Christian Beliefs—Business Attitudes versus Religious Attitudes—Domination of Religion by Business Interests—Attitudes toward War—Attitudes toward Sex / THE MINISTRY. Maintenance of the *Status Quo*—Dilemmas for the Minister—Cultural Lag in Religion.

▶ WHAT IS RELIGION?

DIFFICULTY OF OBJECTIVITY

After a lecture on the social psychology of religion, a college student wrote:

> When we begin to analyze religion, we are lost. Psychologists say a person of emotional maturity should be able to hold judgment in abeyance until he has determined what his new attitudes shall be. Unfortunately, when most people lose the "faith of their fathers," they feel that nothing is left. Personally, I expect to hang on to my old beliefs until I am assured of something better.

This illustrates the difficulties of studying religion objectively. Although many people maintain that religion is the most important force in life, they guard their religious thoughts as if they were state secrets. If we attempt to examine religious values and religious behavior from the viewpoint of psychology, we are likely to be accused either of attacking religion or of attempting to undermine religious beliefs. However, many theologians agree that if the church is to exist as a strong social force in our society, it must be examined objectively in exactly the same way that one would study the family, education, or any other social institution. The persons who become perturbed about an examination of their religious beliefs seem to be not those who are thoroughly sold on their religion, but rather those who have some doubts of their particular brand of religion and, therefore, are afraid to think through their beliefs.

SOCIAL PSYCHOLOGY OF RELIGION

It is small wonder that empirical studies of religion are difficult. Most people lack the objectivity to conduct such studies themselves, because they happen to be tied up with their own particular *brand* of religion. The social psychology of religion deals with the broad aspects of religious life. It is not the psychology of some particular sect such as Congregationalism, Episcopalianism, Methodism, Judaism, or Catholicism, for that is the sort of thing with which theologians concern themselves.

What are the actual functions of religion in our society? It must be emphasized that the present analysis is an objective examination of how religion operates in our culture. Look back at Chapter 2 on the methods of social psychology, especially the discussion of *objectivity,* and you will see why this is so.

SOCIAL AND PERSONAL VALUES OF RELIGION

First of all, what are some of the social and personal values of religion? Historically the church has been responsible for the preservation of knowledge and the transmission of socially desirable culture patterns as has no other institution. There has always been an intimate tie-up between religion and education, and some of the world's greatest scholars have been churchmen. Then, there are the untold benefits of religion as a means of social control. People learn the Ten Commandments and other principles of sound ethics which they attempt to follow in their daily lives. The church is likewise a proving ground for social relationships, carrying on for many parents the training of their young. In fact, young people not only learn moral precepts but also various aspects of social relations in their own organizations, such as the Baptist Young People's Union, the Christian Endeavor, and Sodality.

The lives of millions of people are influenced by religion. Even those who are not churchgoers and who have no firsthand contact with religious patterns of behavior are affected by the religious beliefs and conduct of other members of society. And those who are actually religious may have their whole pattern of life changed because of religious beliefs and ideals. Many are the people whose entire behavior has been transformed after conversion or the adoption of a creed. Religious ideals gradually mold the personalities of countless others and furnish some of the most important motives in life. A famous philosopher has said:

> Religion cannot be made or constructed. It grows up out of life itself, springs out of the basal mood of man in his struggle for life, out of his resolution to

hold fast, under all circumstances, to the validity of that which he has learnt from experience to be of the highest value.[1]

It is little wonder that many clinical psychologists and psychiatrists recommend to various individuals with personality problems that they actually engage in religious work by carrying on Sunday-school or church activities. This is sound psychological therapy for many a person. In fact, Henry C. Link of the Psychological Corporation has maintained in his book, *The Return to Religion,* that religion is the very foundation of personality.[2]

RELIGION AND SCIENCE

Of course, a scientific examination of religious behavior, overt and covert, may be difficult. In fact, a great gulf often exists between the man of science and the man of religion. Einstein has maintained that "a legitimate conflict between religion and science cannot exist."[3] In his book *Human Destiny,* Lecomte du Noüy used a *scientific* approach to support his thesis that man is just beginning his moral evolution.[4] He marshalled data to show that science finds a purpose evident in the history of life which rises above the laws of matter, and that the materialistic approach to man and the universe is no longer tenable.

Certainly many sociologists and psychologists are vitally interested in the same sort of values as the man of religion, and yet because of differences in attitudes and often a lack of understanding by one group as to what the other is like, there is little common ground. The difference between science and theology is well described by Ross:

> The reason why theological controversy so fatally descends into polemic is that *all discussion of things supernal contains the seeds of degeneration.* . . . Theologians are certainly as just and kindly men as scientists, but after they have marshalled in vain their texts and their reasonings, they have nothing else to appeal to. When the scientist has exhausted his ammunition without effect, he can go after fresh evidence. It is not easy to settle by observation the question of the open Polar Sea, the sources of the Nile, or the canals on Mars; but it is child's play compared with getting decisive facts on the question of the nature of the Godhead, or the future state of unbaptized infants.[5]

Those who are worried about people as being irreligious can take solace in the number of religious periodicals published and read in the United States. Magazines in the "general" classification—including the "pulps" and such magazines as the *Ladies' Home Journal, Cosmopolitan, The Saturday Evening Post*—have a total circulation of about 60 million. Religious journals come in a close second with 45 million circulation. Agricultural journals account for only 19 million circulation, and the field of science trails with less than 3½ million.[6] The Bible, which has been translated into 184 languages, is sold in almost every country in the world; it has outsold every book in the United States since 1800.[7] The years after World War II focused particular attention on man's need for a faith to cling to, and many books appeared on the subject of how to integrate religious concepts into one's daily life. In fact, Liebman's *Peace of Mind* was a best-seller.[8]

HISTORY AND DEFINITION OF RELIGION

At least four different phases of religion can be distinguished historically:[9] (1) The first phase consists of belief in mystical reward and punishment in the *present* life. That is, some types of charm, ritual, or taboo are believed to be effective in producing results now, in this life, and the believer acts accordingly. He performs certain rituals in order to attain certain ends *now*. (2) A second set of beliefs revolves around reward and punishment in a *future* life after death. The individual here carries out simple or elaborate sets of rituals which he believes will result in desirable effects after he is dead. He is willing to sacrifice some present values in order to obtain these at a later time. As contrasted with the first set of beliefs, the rewards in the future life are believed to be of greater magnitude and also to last longer, perhaps for eternity. In neither of these two systems is the idea of God essentially involved. (3) A third phase is *theism*. The theistic viewpoint has been expressed in a number of ways, but essentially it involves the satisfaction derived from doing that which pleases God, or "getting into harmony with the underlying plan of the universe." That is, the theist conforms to certain ideals because of the harmony resulting from conforming, and not because of any reward or punishment either now or in the future. (4) A later development in many religions is *humanism*. This involves ethics to the degree of being interested in the welfare or happiness of all mankind, not just with one's own life. Many an individual who talks of his religion in terms of "doing good" or living by the Golden Rule is adopting a humanistic point of view; that is, he is concerned with the welfare of society as a whole, now or in the future.

Most of the major religions involve all four of these stages. Some put greater emphasis on the first two aspects named above. Others of more recent origin seem to put more emphasis on the third and fourth aspects. The first two phases are involved in religious indoctrination; that is, you must perform the ritual in the approved way of this particular church, and you must follow this particular taboo or something unpleasant will happen to you. In other types of religion, these beliefs are not emphasized, or they drop out of the picture completely.

In a broader sense than Christianity, Judaism, or any of the other great faiths, the word "religion" seems to imply: (1) a belief in things and attitudes called "sacred"; (2) a complex set of attitudes; and (3) behavior, a great deal of it ritualistic in nature, which relates to these sacred ideas and attitudes.[10] Another way of describing religion is to say that it includes three things: (1) an official church; (2) a set of beliefs called a creed; and (3) a set of rules of conduct, called morality.[11]

TRANSMISSION OF RELIGIOUS ATTITUDES

In most religious behavior, as in family life and in education, there is indoctrination of the young by their elders. A child of ten or twelve may make a presumably lifelong contract by joining the church, whereas a person is not considered mature enough to make other binding contracts until he is twenty-one.[12] The religious culture patterns are transmitted by causing young people to adopt both covert- and overt-behavior patterns —which conform to those of their parents—both at symbolic and nonsymbolic levels. Thus, we kneel or bow our heads during prayer; we drop our money in the collection plate or pass it on; we listen to the sermon or meditate on last night's party; we "feel happy" because of our presence in the church, or we notice the discomfort of sitting up erect, and begin to attend to the peristaltic contractions of our stomachs. The overt indications do not necessarily square with the covert attitudes. It is simple enough to train the younger people to conform outwardly to the overt behavior of their elders, but not so easy to teach them the covert religious attitudes of their elders.

The only ways in which *covert* attitudes will be transmitted is through the same processes of conditioning to which we have referred again and again: (1) *generalization* of conditioned responses; (2) *differentiation* of conditioned responses; (3) *traumatic experiences* or situations; (4) adoption of the *ready-made opinions* or beliefs of other people. Thus, an individual might develop a set of religious beliefs through many repetitions of varied churchgoing experiences; or as an offshoot from reading philosophy; or through a sudden conversion; or from adopting the beliefs of his parents; or through any combination of these.

MOTIVATION OF RELIGIOUS BEHAVIOR

Try asking your friends this question: "Why does religion play such an important part in American life?" or, "Why are the majority of people in the United States Christians when millions of people in other regions of the world hold different beliefs?" If you will pose such questions, you may find your friends either questioning your sanity or else offering such vague explanations as, "Religion is an instinct inherent in all of us," or, "Christianity is the only real religion." From our previous examination of instincts (Chapter 6), you may question whether religion is instinctive; certainly we cannot isolate any single emotion and find the root of religious behavior. Likewise, it is highly questionable if we can call religion simply an attitude.[13] Rather, religion and religious behavior consist of emotions, attitudes, rituals, ceremonies, conversions, ecstasies, mystical states, gestures, voice inflections, and a whole series of conditioned responses, which are so completely interwoven that to examine any one of these bits gives us only partial information, for we have omitted the other important variables from consideration. As an example, many individuals commit the "nothing but" fallacy.[14] There is little question that a great deal of religious thinking involves superstition, but this does not mean that religion is *nothing but* superstition. Yet many writers on problems of religious behavior are guilty of this fallacy, that is, of reducing a description of religious attitudes simply to one instance of those attitudes, and overlooking other psychological values. For example, friendship, fellowship, community loyalty, patriotism, and even nationalistic feelings are developed in In-group religious atmospheres over and above all elements of the particular religion. There are also indications that those who feel maladjusted in their religious lives tend to be worried about their own personalities.[15]

The reasons for church attendance and other forms of religious behavior are almost innumerable. If you ask an individual why he goes to church, he will probably give you the very simple answer that it is because he is religious. Surveys of attitudes indicate that other reasons may be equally or more important. Thomas's four wishes—the desires for *new experience, security, response,* and *recognition*—are important variables in the complexity of attitudes represented. One person enjoys the beauty of the music and the stained-glass windows—new experience. Worried parents find security and relief from anxieties. Some find that the church is a social means of meeting desirable members of the opposite sex—the desire for intimate response—and similarly others report a sense of fellowship. The desire for recognition is satisfied in the case of the singer who enjoys exhibiting her voice.[16] A study of why people spend money for various wants indicates that money is given to the church primarily to satisfy the desire for security.[17]

SOME RITUALISTIC ASPECTS OF RELIGION

The ideologies which come to be accepted in the church situation are not necessarily the same attitudes which people have in *non*religious situations. People may learn the ritual of giving lip service to particular ideas in order to conform to their religious In-group, but in association with Out-groups these ideologies may be forgotten. Religious rituals serve to promote *autistic* thinking, and those sermons are considered desirable which touch closely on earlier, well-formed attitudes of the hearers and reweave these into what look like new but are essentially the same old patterns.

The ritual of hymn singing is carried on principally because of the appeal of the hymns to childhood attitudes. In an examination of over three thousand Protestant hymns, Kimball Young found that the dominant theme in over one-third was an infantile return to the father or mother situation, and in another fourth, the essential theme was that of future reward for good behavior.[18] This means that well over 50 per cent of the hymns had childhood attitudes as their dominant theme. Such ways of thinking may, of course, be of considerable importance to many of us in a highly complex civilization. It is desirable therapeutically for many of us to engage in types of ritual not only in the church but in fraternal situations, and thus escape temporarily from our daily routine.

E. L. Thorndike has found that cities with the largest percentage of church members are below average in homicides, deaths from venereal disease, and illegitimate births.[19] But they are also below average in good reading, home ownership, and continuance in schools, and above average in illiteracy and amount of child labor. Unless the better communities underreport their church membership or the worst communities overreport theirs, Thorndike suspects that many churches are clubs of estimable people and maintainers of traditional rites and ceremonies rather than powerful forces for human betterment.

THE PROBLEM OF TRANSFER OF BEHAVIOR PATTERNS

This may be accounted for in part by the fact that there is too little transfer of behavior patterns from the church to nonchurch situations.

The transfer is certainly not what the church would have it. Elbert Hubbard once said that he liked the idea of Christianity—that he would like to see it practiced. Others have observed, "You can't tell the difference, from the way they act, between church members and those who don't belong." Perhaps this is because many people do not really believe with their viscera what they confess with their lips.[20] You will recall the study described in Chapter 7 in which Methodists were asked to give their views as to the "proper" method of baptism; as members of the church 90 per cent claimed to believe in baptism by sprinkling, but when asked for their private attitudes, 71 per cent said that either sprinkling or immersion was satisfactory.[21] A reverse relationship was also found in the case of Baptists.

Those who subscribe to a particular church, with its own unique creed and set of beliefs and rules, might be expected to be markedly different from those who belong to a different church. But strangely enough there are relatively few behavior differences in *non*church situations between members of different churches. The various kinds of church creeds and conduct instilled by the many types of religion seem to be equally effective in promoting the same sort of "ways." Furthermore, the differences in moral character between children who attend Sunday school and those who do not are apparently quite small.[22] Although the differences favor the Sunday-school group slightly, we do not know whether this is due to the Sunday school itself or to the type of homes where insistence on Sunday-school attendance is part of the pattern.

There are many instances, of course, where attitudes learned in a religious atmosphere do carry over to nonreligious situations, as was pointed out at the beginning of this chapter. Outstanding cases of righteous and unselfish conduct due to religious motives are well known to everyone, and countless people make it a point to do good deeds primarily because of religious ideals. There is marked evidence of religious ideology in many family situations, social relationships, and some business transactions. Religious patterns of behavior may even extend to athletic games, as in the case of the famous football team known as the "Praying Colonels."

▶ BELIEFS AND CONFLICTS

RELIGIOUS BELIEFS

As Gurnee has pointed out, various means have been developed for securing the good will and favor of a power having ultimate control over human destiny.[23] These means are of five kinds: sacrifice, magic, group ceremonies, prayer, and right conduct.

1. *Sacrifice.* Most primitive religions have entailed sacrifices of animals or even of human beings. In modern Christianity and Judaism, sacrifice is more of a spiritual sort. Instead of animal or human sacrifices, one can give money to the poor, or money and services to the church.

2. *Magical Rites.* The use of magical rites is a way of controlling nature or the gods in primitive religions, but it is not completely absent from civilized religions. Calling on the name of the Lord, quoting a verse from the Bible, burning a candle, are designed to bring good results, whereas evil may befall the person who speaks certain taboo words or talks blasphemously.

3. *Group Ceremonies.* As we have already indicated, ritual is a fundamental characteristic of religion. Religious practices repeatedly engaged in become so ritualistic that deviations become almost sacrilegious. Baptism, initiation into the church, the marriage ceremony, the burial service, the proper ways of bowing the head, standing, kneeling, singing in unison, and other forms of group participation are all essential to the individual's feeling of security.

By engaging with others in acts of religious meaning, the believer experiences a strengthening of his faith and a weakening of any uncertainty he has had about his relations with God. Persons returning from a Sunday morning at church often remark on how much better they feel. Of course, the service has to be one which has acquired the proper religious meaning to the attendant. A small child usually finds the whole proceedings only a bore. Moreover, a Protestant obtains little of religious value in a Catholic mass, or a Catholic in a Protestant hour of worship.[24]

4. *Prayer.* Prayer, a means of directly asking for divine help or favor, is either for material things such as food, shelter, clothing, and health, or for spiritual values such as moral strength. Public prayer enables one to share his problems not only with God but with others.

5. *Right Conduct.* A characteristic teaching of all religions is right conduct. This involves not only ethical principles but moral actions, and the avoidance of certain taboos. In Christianity, character is developed not only by avoiding evil but also by the positive doing of good.[25]

It soon became apparent to intelligent Christian thinkers that man by his own efforts was not capable of achieving that perfection of character which the ideals of Christianity set before him. Even the best of men felt, try as they might, that they often fell short of the commandments of God.

Something else therefore was needed, and the result was the formulation of a doctrine known as "justification by faith." (A similar idea appears in many other religions.) . . . The doctrine maintains that salvation is not something which can be earned but is a gift which a gracious and merciful God bestows upon man as a result of his faith. By trusting God completely, one receives divine favor, much as a child receives the favor and blessing of its benevolent parents by trusting in them.[26]

BELIEFS OF STUDENTS AND SCIENTISTS

A number of studies have centered around the religious beliefs of college students and of scientists. Thurstone and Chave discovered little evidence of loss of respect for the church as students progressed through the University of Chicago.[27] Dudycha found that certain religious propositions were believed almost to the same extent by several hundred college seniors as by the freshmen.[28] For example, 88 per cent of the freshmen and 83 per cent of the seniors believed in the existence of God; 92 per cent of the freshmen and 76 per cent of the seniors believed that the Ten Commandments should be obeyed; 81 per cent of the freshmen and 69 per cent of the seniors believed in the existence of a soul; 82 per cent of the freshmen and 73 per cent of the seniors believed in the divinity of Jesus Christ. Only on such questions as whether or not the world was created in six solar days and whether the devil and hell actually exist were there very great changes in the amount of religious belief.

The most far-reaching study of student attitudes toward religion included responses on four tests of 3,749 students attending eighteen different colleges and universities, thus making a total of almost half a million student responses.[29] The institutions not only were widely distributed geographically, but included state universities and representative institutions of the Lutheran, Society of Friends, Catholic, Methodist, Presbyterian, Seventh Day Adventist, and United Brethren Churches. Attitudes of the students toward Sunday observance, the church, the reality of God, and God as an influence on conduct were in the main favorable; but seniors tended to be somewhat less favorable toward these four variables than the freshmen, and men students less favorable toward them than women students.

In a survey of religious attitudes and practices of college undergraduates at Harvard and Radcliffe, made over a year after the end of World War II, it was reported that:

> Seven out of every ten students feel that they require "some form of religious orientation or belief in order to achieve a fully mature philosophy of life."
>
> By all tests employed women as a group are more religious than men as a group, both in respect to subjective experience and in respect to formal religious observances.
>
> Only one in ten among women and two in ten among men declare definitely that they have no need for religion; and only about 15 per cent deny altogether participating in religious activities, or feeling some religious states of mind, during the preceding six months' period. . . .
>
> The majority are dissatisfied with institutional religion as it exists, so much so that over half do not regard the system of faith in which they were reared as satisfactory to their present needs.[30]

Religious beliefs, like almost all other opinions, undergo examination and revision during college years. With increasing maturity and additional education, this is to be expected. But the various empirical studies of students' beliefs do not indicate that the changes in religious attitudes are nearly so great as many people have believed.

With regard to scientists, Lehman and Witty have found that a smaller percentage of eminent scientists report a church affiliation than do other lesser known scientists—25 per cent as compared with 77 per cent.[31] A number of other observers have been concerned with the extent of religious beliefs or disbeliefs among both students and scientific people. Probably the most complete study in this field is by J. S. Leuba.[32] He asked a large sample of American men of science concerning their beliefs in a personal God and in personal immortality. His subjects included scientists concerned with *inanimate* matter—physicists proper, chemists, geologists, astronomers, engineers, and so forth; scientists concerned with *living* matter—biologists proper, physiologists, bacteriologists, botanists, horticulturists, and so forth; and scientists concerned with society and the individual—sociologists and psychologists. Comparisons were made: (1) between these three groups; (2) between the "greater" and the "lesser" scientists in each field, that is, between those men whose names are and are not starred in *American Men of Science;* (3) between scientists in 1914 as compared with 1933; (4) between students of each of the four classes in college; and (5) between students in 1914 and 1933. The largest proportion of believers in God and in immortality were found in the following categories: (1) the scientists concerned with *inanimate* matter (those concerned with *living* matter came next, and those dealing with society and the individual came last); (2) the *least* eminent men in every branch of science; (3) the scientists of 1914 as compared with those of 1933; (4) the students of 1914 as compared with those of 1933; and (5) the students in the lower college classes.

Of course, belief in God and in immortality are only two aspects of religion. If we should examine the *conduct* of those who do not adhere to these two beliefs, we might find it extremely difficult to distinguish between them and the believers.

CHRISTIAN BELIEFS

Christianity is of particular interest, since it represents a major culture pattern in the United States. When the Lynds asked various people, "What does one believe in if one is a Christian?" the interviewees thought the Lynds were joking. This seemed to reflect the tendency to accept "being a Christian" as practically synonymous with being "civilized" or "an honest man" or "a reputable citizen."[33] Only after a period of time were the Lynds able to determine that Christianity in *Middletown* meant: (1) a confidence in the all-sufficiency for all mankind of Christianity; (2) a belief in the sacredness of the Bible; (3) a belief in God as completely revealed in Jesus Christ; (4) a belief in life after death—in "Heaven" and "Hell"; and (5) a belief in the institution through which these religious habits of thought are taught—hence, the necessity of being a member of the church.[34] A rough pattern of values of religion in *Middletown* consists of the following:

> That Christianity is the final form of religion and all other religions are inferior to it.
>
> But that what you believe is not so important as the kind of person you are.
>
> That nobody would want to live in a community without churches, and everybody should, therefore, support the churches.
>
> That churchgoing is sometimes a kind of nuisance, one of the things you do as a duty, but that the habit of churchgoing is a good thing and makes people better.

That there isn't much difference any longer between the different Protestant denominations.

But that Protestantism is superior to Catholicism.

That having a Pope is un-American and a Catholic should not be elected President of the United States.

That Jesus is the Son of God and what he said is true for all time.

That Jesus was the most perfect man who ever lived.

That God exists and runs the universe.

That there is a "hereafter." "It is unthinkable that people should just die and that be the end." . . .

That God cannot be expected to intercede in the small things of life, but that through faith and prayer one may rely upon His assistance in the most important concerns of life. . . .

That preachers are rather impractical people who wouldn't be likely to make really good in business. (This is the male attitude. Women tend to accept the minister more on the latter's own terms.)

That I wouldn't want my son to go into the ministry. (This again is more a male attitude. Women would be more apt to feel secret pride in a son in the ministry.)

That preachers should stick to religion and not try to talk about business, public affairs, and other things "they don't know anything about."[35]

BUSINESS ATTITUDES VERSUS RELIGIOUS ATTITUDES

In the United States we have the interesting situation of business values and religious values existing side by side, yet with almost no recognition of the conflict between the two. There are any number of contradictions between them.[36] First of all, religion stresses the infinite worth of human personality, that human values are superior to property values, whereas the emphasis in our economic system is primarily on the worth of property, not men. In the second place, religion holds that we should not seek too much individual achievement for ourselves. "He that will be greatest among you must be the servant of all." Our business system, on the other hand, demands individual responsibility and achievement, "rugged individualism." A third theory of religion is that cooperation is the law of life; the brotherhood of man is stressed. Business emphasizes competition between men. A fourth theory of religion is in even more violent contradiction to our economic structure, namely, that service and sacrifice for the common good are desirable. The church's Golden Rule is quite different from business's rule of gold. "The ethics of service and sacrifice for the common good cannot be harmonized with exploitation of the people, large profits for the few and special privilege."[37]

The Gospels nowhere say: Accumulate wealth and save, care for your own and the economic welfare of your family. But they do say: "Take no thought of your life, what ye shall eat, or what ye shall drink; nor yet for your body, what ye shall put on; lay not up for yourselves treasures upon earth, where moth and rust doth corrupt, and thieves break through and steal." . . . We nowhere read: Try to obtain honors, help your friends to achieve fame and position; but we do read: "Blessed are ye when men shall revile you!"[38]

DOMINATION OF RELIGION BY BUSINESS INTERESTS

Logically, it would seem difficult for a person to adapt to these opposite sets of beliefs at one and the same time. Yet most persons are not aware of the conflict between economic power and religious faith, perhaps because of the general present-day domination of religion by business interests. This domination is seen in several important respects.[39] First, the clergy for the most part avoid radical social action and concentrate more attention on theoretical beliefs. A great deal gets into theological books and into sermons about fine points of theology, but discussion of social action is apt to be neglected. Second, business interests tend to keep the liturgy of worship fairly "safe," avoiding "dangerous" doctrines. Third, many churches have even moved away from the geographical areas of greatest social need.

Fourth, the tendency is for many church people to judge the success of the church according to business standards, that is, in terms of buildings, salaries, and money. Finally, the ethical standards of the Christian community conform in general to the ethical standards of business. The old theoretical standards of asceticism are lost in the more modern ones of thrift and individualism.

ATTITUDES TOWARD WAR

Moreover, the Christian Church is in an interesting position on two topics of considerable social importance. One is war, the other sex.

An *ambivalent* attitude exists with regard to war; at least ambivalent attitudes are fostered in many church members when the church adopts a position of both militarism and pacifism at one and the same time. Although the church historically has stood for pacifism and pacifistic principles, it also contains many types of military symbolism. The Christian life is sometimes represented as a great warfare, with a great royal household. Among the favorite hymns are, "Onward, Christian Soldiers," "Fight the Good Fight," "Hold the Fort," and other essentially militaristic themes. The paraphernalia consist of thrones, diadems, armor, and blood-red banners.[40]

Consider the Golden Rule or any of the principles found in the Sermon on the Mount, and you might expect to find all clergymen upholding peace at all costs. Yet an examination of sermons preached in the United States during World War I shows that only a handful of ministers continued to preach pacifism as an example of the brotherhood of man, and that the great majority "presented arms" along with the men in uniform and demanded the isolation of the Hun.[41]

The first months of World War II revealed a tendency in the same direction, with numerous men of religion coming forth in favor of America's entrance into the war.[42] Many continued to preach strict pacifism during 1940, but they comprised a relatively small minority of American clergymen.[43] An analysis by Abrams of religious periodicals and literature, sermons, and material obtained in interviews with religious leaders during the twenty-seven months' period between the time that war broke out in Europe and the time of America's entrance into the war indicated that "the churches and the clergy were hopelessly divided in their attitudes toward the war in Europe."[44] "Up to December 7, 1941, . . . the forces of organized religion were divided into several camps ranging all the way from the absolute pacifists to the interventionists who wanted us to declare war at once."[45]

The survey by Abrams indicates that, after the United States entered the war, Catholic and Jewish religious leaders tended to give active support to winning the war; whereas Protestant clergymen continued to differ widely in their views, although the attitudes of most seemed to be that the war was "a grim necessity—something to be gotten over as soon as possible."[46]

Since World War II the clergy have been active in promoting discussions of peace. Increasingly, sermons have been based on world affairs, politics, international relations, and the need for world peace and security. Many clergymen have militantly opposed war.

ATTITUDES TOWARD SEX

The history of Christian attitudes toward sex is also of interest. The early Christians had the conception of chastity as a religious duty and sex itself as a sin. No place do the Gospels say, "Go and take a wife, and rear able citizens for the state." Instead we read: "There be eunuchs which have made themselves eunuchs for the kingdom of heaven's sake."[47] Under the leadership of Saul of Tarsus—later St. Paul—the early Christians glorified chastity, and any lapse from it even in marriage was considered sinful, although it was admitted that "it is better to marry than to burn." Christians were supposed to work and pray to such an extent that sex passed out of their thoughts; and there are numerous accounts of people both married and unmarried who took the vows of chastity and kept them. Another thing that made the early Christian indifferent to both the pains and pleasures of the body was the belief that the end of the world was imminent.

To some extent the medieval mores of sex continue today, with their two opposite currents of thought—the notion that women are evil, dangerous, and to be shunned, but also the idea that women are lovely, adorable, and worthy of reverence and worship. In the clinic we find many instances of both women and men coming to the marriage relation with the culture patterns of the early Puritans, continuing to believe that there is something unhealthy about admitting that sex may have pleasurable aspects. On the other hand, many ministers have done valuable work in counseling people on various problems of sex and of family relations.

▶ THE MINISTRY

MAINTENANCE OF THE *STATUS QUO*

In any institution, it is important to know what the leaders are like. We saw that the teaching profession is poorly organized, that teachers for the most part are inclined to be meek. Their attitude is largely one of acceptance without question of things as they exist, and education is very much dominated by outside forces and pressure. We might expect, however, in turning to such an old and well-established profession as the ministry to find members of an extremely dominant group who are leaders in movements of social reform.

What do we find? For years churchmen have supported both wittingly and unwittingly the views of our "chieftains" and captains of industry. Even though the demands of the vested financial interests would seem antagonistic to many religions, nevertheless a great many ministers conform to them. Many ministers tend to be pawns of the social and economic forces of their communities.[48] They are considered desirable if they uphold maintenance of the *status quo,* undesirable if they favor social changes, especially in the realms of politics and business. In the famous Johnstown, Pennsylvania, steel strike of 1937, only two of the local ministers openly sympathized with the strikers; the rest either by action or silence upheld the Bethlehem Steel Company.[49]

Even when ministers take action they prefer something that will not antagonize the dominant capitalistic interests. This was well illustrated a few years ago when Professor Webber of Union Theological Seminary tried to get the ministers of a Pennsylvania community to pass a resolution urging that the miners should have the right to put in a check weighman of their own to see that they received an honest weight for the coal they had mined. The ministers refused to take this action but spent considerable time passing a resolution against the right of the miners to play baseball on Sunday.[50]

DILEMMAS FOR THE MINISTER

A number of problems confront the individual minister. The first dilemma which he faces is one of poverty versus salary. According to most religious codes, poverty or lack of material goods is considered desirable. The minister lives, however, in a world which stresses worldly goods and economic dominance. In many a Protestant church he is almost forced by the nature of his occupation to attempt to "get a better church"—which consists not necessarily in ministering to those who are low or unfortunate in the scheme of things, but rather to those people of the greatest wealth who can afford to pay him the largest salary.

A second dilemma for the minister is that of submissiveness versus dominance. The very essence of the religious attitude is one of meekness, submissiveness, brotherly love, and treating others as you would have them treat you. Again, however, the minister must be a practical man living in a practical world where he finds that dominance is the accepted pattern of conduct in his culture. If he behaves too meekly, he may soon find himself without influence in his community.

A third problem which confronts the minister is that of saying or doing anything which is in the least bit new or novel. If his sermons vary from the accepted attitudes of his particular parish, he is likely to be accused of being "newfangled" and may suddenly find himself ministering to nobody. The sermons preached in American churches do not necessarily reflect the views of ministers—who by and large are well-educated men—but rather the fact that they must manipulate over and over again those attitudes considered most desirable in the community.

Your Saturday evening newspaper usually lists the sermon topics for the following day. These are typical: "The Influence of the Bible on the World's Great Literature," "Does It Pay to Be Decent?", "The Man Who Is Able," "The Church Is United," "The Gladdening Soul." Your Monday morning newspaper gives you excerpts from sermons preached the day before. The following headlines are typical: "Self-Love Scorned by Father Gannon," "Pointless Lives Assailed," "Honesty Stressed in Advent Advice," "Child Care Held Important," "Lack of Wisdom in Man Deplored," "Calls Sermons Valuable." Certainly, a social psychologist would tend to mark most of these headlines true on a true-false examination; he, too, would say that too much self-love is bad, honesty is good, lack of wisdom is bad, sermons are no doubt valuable. But he would also ask whether a consideration of such topics should not go farther than the mere bolstering of existing attitudes.

CULTURAL LAG IN RELIGION

In religion we find a greater "cultural lag" than in any institution except the law. Individual ministers with special brands of religion have sometimes been so preoccupied with saving souls that they have failed to attend to the sociological problems of the community about them—problems and conditions which *produce* "lost souls." There has been a lack of understanding among many ministers of the old school of some of the most important problems of the community—the neighborhood, the gang, the school, family life. Add to this the fact that some ministers are mainly concerned with the dissemination of their own particular theological creeds, and the problem is multiplied.

This is not to say that all ministers are unaware of sociological problems. Many of them battle actively to counteract slum conditions, crime, venereal disease, unwholesome family conditions, and inadequate school systems. But large numbers are indifferent to such problems, or else are prevented from acting because of a fear of conflict with powerful members of their congregation.

This, then, is the picture of religion in our society. As was indicated in the preceding chapter on education, it is desirable psychologically to examine all sides of any problem. This has meant an impartial analysis of the church, just as in the case of the family and the school (Chapters 16 and 17), and as with fraternities and clubs, to be considered in the next chapter.

QUESTIONS AND PROBLEMS FOR DISCUSSION

1. *To what extent are science and religion in agreement? in disagreement?*
2. *How much of your attitude toward the church is due to the influence of* (a) *your parents,* (b) *other relatives,* (c) *childhood playmates,* (d) *teachers,* (e) *experiences in the Sunday school or church,* (f) *reading?*
3. *To what extent are your personal opinions or your personal conduct influenced by your attending or not attending religious services?*
4. *What religious values do you want your children to learn? How should these values be taught?*
5. *To what extent does religion supply the personality with a socially acceptable outlet for some childish and self-centered desires?*
6. *Make a psychological analysis of your preference for a particular religious sect or denomination.*
7. *Compare character education in the family, the school, and the church.*
8. *In its past history has the church been more a resister or a leader of movements for social change?*
9. *Should the church adopt or reject modern business methods?*

RECOMMENDED READINGS

Brown, W. A., May, M. A., and Shuttleworth, F. K., *The Education of American Ministers.* New York: Institute of Social and Religious Research, 1934.

Conklin, E. S., *The Psychology of Religious Adjustment.* New York: The Macmillan Company, 1929.

Davis, J., *Capitalism and Its Culture.* New York: Farrar & Rinehart, Inc., 1935.

du Noüy, L., *Human Destiny.* New York: Longmans, Green & Co., 1947.

Höffding, H., *The Philosophy of Religion.* London: Macmillan & Company, Ltd., 1914.

James, W., *The Varieties of Religious Experience: A Study in Human Nature,* Being the Gifford Lectures on Natural Religion Delivered at Edinburgh in 1901-1902. New York: Longmans, Green & Co., 1935.

Liebman, J. L., *Peace of Mind.* Simon and Schuster, 1946.

Ligon, E. M., *The Psychology of Christian Personality.* New York: The Macmillan Company, 1935.

Ligon, E. M., *Their Future Is Now: The Growth and Development of Christian Personality.* New York: The Macmillan Company, 1939.

Link, H. C., *The Return to Religion.* New York: The Macmillan Company, 1936.

Lowie, R. H., *Primitive Religion.* New York: Boni and Liveright, 1924.

Niehbuhr, R., *Does Civilization Need Religion? A Study in the Social Resources and Limitations of Religion in Modern Life.* New York: The Macmillan Company, 1928.

Pratt, J. B., *The Religious Consciousness: A Psychological Study* (second edition). New York: The Macmillan Company, 1928.

Starbuck, E. D., *Psychology of Religion.* New York: Charles Scribner's Sons, 1907.

CHAPTER NINETEEN

FRATERNITIES AND POLITICAL PARTIES

THE FRATERNITY AND CLUB. Initiation—Are You a Joiner?—Classification of Secret Societies—Ritualism—Institutionalism—Fraternal Ideologies—Mutual Aid and Brotherhood—Patriotism—Race and Nationality Restrictions—Religious Ideals—Sexual Morality—Temperance—Retardation of Social Reform—Psychological Values—Union into an In-group—Elimination of Some Prejudices—Role as Pressure Organizations—Economic Advantages—Relaxation and Fellowship—Regression in Ritualism / ALLEGIANCE TO THE POLITICAL PARTY. The Political Party as an In-group—Historical Changes in the Political Scene—Lack of Prestige of Politics—Voters' Prejudices—Analysis of Voters' Groups—(1) "Regular" Party Members—(2) Those Who Vote against Economic Reversals—(3) Radical Voters—(4) Liberal Thinkers Who Vote with Conservative Parties—(5) Voters Subject to Unusual Pressure—Loss of Meaningfulness of the Political Party.

▶ THE FRATERNITY AND CLUB

INITIATION

The "Conductor" puts a heavy chain over the candidate's shoulders, gives him a shepherd's staff, and they proceed to walk a slow, steady step around the hall, while the organ plays *The Knight's Funeral March,* and the members sing together the *Funeral Ode.* When they finish singing the "Conductor" makes one more complete circle around the hall and stops before the "Teacher" in the southwest, who says solemnly:

> Life to us all brings with it happiness and sorrows, its joys and deepest griefs. Tonight you stand in darkness with none save mortal man to guide your steps. And as you stand in silence and in gloom you but represent that condition of man who has no light *within* his soul, a wanderer lost upon the desert, a mariner upon the unknown sea. We welcome you tonight as one who is in search of light. Tear from your breast each thread of fear. Your journey which is before you is unknown to you. Be brave. For fear is the greatest monster man has met to conquer or to be conquered. Clear thy soul, then, of all that would try to mar your journey, and as you pass this way but once let each foot-print left behind be to thy brother who follows a ray of hope to guide his pilgrimage to a safe abode. Fear not. Pass on.

And on they go through all the degrees to the final "tests of boiling metal," in which the candidate is forced to place his hand into a pot of mercury which he supposes to be one of molten lead, thus learning "one of the lessons of life." This is the final step in the ritual of the Supreme Exalted Temple of the Fraternity Sons of Osiris, "an arcane fraternity which has been in existence since 2000 B.C., and which is now teaching humanity the old truths . . ."[1]

In reading this material aloud to a group of college students, a psychologist was once surprised to find that he had revealed some "secrets" of a well-known college sorority—at least, so he was told. The interesting thing about most of these rituals is that the "secrets" must be protected after one has gone through the initiation ceremony. Often the full-fledged member himself, however, may wonder what the secrets are. Figures 34 and 35 illustrate the "mock" and "serious" parts of a certain sorority initiation. Figure 34 shows the pledges, smeared and dirty, lined up in a barn where they were required to recite the Greek alphabet, and the names, addresses, and telephone numbers of the sorority members. In Figure 35, an initiate is shown taking a solemn oath on an open Bible.

ARE YOU A JOINER?

America is a nation of joiners. We join anything and everything. We may belong to the Rotary Club, the Elks, the Moose, the Red Men, the Owls, the Ku Klux Klan, the American Protective Association, the Masons, the Knights of Columbus, the Kiwanis, the Lions, the Knights of Pythias, the Modern Woodmen of America, the Odd Fellows, the Eagles, the Mystic Order of Veiled Prophets, the Daughters of the American Revolution, the Chamber of Commerce, the W.C.T.U., the Military Order of the Caraboa, the Eastern Star, the Colonial Dames, the Daughters of the Prairie, the American Liberty League, Tammany, the Grange, Job's Daughters, the Knights of the Golden Eagle, the Protected Home Circle, ad infinitum. Some of us even form organizations called the Society for the Prevention of Calling Sleeping Car Porters George, the Order of Mules, the Veterans of Future Wars, the Guild of Former Pipe Organ Pumpers, the League for a Woman for President and Other Public Offices, the Benevolent Protective Herd of Buffaloes of the World, the Military Order of the Cootie, and even the Concatenated Order of the Hoo-Hoo!

There are at least 262 different fraternities and sororities in American colleges and universities.[2] Even professional and honorary clubs and organizations invent unique Greek-letter names which mask the character of their activities. Following are ten organizations found in a well-known coeducational university. How many can you identify with respect to their fields of interest?

Fig. 34. A "MOCK" INITIATION IN A SORORITY[3]

FIG. 35. FORMAL INDUCTION INTO THE SAME SORORITY REPRESENTED IN FIGURE 34[4]

1. Alpha Kappi Psi
2. Theta Tau
3. Iota Sigma Pi
4. Phi Chi
5. Alpha Lambda Delta
6. Alpha Chi Sigma
7. Alpha Epsilon Iota
8. Gamma Eta Gamma
9. Kappa Kappa Psi
10. Pi Delta Epsilon

You will do well to guess as many as half correctly. It would never do to call these organizations Chemical Society, Engineers' Club, or Writers' Guild, for it is much more mysterious to have Greek letters and then to invent rituals of initiation. The correct answers are:

1. Professional commerce fraternity
2. Engineering fraternity
3. Honorary chemistry sorority
4. Medical fraternity
5. Freshman women honorary
6. Chemical fraternity
7. Medical sorority
8. Legal fraternity
9. Band honorary
10. Journalism

CLASSIFICATION OF SECRET SOCIETIES

Secrets and rituals involve people of both sexes and in all walks of life. There are at least twelve different kinds of secret organizations: (1) benevolent, beneficial, and philanthropic societies; (2) revolutionary and reformist societies; (3) patriotic societies; (4) professional and occupational societies; (5) mystical and occult societies; (6) religious orders; (7) military societies and orders of knighthood; (8) collegiate "social" and recreational societies; (9) honor societies; (10) abstinence societies; (11) convivial societies; (12) criminal societies.[5]

Such a classification indicates how divergent the various secret groups are in their ultimate aims. Even within the same organization, however, *satellite* societies develop. In fact, it would seem that wherever there is a heterogeneous membership—different ages, nationalities, groups, occupations, and religions—fraternal subgroupings may grow up, carrying along most of the philosophy of the central group with which they are affiliated. The Masonic order with over thirty different organizations, both secret and nonsecret, illustrates on a large scale a characteristic structural pattern of many societies. The Masonic constellation consists of the following:[6]

Orders of Knighthood: Knights Templar; Knights of the Red Cross of Constantine; Royal Order of Scotland.

Convivial Societies: Ancient Arabic Order, Nobles of the Mystic Shrine; Royal Order of Jesters (A Shrine subauxiliary); Mystic Order of the Veiled Prophets of the Enchanted Realm; Tall Cedars of Lebanon; Egyptian Order of Sciots; Order of Rameses.

Women's Auxiliary Societies: Daughters of the Nile; Mysterious Witches of Salem; Order of the Eastern Star; White Shrine of Jerusalem; Heroines of Jericho; Order of the Amaranth; True Kindred; Order of Beauceant.

Collegiate Societies: Acacia; Square and Compass; Scimitar; Gamma Alpha Phi; Phi Omega Phi (women).

Juvenile Societies: Order of De Molay; Order of Builders; Order of Chivalry; Order of the Rainbow; Job's Daughters.

Nonsecret Masonic Clubs: National Sojourners' Club; High Twelve Club.

Honorary: Order of High Priesthood.

This intricate structure is of tremendous importance in strengthening the bonds among the members of the order.

RITUALISM

Reliable estimates indicate that over fifty million of us belong to one or more—usually more—organizations, and the great majority of these are of a "secret" character.[7] Thus we have Maccabees who meet in "Hives," Red Men who meet in "Tribes," Prophets who meet in "Grottos," Watchmen who meet in "Forts," Stags who meet in "Droves," Owls who meet in "Nests," and Eagles who meet in "Aeries."[8] Most of us become tremendously involved in our ceremonies and rituals.

"Our ritual," says the Fraternal Order of Beavers, "stacks up with any Order in existence—brief snappy opening ceremony, including beautiful Patriotic Flag exercises. . . . Special dramatic degree exemplifying the Beavers in the Valley of the Turquemenau and their conflict with the Iroquois."

Perhaps your fancy turns to other lines. "Our ritual," says the Ancient and Illustrious Order of the Knights of Malta, "is the sole repository of the rites and ceremonies practised during the Middle Ages, preserved in their entirety but presented in more exquisite style by the aid of modern invention." [9]

Every secret organization has some ritualistic test of membership. In a famous *sub rosa* college fraternity this test of a "brother" is as follows:

Question: "Have you any freshmen in your house?"
Answer: "Yes."
Question: "How many?"
Answer: "One."
Question: "What's his name?"
Answer: "Nux." (This is a "mystic" word *Xun* spelled backward.)

The members of a chapter of this organization, whose officers have names like "Krusophulax," take the following pledge:

We are one. We rejoice in our strength. We make ourselves leaders. By our union we govern. We revere our stewardship; we keep alive our spirit; we promote loyalty; we strive for fellowship. Our college is the best. We devote ourselves to its welfare and greatness. With no thought of ourselves, we look to the future and build what it may hold. This is our everlasting pledge.

This sort of ritual is by no means limited to college students. For example, the ritual of the Ku Klux Klan permits a Klansman to deny membership for opportunist reasons if he is asked whether he belongs to the Klan, the Ku Klux Klan, or the like, but does not allow him to disclaim membership if he is asked the specific question whether he belongs to the "Invisible Empire, Knights of the Ku Klux Klan," the *official* name of the organization.

The fraternity member loves gaiety and rhythm and color and a good time.[10] A great deal of his behavior is *autistic* and *regressive*. But these terms "autistic" and "regressive" are used here in exactly the same way as in previous chapters (9 and 11), simply as *objective* descriptions of how people behave. Ritualism is no sign of inferiority. It cuts across all members of society, not only in the fraternity, but in the family, school, church, political party, and nation. Ritualism is one of our most important means of transmitting In-group standards and traditions.

INSTITUTIONALISM

Note the egocentric character of the average pledge taken by initiates into a secret society, and the blind devotion to the organization as an institution. The pattern of beliefs is that the institution (1) transcends the members, (2) is superior to other similar institutions, (3) is absolutely right in its aims, and (4) is bound to succeed.[11] Of course, how far-reaching these beliefs may be depends somewhat upon whether an individual member of a secret society is an *institutionalist* or an *individualist*. Katz and Allport termed two-thirds of the members of college fraternities at Syracuse University institutionalists, because the members believed that their particular fraternity was of the order of a superentity or superindividual Being to whom they owed allegiance.[12] The remaining third were classed as individualists, because they looked upon the fraternal organization simply as a group of individual members, and stressed the individual contacts within the organization.

In a study of a local chapter of a national college sorority, these attitudes of institutionalism and individualism show up rather nicely. A sorority member studied the attitudes and ideas expressed by her fellow members, without any of them knowing it, and found that the majority insisted that the organization was supreme, although some few looked on the chapter as no more than a group of individuals. This is indicated by the reasons given by these sorority members for joining: "Thought it was the best national," as contrasted with, "Liked the girls in the sorority," or, "Liked several members in the probable pledge class"; outside pressure from a prominent alumna, as contrasted with an invitation from friends already in the chapter. The reasons for joining given by the pledge class were mostly institutional: "—— is tops most places, and I think it is tops here"; "——'s reputation is excellent the world over"; "I like what —— stands for." (Being a pledge, how can she know what —— stands for, when most of the actual members are vague on this point?) One or two individuals said, "I like the girls." When there was a discussion of which girls should be invited to pledge, the following considerations were raised: "But does she *have* anything?"; "She's a nice girl, but that's all"; "She's not wonderful on looks, but she has plenty of personality"; as contrasted with, "What will she contribute to the chapter?", and "Did you see the good-looking coat she had on? She's already dated up for all the football games." One member went so far as to say, "I haven't any real religion. —— has become my religion."

If you are an institutionalist, you are probably very critical of the individualist, and vice versa. And if you are an institutionalist, you are probably very critical of such an analysis of fraternities—unless you have trained yourself in being *objective*. In either case, however, the prestige factor is of great importance in the fraternity. The prospective "pledge" is always shown the number of trophies won by the fraternity or sorority, and pictures of outstanding athletes over the country. And was there ever a fraternity without a United States Senator or a Representative as an alumnus?

FRATERNAL IDEOLOGIES

In spite of the difference in aims of the various secret societies, there are certain threads of uniformity running through them. Secret societies are primarily morality institutions. They seek to instill and perpetuate the virtues of honesty, unselfishness, loyalty, piety, chastity, nationalism, and friendship. It is characteristic of the In-group—whether it be one's family, gang, school, church, or fraternity—to emphasize those ways of behaving and thinking which are supposed to keep the group strong and able to oppose Out-groups. The morality fostered by the fraternity is principally In-group morality; loyalty to the "house" or "lodge" is emphasized. Certain specific ideologies stand out:[13]

Mutual Aid and Brotherhood. The notion of mutual aid and brotherhood is found particularly in those societies which have insurance features and which maintain homes for their more destitute members; but even in the ceremonies of other organizations the fraternity ritual includes a lecture in which the novitiate is told of the values of assisting fellow members in times of distress. Fraternal kinship and brotherhood are emphasized.

Patriotism. A second ideal is adherence to nationalistic traditions, or patriotism. This is usually brought out in the ceremonial drama that goes with initiation. Some fraternal orders place unusual stress on nationalism—the Junior Order, United American Mechanics; Elks; Daughters of America; Sons and Daughters of Liberty; United Order of Americans; Patriotic Order, Sons of America; and the Fraternal Patriotic Americans.

Race and Nationality Restrictions. For those who belong to the dominant culture groups, membership is rather strictly limited to their own kind. Barriers are raised against people with black, brown, yellow, or red skin, or people of Jewish or Catholic faiths, and so on. The Improved Order of Red Men, whose ritual is based upon the supposed customs of American Indians, excludes Indians from membership. Vincent Sheean, of Irish descent, broke his pledge to a "Jewish" fraternity in college because of the danger of being ostracized from the life of the Gentile part of the undergraduate body.[14]

Religious Ideals. In the framework of the ritual is usually found material on the God concept—usually dealt with as an omnipotent, omniscient, and anthropomorphic deity. If a potential member should deny or question the existence of a Supreme Being, this is sufficient to exclude him from membership. Secret societies break into a number of categories on religious lines. Protestant, Catholic, and Jewish societies are in agreement on certain canons of moral conduct, yet differentiated on religious issues. Some even stress opposition to some other religious group; for example, the following societies are opposed to Catholicism —the Sons and Daughters of Liberty, the Loyal Orange Institution, the Ancient and Illustrious Order of Knights of Malta, and the Junior Order, United American Mechanics.

Sexual Morality. Sexual ethics are frequently stressed in the initiation; that is, the members pledge themselves to uphold the prevailing standards of sexual morality. However, the oath concerning sexual irregularities appears to be more characteristic of men's than women's organizations.

> Whenever sex morals are specifically mentioned in the rituals, the reference is to relations between a member and a female relative or dependent of a fellow fraternalist. Some fraternal orders include in their ritualistic obligation a promise that the new member will not "violate the chastity" of a wife, sister, mother, or daughter of a member of the order. Beyond the circle of fraternalism, however, there are usually no stated taboos against illicit sex relations.[15]

Temperance. In addition to sex morality a great many organizations emphasize temperate values—both in their rituals and in certain public functions. The rules of conduct to which a member gives lip service in the institution, however, do not always square with convivial types of conduct carried on outside.

Retardation of Social Reform. Because of the nature of their functions and the desirability of promoting their own In-group standards of conduct, most fraternal organizations disapprove of social change. In order to maintain the *status quo,* they will actively resist any attitudes which come in conflict with their own ideologies. The fact that millions of Americans belong to various secret societies cannot be overlooked as a tremendous force for conservatism in our society.

PSYCHOLOGICAL VALUES

There are certain psychological values in the existence of clubs and societies, whether secret or not:

Union into an In-group. In the first place, membership in these societies unites people into a strong In-group with common ideals, to an extent that is otherwise impossible. In our democracy, with its strong community and state allegiance, it has been extremely difficult to develop the same feelings of loyalty and patriotism as in the "brotherhoods" and "sisterhoods." Here are symbols of united emotion and allegiance which no other institution except the church supplies.

Elimination of Some Prejudices. In the second place, and paradoxically enough, these In-groups tend to break down certain kinds of prejudices. For example, in one of the service clubs a Jewish President of a Kiwanis club used money from the treasury, which had been contributed in part by Catholics, to buy a Christmas tree for the children of a Norwegian Lutheran orphanage![16] When a group cuts across the In-group lines of Jews, Catholics, and Lutherans, this has considerable social significance. What is true of the service organizations is likewise typical of many another club. Many groups have devoted themselves to giving special aid to the needy at Christmas time; to carrying on a particular charity within the community, such as an orphans' home; to securing camp sites for boys; or, as in the case of the D.A.R., to supporting deserving students in schools and colleges.

Role as Pressure Organizations. A third advantage of the tremendous number of organizations in the United States is that they can serve as pressure organizations for the beliefs of the individual members. In a democratic society, it is of the utmost importance that members of particular groups have a means of fostering their beliefs and of trying to influence the opinions of other individuals. For example, on the letterhead of a communication appear the names of forty participating organizations. By combining for a given goal—in this case "National Defense for an Enduring America"—they can carry on activities on a scale that could not be fostered by individual groups. Here are some of the forty organizations:

American Gold Star Mothers, Inc.
American Legion Auxiliary
American War Mothers
American Women's Legion of the World War
Auxiliary to Sons of Union Veterans of the Civil War
Dames of the Loyal Legion of the U.S.A.
Daughters of the Defenders of the Republic, U.S.A.
Daughters of Union Veterans of the Civil War, 1861–65
Florida Society of Patriots
Guadalupe Club of 1848
Ladies Auxiliary to the Veterans of Foreign Wars of the U.S.
Ladies of the Grand Army of the Republic
National Auxiliary, United Spanish War Veterans
National Patriotic Council
National Ladies' Auxiliary to the Jewish War Veterans
National Society of Colonial Descendants of America
National Society, Daughters of Founders and Patriots of America
National Society, Daughters of the Revolution
National Society, Daughters of the Union, 1861–65, Inc.
National Society, Patriotic Women of America
National Society of New England Women
National Society, United States Daughters of 1812
National Society, Women Descendants of the Ancient and Honorable Artillery Company

Economic Advantages. A fourth advantage is the economic one. This has two aspects: joining an organization which has insurance features, and joining one for business reasons. Men dress themselves up as Algerian Zouaves, wear flaming plumes, and engage in group singing partly because they stand to reap some gains in business and prestige.

Relaxation and Fellowship. There are, in the fifth place, certain nonmaterial gains involving relaxation and fellowship inherent in belonging to clubs and societies. They serve as an excellent means of escape for most citizens from the humdrum activities of daily living—the Kill Kare Club, the Jolly Eight, the Happy Twelve. Even though the names of some imply that they are "study" groups, a realistic examination of what goes on at the average club meeting indicates that most societies are more concerned with social participation, "good times," and refreshments. For example:

I belong to a new group who get together to do a little study on infants—it's a sort of Pre-Mama Club—purely theoretical and nothing but optimism on the part of most of us, but still it's rather interesting. No one who has an actual offspring can belong, and perhaps most of us are studying in vain, but anyhow we have *marvelous* refreshments!

The mottoes of "mutual, mental improvement" and "progress" turn out in many instances to be nothing more than verbal symbols. Within one year the program of one federated club included such amazingly diverse topics as "Recent Religious Movements; Christian Science and New Thought," "The Dictograph," "Mural Paintings," "The Panama Canal," "The Drama," "Hull House," and "Dresss."[17] These were simply verbal titles around which people could rally for other reasons. The same is true of most college "honor" societies. As we have already indicated, this does not mean that such societies are worthless; as a matter of fact, they are extremely valuable as a means of providing relaxation and of fostering social solidarity.

Regression in Ritualism. The satisfactions of belonging to a cohesive group are well illustrated in secret societies, where one may not only escape from his daily routine but even engage in infantile types of play behavior without criticism from his fellows—in fact, with their complete approval. He may not only regress in the lodge meeting itself, but may march down the street with bands blaring, wearing strange-looking garments admired by the bystanders. The ritualism of the church may even be supplanted; one may become a Kleagle or a Maharajah. The officers in a chapter of the Military Order of the Cootie are Blanket Bum, Seam Squirrel, Hide Gimlet, Provost Marshal, Tight Wad, Keeper of the Crummy Duffle Bag, and Hungry Cootie.

To live in a modern world and be an ancient; to live in a humdrum world and be a knight; to live in a gabby world and have a secret—all this is possible. It is the essence of fraternalism that it does its best to make it possible. An illustrious name is only a beginning. When the password is given and the inner door swings back, it is upon a world as different from the world outside as ingenuity can make it.

No mere Presiding Officer sits [there] . . . On the dais sits a Monarch or a Master, a Supreme Seignior, an Illustrious Potentate, a Grand Illuminator or a Maharajah. No secretary is a secretary in this world of dreams come true: he is a Thrice Illustrious Scribe. No treasurer is a treasurer: he is an August Keeper of the Strong-Box. No citizen is a citizen: he is a knight, a monk, a priest, a dervish or an ogre.

Never mind if the light is bad and the toga needs a safety-pin; whose hands have never trembled as he tied a mask behind his ears or combed the fine gold fringe of a glossy pair of epaulettes or stuck in his hat the splendid plume that made of him a Don Quixote? . . . All over America, six nights a week, from one to five million men and women are dressing themselves as brahmins, pharaohs, Vikings, princes, furies, hermits, druids, Galahads, sorcerers, Maltese and Tibetans.[18]

All of this has tremendous social value, and means that American ritualism has introduced into our routine daily affairs something agreeably different.

▶ ALLEGIANCE TO THE POLITICAL PARTY

THE POLITICAL PARTY AS AN IN-GROUP

Membership in fraternities and clubs has replaced for millions of Americans the allegiance which was formerly given to the small local community and to the church. Historically the political party, too, had many characteristics of the club. Here also the same types of In-group attitudes were fostered—loyalty to the group, cooperation, social solidarity. The Out-group consisted of those "other" people who by reputedly corrupt methods were always trying to get in power.

HISTORICAL CHANGES IN THE POLITICAL SCENE

Political ideology has, of course changed with our history. In early pioneering times political attitudes depended, first, upon equality of ability in citizenship and, second, upon locality. In the days when the majority of people were engaged in much the same sorts of occupations, such as tilling the soil, lumbering, and fishing, and when there were not great diversities within a given community, it was possible for citizens to know a great deal about their political affairs and the men who were eligible for public office.

The town meeting and personal participation in political life in the community became the rule. Here the individual was aware of the needs of his village. He knew his neighbors well. He had a common interest in schools, roads, fire and police protection, and moral control. It was assumed that the person could make adequate judgments on political questions and decide issues through voting directly on them or by choosing representatives to settle these matters for him and his fellow-citizen. The basic interest was the immediate locality. People in a certain area had common concerns.[19]

Today, with modern communication, transportation, and specialization in particular fields of industry, equal ability in citizenship does not exist on the same level as previously, nor is it likely in our urban civilization that all citizens will be well informed on the ways of thinking and acting of all candidates for public office. Ours are much more "touch-and-go" contacts than in the early history of our country. Voters are influenced in their judgments by machine politics, newspapers, radio programs, movies, schools, churches, clubs, lodges, public meetings, music, speeches, magazines, billboards, handbills, over-the-fence and over-the-lunch gossip, and a hundred other ways of thinking and acting. The personalities of the candidates may mean more than the issues. One analysis of elections for four different presidential-election years revealed no clear relationship between the choices by newspapers of presidential candidates and the final behavior of the voters at the polls—one indication that in a democratic society there are a great many variables that help to determine how a citizen will vote.[20]

LACK OF PRESTIGE OF POLITICS

The lack of prestige of American politics is one of the principal reasons why there is not greater allegiance directly to the political club or political party. Apparently, most Americans have stereotyped ideas about politics being "corrupt, rotten, and dirty." One investigation revealed that the prestige value of positions in the municipal government in Chicago was far down the scale as compared with comparable types of work carried on in a private enterprise.[21] A *Fortune* survey has shown that the average American would rather be employed by private business than by the Government.[22]

As citizens, we have developed something of an *ambivalent* attitude toward the political scene. We give lip service on the one hand to the notion that we and our fellow citizens are intelligent and can make up our minds for ourselves; yet at the very same time we recognize full well the extent to which individual opinions in the mass can be manipulated by emotional techniques. People realize that the majority of voters —other voters, of course, not themselves—are easily swayed by emotional appeals and are constantly prejudiced by misinformation.[23]

VOTERS' PREJUDICES

That citizens vote under the influence of many prejudices, that their political behavior is irrational like much of the rest of their behavior, is indicated by a unique study by Vaughan.[24] An analysis of 762 letters in a newspaper, written by voters stating reasons for their choices in a presidential campaign, showed they were mere rationalizations in defense of the writers' many prejudices. Not one letter was free from this, and no writer even hinted at the possibility that he might be mistaken.

The element of pure personal conviction based on individual thinking is small compared with impressions from others. Gundlach has found the socioeconomic and political views of college students to be extremely inconsistent, largely reflecting undigested and contradictory clichés of the daily press.[25] Instead of every citizen having rationally thought out definite opinions concerning the principles of government, beliefs revolve around definite prejudices, and elections around unanalyzed catchwords. Meier studied voting motives by testing over a thousand university students and citizens in four Midwest states, and found that the most successful campaign material dealt with simple appeals arousing specific emotional habit patterns.[26] Hartmann was interested in determining the vote-getting effect of emotional as compared with rational political material when he ran on the Socialist ticket of Allentown, Pennsylvania.[27] He divided the town into three election districts: (1) an area in which an "emotional" plea for votes was distributed; (2) an area in which a "rational" pamphlet was distributed; and (3) a control district in which no Socialist material was distributed. Election returns showed the greatest increase in votes where the emotional literature had been given out. Menefee and Granneberg found that emotional editorials with respect to American foreign policy were more effective in swaying the opinions of college students than were rational or non-emotional editorials.[28]

Lazarsfeld, with two colleagues, has reported one of the most significant analyses ever made on "how the voter makes up his mind in a presidential campaign."[29] A detailed survey was made of approximately three thousand voters in Erie County, Ohio. Repeated interviews were made over several months in order to trace the effects of political propaganda statistically, especially as to who changes his thinking during an election year and why. Preconvention attitudes were sampled, and then changes in attitudes as the campaign progressed, right up to election day. Psychologically, the most useful material is the discussion of the vote decision, especially of three important factors: (1) the *activation* effect, (2) the *reinforcement* effect, and (3) the *conversion* effect.

(1) *Activation.* . . . While people hesitate and meditate and imagine that they decide rationally on the better road to take, it would often have been possible to predict at the outset what they would decide to do in the end. Knowing a few of their personal characteristics, we can tell with fair certainty how they will finally vote: they join the fold to which they belong. What the campaign does is to activate their political predispositions.[30]

(2) *Reinforcement.* Half the people knew in May, before the campaign got underway, how they would vote in November, and actually voted that way. But does that mean that campaign propaganda had no effect upon them? Not at all. . . . It kept the partisans 'in line' by reassuring them in their vote decision; it reduced defections from the ranks. It had the effect of reinforcing the original vote decision.[31]

(3) *Conversion*. . . . The people who did most of the reading and listening not only read and heard most of their own partisan propaganda but were also most resistant to conversion because of their strong predispositions. And the people who were most open to conversion—the ones the campaign managers most wanted to reach—read and listened least. Those inter-related facts represent the bottleneck of conversion.[32]

Studies of this type give considerable insight into voting behavior, and should be of very practical value to politicians.

ANALYSIS OF VOTERS' GROUPS

Without stereotyping voters too much, it is possible to divide them into certain groups: (1) "regular" party members; (2) those who vote against candidates or parties they feel are responsible for economic reversals; (3) radical voters; (4) liberal thinkers who vote with conservative parties; (5) those voters subject to unusual pressure.

1. *"Regular" Party Members.* Politics, like religion, is already determined for many voters by their early family conditioning. Many are never concerned about campaign issues because they know that they are going to vote for the same party they did last time and the time before that—which is the same party that their fathers voted for before them. In a study of 375 students at Dartmouth, Gordon W. Allport found that 79 per cent voted for the candidate of the party indicated as their fathers' affiliation.[33] There are some indications, however, that the old-time tradition of blind party loyalty is breaking down, and that there are many independent voters who swing from one party to another.[34]

2. *Those Who Vote against Economic Reversals.* Some voters desert their party if it is in power during a depression period. Politicians are agreed that business conditions decidedly affect votes. In this connection, a survey of the literature indicates, with few exceptions, that economic contentment as reflected by higher incomes tends to be associated with greater political and economic conservatism.[35]

Persons in all economic levels were adversely affected by the 1929 "crash," and many relieved some of their tension by voting against the Republican party in 1932.[36] One study of independent voters showed that the greatest party fluctuation took place in groups whose members had experienced the least increase in wages since the last election.[37] Another investigation has shown a positive relationship between the popularity of political parties and good business conditions; the party affiliations of representatives elected by 94 Congressional districts in nine states for the period 1875-1902 were compared with selected points on a curve of business activity.[38] The number of votes given to representatives in power increased with prosperity, but declined with bad business. A study of voters by Hayes indicates, however, that those who bolt from one political party to another do so because of differences in attitudes toward specific policies, rather than just to "vote for the man" or to "jump on the band wagon."[39]

3. *Radical Voters.* Then, there is a small but vociferous minority of voters who are "radical." They advocate drastic and immediate changes by "going to the roots" of problems. Both the "intellectual radicals" and those who have become radical because of actual hunger or discrimination sometimes undergo active persecution in defense of their beliefs. Radicalism tends to grow up during financial depressions and as a result of labor conflicts, and those who support radical candidates and platforms are indicating that they are not "quitters." Although active in practically all elections, radicals have succeeded in electing few candidates.

4. *Liberal Thinkers Who Vote with Conservative Parties.* Of great psychological significance is the fact that large numbers of voters think liberally on certain social issues, yet go to the polls and vote for conservative parties. Conservatism seems to increase toward election time.[40] In Gordon W. Allport's study of Dartmouth students at the time of a national election, he found many individuals with liberal views on specific issues who followed the conservative party labels.[41] He believes that the phenomenon of radical thinkers continuing to vote the conservative ticket may be due to lack of efficient organization of the liberal movement, timidity of action, or lack of integration of radical attitudes with actions.

A further explanation is in terms of the emotional components of certain words (compare Chapter 8 on language). The label "Communism," for example, is sufficient to damn many a liberal belief. Hartmann demonstrated that the feeling tone for the major-party labels does not agree with the amount of endorsement of the specific items which constitute their programs.[42] Again, in a study of Fascist attitudes, Stagner showed that many of the people who were in agreement in rejecting the label "Fascism" actually were in favor of many of the specific things for which Fascism stands.[43] In one of Menefee's studies, about a third of the persons who endorsed certain statements of national policy rejected these same statements when they were labeled "radical," "Fascist," or "Communist."[44] These general results have also been confirmed by other investigators.[45]

Closely related to this is the tendency of many voters to subscribe to mutually contradictory statements; that is, they will favor a certain proposition, and *at the same time* a proposition almost the opposite of it! This has been demonstrated in studies by Hayes, who obtained data on the political attitudes of over eight thousand voters scattered through thirty-seven states, prior to a national election.[46] A total of 1,133 persons accepted *both* of the following statements: "The United States should maintain an army and navy at least equal to those of other great powers," and "The United States should lead the way to peace by reducing her army and navy." Altogether 917 persons believed *both* that "The rich should bear a larger proportion of the burden of taxation," and that "High taxes on the rich will retard recovery of prosperity." There were 1,230 persons who agreed *both* that "The currency of the United States should be kept sound at all hazards," and that "What this country needs is a liberal policy in issuing money." While some people no doubt could reconcile these apparent inconsistencies, most of the subjects who answered affirmatively apparently did so because they accepted the stereotyped phrases and ideas uncritically. Hayes has further demonstrated that a general attitude of both "liberalism-and-conservatism" characterized the political thinking of voters of every party in the 1932 elections.[47] Like all men, voters are often irrational on logical matters.

5. *Voters Subject to Unusual Pressure.* When under pressure, economic or otherwise, the interrelations of political attitudes and actions are greatly altered. The Lynds found that although a person's political party, like his religion, is usually determined by his family, there are economic considerations which "override the accident of birth."[48]

In other words, there are innumerable instances where persons vote contrary to their own attitudes because of political and economic pressure. This is one more example of lack of agreement between covert and overt behavior discussed in Chapter 7.

LOSS OF MEANINGFULNESS OF THE POLITICAL PARTY

The political party has little of the meaningfulness that the fraternity and lodge have for the average citizen. In the early history of our country the political party was a closely knit organization which aroused the enthusiasms of many citizens, but in our modern "machine age" there are many other loyalties. For some, *the* party transcends its members, is superior to other parties, is absolutely right in its aims, and is bound to succeed; but for countless others allegiance to any political party is superficial. The average man and woman are busy being elected to the office of Maharajah or of Grand Illuminator in a little world of politics all their own, where the issues are not too complex.

QUESTIONS AND PROBLEMS FOR DISCUSSION

1. *What are the psychological factors that build up the prestige of a fraternity?*
2. *Make a* social-psychological *analysis of your club or fraternity. Can you distinguish between attitudes of institutionalism and individualism in the other members?*
3. *List in two columns the advantages and disadvantages of ritualism.*

4. *Analyze your own attitudes in the last major political campaign. How did you get those particular attitudes?*
5. *What is the significance for political theory of individual differences?*
6. *What do you think might be meant by the "psychopathology of politics"?*
7. *What are the psychological and economic values of fraternal organizations?*

RECOMMENDED READINGS

Albig, W., *Public Opinion,* New York: McGraw-Hill Book Company, Inc., 1939.

Arnold, T. W., *The Symbols of Government.* New Haven: Yale University Press, 1935.

Ferguson, C. W., *Fifty Million Brothers: A Panorama of American Lodges and Clubs.* New York: Farrar & Rinehart, Inc., 1937.

Key, V. O., Jr., *Politics Parties and Pressure Groups.* New York: Thomas Y. Crowell Company, 1942.

Lasswell, H., *Psychopathology and Politics.* Chicago: University of Chicago Press, 1930.

Lazarsfeld, P. F., Berelson, B., and Gaudet, H., *The People's Choice: How the Voter Makes Up His Mind in a Presidential Campaign.* New York: Duell, Sloan and Pearce, 1944.

Odegard, P. H., and Helms, E. A., *American Politics: A Study in Political Dynamics.* New York: Harper & Brothers, 1938.

Rice, S. A., *Quantitative Methods in Politics.* New York: Alfred A. Knopf, Inc., 1928.

Salter, J. T., *The Pattern of Politics: The Folkways of a Democratic People.* New York: The Macmillan Company, 1940.

Smith, C. W., Jr., *Public Opinion in a Democracy: A Study in American Politics.* New York: Prentice-Hall, Inc., 1939.

*Newcomb, T. M., Hartley, E. L., and others (editors), *Readings in Social Psychology.* New York: Henry Holt and Company, Inc., 1947: —Lazarsfeld, P. F., Berelson, B., and Gaudet, H., "Social Factors in Voting," pp. 605-617.

CHAPTER TWENTY

OCCUPATIONAL GROUPS

PROFESSIONAL GROUPS. Economic Specialization—Necessity of Stereotyping—Professional Egocentrism—The Engineering Profession—The Medical Profession—The Legal Profession/ OTHER OCCUPATIONAL GROUPS. Horizontal Differences—Vertical Differences between Employed and Unemployed—Vertical Differences among the Employed—Occupational Egocentrism—Cultural Factors—"Working Class" Versus "Business Class"—Attitudes of the Business Class—Attitudes of the Working Class—Development of the Labor Movement—Reasons for Development of Labor Movement—Conflicts between Unions and Employers—A.F. of L.-C.I.O. Conflict—The American Economic System.

▶ PROFESSIONAL GROUPS

ECONOMIC SPECIALIZATION

Besides belonging to a community, growing up in a family, coming in contact with an educational system, belonging to clubs or fraternities, and being involved in the political scene, most people are also members of an occupational group. In many ways economic status and membership in occupational groups determine their other activities—which schools they attend, which fraternities and clubs they belong to, and even how they vote. Some insight into this will be gained by a psychological analysis of the attitudes of some of these occupational groups.

Our present economic structure is largely based upon the activities of individuals and of groups who have produced or promoted the production and exchange of various types of goods and services. In pioneering days, a man could carry on any number of different occupations. For example, farmers were not only producers of grain and livestock but also manufacturers of flour, leather, liquors, and other products, as well as boat builders, boatmen, and merchants. But farming gradually became specialized, and today nonfarmers carry on manufacturing, transportation, and merchandising, each of which activities has also become highly specialized.[1] What is true of these pursuits is true of others as well. Our economic structure has become exceedingly complex because of the many specialized activities performed by persons in different types of work.

NECESSITY OF STEREOTYPING

Unique occupational attitudes have also grown up as these fields of specialization have developed. In the present chapter we are concerned with what some of these attitudes are like, first, in the professions, and then in other occupational groups. Among the professions where In-group attitudes exist are teaching, the ministry, engineering, medicine, and the law. Although there are great individual differences within each group, it is necessary to stereotype to some extent, in order to interpret the characteristic attitudes of their members. These attitudes tend to differ not only according to the type of work but also with differences in economic and social status.

Already at the age of twenty-five you see the professional mannerism settling down on the young commercial traveller, on the young doctor, on the young minister, on the young counsellor-at-law. You see the little lines of cleavage running through the character, the tricks of thought, the prejudices, the ways of the 'shop,' in a word, from which the man can by-and-by no more escape than his coat-sleeve can suddenly fall into a new set of folds.[2]

PROFESSIONAL EGOCENTRISM

There is professional egocentrism within each group. In those occupations which are at the same social level, there are interesting "horizontal differences"; that is, the members of the professional groups stand out "vertically" above other occupational groups in prestige, but each differs somewhat from the others in certain respects. Either from differences in training or because of their types of work, the members develop particular allegiances and loyalties to their own In-groups which make for a lack of understanding of the ways of thinking and acting of other groups. In Chapters 17 and 18, we have already seen the extent to which teachers and ministers have their own In-group attitudes. Characteristic attitudes are also found in the case of engineers, physicians, and lawyers.

All five of these professions might be expected to contribute leadership in social changes. Actually many of the members of these groups prefer maintenance of the *status quo,* of the group and of society.

THE ENGINEERING PROFESSION

Neither ministers nor teachers are particularly well united. Physicians and lawyers are. The engineering profession stands some place between these two extremes in "social solidarity." In their professional associations engineers have even begun to develop "tribe" standards in much the same way as other groups. Although they have a great many individual attitudes, these have been culturalized in terms of professional training. Largely because of the type of education engineers receive, they tend to be more analytical and mechanistic than members of other groups. Perhaps the most striking thing about engineers, especially the successful ones, is that they associate themselves almost wholly with the captains of industry, not with labor.

THE MEDICAL PROFESSION

Physicians not only tend to have views toward life somewhat different from members of other professions, but these views are found in culturalized form in professional associations such as the American Medical Association. Thus, there is considerable agreement—at least among the *older* physicians—that socialized medicine is dangerous, that people in other professions are not as learned, that science is the standard measure of values. Although there is some disagreement within the profession about such matters, general adherence to the standards of the group is important for self-protection.

The individual physician usually develops characteristic ways of behavior. The rigorous study and analysis necessary to complete medical school leaves a lasting imprint on many a young student. The physician learns to be a more drastic person than the minister, and a more realistic person than the teacher. Through the mechanisms of his various societies and contacts, certain rites and habits are solidified and perpetuated. Eventually he is likely to develop a more reticent and reserved character than his brother the lawyer; and between these two the horizontal differences show up. Although physicians and lawyers are social equals, they are not alike in attitudes.

> The doctor is incensed by the noisy manners of the lawyer; this is most trying to the physician's reserved dignity. If he cannot maintain silent contempt, he may with cynical disgust bestow the appellation of "windbag" upon the verbose advocate, of which the latter, if not unaware of the owlish fluff of the medical man, is self-satisfiedly tolerant.[3]

THE LEGAL PROFESSION

Lawyers are another group of individuals who, on the basis of precedent, training, and type of work, are more conservative and conventional than might be expected. One might suppose that lawyers would be great social engineers or specialists in sociological planning.[4] Since they have studied individual and group behavior, and have engaged in legal work which is essentially social-psychological in nature, one would expect them to be interested in progressive or even "liberal" movements.[5] On the contrary, men of law on the whole are champions of the existing ways. Because of their legalistic training, many lawyers and judges do not realize the necessity of some modifications in our nonmaterial culture patterns. It is difficult for some of them to see that a particular idea is out of date and needs to be changed. They tend to be absorbed with the question, "What is the law?"

> In the professional school of law, men are not trained primarily to see social problems but only to study situations which are in the past and the "rules" of law which apply to those situations. . . .
>
> The legal education of lawyers and judges tends to give them an attitude of caution and conservatism. Their other-than professional education has sometimes ceased completely. Hence, their thinking tends to run upon precedent, upon the forms and practices of the past, rather than upon future improvement in the present growth of the law.[6]

An examination of the group loyalties as expressed in the American Bar Association shows that a great deal of "talking" and committee work is done year after year, but that the changes discussed seem to materialize only after years of talking, if at all. In this professional group we find conservatism to an outstanding degree.

A great many lawyers are noted for their good judgment, reserve, and interest in the welfare of others. It is important to recognize that a high percentage are conscientious, honest, and ethical. But some have developed overconfident and rather boisterous mannerisms and have acted in such ways as partially to deserve the common stereotypes of "shyster," "corrupt," and "scheming."

In one study of thirteen lawyers, the following characteristics seemed outstanding: intellectualism, or emphasis on mental processes; stress of words and definitions ("the lawyer becomes particular almost to a fault not only about the words he uses for his own expressions but also about the meaning of language addressed to him by others"); combativeness and competitiveness, that is, the tendency to make of any proposition a battle of wits; skepticism, of everything except what is on his own side; formality, and the use of long-established ways; money considerations, principally of self-support, and almost negligibly service to mankind; reputation, or desire to be known to the public; politics, both in the community and in bar associations.[7] An outstanding legal scholar says:

> People resent the existence of lawyers as a profession in a way they do not resent the existence of any other specialized profession. They do not see why there should be any lawyers at all. They do not resent the existence of physicians and surgeons and dentists, although they grumble at the fees they must pay for their services. They rarely suppose they can get along without them. They do not resent the existence of trained engineers. It is not everybody who can design and construct a bridge. But what do lawyers do, that anybody else could not do? And resentment is particularly strong whenever attention is called to the fact that the law is supposed to have justice at its end.[8]

However, when most people get into a difficult situation regarding business affairs or property rights, they discover that a lawyer is a very necessary person, the one person, in fact, who knows the answers and can give sound advice.

▶ OTHER OCCUPATIONAL GROUPS

HORIZONTAL DIFFERENCES

Members of the professions owe loyalty and allegiance to their own In-groups and look with avoidance and suspicion on other professional groups. Thus, members of Out-groups on the same professional level may look on the teacher as a "theorist," the minister as a "softy," the engineer as uncouth and crude, the physician as a "quack," the lawyer as a "shyster." These are examples of *horizontal* differences. Such differences are likewise found in nonprofessional groups. For example, among carpenters, plumbers, steel workers, electricians, and other skilled craftsmen there are strong allegiances to one's own group, and sometimes suspicion and psychological avoidance of other groups. This helps to encourage "jurisdictional disputes" between skilled workers' unions.

VERTICAL DIFFERENCES BETWEEN EMPLOYED AND UNEMPLOYED

The *vertical* differences between various groups are even more apparent. There is a regular hierarchy of psychological or social distance between members of the "upper" classes continuing gradually down through to the "lower" classes. First of all, we can distinguish all those in the ranks of the employed from those who are without jobs. In pioneer days, men lost prestige if they did not engage in the traditional male activity of getting a living. The reasons are perfectly obvious. Those not working for themselves and for the community were liabilities. There has been an interesting carry-over of this idea to the present.

VERTICAL DIFFERENCES AMONG THE EMPLOYED

Those who work may be differentiated from each other by the *amount* of wealth and income, by the *source* of the income, or by *occupational categories*.[9] One possible classification according to occupational standards is shown in Table 16.

These general categories indicate a hierarchy of vertical differences which shows up both in the business and social aspects of life. The character of an individual's work colors his status in his community more than anything else, more even than the amount of money that he makes. For example, clerical work may mean lower pay than skilled craftsmanship,

TABLE 16

Categories of Vertical Differences by Occupations

1. Bankers, large manufacturers, managers of big business, and some professional persons
2. Officials, smaller manufacturers, and most professional persons
3. Small officials, salesmen, clerical workers, small retail business, and civil servants
4. Best skilled labor, skilled craftsmen, foremen
5. Farmers, bakers, painters, barbers
6. Semiskilled workers, chauffeurs, truckmen, teamsters, waiters, porters, servants
7. Unskilled workers and unemployed

but often it carries more prestige. But, if one's income is large enough, he may drive a Packard instead of a Ford, increase his prestige by playing golf instead of pool, join a "service" club instead of limiting himself to membership in his union, belong to a church which has greater wealth. The amount of money one makes tends to be related to whether he votes the Republican or the Democratic ticket, belongs to the Episcopalian or the Baptist church, "dresses up" or not. Perhaps the most distinguishing mark of our vertical differences is the presumption that the children in the different groups may not intermarry. As Walter Lippmann has said:

> To marry outside the set involves, at the very least, a moment of doubt before the engagement can be approved. Each social set has a fairly clear picture of its relative position in the hierarchy of social sets. Between sets at the same level, association is easy, individuals are quickly accepted, hospitality is normal and unembarrassed. But in contact between sets that are "higher" or "lower," there is always reciprocal hesitation, a faint malaise, and a consciousness of difference.[10]

OCCUPATIONAL EGOCENTRISM

The recognition of the differences between groups tends to increase the feelings of occupational egocentrism. A person who has enjoyed his work in a given occupation and has succeeded in it is likely to feel that his kind of work is the most important of all. Thus, the farmer may console himself for his meager rewards by reflecting that but for him the people in the cities would starve. The policeman on his beat may flatter himself that no one could sleep soundly but for him. Coal miners can see the limits of their job up there where factories would stop and children would freeze unless "we send 'em their coal." The miller may feel that the wheat grows in order to keep his mill going. The clergyman enjoys the role of "God's ambassador." Unappreciated schoolteachers find comfort in the proverb, "Just as the twig is bent, the tree's inclined." The secretary of a hoboes' union exclaims, "The country can't get along without us! If we don't hop from the Northwest timber-camp in the winter to the Oklahoma wheatfields in the summer—and get there on time, mind you—w'y, crops go to waste and millions o' dollars are lost!"[11]

CULTURAL FACTORS

The cultural factors of our society seem largely responsible for these occupational attitudes. We could examine the details of the nervous system, the physiological aspects of sex and hunger drives, but would fail to find explanations of social distance. College students have grown up in a society which tends to give less prestige to those individuals who do things with their hands. In pioneering times the man who was skilled with his hands, the master craftsman, was respected as he is not always today in a culture which emphasizes skill and adroitness in the art of putting one word after another.

There is a tendency for sons from lower strata to choose vocations above rather than below the level of the father.[12] Parents are largely responsible for this attitude, wanting their children to achieve the goals which they never attained. Both parents and children have a "level of aspiration" above their present status. This "level of aspiration" is apt to be not the highest goal, but an intermediate step in that direction.[13] When people were asked how large an income they needed in order to be happy, they tended to put the figure at about one-third more than their present income, no matter whether that income was $1,000 or $10,000 a year.[14]

Two other studies are of importance in this connection. The first involved tests of the social status of forty-five different occupations.[15] American children ranked the occupation of banker as highest and ditch digger last. However, with similar tests on Russian children, peasant ranked first in prestige and banker among the lowest. The occupation of clergyman ranked fourth with young Americans but stood last with young Russians. The "prosperous businessman" stood sixth in the American list, but forty-fourth on the Russian list. This experiment indicates that it is thoroughly possible by proper conditioning to get people to believe anything, to respect anyone, and to hold in contempt anything or any person. We are taught to respect the man of wealth, such as the banker or the broker; Russian children are taught to respect the worker and to hold in contempt the aristocrat.

Another study concerned the prevocational attitudes of 861 college students.[16] The majority were willing to accept the teacher, doctor, and lawyer into their church or club, even into their family. Nearly all were willing to accept day laborers, factory workers, servants, and waiters as fellow citizens, but few stood ready to accept them into their club or into their family. Toward the farmer there was little sense of social distance. Feelings toward the dance-hall keeper, dance-band musician, vaudeville dancer, and actor varied with the student group, suggesting that the place of these had not been settled in the mores. Vertical differences between occupations are related to the prestige and social status which these occupations possess among persons outside their own In-groups.

"WORKING CLASS" VERSUS "BUSINESS CLASS"

People are sometimes divided into two groups, "working class" and "business class." Because this sort of rough distinction is commonly made among most people, it becomes a *useful psychological stereotype.* Table 17 shows in general the distinctions between the two groups.

TABLE 17

Differentiation of Working Class and Business Class[17]

Working Class	*Business Class*
Address their activities to *things*..........	Address their activities to *persons*
Work with their *hands*..................	Work with their *tongues*
Make things	*Sell or promote* things and ideas
Use *material* tools......................	Use *non-material* institutional devices

The mere fact of being born upon one or the other side of the watershed roughly formed by these two groups is the most significant cultural factor tending to influence what one does all day long throughout one's life; whom one marries; when one gets up in the morning; whether one belongs to the Holy Roller or Presbyterian church; or drives a Ford or a Buick; whether or not one's daughter makes the desirable high school Violet Club; or one's wife meets with the Sew We Do Club or with the Art Students' League; whether one belongs to the Odd Fellows or to the Masonic Shrine; whether one sits about evenings with one's necktie off. . . .[18]

Such a division is apparent in the majority of American communities and is probably a more useful one than that of "capital" versus "labor." One *Fortune* survey indicated that 79.2 per cent of the people thought of themselves as "middle class."[19] In an analysis of a representative cross section of the national population, Cantril has also found that the majority identify themselves both *socially* and *economically* with the middle class.[20] There is no one-to-one correspondence between social and economic identification; in fact, there is a tendency to regard one's social class as higher than one's economic class.

Although logically they fit into the ranks of labor in ways of earning income, the great majority of small officials, clerical workers, and shopkeepers like to think of themselves as lined up with "capital." The white-collar clerk, who may earn less than a skilled mechanic, usually feels himself "above" the ranks of labor and identifies himself with the management and employing group.

Social distances between the two groups exist, even though physical contact is great. People who think of themselves as belonging to the "upper" group feel that they know all the worth-while people in their community and often adopt a condescending attitude toward those engaged in work with their hands. Strangely enough, those who work with their hands often help to foster this very type of class consciousness by a subservient attitude to those who work with their tongues. Only the magic symbol of education for the children can supposedly bridge the gap. "We want them to have a good education so they can get along easier than their father," and, "If they don't have a good education, they'll never know anything but hard work."[21] Yet polls have indicated that college students expect to receive much higher incomes than there is any probability they will receive.[22] Also, almost half of the business and industrial jobs require no more formal education than the ability to speak, read, and write.[23] Probably 60 to 70 per cent of all jobs in the United States are of a routine mechanical sort which can be learned in very short order. An unwillingness is even found among many young workers to learn more than is necessary in their particular trade because of a desire to do something else which has greater social prestige. At the beginning of the 1940 national-defense program, there was an actual scarcity of available *skilled* workmen.

Differences in social attitudes are illustrated in the results of a survey of 1,700 persons in Akron, Ohio.[24] A random sample of people chosen from the city directory, and also special groups, were interviewed. The questionnaire consisted essentially of eight little stories describing real or realistic incidents which involved conflict between corporate property rights and several varieties of personal rights; and each person was asked to express degree of approval or disapproval of certain actions described. As might be expected, the attitudes of business leaders and industrial executives were the most favorable to corporate property. Attitudes of the working class were less favorable, but were more like those of professional men, office workers, and small businessmen. However, what might be termed "middle class" ideas tended to predominate in the survey, which indicated that old ideas of respect for property in general have not drastically weakened.

ATTITUDES OF THE BUSINESS CLASS

The business class as a group is strikingly unaware of the ways of thinking and acting of the working class, and vice versa. The members of one group ordinarily have never had the opportunity to live and think as members of the other and therefore fail to appreciate their point of view. Thus, the proposal that daylight-saving time be introduced in *Middletown* resulted in a complete conflict between the two groups:

. . . The working class majority overwhelmed the measure before the city officials on the plea that in summer their small dwellings cool off slowly, often remaining warm until after midnight, and that they can ill spare an hour of cool early-morning sleep before they must get up to work. The business men, on the other hand, urged the need of daylight time because of golf and because standard time put local business at a two-hour disadvantage in dealing with Eastern business. Each group thought the other unreasonable.[25]

But the attitudes of employers toward the employed have changed remarkably during the present century. Within the last two decades have come changes and innovations in terms of recreational facilities, educational opportunities, better living conditions, and principally improved working conditions—greater numbers of safety devices, better ventilating systems, cleaner rest rooms, better types of food. Yet many employers still oppose factory inspection, workmen's compensation, and wage-hour laws.

ATTITUDES OF THE WORKING CLASS

The working people are not without their prejudices. In a country which emphasizes "equal opportunity for all," parents attempt to force their children into occupations which will advance both their economic and social status. In fact, a child of working-class parents may have feelings of guilt if he does not subscribe to the golden theory of personal progress in a material respect. This often has end results in psychological conflicts.

S is a young man of Jewish background. His father was a carpenter and was determined that his son become a "professional man." At graduation from high school *S* was given the choice of studying law or medicine and chose the former.

After he had passed the New York bar examinations, his father, a man of slight means, sacrificed almost all of his material resources in order to establish the boy in an office. After doing this he felt his end had been attained.

S struggled at being an attorney for two years and was then forced to give up his small practice. He is now unemployed and feels that it is too late to "start over again."

These desires to rise in the social scheme are traceable in large measure to the complexities of a machine civilization. In pioneering days there was not only respect for craftsmanship but also pride in one's work as the finished product shaped up. In a machine civilization, however, where the majority of workers are carrying on purely routine operations, and with little knowledge of the end result, the problem is different. Working at routine tasks, either in the factory or the office, may prevent an employee from carrying out creative impulses, especially if any deviation from the routine is penalized. This results in loss of pride in his work. Working groups tend to develop antagonistic attitudes toward employers, especially during depressions, when there is so little satisfaction of the wishes for recognition and new experience in their work.

During periods of economic conflict, external evidences of great wealth and show on the part of the upper socioeconomic groups are usually resented by those in the lower-income brackets. This is not surprising in view of the tremendous gap between the salaries received by executives of big corporations and the wages paid to employees.

On the other hand, compensation or base pay, surprisingly enough, is not the first factor of importance to most workers, as has been shown in a number of different surveys.[26] Actually job security is the foremost factor affecting attitudes toward work and toward the company. In this connection, Roethlisberger and Dickson found in their twelve-year investigation among over twenty thousand employees of the Hawthorne Plant of the Western Electric Company that the program of the plant as "blueprinted" by the management had little relation to the actual informal social patterns developed among the workers.[27] The operating plans had been developed on the erroneous assumption that workers were interested primarily in the amount of money earned, whereas the culture patterns of the groups showed that other values were of even greater importance. Similarly, in the engineering department of another large company, an investigation into the causes of bad morale revealed that the theoretical organization of the company did not correspond to the way things actually got done.[28]

DEVELOPMENT OF THE LABOR MOVEMENT

The antagonistic attitudes of employers and employees have been reflected in the frequent conflicts between employer groups and organized labor. Only after years of bitter opposition and oppression have labor groups finally secured a recognized place in our economic order. The Knights of Labor, founded in 1869, was an amorphous body which included both employers and workers. The American Federation of Labor (A.F. of L.), formed in 1881, was the first strong trade-union organization on the American scene. The A.F. of L. was built up on the principle of "craft" unionism, that is, of uniting in all sorts of different industries those who engaged in the same types of skilled work. In 1935 the Congress of Industrial Organizations (C.I.O.) came to the fore. It emphasized the principle of "industrial" unionism, that is, of uniting all those who worked in the same industry even though they engaged in different types of work. There are also thousands of independent labor groups unaffiliated with either of these large national organizations.

REASONS FOR DEVELOPMENT OF LABOR MOVEMENT

There are a number of reasons why the development of an organized labor movement was inevitable.[29] Our democratic system of education produced workers and labor leaders of a sort able to bargain for higher wages and better working conditions. Both the press and radio also contributed to the education of great masses of people concerning the aims and ideals of the labor movement. The development of the telegraph, the telephone, the railroad, and other systems of rapid communication and transportation helped to unite the labor groups. The influx of immigration, and the western movement of population, had far-reaching effects for the cause of labor.

Most important of all, however, was the growth of the factory system and the accompanying development of "big business," which produced sharp economic cleavages between employer and employee. First, the development of machines reduced many skilled workmen to the ranks of unskilled men with lower pay, and eventually technological unemployment began to be felt, causing unrest. Second, the growing size and power of employers and business organizations stimulated labor groups and employees to increase their own strength. Collective bargaining grew up because of strong organizations on *both* sides.

CONFLICTS BETWEEN UNIONS AND EMPLOYERS

Labor organizations are effective today in securing higher wages, better working conditions, workmen's compensation laws, and other benefits for workers. But they have had a long difficult struggle to maintain their existence.

Unions and employers are still in open or undercover conflicts. The principal weapon of the unions has been the strike, including the "sit-down" technique which developed to a high point of popularity in 1936-1937. Manufacturers and "big business" have tried to suppress labor unions by firing of employees, lockouts, strong-arm methods, and espionage. The Senate La Follette Civil Liberties Committee of the 1930's reported that it was quite clear that the employment of labor "spies" had become "the habit of American management."[30] From 1933 to 1937, over $9,000,000 was spent by industrial firms and corporations on espionage, munitioning, and strikebreaking.[31] A partial list of industries serviced by the Pinkerton Detective Agency alone included ninety-eight companies.[32]

Since the psychology of industrial conflict cuts across so many aspects of present-day society, the federal government has naturally taken more and more of a hand in adjusting relations between employers and workers. The passage of the National Labor Relations Act in 1935 was a sharp departure from previous governmental policies, recognizing as it did the *right* of workers to determine by a majority vote whether or not they want to bargain collectively and which labor union they wish to represent their interests. In spite of the fact that strikes diminished greatly after the N.L.R.A. was given the stamp of constitutionality, employers still fought vigorously for the repeal or emasculation of this law.

A.F. OF L.-C.I.O. CONFLICT

A conflict also exists within the ranks of labor—between the A.F. of L. and the C.I.O. Few American social problems have received more attention in the past few years in press, pulpit, radio, courts, and administrative tribunals than the factional labor dispute between these two groups. There are two outstanding views of the causes of the division between them, and of the necessary procedure to follow to bring about a reunited labor movement. On the one hand are those who picture the conflict as essentially one between industrial unionism (C.I.O.) and craft unionism (A.F. of L.). In this sense, we have an institutional conflict.[33] On the other hand, there are those who view the dispute as one of "power politics" between the leaders of the rival organizations for control of the labor movement. Although there may be some truth to both of these positions, neither one of them is a complete explanation of the division between the two organizations.[34]

Negotiations for peace between the two groups broke down in 1937, since the leaders and members of each organization seemed to fear that the opposing group would gain more advantages.[35] Since then, other peace proposals have been caught on the sharp horns of the dilemma of uniting the labor movement, and at the same time preserving "face" for all concerned. Investigations involving members of both groups have shown rather considerable understanding of common goals and purposes.[36]

If the A.F. of L. and the C.I.O. were united, their total membership would be a powerful force in American politics and social life. However, probably only about a fifth of eligible American workers are organized into unions—a much smaller proportion than in England, France, and many other countries where class stratifications are more rigid than in America. Resistance to unions and unionization among American workers—especially among the middle-class "white-collar" workers—is largely due to our individualistic traditions.

THE AMERICAN ECONOMIC SYSTEM

During 1948 the Advertising Council conducted a nation-wide campaign to give Americans the "facts of life" about the American economic system.[37] The program, which had active support of *both* management and labor groups, was designed "to show the reasons why, in spite of its shortcomings, the American system has given us the highest standard of living and the greatest freedom in the world." Ten points stressed in the campaign were these:

1. Freedom of the individual to work in the callings and localities of his choice.

2. Freedom of the individual to contract about his affairs.

3. Freedom of the individual owner of private property to start and manage an enterprise, to invent and profit thereby, to invest in a profit and loss system, to buy and to sell in a free market—in so far as this freedom does not conflict with the public interest.

4. Freedom to speak, to inquire, and to discuss.

5. Protection for the individual—by public or private means—against the basic hazards of existence over which he may have no control.

6. Government action in economic affairs when necessary to ensure national security or to undertake socially desirable projects when private interests prove inadequate to conduct them.

7. Freest possible competition consistent with the public welfare.

8. Free collective bargaining—the right of labor to organize and to bargain collectively with employers.

9. Expanding productivity as a national necessity.

10. Increased recognition of human values a prerequisite to better living.

It is facts of this kind which are unique to the economy of the United States. Most members of our various occupational groups would probably agree on them. However, the problems of employers and employed, and divisions within the ranks of labor, still represent serious social conflicts.

In the remaining section of this book (Part VI), we shall treat some other major social conflicts in some detail. We shall examine the social psychology of delinquency, race differences, prejudices against minority groups, nationalism, and war.

QUESTIONS AND PROBLEMS FOR DISCUSSION

1. *What is meant by* (a) *horizontal differences and by* (b) *vertical differences in occupational groups?*
2. *Try writing a social-psychological analysis of the engineering profession.*
3. *List in two columns the psychological advantages and disadvantages of machine production.*
4. *Why are symbols important in class struggles?*
5. *Get some factual information about the National Labor Relations Board. To what extent is it applying sound psychological principles?*
6. *Give specific examples and illustrations of factors unique in the American economic system.*

RECOMMENDED READINGS

Bell, H. M., *Matching Youth and Jobs.* Washington, D. C.: American Youth Commission, 1940.

Brown, E. L., *Physicians and Medical Care.* New York: Russell Sage Foundation, 1937.

Brown, E. L., *Lawyers and the Promotion of Justice.* New York: Russell Sage Foundation, 1938.

Daugherty, C., *Labor Problems in American Industry* (revised edition). Boston: Houghton Mifflin Company, 1938.

Hartmann, G. W., and Newcomb, T. (editors), *Industrial Conflict: A Psychological Interpretation.* New York: The Cordon Company, 1939.

Hoover, T., and Fish, J. C. L., *The Engineering Profession.* Palo Alto: Stanford University Press, 1941.

Robinson, E. S., *Law and the Lawyers.* New York: The Macmillan Company, 1935.

Roethlisberger, F. J., and Dickson, W. J., *Management and the Worker.* Cambridge: Harvard University Press, 1939.

Williams, W., *What's On the Worker's Mind.* New York: Charles Scribner's Sons, Inc., 1920.

*Newcomb, T. M., Hartley, E. L., and others (editors), *Readings in Social Psychology.* New York: Henry Holt and Company, Inc., 1947. (The following selections are listed according to the sequence of related discussions in the chapter you have just read.)

- McGregor, D., "Conditions of Effective Leadership in the Industrial Organization," pp. 427-435.
- Katz, D., and Hyman, H., "Morale in War Industries," pp. 437-447.
- Homans, G. C., "Group Factors in Worker Productivity," pp. 448-460.
- Golden, C. S., and Ruttenberg, H. J., "Labor and Management Responsibility for Productive Efficiency," pp. 461-465.
- Davis, A., Gardner, B. G., and Gardner, M. R., "The Class System of the White Caste," pp. 467-475.
- West, J., "Learning the Class System in Plainville, U. S. A.," pp. 475-477.
- Warner, W. L., and Lunt, P. S., "The Family in the Class System," pp. 477-479.
- Centers, R., "The American Class Structure: A Psychological Analysis," pp. 481-493.

PART SIX

SOCIAL CONFLICTS

► CONFLICTS of occupational groups were described in the preceding chapter. The present section deals with some other major social conflicts of the modern world.

First of all, the bases for delinquency patterns in the community are analyzed. This is done by describing both the social and the psychological factors of gang life and delinquency areas in the modern city.

Since another major conflict centers around the question of race, a scientific analysis is given of the meaning of the term. Several popular fallacies are then discussed, especially those based on theories of racial superiority and inferiority.

This leads to a discussion of prejudices against minority groups in the United States. The psychological bases of prejudices against Negroes, Orientals, Catholics, and Jews are explained in considerable detail.

The next chapter deals with nationalism and war. The foundations of nationalistic prejudices are given in some detail, including a brief analysis of the Nazi regime. This furnishes the necessary background for a psychological analysis of modern war.

In the final chapter in this book, the question is raised, Is society logical or illogical? Various instances of social inconsistencies and conflicts are described. What can we do about them?

CHAPTER TWENTY-ONE

DELINQUENCY PATTERNS

THE COMMUNITY. The Impact of the Community—Influence of Social Groups on Personality—The City—The Nation's Capital / DELINQUENCY. The Gang—Studies of Gang Life—Attempted Solutions—Delinquency Areas—Social-Psychological Factors in Delinquency—Is Punishment the Answer?—Individual and Social Welfare—Time and Crime—Education for Crime Prevention.

▶ THE COMMUNITY

THE IMPACT OF THE COMMUNITY

The problems of the community might be broken down into a number of different considerations—neighborhood, school life, religious life, gang life, club life, village life, all the mechanisms of gossip and social interaction which go to make up the places where people exist. The neighborhood in which one lives and the play group into which he drifts are *primary* groups with intimate face-to-face associations not consciously organized. It is here that the child learns ways of behaving and thinking which are not necessarily taught him at home, and it is here that he comes into conflict with "ways" which are definitely different from the "correct" ones which he has learned in the family situation. Having previously gone through a training period of becoming "civilized" in his family group so that he can take nourishment with passable table manners, control his habits of elimination, and avoid the use of "naughty" words, he now has his personality influenced by direct contact with members of the community who are his own age or older. They define "good" and "bad" behavior, and introduce the child to the myriad of social pressures to which he must conform.

The family is the smallest social unit and the primary defining agency. As soon as the child has free motion and begins to pull, tear, pry, meddle, and prowl, the parents begin to define the situation through speech and other signs and pressures: "Be quiet," "Sit up straight," "Blow your nose," "Wash your face," "Mind your mother," "Be kind to sister," etc. . . . His wishes and activities begin to be inhibited, and gradually, by definitions within the family, by playmates, in the school, in the Sunday School, in the community, through reading, by formal instruction, by informal signs of approval and disapproval, the growing member learns the code of his society.[1]

The community in which one grows up is composed of both structural and functional elements. Structurally, a community is a consciously organized aggregation of people living in a specified area or locality endowed with political autonomy, supporting such primary institutions as schools and churches, and among whom certain degrees of interdependency are recognized. Functionally, a community is any process of social interaction which gives rise to more intensive or extensive attitudes and practices of interdependence, cooperation, collaboration, and unification. The structural factors are easily recognized, but because the other elements tend to be implicit rather than explicit, their psychological importance might be overlooked.

INFLUENCE OF SOCIAL GROUPS ON PERSONALITY

In a study of male, white, native American men who had graduated from college subsequently to 1920, elaborate data were collected by personal interviews, questionnaires, check lists, correspondence, autobiographical notes, and college records.[2] The data showed that the larger intimate groups of the church, the mixed social group, the scholastic club or social group, and the fraternity, all had tremendous effects on the personalities of these college men. Thus, in childhood and adolescence these larger intimate groups are mediums in the process of alienation from the family, acutally supplanting it in influencing personality development. By the time the youth reaches college age, these groups are the centers around which problems of social status revolve, resulting in frustration or adjustment. In all periods they are socializing agencies making for broader viewpoints, expanded contacts, balance, and a definition of status. On the less favorable side, these groups in the community may cause persons to become absorbed in nonconstructive activities, and competition between some of these groups may result in a superficial sophistication.

The contacts developed in the neighborhood and community have a great deal to do with the later personality development of the given individual, largely through the process of *conditioning*. Whether one is a farm boy or a city boy may determine not only his attitudes toward life but the activities in which he later engages. Lehman and Witty, for example, have found significant differences between the number of play activities engaged in by city boys and country boys.[3]

THE CITY

Some of our greatest social problems at the present time center around the city and city development. The types of culture traits found among city dwellers are quite different from those in rural communities. Not only are our cities swollen to monster proportions, but Mumford and others believe that modern city life is having very deleterious effects upon modern men and women.[4] In cities, elevators and skyscrapers make it possible to squeeze an incredible number of people into a space intended for a very few; and buses, streetcars, and subways allow people to spend hours and hours per week "upon an activity that has flatly no value in itself." Millions of Americans daily die the small death of the rush hour.

Instead of resorting to the usual recreational and play aspects of community life of the smaller towns and country, millions of city dwellers have fallen back on passive sedentary activities of reading, radio listening, going to the movies, and watching but not participating in sports.[5] Are these the most desirable activities available in our culture, for adequate personality development?

A factor in city life which has received the greatest amount of attention has been that of city planning, particularly with relation to slum life. Strangely enough, the principal reforms in housing have occurred only within the last thirty or forty years. With our theories of a democratic society, it formerly was not considered to be the business of the members of the community if some people therein happened to live in poverty and filth. Recently, however, through the work of government and private agencies, we are coming to realize that poverty not only has significant effects upon personality development, but that from a selfish standpoint this affects our welfare as a nation. Compare the "before-and-after" scenes shown in Figure 36.

THE NATION'S CAPITAL

Consider your national capital, Washington, D. C. If any city in the country should be free of slums, this is it. What is it actually like?

> On your right, . . . you have Washington the beautiful, a city of lush parks, broad avenues and magnificent marble monuments; a city well fitted to be the capital of a great nation. "Gateway to God," it's called in a song popular at civic celebrations.
>
> On your left you have Washington the filthy. You have a city of slums, blighted areas that give Washington one of the highest death rates in the country; areas that make it, along with the health centers of Arizona and New Mexico, one of the focal points of tuberculosis; areas that foster venereal diseases at the estimated rate of 27,000 new cases a year; areas that produce criminals in such quantities that the city [in 1937] ranked fifth among American cities in the number of burglaries, seventh in robberies and auto thefts, eighth in assaults, thirteenth in murders and among the first five in larcenies.[6]

Housing authorities have said that the slums of the nation's capital are the worst of any city in the world. Thousands of homes in the District of Columbia are illuminated only by candles or oil lamps, have no inside baths, and no sewage outlets. Neighborhood poverty and comfort exist virtually arm in arm.

Before . . . An alley slum in Charleston, S. C.

After . . . Replaced with well-built, attractive homes

FIG. 36. THE TRANSFORMATION OF A SLUM INTO AN ATTRACTIVE COMMUNITY [7]

DELINQUENCY

THE GANG

The objections which social psychologists have to slums are based not only upon their unsavory health conditions and the poverty prevailing there, but also upon the limited personality development which can be expected of the citizens produced under such conditions. One of the most serious psychological problems in the modern city, and particularly in the slum areas, is the social group known as "the gang."

What is a gang? The gang is the result of collective action and particularly conflict. Its development may be traced at first to the play group itself. In the overcrowded sections of the city where there is no playground, the children who play together in the street eventually organize into gangs. Thrasher reports a case where the children who lived on the left-hand side of the street formed a gang to fight another gang of children who lived on the other side of the street.[8] This is an illustration of the gang in its most elementary form. A gang, then, is simply a group of children or adolescents who band together to fight some other group like themselves. The gang is one of the few outlets available to break the routine existence of many boys.

Here is a type of *primary* group with intimate face-to-face contacts, and with all the attributes of the *In-group*—loyalty, cooperation, social solidarity, feeling of oneness or unity. It is a group concerned with play activities, and play has long been considered psychologically desirable.[9] Then, what is there about this primary group which makes it a social problem? A great deal of material in educational psychology has demonstrated the value of that phenomenon known as *transfer of training,* so that ways of behaving and attitudes learned in one situation may be carried over or "transferred" to a later situation. For example, if a group of subjects have mastered one maze, it is highly probable that they will do better in mastering a second maze because of their previous experience in the first maze situation. Why should it not also be true that boys growing up in a gang where loyalty, social solidarity, and cooperation are fostered as attitudes should carry over or transfer these attitudes to their adult life so that they will be better citizens? Theoretically, would it not seem probable that these attitudes, the very ones which we are demanding of adult citizens, would be best developed in gang activities? Whether this occurs depends very largely on the type of gang involved.

STUDIES OF GANG LIFE

Puffer, Furfey, and Thrasher have made elaborate investigations of gang life, and all have demonstrated that the type of gang prevalent in cities, particularly in the crowded areas, has definite antisocial aspects.[10] Studying over 1,300 gangs in Chicago, Thrasher found that they were located wherever there were slums, overcrowding, and poverty. The gang touches in one way or another almost every vital problem in the community. It is very closely connected with crime in all its aspects, corrupt politics, race riots, and delinquencies of all kinds.

On the other hand, it is also true that some "gangs" may be of a very high type and may work for the welfare of the community. The difference lies in the background and environment of the individuals who constitute the gang. You are an exception if at some time as a boy or girl you did not belong to some particular gang or close-knit play group. As to whether the group was socially desirable or not, that depended upon the activities in which you engaged. In many instances gangs have formed antisocial purposes after developing a hangout, which may be a poolroom, a deserted shack, or even a street corner.

> The neighborhood in [one case] was in a suburb of northeast Washington, D.C. Family providers, except for a doctor, were laborers. Economic status varied from low average to outright poverty. In several of the families *Ww* knew of constant friction. Alcoholism in one or both parents was common. Many of the children grew up with little or no parental guidance.
>
> Near this neighborhood were a slaughterhouse and barns in which race horses were wintered. When they were about 10 years of age many of the boys were accustomed to play about these places. Some of the group were initiated into bestiality by the laborers around the slaughterhouse. Some were also seduced into homosexual practices by men about the barns. Before *Ww* was 13 a ring of the boys from this neighborhood had formed in which these perversions were continually indulged. The homosexual practices were continued longer, and the ring was not dissolved until . . . most of the group were nearing the age of 20.[11]

Puffer found that the typical gang age is from ten to sixteen. The names which gangs attribute to themselves give some indication of the attitudes of their members: The Hicks Street Fellows, Wharf Rats, Egg-men, Dowser Glums. Most have a regular time and place of meeting, and recognized leaders. Leadership is determined very largely by who is the strongest or who is the most adept at stealing or fighting. These are interesting parallels to the dominance behavior which we have examined in infrahuman primates (Chapter 13).

The gang adopts the patterns of behavior which have prestige in its own particular environment. Since a large number of the boys live in socially isolated neighborhoods and do not come in contact with groups with different ideals, they naturally adopt unique social patterns. The language may be different, and the customs and religion may be opposed in many respects to the culture patterns of groups in other neighborhoods. The environment determines very largely the entire structure of the gang, its leaders, its activities, and any or all parts of its life as a gang. As the boys grow up, the gangs may even continue over into adult years and develop into vice rings, gambling groups, bootlegging gangs, and engage in various types of crime, involving perhaps political corruption. Of those persons from slums arrested for such crimes as burglary, robbery, and larceny, the percentage under the age of twenty-one is far above the percentage of persons arrested under twenty-one from the general population.

ATTEMPTED SOLUTIONS

These activities have existed as long as have large cities, but it is only quite recently that any very serious attempts have been made to remedy the situation. It was as late as 1868 that the first directed public playground was opened in this country, in Boston. The first boys' club which has continued in operation came into existence in 1869, but the Boys' Club movement has actually developed only in the last twenty or twenty-five years. The Society for the Prevention of Cruelty to Children had its origin in 1875. It was not until the turn of the century that juvenile courts were established in two or three cities to deal with problems of delinquency. The first White House Conference on Child Welfare was called in 1909, and not until 1912 was the Children's Bureau established by act of Congress. Even now there is considerable *cultural lag* in coping with the problems of crime and delinquency which are found in the city. Sociologists and social psychologists know what some of the solutions are, but the majority of citizens find it simpler to eliminate some of the symptoms of the "disease" by putting people in jail, by building "bigger and better" reform schools, and by having a larger police force.

The main reason for the gang's formation, as indicated, lies in the environment of the city. It is here that the attitudes, ideas, habits, and general behavior patterns of gang members are determined. We have within the gang a picture of the same sort of habits, the same sort of codes, the same desires as are found anywhere in any other group. It is an In-group banded together in conflict with other similar groups where In-group attitudes are likewise fostered. The particular turn which these In-group attitudes will take is determined by the kind of conflicts in which the gang engages, whether it is a conflict with other gangs or with the police.

DELINQUENCY AREAS

Many people seem to think that gangs are made up entirely of foreign populations and that crime is fostered in America largely by Immigrants. Interestingly enough, immigrants do not commit crimes in as high a proportion of cases as do the native-born.[12] On the other hand, the *children of immigrants* apparently contribute more than their share of delinquency. The reasons for this seem fairly obvious. Children of newcomers to our country often find themselves caught in the conflict between the culture pattern of their parents to which allegiance is demanded, and the new culture pattern found in the United States to which loyalty is also demanded by native Americans. The children of immigrant groups find themselves in a difficult psychological position because of the loyalties and ideals of the old country may conflict with the ways which obtain in America. The new *material-culture* patterns are relatively easy to learn—such as the use of mechanical refrigerators, vacuum cleaners, and the latest type radio. It is much more difficult, however, to adjust to attitudes which involve new types of patriotism, new rituals, new ways of dealing with political problems.

Delinquency areas are found in every city in those regions where there is crowding and poverty. There is less criminality, delinqency, and disease as we go out from these areas where there are adequate playgrounds, sufficient ventilation, and small numbers of people living together in one room. See Figure 37.[13] Studies have shown that children from poorer homes tend to cheat and steal more than those from more fortunate homes, and they may tend to greater neuroticism.[14] Other investigations have revealed a higher incidence of mental disorders in the population from the disorganized areas near the center of cities, as contrasted with the residential sections near the outskirts.[15]

The outstanding investigations of delinquency areas have been made by Clifford R. Shaw.[16] His original study—made under the auspices of the Chicago Institute for Juvenile Research with the cooperation of the University of Chicago, the Chicago Department of Education, the Juvenile Court, and the Police Department—covered a period of eight years, and involved data on over 100,000 individuals. In addition to his statistical data, which were taken directly from the records of the juvenile courts, schools, probation records, boys' court, and jail, a number of life histories were also secured. Rates and ratios of delinquency were computed in comparison with the total population of similar age and sex in each section. In this way the geographical distribution of truants, juvenile delinquents, and adult offenders in Chicago was determined.

Chicago had grown from a village of about two hundred to a city of more than three millions in less than a century, and at the time of the study covered over two hundred square miles. An area of heavy industry extended from the center of the city along the north and south branches of the Chicago River with other large industrial areas in the southeastern and southwestern parts of the city. These areas were fringed by light manufacturing and commerical districts which were steadily

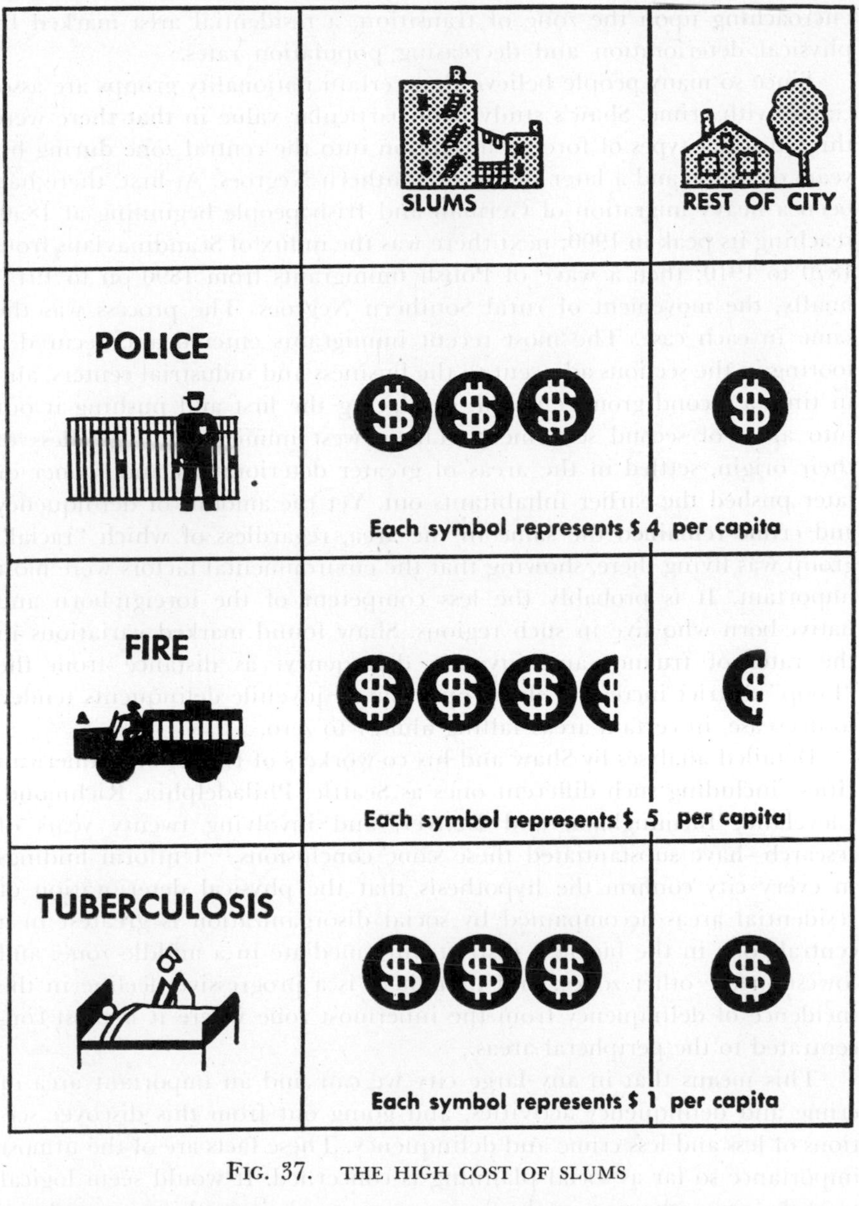

FIG. 37. THE HIGH COST OF SLUMS

The charts on this page (from Pictorial Statistics, Inc., for *Survey Graphic*) illustrate the high costs of Cleveland slums, in terms of police and fire protection, and incidence of tuberculosis. What is true in Cleveland is true in scores of other American cities. Slums cost local taxpayers a tremendous sum each year in city services.

encroaching upon the zone of transition, a residential area marked by physical deterioration and decreasing population rates.

Since so many people believe that certain nationality groups are associated with crime, Shaw's study is of particular value in that there were three distinct types of foreign migration into the central zone during his years of study, and a later influx of Southern Negroes. At first, there had been a heavy migration of German and Irish people beginning at 1850, reaching its peak in 1900; next there was the influx of Scandinavians from 1870 to 1910; then a wave of Polish immigrants from 1890 on to 1914; finally, the movement of rural Southern Negroes. The process was the same in each case. The most recent immigrants entered and secured a footing in the sections adjacent to the business and industrial centers, and in time a second group entered, displacing the first and pushing it out into areas of second settlement. The newest immigrants, regardless of their origin, settled in the areas of greater deterioration and sooner or later pushed the earlier inhabitants out. Yet the amount of delinquency and crime remained the same in the area, regardless of which "racial" group was living there, showing that the environmental factors were most important. It is probably the less competent of the foreign-born and native-born who live in such regions. Shaw found marked variations in the rates of truancy and juvenile delinqency; as distance from the "Loop" district increased, the proportion of juvenile delinquents tended to decrease, in certain areas falling almost to zero.

Detailed analyses by Shaw and his co-workers of twenty-one American cities—including such different ones as Seattle, Philadelphia, Richmond, Cleveland, Birmingham, and Denver, and involving twenty years of research—have substantiated these same conclusions.[17] Uniform findings in every city confirm the hypothesis that the physical deterioration of residential areas accompanied by social disorganization is greatest in a central zone in the business district, intermediate in a middle zone, and lowest in the other zones; and that there is a progressive decline in the incidence of delinquency from the innermost zone where it is most concentrated to the peripheral areas.

This means that in any large city we can find an important area of crime and delinquency activities, and going out from this discover sections of less and less crime and delinquency. These facts are of the utmost importance so far as social planning is concerned. It would seem logical to make some changes in the community, to do something toward the eradication of crime and delinquency. This can be accomplished to a large extent by elimination of "sweatshop" conditions, by zoning, by the construction of more playgrounds and parks, by slum clearance projects, and by modern housing developments. Delinquency can be eliminated only by getting at the causes.

SOCIAL-PSYCHOLOGICAL FACTORS IN DELINQUENCY

Of course, the type of neighborhood is not the sole cause of delinquency or crime. After all, the problem of *which* individuals become delinquent must not be overlooked.

Why do children react in such different ways to the features of their environment? Why are some able to resist the influences of bad companions and the temptations provided by unlocked automobiles, easily entered windows, alluring displays of finery, suggestions derived from newspapers and movies, or unhappiness or poverty at home, and countless other factors which contribute to make other children delinquent? Why are other children unaffected by the "temptations to right-doing" which should serve to immunize them against possible stimuli to bad conduct?[18]

When business and industry invade a neighborhood, the traditional norms and standards that formerly prevailed, because of the continuity of the groups in residence areas, tend to weaken and disappear, and the community itself ceases to be an effective means of social control. A process of selection leaves the less capable, the shiftless, and even antisocial in the community, although bad luck and physical mishaps may also keep many capable persons there. Even though some of the persons who live in these transition areas are from cultural and social backgrounds which differ widely from the new situation, the conflicts between "old" and "new" ideals tend to break down the traditional family controls. Delinquent behavior becomes tolerated in some circles, or even accepted and approved, and is transmitted just as are other cultural traits in any community.

There is also the factor of stimulation to delinquent conduct produced through association with persons with criminal tendencies. A delinquent is not so likely to commit a misdeed alone as with someone else. In 90 per cent of six thousand cases of stealing, Shaw reported that two or more boys were involved in the act.[19] According to Sheldon and Eleanor Glueck, about 95 per cent of criminals have associated with poolroom habitués, professional gamblers, habitual drunkards, or criminals.[20] It is also interesting to find that, of 953 juvenile delinquent boys followed up and investigated by the Gluecks for many years, almost 40 per cent had ceased to be criminals by the time they had reached an average age of twenty-nine.[21] However, chronological age apparently was *not* the determining factor; instead, the length of time that the tendency toward crime had lasted seemed to determine its end.

Apparently abandonment of criminal conduct does not occur at any specific chronological age-level, but rather after the passage of a certain length of time from the point of first expression of definite delinquent trends. On the whole, if the acts of delinquency begin very early in life they are apparently abandoned at a relatively early stage of manhood, provided various mental abnormalities do not counteract the natural tendency to maturation.[22]

We see, then, that *both* neighborhood and individual patterns of behavior are important in accounting for delinquency. As suggested before, community planning—such as slum clearance and the building of parks and playgrounds—is desirable in eliminating breeding places of crime and delinquency. But we must also take account of the individual. His family and his educational and religious background are of the utmost importance in determining whether he will be adequately adjusted to the standards of his society. In fact, no solution of the crime problem is possible which fails to take into consideration both the social and the individual factors.

IS PUNISHMENT THE ANSWER?

From the standpoint of social psychology, crime or delinquency is any act which violates rights of persons or property, and which is so contrary to the mores of a particular society that *if* the act were known to the members of the community, the act would be considered hazardous to the general welfare.[23] The state has punished criminals and delinqents for thousands of years, but crime is still with us on a large scale. These ideas of punishment grew up along "transcendental" and political lines.[24] According to the transcendental notion, it is a religious duty to punish criminals; this is the fulfillment of the divine mission of the state. The "stain of guilt" must be washed away by suffering. Coupled with this has been the political theory of punishment. This has been based on ideas of: (1) *retribution* or revenge—"an eye for an eye, and a tooth for a tooth"; (2) *determent*—if a criminal is punished, this will deter or prevent other criminals or potential criminals from committing similar acts; and (3) *protection*—if the criminal is locked up, he is not a menace to society. A fourth theory has also gained acceptance: (4) *reformation*—if the criminal's background and behavior are studied under a controlled environment, perhaps he can be reformed and prevented from carrying on other criminal activities.

Little can be said in justification of the theory of retribution, and there is no overwhelming body of *factual* evidence to demonstrate that punishment serves as a deterrent to crime. One study, comparing the records of prisoners in a Delaware county who had been whipped, with a group committing similar crimes but not punished by whipping, revealed that whipped prisoners were again convicted of crimes with a somewhat greater frequency than unwhipped prisoners.[25]

The third theory, of protection for society, has more to be said for it, especially in the cases of those who are psychopathic (insane) or habitual criminals. (A distinction should be made between the habitual or chronic criminal, and the "accidental" criminal who commits an offense through ignorance of the law or under extraordinary circumstances.) However, it is largely in the last approach—reformation of the criminal—that hope lies for bettering the situation. We get no place in solving the problem of crime so long as we merely become angry at those who violate the law and punish them by rule of thumb. The fact that two persons have committed the same crime does not mean that they should be dealt with alike. They may have behaved as criminals for completely different reasons. If *A* and *B* have each separately stolen $100, their legal guilt is the same, but they should be studied carefully as individuals to determine what sort of treatment each should receive.[26] *A* may be a married man who has a good record of work and has supported his family, but who has been unemployed for a long period and has become depressed, whereas *B* may be a man who has abandoned his family and for years has lived by petty crime. *A* may profit most from a suspended sentence, *B* from being institutionalized and studied.

It would be utterly absurd for a physician to say to each patient who has the grippe, "Go into the hospital and stay two weeks." "But what if I'm cured before that?" "Stay two weeks anyhow." "But supposing I'm not well in two weeks?" "Out you go just the same."[27] This would be somewhat comparable to our present system of letting the punishment fit the crime instead of the criminal.

INDIVIDUAL AND SOCIAL WELFARE

Our existing agencies for handling criminals are not well coordinated. Each is primarily concerned with its own special functions. For example, many police forces consider that they have done their work when they have made arrests; prosecutors are likely to feel that they have completed their jobs when they have secured convictions; and prison officials may believe that their tasks are well done if they have kept people in jails without letting them escape. These various legal restraints, important though they are, need to be linked throughout with study and analysis of those human beings who commit crimes and with study of how their antisocial conduct may best be controlled, directed, or eliminated.

One way this can be done is to have legal agencies decide only one thing—whether the person has committed the criminal act—and if the answer is "yes," to turn him over to a diagnostic board to determine what is to be done with him.[28] This is what has been proposed by a committee of the American Law Institute with reference to youthful offenders.[29] It is recommended that the diagnostic board or "Youth-Correction Authority" should consist of at least three members: an administrator, such as a lawyer; a sociologist, psychologist, or psychiatrist; and a specialist in problems of delinquency.

Not only do we need to give greater attention to the offender himself as a *human being,* to be studied and helped psychologically, but we must consider also the entire problem of community and individual welfare. We need to realize that much crime and delinquency have their bases in feelings of insecurity which can be remedied only by greater economic benefits and by a stimulating social life for all the people. This means the development of an adequate social-welfare program in such fields as sanitation, health, education, recreation, housing conditions, and industrial working situations.

Crime, of course, will never be eliminated by improved sanitary conditions *alone* or by better housing conditions *alone.* Nor will recreation programs be a nearly adequate solution unless the programs are well integrated. Thus, a community might be well equipped with playgrounds for children up to the teen age, but make no provision for the recreation of its youth. Young people eager to dance, to meet each other socially, and to begin to function in adult patterns can scarcely be expected to find stimulating training in the swings, the seesaws, and the sand piles of infancy. Sand piles *may be* a partial answer to the problems of a certain age; but there should also be boys' clubs, girls' clubs, and boy-and-girl clubs. And provisions should be made for adults as well. The point is that there must be a true cooperation of all agencies in a united program if the amount of crime is to be lessened.

TIME AND CRIME

But such a program takes time, and there is constant pressure to solve the *present* crime problem *now.* Yet the quickest solution is not necessarily the best one. To take an aspirin may give temporary relief from pain but does not necessarily cure disease. To lock people up may give temporary relief from crime but does not cure us of the social problems of crime.

There are three major fields of endeavor in treating problems of delinquency and crime: (1) *apprehension* of delinquents and criminals; (2) *correction* or treatment; and (3) *prevention* of crime, by studying its causes and trying to control them. Each of these fields is closely bound up with the other two. A program in any one is not very effective unless the other two fields are taken into consideration. Why apprehend delinquents and criminals without treating them? Why bother to treat them unless the causes of crime are studied so that we can treat them intelligently?

EDUCATION FOR CRIME PREVENTION

Many people are unaware of the basic causes of crime, just as men used to overlook the causes of certain diseases. When the origins of smallpox, diphtheria, and bubonic plague were not understood, these diseases were frequently attributed to some fault or "evil" in the individuals who had them; and the sick were often shunned and segregated, sometimes neglected. Only after large sections of the public had been educated about the true nature of these diseases were physicians supported with sufficient funds so that the diseases could be practically subdued. Many of the causes of crime have been known for a long time; but a truly educated and informed citizenry is necessary before any program of crime eradication can become effective.

Medical men might have been content to apprehend and "swat" yellow-fever mosquitoes indefinitely. In this way they might have relieved their anger, but would not have stamped out yellow fever. Instead, they found it necessary to study mosquitoes and yellow-fever germs. Shall we be content to "swat" criminals, or shall we also study the "germs" of crime? The answer depends on the extent to which we become informed and educated about individual and social conditions in our communities. Education for crime reduction is not just information or retention of facts (compare Chapter 17 on Education). The threefold program of apprehension, correction, and prevention of crime must affect our attitudes; for only when we become intelligently aroused about crime, its causes, and its cures can we act effectively to prevent its development and recurrence.

QUESTIONS AND PROBLEMS FOR DISCUSSION

1. *Why do the primary group loyalties of the gang not always carry over to wider social contacts?*
2. *How would you study scientifically the differences in attitudes of city dwellers and of country people?*
3. *Get a map of your own community, and see if you can plot in the high-delinquency and low-delinquency areas. From what you already know of your community, explain.*
4. *Outline a practical program of crime prevention for your own community.*

RECOMMENDED READINGS

Barnes, H. E., and Teeters, N. K., *New Horizons in Criminology: The American Crime Problem.* New York: Prentice-Hall, Inc., 1943.

Cantor, N. F., *Crime and Society: An Introduction to Criminology.* New York: Henry Holt and Company, Inc., 1939.

Carr, L. J., *Delinquency Control.* New York: Harper & Brothers, 1941.

Glueck, S., and Glueck, E. T., *One Thousand Juvenile Delinquents.* Cambridge: Harvard University Press, 1934.

Glueck, S., and Glueck, E., *Juvenile Delinquents Grown Up.* New York: Commonwealth Fund, 1940.

Harrison, L. V., and Grant, P. M., *Youth in the Toils.* New York: The Macmillan Company, 1938.

Hunt, J. McV. (editor), *Personality and the Behavior Disorders: A Handbook Based on Experimental and Clinical Research.* New York: The Ronald Press Company, 1944 (2 volumes).

Mumford, L., *The Culture of Cities.* New York: Harcourt, Brace and Company, 1938.

Shaw, C. R., with the collaboration of Zorbaugh, F. M., McKay, H. D., and Cottrell, L. S., *Delinquency Areas: A Study of the Geographic Distribution of School Truants, Juvenile Delinquents, and Adult Offenders in Chicago.* Chicago: University of Chicago Press, 1929.

Shaw, C. R., McKay, H. D., and others, *Juvenile Delinquency and Urban Areas.* Chicago: University of Chicago Press, 1942.

Sutherland, E. H., *Principles of Criminology* (3rd edition, revised). Philadelphia: J. B. Lippincott Company, 1939.

Tannenbaum, F., *Crime and the Community.* Boston: Ginn and Company, 1938.

Thrasher, F. M., *The Gang: A Study of 1,313 Gangs in Chicago.* Chicago: University of Chicago Press, 1927.

Wood, A. E., and Waite, J. B., *Crime and Its Treatment: Social and Legal Aspects of Criminology.* New York: American Book Co., 1941.

*Newcomb, T. M., Hartley, E. L., and others (editors), *Readings in Social Psychology.* New York: Henry Holt and Company, Inc., 1947: —Sutherland, E. H., "The Professional Thief," pp. 394-402.

CHAPTER TWENTY-TWO

RACE DIFFERENCES

WHAT IS RACE? Scientific Meanings of "Race"—No Psychological or Cultural Connotations—Popular Fallacies Regarding Race—(1) The Fallacy of the "Racial Average"—(2) The Fallacy of Confusing Race and Nationality—(3) The Language Fallacy—(4) The Fallacy of Confusing Race and Culture / THE QUESTION OF RACIAL INFERIORITY. Motivation of Theories of Racial Inferiority—Universal Beliefs of Superiority—History of "Races"—Recent Changes in Technology—Intelligence Testing of Races—(1) Motivation—(2) Rapport—(3) Culture—(4) Social and Economic Status—(5) Language—(6) Schooling—(7) Sampling—(8) City versus Country—(9) The Test Habit—No Superior Intelligence of Any One Race.

▶ WHAT IS RACE?

> The future peace of the world largely turns on the question whether we have, as is sometimes said and often assumed, an *instinctive* affection for those human beings whose features and colour are like our own, combined with an *instinctive* hatred for those who are unlike us. [Italics ours.] [1]

Our examination of instincts in Chapter 6 indicated that the existence of prejudices between groups is no sign that such prejudices are instinctive or unlearned. Rather, prejudices are primarily products of the environment, both individual and social. Before examining the question of what is meant by race, try filling in the blanks in Figure 38. This may give you some idea of how good you are in judging "racial" differences.

SCIENTIFIC MEANINGS OF "RACE"

According to anthropologists, there are two facts alone which are important for any definition of race. A race is a large group of people possessing in common (1) certain distinctive *physical characteristics* which are (2) *determined by heredity.*[2] Only when both of these facts can be demonstrated do we have a true race. The physical characteristics used are many: skin color, hair texture, hair color, eye form, eye color, stature, head form, nasal form, blood groups. The difficulty is that the complexities of these physical characteristics from one group to another are so great, and the individual differences within the same group are so tremendous, that no one "race" has yet been found which can be said to be true or "pure."

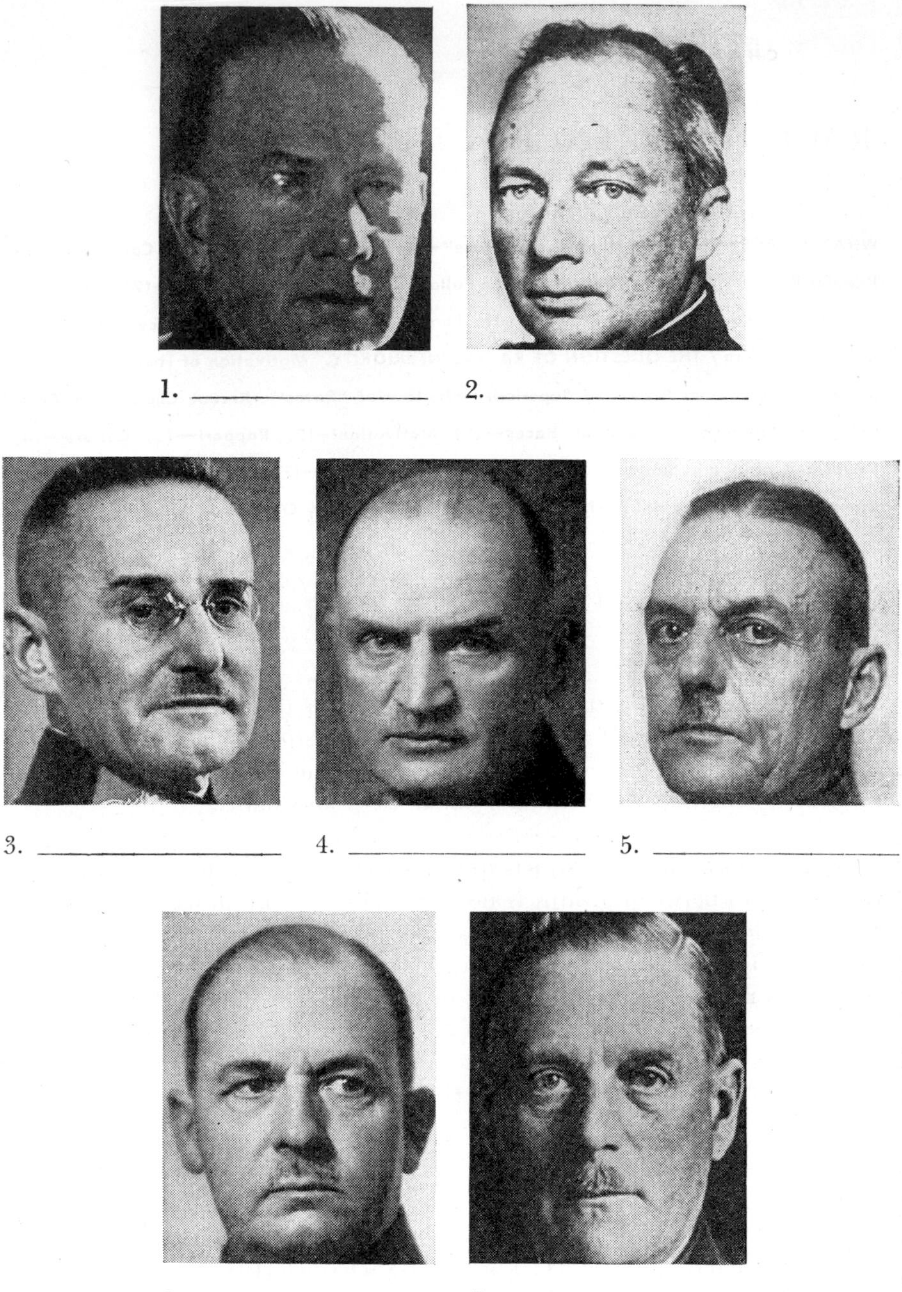

FIG. 38. A PROBLEM IN JUDGING "RACE" DIFFERENCES[3]

In each of the seven spaces, write what "race" or nationality you think the man is (answers will be found at the end of the chapter).

One investigator lists seventeen main races and twenty-nine subraces.[4] By various arbitrary divisions, classifications may vary from three to three hundred.[5]

Take, for instance, *head shape*. Certain Africans and northern Europeans are very much alike in this respect. As to *skin color*, many north and central Europeans are alike, as are certain Negroes and native Australians. In *hair* texture, Australians and Mongolians are much alike. Accordingly, most anthropologists now limit themselves to a description of races in terms of three stereotyped forms, namely, the Negroid or "black," the Mongoloid or "yellow-brown," and the Caucasian or "white."[6] In doing this, they are perfectly aware that they are engaging in the *stereotyping* process, and that it is impossible to find a "pure" white, yellow-brown, or black race.

NO PSYCHOLOGICAL OR CULTURAL CONNOTATIONS

Anthropologists are even more convinced, however, that a differentiation of races in terms of cultural and psychological characteristics will not hold water. There may be some *psychological* differences between races, but they are so small and there is so much overlapping from one group to another as not to warrant any discrimination on account of race. No conclusive evidence has yet been found for innate racial differences in either intelligence or personality. For political and economic reasons, some people—not anthropologists—have insisted that a common habitat or a common type of language will differentiate one racial group from another; yet these are cultural characteristics which shift from one period of time to another, and from one part of the world to another. In Germany during Hitler's regime, the "pure" Germans were supposed to be psychologically superior to the scapegoats, the German Jews, while in our country the supposedly superior psychological characteristics of white Americans are often contrasted with those of Negroes.

As we shall see, a scientific, *objective* examination reveals that these notions are untrue. Anthropologically, there is no such thing as pure race in the sense in which the word "race" is popularly used. And there are comparatively few groups that are relatively "pure" in the sense of no intermarriage with members of other groups. The following resolution was passed unanimously some years ago by the American Anthropological Association: "Race involves the inheritance of similar physical variations by large groups of mankind, but its psychological and cultural connotations, if they exist, have not been ascertained by science."[7] In spite of anthropological resolutions, however, the term race exists and will no doubt continue to exist in the popular sense, that is, including supposed psychological and cultural differences.

POPULAR FALLACIES REGARDING RACE

There are a number of popular fallacies regarding race which should be considered in some detail.

1. *The Fallacy of the "Racial Average."* First of all, there is the fallacy of the "average individual."[8] Simply to know what the averages of two groups are, without knowing anything about the individual differences within each group, means little. Because the average score of one group on some characteristic differs from the average of another group, it does *not* follow that all members of one group differ from members of the other. Take such a simple example as physical height:

> If we are told that in a group of, say, twenty individuals "the average height is 5 feet 6 inches" we know nothing of the composition of the group. It may, for instance, consist of ten giants of 6 feet 6 inches and ten dwarfs of 4 feet 6 inches. If to the statement is added the additional qualification that the extremes are 5 feet and 6 feet, we still know nothing definite of the group except that it contains no dwarfs and no giants. It may consist of ten tall individuals of 6 feet and ten short individuals of 5 feet or it may contain one individual of 5 feet, one of 6 feet, and eighteen of 5 feet 6 inches. And there is an infinity of possibilities between these extremes.[9]

Another example is that of a track meet or horse race. You are much more concerned with what your favorite does in a particular race than with what the average running time is for *all* the contestants. The point is that in giving results on particular groups, a mere statement of what the average, or mean, is with regard to some physical or psychological characteristic tells you little about the characteristics of the group as a whole, or about one member of the group. Yet in this matter of racial differences, a tendency exists to talk in terms of averages, even though no average individual exists. There are certain physical characteristics which are supposed to be found among Swedes, Italians, South Africans, Australian Bushmen, or Chinese, for example. But when we examine the characteristics within each group, we find that there is a greater tendency toward differences within the group than there is a tendency of all members of the group to be alike. Scandinavians are thought of as tall, blond, and long-headed. Yet in one study of Swedish army recruits, only 11 per cent of the entire group were found to be "typical" Nordics; and in another investigation using less rigorous criteria the figure was 30 per cent.[10]

> When two races are described as differing in any particular physical feature—for example, in stature—strictly speaking, this ought to mean that every member of the one race differs in that respect from every member of the other. Actually, when Mongoloids (for example, Japanese) are described as short, and North Europeans (for example, Swedes) as tall, this does not mean that all Japanese have the same (short) stature, nor that every Japanese is shorter than every Swede. Japanese vary greatly, and so do Swedes, and there is a great deal of

overlapping—that is to say, there are many Japanese who are taller than many Swedes.[11]

In other words, tremendous individual physical differences exist in any one group with regard to a given factor. Each group also runs the gamut from idiots to geniuses, with the majority falling somewhere in between. Since overlapping is always found between two groups with regard to any given characteristic, it becomes practically impossible to make any sweeping generalizations about one racial group which will not apply to some others as well. Race theories exist for most of us in order that we may pigeonhole our ideas and reactions to large groups of people. Objective thinking is difficult; it is simpler to have neat little categories into which other persons can be classified, even though all do not conform to the stereotype.

2. *The Fallacy of Confusing Race and Nationality.* A second false belief may be called the nation fallacy; that is, "race" is equated with "nation." This represents a confusion between genetic and political concepts. Race is based on physiological characteristics. Nation is a political term, implying boundaries and government.

> A nation is a group of people with a common tract of country, bound together in a common State by common history, common sentiment and traditions, common social organization, and usually (though not always, as for example Belgium or Switzerland) by common language.[12]

Again, however, the mere fact that nation and race do not square with each other does not prevent people from thinking of national boundaries as representing racial groups. The average person thinks of a British, German, Italian, or Japanese "race" largely because of political boundaries which represent nationality classifications, plus language and culture differences. Although there are no *pure* races among modern nations, few people are in danger of mistaking a *group* of Orientals for Occidentals, or for that matter a *group* of Spaniards for Swedes.

3. *The Language Fallacy.* A third fallacy is that of language as a means of differentiating races. There is a common misconception that language, or means of communication, may be regarded as a criterion of race. Three outstanding examples are the "Latin race," the "Aryan race," and the "Semitic race." The Latin race seems to include popularly French, Italians, Spaniards, Portuguese, Rumanians, Mexicans, and other "Latin Americans." Yet an examination of these groups reveals tremendous *cultural* differences among them. And so far as physical characteristics are concerned, it is impossible to distinguish a *pure* racial type in any of these nationalities.

A second instance of the same fallacy concerns the supposed Semitic race. All that the term "Semitic" means scientifically is a type of language which has been common historically both to Arabic and Hebrew groups. There are so many individual differences within the various Arabic and Jewish groups scattered over the face of the earth, both as to physical characteristics, and more especially as to cultural characteristics, that it is impossible ethnologically to speak of a pure Jew or pure Arab.

Perhaps the most blatant instance of this fallacy is the one long current in Germany concerning an "Aryan" race which was supposed to have existed in pure form long, long ago but to have been contaminated by "foreign" elements. Actually the word "Aryan" has no meaning scientifically so far as physical characteristics are concerned, but refers to a *language*. It would be just as sensible to speak of a long-headed dictionary or a wide-headed grammar as to talk of Aryan race, Aryan blood, Aryan eyes and hair.[13]

4. *The Fallacy of Confusing Race and Culture.* In addition to confusing language differences with racial differences, there is also the mistaken notion that races can be distinguished from each other by differences in culture. Differences in traditions, folkways, techniques of using machines, ways of dressing, the social institutions of the state, the school, the church, the club, and all of those culture patterns which we have previously examined, are supposed to indicate innate race differences. But there is no basis whatsoever for speaking of any of these differences as innate or racial. Different "ways" are learned in the environment in which a particular individual or group lives.

The supposed Jewish race is a case in point. Jews living in Spain, Germany, France, England, and the United States have culture characteristics which are very much like the patterns of the society in which they live. Although Jews have maintained a certain common identity over many, many generations, the majority of their characteristics can be traced to matters of a religious and, therefore, cultural sort—traditions which continue to be found in various nations over the world but which also contain an infiltration of the culture characteristics of the nations in which they live. The word "Jewish" refers to a *religion,* and the word "Hebrew" to one of the Semitic *languages.* (But these are far from universal among the younger generation of Jews.) Racial traits are even less homogeneous than religion and language.

▶ THE QUESTION OF RACIAL INFERIORITY

MOTIVATION OF THEORIES OF RACIAL INFERIORITY

A belief of far-reaching import is that of the supposed *racial* inferiority of certain groups. This is perhaps best illustrated by the recent history of mankind, where white peoples have tended to dominate those with black skins. Domination has been taken as evidence not only that Negroes are mentally inferior to white persons, but that they never can be raised to the level of whites. People have thus been able to dominate blacks and then rationalize cruel or discriminatory treatment by explaining that Negroes are after all not only totally different from other species of men, but actually are lower forms of human life.

The most curious example of the belief in racial inferiority is the notion that of the three great "racial" groups—the Mongolian, Negroid, and Caucasian—the Negroes stand so low in the scale of development that they are closely related to the ape form. This notion has grown up since doctrines of evolution have been widely preached. Yet if we classify Negro, Caucasian, and Mongolian groups according to their physical characteristics, many in each group have physical traits that make them seem more physically like the ape forms of life than representatives of the other groups.[14]

UNIVERSAL BELIEFS OF SUPERIORITY

The tendency to look upon Negroes as a mentally inferior group is simply one striking instance of the universal belief that those who differ from us physically are inferior persons. Where language or other culture characteristics, such as manner of dress or ornamentation, seem to differentiate one group from another, people tend to believe that the groups are biologically different, even though there is no real evidence for this. Furthermore, people tend to believe that those groups over the world who resemble them in language, political behavior, or any cultural characteristics, are superior to those who differ from them. The next step is simply to believe that the supposed inferiorities of these other groups are due to biological differences which cannot be overcome. The Aryan myth in Germany during World War II was an excellent example of this. Just as Americans tend to think of themselves as superior to all other peoples, the people of Germany were taught to believe to an even greater extent that persons not of Germanic origin were inferior to them. (See Chapter 24 for an explanation.) The *Nazi Primer* and *Mein Kampf* are full of examples of this belief.[15]

HISTORY OF "RACES"

People take it for granted that because one particular nationality or culture group is now prominent that it is, therefore, biologically superior to other groups. History reveals, however, that many of the supposedly inferior groups of several hundred years ago are now, in the twentieth century, "superior" groups. In ancient times, the people of the Italian peninsula lived in fear of the "inferior" invaders from the North. In the early history of Germany, people worried about the "horrible Huns" who were invading the region. Differences in development in a few hundred, or even a few thousand, years are insignificant as compared with the age of mankind; a relative backwardness of a people today does not prove that they are biologically inferior. The so-called proofs of inborn inferiority of any one race as compared with any other have usually been invented for political and economic reasons, or else are beliefs which we naïvely take for granted.

RECENT CHANGES IN TECHNOLOGY

Because we live in a machine civilization with tremendous natural resources, we tend to regard ourselves as intellectually superior to those groups that are called "primitive." But stop a moment to consider how very recent are many of the changes in our own civilization. You live in a type of world which is completely different from that of your great-great-grandmothers. In fact, there were so few technological changes from the time of Aristotle until the latter part of the nineteenth century that in many respects your great-great-grandparents were living under almost the same sort of primitive conditions which existed many hundreds of years ago. We have brought about technological changes with an amazing rapidity in the last three generations, but this does not necessarily indicate that we have suddenly developed a *biological* superiority as compared with the more primitive groups, which have simpler patterns of material culture.

"Inventions and discoveries of practical value to the race were few and far between until the dawn of the nineteenth century. Then, it seemed, the floodgates opened and in rapid succession we acquired the cast-iron plow, the cotton gin, the high-pressure steam engine, the screw propeller, the electromagnet, the telegraph, vulcanized rubber, the sewing machine, the electric locomotive, the air-brake, celluloid, the quadruplex telegraph, the telephone, the talking machine, the typewriter, the incandescent lamp, the trolley car, the automatic knot-tying harvester machine, the transparent photograph film, electric welding, calcium carbide, carborundum, electrolytic alkali production, the motion-picture machine, disk plows, high-speed steel, the airplane, wireless telegraphy—to say nothing of monstrous devices for havoc and destruction in war."

During this period of a hundred years, it is certain that more inventions were registered in the patent offices than had appeared before in the history of the world, and it is incredible that in so short a time the inventive ability of the white race should have improved in proportion to the variety and complexity of these inventions. It means only that a greater number of men were working on these problems in a specialized way, with superior techniques, on the basis of a greater body of accumulated data.[16] [See last section of Chapter 14 on invention.]

. . . .

> When the white man came into possession of gunpowder and the gun the fate of the [primitive] races was sealed; you cannot hold out with slings, spears, clubs, blowguns, and bows and arrows against rifles. And yet the ingenuity incorporated in the blowgun and bow and arrow is not inferior to that of the gun. The natives of the Amazon-Orinoco region and of the Malay Peninsula who puffed through the stalk of bamboo a tiny arrow no larger than a knitting needle but tipped with the deadly curare or the juice of the upas tree had developed a device involving as much "mind" as the one where a bullet is projected through a metal tube by a puff of powder.
>
> When, in fact, we consider that inventions emerge in proportion to the materials and techniques already accumulated by a society it is more difficult to understand the invention of the bow and arrow than that of the gun. . . . No one has been able to suggest any model in nature from which the clever contrivance of bow and arrow could have been derived.
>
> Similarly the West Africans invented a system of distant speaking which showed as much or more original "mind" than modern telegraph. Taking advantage of the tonal quality of their language, the natives were able to communicate at a distance, literally speak, by means of a drum language. We shall never be able to do this because our language lacks the tonal quality.[17]*

As for modern mankind, racial inferiority of any group is difficult to demonstrate. In a well-controlled study of Europeans, Klineberg found no significant differences in intelligence between Nordic, Alpine, and Mediterranean groups.[18] Many a tourist has found that there are differences in behavior from one part of Europe to another, but this is no proof of any *innate* differences in intelligence or of biological differences of any kind.

INTELLIGENCE TESTING OF RACES

Intelligence tests have produced interesting differences in *average* scores between races. But this evidence is not conclusive. Many people seem to believe that intelligence tests are no good at all, or else that they are foolproof. The truth lies some place between these extremes. This is largely because the administration and scoring of intelligence tests is a social-psychological problem; that is, the attitudes and ways of behaving of both the tested and the testers affect the scores of individuals and of groups. Among the many factors which may account for apparent differences in intelligence-test scores between groups, the following are especially important:

1. *Motivation.* As an example, Klineberg discovered that among the Dakota Indians, it is considered rather bad form for an individual who is being tested to answer a question in the presence of someone who does

not know the answer.[19] Such factors of motivation might seriously affect intelligence scores.

2. *Rapport.* Klineberg also tells of administering intelligence tests in Italy; a teacher showed him what one boy had written as his daily theme:

> Today a foreign doctor came to the school and the teacher told me to go alone with him into another room. I was terribly afraid and commended myself to the Holy Virgin. As I left the classroom I asked Pietro to say an Ave Maria for me. But the doctor only wanted me to do some puzzles for him.[20]

With such an attitude on the part of the person tested, it would seem doubtful if the score obtained was representative of his true intelligence level. This same problem sometimes arises with the administration of intelligence tests to Negro children. A white tester may not have the same rapport with Negro subjects as a Negro tester. Would it make any difference in your performance if an intelligence test were administered to you, a white person, by a very dark Negro?

3. *Culture.* Various test questions illustrate how much culture patterns influence test scores. The following completion question on one test assumes a definite cultural background: " — should prevail in churches and libraries." Various Southern Negro children do not necessarily consider "silence" to be the correct answer, for after all they have observed that silence is neither expected nor desired in church situations. "Why should all parents be made to send their children to school?" The correct answer is that "school prepares the child for his later life"; but various American Indian groups have found that this is not true, that schooling has unfitted them for life on an Indian reservation. In a picture-completion test, a house is shown lacking a chimney, and the child is required to draw the missing part. A Sicilian child drew in a crucifix, since his experience had taught him that no house was complete without one.[21]

> Speed is regarded as a value in western, and particularly in American, civilization. Children learn very rapidly that the "race is to the swift," and they will tend to work quickly at their tasks, even when there is no special instruction to hurry. In other communities, for example, among the American Indians, children may be specifically taught to think carefully before they act, and not to answer before they are sure of what they say. [In a study] in which White and Indian children were compared by means of a series of performance tests in the Pintner-Paterson scale, there was a very striking qualitative difference in the way the two groups worked. Typically, the White child jumped at the task, tried out a piece quickly in a succession of positions until he had hit upon the right one, finished the test rapidly, but with a relatively large number of errors. The Indian child, though he received the same instructions, looked at

the problem very carefully, slowly and cautiously picked up one of the pieces, put it in the right place, and slowly and cautiously went on to the next. He usually took much longer than the White child, but he made fewer errors.[22]

4. *Social and Economic Status.* Differences in intelligence-test scores may likewise be attributed in part to differences in social background and environmental influences. For example, familiarity with books—more characteristic of some cultures than of others—is an aid to language facility and speed on many intelligence tests. There is a close correspondence between standing in terms of intelligence scores and status in terms of socio-economic groupings.

5. *Language.* The language of the test itself, and the instructions of the examiner as well, are important in determining what intelligence-test scores will be. The mere translation of an intelligence test into another language does not mean that the culture characteristics of another group have been taken into account. Language involves more than mere grammar and sentence construction. Consider whether there would be any differences in your performance on an intelligence test if the test instructions were given orally by a Scotsman with a decided accent as compared with a native of your community.

6. *Schooling.* It has sometimes been jokingly said that intelligence tests test whatever it is that the tests test. Certainly there is abundant evidence that the tests include many of the same factors as those involved in schooling. "It is estimated by Kelley that some ninety per cent of a general intelligence test and an all-around achievement (i.e., scholastic) test measure the same thing."[23] This accounts in part for the very high relation between intelligence-test scores and grades in school.

Are the intelligence-test scores, then, to be taken as final answers to the question of differences in intelligence when one group has had a type of schooling different from that of another group? As an example, four years in a Southern rural Negro school are far from equivalent to four years in a white school in Chicago.

7. *Sampling.* The problem of selecting a group of individuals in one culture who may be considered sufficiently typical to compare with a "representative" group of another culture is a difficult one to solve. Suppose that you make a comparison of a thousand Chinese and a thousand English children on test scores. This is no guarantee that you have groups who are representative of all Chinese or Englishmen—the Chinese children might be from the families of coolies and peasants, the English children from the families of the English landed gentry. In other words, this would not be a typical cross section of either Chinese or English.

8. *City versus Country.* There are many instances where items on intelligence-test scores are fairer to persons with a city background than to those with a rural background.

The comprehension questions at year VI are specifically difficult, and somewhat unfair, for a rural group. The child is asked, "What is the thing for you to do,

(*a*) If it is raining when you start to school,
(*b*) If you find that your house is on fire,
(*c*) If you are going some place and miss your car (or trolley, or bus, according to local usage)?"

The city child is much more likely to have experienced a definite regime in connection with the first question; experience with fires and fire engines is more common in the city, as is also experience with electric cars. These rural children are all familiar with automobiles, but many of them have never heard of cars or busses as common carriers.[24]

Studying Negro children coming from the South to live in Harlem, Klineberg found a close relation between higher intelligence-test scores and length of residence in New York, at least for the first five or six years after moving there.[25]

9. *The Test Habit.* American children, especially in the cities, have been bombarded with all sorts of tests through grade and high school. They become "test-wise." There is consequently real difficulty in comparing their test scores with those of people in other cultures who are experiencing the tests for the first time.

NO SUPERIOR INTELLIGENCE OF ANY ONE RACE

These factors are given so that you may take them into account in making any sort of objective comparisons between various groups. Many intelligence tests are both reliable and valid, but there is no conclusive evidence as yet for any great differences between various races in terms of intelligence-test scores. "We may fairly say that if we were to select the best third of mankind, according to intellect and personality, every one of the large races would be represented in that group."[26]

QUESTIONS AND PROBLEMS FOR DISCUSSION

1. *Is it instinctive for human beings to like persons like themselves and to hate persons unlike themselves?*
2. *Why does the word "race" mean so many different things to different people?*
3. *What are the foundations of most of the prejudice that exists regarding questions connected with race?*
4. *Why do you think that your own "race" is more intelligent than others?*
5. *What are some of the reasons for* social distance *between races?*

RECOMMENDED READINGS

Barzun, J., *Race: A Study in Modern Superstition.* New York. Harcourt, Brace and Company, 1937.

Benedict, R., *Race: Science and Politics.* New York: Modern Age Books, Inc., 1940.

Benedict, R., and Weltfish, G., *The Races of Mankind.* Washington, D. C.: Public Affairs Pamphlets, 1943, No. 85, pp. 31.

Benedict, R., and Weltfish, G., *In Henry's Backyard: The Races of Mankind.* New York: Henry Schuman, 1948.

Boas, F., *The Mind of Primitive Man* (revised edition). New York: The Macmillan Company, 1938.

Hankins, F. H., *The Racial Basis of Civilization: A Critique of the Nordic Doctrine* (revised edition). New York: Alfred A. Knopf, Inc., 1931.

Huxley, J. S., and Haddon, A. C., *We Europeans: A Survey of "Racial" Problems.* New York: Harper & Brothers, 1936.

Klineberg, O., *Race Differences.* New York: Harper & Brothers, 1935.

Linton, R. (editor), *The Science of Man in the World Crisis.* New York: Columbia University Press, 1945.

*Newcomb, T. M., Hartley, E. L., and others (editors), *Readings in Social Psychology.* New York: Henry Holt and Company, Inc., 1947: —Klineberg, O., "Negro Intelligence and Urban Residence," pp. 24-33.

The men in Figure 38 are all Germans; they were generals and commanders in the German army during World War II.

CHAPTER TWENTY-THREE

PREJUDICES AGAINST MINORITY GROUPS

FOUNDATIONS OF PREJUDICE AGAINST MINORITY GROUPS. Psychological Reality of Race—Reality of Race Prejudice—Bases of Prejudices—Minority Groups—Frustration and Aggression—Can Prejudices Be Changed?—Difficulties of Changing Prejudices / PREJUDICES AGAINST NEGROES. Difficulty of Objectivity—Two Questions—Stereotyped Beliefs—Constant Reinforcement of Stereotypes—Educational Status of Negroes—Inequality of Opportunity—Cultural Factors Affecting Intelligence-test Scores—"Mixed Blood"—Development of Prejudices against Negroes—Northern and Southern Attitudes—Violence against Negroes / PREJUDICES AGAINST ORIENTALS. Immigration of Chinese—Immigration of Japanese—The Chinese as an Out-group—The Japanese as an Out-group—Economic Competition / ANTI-CATHOLIC AND ANTI-SEMITIC PREJUDICES. Various Types of Religious Prejudice—Anti-Catholicism and Anti-Semitism—The Spread of Anti-Semitism—Bases of Anti-Catholicism and Anti-Semitism—Psychological Analysis of Anti-Semitism—(1) Distinguishing Characteristics of Jews—(2) History of Jews—(3) Competition—(4) Projection and the Scapegoat Mechanism—(5) Recent European History—(6) Jews Represented Both as Capitalists and as Communists—(7) Propaganda Devices—Conclusion.

▶ FOUNDATIONS OF PREJUDICE AGAINST MINORITY GROUPS

PSYCHOLOGICAL REALITY OF RACE

In spite of all that has been said in the preceding chapter, *race* is very real to most people, and so is race prejudice. Why? The answer is a psychological one. Even though certain things do not exist logically, if most people believe these things to exist, they have psychological reality for them. Even though the notions of sharp distinctions between so-called races can be disproved by objective measurement, a given race is a reality to those who think of the people as a race. The word "race" is an abstraction which represents a mythical average which we conjure up for ourselves.

. . . A word is not to be defined by what it should mean but rather by what people have come to use it to mean. . . . Political leaders, agitators, men in the street certainly have a definite idea of what they mean by race. A concept, however erroneous, is of major sociological significance when it has become so vital that men will die in its defense.[1]

REALITY OF RACE PREJUDICE

Racial prejudice likewise has tremendous reality. The shapes of noses, the colors of skins, the textures of hair, prove very convenient ways for most people to think of their fellows, and serve as pegs on which to hang the cultural characteristics of various groups. And people think that they *know* what the supposedly inferior characteristics of various races are. Social psychologists can—and sometimes do—talk themselves blue in the face, unsuccessfully attempting to convince other persons that *innate* psychological differences in racial groups have not as yet been clearly demonstrated.

BASES OF PREJUDICES

Of course, the existence of racial and religious prejudices is not surprising. Throughout this book we have seen the bases for them. Some of these are: *generalization* of conditioned responses, *differentiation* of responses, *traumatic experiences,* and acceptance of *ready-made attitudes;* the desires for *security* and for *recognition;* propaganda, and the growth of *myths* and *legends; subliminal stimulation* and *stereotyping; compensation, rationalization, identification, regression, projection, suggestion,* and *imitation; crowd and audience behavior, crazes, fads,* and *fashions;* factors of *dominance* and *prestige;* and the *influence of leaders.* These various influences have been felt principally through the medium of the *social institutions*—especially the *family, school, church, fraternity* and *club, political party,* and *occupational group.*

MINORITY GROUPS

Since people have so naturally come to hold their beliefs and prejudices about other groups, they can then use these beliefs as justification for aggression against other races and religions, especially against minority groups. Wherever minority groups exist, prejudices and conflicts arise.[2]

> Somebody should write a handbook on how to create a minority group. . . . Actually there are definite rules in the game of creating them. First you have to label them, and you may choose a classification by skin color, by sex, by religion, by occupation, by whether they live north or south of the Mason and Dixon Line, or on the wrong side of the tracks, or whether they came to America before or after 1890. According to your taste, you can put one hundred people in one pigeonhole or distribute these same people into a hundred differently labeled pigeonholes. However arbitrary the classification, you write your label with a capital letter, and your description as if everybody in the group could be identified by the same traits. You give this group special treatment, special dis-

abilities, special taboos—and, sure enough, it becomes special. It does not take long. Lines of cleavage emerge under your eyes; both sides take up the cudgels. Obviously you were right in the criteria you chose for your minority group, for now the minority group is fenced off and fighting. The schism grows.[3]

This is a special instance of rivalry between the In-group and the Out-group. It is a two-way process, those in the minority being in conflict with the more dominant In-group, as well as vice versa. Differences in culture patterns cause mutual antagonism. The major culture pattern in this country has always been *white-Occidental-Protestant.* Most people of this dominant group in American life manifest various prejudices against "outsiders" who do not conform to the more prevalent racial and religious standards. We shall be concerned in this chapter with the attitudes of the majority group directed against Negroes, Orientals, Catholics, and Jews.

FRUSTRATION AND AGGRESSION

Where the rivalry between any of these groups and the dominant group becomes acute, the result is a feeling of *frustration* by members of both groups. And reactions to frustration may be as diversified as shame and embarrassment, withdrawal, regression, feelings of guilt and remorse, resistance, anger, or aggression.[4] In a great many instances of frustration, aggression is quite marked.[5] For example, at a boys' camp subjects were forced to take a long, tedious examination and were not allowed to attend the movies; their ratings of Japanese and Mexicans before and after the examination were much lower in the second instance. Again, after undergoing some very annoying social experiences and frustrations, subjects rated their friends much lower on a personality scale than did a control group who had not been subjected to these experiences. Lippitt and others, studying groups of boys placed under autocratic, democratic, and "laissesz-faire" leadership, found that hostility, aggression, and apathy were much more common while autocratic control was operating.[6] Much of the aggression was directed toward "scapegoat" members of the group rather than toward the autocrat. The point is that where tensions and conflicts arise, there is often the necessity for someone or something "to take it out on." In the case of prejudices, the scapegoat is usually some convenient minority group.

CAN PREJUDICES BE CHANGED?

Can anti-Negro, anti-Oriental, anti-Catholic, and anti-Jewish attitudes be changed? Most people with such views cannot be changed in their prejudices. The main possibility is a change of attitudes with new generations; that is, little can be done about prejudices against minority groups until a new generation comes along. Present-day prejudices can be decreased, however, by removing economic sources of rivalry and friction, and by education of children from the cradle on in certain ways of believing. In an analysis of the development of nationality and racial attitudes, Meltzer has found that children with the largest number of intense dislike reactions have a deep sense of personal insecurity.[7]

In Chapter 7 experiments were reported in changing attitudes by movies and editorials. But deep-seated prejudices are not altered suddenly by any one panacea. Living as neighbors with Negroes and going to a mixed school, for example, have been found insufficient to overcome prejudices against Negroes.[8] And adolescent years are apparently too late to do much about changing prejudices; at least, college courses dealing with American race problems have had little or no measurable effect in changing the attitudes of students.[9]

There is one experiment, however, which has demonstrated a slight change in attitude by association with an Out-group.[10] White students in New York City were invited to participate in two week-end visits to Harlem in which they were to come in close contact with Negroes. Forty-six of 354 students accepted the invitation, and for two successive week-ends heard addresses by a prominent Negro editor, a Negro surgeon, and a Negro novelist; had tea with Negro college groups; ate lunch at a Negro social worker's club; visited Negro churches and hospitals; went to a party at the home of a distinguished Negro where they met three outstanding Negroes—a poet, an artist, and a musician. Comparison of these subjects with forty-six individuals who did not accept the invitation showed statistically significant changes in the direction of favorable attitude toward Negroes. One criticism of the study is, of course, that perhaps those individuals who accepted the invitations were already somewhat predisposed to have their attitudes changed in this direction.

DIFFICULTIES OF CHANGING PREJUDICES

One great obstacle in the way of any change in attitudes is the fact that the members of the majority group have not lived as members of the minority groups. For example, no white person has ever lived as a Negro, growing up in a Negro family and being treated as a Negro, and therefore, cannot ever completely understand the Negro point of view. Where someone has grown up surrounded by people of another group, his point of view may be unique. Pearl Buck grew up in China among Chinese and says of this background:

> This has given me an invaluable training in detachment, so that I am able to look at white people as though I were not one of them. Indeed, there have been times when I wished I were not one of them, when I wished I had not a drop of white blood in my veins. I have seen white men and women so stupid in their ignorance and arrogance, so much a disgrace to the very race in

which they took pride, that I have despised them and been ashamed that my skin was like theirs.[11]

Most people in the majority group not only have not lived with members of minority groups, but ordinarily they never come in contact with them except in business transactions. They know almost nothing of the home life, religious values, customs, and beliefs of the other peoples except by hearsay and fictionalized accounts. How many white Protestant Americans, for example, ever discuss community problems with a Negro, consult a Chinese or Japanese physican, go to school to members of Catholic orders, or eat dinner in the homes of Jews?

PREJUDICES AGAINST NEGROES

DIFFICULTY OF OBJECTIVITY

As we have emphasized previously, man is not always a logical animal; at least, he is logical only on those subjects on which he wishes to be, and not always even then. When people discuss subjects on which their minds are already made up, or on which they already have a set of prejudices and definite beliefs, they may behave in the most irrational fashion. For this reason it is difficult for a great many persons to consider the problem of anti-Negro prejudice objectively.

TWO QUESTIONS

Ask yourself two questions, and you can determine whether you are going to be objective. First of all, what is the connotation for you of the word "black"? For many people it seems that the word "black" or "dark" is associated with evil, misery, dirt, filth, and related items; whereas "white" tends to be associated with purity, nobility, uplift, and cleanliness. In discussing people with "black" skins, this association should not carry over.

Second, ask yourself some questions concerning your actual acquaintanceship with individual Negroes. These people, just as much as whites, range in occupations from those who perform the most menial tasks to those in the professions. Now, how many Negroes have you known who are engaged in menial performances—cooks, charwomen, car washers, bus boys, house servants, janitors, and the like? Your answer may easily be in the dozens. Now, ask yourself a related question—how many individual Negroes have you known in such occupations as teaching, engineering, law, medicine, advertising, and selling? Your answer to this question may approximate zero. Does this selective acquaintanceship influence your appraisal of the abilities of Negroes?

STEREOTYPED BELIEFS

The reason for these questions is that it is important for you to base your judgments not simply upon those individual Negroes with whom you have come in contact but also on the other Negroes who fall at various positions along the occupational scale. Judgments by white persons of Negroes often fail to take account of the Negro tradesmen, independent workmen, and professional persons, who differ as much from the domestic servants as the white physician or tradesman differs from the white unskilled laborer. It would be equally unfair, of course, to base judgments only on those Negroes who are in the professions. In either instance the stereotyping fallacy would be committed.

Most of the common stereotyped beliefs about the Negro, however, tend to be based on the characteristics of those at the lower end of the economic scale. According to the popular stereotype, the Negro is an individual of very low mentality. He is considered immoral, or else "unmoral," and is regarded as having criminal tendencies, being physically unattractive, highly emotional, lazy, happy-go-lucky, boisterous, bumptious, overassertive, and "childish." The terms sensual, shiftless, mentally inferior, filthy, untruthful, undependable, savage, careless, are common stereotypes.[12] Some other commonly accepted beliefs about Negroes are:

> That a Negro's vote may always be readily bought for a dollar.
>
> That all male Negroes can sing.
>
> That whenever a Negro is educated he refuses to work. . . .
>
> That all Negroes who show any intelligence are two-thirds white. . . .
>
> That a Negro ball always ends up in a grand free-for-all fight in which several Negroes are mortally slashed with razors.[13]

Stereotyping of Negroes in terms of personal views sometimes occurs even in scientific books. Thus, one student of behavior lets his prejudices run away with him—a social psychologist's reactions are added in brackets:

> Like a child the negro is ordinarily cheerful and good-natured; childlike, too, is his speedy recovery from grief or depression. [Is this true only of Negroes?] . . .
>
> The superstition of the negro is probably largely due to his ignorance and to his great emotional excitability. The negro has a firm belief in charms to entice "Lady Luck" or to keep away evil spirits. [Did you ever carry a good-luck piece?] . . .
>
> Negroes are especially gregarious, loving big crowds and much display. Secret organizations flourish among them. [When is your next fraternity meeting, and do you like to go to the circus?] . . .

> The negro love of display is shown by the bright colors, extreme styles, and flashy jewelry worn by them on gala occasions. [Have you been to any formal dances recently?] . . .
>
> The colored race is especially fond of music and dancing. [What about you?] The white child has to learn to dance, but the little pickaninny apparently dances instinctively. [See Chapter 6 above.] . . .[14]

This shows that formal education of an intelligent person is no guarantee that his early childhood prejudices will be overcome sufficiently for him to deal objectively with certain topics.

CONSTANT REINFORCEMENT OF STEREOTYPES

Such beliefs are fostered by myths and legends which have become a part of our culture. Americans are interested in the folk tales of European countries, yet fail to realize the extent of our own folklore, particularly as concerns Negroes. We have legendary stories dealing with Negroes under slavery, ranging from *Uncle Tom's Cabin* to *Gone with the Wind*. Stories of savage Negro life in Africa also tend to reinforce whatever notions people may have about the primitive nature of Negroes. In the theater and the movies the personality of the Negro provides a stereotype for amusement and derision. The old-time minstrel show and the modern Amos and Andy are examples. With the popular use of such terms as "nigger," "darky," "coon," "pickaninny," "mammy," and the habit of speaking of adult colored men as "boys," we have constant reinforcement of the notions that Negroes are unintelligent, lazy, undependable, childish, and in every way inferior to white persons.

EDUCATIONAL STATUS OF NEGROES

What are the actual facts concerning the educational status and intelligence of Negroes? First of all, the educational problem always has been and still remains a very real one. It is estimated that in 1866 only 10 per cent of Negroes were literate enough to read and write. Today probably over 80 per cent are literate, although this figure tells us little of their actual educational progress. From 1826 to 1936, during a period of 110 years, over 40,000 Negroes graduated from colleges and professional schools in America. Among outstanding Negroes have been such people as Charles W. White, who graduated with highest scholastic distinction at Harvard University; Dr. Alain Locke, Harvard graduate, Rhodes scholar, noted professor and author; Professor George Washington Carver of Tuskegee Institute, famed agricultural chemist; and Paul Robeson, Phi Beta Kappa, All-American football star, famous singer and actor. There are thousands of Negroes in such professions as teaching, social work, law, and medicine, and in such occupations as real estate and insurance. The point is that as greater educational opportunities open up for Negroes, an even larger proportion of them do not fit the common stereotyped ideas of white people.

Take the single notion that Negroes are shiftless and do not save money or acquire property. A survey of Negro college graduates some years ago showed that 53 per cent were property owners with median holdings valued at over $5,000, that 80 per cent out of school for forty years were property owners, and that 15 per cent owned property valued at more than $10,000.[15] These figures are given simply to show the other side of the picture, a side not usually known nor often presented.

INEQUALITY OF OPPORTUNITY

The primary reason that even greater educational advances have not been made by Negroes is because they are for the most part living in a white man's world, where the educational system is controlled by whites. Negroes make up a tenth of our population—most of this population being located in nineteen states—but an examination of teachers' salaries, public-school property, length of the school term, and transportation facilities shows that educational opportunities are distinctly not the same for Negroes as for whites.[16]

An absolutely fair comparison of Negroes and whites is impossible because in American culture there is *not* equal opportunity for whites and "blacks." White people criticize Negroes for lack of progress in the professions, literature, art, and science; and the typical white point of view is that Negroes are *innately* inferior because the number who have achieved distinctions in these fields is not great. But a group of people, who less than a century ago were only 10 per cent literate, can hardly be expected to produce many examples of literature, art, or scientific achievement equal to those of white people in a white culture. In occupational pursuits, Negroes do not have the same expectation of rewards to motivate them as do whites.

> Negro labor in Middletown has fairly steady employment at the harder, meaner type of job in certain of Middletown's factories, as hod carriers and similar unskilled labor in the building trades, on road gangs, and, in exceptional cases, where a Negro's character is above question, as janitors. But the only thing a Negro man can do beyond that is a long step up from there to the professional class serving his own race.[17]

The careful analytical studies of Negro life by E. Franklin Frazier,[18] Charles S. Johnson,[19] and Howard W. Odum[20] have demonstrated the great *futility* of life for large segments of our Negro population. Historically millions have had little or no opportunity to achieve greater social or economic status; and Negro youth finds itself today "at the crossways."

CULTURAL FACTORS AFFECTING INTELLIGENCE-TEST SCORES

Such facts give the problem of Negro intelligence its proper setting. In the preceding chapter we saw that motivation, rapport, culture, socio-economic status, educational background, and related factors were important in determining scores on intelligence tests. Considering the fact that educational advantages for Negroes and whites are not the same, it is not surprising to find that the average score for whites is somewhat higher on intelligence tests than that for Negroes. Whites tend to be superior to Negroes on intelligence tests developed by white people in a white culture and administered primarily in school situations. The "average" white person's environment is more conducive to the development of certain abilities which help him to test as more intelligent than the "average" Negro.[21] However, even though there is a difference in the central tendencies or averages of intelligence-test curves for Negroes and whites, the two distributions actually overlap considerably. This means that there are many individual whites who have higher scores than individual Negroes, and also others who have lower scores than some Negroes; and vice versa, there are many individual Negroes who have higher scores than the average for whites, as well as others who have lower scores than whites.

Among a group of Southern adults, 63 per cent thought that the "typical" Negro was not over 25 per cent as bright as the "typical" white man.[22] One man, in discussing these facts, said that he did not care what the tests showed, he was convinced that no Negro is as intelligent as any white man. When it was then pointed out to him that this would mean that a Negro professor of mathematics at Howard University would be less intelligent than a white handy man, he simply lost his temper. Most of us prefer to be irrational and illogical in dealing with such questions.

Klineberg points out the difficulty of getting groups who will compete with equal eagerness for the possible results.[23] Culturally conditioned attitudes vary from group to group and prevent equal motivation. For example, cultural resistance to speed is to be noted in many Negro groups, and Negroes have to overcome additional handicaps in the test situation because of social and economic status.

> The direct comparison between Negroes and whites will always remain a doubtful procedure because of the impossibility of controlling the various factors which may influence the results. *Intelligence tests may therefore not be used as measures of group differences in native ability, though they may be used profitably as measures of accomplishment.* When comparisons are made within the same race or group, it can be demonstrated that there are very marked differences depending upon variations in background. These differences may be satisfactorily explained, therefore, without recourse to the hypothesis of racial differences in mental ability. [Italics ours.][24]

In a study of the relation between intelligence and educational opportunities, Klineberg found that Negroes living in New York City with educational advantages almost equal to those of white children, test markedly higher than Negroes in some of the Southern communities which have segregated schools.[25] Moreover, the intelligence rating of Southern colored children who moved to New York City increased on the average every year while there, until they had been residents four or five years. Such a study shows either that the tests do not measure pure intellectual ability but rather a mixture of intelligence and cultural achievement, or else that intelligence is not entirely an innate ability but is capable of development under favorable conditions of training. In either case Klineberg's study seriously challenges the conclusions that the "white race" is born superior in mentality to the colored. We have little evidence that Negroes as a group are *innately* less intelligent than white people as a group.

To summarize the evidence on intelligence differences between Negroes and whites, we may say that on our present forms of intelligence tests, Negroes make much lower scores than do whites, but that schooling and length of residence in the city seem to affect the ratings of Negroes to such a great extent that we cannot determine from present data what the actual difference would be if environmental differences were eliminated.[26]

"MIXED BLOOD"

Another interesting consideration is that of race mixture. About one-tenth of our population is classed as Negro, although a large percentage of these persons are part "white." Mulattoes made up 11.2 per cent of the total Negro population in 1850, 12.0 per cent in 1870, 15.2 per cent in 1890, and 20.9 per cent in 1910. In later censuses mulattoes have not been differentiated from other Negroes, probably because the figures were thought to be too unreliable; but there is no doubt that the number of mulattoes is increasing.

Most Americans tend to think of a separate Negro race, dark brown or black in color, characterized by frizzly hair, thick lips, broad flat nose, long arms and legs.[27] But scientifically we cannot refer to American Negroes as a separate "race," if we mean a group which possesses a set of *innate* psychological and physical characteristics. Negro college students in New York City and Washington, D. C., were measured in supposedly Negroid traits—width of nostril, thickness of lips, white element in skin color, and black element in skin color—and were given intelligence tests.[28] No significant relationships showed up between test scores and these physical traits.

In a survey of 263 prominent and influential Negro teachers, 241 were of "mixed blood" and only 22 were pure "black."[29] Of 495 Negro preachers, the ratio of mulattoes to blacks was 6 to 1; and, of 171 well-known Negro musicians, 158 were mulattoes and only 13 were full-blooded. Of 139 Negroes selected as outstanding, 124 of the men and 8 of the women were of "mixed blood." Such facts are likely to lead one to the immediate conclusion that an admixture of white blood produces greater mental ability and general superiority, and, therefore, that this proves the white race to be much superior. Such a conclusion, however, overlooks the importance of American culture patterns. Do these people of mixed bloods attain prominence because of the physical fact of white ancestry, or because lighter skinned Negroes can much more easily escape from the racial taboos than their darker brethren? Interviews with several thousand Negroes, by Warner and his colleagues, have indicated that shade of skin color is definitely associated with social or class position.[30]

DEVELOPMENT OF PREJUDICES AGAINST NEGROES

Where do prejudices against Negroes come from? The answer is, from environmental factors. Most of these were mentioned in the third paragraph of the present chapter. Although there is no innate or instinctive prejudice against Negroes, avoidance and antagonism tend to be built up at an early age out of fear, combativeness, ridicule, and similar factors.[31] These prejudices are determined not simply by contact with Negroes, but by contact with the prevailing attitudes toward Negroes. Certainly many an individual who has lived in a Northern community almost entirely without Negroes has grown up with definite prejudices toward them because of the acceptance of cultural attitudes. Here is the way that prejudice against Negroes grew up for one individual:

> I had never seen a Negro until about my third year in grammar school. Our public school system did not maintain separate housing for Negro students. Outwardly Negroes were equal in the matter of getting an education in our urban society. In spite of the efforts of the school to maintain a basis of social equality, there grew up in me an attitude of dislike for Negroes because of my parents.
>
> At home such expressions as, "lazy as a nigger," "smells like a nigger," "unreliable as a nigger," and "work like a nigger slave," were terms often used in reproachment. This was climaxed by an emotional experience. I was forced to sit beside a Negro student as part of a stupid gesture of punishment. To this day physical contact or nearness to Negroes places me mentally in the category of one being punished.

This traumatic experience may be contrasted with a more generalized sort of experience typical of many a person who has lived in the South with Negroes for servants:

For four years, we had our washing done by an old colored woman named Minnie. Another one, Willie Mae, was a general housemaid for our last few months in Georgia. In the move, it was necessary to discard a lot of old belongings. Minnie and Willie Mae were to share them. This caused discord between the two and I could hear them arguing. Minnie said, "They's been my folks longer than they has yours." Willie Mae replied, "But they's the only folks I got." It greatly amused me to hear them call us their "folks."

Note the attitudes of superiority and amusement in this social situation. Such attitudes are easily carried over to all situations where Negroes are involved. Here is a case in point:

A Negro lost control of his automobile, and it went over a curb and hit a tree. A few people were sympathetic. One woman remarked that it was too bad, but that "accidents could happen to anyone." A man, apparently her escort, asked the driver if he was sure that he was not hurt. Another man, attempting to take charge of the situation, wanted to know how he happened to drive off such a wide street. A man in the outskirts of the crowd said, "Hell, he was drunk." A colored man heard the remark and said, "I just seen him down at ——— and he hasn't had a drink." The man who had made the original remark said, "One 'nigger' will lie and the other one will swear to it." A woman said, " 'Niggers' shouldn't be allowed to drive; they're too dangerous." Still another man said, "That's right, they never have much of an equity in the car, so they get drunk and don't care a damn."

This story clearly demonstrates how our stereotyped notions may prevent a clear conception of incidents involving members of an Out-group.

In a survey of white pupils in grades 4 to 11 of a Virginia school, it was found that unfavorable attitudes toward Negroes were acquired at an early age.[32] This is similar to the results of an earlier investigation, which showed that prejudices against Negroes develop at a very early date for most children and do not change very readily.[33] The experimenter tested the attitudes of white boys, kindergarten through the eighth grade, in New York and in the South, toward Negro boys. Photographs of white and Negro boys individually and in social situations were shown. In a rank-order test the children were asked to indicate their order of preference from among a mixed assortment of white and Negro faces. The colored faces were of various degrees of skin color, but all had been judged racially typical by several adults. In a "Show-me" test, the children were asked to point out which individual boys they would like to play ball with, bring home to lunch, and similar activities. In the "social situations test" they were asked to point out those social groups with which they would like to "join in"—one with Negro children and one without them. The investigator found prejudice against Negroes strong even among many of the younger children.

Interestingly enough, when a fairly popular Negro boy was put with other boys in the fourth grade, the amount of prejudice did not change to any measurable extent. In a great many situations, one Negro may be tolerated; but, if the number increases, they may become a "problem," and mild dislike may crystallize into open antagonism and even conflict.

J. L. Moreno has demonstrated this experimentally in his work at the Hudson School for Girls, a New York State correctional institution. The girls are grouped by houses with six or eight in a house. Moreno has found that one Negro girl can be inserted in a white group with little or no racial resentment appearing on the part of the white girls, but when the number of Negroes in a house group is increased antagonism increases at a more rapid rate than the mere addition of a second or third Negro girl would seem superficially to warrant.[34]

NORTHERN AND SOUTHERN ATTITUDES

The fact that antagonism tends to increase with an increase in numbers of Negroes helps to explain the greater amount of prejudice in the South than in the North. Of course, in those Northern cities where there are an unusally large number of Negroes competing for jobs, the antagonism against them is great. Chicago today is an example.[35] Negroes are much more of an economic threat in those sections where they live in great numbers. Both white employers and white workers have resented the desire of Negroes for higher wages.

Prejudices toward Negroes differ in the North and in the South not only in intensity but in kind. Northerners often tend to dislike individual contacts with Negroes, while maintaining that they believe in racial equality. In the South, on the other hand, contacts with individual Negroes are perfectly all right provided they are servants, but Negroes are not considered at all equal. Both demonstrate *ambivalent* attitudes —Northerners tending to like Negroes as a group but disliking the individual Negro, Southerners tending to like the individual Negro but disliking Negroes as a group. It is in the South, however, that the issue of "white supremacy" has had the greatest political emphasis.

VIOLENCE AGAINST NEGROES

Dislike of Negroes takes the form of open discrimination against them in most sections of the country, but especially in the South. Sometimes there is actual physical violence. Of over 4,500 persons lynched in the United States in the last sixty years, about four-fifths have been Negroes, and most of these lynchings have occurred in the southern states. Although the reduction in the number of lynchings has been very great during recent years, this does not indicate that the tensions do not still exist. The possibility of future lynching is still present so long as attitudes in the South do not change.

What is the principal crime with which lynched Negroes have been charged? Your answer will probably be rape. Yet the figures show that this is not the case. In only one-fourth of all the lynchings of Negroes has there been any accusation of rape or attempted rape. Other accusations involved have been theft, murder, felonious assault, insulting white persons, throwing a pebble against the courthouse window, sudden racing of an automobile engine, being too prosperous.[36]

Studies of the communities in which lynchings occur demonstrate that the problem is an intricate one, with sociological, psychological, and economic causes. In general, lynchings have occurred in communities that were either on the starvation line or headed in that direction. For the most part, they have not occurred in cities of any size, and the towns that have seen them have tended to be on the downgrade economically. In general, better educated Southerners and those with financial security are not lynchers. Violence may be encouraged, however, by members of the Ku Klux Klan—who can remain anonymous. Lynchings usually have taken place in drab rural sections without libraries, museums, movie houses, or other means of changing the tedious routine of daily life. A comparison of the counties in which twenty-one lynchings took place in 1930 with other counties in the same states, showed that they were considerably below average.

> In approximately nine-tenths of these counties the per capita tax valuation was below the general state average; in almost nineteen-twentieths the bank deposits per capita were less than the state average; in three-fourths the per capita income from farm and factory was below the state average, in many cases less than one-half; in nine-tenths fewer and smaller income tax returns were made per thousand population than throughout the state; in over two-thirds, the proportion of farms operated by tenants was in excess of the state rate; and in nearly three-fourths of the counties, automobiles were less common than in the state.[37]

The deadly monotony of life in a rural community where people desire excitement and something new, plus *the extremely important factor of economic competition between Negroes and "poor whites,"* is sufficient to produce an outbreak. People living a varied life do not need an emotional outburst as do those who find escape from dull boredom in emotional distortion. Following a lynching the community can settle down to a period of "normality" and relive vicariously the emotional orgy and the feelings of superiority afforded by the lynching experience.

Mob violence has also occurred in Northern communities, but lynchings are extremely rare. The acts of violence in the rural communities of the agricultural South occasionally have their counterpart in riots in the cities of the more industrial North. Open hostilities have resulted especially when Negroes have migrated northward by the thousands to take jobs in mills and factories. When the economic tensions have been very great, it has taken only an "incident" to set off the spark which produces a race riot.

> One sultry afternoon in the summer of 1919 a seventeen-year old colored boy was swimming in Lake Michigan by a Chicago bathing-beach. Part of the shore had been set aside by mutual understanding for the use of the whites, another part for the Negroes. The boy took hold of a railroad tie floating in the water and drifted across the invisible line. Stones were thrown at him; a white boy started to swim toward him. The colored boy let go of the railroad tie, swam a few strokes, and sank. He was drowned. Whether he had been hit by any of the stones was uncertain, but the Negroes on the shore accused the whites of stoning him to death, and a fight began. This small incident struck the match that set off a bonfire of race hatred. The Negro population of Chicago had doubled in a decade, the blacks had crowded into white neighborhoods, and nerves were raw. The disorder spread to other parts of the city—and the final result was that for nearly a week Chicago was virtually in a state of civil war; there were mobbings of Negroes, beatings, stabbings, gang raids through the Negro district, shootings by Negroes in defense, and wanton destruction of houses and property. . . .[38]

Serious race riots occurred in 1943 in Detroit, New York, and Los Angeles. As Lee and Humphrey have pointed out, the Detroit riot developed from a whole series of variables: heavy migration of Negroes to Detroit, overcrowding, a high delinquency and crime rate, discriminatory police behavior, minor racial frictions, demagogic groups, segregation of Negroes in the armed services, competition for jobs.[39] All of these factors furnished the necessary background for a flare-up of violence. Orlansky's analysis of the Harlem riot in which Negroes made mass attacks on white property was that long-time frustrations eventually resulted in aggression, which was misplaced in that it struck "not at the ultimate causes of Negro deprivation," but only at its immediate agents, namely, storekeepers and policemen.[40]

Mob violence serves psychologically to do for a community what any sort of crisis does; that is, it releases people from the monotony of their daily routine lives. The psychology of war, of some strike situations, and of violence involving Negroes, are alike in this pattern of release. People are enabled to engage in emotional behavior and to escape objective, realistic thinking.

After a comprehensive survey for the Carnegie Corporation of the problems facing American Negroes, Gunnar Myrdal, distinguished Swedish sociologist, published his results under the title, *An American Dilemma.*[41] As *Life* magazine pointed out in an editorial: "The dilemma, of course, is this: the basic tenets of the American creed make all men free and equal in rights. Yet in fact we deny equal rights to our largest minority, and observe a caste system which we not only criticize in other nations but refuse to defend in ourselves."[42]

▶ PREJUDICES AGAINST ORIENTALS

IMMIGRATION OF CHINESE

Prejudice against Negroes in Southern states is very nearly matched by prejudice against Orientals in the Far West, where economic rivalry exists between whites and Orientals. Chinese coolies first came to California during gold-rush days, as cooks and laundrymen. In the 1860's they were imported or "shanghaied" in great numbers, especially as contract laborers for the Central Pacific Railroad. By 1882 there were 132,000 Chinese on the Pacific coast. Because of the economic competition between the mass of Chinese left after the railroads were built and the white laborers, Congress passed an act in 1882 which barred Chinese laborers from entering the United States for the next ten years.[43] William Randolph Hearst's San Francisco *Examiner* took up the battle against Orientals, and other exclusion laws were passed during the latter part of the century. By 1900 many Chinese had returned to China and, as others found their places in lines of work in which they did not compete too directly with the whites, feeling against them declined.

IMMIGRATION OF JAPANESE

The Japanese were never imported in great numbers for contract labor. They entered gradually, often to become truck farmers in California. As they became active competitors of whites, prejudice arose against them. As early as 1906 the San Francisco School Board adopted a resolution requiring all Japanese pupils to attend a separate Oriental school, although the edict was later withdrawn. By 1908 Japanese immigration was restricted almost as completely as Chinese. In 1913 California passed legislation denying aliens the right to acquire agricultural lands or leaseholds for more than three years; and in 1920, since children born to Japanese in the United States would be American citizens, the law was extended to make it impossible for aliens to act as guardians for minors possessing agricultural properties. Other Western states adopted similar legislation. In 1924 "aliens ineligible to citizenship" were excluded from further entry into the United States. From that time on, anti-Japanese feelings tended to subside.[44] Naturally, they flared up again in December, 1941, when Japan attacked the United States at Pearl Harbor. In 1942 tens of thousands of Japanese were evacuated from the West coast military zone to relocation centers for the duration of the war.

THE CHINESE AS AN OUT-GROUP

The Chinese on the West coast represented distinct Out-groups, with characteristics which set them apart from the native American In-group. They retained their dress, habits, religion, and methods of work throughout their lifetime. In other words, a Chinese remained a "Chinaman" as long as he lived, and usually looked with scorn upon American ways, considering them to be inferior to his own. This was partly a defense reaction to the discrimination against Chinese in white communities. The Chinese did not apply for citizenship in great numbers, and sent home any extra money they earned, hoping to follow the money themselves as soon as they became independent. They were ultraconservative, secretive, and clannish, and organized secret trade societies or "tongs." Their low standards of living were believed to be a menace to public health. They refused for the most part to cooperate in improvement projects sponsored by whites, and this had a twofold result. While it aroused antagonism against Chinese at first, it also kept them in their own communities where friction with the whites was at a minimum.

THE JAPANESE AS AN OUT-GROUP

The Japanese were different. They adopted American dress, customs, and manners as soon as possible. They were ambitious and eager to get into the ranks of skilled American workers. They became interested in securing an education, and learned the English language fairly quickly. Whereas the Chinese were looked on with suspicion because they were so different, the Japanese were becoming so much like Americans that they were an economic and social threat.

ECONOMIC COMPETITION

Competing white labor found both groups a menace. Orientals were accused of taking jobs away from the whites, and also of cutting prices on small businesses such as laundry and farm produce. Property values dropped because these people would live—or were forced to live—in places that white people refused to accept. (This has an interesting parallel to living conditions for Negroes in the South.) Stereotypes rapidly grew up of "tricky," "cunning," and "crafty." These prejudices have spread to other sections of the country.

After Japanese immigration was stopped, employers of agricultural and other unskilled labor began to import Mexican and Filipino labor. Again, white laborers became incensed at the new competitors, and violent prejudices arose. New stereotypes were bandied about for these newcomers, such as "Mexicans are shiftless," and "Filipinos have tails." Actual cases of physical violence occurred on a number of occasions. *Once more, we see the close parallel between economic competition and violent race prejudice.* Economic factors are of the utmost importance in helping to explain prejudices against all minority groups.

▶ ANTI-CATHOLIC AND ANTI-SEMITIC PREJUDICES

VARIOUS TYPES OF RELIGIOUS PREJUDICE

Prejudices exist toward religious as well as racial minorities. Although many types of religious prejudice might be profitably discussed, particularly between various brands of the same religion—for example, Baptists versus Methodists, or Orthodox Jews versus Reformed Jews—our concern here is with the conflicts between the majority and the minority patterns.

ANTI-CATHOLICISM AND ANTI-SEMITISM

The two outstanding examples are symbolized by anti-Catholic and anti-Semitic prejudice. In other words, the predominant religious pattern in the United States is Protestant. The number of Catholics and Jews, although numerically large, is small in proportion to the total population. One person analyzes his childhood prejudices against Catholics as follows:

> In my own childhood, . . . brought up in a strict Protestant family, I was conditioned to regard Catholics with fear and suspicion. I can recall in my early boyhood, coming home from school at twilight, crossing to the other side of the street when I passed a Catholic church and running as hard as I could. I did not know what evil thing might reach out for me but I knew there was evil there. It was not until I mingled with Catholic boys and girls in high school and later in college that I learned that they were as kindly, as good, as bad, and as mischievous as the Protestants among us. I learned that some of them had been conditioned to fear and suspect Protestants.[45]

Another person explains his prejudices against Jews:

> From the very beginning of my Sunday School days I can well remember the story of the Jews clamoring for the crucifixion of Jesus and their final success in the horrible undertaking. Surely a race that refused to espouse the cause of

the Saviour and even after that killed him was worthy of nothing better than eternal damnation. This was constantly the teaching I received from ——— church of which I am a member.

I seldom think of Jews as including Einstein, Disraeli, Dr. Stephen S. Wise, or the famous Rothschild family. I come more in contact with the junk peddler, the fish monger, or the pawn broker and am content to think of these men as representative of their race and religion. . . . It seems that those that are the most vituperative are the last in any way to attempt to correct their impressions. They are satisfied with the very expressive phrase, "He's a damn Jew," and let it go at that. I know because I have said the same thing.

Many Protestants seem to consider themselves authorities on the Catholic and the Jew. Yet these same persons would resent a Catholic or a Jew setting himself up as an expert on the Protestant Gentile. In fact, it is interesting that the members of *any dominant group* always tend to take their own superiority for granted and not to turn the searchlight of criticism on themselves. For example, when Protestants happen to be aggressive, arrogant, bad-mannered, clannish, close-fisted, greedy, money-grabbing, noisy, or rude, they do not stop to say to themselves, "Dirty Protestants!" or "Dirty Gentiles!"

THE SPREAD OF ANTI-SEMITISM

In the 1930's, news and propaganda from Germany, Italy, and other countries encouraged Americans who already had pre-existing anti-Semitic attitudes to become more outspoken in their views. In fact, the frequency of appearance of newspaper want ads which requested "Christians" or "Gentiles" was apparently closely related to the amount of current propaganda against Jews.[46] Also, the economic depression increased distrust and suspicion toward minority Out-groups, and this developed into open antagonism when competition for jobs and financial success became very keen.

Probably a majority of Protestant Americans today would agree with *The Nazi Primer* that, "A Jew both in Germany and in all other countries remains only a Jew."[47] This feeling extends even to the well-educated professional classes.

A distinguished committee of Harvard professors . . . in submitting a report on "Some Problems of Personnel in the Faculty of Arts and Sciences" on March 25, 1939, made important findings on "sectional, racial and religious discrimination" in that university. The committee stated that it was difficult to assess the extent of anti-Semitic bias in the making of faculty appointments, but that "those who raised the issue seemed in agreement, to use the words of one of them, that 'racial prejudice is so thoroughly ingrained and taken for granted that no one takes much notice of it except in particularly flagrant cases.' "[48]

Meenes has presented evidence from a variety of sources that anti-Semitic attitudes are found in all parts of the United States.[49]

BASES OF ANTI-CATHOLICISM AND ANTI-SEMITISM

Both anti-Catholic and anti-Semitic prejudices exist on a wide scale in the United States. A review of the first section of Chapter 10, *Our Judgments of Other Persons,* and of the first section of the present chapter furnishes the necessary background to explain these prejudices.

However, since prejudices against Catholics apparently have not increased or decreased in scope of late, whereas anti-Semitism has spread rapidly in the United States, a special analysis will be made of some of the unique psychological factors involved therein. Attitudes toward Catholics are rather vague ones of slight suspicion or distrust. The general notion seems to be—despite all the evidence to the contrary—that a Catholic's political and social beliefs are rigidly determined by the Church. But there have been relatively few instances of open discrimination, as in the case of Jews.

PSYCHOLOGICAL ANALYSIS OF ANTI-SEMITISM

On the other hand, a tremendous amount of anti-Semitic propaganda exists in this country and finds a receptive audience. Several psychological investigations have been directly concerned with the question of how anti-Semitic attitudes develop. One study of college students suggested that anti-Semitic college women had "restricted, narrow" personalities or points of view and tended toward stereotyped thinking.[50] Careful analysis by Levinson and Sanford has resulted in the development of an actual scale for the measurement of anti-Semitism.[51] "Depth" interviews and projective techniques have been utilized in several studies, in an attempt to obtain greater insight into anti-Semitic manifestations and the relations of these prejudices to other attitudes.[52] Jahoda and Ackerman have presented evidence indicating that at one extreme anti-Semitic attitudes come into existence as the result of conformity to the attitudes of dominant groups, and at the other extreme they are motivated by specific personality conflicts "which are related to specific items in the content of the culturally developed negative stereotype of the Jew."[53]

Why does anti-Semitism exist to such a great extent? There is no single explanation, but rather a complexity of causal factors.[54]

1. *Distinguishing Characteristics of Jews.* In the first place, the Jewish group is one of the most distinguishable of the white groups in the United States. Although Jews do not constitute a biological race, there are enough who have similar features to confirm the stereotyped notion of a Jewish "type." The negative findings of anthropologists concerning pure racial types have led to a tendency among the sophisticated to overlook the real physical differences between *some* Jews and most Gentiles.

But among most people, it requires only partial confirmation of discernible differences to accept the belief in the racial distinctiveness of the Jew. This belief is further supported by the religious and cultural differences between the Jewish group and other American patterns. Other immigrant groups differ culturally from the prevailing American picture, but ordinarily do not in addition possess a distinctive religion.

Of all the white-skinned groups, Jews stand out as the most distinctive against the background of the rest of the population. The supposed combination of physical, cultural, and religious differences results in considerable prejudice against Jews. Easily discernible differences in themselves do not necessarily result in prejudices, but they tend to reinforce prejudices once they come into existence. Moreover, most groups of a religious and cultural nature preach a doctrine of the superiority of their own group. Hence, Jews run counter to other religions and nationalities. Furthermore, they have to face the "residual emotion" from historical religious conflicts as well as the present hostility to foreign cultural habits; and since they can be differentiated after a fashion, by their physical appearances, it is easy to associate them as a group with *any* undesirable act of *any* Jew. If one is jostled in the subway or bus by a person of nondescript appearance, the reaction is directed toward him as an individual; but if one is jostled by a person who looks Jewish, the action is set down as proof of the aggressiveness of the Jewish people.

The distinctiveness which is attributed to the Jewish group is both a cause and an effect of racial prejudice. Because of the long-standing history of the problem of anti-Semitism, the process has become circular—in fact, a vicious circle. Prejudice against Jews brings them together in self-defense, and this creates more prejudice.

Any discussion of the question of interracial relations should not overlook the vast number of Jews who have been assimilated culturally and who have been incorporated biologically into the American nation. Many are not recognized by Gentiles as Jews. The Jews who resemble non-Jews most closely may be the first to intermarry and to be assimilated into the American population. Those who stand out as more distinctive, either because of physique, language behavior, gesture behavior, or adherence to old religious values, are selected out by Gentiles as being typical of all Jews.

2. *History of Jews.* A second factor which makes for anti-Semitic prejudice stems from the history of the Jewish group. Jewish culture has emphasized learning and scholarship; and Jews for centuries have been an urban people. One reason for this is that in many European countries for centuries Jews were not allowed to own land. They are even now heavily concentrated in business and the professions, and have competed successfully with Gentiles in the cities. This has had two results.

As successful people they are very much in evidence, and non-Jews feel that these Jewish "outsiders" occupy too many good positions. Also, our city populations are recruited in part from the farms and small towns, and these residents carry with them some of the rural prejudices against the old type of city dweller. Jews, as a city type, bear the full brunt of these prejudices.

In short, Jews are not only a distinctive group; they are an urban group which draws the fire of nonurban persons. Some of them are, moreover, outstandingly successful in certain urban businesses, such as the clothing trade, and this places them in the public eye. Their traditional urbanism also means that Jewish children usually have different educational values from non-Jews. Jewish students are likely to be less interested in athletics than others, and more interested in scholarship, debating, and journalism. Hence, on many a college campus they come to the fore as honor students, debaters, and leaders in literary activities. Not only do they stand out in these activities, thereby incurring the jealousy of less successful non-Jews, but they also defy the convention of the all-around personality by the unrepresentative character of their activities.

3. *Competition.* A third factor in explaining anti-Semitism is competition. Given a Jewish group which is readily distinguished as a people having different cultural values, emphasizing different activities, and confining itself to urban occupations, the basis is well laid for hostile attitudes. The actual hostility builds up into serious animosity, however, only under the proper motivating conditions. People traveling abroad do not object to foreign groups no matter how different their customs; the foreign ways in such circumstances seem interesting or even amusing. However, when easily identified members of an Out-group living in the United States become economic competitors, attitudes of interest and amusement give way to resentment and hate.

The rise in anti-Semitism bears a direct relation to the increased competition for jobs and for the "good things of life." Propaganda represents Jews as running America, and as having a monopoly on the good jobs and the spare cash. This appears to be plausible to some people, because the Jews as a city people have appeared in vocations which place them in conspicuous positions as lawyers, physicians, merchants, scientists, and teachers. Hence, to the insecure and to the unemployed, it may appear that Jews have been far too successful in establishing themselves in desirable positions and generally "running the country."

The situation regarding the Jews is similar to that which developed on the Pacific coast in the 1920's with respect to the Japanese. As a distinct and different group, the Japanese were already convenient objects for attack; when they became a serious economic threat by acquiring land through hard work, shrewd business methods, and a willingness to tolerate low standards of living, resentment developed into intense, active, and open hatred.

4. *Projection and the Scapegoat Mechanism.* Anti-Semitism also has furnished an outlet for the thwarted lives of people whose aspirations are developed to a higher level than their abilities or achievements justify. In our modern complex way of life, the direct satisfactions of the old family and community ways have diminished. We live in cities, and most of us work at mechanical or fairly routine jobs. Our satisfactions are in good part derived from ego enhancement by showing our status, and by having expensive clothes, automobiles, and other displays of conspicuous consumption.

However, since only relatively few can really achieve these material signs of importance, many people remain frustrated. Under such circumstances, psychological relief is afforded if people can look down upon some other group as inferior to themselves, and then vent their repressed hatreds upon its members. This is especially satisfying if members of the hated group have been enjoying the very things which other people want. This is the *scapegoat mechanism* so familiar in Germany, where the Jews were made scapegoats for the loss of the first World War, for the depression, and for all the misfortunes of the German people. This mechanism is the psychological expression of economic competition, as well as of other strains in modern living. Where there are not enough jobs to go around, and where Jews are localized as the causes of economic thwarting, the inference is drawn that there would be more jobs if the Jews were dispossessed. In other words, the scapegoat phenomenon goes hand in hand with economic competition.

5. *Recent European History.* As mentioned earlier, European events and movements have also contributed to anti-Semitism in America. The former organized persecution of Jews abroad has furnished the inspiration to self-seeking leaders in this country who are eager to capitalize upon any type of sentiments which can be aroused. Also, the organized pogroms abroad have not been without their anti-Jewish effect in this country. Although the majority of Americans were shocked by the excesses of the Nazis, many felt that there must be something to the accusations against the Jews.

It is an old technique to confront people with the *fait accompli,* for they tend to accept as right and proper whatever actually exists. Since persecution of the Jews was the accomplished fact abroad, many Americans were thereby encouraged in their own anti-Semitic attitudes. If the Jews have been dealt with harshly in Europe, they must either be a wicked or a weak people—this is the inference that many people draw. "Where there's smoke, there must be fire."

Furthermore, persecution in Europe has sent a steady stream of refugees to this country. Not all of these refugees have been Jewish, but the idea has been built up that most of them are. Many of these victims of totalitarian aggression have been from the professional and business groups, the very fields in which native American Jews are already well represented. Hence, feelings of sympathy for refugees have been confusedly mixed with fears of being overrun by foreigners.

6. *Jews Represented Both as Capitalists and as Communists.* Paradoxically anti-Semitism is associated both with the evils of capitalism and with measures for its reform or abolition. Because the Jews have been a city people engaged in business pursuits, they have been identified with the worst features of capitalism. They are accused of crafty bargaining, shrewd manipulations, "international banking," and unscrupulous exploitation of other people. On the other hand, as a city people interested in *ideas* as well as *things,* Jews have been conspicuous in social reforms and liberal movements. Not only are the Jews accused of being the personal devils who make the system vicious, but their supposed deviltry is also evidenced in the "ungodly" talk of some Jews about changing the system.

Thus, we have the paradox of anti-Semitic propaganda which pillories the Jews *both* as capitalists and as Communists. Logically the two charges are contradictory, but psychologically they represent an integration of prejudices. Our social institutions are all right in spite of the criticisms of Jewish "radicals" and "Communists," reasons the person who has accepted anti-Semitic propaganda, and it is only the "Jewish capitalists" and "international bankers" who are wrong.

7. *Propaganda Devices.* Dozens of anti-Semitic organizations have flourished in all parts of the United States, especially during the 1930's.[55] A survey in the late 1940's, however, indicated that, while anti-Semitic prejudice was more widespread than formerly, *organized* anti-Semitism was decreasing.[56]

One device in all anti-Semitic propaganda is simply to see to it that the words "Jews" and "Jewish" come to be associated with whatever is already disliked. This is the *conditioning* process, discussed in Chapter 6.[57] Most people have well-developed negative attitudes against Communism on the one hand, and against excessive profiteering on the other. Therefore, both the name-calling and transfer devices are resorted to (compare Chapter 9)—Jews are linked with Communism by constant repetition of the idea that Communism is Jewish, and at the same time with profiteering by constant repetition of the notion that Jews are "international bankers." It makes little difference that both kinds of statements are factually untrue. Since most non-Jews already have developed some distrust or suspicion of individual Jews, or of Jews as a group, they are only too ready to accept these ready-made associations and to scoff at any contradictory facts.

What are the facts regarding Communism? It was estimated by *Fortune* magazine in 1936 that probably less than 1/10 of 1 per cent of the 4½ million Jews in the United States were members of the Communist party.[58]

What about the notion of Jews as "international bankers"? An analysis in 1939 indicated that only about 4.8 per cent of the 80,000 directors of American corporations were Jews, and there was only one Jewish firm which had done any substantial amount of "international banking."[59] With the largest Jewish population in this country living in New York City, only 7 per cent of the directors of the New York Clearing House, and only 18 per cent of the members of the New York Stock Exchange were Jews. In other large cities the percentages are even less, in many instances being almost negligible.

Additional facts might be marshaled in detail, but they would matter little to those with a "will to believe." Our modern world has become so complex that we rely on the stereotyped ideas fed to us by others, most of them mere word formulas, or else we cite a single specific instance to "prove" a generality. "After all," says the man in the street, "you can't tell me—I know of a case where . . ."[60]

CONCLUSION

The problem of prejudices against minority groups will probably not be solved in our lifetime but only in the far distant future. Over a period of many generations, intermarriage may automatically solve some of the problems. Also, education in the early years of life, and improvements in our economic system, may keep such prejudices at a minimum. If we are to make democracy work and preserve civil liberties, it becomes increasingly important for young persons to maintain tolerant behavior toward representatives of other groups.

QUESTIONS AND PROBLEMS FOR DISCUSSION

1. *Why is there more prejudice by white Americans toward Negroes than toward Indians?*
2. *"Northerners tend to accept the Negro as a race, but not as a person." To what extent do you think this is true?*
3. *Talk with some Northerners and with some Southerners about their attitudes towards Negroes. To what extent is each group correct?*
4. *Give a complete social-psychological explanation of lynching.*
5. *What are some practical solutions of the Negro problem?*
6. *Write a social-psychological analysis of anti-Catholic attitudes of many Protestants. Make a similar analysis of anti-Protestant attitudes of many Catholics.*
7. *What are some of the underlying myths and legends that cause friction between Jews and non-Jews?*

8. *To what extent are all prejudices against minority groups economic in origin?*

RECOMMENDED READINGS

Baron, S. W., *A Social and Religious History of the Jews* (3 vols.). New York: Columbia University Press, 1937.

Belloc, H., *The Jews* (3rd edition). Boston: Houghton Mifflin Company, 1937.

Broun, H., and Britt, G., *Christians Only: A Study in Prejudice.* New York: The Vanguard Press, Inc., 1931.

Davis, A., and Dollard, J., *Children in Bondage.* Washington, D. C.: American Council on Education, 1940.

Dollard, J., *Caste and Class in a Southern Town.* New Haven: Yale University Press, 1937.

Drake, St. C., and Cayton, H. R., *Black Metropolis.* New York: Harcourt, Brace and Company, 1945.

Frazier, E. F., *The Negro Family in the United States.* Chicago: University of Chicago Press, 1939.

Frazier E. F., *Negro Youth at the Crossways.* Washington, D. C.: American Council on Education, 1940.

Graeber, I., and Britt, S. H. (editors), *Jews in a Gentile World: The Problem of Anti-Semitism.* New York: The Macmillan Company, 1942.

Herskovits, M. J., *The American Negro: A Study in Racial Crossing.* New York: Alfred A. Knopf, Inc., 1928.

Herskovits, M. J., *The Myth of the Negro Past.* New York: Harper & Brothers, 1941.

Johnson, C. S., *Growing Up in the Black Belt: Negro Youth in the Rural South.* Washington, D. C.: American Council on Education, 1941.

Klineberg, O. (editor), *Characteristics of the American Negro.* New York: Harper & Brothers, 1944.

Lasker, B., *Race Attitudes in Children.* New York: Henry Holt and Company, Inc., 1929.

Lee, A. M., and Humphrey, N. D., *Race Riot.* New York: Dryden Press, 1943.

McWilliams, C., *Brothers under the Skin.* Boston: Little, Brown & Company, 1943.

Myrdal, G., and others, *An American Dilemma: The Negro Problem and Modern Democracy.* New York: Harper & Brothers, 1944.

Odum, H. W., *Race and Rumors of Race: Challenge to American Crisis.* Chapel Hill: University of North Carolina Press, 1943.

Raper, A. T., *The Tragedy of Lynching.* Chapel Hill: University of North Carolina Press, 1933.

Ruppin, A., *The Jews in the Modern World.* London: Macmillan and Co., Ltd., 1934.

Stonequist, E. V., *The Marginal Man: A Study in Personality and Culture Conflict.* New York: Charles Scribner's Sons, 1937.

Strong, D. S., *Organized Anti-Semitism in America: The Rise of Group Prejudice During the Decade 1930-40.* Washington, D. C.: American Council on Public Affairs, 1941.

Sutherland, R. L., *Color, Class, and Personality.* Washington, D. C.: American Council on Education, 1942.

Valentin, H. M., *Antisemitism Historically and Critically Examined* (translated by A. G. Chater). London: Victor Gollanz, Ltd., 1936.

Warner, W. L., Junker, B. H., and Adams, W. A., *Color and Human Nature: Negro Personality Development in a Northern City.* Washington, D. C.: American Council on Education, 1941.

*Newcomb, T. M., Hartley, E. L., and others (editors), *Readings in Social Psychology.* New York: Henry Holt and Company, Inc., 1947. (The following selections are listed according to the sequence of related discussions in the chapter you have just read.)

- Marks, E. S., "Skin Color Judgments of Negro College Students," pp. 116-121.
- Miller, N. E., Sears, R. R., Mowrer, O. H., Doob, L. W., and Dollard, J., "The Frustration-Aggression Hypothesis," pp. 257-258.
- Dollard, J., Doob, L. W., Miller, N. E., Mowrer, O. H., and Sears, R. R., "Definitions and Principles," pp. 258-261.
- Sears, R. R., Hovland, C. I., and Miller, N. E., "Adult Reactions in a Frustrating Situation," pp. 261-263.
- Levy, D. M., "The Hostile Act," pp. 263-266.
- Bateson, G., "The Frustration-Aggression Hypothesis and Culture," pp. 267-269.
- Dollard, J., "Hostility and Fear in Social Life," pp. 269-281.
- Maslow, A. H., "Deprivation, Threat, and Frustration," pp. 281-282.
- Lippitt, R., and White, R. K., "An Experimental Study of Leadership and Group Life," pp. 315-330.
- Bogardus, E. S., "The Measurement of Social Distance," pp. 503-507.
- Clark, K. B., and Clark, M. P., "Racial Identification and Preference in Negro Children," pp. 169-178.
- Sims, V. M., and Patrick, J. R., "Attitudes toward the Negro of Northern and Southern College Students," pp. 358-365.
- Horowitz, E. L., "Development of Attitude toward Negroes," pp. 507-517.

Information and Education Division, U. S. War Department, "Opinions about Negro Infantry Platoons in White Companies of Seven Divisions," pp. 542-546.

Campbell, A. A., "Factors Associated with Attitudes toward Jews," pp. 518-527.

Frenkel-Brunswik, E., Levinson, D. J., and Sanford, R. N., "The Antidemocratic Personality," pp. 531-541.

CHAPTER TWENTY-FOUR

NATIONALISM AND WAR

NATIONALISTIC PREJUDICES. Nationalism—Nationalism as a Religion—Nationalistic Feelings of Superiority—Extent of Nationalistic Prejudices—Psychological Bases of Nationalistic Prejudices—(1) Differences in Appearance—(2) Distrust and Fear of the Strange—(3) Separation or Isolation—(4) Ignorance—(5) Personal Experience—(6) Economic and Social Competition—(7) Differences in Culture—(8) Stereotyping—(9) Propaganda Devices—(10) Jingoism—(11) Patriotism and Community Loyalty—(12) Nationalistic Indoctrination in Social Institutions—Fascism—The Nazi Program—Growth of the Nazi Regime—German Racial Doctrines—The Russian Problem—Communism / THE SOCIAL PSYCHOLOGY OF WAR. Nationalism as a Basis of War—The Supposed Inevitability of War—The Munitions Makers—Other Supposed Causes of War—Wishful Thinking—Other Psychological Factors in War / SOME PSYCHOLOGICAL ASPECTS OF WORLD WAR II. The Development of War-nationalism in Germany—Propaganda in Totalitarian and Democratic Nations—Aims of War Propaganda—Use of the Conditioned Response in War Propaganda—Conditioning in Terms of Emotional Symbols—American Attitudes during Early Part of World War II—Symbolic Significance of Finland—Propaganda from Germany and England—The Fall of France—Changes in American Attitudes—Anti-Japanese Feelings—Pearl Harbor—The Atom Bomb—The Costs of War—Attitudes about War Costs and International Affairs—Psychological Bases of Permanent Peace—The Psychologists' Manifesto.

▶ NATIONALISTIC PREJUDICES

NATIONALISM

Whether any nation can attain complete supremacy in this interdependent modern world is doubtful. Nevertheless, the people of nearly all modern nations act as if their own nation were better than all other nations. The nation-state demands and receives the highest loyalty. It is the largest of all In-groups, containing in some instances tens of millions of members or citizens.

In their efforts to maintain supremacy—or the illusion of supremacy—nations are engaged in an eternal struggle for power or for survival. Competition between nations in its extreme form is manifested in war and in diplomacy (which depends upon the threat of war for its strength). A loyal citizenry is, therefore, necessary for the success and continued life of any nation. It is of first importance to the life of every nation that it command unquestioned obedience from its subjects in the event of any international struggle.

NATIONALISM AS A RELIGION

The modern nation-state contains within itself many of the characteristics of religion, and nationalism has been termed the religion of the state. In fact, man's traditional religion is even threatened by the religion of nationalism—a supreme devotion to state rather than a personal God. This type of nationalism is not simply patriotism. It is not only love of country. Nationalism of this kind consists of being obsessed with the supreme importance of one's country above all else.

It has its hymns of praise, its days of feasting, its altars of freedom. The quality of self-sacrifice demanded for the state often takes on religious aspects. Piety is sought from its members, and adoration for its national heroes and martyrs. It is famous for its missionary spirit, and represents the cult of the nation.

NATIONALISTIC FEELINGS OF SUPERIORITY

To insure devotion from the citizens, much time is spent in conditioning the people in their attitudes and feelings of superiority over other nations. These feelings are by-products of the belief that the continued existence and well-being of the nation is one of the principal objects of the life of the citizens. There is scarcely a people that does not think its culture superior to that of every other.[1] The Japanese have thought of themselves as the race chosen to rule. The Chinese for ages have referred to themselves as the Middle Kingdom—the center of the earth. The Russians have called the western Europeans the "nemei," or dumb nations. The German Nazis and Italian Fascists were notorious for their exalted notions of superiority. And in America we consider our nation to be the best and the most powerful in all history, and the hope of the world to preserve democracy. There are millions of patriotic Americans and hundreds of societies devoted primarily to patriotic ideals, although their feelings of nationalism do not reach the extremes of people in totalitarian countries.

Yet in an analysis of eleven kinds of *outstanding* contributions to science and art, Lehman has found that no one nation has ranked first during the last four centuries in its total number of creative contributions to all eleven fields of endeavor.[2]

EXTENT OF NATIONALISTIC PREJUDICES

Nationalistic prejudices frequently cut across all other prejudices. Thus, strong feelings against other nationalities are found within a nation which includes Catholics, Jews, Protestants, and Buddhists. Likewise, strong nationalistic feelings exist in countries with more than one language. In old Austria-Hungary, depending on the geographical location, court proceedings were carried on in three languages; in present-day Switzerland German, French, and Italian are all spoken; and in the United States many languages are spoken by different people who are proud of their American citizenship. In fact, the only means of determining the nationality of a person is to ask him—for his answer may indicate how he feels.[3]

PSYCHOLOGICAL BASES OF NATIONALISTIC PREJUDICES

What are the bases of these strong feelings of nationalism? All those factors mentioned in the third paragraph of Chapter 23 apply here, but there are certain items which should be specifically mentioned. Although our main concern here is with our own prejudices against other nationalities, nationalistic prejudices exist in all cultures, and many of the factors mentioned below could easily be duplicated in countries other than the United States. For example, ignorance of other peoples (page 559) is by no means limited to Americans; most Turks and Chinese know as little about Americans—except through erroneous ideas picked up in the movies and contact with American servicemen in World War II—as most Americans know about them. Similarly, the stereotyping fallacy (page 561) is by no means limited to Americans with their conceptions of "volatile Italians" or "immoral Frenchmen"; but these other peoples also have stereotyped notions about "money-chasing, aggressive Americans." And feelings of *intense uncompromising nationalism* are *deliberately fostered* to a far greater extent in totalitarian nations than in the democracies.

1. *Differences in Appearance.* We have previously noted that people whose appearance is different from other groups are looked at askance. For this reason many Americans look down on people of other nationalities who dress or ornament themselves differently from ourselves. For the same reason, people in the Orient are often suspicious of Americans and other Caucasian groups who come into their country.

2. *Distrust and Fear of the Strange.* A strange group is considered an enemy group or an inferior group until its members prove themselves otherwise. Those individuals with whom we have not been acquainted before, whose ways we have not known, are looked upon with distrust and even fear, especially if they become our competitors. People born in the United States whose names are of Polish, Slavic, or Italian origin report difficulties in being accepted by "native American" groups because of their names. Differences in language behavior—including accent—increase feelings of prejudice. Aliens and alien methods are made to appear ridiculous or perhaps dangerous, while the familiar methods of one's own culture tend to be accepted as "natural" or even God-given.

3. *Separation or Isolation.* Individuals who have not traveled in a foreign country or who have not known individuals of another nationality group look on members of that group with suspicion because they act and think differently. This separation or isolation is not necessarily a physical one. It may simply be "social distance," in the very community in which you live. Recent immigrants from Europe, for example, even though living on the same street with "natives," may be set apart socially almost as much as if they had remained in the old country.

4. *Ignorance.* Lack of knowledge of what other nationalities are like is often due to false standards of education, and to an emphasis on the traditions of one's own country to the exclusion of others. Again, this is not unique in the United States. Every nationality emphasizes its own culture, while the ways of other nationalities are of little interest other than as a source of comparison and sometimes amusement.

In one ingenious experiment, students were asked to rate ten nationality groups—Chinese, French, Greek, Japanese, Russian, English, German, Hindu, Norwegian, American—in respect to various attributes.[4] The students were then classified according to their amount of travel in foreign countries. There was a definite gradation in favor of those nationalities in whose countries the students had traveled, in fact, a consistent lessening of prejudice as the students' travel experience varied from no travel, to travel less than one week, one week to six months, and six months or more. That is, more favorable attitudes were expressed toward a particular nationality by those who had traveled in that country. Furthermore, the average position of all the groups among which the given subject had no intimate acquaintances was 6.14 on a ten-point scale in which a high score represented prejudice or dislike. For those who had one acquaintance, the rating was 5.07; two acquaintances, 4.50; three acquaintances, 3.19; four acquaintances, 2.65. In other words, both travel in a foreign country and acquaintance with members of some foreign group meant greater liking of the particular nationality. This tendency is to be contrasted with the unfavorable attitudes toward Outgroups when they live in the United States and are a source of economic competition. Some of these attitudes were analyzed in the preceding chapter.

5. *Personal Experience.* Again and again we have mentioned various bases of individual *conditioning*. Rather than list these once more, two examples of *traumatic conditioning* against particular nationalities will be given. The first concerns Chinese:

When I was about five years old a friend of mine said that her mother had told her that if she ever called a Chinese laundryman a "Chinky Chinky Chinaman," he would chase her with a hot iron, and if he caught her he would brand her on the back. This excited us, and we decided to see what would happen.

We would pass the laundry on the way home from school every day and open the screen door and scream at the top of our lungs, "Chinky Chinky Chinaman." Nothing happened at first, but one day when we screamed at the laundryman, he picked up the iron and started for the door. By the time he got to the door we must have been almost home, but whether he picked up the iron with malicious intent or not, he rid himself of us forever, and I hate to this day to go into a Chinese laundry by myself.

The second concerns Italians:

When I was a youngster there was an Italian huckster who peddled his vegetables each day in our neighborhood, and it was the favorite sport of my playmates to torment him while he went from door to door. During the barrage of boyish disparaging invectives hurled at him there were, of course, among them certain phrases and comments not particularly complimentary to the Italian race. One day the huckster had apparently borne the abuse to the breaking point, so he grasped a hatchet that he used for opening produce and fruit crates and threw it at us. Fortunately the weapon was not well aimed and did not strike any of us, but we scattered and ran, scared to death. Since that boyhood experience I have classed all Italians as very hot tempered, lacking in emotional constraint, and quite willing to commit serious bodily attack. This experience has caused me to hold all Italians at a distance, and when I do occasionally come into contact with them I am particularly careful to handle them with discretion and diplomacy.

6. *Economic and Social Competition.* The manifestations of prejudice vary considerably from one section of the United States to another. In southern Texas, prejudice is manifested toward Mexicans; on the West coast formerly toward the Chinese, and more recently toward the Japanese; in northern New York State toward the French "Canucks"; in parts of Michigan toward the Dutch. Wherever competition for jobs is fairly keen, prejudice arises among the people who are competing. This is enhanced considerably if the minority competitors have a lower standard of living and will work for lower wages. The prejudices often begin with the lower economic groups because of actual competition, but then spread to the upper economic brackets as well. Social competition is not severe at first, but may become so after a group has become fairly well assimilated. After a foreign group has been in the United States for a generation or so and adopted American folkways and mores, prejudice is directed against its members because they do not have "native American" or Anglo-Saxon names.

7. *Differences in Culture.* Material culture traits are rather quickly adopted by immigrant groups; and they learn to buy and drive automobiles, purchase vacuum cleaners on the installment plan, and own electric

refrigerators, electric irons, and washing machines.[5] Yet when it comes to the *nonmaterial* culture traits, difficulties may arise. For example, it may be hard for members of an immigrant group to develop strong anti-Negro feeling when they have not experienced Negroes before and do not have a long tradition concerning the War between the States. Similarly, it is difficult for them to give up the traditions and ways of the old country and adopt American ways.

8. *Stereotyping.* Everyone has definite notions of what people of other nationalities are like. The French are believed to be emotional and somewhat immoral; Italians are supposedly excitable and liable to engage in criminal careers; Germans are scientific but also war-hungry; Russians are "radicals"; the English have no sense of humor.

> To the average American, the average Englishman seems affected, patronizing, humorless, impolite, and funny. To him also the Englishman wears spats and carries an eyeglass; to him also he is slim and neatly dressed; yet the American . . . is not impressed by these elegancies; he considers them ridiculous. . . .[6]

Many an American who has traveled in England has had some Englishman say to him, "But you are not at all like most Americans." This simply means that the person does not conform to the stereotyped notion which an Englishman may have of noisy, gum-chewing, aggressive, gin-drinking, gun-toting Americans. In answer to the question, "When you think of an American, what kind of person do you think of?" at least one-third of the British indicate that they think of a boaster, one who is loud voiced, cocksure, and opionated.[7] Similarly, an American may say in amazement to an Englishman, "But you don't speak so differently from me," which means that the American had strange notions of how Englishmen actually talk. Our ideas of our neighbors to the south are likewise illuminating:

> There are some things which any American knows about all Mexicans: Mexicans are bandits, they carry guns, they make love by moonlight, they eat food which is too hot and drink which is too strong, they are lazy, they are communists, they are atheists, they live in mud houses and play the guitar all day. And there is one more thing which every American knows: that he is superior to every Mexican.[8]

9. *Propaganda Devices.* The various propaganda devices described in Chapter 9 are important in reinforcing nationalistic prejudices. For example, the use of bad names in describing other groups helps to create and to keep alive antagonism.[9] Children may hear adults or older children use nicknames of disgust—"Wop," "Greaser," "Frog," "Limey," "Squarehead," "Kraut," "Hunkie," "Chink"—and become conditioned to the label as representing unfavorable characteristics of the particular nationality.

10. *Jingoism.* Every nationality group has some "superpatriots" who deliberately stir up prejudice against other groups, sometimes with the definite purpose of involving their own country in war. William Randolph Hearst has been an outstanding example of a jingoist in our own country. The Spanish-American War, for example, has been traced by some observers in part to certain of Hearst's activities. There are always persons, and even organizations, deliberately trying to create prejudices against other countries. Some of these people, of course, are paid propagandists.

11. *Patriotism and Community Loyalty.* One majority culture pattern in the United States involves traditions many generations old. Thousands of Americans make a fetish of "ancestor worship." Although all groups in the United States save the American Indians were originally immigrants, there is considerable prestige in having had early pioneer farmers and woodsmen for ancestors as compared with more recent European ancestry.

"Native Americanism" is fostered by various organizations. Although the psychological functions which such groups perform are useful, many of the members tend to overlook what American culture is actually like today. Plymouth Rock and Jamestown were important, but so is Ellis Island. The culture of the United States today is not simply an extension of Anglo-Saxon life from the British Isles, but it is part of European and even of Asiatic and African culture. At least one-third of our population is *not* of Anglo-Saxon origin. Present-day America is as much the result of the labor and the genius of immigrants who have come over in the last seventy or eighty years as it is of the early Anglo-Saxon strain.

Most Americans agree that "the white race is the best on earth" and that "the United States is unquestionably the best country in the world."[10] And one who lives in a large city becomes impressed with the loyalty and allegiance of all peoples to the state in which they originated —"back home" is a frequent phrase. An outstanding *Middletown* clubwoman said to a group of children:

> You must have community spirit. You must think that there is no finer town in the whole United States than this. There is no finer school than yours, no finer parents than yours, no finer opportunities anywhere than you have right here. People talk of California where there is sunshine all the year round, but I've lived in California, and give me Middle Western rains! I tell you there's no lovelier place on God's footstool than this old state of ours.[11]

12. *Nationalistic Indoctrination in Social Institutions.* Any number of social institutions contribute to the promotion of nationalistic feelings.[12] This conditioning begins almost at the time a child draws his first breath, before he is "awake" to his world. Parents pass on their patriotic attitudes to the children. In the educational system, considerable emphasis

is placed on the superiority of white groups, and especially of Americans. Many textbooks that consider critically the causes of a major war or criticize the myths and legends surrounding the lives of national heroes encounter the wrath of various patriotic societies.[13] An examination of 160 high-school texts in geography, history, civics, and biology on the accredited lists of various school systems showed that 66 per cent use the word "race" where "nationality" or "people" is meant, and that 20 per cent contain teachings of "racial" superiority.[14] Feelings of nationalism are likewise instilled in many church situations. "In Sunday School classes and in sermons, pictures of the benighted heathen peoples are added to other images and stereotypes about other nations and races."[15]

The glory of the state is also demonstrated by outstanding personalities of the Army, Navy, and civil services, and in the ceremonies and rituals surrounding them. We have already seen (Chapter 19) that most secret societies foster feelings of nationalism. This is, of course, an important function of all patriotic groups. In addition, various youth organizations such as the Boy Scouts, Girl Scouts, and Camp Fire Girls, condition people at early ages to be supremely loyal to the state and nation. The political party also serves as a rallying force for the nation, and acts as a focus for the discussion of national problems.

The modern newspaper has tremendous influence in molding nationality prejudices. Over a period of years it impresses upon citizens the traditions, symbols, and maxims of the nation. The wide use of political cartoons has strong effect in stereotyping foreign nations; and we have our nationalistic stereotypes further reinforced by modern movies and radio programs.

FASCISM

Extreme nationalistic feelings grew up in several European countries in the 1930's under Fascist ideologies. Fascism was first developed in Italy under the leadership of Benito Mussolini. Its influence soon spread beyond Italy, and many of its principles were the basis for Hitler's National Socialist party. With its philosophy of a strong military state, government by force, and sacred national egoism, Fascism grew from a political party movement to be the ruling force in the government of Italy. However, the Nazi regime of Germany was eventually influencing and dominating Mussolini and his Fascist dictatorship in Italy; and many of the same kinds of organizations and propaganda techniques, developed under the Nazis, also grew up in Italy.

In 1936 the Rome-Berlin "Axis" came into being, a collaboration avowedly to oppose the spread of Communism. Japan joined the Axis the following year in a pact for political, cultural, and economic cooperation; and the Axis "war of nerves" was under way, eventually developing into World War II.

THE NAZI PROGRAM

The former Nazi regime in Germany is of particular interest because it went further than any other government in stimulating extreme nationalism and exalted notions of superiority. The feelings of nationalism developed in a democracy are in the direction of unity, but they are not so likely to result in war as in Fascist nations where those in power stimulate feelings of intense nationalism in order to get support for policies which imply unrestricted use of force and risk of war. Patriotism and loyalty are aims of nationalistic programs in the United States, but not ultimate warfare. In Nazi Germany, on the other hand, nationalism was built up and intensified with one aim and one alone—political and economic domination of other countries. This Nazi program was based on ideas of: (1) a common enemy; (2) common sacrifice; (3) a common scapegoat; (4) the elimination of all counteragitators; (5) national unity; (6) community good will; (7) the removal of vice; (8) acts of national prestige; (9) the provision of disciplined leadership for all groups.[16] And the ultimate goal was conquest and mastery.

> Here were men . . . who were deliberately cultivating war as the central framework of society. They had made it the operating principle of the state, the primary social institution binding all others together. War was as fundamental to the totalitarian state as the concept of majority rule or legal process was to the democratic type of social organization. Their economy was based on armament orders; their politics on military discipline; their social aims on imperial conquest; their foreign policy on . . . cruel myths—racial superiority, survival of the fittest, population pressure, the necessity to expand and so on . . .[17]

That such indoctrination had a very real effect on German youth was demonstrated by McGranahan in a survey made after the surrender of Germany.[18] A comparison of responses from American and German youth to anonymous questionnaires on social and ethical attitudes showed that the German boys and girls placed much higher values on obedience to authority, honor, and loyalty to the state; they also expressed more faith in their national superiority than American youth, and expressed less tolerance and respect for individuals.

GROWTH OF THE NAZI REGIME

The National Socialist regime grew up in Germany largely because of the country's economic instability. Defeat in the first World War, and the world depression of the late 1920's, had together resulted in unemployment and misery for millions of Germans. A fertile soil had thus been provided for the growth of new ideologies, and conditions were ripe for a new leader in the form of Adolf Hitler, presented to the German people as their savior.

The Nazi program was put into effect with the financial help of powerful industrialists who feared communism; and the device for winning popular support was through a huge propaganda campaign reinforced by acts of terrorism against the "nonbelievers" and the "scapegoats" (Jews). All the propaganda devices mentioned in Chapter 9 were used over and over again.[19] *Name-calling* attacks were made on "alien enemies," especially the Jews. *Glittering generalities* were contained in appeals such as those for the "welfare of the community." The establishment of Hitler as a quasi divinity to whom the religious feelings of German people could be transferred was an instance of the *transfer technique.* The *testimonial device* is illustrated by the statement that, "The Führer knows the goal and knows the direction." The fact that Hitler was a "man of the people" who wore simple clothes, ate plain food, and led a quiet, secluded life, represented the *plain-folks technique. Card stacking* was twofold: rigid censorship, including an elaborate spy system and the use of concentration camps; and falsehoods and misrepresentations, especially through the government-controlled press and radio. The *band-wagon device* is illustrated by the fact that lack of outward sympathy with the Nazi program was akin to treason.

Eventually the Nazi party grew into a great secret society, perhaps the largest of all times. It had its mysterious swastika, its parades, its officers, its "Third Reich," its esoteric "wisdom," its solidarity achieved by familiar symbols and uniforms; and it was elaborately organized with even a women's auxiliary, children's groups, and youth divisions.[20] Among the Nazi organizations were the Elite Guard or SS, Storm Troops, National Socialist Motor Corps, Order Police, City Guards and Rural Guards, Factory Guards, Railroad Militia, Labor Service, Todt Organization, Ex-Soldiers' Organization, and Hitler Youth.

GERMAN RACIAL DOCTRINES

The racial theories of Nazi Germany were actually developed, and had been accepted by many Germans, long before the advent of Hitler. But these racial doctrines were made an essential part of the state's philosophy when the political government of Germany changed hands in 1933. According to this racial credo, Germans belonged to a Nordic or "Aryan" race—a group of supermen, tall, long-legged, and slender, with broad shoulders, narrow hips, blond hair, fair skins, and pale eyes, usually blue or blue-gray.

Actually Germany consists of one of the most mixed stocks in Europe, and it is scientifically untrue that there is any "Germanic race." Germans are a blend of many early groups. There is no more a German race than there is an English or an American race. But, as we have indicated more than once, *if people want to believe certain things to be true, then they are true for them.* Thus, the Aryan stereotype was accepted by millions of

Nazis even to the extent of overlooking the fact that it did not fit their own leaders. Look at photographs of the Nazi leaders, and ask yourself how you would look if you were as blond as Hitler, as slender as Goering, as manly as Streicher, as tall as Goebbels, or as long-headed as Rosenberg.[21]

The social sciences eventually collapsed in Germany. Many of the "scientific" publications of Nazi Germany would be laughable if they were not so tragic. An experiment was reported in a German psychological journal in 1939 which was supposed to show that the superiority of "Nordic races" is reflected in race differences among chickens![22] The Nordic chicken was said to be inwardly integrated, better behaved, and more efficient in feeding than the Mediterranean chicken, thus paralleling certain supposed typological differences among humans. In another German journal of the same period the writer of an article dealing with "the deeper meaning of pure and mixed blood" came to the conclusion that the Germans and a few millions of related peoples were the last reserve of creative humanity, and that the influence of uncreative non-Germans must be kept away from their youth.[23]

THE RUSSIAN PROBLEM

Concurrently with the development of the Nazi regime, a strong Socialist state had grown up in Russia (the Union of Soviet Socialist Republics) under Joseph Stalin. Although Russia and the United States of America had been military allies during World War II—and there had been important diplomatic conferences between the leaders of the two nations together with Britain's wartime minister—the end of the war was the beginning of a period of mutual distrust and suspicion. The lack of confidence by the representatives of the two nations in each other was illustrated dramatically again and again in sessions of the United Nations, where Russia and the United States were repeatedly in opposition.

Undoubtedly a great deal of this was due to exalted feelings of nationalism on the part of the Russians, or perhaps feelings of inferiority which could be covered up or concealed only by rude or bluff tactics. This manifested itself even to the extent of holding back information to America or any Western power on any aspects of life back of Russia's "Iron Curtain," and refusal to let outsiders enter this forbidden Russian territory which began to expand westward in a "cold war" and encompass in rapid succession Yugoslavia, Albania, Bulgaria, Hungary, Rumania, Czechoslovakia, and Finland. (As early as 1939 and 1940, Stalin had seized Estonia, Latvia, and Lithuania; and after the war had become complete master of Poland.)

The foreign-news editor of the United Press pointed out in 1947 that much of the conflict between Russia and the United States could be explained by the complete *misconceptions* which people in each nation had about the other country.[24] Russians, for example, were likely to believe that: the United States was a "capitalist, imperialist state"; that the "capitalist imperialist states," headed by the United States, encircled Russia and plotted against her; that the United States was the world's leading *militaristic* power; and that America's relations with the world were basically hypocritical. This same writer listed the following as basic American fallacies: that Russia was a completely Communist state; that Russia's major preoccupation was "world revolution"; that Russia was a strong and *aggressive* state; and that Russian diplomacy was "a riddle wrapped in a mystery inside an enigma."

Regardless of the extent to which any of the beliefs on either side were based in whole or in part on fact, the point is that the people in both nations developed *even greater feelings of nationalism.* Russia's policy of non-cooperation seemed to increase with each new issue in international affairs. Her opposition to the Marshall Plan for European Recovery, and her continuing moves of aggression, as evidenced especially in the cases of Czechoslovakia and Finland, increased the fears of Americans of an eventual showdown between Russia and the United States.

Along with Russian refusal to cooperate on free exchange of newspapermen and radio representatives, there began an increase of distortion and misrepresentation of American news and views. By 1948, the United States and Russia were engaged in psychological warfare on an extensive scale, including propaganda broadcasts beamed at people in other nations, especially in Europe. The possibilities that the two powers might be involved in a world conflict led each one to increase its military strength considerably during 1948.

COMMUNISM

Attitudes of the American people, as indicated in various studies conducted by the Survey Research Center of the University of Michigan during 1946 and 1947, may be briefly summarized as follows:

> Most Americans believe that Russia is behaving badly. They feel that Russia has been obstinate and uncompromising in her dealings with this country since the war. They believe that she has been unreasonable in her insistence on her own way in the various international conferences. This criticism comes about equally often from all of the broad classifications within the American public; it is not confined to any particularly anti-Russian group. . . . Only a very small minority feel with assurance that the United States can count on a cooperative spirit on the part of Russia in settling world problems. For the most part, Americans regard themselves as unfriendly toward the Soviet Union.[25]

This does not imply, however, that most people were generally well informed regarding Russia. In fact, the contrary was true. The great majority of people do not follow international problems and news sufficiently to grasp and retain more than the broadest facts. Surveys showed that most people had only the most elementary notions of the political and economic structure of the Soviet Union, or of the life of the Russian people; the single concept which had made the greatest impression on American people was the *dictatorial* character of the Russian state.[26]

This meant that problems of nationalism developed into an even broader and more important international question. This involved a fundamental conflict between two entirely different ideologies and ways of life—the Russian totalitarian system, with its emphasis on the supremacy of the state; and the American democratic system, with its emphasis on the individual, his rights, and his freedom. Americans developed a hatred of Communism even greater than their previous hatred of Nazism, for their fears were greater for themselves—fears that Communism might sweep the world, and that Stalin and his lieutenants would be the dictators.

Americans had always disliked Communism, but now they became increasingly fearful of the Communists in the United States, and of the possibility that such a group could develop into a powerful organization which might try to overthrow the United States government by force or violence. The many misgivings held by Americans about Communist ideologies were added to when the Chairman of the Communist Party of the United States testified before a Senate Judiciary subcommittee that American Communists would not support the United States in any conceivable war with the Soviet Union.[27]

All over America, and throughout the world, people wondered whether there would be such a war.

▶ THE SOCIAL PSYCHOLOGY OF WAR

NATIONALISM AS A BASIS OF WAR

The causes of war are many and complex. It is a mistake to look for a *simple* answer to the question: Why do wars arise between the nations of the world? Involved are matters of competing national interests—economic, political, cultural—competing ideologies, and the failure *so far* of any international organization to cope successfully with disputes between nations and to guarantee to the peoples of the nations their basic liberties.

Before a nation goes to war, its people must be prepared to fight. An aggressive nationalism predisposes a nation to war. If other causes are also operative, war will likely result. A nation with less virulent nationalistic sentiments will tend to seek peaceful adjustment of international disputes so as to avoid war. When war seems imminent, or has actually broken out, then strong nationalistic feelings on the part of the citizens become an important factor in gaining victory.

The development of *intense* and *uncompromising* feelings of nationalism is usually a fundamental step toward preparation for war. And the morale of the people holds up better during wartime if these feelings of nationalism and patriotism have been fanned to a white pitch comparable to that of religious fervor and excitement. This is in no place better illustrated than in Nazi Germany of the late 1930's and early 1940's. The fanatical development of nationalism there is to be contrasted with patriotic conditioning in the United States due largely to the democratic way of life itself. *The essence of democracy is freedom,* not suppression and coercion. Americans have become devoted to their traditions and practical forms of living, and to the nation that represents the fullest expression of this way of life. But this democratic nationalism is not directed toward war as its goal, although it may result in willingness to go to war if the representatives of another nation explicitly challenge its right to existence as a democracy,

THE SUPPOSED INEVITABILITY OF WAR

You may say, then, that war must be inevitable. A great many people believe this. Three reasons in particular have been advanced for the inevitability of war: first, that war is a "divine institution"; second, that, since there have always been wars, there will always be war; third, that "human nature" is unchangeable.[28]

But what are the facts of the case? First, the notion of war as a divine institution may be scotched at once. There is certainly no evidence that God is a warmonger or favors one side more than the other—except in the propaganda materials.

Second, the notion of the universality of war is not strictly true. Within recent years primitive groups have been discovered to whom war is unknown, and there is evidence from some ancient civilizations which indicates that the people were entirely pacific.

The third argument, that human nature cannot be changed, is one phase of the old instinct theory. According to this belief, there is a fighting or pugnacious instinct in mankind which cannot be eradicated. In Chapter 4 we saw how variable is "human nature" from one group to another, and in Chapter 6 we indicated that fighting is *learned,* rather than instinctive. It is true that fighting is found in many species throughout the animal kingdom, and that the phenomenon of war—in the sense of organized intra-specific group fighting—is confined to men and a few species of ants.[29] But this does not mean that war is "instinctive." War-ing can be changed just as can other learned patterns of behavior. For example, consider such an activity as that of taking a bath:

> From the instinct point of view, our tribal ancestors had a nonbathing instinct; but, although bathing is not yet as popular as it might be, we have made considerable progress towards doing away with the nonbathing instinct and the substitution of a bathing instinct. It would have been no more foolish to say, a thousand years ago, that since men had generally been dirty, there was no hope of their ever becoming cleanly in their habits, than it was to say thirty years ago that since men did make war, nothing could change them into peaceful people.[30]

War is somewhat akin to religious persecution and to dueling. So long as these activities were taken for granted, it was easy to say that, although they were "bad," they were part of human nature, and, therefore, could not be eradicated. Today both dueling and active religious persecution have practically disappeared in this country. The prestige factors in dueling and the scapegoat mechanism in religious persecution are satisfied in other ways. Of course, war is infinitely more complex; but this very complexity is another indication that it consists of many different *learned* patterns of behavior.

This theme is well developed by Mark A. May in his book, *A Social Psychology of War and Peace.*[31] He challenges the popular notion that the underlying causes of war are found in man's fighting instincts; but instead shows that human nature is affected by various types of bias in man's environment. War and peace are dependent on the conditioning and habit patterns learned by men. This type of education is a *long-term* process. Nicholas Murray Butler is reported to have said in the 1930's that *nothing* could be done to stop the next war, but that the Carnegie Endowment for International Peace, of which he was President, was engaged in "trying to stop the war a hundred years from now."[32]

THE MUNITIONS MAKERS

Another theory of modern war, especially popular after World War I, is that the munitions makers and the bankers purposely bring about war in order to line their own already overflowing purses. This exaggerated belief implies that the "merchants of death" are personal devils. There is no question that individuals here and there have favord war for their own private gains, either in money or prestige.[33]

However, as for the great majority of businessmen, bankers, and investors, the weight of the evidence is that as individuals they have been opposed to war.[34] Obviously war means wholesale speculation and lack of prediction, whereas peace means greater stability and reasonably accurate forecasting. Even though some makers of war materials favor "preparedness" campaigns in order to stimulate orders, actual war is opposed by most businessmen.[35]

OTHER SUPPOSED CAUSES OF WAR

The list of supposed causes of war goes on indefinitely. First one factor and then another has been seized on as being wholly responsible. The causal factors suggested by various persons have been as diversified as: sunspots, climate, and the arrangements of the planets; overpopulation and underpopulation; high birth rates and low birth rates; high death rates and low death rates; the "universal law of struggle for existence"; psychological factors such as fear, the fight for freedom, the lust for power, and man's vanity; philosophical abstractions like "Destiny" and "Providence."[36]

Like many social phenomena, no one factor is by itself the entire cause. There is little question, for example, that a social and economic structure oriented toward imperialism is more likely than not to lead to tensions which may eventually result in warfare. Yet however true it may be that basic economic problems in our social system may produce acts of aggression, including war, we must remember that the "social system" is not some sort of a super-entity entirely separated from *men*. It is men, after all, who make any social system; our social institutions do not exist apart from us as if they were external forces controlling us.

WISHFUL THINKING

Many people approach the problem of the prevention of war with little more than pious hopes and a feeling of helplessness. We have endless portrayals of the horrors and the futility of war—in plays, short stories, movies, novels, radio dramas, speeches, articles, and newspaper accounts. We have had elaborate organizations such as the National Council for the Prevention of War, World Peaceways, the National Committee on the Cause and Cure of War, and the Women's International League for Peace and Freedom. The rest of us say that we are against war, and yet engage in little more than wishful thinking about peace. Perhaps we have resorted too much to the simple technique of name-calling. We have denounced war and warmongers, and this has made us feel better.

Modern mankind in the main has fallen prey to a militaristic set of attitudes, although most men prefer to deny this. Men lay the foundations for militarism and for war, and then bemoan the fact that they are killing and being killed. Even before the hostilities begin, many a person fatalistically chalks up a war on his private calendar, but at the same time argues to himself that "my number isn't coming up." Men manage to want the conditions of peace and the situations that lead to war at the very same time. Even the United States has engaged in a war of some sort about once every twenty-five years.

OTHER PSYCHOLOGICAL FACTORS IN WAR

While peace is drab and empty for millions of people, war is exciting. When large numbers of individuals in any country have been thwarted in their desires, war may come as a welcome relief. People can escape; they can engage not only in mental but in physical *regression* and carry on all sorts of play activities and ritualism ordinarily not permitted. If one is a soldier or sailor and there are dangers to be met, there is always the possibility of "fun" on a furlough with wine, women, and song; the taboos of "back home" can be violated. The dreams of heroism require little effort and give considerable pleasure. And some of the pleasures are quite tangible.

> The army offers the thrill of the uniform, the vanity of chevrons, the pride of decorations for bravery. There is the irresistible excitement of the drums and the intoxicating pleasure of . . . the military band. There is the melodrama of flags, pageants, parades, extravagant oratory, and the glorious thrill of being worshipped by mothers, sweethearts, and the multitudes that line the boulevards.[37]

In spite of the efforts of many women's groups in peace work, the great majority of American women have been nursed on the "Girl I Left Behind Me" type of slogan, and taught the glamour of being war brides (either as civilians or as servicewomen). Along with men they have grown up learning to believe that somehow war is inevitable, and that it is woman's place to be strong and courageous and smiling as she carries on *volunteer* activities.

In spite of this traditional background, however, women the world over participated in the second World War in a greater measure than in any war in history; and American women for the first time in any number served in all the armed services of the country. On the home front, aside from volunteer activities, women's organizations took a more active political interest in the problems of making and maintaining the peace, working for the organization of the United Nations and its special agencies, and seeking to get women represented on the various councils of such agencies.

We may be shocked when a Mussolini tells Italians that their war is to be one of religion, that is, "religion of humanity and civil progress" against disorders.[38] But we cannot afford to be shocked when we ourselves are at war or contemplating war. The psychological factor of *suggestion* is one of the many important factors in building up the feeling that war is necessary. When a few members of a group are stimulated to emotional behavior, the other members receive stimulation from those already aroused, and themselves become stimulated. In this case the environmental situation is loaded with suggestion. This means that feelings of national unity can be achieved during wartime far better than in peacetime. During a war, people are sometimes willing to give up their election rights and practically to turn over their private enterprises to the government, as in the case of the English in World War II.

Similarly, *imitation* enters into the picture quite easily, because of the common experiences, customs, and mores of the people within a nation. Since their attitudes are often based on history that is a history of the group as a whole, on customs that are somewhat common to all, and on stereotyped ideas of what they as a people are, reactions to a common danger are quite similar. Being banded together in a common enterprise of "all for one, and one for all," each person can *identify* himself with the leaders and the heroes, and even with the cause itself. One may be able to experience vicariously the thrills of war without necessarily being involved in *all* the dangers. At the same time everyone, serviceman or civilian, can *project* all sorts of repressed and hateful characteristics onto the representatives of the enemy. This becomes much simpler if one person or idea can be seized upon as the living embodiment of the enemy —such as Hitler or Nazism. For everyone, the desires for *new experience, security, response,* and *recognition* affect wartime behavior.

▶ SOME PSYCHOLOGICAL ASPECTS OF WORLD WAR II

THE DEVELOPMENT OF WAR-NATIONALISM IN GERMANY

The place of nationalism in the development of the war situation is clearly seen in the sequence of events leading up to September, 1939. On the one hand, people in the democracies showed a pacifistic tolerance and a desire to appease, based upon an unwillingness to accept war as a part of modern civilized existence and upon a fear of the consequences of war should it befall them. On the other hand, under the tutelage of the National Socialist party in Germany and the Fascist regime in Italy, people in those countries had come to accept war as a necessary part of national policy, as the fulfillment of national destiny.

The idealism of citizens in a democracy may be contrasted with the ideologies of the people living under the Nazi regime, which slowly culminated in one of the most closely knit nationality groups of all history. When the second European war began in 1939, there could be no letdown in this philosophy; and feelings of fervent nationalism were constantly strengthened in preparation for the *Blitzkrieg* against England in 1940. There were at least nine different mental processes, common to most people, to which Hitler and his propagandists appealed in order to keep the people strongly nationalistic and war-minded:[39]

1. *Custom.* Most persons tend to believe and act according to traditional patterns of home, school, church, and community. Accordingly, Hitler's propaganda continued to be in terms of traditional German patriotism. It also included public condemnation of big business and international banking, and praise of small business enterprises, although privately big industrialists were supported.

2. *Simplification.* Most people cannot understand complex explanations of events. They need simple formulas and concrete examples. Hence, the attack continued on the simple basis of blaming the "English beast," the Jews, and "Jewish communism" for supposed wrongs.

3. *Frustration.* When people are frustrated, they need all sorts of outlets for their feelings. If they vent their hatred on a common enemy, there is less danger of unrest within the country. The British were pointed to as the ones who had started the war and who were out to destroy Germany completely and forever. Churchill was named as the man responsible for England's policy.

4. *Anxiety.* When we anticipate trouble, we become worried and anxious. If we can find relief from our anxiety, we feel better. Hitler was a past master at building up anxiety among his people and then relieving it. Thus, acts of terror were carried out by Brown Shirt squads and by secret police, especially in the form of imprisonment in concentration camps and of death sentences. But relief from anxiety was produced on numerous occasions by sudden surprises, such as the Russo-German pact, the fall of France, and by tremendous gala affairs where the Führer appeared in all his glory. Meanwhile, anxiety was created abroad by propaganda barrages calculated to inspire terror and to demoralize the enemy—Germany bragged of her secret weapons, and it was claimed that a lightning war could blot out the English in only a few days.

5. *Reinforcement.* In order that some attitudes be maintained, they must constantly be reinforced. Hence, the technique of repetition was used. Nazi slogans were endlessly repeated, and the swastika symbol was constantly displayed on every hand.

6. *Association.* Association of ideas is one of the most basic types of conditioning (to be discussed in greater detail below). Two words or ideas are coupled together so many times that one calls forth an association with the other. For example, prior to the Russo-German pact Hitler associated democracy with communism, later with "Jewish capitalism."

7. *Universals.* The generalizations which apply to all objects or to all persons of a given class are called universals. They are one variety of *stereotyping* (compare Chapter 10). Universals were used astutely in Germany, by building up the notion that *all* German "Aryans" were a superior group, and that *all* Jews were "parasites."

8. *Identification.* Most of us want to be "big shots," or at least to be acquainted with people who are important. Hitler became a visible

symbol of the German people, and they identified themselves with him. Their exploits were his exploits, and his life was theirs.

9. *Rationalization.* We often cover up our faults and mistakes, and invent socially acceptable reasons for them. Not only did Hitler blame the outcome of World War I on the Jews, Communists, and Woodrow Wilson, but after World War II had broken out, he easily "explained" away every act which might reflect on the Nazi regime. The argument ran somewhat as follows:

> The Nazi leaders did not want to invade Norway, but they had to prevent the British from invading it. The Führer doesn't want to kill helpless people in England, but the evil Churchill won't make peace. The German soldiers hated to kill refugees on the roads of France, but the cruel and heartless French generals deliberately put the refugees there to block the Nazi advance.[40]

PROPAGANDA IN TOTALITARIAN AND DEMOCRATIC NATIONS

In common parlance the word "propaganda" has come to have an essentially sinister significance, and is frequently used to discredit any idea or set of ideas that are disliked. Actually, propaganda means the selective utilization of either truth or falsehood in order to influence the attitudes and opinions of others. *"Propaganda consists of the planned use of any form of public or mass-produced communication designed to affect the minds and emotions of a given group for a specific purpose, whether military, economic, or political."*[41]

Certain propaganda devices, already discussed, seem to be more effective than others. The ideas advanced may or may not be open to free and impartial investigation; and to a large extent this depends on whether the nation is a democratic or a totalitarian one, and whether peace or war exists.

In a totalitarian system, there is rigid governmental control of the agencies engaged in disseminating news and forming opinions. Reports of events within the nation and in the outside world are strained through the sieve of censorship so that the mass of the people receive only what the government leaders mean for them to receive. With press and radio entirely controlled, with strict penalties for listening to foreign broadcasts, with public meetings and free discussion barred, the people have little or no access to the true facts of their national life or to the movement of events in the world outside. Their judgments are formed, their actions as citizens motivated, by government-dictated or government-inspired statements. The coming of war has the effect merely of tightening still more an already tight censorship, and of itensifying an already thick barrage of nationalistic propaganda.

The situation is different in a democracy. Although nationalistic conditioning proceeds in peacetime, the relative freedom of the press, the radio, and public discussion places a definite limitation on the power of propaganda. Stories released by any group or agency to further a particular cause can be checked for accuracy. In the event of war, however, the citizens do not have the same means of checking the accuracy of news and of analyzing the factual bases of propaganda; and the emergence of censorship as a necessary part of national policy destroys to a considerable degree the freedom of the press and of public discussion. But the censorship, enforced or voluntary, does not reach the extremes of a dictatorship. Foreign-news broadcasts may still be listened to, foreign newspapers and magazines distributed, and relatively free discussion may even take place in public meetings and legislative bodies. Many people come to be "propaganda wise." Incidentally, the continuance of this measure of freedom makes news coming out of a democracy more authentic than that emanating from a totalitarian country.

AIMS OF WAR PROPAGANDA

The problem of maintaining morale has existed in every major conflict in history, but never on so large a scale as in modern warfare. Battles are won not only with bullets and bombs, but also with propaganda and publicity. Morale among the armed forces is only a small portion of this problem, for in any nation at war constant propaganda activities must also be carried out on three additional fronts: (1) to mobilize hatred against the enemy among the *civilian population* at home; (2) to preserve the friendship of citizens of *neutral nations* and of *allies;* and (3) to demoralize both the civilian populations and armed forces of *enemy countries.*[42]

In World War I Americans made the Kaiser the scapegoat. We were out to "Beat the Kaiser" as a hated symbol of *Kultur,* and people found that for once they could openly express feelings of hatred not only as good citizens but also as religious persons. During the first two years of the war we were bombarded with appeals from both the Allies and the Germans to see their side of the war and to aid them in their struggle to preserve civilization. Once we allied ourselves with Great Britain and France, we were reminded again and again of our own Anglo-Saxon culture, and of the fact that Lafayette and the French had aided us in our own war for independence. Later on we carried our propaganda into Germany, telling both citizens and soldiers there that it was futile for them to continue the war. And we "kept the home fires burning" with carefully planned campaigns and drives. Most of our propaganda activities were centered in a "Committee of Public Information."[43]

The three aims of war propaganda, mentioned above, can also be demonstrated in World War II. The Office of War Information, the

Office of Strategic Services, various branches of the War and Navy Departments, and other Federal agencies carried on propaganda activities of numerous kinds.[44]

1. The first aim of war propaganda is to establish firmly among the *whole population* the idea that *the war comes first*. This is more readily achieved in a totalitarian nation, where economic and political centralization is already accepted, than in a democratic nation. In a democracy, it involves the subordination of personal, social, and economic interests to the paramount claims of the prosecution of the war. This aim is partly achieved by stressing the threat to national existence from the enemy, and by fostering hatred for that enemy and for its leaders. Since hatred is more easily directed against an individual than against a nation, a person is usually selected to symbolize the "evil thing" that menaces—such as Hitler. But ideological hatreds also play a large part, and such terms as "Nazi" and "Red" have been widely used to arouse hatred.

2. An equally important aim is to preserve the friendship of the citizens of *neutral countries* and of *allies,* and to secure their cooperation. German propagandists made good headway among the Italians and Japanese, partly because those peoples shared totalitarian aims similar to those of the Third Reich. But the Nazis "jammed" in their American propaganda because of their prior thesis—theirs as well as ours—that the democratic and totalitarian ways of life are unalterably opposed. The people of Great Britain, on the other hand, had the immense advantage of using the same language that we do, of having government and social institutions more similar to our own, and memories of British and Americans engaged in a common cause in World War I.

3. A third aim of war propaganda is to demoralize both the civilian populations and armed forces of *enemy countries*. In modern warfare this may be done by dropping propaganda leaflets from airplanes—as has been done on many fronts—and by a sustained barrage of foreign-language broadcasts. "Lord Haw-Haw" and "Tokyo Rose" became famous radio characters during the second World War. The actual effectiveness of some of this propaganda is open to question, for the majority of people on each side continue to believe that they cannot be beaten. However, some of the most strategically important victories of World War II were won *before* a shot was fired. High-powered propaganda was laid down by the totalitarian leaders with the accurate deliberation of an artillery barrage *prior to* the movements of troops into a country. This was the story of Austria, of the Rhineland, of the Sudetenland and the rest of Czechoslovakia. And the "fifth-column" technique, perfected by Franco in the Spanish Civil War, was put to effective use in Norway, Holland, Belgium, and even in France. Organized Nazi sympathizers in these countries spread the word of the inevitability of Nazi conquest, of the futility

of resistance. When the blow fell, a sufficient number of the defenders were so thoroughly prepared for defeat that military conquest was much easier than it otherwise would have been.

USE OF THE CONDITIONED RESPONSE IN WAR PROPAGANDA

The technique of forming *conditioned responses* (compare Chapter 6) is essential in effective war propaganda. If the original stimulus, which will ordinarily evoke a response, is presented together with the conditioned stimulus over and over again, usually the response produced by the original stimulus is finally obtained by presenting the conditioned stimulus alone. Similarly, through the constant association of disagreeable words with the people of some nation, feelings of unpleasantness originally elicited by the disagreeable words will finally become associated with the mere mention of the particular nationality group. People of this other nationality become "baby killers" or "murderers." Before Hitler invaded Czechoslovakia and Poland, the way was carefully prepared by "documented" reports of atrocities committed against German nationals living in those countries.

This technique of circulating atrocity stories is one of the oldest propaganda devices, as a means of conditioning and of arousing anxiety. If the stories involve women and children, the results are particularly effective. But, if propaganda of this sort is to be effective in another country, the culture of that country must be well understood by the propagandists. Many of the efforts of the Germans were not subtle enough and were the subject of jokes and amusement. In World War I, German agents spread stories in the United States of "sniping" done by Allied soldiers; but, instead of stimulating the expected indignation among Americans, the stories had the opposite effect. Among a people such as ourselves, whose history has many tales that glorify frontier fighting and guerilla warfare, the attitudes toward sniping were not those of universal disapproval. Again, in World War II, German movies of the *Blitzkrieg* in Poland did not serve to create admiration of Americans for Nazi methods or ideologies.

CONDITIONING IN TERMS OF EMOTIONAL SYMBOLS

Conditioning in wartime is particularly effective when tied up with emotional symbols. Vague and ill-defined feelings of patriotism come to be identified with specific nationalistic symbols, especially with the flag and the national anthem. Rallying around such symbols as a focal point, it becomes relatively easy to stir up hatred for any person or anything opposed to these symbols. All features of *institutional* ideology are fostered (compare Chapter 15): that the nation is a supreme entity which transcends the citizens themselves, that the nation is superior to other nations, that it can do no wrong, and that it is bound to win. These ideas are constantly reinforced both by deliberately planned propaganda and by the spread of excitement among the citizens.

Most people have little or no personal contact with their enemy. Therefore, they identify themselves with the state; and the aims of the state become oversimplified, personalized, and moralized into a conflict of Good versus Evil.[45] Once such a philosophy has been accepted, it is easy for most persons openly and publicly to admit their hatred of people —thought of as very different from themselves—who live in enemy countries, and then to rationalize their hatred as being for the public good.

> The history of nearly all war, from the most remote to the most recent, reveals one hackneyed peculiarity. Even when they start on both sides with great professions of "no hate against the enemy people," that attitude undergoes a rapid change as the result of stories of atrocities for which the whole enemy people are held to be responsible. Half a dozen cases, if only of the right degree of obscenity and horror, will suffice to place the enemy people outside the pale, to close our minds, to make impossible any sane and responsible attitude, and any workable peace.[46]

Incidentally, to recognize this technique of war propaganda does not eliminate from consideration the moral issues in war. However, the conflict is usually between two different conceptions of what is good or, at least, practically attainable.

AMERICAN ATTITUDES DURING EARLY PART OF WORLD WAR II

At the outbreak of World War II, most people in the United States, although sympathetic to the Allies, were isolationist with reference to any participation in the "European struggle." And they were very wary of propaganda. Newspaper readers were warned that war stories and communiqués were censored at the source. Radio listeners learned to take with a grain of salt the reports of commentators broadcasting from European capitals. Except in already sympathetic circles, it is doubtful whether either the hundreds of thousands of dollars spent by the German Library of Information for the distribution of leaflets and pamphlets in this country, or the amounts spent on releases by the British Library, were very effective. Most Americans did not like the Nazis, but did admire the English and French and hoped they would win. Yet Americans were determined that they were not going to be sold a bill of goods in favor of either side to the point of American participation in the war.

But when the citizens of a country are not themselves engaged in war, they may feel that they can "sit on the sidelines" comfortably and watch other nations at war, cheering for one side and booing the other. That is what most Americans did during the latter part of 1939 and the early months of 1940. Because of lulls in actual fighting, many Americans began to talk of the conflict as a "phony war." We had not yet become aware of the extent to which modern war consists of political, economic, and psychological warfare, with long-time advance planning and preparation for attack and defense. However, we read the morning headlines, saw the pictures in the newsreels, and "tuned the war in" on our radios, and our apprehensions increased as the months went by.

SYMBOLIC SIGNIFICANCE OF FINLAND

The principal break in our feelings of aloofness came with the Soviet invasion of Finland. When the Russians marched into Finland late in 1939, our dislike of Communism broke into open hatred of "Red Russia"; and our general liking of the Finns grew into open adoration of "little Finland." Finland was looked upon as being the ultimate democracy, while Russia was brutal inhumanity incarnate. The Finns were God-fearing people, the Russians "godless unbelievers." Finland made the front pages by paying the latest installment on her debt to the United States—as usual. The newspapers and radio commentators were overwhelmingly sympathetic to "the underdog." Society balls and sporting benefits swelled the coffers. Movie stars actively campaigned for Finnish relief. The cause was espoused by such diverse personalities as Franklin D. Roosevelt, Herbert Hoover, and Father Charles E. Coughlin. More money was raised for Finland privately in a few weeks than had been raised privately for China in three years, in spite of almost universal sympathy for the Chinese in their war with the Japanese. The news of the collapse of Finnish resistance under overwhelming Russian pressure carried the weight of a personal disaster to countless Americans.

PROPAGANDA FROM GERMANY AND ENGLAND

In the meantime, both the English and the Germans had for months been making concerted propaganda drives to stir up Americans in their favor. Both groups felt that they were "in the right." The members of warring nations always do. And they also believed that God was on *their* side.

> In the first month of the war, the French newspaper *Le Temps* published forty-eight separate articles which sanctified the Allied cause in the name of God and with the blessing of His churches, or implied divine disapproval of the Reich. *The Times* of London published thirty-three such articles; the *Manchester Guardian,* thirty-one . . .
>
> Conversely, the German *Angriff* published eleven articles enlisting religion on Hitler's side; the *Frankfurter Zeitung,* thirteen.[47]

With intense feelings of nationalism and religion combined in a war which each side believed to be one of self-preservation, the activities of the

United States, "the greatest neutral," became of the utmost importance. The German propagandists realized that there was almost no chance of enlisting American help on behalf of Germany, and hence concentrated their efforts on verbal attacks on the British, in the hope that we would remain neutral and thus not give active aid to the Allies. But as in World War I, propaganda activities were difficult for the Germans because of cultural differences, especially in language. One could not be too impressed by an appeal in behalf of "help- and defenceless German civilians." Yet the daily short-wave broadcasts from Germany, given in English, may have had some effect.

Various propaganda organizations, such as the *Deutscher Fichte-Bund* of Hamburg and the organization publishing *News from Germany,* continued to bombard thousands of Americans with their leaflets. The thesis of this literature was that the British were actually to blame for the war; that the Germans were protecting themselves against "encirclement" by other countries; that the Germans had been the aggrieved rather than the aggressors in Poland; and that, even after the war started, it was the British who were responsible for its continuance, not the Germans. The Germans were in need of what they called "space for living," and they claimed to have no alternative but to "meet force with force."

However, the majority of Americans remained unconvinced, and the Gallup poll consistently showed an overwhelming sympathy for the English. The choice between German National Socialism and British democracy was not very difficult for most people to make. With pre-existing attitudes favorable to the English because of a common language and similar traditions, the foundation was already well laid for convincing Americans that they belonged on the side which was "fighting America's battle for her." Even before the outbreak of hostilities, Captain Sidney Rogerson, an Englishman, said in his book, *Propaganda in the Next War,* that the English could be entirely sincere with Americans "as our main plank will be the old democratic one."[48] During the early days of the war Americans were subjected to many an appeal concerning the preservation of British democracy. The British were fighting to smash Hitlerism, and if they were not successful, our democracy as well as theirs might perish.

Even before the war began we had been visited by their Majesties, the King and Queen. And the center of Britain's exhibit at the New York World's Fair was the Magna Charta, from which America's liberties are partly derived, while near by was a huge chart of George Washington's family tree, showing quite definitely that the Father of Our Country was of British stock. The British Commissioner-General to the Fair said:

> . . . Our national contribution would be incomplete without some reference to the foundations in the past in which both of the great English-speaking

democracies have their roots. Accordingly a series of exhibits are designed to illustrate in graphic form the storied past which we share in common with the people of the United States.[49]

The increase in our pro-British feelings was reinforced by the dozens of prominent Englishmen who came to this country during 1939.[50] English lecturers and members of the socially elite traveled over "the States," spoke in public, and dined and chatted with important businessmen, public officials, publishers, college professors, and ministers. Those who visited us included lords and laborites, soldiers and statesmen, politicians and professors. Certainly there was no concerted plot to entrap the United States into a war, but there were definite efforts both by prominent Americans and Englishmen to bolster our already pro-British feelings. A *Fortune* survey made during this period showed that almost 40 per cent of the people felt that the British are our blood brothers and codefenders of democracy.[51]

THE FALL OF FRANCE

At the outbreak of hostilities, Americans were definitely sympathetic to the English and French, but only in a passive way. They were definitely pro-Ally, but not enough so to take any active steps. They were unwilling to do more than express pious hopes that democracy would triumph; and they could rationalize their lack of activity by saying that the Allies would win in the long run anyway. But the rapid conquest by Germany of the smaller European countries—Denmark, Norway, Holland, Belgium, countries which had contributed hundreds of thousands of citizens to the United States—could not be ignored. On this side of the Atlantic we were watching the destruction of ways of living that we understood. The Nazi power was no longer a legend, and the Nazi "lightning war" was actually taking place. About this time the pressure for increased aid for the Allies began, linking the protection of this hemisphere to Allied victory. *Then came the fall of France* in June, 1940.

It is difficult to estimate the shattering effect upon American morale of this event. Even up to the last moment we had still insisted that the Allies would win—it might be a long war, but ultimately Germany would be defeated. So we said. But now that was ended. Probably more important than anything else in galvanizing our sympathies into definite action was the growing realization by millions of Americans of the genuine threat to our interests and to our democratic ways of life by the Nazis. No longer did newspaper headlines, press dispatches, newsreels, and radio talks pretend neutrality. At the beginning of the war, occasional bows had been made in the direction of impartiality, but now Americans knew where their sympathies were, and so did the politicians, newspaper editors, radio commentators, and movie producers. Whereas a year or two before Hollywood producers had not wanted to offend the Germans—in *Idiot's Delight* Esperanto had to be spoken—the lid was off in 1940, and people packed the movie houses to see *The Great Dictator, Foreign Correspondent, Escape,* and other anti-Nazi films long in preparation.

CHANGES IN AMERICAN ATTITUDES

After France's collapse, it seemed certain that England would be invaded at any moment, that Great Britain might be doomed, and that Hitler, as master of Europe, might soon be in a position to challenge the world. The outcome in the United States was a gigantic program of American national defense, resulting in the voting of an unprecedented peacetime budget, a large increase in the national guard, and, late in the summer of 1940, the voting of compulsory registration for military service of all men twenty-one to thirty-five years of age. At first, this defense program was considered in hemispheric terms, and in midsummer a joint defense pact was made with Canada to insure the northern half of the continent against attack. But gradually the defense of America became linked with aid to England. The removal of Chamberlain from the office of Prime Minister of England, and the rise of Churchill's power, had done much to lessen suspicions of Britain; and the attempted *Blitzkrieg* against England in the summer of 1940 had its effect on our sympathies. Actually, the evacuation from Dunkerque, the fall of France, and the bombings of London probably had more to do with most Americans' convictions that we should back the British than any British propaganda. In the autumn of 1940, we sent fifty outmoded destroyers to England in exchange for air bases; and from then on planes, materials of war, and supplies of all kinds began to be shipped on a fairly large scale by American manufacturers.

A national survey covering the period from midsummer to mid-fall, 1940, indicated that Americans had swung sharply toward greater aid to Britain and a firmer stand against Japan in the Far East; the isolationist group had lost about half its supporters, while the interventionist group had grown in size considerably.[52] However, while Gallup polls during the first months of 1941 showed increasing sentiment in favor of a plan to lease or lend war materials to Britain,[53] they also revealed that the majority of people were against our *active* entrance into the war;[54] were opposed to any military aid to Britain, whether from our Army, Air Forces, or Navy;[55] and in May, 1941, 50 per cent of the people were against our entry into the war even if the Nazis should sink an American ship.[56]

Yet two ideas emerged with increasing clarity among many people in the United States: (1) America was probably in serious danger from actual attack if the British fleet were sunk or surrendered. (2) The ways of life enjoyed by Americans in a free democracy were believed to be threatened with destruction if the Axis powers triumphed. From the summer of 1940 through the spring of 1941, the American people were subjected to a bombardment of propaganda, both pro and con, which in itself was an excellent demonstration of democracy at work. Committees were formed to "defend America by aiding Britain," to "keep America out of war," to advocate "America first," to proclaim "no foreign war" for Americans. This debate on a national scale, which reached the floor of Congress in the discussion of the Lend-Lease bill in January and February, 1941, served to clarify the main issue. The passage of the Lend-Lease bill in March after full and free discussion in both houses of Congress marked an abandoment of our previous police of neutrality, and the open acceptance of a policy of all aid short of "active war."

ANTI-JAPANESE FEELINGS

Even the sympathies of Americans for the Chinese in their struggle against Japan were revived. Most Americans had paid little attention when Japan seized Manchuria in 1931-32 and Japanese armies had penetrated, almost without resistance, into north China; but many had become concerned in 1937 and 1938 when the war in China became a real "shooting war." In 1939 and 1940, however, people had become so interested in the European scene that they had almost forgotten about the war in the East. The Japanese propagandists had done their best to make us believe that China was a "violator of treaties," and the Chinese had built up a picture of "Japan the Aggressor."[57] Although our sympathies had been almost wholly for the Chinese, these feelings were much less intense than those we felt for the British, who were white and spoke the same language we did. But, as we began gradually to favor coming to the rescue of Britain with credits and supplies, we also began to feel that we ought at the same time to give more tangible aid to China. Not only did we send money and actual supplies to the Chinese, but we also terminated our shipments of scrap iron and practically all iron and steel products to Japan.

PEARL HARBOR

Although our anti-German and anti-Japanese feelings grew even stronger during the last half of 1941, and although we speeded up our national defense program, it was not until Sunday, December 7, 1941, when the Japanese attacked Pearl Harbor that the American people were galvanized into action. The very next day the United States declared war on Japan, and three days after that on Germany and Italy following earlier Axis declarations.

Overnight the American people went into action. For almost the next four years they "tightened their belts," rationed themselves, volunteered for all kinds of war activities, ran the factories twenty-four hours a day, and as a nation built the largest and strongest fighting force in all history.

Many were the times of indecision as to which side might eventually win the war; but the original Axis powers finally were completely defeated in May, 1945, and Japan in September of the same year. The Fascist ideologies were by no means dead, however, as our occupation troops in Europe soon learned; and even in his surrender message to his people the Emperor of Japan said that Japan "declared war on America and Britain out of our sincere desire to insure Japan's self-preservation and the establishment of East Asia, it being far from our thought to infringe upon the sovereignty of other nations or to embark upon territorial aggrandizement."[58]

THE ATOM BOMB

One of the greatest scientific achievements, and perhaps the most powerful psychological weapon of the war, was the atomic bomb which was dropped on Hiroshima on August 6, 1945. This, and the later one dropped on Nagasaki, were primarily responsible for bringing the war to an end, and opened a new era in man's understanding of warfare. As Dr. Karl T. Compton said, "It was not one atomic bomb, or two, which brought surrender; it was the experience of what an atomic bomb will actually do to a community, *plus the dread of many more,* that was effective."[59]

Atomic scientists have pointed out that nuclear knowledge of this kind cannot forever be kept secret, and that no adequate defenses are known or can be devised![60] It is also conceded that the use of atom bombs in another war could mean the end of civilization as we know it. Because of the enormity of the implications of these new scientific developments, plans were immediately formulated for the development and control of atomic energy for *peaceful* uses. One of the tests made on the bomb after the war, known as Operation Crossroads, may well have been significantly named—man's choice of the use of atomic energy for peace or war. On a purely rational basis, the decision would seem clear.

As a psychological factor, the atom bomb had an indisputable effect on the whole world. All the old concepts of war were changed overnight, and a covert fear gripped people of all nations, including those of the United States, which was at that time the only country in possession of atom bombs, or of the "secret" of producing them. The existence of the bomb imposes a great moral obligation on all nations to outlaw its use for war; and the means of its ultimate control rests with a strong international organization.

This was certainly the view of most physicists and atomic scientists; and it was not long before organizations were formed such as the Emergency Committee of Atomic Scientists, and the Association of Education for Atomic Energy. The remarkable thing is that the majority of American people during the immediate postwar years did not become *actively* concerned about the atom bomb, except to express feelings of helplessness.[61] Surveys indicated that only a small proportion expressed great worry about the bomb; in fact, half of the people polled, when asked, "How worried do you think people in this country are about the atomic bomb? How about yourself?", replied that they were not at all worried. "*The principal significance of the answers to this question, however, is not that so many denied worry but that so few of those who did so indicated any feeling of security about the bomb.*"[62] Even those people who were relatively well informed about world affairs were as likely as the poorly informed to say they were not worried because "worry is useless." People felt so completely helpless that they refused to deal with the problem on any logical basis, and preferred to leave the entire problem up to the "leaders," the "experts," or the "government."[63]

THE COSTS OF WAR

The costs of modern warfare are simply stupendous, in terms of both lives and money.

The three-year "civil war" in Spain in the late 1930's resulted in the deaths of almost one million men, women, and children.[64] The first three years of the Sino-Japanese war resulted in more than two million deaths. As for the first World War, the cost in terms of deaths, according to the League of Nations, was: almost ten million known dead, another three million presumed dead, over six million seriously wounded, and another fourteen million otherwise wounded. Over one million men were killed in the battlefields around Verdun alone.[65] As a result of World War II, millions and millions of people are known to have died—certainly several times as many as in World War I—but actually how many is pure speculation.

As for money costs, when a single flying-fortress bomber cost a quarter of a million dollars in the late 1930's and one modern fully equipped battleship sixty million dollars, it is obvious that the total amount spent in World War II was stupendous! A fairly accurate figure can be given of the costs of World War I—about 190 billion dollars.[66] When the costs of property destroyed and of interruptions to trade and similar items are included, the actual figure runs close to 400 billion dollars. Since you may not find this figure too meaningful, suppose we translate:

> It means that the war, throughout its duration, was costing mankind a rough average of $260,000,000 a day, $10,800,000 an hour, $180,000 a minute, or $3,000 a second. It means that the belligerents were using about half their resources for destruction. . . . It means that they lost an amount equal to four and a half times their combined national wealth. Translating the sum . . . into "the things

given up in order to have the war," we find that four hundred billion dollars would be enough to buy:

"A $3,500 furnished home on 5 acres of land for every family in the United States, Canada, Australia, Great Britain, France, Germany, and Russia. . . .

"AND a $10,000,000 university and a $5,000,000 library for each city of 200,000 in the countries named. . . .

"PLUS $1,000 annual salary for *all time* to 125,000 teachers and 125,000 nurses. . . .

"AND have enough left to buy *everything* of value in France and Belgium."[67]

In World War II, Great Britain alone was spending some six million pounds a *day* on the war during 1940, and the loss in property and trade could not possibly be estimated.[68] At the end of the European phase of the war in May, 1945, the total costs were estimated at one trillion (one thousand billion) dollars.[69] This was over *five times* the estimated cost of World War I, but does *not* take into account the costs of the remainder of the war in the Pacific.

The costs to social betterment have become perfectly obvious in Great Britain, Germany, France, Japan, and every other nation at war. The more spent on armaments, the poorer each nation became. If the same amounts could have been spent on education, research, public health, new highways, and other public projects, the benefits to society would have been untold. Not only was the money not spent in this way, but the amount which would ordinarily have gone to support such projects even on a small scale had to be diverted to carry on the war. Most of the nations involved ended up poverty-stricken and almost bankrupt.

ATTITUDES ABOUT WAR COSTS AND INTERNATIONAL AFFAIRS

And yet, following the war, the people of the United States and their elected representatives felt that they had little choice—simply for their own protection—other than to spend enormous sums for national defense. Total war costs for the United States for the fiscal year 1949—including the cost of defense, veterans' aid, foreign aid, and the interest on the national debt—were budgeted at over thirty-one billion dollars.[70] Spending for military defense alone was estimated at close to thirteen billion dollars. According to the *U. S. News and World Report,* this amount was greater than for all nineteen years from 1922 through 1940; and it was also "50 per cent larger than the entire cost of Government in the most expensive New Deal year."[71]

Still these expenditures did not excite unusual interest or discussion by very many people. The great majority were much more concerned about the bullish tendencies of the stock market, the batting averages of baseball players, plans for summer vacations, and later in the year with the varied abilities of different groups of eleven college men in colored sweaters to carry a pigskin ball over a white line protected by eleven other men in different colored sweaters. Public-opinion surveys show that "a large part of the American public lacks the information which would be necessary for them to understand even the broadest aspects of the decisions the nation must make on foreign policy."[72] In general, most American people did not "do much" about foreign affairs because:

1. They don't believe they could exercise any influence if they did become interested.
2. Other more pressing personal interests (such as child-rearing and jobs) compete for their time.
3. The problems seem too difficult for any ordinary person to grasp. Consequently, people feel that they should "leave it to the experts."
4. They lack experience—have no habits for dealing with such matters.[73]

In other words, people avoid thinking about international affairs—just as in the case of the atomic bomb—because the problems are too complex, and too frightening.

PSYCHOLOGICAL BASES OF PERMANENT PEACE

History has shown us more than once that one war-making nation can disrupt the peace of the whole world. The denunciation of war, then, accomplishes little so long as conditions exist *throughout the world* which produce war. Merely to pass resolutions against war or to say that you are opposed to it may be about as useful as the incantations of a medicine man over a suffering tribesman; everyone feels better, but the man is not cured. With certain other social problems, however, we have not been content with incantations. For example, we have practically stamped out tuberculosis, not by calling the tuberculous wicked people, but by making a frontal attack on all *those conditions which tend to produce* tuberculosis. Campaigns against venereal diseases would have made no headway if we had continued blindly to say that they were "dirty"; instead we resorted to a direct approach to *the factors which tend to produce* these diseases.

Imperialistic policies foment war; and economic insecurity, poverty, miserable living conditions, monotony of work, and feelings of frustration all go to make the melodrama of war welcome. These were the conditions that existed in Germany on a wholesale scale in the 1930's, and they served as a foundation for the mighty militaristic machine developed by the Nazis. Only some sort of *international* organization could have alleviated many of the economic and social conditions and thus made the building up of warlike policies less likely. This would mean bringing under control both the economic and social factors which tend to cause war. It would also mean the alleviation of psychological causes of unrest that exist during peacetime. It would imply more careful planning *over the entire world* with reference to social welfare, public health, and economic benefits. It would include such activities as slum clearance, public welfare projects, recreational activities, and adequate educational facilities. As Mark A. May has well said:

Laying the psychological foundations for peace is mainly a job of education broadly conceived. The task is a gigantic one of reconditioning the minds of men, changing their attitudes toward one another, and equipping youth with habits of belief and action that are compatible with world citizenship. This cannot be accomplished by preaching pacifism or persuading people to sign pledges refusing to participate in war or [merely] agreeing to join and support a league of nations. It requires building into the lives of people new understandings, outlooks, motivations, and conceptions.[74]

In other words, times of peace everywhere in all nations must be so enriched as to offer men all the benefits, both physical and psychological, without which they might be tempted toward war. Some of the specialized agencies within the United Nations organization designed to achieve social and economic cooperation are the following: World Health Organization (WHO), United Nations Educational, Scientific, and Cultural Organization (UNESCO), Food and Agriculture Organization (FAO), International Labor Organization (ILO), International Bank for Reconstruction and Development, and International Monetary Fund.

The extent to which the United Nations organization and its agencies will be successful in remedying some of the conditions that lead to war, only time will tell. Certainly we should not make the mistake of thinking that merely because an international organization of this kind exists it is a *guarantee* of international peace. To desire certain goals does not necessarily mean that they will be achieved; and there are many types of "one world" organization. Most Americans, in fact, are in favor of some kind of world organization, much in the same way that they favor peace, prosperity, and happiness. The important questions, however, concern the types and methods of organization; and these need careful scientific investigation.[75]

It was after years of frustrating social and economic conditions that the Germans were finally led to war. Ideals of war and conquest were deliberately fostered among them until they were ready to make almost any sacrifices for the state and for "living space." Then, with the invasion of Poland, the peoples of other nations were hopelessly drawn into the maelstrom of conflict. Policies of appeasement rapidly became out of date as more and more countries were attacked or invaded: Denmark, Norway, Luxembourg, Holland, Belgium, France, England, Hungary, Rumania,

Bulgaria, Yugoslavia, Greece, Crete, Russia. Suddenly a difficult choice was forced on people in many nations—a choice of meeting war with war, or of surrendering their personal rights to the might of the totalitarian war machine.

> Here was the demonstration, and here was the dilemma. One had either to fight war by making oneself warlike—by embracing all the cruelties, the suppressions, the agonies which we had detested—or one had to surrender to it and see it enthroned in the world as the central institution of Western civilization. . . .[76]

Of the greatest importance, therefore, is the development of a satisfactory *international organization*. Whether it is called the "United Nations" or some other name, this means an organization which can effectively *police* the world against aggression. If the entire political and social philosophy of one nation is challenged sufficiently by a second nation, and if there are acts of aggression against the first nation, its people probably will fight, regardless of how much as individuals they prize peace. In the future we need to build up a community of nations in which the people of no country need to fear force and aggression from those of other countries.

This does not mean that there must be a wholesale eradication of national pride and national allegiance, and that instead there must be loyalty to a higher world order, above any individual nation. (In the United Nations, for example, the nations of the world are not part of an organization with unlimited world authority, or one that can regulate internal affairs of a nation only of domestic concern.) Nationalism serves a useful purpose if it does not go to extremes; it makes for greater cohesion of the citizens of a nation, and it often serves to counteract selfish absorption in purely personal interests and to lead to disinterested community service. But it becomes dangerous when it is exclusive, emphasizing the superiority of one nation over every other nation in the world.

This narrow nationalism has frequently resulted in the frustration of attempts, partly idealistic and partly practical, to organize world peace on a permanent basis. Any satisfactory world order of the future will mean a drastic restriction on the conception of national sovereignty and the consequent extension into the international field of the conception of national loyalty. The maintenance of permanent peace will require the building of a *world order* with adequate machinery to settle international disputes, with sufficient authority and sanctions to enforce its decisions, and with enough control over the economic life of the world to insure access of the world's peoples to their means of livelihood.

To summarize, a true world order and international peace will require "first, international law and police force; second, the building up of an international code of conduct as the basis for the use of sanctions; and third, the development of an international conscience in a large number of people."[77] We might even say that such a world order would represent the extension into the world of nations—now a comparatively small world—of those principles of democratic government that have been tested by free peoples and found satisfactory.

THE PSYCHOLOGISTS' MANIFESTO

During World War II over two thousand American psychologists signed and released to the press a statement of ten principles which necessarily must be put into practice if a *true* peace was to be won.[78] In this "Psychologists' Manifesto" it was pointed out that neglect of these basic principles may breed new wars, no matter how well intentioned are our political leaders:

1. *War can be avoided: War is not born in men; it is built into men.* No race, nation, or social group is inevitably warlike. The frustrations and conflicting interests which lie at the root of aggressive wars can be reduced and re-directed by social engineering. . . .

2. *In planning for permanent peace, the coming generation should be the primary focus of attention.* Children are plastic; they will readily accept symbols of unity and an international way of thinking in which the evils of imperialism, prejudice, insecurity, and ignorance are minimized. . . .

3. *Racial, national, and group hatreds can, to a considerable degree, be controlled.* Through education and experience people can learn that . . . members of one racial, national, or cultural group are basically similar to those of other groups, and have similar problems, hopes, aspirations, and needs. Prejudice is a matter of attitudes, and attitudes are to a considerable extent a matter of training and information.

4. *Condescension toward "inferior" groups destroys our chances for a lasting peace.* The white man must be freed of his concept of the "white man's burden." The English-speaking peoples are only a tenth of the world's population; those of white skin only a third. . . .

5. *Liberated and enemy peoples must participate in planning their own destiny.* Complete outside authority imposed on liberated and enemy peoples without any participation by them will not be accepted and will lead only to further disruptions of the peace. . . .

6. *The confusion of defeated people will call for clarity and consistency in the application of rewards and punishments.* . . . A clear-cut and easily understood definition of war-guilt is essential. Consistent severity toward those who are judged guilty, and consistent official friendliness toward democratic elements, is a necessary policy.

7. *If properly administered, relief and rehabilitation can lead to self-reliance and cooperation; if improperly, to resentment and hatred.* Unless liberated

people (and enemy people) are given an opportunity to work in a self-respecting manner for the food and relief they receive, they are likely to harbor bitterness and resentment, since our bounty will be regarded by them as unearned charity, dollar imperialism, or bribery. No people can long tolerate such injuries to self-respect.

8. *The root-desires of the common people of all lands are the safest guide to framing a peace.* Disrespect for the common man is characteristic of fascism and of all forms of tyranny. The man in the street . . . can be studied (by adaptations of the public opinion poll). His expressed aspirations should even now be a major guide to policy.

9. *The trend of human relationships is toward ever wider units of collective security.* From the caveman to the twentieth century, human beings have formed larger and larger working and living groups. Families merged into clans, clans into states, and states into nations. The United States are not 48 threats to each other's safety; they work together. At the present moment the majority of our people regard the time as ripe for regional and world organization. . . .

10. *Commitments* now *may prevent postwar apathy and reaction.* Unless binding commitments are made and initial steps taken now, people may have a tendency after the war to turn away from international problems and to become preoccupied once again with narrower interests. This regression to a new postwar provincialism would breed the conditions for a new world war. . . .

These are fundamental psychological principles. They should be re-read and analyzed as a basis for social action. But the extent to which they will be followed in the years ahead is a problem for future historians.

QUESTIONS AND PROBLEMS FOR DISCUSSION

1. *How do feelings of nationalism differ from feelings of race.*
2. *Show the differences between the development of nationalism in a Fascist state and in a democracy.*
3. *Can war be explained in terms of racial differences?*
4. *Make a comparison of our basic culture patterns in times of peace and of war.*
5. *Show the importance of ambivalent habits and attitudes in times of war.*
6. *What is the effect of war on democratic processes?*
7. *Develop in detail what you would consider a workable plan for the prevention of war.*

RECOMMENDED READINGS

Arne, S., *United Nations Primer* (revised edition). New York: Rinehart & Company, Inc., 1948.

Barnes, H. E., *The Genesis of the World War: An Introduction to the Problem of War Guilt.* New York: Alfred A. Knopf, Inc., 1926.

Brogan, D. W., *The English People: Impressions and Observations.* New York: Alfred A. Knopf, Inc., 1943.

Bruntz, G. G., *Allied Propaganda and the Collapse of the German Empire in 1918.* Palo Alto: Stanford University Press, 1938.

Churchill, W., *The Gathering Storm.* Boston: Houghton Mifflin Company, 1948.

Creel, G., *How We Advertised America: The First Telling of the Amazing Story of the Committee on Public Information That Carried the Gospel of Americanism to Every Corner of the Globe.* New York: Harper & Brothers, 1920.

Farago, L. (editor), *German Psychological Warfare.* New York: G. P. Putnam's Sons, 1942.

Fay, S. B., *The Origins of the World War* (2 volumes). New York: The Macmillan Company, 1930.

Hayes, C. J. H., *Essays on Nationalism.* New York: The Macmillan Company, 1926.

Hayes, C. J. H., *The Historical Evolution of Modern Nationalism.* New York: Richard R. Smith, 1931.

Hitler, A., *Mein Kampf.* New York: Reynal & Hitchcock, Inc., 1939.

Knight, B. W., *How to Run a War.* New York: Alfred A. Knopf, Inc., 1936.

Lasswell, H., *Propaganda Technique in the World War.* New York: Alfred A. Knopf, Inc., 1927.

Lavine, H., and Wechsler, J., *War Propaganda and the United States.* New Haven: Yale University Press, 1940.

Linebarger, P. M. A., *Psychological Warfare.* Washington: Infantry Journal Press, 1948.

Lippmann, W., *U. S. Foreign Policy: Shield of the Republic.* New York: Pocket Books, Inc., 1943.

Lochner, L. P. (editor), *The Goebbels Diaries.* New York: Doubleday & Company, Inc., 1948.

May, M. A., *A Social Psychology of War and Peace.* New Haven: Yale University Press, 1943.

Merriam, C. E., *The Making of Citizens.* Chicago: University of Chicago Press, 1931.

Millis, W., *Road to War: America 1914-1917.* Boston: Houghton Mifflin Company, 1935.

Mock, J. R., and Larsen, C., *Words That Won the War.* Princeton: Princeton University Press, 1939.

Murphy, G. (editor), *Human Nature and the Enduring Peace: Third Yearbook of the Society for the Psychological Study of Social Issues.* Boston: Houghton Mifflin Company, 1945.

Peterson, H. C., *Propaganda for War: The Campaign Against American Neutrality, 1914-1917.* Norman, Oklahoma: University of Oklahoma Press, 1939.

Schuman, F. L., *The Nazi Dictatorship: A Study in Social Pathology and the Politics of Fascism* (2nd edition revised). New York: Alfred A. Knopf, Inc., 1936.

Schuman, F. L., *Night Over Europe: The Diplomacy of Nemesis 1939-1940*. New York: Alfred A. Knopf, Inc., 1941.

Tansill, C. C., *America Goes to War*. Boston: Little, Brown & Company, 1938.

*Newcomb, T. M., Hartley, E. L., and others (editors), *Readings in Social Psychology*. New York: Henry Holt and Company, Inc., 1947. (The following selections are listed according to the sequence of related discussions in the chapter you have just read.)

Fromm, E., "Hitler and the Nazi Authoritarian Character Structure," pp. 413-427.

Bettelheim, B., "Individual and Mass Behavior in Extreme Situations," pp. 628-638.

Kluckhohn, C., "Anthropological Research and World Peace," pp. 657-663.

Cantril, H., "Public Opinion in Flux," pp. 591-605.

Allport, G. W., and others, "The Psychologists' Manifesto," pp. 655-657.

CHAPTER TWENTY-FIVE

KNOWLEDGE FOR WHAT?

ILLOGICAL ASPECTS OF SOCIETY. A Contrast—Social Problems—Purpose or Pretense?—Conflicts in Our Society / WHAT SHALL WE DO ABOUT IT? A Healthy Skepticism—Social Psychology and Democracy—Expert Social Scientists—Knowledge for What?

▶ ILLOGICAL ASPECTS OF SOCIETY

A CONTRAST

The history of the United States is one of great physical, economic, and social growth. We have developed unusual skills and techniques of production, and are able to turn out more goods and services in every hour we work than any other people in the world. We operate under a system of political democracy—with freedom of speech, freedom of religion, freedom of press, and freedom of work. As a nation, our accomplishments are many. Within the last hundred years, for example, we have:

Increased our output per man-hour of work more than five times—from 27 cents to $1.41 (in terms of today's purchasing power);

Reduced our average work-week from 70 hours to about 40 hours;

Increased our national income 26 times, with a working force that has increased only about 8 times;

Given ourselves the highest standard of living ever known by any people in any country at any time.[1]

Hundreds of examples might be given of improvements in life in modern America. For example, in 1910 only 44 out of each 100 boys and girls of high-school age actually went to high school; but by 1940 there were 65 out of 100, and the proportion is still rising. The death rate per 1,000 persons fell from 17 in 1900 to less than 11 in 1945. During the same period, life expectancy was raised from an average of 49 years to an average of 66 years. The list could be extended to include successful campaigns in special fields of public health, better community planning in many cities, increase in literacy, better recreational facilities than at any time in our history, and so on almost indefinitely.

But, after this survey of social psychology, would you say that ours is "the best of all possible worlds"? And would you say that social behavior is primarily rational and logical? In answering these questions, consider once more the problem of "cultural lag" in certain parts of our culture (Chapters 5 and 14); and re-examine the social conflicts described in the chapters immediately preceding this one. Although society has many logical aspects, the significance of these illogical types of behavior is sometimes overlooked.

SOCIAL PROBLEMS

We say that slums are not "pretty," but we do not worry too much about their effects on public health; only recently have we become concerned about eliminating them and substituting modern housing. Look about you and observe poverty and suffering alongside great wealth and comfort, an inexplicable situation to various "primitive" groups who feel that the white man surely cannot be that irrational. Historians of the future may write about us:

> Houses and buildings were set side by side in square blocks, without relationship to each other and without any plan or specific reason for their being in any given place. Ramshackle slums nudged towering 'skyscrapers,' and residential areas were indescribably mingled with the smoking, clamorous factory districts. The streets were fifthy.[2]

Fresh-air camps have been established near most cities where slum children may be sent for a couple of weeks each year to give them a taste of how the other half lives. Yet little attempt is made to deal with the slum problem during the other 50 weeks of the year on a logical basis. The argument is that it would cost so much. Consider our high rates of infant mortality, venereal disease, tuberculosis; only within very recent years have these problems even begun to be approached on a rational basis.

If this were a rational society, we could expect social and economic conflicts to be worked out on a logical basis and not by force and aggression. Of over 45 million families in the United States, over 27 per cent of them receive less than $1,000 a year, and over 47 per cent less than $2,000.[3] Consider the constant threat of great unemployment, and the necessity of public and private relief. As for our vagrant population, little has been done to deal with these individuals in a logical way. Every summer in New York City, for example, men from the Bowery are taken on a day's outing up the Hudson River, with little consideration to an adequate solution of the problem of homeless men. Our ability to foresee, manage, and control our social structure has not kept pace with the rapid increases in the complexity of life. As a former president of the American Bar Association said:

> Imagine a nation with only 6% of the world's area and 7% of its population, owning 33% of its railroads, using 48% of its coffee, 56% of its rubber,

owning 60% of its telephone and telegraph lines, consuming 70% of its oil, 72% of its silk, using 80% of its motor cars, having one-half of its monetary supply, fifteen billions in gold, and two-thirds of its banking resources and yet, due to obvious maladjustments, discontented and in many quarters bitter.[4]

PURPOSE OR PRETENSE?

During the early 1930's, the English spent approximately $60,000,000 annually on fox hunting.[5] Each year approximately 15,000 foxes were killed at a cost of $4,000 per fox. This is accounted for by the fact that 200 packs of fox hounds, 9 packs of stag hounds, 39 packs of harriers, and 50,000 horses have been necessary for this sport, as well as the costs of fodder, shoeing, labor, veterinary fees, saddlery, stable equipment, hunt servants, grooms, and clothes. An English sportsman was asked the object of fox hunting, and said, "To kill the fox." When it was suggested that this could be achieved quite simply by rounding up all the foxes and killing them off once and for all, thus saving this cost of $60,000,000 per year, he was, to say the least, perplexed. "After all," he said, "that would spoil the fun of the game." Obviously the object is not really to kill off the foxes.

Much of the irrationality of our society is comparable to the English fox hunt. For example, we are content to spend money for bigger prisons and to adopt the philosophy that "the criminal is a rat," rather than to concern ourselves with actual *solutions* of the problem of crime. Or, take the matter of "cultural lag" in our legal setup. Most people agree that many legal concepts are outmoded. Yet when rational solutions are suggested, the answer is that the law is the law and must be preserved.[6] In general, people wish to preserve the *status quo*.

Actually, the modern world around us is too complex for most of us to understand. The need for better *physical* facilities alone is tremendous—for better schools and libraries; recreational buildings, parks, playgrounds, and athletic fields, hospitals and maternal-care centers; highways, roads, and streets; bridges and viaducts; incinerator plants and sewage plants; conservation dams and irrigation systems. Yet as a society we have not made any unified attack on such important problems. Instead of being capable of organizing ourselves to solve such matters, most of us "grouse" or complain, and remain frusrated.

CONFLICTS IN OUR SOCIETY

The conflicts in our society are varied and extreme. For example, we hold to the notion that our democracy is based on the principle of freedom of speech, yet we try to prevent people from expressing "dangerous" opinions.

One frequently gets a sense of people's being afraid to let their opinions become sharp. They believe in "peace, but—." They believe in "fairness to labor, but—." In "freedom of speech, but—." In "democracy, but—." In "freedom of the press, but—."[7]

We talk a great deal about equality in the United States, yet tolerate a tremendous amount of social inequality.[8] We discourse about democracy, yet talk about "upper" and "lower" classes as if they were innate, worry about our ancestors, and join various societies to prove our social prestige. We pretend that we have respect for law and order, yet we tolerate racketeering, bribery of officials, falsification of tax returns, and various forms of vice. We give lip service to the notion that women and men are equals, yet most employed women must work for less money than men at similar jobs. We condemn birth control, yet practice it. We claim to be a monogamous society, yet accept infidelity and divorce all about us. We call ourselves a Christian nation, yet half of us belong to no church at all. We claim to believe in a God of peace, yet pray to Him for victory in time of war. Sometimes we starve in the midst of plenty. "We praise competition, but practice merger and monopoly. Everybody has equal economic opportunity, except Negroes, immigrants, women . . ."[9]

The outright conflicts in our society involve Negroes *versus* whites, old *versus* young, the educated *versus* the ignorant, city *versus* country, individual medical practice *versus* socialized medicine, public *versus* private education, men *versus* women, 100 per cent Americans *versus* aliens, pacifists *versus* militarists.[10] Such facts indicate the amount and intensity of our own cultural contradictions.

As a report of the Rockefeller Foundation has indicated:

> We have created a society so interdependent that issues are no longer simple, individual and local; they are complex, social and world wide. And they are beyond the experience of most of us. Money and credit, fiscal policy, international relations, international trade and finance, national income and its distribution, wages, profits, prices, monopoly, purchasing power, savings and investment, employment and unemployment, social security, collective bargaining, housing, public opinion, propaganda, public administration, the relations between government and business, individual and social adjustment, crime, social welfare, education, population, social justice in an interdependent society —here is merely a brief list of some of the urgent issues.[11]

▶ WHAT SHALL WE DO ABOUT IT?

A HEALTHY SKEPTICISM

We have ideals of a logically organized society and of avoidance of social conflicts; but the only way that this can be accomplished is in terms of actual societal planning or "social engineering." What, then, are you likely to do about it?

First of all, if you are content with the *status quo,* you will do nothing about it. If you believe that the ways of your grandfather are good enough for you and that, "It's a pretty good old world after all," then for you there is no problem of a logical society.

An attempt has been made in this book, however, to engender a certain degree of *healthy skepticism.* The word "skepticism" is used to denote an intellectual curiosity about the society in which we live. As was pointed out in Chapter 2, *skepticism should not be confused with cynicism—they are not at all synonymous.* The word "healthy" in healthy skepticism may be explained by an analogy. If you are occasionally skeptical about your own good health, a careful physical examination may reveal certain changes in your living which will be desirable. Likewise, an objective examination of society may suggest certain desirable social changes. This book is in no sense intended to suggest that society as a whole is illogical or abnormal. In fact, we have examined many phases of both normal and abnormal behavior, and of both rational and irrational behavior.

A famous teacher once said that if he could not upset the views of a student who came into his class and make him think for himself, then it was a waste of the student's time to come. The same thing may be said for this book on social psychology. Unless you have been forced to think about some old problems and have worried a little bit about them, your time has been wasted. No attempt has here been made at indoctrination in favor of any one "philosophy of life." Instead, stress has been laid upon a scientific examination of your own attitudes and behavior in relation to your fellows.

One difficulty with any analysis is that the one who makes it may be accused of attacking society. Again, an analogy may be useful. Suppose that this were a book on the physiology of teeth. Critics might say: "This man is attacking teeth for he does not show up their beautiful characteristics. He does not say much about the good that teeth do, and he offers us no substitute."[12] That would be analogous to a belief that the present book is an attack on society, because we have not always "pointed with pride" but have realistically examined our social behavior.

SOCIAL PSYCHOLOGY AND DEMOCRACY

The question of what we can or will do about our society always depends upon our aims and ideals. Social psychologists are strong believers in democratic principles.

A critical examination of the word "democracy," not as a mere shibboleth or catchword, should suggest a great many things to you concerning your present-day society. Democracy is not only institutional and external to ourselves, but is a way of life. Questions of freedom of speech, equality of the sexes, lack of racial and religious discrimination, the solution of economic problems, the elimination of social diseases, all should be problems with which you are concerned. These problems can eventually be solved if our democracy functions in a truly logical way.

EXPERT SOCIAL SCIENTISTS

Expert social scientists—historians, economists, political scientists, anthropologists, sociologists, psychologists—probably know better than most other people what to do about *social* problems. Experts should know most about the problems in their own field. When you suffer from a physical ailment, you consult your physician and not your laundryman. When you have a legal problem, you see your lawyer and not your butcher. When you are interested in questions of laundry or meat prices, you do consult your laundryman or butcher.

But when it comes to problems of society, every man considers himself an expert. One reason is that most people have no accurate conception of what is meant by *social science*. "They confuse psychology with psychoanalysis, economics with capitalism, communism, or some other ideology, and sociology with everything from Christian socialism and social work to transcendental philosophy."[13] A second reason is:

> . . . Most people feel they already know the answers to problems of human relations. What are some of these solutions? Why—"an honest day's work for an honest day's pay"; "the Ten Commandments"; "the Golden Rule"; socialism; free enterprise; communism; cooperation; another World Conference; World Union; and so forth.[14]

Finally, most "brain trusters" are suspect by the average businessman and politician. Historians, economists, political scientists, anthropologists, sociologists, and psychologists are not always consulted, even though they probably know what the answers are to many of our social ills.

> The fact is that the course of events following World War I, down to and including the present, was predicted with great accuracy by large numbers of social scientists. That nothing was done about it is not the special responsibility of social scientists. "Doing something about it" is the common responsibility of all members of a community, including scientists, and especially of those who specialize in mass education, mass leadership, and practical programs.[15]

Social scientists, then, should not be afraid to step outside the "ivory tower." They should stand ready to make recommendations after they have carefully and *objectively* analyzed alternate possible courses of action. In their capacity as citizens, they may then join with other citizens in advocating various solutions to social problems.

KNOWLEDGE FOR WHAT?

But the problem of what to do is not one for the social scientists alone. It is one for other persons, too, those who read the books on social science. Suppose that you have examined your society and dissected it. What good is this information? "Knowledge for what?" is a real question.[16]

This book began with a plea for *objectivity,* that is, for an impartial scrutiny of all the facts concerning any problem. Objectivity, however, should not make you colorless, neutral, or completely lukewarm. The demand is simply that you make up your mind about a problem, not in terms of impulses and prejudices, but through an objective analysis of all sides of the question. After such an analysis, you are entitled to carry your thoughts into action. In a democracy you have a right, like other citizens, to "do something about it."

QUESTIONS AND PROBLEMS FOR DISCUSSION

1. *What differences would there be between a benevolent society and a rational society? Give concrete examples.*
2. *Is the nonconformist necessarily antisocial?*
3. *As an individual, what do you think you can or should do about any of the social conflicts of the society in which you live?*

RECOMMENDED READINGS

Bossard, J. H. S., *Social Change and Social Problems* (revised edition). New York: Harper & Brothers, 1938.

Bridgman, P. W., *The Intelligent Individual and Society.* New York: The Macmillan Company, 1938.

Elliott, M. A., and Merrill, F. E., *Social Disorganization* (revised edition). New York: Harper & Brothers, 1941.

Frank, L. K., *Society as the Patient: Essays on Culture and Personality.* New Brunswick: Rutgers University Press, 1948.

Gillin, J. L., Dittmer, C. G., Colbert, R. J., and Kastler, N. M., *Social Problems* (3rd edition). New York: D. Appleton-Century Company, 1943.

Lundberg, G. A., *Can Science Save Us?* New York: Longmans, Green & Co., 1947.

Lynd, R. S., *Knowledge for What? The Place of Social Science in American Culture.* Princeton: Princeton University Press, 1939.

Wylie, P., *Generation of Vipers.* New York: Farrar & Rinehart, Inc., 1942.

*Newcomb, T. M., Hartley, E. L., and others (editors), *Readings in Social Psychology.* New York: Henry Holt and Company, Inc., 1947: —Hartley, E. L., and Hartley, R. E., "Tolerance and Personality Traits," pp. 527-531.

APPENDIXES

APPENDIX A

LITERATURE CITED

The numbers refer to the superscripts in the text of each individual chapter.

▶ *Chapter One* THE SOCIAL PSYCHOLOGY OF EVERYDAY LIFE

(Pages 3-11)

1. Compare H. Cantril, "The Social Psychology of Everyday Life," *Psychological Bulletin,* 1934, *31,* 297-330.
2. *The New York Times,* July 2, 1939.
3. *Washington Star,* Aug. 20, 1939.
4. Compare S. H. Britt, "Social Psychologists or Psychological Sociologists—Which?," *Journal of Abnormal and Social Psychology,* 1937, *32,* 314-318; also, *American Sociological Review,* 1937, *2,* 898-902.
5. R. S. Lynd, *Knowledge for What? The Place of Social Science in American Culture.* Princeton: Princeton University Press, 1939, p. 162.
6. J. Dewey, "The Need for Social Psychology," *Psychological Review,* 1917, *24,* 266-277, p. 267.
7. J. R. Kantor, "The Current Situation in Social Psychology," *Psychological Bulletin,* 1939, *36,* 307-360, p. 329.
8. F. H. Allport, *Social Psychology.* Boston: Houghton Mifflin Company, 1924, p. 4.
9. G. Murphy, L. B. Murphy, and T. M. Newcomb, *Experimental Social Psychology: An Interpretation of Research upon the Socialization of the Individual* (revised edition). New York: Harper & Brothers, 1937, pp. 22-23.
10. F. H. Allport, "The Subject Matter and Methods of Social Psychology. I. Introduction: The Hanover Round Table and Social Psychology of 1936," *Social Forces,* 1937, *15,* 455-495, at 455-462, p. 464.
11. Compare R. B. Liddy, "The Field of Social Psychology," *Journal of Psychology,* 1942, *13,* 21-29.
12. Compare M. P. Crawford, "The Social Psychology of the Vertebrates," *Psychological Bulletin,* 1939, *36,* 407-446.
13. Compare K. L. Smoke, "The Present Status of Social Psychology in America," *Psychological Review,* 1935, *42,* 537-543.
14. Compare C. Bird, *Social Psychology.* New York: Appleton-Century-Crofts, Inc., 1940. S. H. Britt, *Social Psychology of Modern Life* (revised edition). New York: Rinehart & Company, Inc., 1949.

J. F. Brown, *Psychology and the Social Order*. New York: McGraw-Hill Book Company, Inc., 1936. E. Faris, *The Nature of Human Nature and Other Essays in Social Psychology*. New York: McGraw-Hill Book Company, Inc., 1937. E. Freeman, *Social Psychology*. New York: Henry Holt and Company, Inc., 1936. H. Gurnee, *Elements of Social Psychology*. New York: Rinehart & Company, Inc., 1936. D. Katz, and R. L. Schanck, *Social Psychology*. New York: John Wiley & Sons, Inc., 1938. O. Klineberg, *Social Psychology*. New York: Harper & Brothers, 1940. D. Krech and R. S. Crutchfield, *Theory and Problems of Social Psychology*. New York: McGraw-Hill Book Company, Inc., 1948. M. H. Krout, *Introduction to Social Psychology*. New York: Harper & Brothers, 1942. R. T. LaPiere and P. R. Farnsworth, *Social Psychology*. New York: McGraw-Hill Book Company, Inc., 1936. Murphy, Murphy, and Newcomb, same citation as note 9 above. J. M. Reinhardt, *Social Psychology*. Philadelphia: J. B. Lippincott Company, 1938. M. Sherif, *Outline of Social Psychology*. New York: Harper & Brothers, 1948. R. H. Thouless, *General and Social Psychology* (revised edition). London: University Tutorial Press, 1937. W. F. Vaughan, *Social Psychology*. New York: The Odyssey Press, 1948. K. Young, *Social Psychology* (second edition). New York: Appleton-Century-Crofts, Inc., 1944.

15. T. S. Harding, "The Alleged Ignorance of Social Scientists," *American Sociological Review*, 1938, *3*, 850-854, pp. 851-852.
16. Same citation, p. 850.
17. *The New York Times*, Oct. 20, 1938.
18. H. Cantril and Research Associates, *Gauging Public Opinion*. Princeton: Princeton University Press, 1944.
19. See C. W. Bray, *Psychology and Military Proficiency: A History of the Applied Psychology Panel of the National Defense Research Committee*. Princeton: Princeton University Press, 1948.
20. A. J. N. Schneider, C. W. LaGrone, E. T. Glueck, and S. Glueck, "Prediction of Behavior in Civilian Delinquents in the Armed Forces." *Mental Hygiene*, 1944, *28*, 1-20, p. 18.
21. F. L. Ruch, *Psychology and Life*. Chicago: Scott, Foresman & Company, 1937, pp. 410-411.

▶ *Chapter Two* THE METHODS OF SOCIAL PSYCHOLOGY

(*Pages 12-22*)

1. S. H. Britt, "The Subject Matter and Methods of Social Psychology. II. Past and Present Trends in the Methods and Subject Matter of

Social Psychology," *Social Forces,* 1937, *15,* 455-495, at 462-469, pp. 464-465.
2. L. M. Terman and others, *Genetic Studies of Genius* (3 vol.). Stanford: Stanford University Press, 1925-1930.
3. H. Hartshorne, M. A. May, J. B. Maller, and F. K. Shuttleworth, *Studies in the Nature of Character* (3 vol.). New York: The Macmillan Company, 1928-1930.
4. L. W. Doob, *Propaganda: Its Psychology and Technique.* New York: Henry Holt and Company, Inc., 1935.
5. H. Cantril and G. W. Allport, *The Psychology of Radio.* New York: Harper & Brothers, 1935.
6. E. S. Robinson, *Law and the Lawyers.* New York: The Macmillan Company, 1935.
7. F. S. Keller, *The Definition of Psychology.* New York: Appleton-Century-Crofts, Inc., 1937, p. 64.
8. R. A. Fisher, *The Design of Experiments.* London: Oliver & Boyd, 1935.
9. A. Myerson, *Social Psychology.* New York: Prentice-Hall, Inc., 1934, p. 21.
10. G. Murphy, "The Research Task of Social Psychology," *Journal of Social Psychology,* 1939, *10,* 107-120, pp. 114-115.
11. H. Gurnee, *Elements of Social Psychology.* New York: Rinehart & Company, Inc., 1936, pp. 16-17.
12. W. Miller, *I Found No Peace.* New York: Simon and Schuster, 1936, pp. 317-318, copyright, 1936, Webb Miller.
13. F. H. Allport, "The Influence of the Group upon Association and Thought," *Journal of Experimental Psychology,* 1920, *3,* 159-182.
14. S. A. Rice, *Quantitative Methods in Politics.* New York: Alfred A. Knopf, Inc., 1928.
15. Britt, same citation as note 1, pp. 466-469.
16. J. K. Folsom, *Social Psychology.* New York: By permission of Harper & Brothers, 1931, pp. 1-7, copyright, 1931, Harper & Brothers.
17. R. S. Mulliken, "Science and the Scientific Attitude," *Science,* July 23, 1937, *86,* 65-68, p. 66.
18. E. T. Bell, *Man and His Lifebelts.* New York: Reynal & Hitchcock, Inc., 1938, p. 95, copyright, 1938, The Williams & Wilkins Co.
19. R. B. Fosdick, *The Rockefeller Foundation: A Review for 1940.* New York: The Rockefeller Foundation, 1941, pp. 43-44.

▶ *Chapter Three* BIOLOGICAL BASES OF HUMAN BEHAVIOR

(Pages 25-40)

1. J. R. Kantor, "The Current Situation in Social Psychology," *Psychological Bulletin,* 1939, *36,* 307-360, p. 327.

2. H. H. Newman, F. N. Freeman, and K. J. Holzinger, *Twins: A Study of Heredity and Environment.* Chicago: University of Chicago Press, 1937.
3. S. Lewis, *Work of Art.* New York: Copyright, 1934, pp. 310-311, reprinted by permission of Doubleday & Co., Inc., 1934.
4. J. P. Guilford, *General Psychology.* New York: Courtesy of D. Van Nostrand Company, 1939, p. 310 (adapted from Cannon).
5. Compare also A. Kuntz, *The Autonomic Nervous System* (second edition). Philadelphia: Lea & Febiger, 1934.
6. G. W. Allport, *Personality: A Psychological Interpretation.* New York: Henry Holt and Company, Inc., 1937, pp. 115-116.
7. D. J. Ingle, "Endocrine Function and Personality," *Psychological Review,* 1935, *42,* 466-479.
8. L. K. Frank, "Physiological Tensions and Social Structure," *Publications of the American Sociological Society,* 1927, *22,* 74-82. L. K. Frank, "The Concept of Inviolability in Culture," *American Journal of Sociology,* 1931, *36,* 607-615.
9. L. K. Frank, "Physiological Tensions and Social Structure," *Publications of the American Sociological Society,* 1927, *22,* 74-82, p. 81.
10. G. Murphy, L. B. Murphy, and T. M. Newcomb, *Experimental Social Psychology* (revised edition). New York: By permission of Harper & Brothers, 1937, p. 91, copyright, 1931, 1937, Harper & Brothers.
11. Compare C. R. Griffith, *Psychology Applied to Teaching and Learning.* New York: Rinehart & Company, Inc., 1939, p. 103.

Chapter Four SOCIAL ANTECEDENTS OF BEHAVIOR

(*Pages 41-61*)

1. W. Bagehot, *Physics and Politics.* New York: Appleton-Century-Crofts, Inc., 1902.
2. W. Wundt, *Elemente der Völkerpsychologie.* Leipzig: Alfred Kröner Verlag, 1912. Translated by E. L. Schaub, *Elements of Folk Psychology.* New York: The Macmillan Company, 1916.
3. W. I. Thomas, *Primitive Behavior: An Introduction to the Social Sciences.* New York: McGraw-Hill Book Company, Inc., 1937, Chap. 14.
4. J. K. Folsom, *Social Psychology.* New York: Harper & Brothers, 1931, p. 520.
5. J. Gunther, *Inside Asia.* New York: Harper & Brothers, copyright 1938, 1939, pp. 2-3.
6. H. McCombs, "Pistols at 50 Paces," *Life,* March 20, 1944, 16, 11-12 and 14, p. 11.

7. Folsom, same citation as note 4.
8. B. Malinowski, *Sex and Repression in Savage Society*. New York: Harcourt, Brace and Company, 1927.
9. Same citation, p. 9.
10. Same citation.
11. Compare B. Malinowski, *Crime and Custom in Savage Society*. New York: Harcourt, Brace and Company, 1926.
12. B. Malinowski, *The Sexual Side of Savages*. London: George Routledge & Sons, Ltd., 1929.
13. Malinowski, same citation as note 11.
14. R. Benedict, *Patterns of Culture*. Boston: Houghton Mifflin Company, 1934.
15. Same citation, p. 118, copyright, 1934, Ruth Benedict.
16. Same citation, p. 60.
17. Same citation, p. 74, copyright, 1934, Ruth Benedict.
18. Same citation, p. 143, copyright, 1934, Ruth Benedict.
19. Same citation, p. 190, copyright, 1934, Ruth Benedict.
20. F. Boas in Foreword to M. Mead, *Coming of Age in Samoa* (in—*From the South Seas*). New York: William Morrow & Company, 1928, p. xiv.
21. Same citation, p. xv.
22. Mead, same citation as note 20.
23. Same citation, p. 221.
24. Same citation, p. 207, copyright, 1928, Margaret Mead, by permission of William Morrow & Company.
25. M. Mead, *Growing Up in New Guinea*. New York: William Morrow & Company, 1930; M. Mead, *Sex and Temperament* (in—*From the South Seas*). New York: William Morrow & Company, 1935.
26. Mead, *Sex and Temperament*, same citation as note 25, p. 164.
27. Same citation, p. 280.
28. Same citation, p. 189.
29. Same citation, p. 279, copyright, 1935, Margaret Mead, by permission of William Morrow & Company.
30. Same citation, copyright, 1935, Margaret Mead, by permission of William Morrow & Company.
31. G. K. Chesterton, *The Man Who Was Chesterton*. New York: Dodd, Mead & Company, Inc., 1937, p. 104.
32. E. D. Monachesi, "Sociology and Culture." In E. P. Schmidt (editor), *Man and Society: A Substantive Introduction to the Social Sciences*. New York: Prentice-Hall, Inc., 1937, Chap. 1, pp. 3-4, copyright, 1937, Prentice-Hall, Inc.
33. Data from J. P. Shea.
34. C. Merz, *The Great American Band-Wagon*. New York: The John Day Company, 1928, pp. 162-163, copyright, 1928, by Charles Merz, copyright, 1926, 1927, 1928, Harper & Brothers.

35. S. Pribichevich, "In an American Factory," *Harper's Magazine*, 1938, *177*, 362-373, p. 362, copyright, Harper & Brothers.
36. O. Klineberg, *Race Differences*. New York: Harper & Brothers, 1935, pp. 341-342.
37. Same citation, p. 342.

▶ *Chapter Five* THE NATURE OF CULTURE

(*Pages 62-80*)

1. A. Myerson, *Social Psychology*. New York: Prentice-Hall, Inc., 1934, pp. 3-6, copyright, 1934, Prentice-Hall, Inc.
2. J. K. Folsom, *Social Psychology*. New York: Harper & Brothers, 1931, p. 405.
3. W. I. Thomas, *Primitive Behavior: An Introduction to the Social Sciences*. New York: McGraw-Hill Book Company, Inc., 1937, p. 8.
4. K. Young, *Social Psychology: An Analysis of Social Behavior*. New York: Appleton-Century-Crofts, Inc., 1930, p. 676.
5. H. Cantril, "The Place of Personality in Social Psychology," *The Journal of Psychology*, 1947, *24*, 19-56, p. 24.
6. J. O. Hertzler, "Some Notes on the Social Psychology of Regionalism," *Social Forces*, 1940, *18*, 331-337.
7. Same citation, pp. 334-335.
8. Folsom, same citation as note 2, p. 472.
9. C. Wissler, *Man and Culture*. New York: The Thomas Y. Crowell Company, 1923, p. 74, copyright, 1923, The Thomas Y. Crowell Company.
10. W. F. Ogburn, *Social Change*. New York: B. W. Huebsch, 1922, p. 201.
11. Wissler, same citation as note 9, Chap. 1.
12. W. G. Sumner, *Folkways*. Boston: Ginn and Company, 1906, p. 28.
13. *This Week*, Oct. 23, 1938, p. 6, photos by Wallenberg of Three Lions.
14. Same citation.
15. *Life*, Feb. 17, 1941, *10*, 38 and 41, photos by Walt Sanders from Black Star.
16. *Laws and Liberties of Massachusetts*. Cambridge: Harvard University Press, 1929, p. 37; reprinted by permission of the President and Fellows of Harvard College.
17. B. Malinowski, *The Father in Primitive Psychology*. London: Kegan Paul, Trench, Trubner Company, 1927, p. 87.
18. R. T. LaPiere and P. R. Farnsworth, *Social Psychology*. New York: McGraw-Hill Book Company, Inc., 1936, p. 68.
19. G. Murphy, L. B. Murphy, and T. M. Newcomb, *Experimental Social Psychology* (revised edition). New York: By permission of Harper & Brothers, 1937, p. 327, copyright, 1931, 1937, Harper & Brothers.

20. R. S. Lynd and H. M. Lynd, *Middletown: A Study in Contemporary American Culture.* New York: Harcourt, Brace and Company, 1929, p. 427.
21. B. Mauldin, *Up Front.* New York: World Publishing Co., 1945 (copyright by Henry Holt and Company, Inc.), pp. 12-14.
22. Courtesy of *Time,* copyright Time, Inc., May 21, 1945, *45,* 44 and 46.
23. K. Davis, "Mental Hygiene and the Class Structure," *Psychiatry,* 1938, *1,* 55-65.

▶ *Chapter Six* UNLEARNED AND LEARNED BEHAVIOR

(*Pages 83-111*)

1. A. Smith, *Wealth of Nations.* New York: E. P. Dutton & Company, Inc., 1933.
2. W. Trotter, *Instincts of the Herd in Peace and War.* London: T. F. Unwin, Ltd., 1920.
3. Compare E. Faris, "Are Instincts Data or Hypotheses?" *American Journal of Sociology,* 1921, *27,* 184-196, p. 187.
4. L. L. Bernard, *Instinct: A Study in Social Psychology.* New York: Henry Holt and Company, Inc., 1924, Chap. 8.
5. Compare Faris, same citation as note 3.
6. L. L. Bernard, *An Introduction to Social Psychology.* New York: Henry Holt and Company, Inc., 1926, p. 132, copyright, 1926, Henry Holt and Company.
7. *Time* magazine, May 6, 1940, *35,* p. 50.
8. H. Howland, *Theodore Roosevelt and His Times.* New Haven: Yale University Press, 1921, p. 78.
9. W. McDougall, *An Introduction to Social Psychology.* Boston: John W. Luce & Comapny, 1926.
10. W. McDougall, *Outline of Psychology.* New York: Charles Scribner's Sons, 1923, Chap. 5.
11. Bernard, same citation as note 4.
12. Bernard, same citation as note 6, p. 126.
13. Same citation, p. 133.
14. Same citation, pp. 135-136.
15. O. Klineberg, *Race Differences.* New York: Harper & Brothers, 1937, pp. 263-272.
16. Same citation, p. 274.
17. Bernard, same citation as note 6, p. 116.
18. W. James, *Psychology: Briefer Course.* New York: Henry Holt and Company, Inc., 1892, pp. 143-144; copyright, 1920, by Alice H. James.

19. E. R. Hilgard and D. G. Marquis, *Conditioning and Learning.* New York: Appleton-Century-Crofts, Inc., 1940.
20. Compare I. P. Pavlov, *Lectures on Conditioned Reflexes.* (Transl. by W. H. Gantt.) New York: International Publishers, 1928.
21. S. H. Britt, "Tonal Sensitivity in the White Rat," *Journal of Comparative Psychology,* 1935, *19,* 243-264.
22. J. B. Watson and R. Rayner, "Conditioned Emotional Reactions," *Journal of Experimental Psychology,* 1920, *3,* 1-14.
23. C. W. Valentine, "The Innate Basis of Fear," *Journal of Genetic Psychology,* 1930, *37,* 394-420.
24. H. B. English, "Three Cases of the 'Conditioned Fear Response,'" *Journal of Abnormal and Social Psychology,* 1929, *24,* 221-225.
25. W. Dennis, "Infant Reaction to Restraint: An Evaluation of Watson's Theory," *Transactions of the New York Academy of Sciences,* 1940, *2,* 202-218, pp. 214-215.
26. E. Bagby, "The Etiology of Phobias," *Journal of Abnormal and Social Psychology,* 1922, *17,* 16-18, p. 17.
27. R. L. Duffus, "Where Do We Get Our Prejudices?" *Harper's Magazine,* 1926, *153,* 503-508, p. 505, copyright, Harper & Brothers.
28. B. Hart, *The Psychology of Insanity.* New York: By permission of The Macmillan Company, 1934, pp. 88-89, copyright, 1931, The Macmillan Company.
29. R. W. Husband, *Applied Psychology.* New York: By permission of Harper & Brothers, 1934, p. 137, copyright, 1934, Harper & Brothers.
30. Reprinted by permission from *Social Psychology* by D. Katz and R. L. Schanck, published by John Wiley & Sons, Inc., New York, 1938, p. 508, copyright, 1938, by Daniel Katz and Richard L. Schanck.
31. G. Murphy, L. B. Murphy, and T. M. Newcomb, *Experimental Social Psychology* (revised edition). New York: By permission of Harper & Brothers, 1937, p. 331, copyright, 1931, 1937, Harper & Brothers.
32. G. W. Allport, "Attitudes." In C. Murchison (editor), *A Handbook of Social Psychology.* Worcester: Clark University Press, 1935, Chap. 17, p. 811, copyright, 1934, 1935, Clark University.
33. G. B. Vetter and M. Green, "Personality and Group Factors in the Making of Atheists," *Journal of Abnormal and Social Psychology,* 1932, *27,* 179-194.
34. M. H. Means, "Fears of One Thousand College Women," *Journal of Abnormal and Social Psychology,* 1936, *31,* 291-311.
35. D. H. Yates, "An Association-Set Method in Psychotherapy," *Psychological Bulletin,* 1939, *36,* 506.
36. C. R. Griffith, *An Introduction to Applied Psychology.* New York: The Macmillan Company, 1934, pp. 31-32.
37. O. Klineberg, *Social Psychology.* New York: Harper & Brothers, 1940, pp. 160-161.

38. Murphy, Murphy, and Newcomb, same citation as note 31, pp. 98-99.
39. G. W. Allport, *Personality: A Psychological Interpretation.* New York: Henry Holt and Company, Inc., 1937, p. 194, copyright, 1937, Henry Holt and Company, Inc.
40. Murphy, Murphy, and Newcomb, same citation as note 31, pp. 104-105.
41. W. I. Thomas, *The Unadjusted Girl.* Boston: Little, Brown & Company, 1923.
42. M. H. Krout, "Wish and Behavior," *Journal of Abnormal and Social Psychology,* 1934, *29,* 253-268.
43. S. Freud, *The Basic Writings of Sigmund Freud.* (Transl. by A. A. Brill.) New York: Random House, Inc. (Modern Library, Inc.), 1938.
44. Allport, same citation as note 39, p. 193.

▶ *Chapter Seven* BEHAVIOR, TRAITS, AND ATTITUDES

(Pages 112-137)

1. G. W. Allport, "Attitudes." In C. Murchison (editor), *A Handbook of Social Psychology.* Worcester: Clark University Press, 1935, Chap. 17, pp. 798-844, p. 810. But compare E. Nelson, "Attitudes: I. Their Nature and Development," *Journal of General Psychology,* 1939, *21,* 367-399.
2. R. S. Lynd and H. M. Lynd, *Middletown: A Study in Contemporary American Culture.* New York: Harcourt, Brace and Company, 1929, p. 247.
3. Same citation, p. 336.
4. V. O. Weber, "Moral Judgment in Female Delinquents," *Journal of Applied Psychology,* 1926, *10,* 89-91.
5. L. M. Terman, "The Measurement of Personality," *Science,* 1934, *80,* 605-608, p. 605.
6. D. D. Droba, "The Nature of Attitude," *Journal of Social Psychology,* 1933, *4,* 444-463, p. 458.
7. D. Katz and R. L. Schanck, *Social Psychology.* New York: John Wiley & Sons, Inc., 1938, p. 428.
8. G. Murphy, L. B. Murphy, and T. M. Newcomb, *Experimental Social Psychology* (revised edition). New York: Harper & Brothers, 1937, pp. 780-781.
9. Same citation, p. 781; by permission of Harper & Brothers, copyright, 1931, 1937, Harper & Brothers.
10. G. W. Allport and H. S. Odbert, "Trait-Names: A Psycho-lexical Study," *Psychological Monographs,* 1936, *47,* No. 211, pp. 171.

11. J. B. Watson, *Behaviorism* (revised edition). New York: W. W. Norton & Company, 1930, p. 278, copyright, 1930, W. W. Norton & Company.
12. N. L. Munn, *Psychological Development.* Cambridge: The University Press, 1938, p. 517.
13. Murphy, Murphy, and Newcomb, same citation as note 8, p. 872.
14. J. P. Guilford and K. Braly, "Extroversion and Introversion," *Psychological Bulletin,* 1930, *27,* 96-107.
15. J. P. Guilford and R. B. Guilford, "Personality Factors S, E, and M, and Their Measurement," *Journal of Psychology,* 1936, *2,* 109-127.
16. J. P. Guilford and R. B. Guilford, "An Analysis of the Factors in a Typical Test of Introversion-Extroversion," *Journal of Abnormal and Social Psychology,* 1934, *28,* 377-399.
17. J. V. Hanna, "Clinical Procedure as a Method of Validating a Measure of Psychoneurotic Tendency," *Journal of Abnormal and Social Psychology,* 1934, *28,* 435-445.
18. Compare L. L. Bernard, *An Introduction to Social Psychology.* New York: Henry Holt and Company, Inc., 1926, p. 246.
19. C. Kirkpatrick, "Assumptions and Methods in Attitude Measurement," *American Sociological Review,* 1936, *1,* 75-88.
20. R. T. LaPiere, "The Sociological Significance of Measurable Attitudes," *American Sociological Review,* 1938, *3,* 175-182.
21. Same citation, p. 176.
22. Compare Droba, same citation as note 6.
23. K. Duncker, "The Influence of Past Experience upon Perceptual Properties," *American Journal of Psychology,* 1939, *52,* 255-265.
24. Compare F. H. Allport, *Social Psychology.* Boston: Houghton Mifflin Company, 1924, Chap. 13. Also D. W. MacKinnon, "Violation of Prohibitions." In H. A. Murray (editor), *Explorations in Personality: A Clinical and Experimental Study of Fifty Men of College Age.* New York: Oxford University Press, 1938, pp. 491-501.
25. G. C. Myers, "Affective Factors in Recall," *Journal of Philosophy, Psychology, and Scientific Methods,* 1915, *12,* 85-92.
26. R. W. Husband, *Applied Psychology.* New York: By permission of Harper & Brothers, 1934, p. 468, copyright, 1934, Harper & Brothers.
27. S. A. Rice, "Contagious Bias in the Interview," *American Journal of Sociology,* 1929, *35,* 420-423.
28. M. Zillig, "Einstellung und Aussage," *Zeitschrift für Psychologie,* 1928, *106,* 58-106.
29. M. Sherif, "An Experimental Study of Stereotypes," *Journal of Abnormal and Social Psychology,* 1935, *29,* 371-375.
30. M. Saadi and P. R. Farnsworth, "The Degrees of Acceptance of Dogmatic Statements and Preference for Their Supposed Makers," *Journal of Abnormal and Social Psychology,* 1934, *29,* 143-150.

31. M. Sherif, *The Psychology of Social Norms.* New York: Harper & Brothers, 1936.
32. B. Malinowski, *The Father in Primitive Psychology.* New York: W. W. Norton & Company, Inc., 1927, pp. 87-92.
33. J. O. Chassell, *The Experience Variables.* Rochester, New York: The Author, 1928.
34. L. B. Murphy, *Social Behavior and Child Personality: An Exploratory Study of Some Roots of Sympathy.* New York: Columbia University Press, 1937.
35. J. L. Moreno, *Who Shall Survive? A New Approach to the Problem of Human Interrelations.* Washington, D. C.: Nervous and Mental Disease Publishing Company, 1934.
36. A. Anderson and B. Dvorak, "Differences between College Students and Their Elders in Standards of Conduct," *Journal of Abnormal and Social Psychology,* 1928, *23,* 286-292.
37. R. L. Schanck, "A Study of a Communuity and Its Groups and Institutions Conceived of as Behaviors of Individuals," *Psychological Monographs,* 1932, *43,* No. 195, pp. 133.
38. H. Meltzer, "Students' Adjustments in Anger," *Journal of Social Psychology,* 1933, *4,* 285-309.
39. E. S. Robinson, "Are Radio Fans Influenced?", *Survey Graphic,* 1932, *68,* 546-547.
40. A. D. Annis and N. C. Meier, "The Induction of Opinion through Suggestion by Means of Planted Content," *Journal of Social Psychology,* 1934, *5,* 65-81.
41. R. C. Peterson and L. L. Thurstone, *Motion Pictures and the Social Attitudes of Children.* New York: The Macmillan Company, 1933.
42. F. H. Lund, "The Psychology of Belief," *Journal of Abnormal and Social Psychology,* 1925, *20,* 63-81 and 174-196.
43. H. Cantril, "The Prediction of Social Events," *Journal of Abnormal and Social Psychology,* 1938, *33,* 364-389.
44. D. McGregor, "The Major Determinants of the Prediction of Social Events," *Journal of Abnormal and Social Psychology,* 1938, *33,* 179-204.
45. H. S. Carlson, "Information and Certainty in Political Opinions: A Study of University Students during a Campaign," *University of Iowa Studies: Studies in Character,* 1931, *4,* No. 1, pp. 48.
46. E. L. Thorndike, "Science and Values," *Science,* Jan. 3, 1936, *83,* 1-8.
47. Same citation, p. 5.
48. T. E. Coffin, "Some Conditions of Suggestion and Suggestibility: A Study of Certain Attitudinal and Situational Factors Influencing the Process of Suggestion," *Psychological Monographs,* 1941, *4,* No. 241.

49. T. M. Newcomb, *Personality and Social Change*. New York: Dryden Press, 1943.
50. H. B. Lewis, "An Approach to Attitude Measurement. I," *The Psychologists League Journal,* 1938, *2,* 64-66, p. 65.
51. Allport, same citation as note 1, pp. 828-832.
52. D. Katz and F. H. Allport, *Students' Attitudes.* Syracuse: Craftsman Press, 1931.
53. E. S. Bogardus, "Social Distance and Its Origins," *Journal of Applied Sociology,* 1925, *9,* 216-226. E. S. Bogardus, "Measuring Social Distances," *Journal of Applied Sociology,* 1925, *9,* 299-308.
54. L. L. Thurstone and E. J. Chave, *The Measurement of Attitude: A Psychophysical Method and Some Experiments with a Scale for Measuring Attitude toward the Church.* Chicago: University of Chicago, Press, 1929.
55. R. K. Merton, "Facts and Factitiousness in Ethnic Opinionnaires," *American Sociological Review,* 1940, *5,* 13-28.
56. Compare B. L. Riker, "A Comparison of Methods Used in Attitude Research," *Journal of Abnormal and Social Psychology,* 1944, *39,* 112-117.
57. R. Stagner, "Methodology of Attitude Measurement." In J. D. Black (editor), *Research in Social Psychology of Rural Life.* New York: Social Science Research Council, Bulletin No. 17, 1933, 115-127, p. 123.
58. L. W. Ferguson, "The Requirements of an Adequate Attitude Scale," *Psychological Bulletin,* 1939, *36,* 665-673.
59. Kirkpatrick, same citation as note 19, p. 76.
60. LaPiere, same citation as note 20, pp. 176-177.
61. Same citation, p. 177.
62. H. B. Lewis, "An Approach to Attitude Measurement. II," *The Psychologists League Journal,* 1939, *3,* 10-12, p. 11.
63. Allport, same citation as note 1, p. 832.
64. W. E. Deming, "On Errors in Surveys," *American Sociological Review,* 1944, *9,* 359-369.
65. Stagner, same citation as note 57, p. 116.
66. D. Katz and H. Cantril, "Public Opinion Polls," *Sociometry,* 1937, *1,* 155-179.

▶ *Chapter Eight* THE SOCIAL PSYCHOLOGY OF LANGUAGE

(*Pages 138-165*)

1. R. S. Woodworth, *Contemporary Schools of Psychology*. New York: The Ronald Press Company, 1931, p. 72.

2. H. C. Warren (editor), *Dictionary of Psychology*. Boston: Houghton Mifflin Company, 1934, pp. 149-150.
3. R. M. Yerkes and A. W. Yerkes, *The Great Apes*. New Haven: Yale University Press, 1929, p. 307.
4. R. Paget, *Human Speech*. New York: Harcourt, Brace and Company, 1930.
5. C. H. Judd, *The Psychology of Social Institutions*. New York: The Macmillan Company, 1926, p. 195.
6. E. L. Thorndike, "The Origin of Language," *Science*, July 2, 1943, *98*, 1-6, pp. 3-4.
7. O. Jespersen, *Language: Its Nature, Development, and Origin*. New York: Henry Holt and Company, Inc., 1928.
8. S. S. Newman, "Further Experiments in Phonetic Symbolism," *American Journal of Psychology*, 1933, *45*, 53-75.
9. Judd, same citation as note 5, p. 200.
10. M. Smith, "An Investigation of the Development of the Sentence and the Extent of Vocabulary in Children," *University of Iowa Studies in Child Welfare*, 1926, *3*, No. 5, pp. 92.
11. O. C. Irwin and H. P. Chen, "Development of Speech during Infancy: Curve of Phonemic Types," *Journal of Experimental Psychology*, 1946, *36*, 431-436.
12. F. M. Young, "An Analysis of Certain Variables in a Developmental Study of Language," *Genetic Psychology Monographs*, 1941, *23*, 3-141.
13. Judd, same citation as note 5, p. 198, copyright, 1926. The Macmillan Company.
14. J. B. Watson, *Behaviorism*. New York: W. W. Norton & Company, 1930, p. 227.
15. R. T. LaPiere and P. R. Farnsworth, *Social Psychology*. New York: McGraw-Hill Book Company, Inc., 1936, p. 112.
16. J. B. Wolfe, "Effectiveness of Token-rewards for Chimpanzees," *Comparative Psychology Monographs*, 1936, *12*, No. 60, pp. 72.
17. F. L. Ruch, *Psychology and Life*. Chicago: Scott, Foresman and Company, 1937, p. 279, copyright, 1937, Scott, Foresman and Company.
18. C. L. Hull, "Quantitative Aspects of the Evolution of Concepts," *Psychological Monographs*, 1920, *28*, No. 1, pp. 86, pp. 5-6.
19. LaPiere and Farnsworth, same citation as note 15, p. 115.
20. Compare *Time*, Nov. 25, 1946, *48*, 69.
21. W. I. Thomas, *Primitive Behavior: An Introduction to the Social Sciences*. New York: McGraw-Hill Book Company, Inc., 1937, p. 52, copyright, 1937, McGraw-Hill Book Company, Inc.
22. G. W. Allport and H. Cantril, "Judging Personality from Voice," *Journal of Social Psychology*, 1934, *5*, 37-55. Also, compare P. J. Fay and W. C. Middleton, "Judgment of Kretschmerian Body

Types from the Voice as Transmitted over a Public Address System," *Journal of Social Psychology,* 1940, *12,* 151-162.

23. S. H. Britt, "Learning and Retention." In C. S. Marsh (editor), *Educational Broadcasting 1936.* Chicago: University of Chicago Press, 1937, 236-244, pp. 243-244, copyright, 1937, The University of Chicago.
24. Quoted by E. Horn, *Methods of Instruction in the Social Studies.* Report of the Commission on the Social Studies, American Historical Association, Part XV. New York: Charles Scribner's Sons, 1937, pp. 187-188, copyright, 1937, Charles Scribner's Sons. From J. C. Dewey, *Reading Comprehension Difficulties in American History,* Chap. 5 and 6.
25. Horn, same citation, p. 190, citing H. C. Short, *Concepts of Certain Quantitative Terms Used in Seventh Grade Social Science Materials,* Master's thesis, State University of Iowa, 1933.
26. Horn, same citation, p. 189, citing A. M. Ayer, *Some Difficulties in Elementary School History.* New York: Teachers College, Columbia University, 1926, pp. 36-37.
27. R. Gans, *A Study of Critical Reading Comprehension in the Intermediate Grades.* New York: Teachers College, Columbia University, 1940.
28. E. A. Schuler, "*V* for Victory: A Study in Symbolic Social Control," *The Journal of Social Psychology,* 1944, *19,* 283-299.
29. O. Klineberg, *Race Differences.* New York: Harper & Brothers, 1935, Chap. 15.
30. G. Murphy, L. B. Murphy, and T. M. Newcomb, *Experimental Social Psychology* (revised edition). New York: By permission of Harper & Brothers, 1937, pp. 153-154, copyright, 1931, 1937, Harper & Brothers.
31. Klineberg, same citation as note 29, p. 283.
32. Same citation, pp. 285-286.
33. Same citation, pp. 286-287; by permission of Harper & Brothers.
34. D. Efron and J. P. Foley, Jr., "A Comparative Investigation of Gestural Behavior Patterns in Italian and Jewish Groups Living under Different as Well as Similar Environmental Conditions," *Zeitschrift für Sozialforschung,* 1937, *6,* 151-159.
35. J. Piaget, *The Language and Thought of the Child.* New York: Harcourt, Brace and Company, 1926.
36. Same citation, p. 9.
37. D. McCarthy, "Language Development." In C. Murchison (editor), *A Handbook of Child Psychology* (revised edition). Worcester: Clark University Press, 1933, Chap. 8.
38. D. McCarthy, *The Language Development of the Pre-school Child.* Minneapolis: University of Minnesota Press, 1930, Institute of Child Welfare Monograph Series, No. 4.

39. H. Rugg, L. Krueger, and A. Sondergaard, "Studies in Child Personality. I. A Study of the Language of Kindergarten Children," *Journal of Educational Psychology,* 1929, *20,* 1-18.
40. F. L. Goodenough, "The Use of Pronouns by Young Children: A Note on the Development of Selfawareness," *Journal of Genetic Psychology,* 1938, *52,* 333-346.
41. M. Henle and M. B. Hubbell, "'Egocentricity' in Adult Conversation," *Journal of Social Psychology,* 1938, *9,* 227-234.
42. H. T. Moore, "Further Data Concerning Sex Differences," *Journal of Abnormal and Social Psychology,* 1922, *17,* 210-214.
43. M. H. Landis and H. E. Burtt, "A Study of Conversations," *Journal of Comparative Psychology,* 1924, *4,* 81-89.
44. W. J. Baker and D. McGregor, "Conversation as a Reflector of Social Change," *Journal of Social Psychology,* 1937, *8,* 487-490.
45. Same citation, p. 488.
46. C. Landis, "National Differences in Conversation," *Journal of Abnormal and Social Psychology,* 1927, *4,* 354-357.
47. J. S. Carlson, S. W. Cook, and E. L. Stromberg, "Sex Differences in Conversation," *Journal of Applied Psychology,* 1936, *20,* 727-735.
48. R. F. Griggs, "Nicotinic Acid," *Science,* Feb. 13, 1942, *95,* 171.
49. J. R. Enright, "Nicotinic Acid," *Science,* July 24, 1942, *96,* 84.
50. H. Blumer, "The Problem of the Concept in Social Psychology," *American Journal of Sociology,* 1940, *45,* 707-719.
51. E. Browder, *What Is Communism?* New York: Workers Library, 1936, p. 21, copyright, 1936, Earl Browder.
52. E. R. Hunter and B. E. Gaines, "Verbal Taboo in a College Community," *American Speech,* 1938, *13,* 97-107.
53. W. La Barre, "The Psychopathology of Drinking Songs," *Psychiatry,* 1939, *3,* 203-212.
54. J. M. Steadman, Jr., "Affected and Effeminate Words," *American Speech,* 1938, *13,* 13-18.
55. G. W. Hartmann, "The Contradiction between the Feeling-Tone of Political Party Names and Public Response to Their Platforms," *Journal of Social Psychology,* 1936, *7,* 336-357.
56. S. C. Menefee, "Stereotyped Phrases and Public Opinion," *American Journal of Sociology,* 1938, *43,* 614-622.
57. Compare R. H. Thouless, *Straight and Crooked Thinking.* New York: Simon and Schuster, 1932, pp. 16-18.
58. C. K. Ogden and I. A. Richards, *The Meaning of Meaning.* London: Kegan Paul, Trench, Trubner & Co., 1923.
59. S. Chase, "The Tyranny of Words," *Harper's Magazine,* 1937, *175,* 561-569, p. 567, copyright, Harper & Brothers.
60. *The New York Times,* July 16, 1938, quoting James A. Farley.
61. Reported in *Washington Post,* June 26, 1940.

62. Governor Robert S. Kerr speaking to Democratic Convention, as reported in *The New York Times,* July 20, 1944, p. 11.
63. Governor Earl Warren speaking to Republican Convention, as reported in *The New York Times,* June 27, 1944, p. 10.
64. W. J. Cameron, *Thanks and Discontent.* Dearborn, Michigan: Ford Motor Co., Nov. 21, 1937, pp. 4.
65. *Washington Post,* March 9, 1939, quoting Jerome Frank.
66. *The New York Times,* June 8, 1939.
67. *The New York Times,* Sept. 3, 1939.
68. T. W. Arnold, *The Symbols of Government.* New Haven: Yale University Press, 1935, p. 95.

▶ *Chapter Nine* THE PSYCHOLOGY OF IRRATIONALITY

(*Pages 166-198*)

1. H. Blumer, *Movies and Conduct.* New York: The Macmillan Company, 1933.
2. E. S. Robinson, *Man as Psychology Sees Him.* New York: By permission of the The Macmillan Company, 1932, p. 164, copyright, 1932, The Macmillan Company.
3. Same citation, p. 163.
4. E. D. Martin, *Psychology: What It Has to Teach You about Yourself and Your World.* New York: People's Institute, 1924, p. 120.
5. See Publications of Institute for Propaganda Analysis, Inc., of New York, especially Vol. 1, Nos. 2 and 3, November and December, 1937. Also, A. M. Lee and E. B. Lee, *The Fine Art of Propaganda.* New York: Harcourt, Brace and Company, 1939.
6. Quotation from Thomas, given by K. Young, *Social Psychology: An Analysis of Social Behavior.* New York: Appleton-Century-Crofts, Inc., 1930, p. 397, copyright, 1930, Kimball Young.
7. Young, same citation, pp. 440-441.
8. C. Kirkpatrick, "A Tentative Study in Experimental Social Psychology," *American Journal of Sociology,* 1932, *38,* 194-206.
9. J. F. Dashiell, "Legal Rules of Evidence as a Neglected Experimental Field," *Psychological Bulletin,* 1931, *28,* 576. J. F. Dashiell, "Experimental Studies of the Influence of Social Situations on the Behavior of Individual Human Adults." In C. Murchison (editor), *A Handbook of Social Psychology.* Worcester: Clark University Press, 1935, Chap. 23, pp. 1141-1144.
10. F. C. Bartlett, *Remembering: A Study in Experimental and Social Psychology.* Cambridge: Cambridge University Press, 1932, pp. 118-185.

11. A. Train, "Are You 'Psychic'?", *Scribner's Magazine,* 1936, *99,* 153-160, p. 156, footnote.
12. *The Commentator,* July, 1938, *3,* 69-70.
13. A. Nevins, *The Gateway to History.* New York: Appleton-Century-Crofts, Inc., 1938, p. 119 and p. 130.
14. Same citation, p. 121.
15. H. Jennings, C. Madge, and others (editors), *May the Twelfth.* London: Faber & Faber, Ltd., 1937.
16. Nevins, same citation as note 13, pp. 139-140, copyright, 1938, D. C. Heath & Co.
17. Same citation, pp. 161-162, copyright, 1938, D. C. Heath & Co.
18. P. Van Paassen, *Days of Our Years.* New York: Hillman-Curl, Inc., 1939, pp. 103-104, copyright, 1939, Hillman-Curl, Inc.
19. K. Young, "The Psychology of Hymns," *Journal of Abnormal and Social Psychology,* 1926, *20,* 391-406.
20. S. J. Case, *The Millennial Hope.* Chicago: University of Chicago Press, 1918, p. 2.
21. Advertisement in *Washington Post,* Oct. 3, 1936.
22. *The New Republic,* Jan. 8, 1940, *102,* p. 53.
23. W. Albig, *Public Opinion.* New York: McGraw-Hill Book Company, Inc., 1939, pp. 131-134.
24. *Time* magazine, Nov. 27, 1939, *34,* p. 18.
25. Taken from *Washington Star,* Jan. 8, 1939.
26. A. Machen, *The Angels of Mons.* London: Simpkin, Marshall, Hamilton, Kent, 1915.
27. W. Irwin, *Propaganda and the News.* New York: McGraw-Hill Book Company, Inc., 1936, p. 141.
28. Same citation, pp. 142-144.
29. *Time* magazine, Jan. 8, 1940, *35,* p. 47.
30. *Washington Post,* Sept. 12, 1939.
31. *The New York Times,* Sept. 4, 1939.
32. Compare Associated Press report in *Washington Post,* Sept. 20, 1939, with International News Service account in Washington *Times-Herald,* Sept. 19, 1939.
33. *Somebody Is Wrong,* Special Bulletins on War Propaganda of Institute for Propaganda Analysis, Inc., No. 2, Oct. 31, 1939, p. 1.
34. *The "Fifth Column,"* Bulletin of the Institute for Propaganda Analysis, Inc., *3,* July 8, 1940, p. 1.
35. Courtesy of *Time,* copyright Time Inc., March 23, 1942, *39,* 15.
36. *Time,* April 13, 1942, *39,* 2.
37. Courtesy, *Washington Daily News,* Feb. 27, 1945, p. 19.
38. Compare column by Jerry Klutz, *Washington Post,* Nov. 6, 1942, and *Washington Star,* Nov. 7, 1942.
39. *Washington Post,* Aug. 10, 1942.

40. *Washington Star,* Aug. 11, 1942; and *Washington Post,* Aug. 13, 1942.
41. *Washington Star,* May 11, 1943.
42. W. F. Colville, *The Philosophy and Psychology of Human Relations.* Ocala, Florida, 1914, pp. 7-8.
43. L. B. Barratt, "Your Fortune in Your Eyes," *The American Magazine,* January, 1938, *75,* 48-49 and 100-102, p. 49, copyright, Crowell-Collier Publishing Company.
44. R. S. Lynd and H. M. Lynd, *Middletown: A Study in Contemporary American Culture.* New York: Harcourt, Brace and Company, 1929, pp. 298-299, copyright, 1929, Harcourt, Brace and Company.
45. A. Carrel, *Man the Unknown.* New York: Harper & Brothers, 1935. Reviewed by R. Bain, *American Sociological Review,* 1936, *1,* 814-817.
46. C. Withers, "The Folklore of a Small Town," *Transactions of the New York Academy of Sciences,* 1946, *8,* 234-251, p. 238.
47. Washington *Daily News,* Nov. 19, 1937.
48. *Washington Star,* Sept. 19, 1937.
49. W. James, *Some Problems of Philosophy.* New York: Longmans, Green & Co., 1911, p. 224.
50. C. Spearman, "Normality." In C. Murchison (editor), *Psychologies of 1930.* Worcester: Clark University Press, 1930, Chap. 24.

▶ *Chapter Ten* OUR JUDGMENTS OF OTHER PERSONS

(*Pages 201-238*)

1. Compare W. B. Pitkin, *The Art of Learning.* New York: McGraw-Hill Book Company, Inc., 1931, pp. 219-220.
2. W. F. Ogburn, "Bias, Psychoanalysis, and the Subjective in Relation to the Social Sciences," *Proceedings of the American Sociological Society,* 1922, *17,* 62-74, p. 62.
3. H. Gurnee, *Elements of Social Psychology.* New York: Rinehart & Company, Inc., 1936, p. 125, copyright, 1936, Herbert Gurnee.
4. S. H. Britt and M. M. Balcom, "Jumping-rope Rhymes and the Social Psychology of Play," *Journal of Genetic Psychology,* 1941, *58,* 289-306.
5. B. Lasker, *Race Attitudes in Children.* New York: Henry Holt and Company, Inc., 1929.
6. *Can You Name Them?* New York: American Committee for Democracy and Intellectual Freedom, 1939.
7. G. Murphy, L. B. Murphy, and T. M. Newcomb, *Experimental Social Psychology* (revised edition). New York: Harper & Brothers, 1937, p. 979.

8. Quoted by C. R. Miller (President of Institute for Propaganda Analysis, Inc.), *How to Detect and Analyze Propaganda*. New York: Town Hall, 1939, p. 12.
9. W. D. Wallis, "Social Anthropology." In E. P. Schmidt (editor), *Man and Society: A Substantive Introduction to the Social Sciences*. New York: Prentice-Hall, Inc., 1937, Chap. 3, pp. 93-94, copyright, 1937, Prentice-Hall, Inc.
10. K. Young, *Social Psychology: An Analysis of Social Behavior*. New York: Appleton-Century-Crofts, Inc., 1930, p. 528, copyright, 1930, Kimball Young.
11. M. Sherman, "The Differentiation of Emotional Responses in Infants: I. Judgments of Emotional Responses from Motion Picture Views and from Actual Observation," *Journal of Comparative Psychology*, 1927, *7*, 265-284.
12. M. Sherman, "The Differentiation of Emotional Responses in Infants: II. The Ability of Observers to Judge the Emotional Characteristics of the Crying of Infants and of the Voice of an Adult," *Journal of Comparative Psychology*, 1927, *7*, 335-351, p. 335.
13. A. M. Feleky, "The Expression of the Emotions," *Psychological Review*, 1914, *21*, 33-41. Also A. M. Feleky, *Feelings and Emotions*. New York: Pioneer Publishing Company, 1922.
14. H. S. Langfeld, "The Judgment of Emotion by Facial Expression," *Journal of Abnormal Psychology*, 1918, *13*, 172-184.
15. C. Landis and R. Gullette, "Studies in Emotional Reactions: III. Systolic Blood Pressure and Inspiration-Expiration Ratios," *Journal of Comparative Psychology*, 1925, *5*, 221-253.
16. C. Landis, "Studies in Emotional Reactions: II. General Behavior and Facial Expression," *Journal of Comparative Psychology*, 1924, *4*, 447-509.
17. R. C. Davis, "The Specificity of Facial Expressions," *Journal of General Psychology*, 1934, *10*, 42-58.
18. C. Landis, "The Interpretation of Facial Expression in Emotion," *Journal of General Psychology*, 1929, *2*, 59-72.
19. F. H. Allport, *Social Psychology*. Boston: Houghton Mifflin Company, 1924, Chaps. 9 and 10.
20. A. Jenness, "The Effects of Coaching Subjects in the Recognition of Facial Expressions," *Journal of General Psychology*, 1932, *7*, 163-178.
21. K. Dunlap, "The Rôle of Eye-Muscles and Mouth-Muscles in the Expression of the Emotions," *Genetic Psychology Monographs*, 1927, *2*, No. 3, 196-233.
22. W. Wolff, *The Expression of Personality; Experimental Depth Psychology*. New York: Harper & Brothers, 1943.
23. N. L. Munn, "The Effect of Knowledge of the Situation upon Judg-

ment of Emotions from Facial Expressions," *Journal of Abnormal and Social Psychology,* 1940, *35,* 324-338.

24. N. L. Munn, "The Effect of a Knowledge of the Situation upon Judgment of Emotion from Facial Expressions Aroused in Everyday Life," *Psychological Bulletin,* 1939, *36,* 568-569.
25. W. A. Hunt, "Recent Developments in the Field of Emotion," *Psychological Bulletin,* 1941, *38,* 250-276, pp. 261-262.
26. First four photos of Gene Tierney, *Life* magazine, Feb. 19, 1940, *8,* p. 36, by Hart Preston; last four photos, *Life* magazine, Nov. 27, 1939, *7,* p. 88, from scenes in the Warner Bros. picture, *We Are Not Alone,* starring Paul Muni and Jane Bryan.
27. B. Sidis, *The Psychology of Suggestion.* New York: Appleton-Century-Crofts, Inc., 1898, pp. 372-373.
28. H. L. Hollingworth, *Advertising and Selling: Principles of Appeal and Response.* New York: Appleton-Century-Crofts, Inc., 1913, pp. 229-232.
29. L. E. Baker, "The Influence of Subliminal Stimuli upon Verbal Behavior," *Journal of Experimental Psychology,* 1937, *20,* 84-100.
30. A. C. Williams, Jr., "Perception of Subliminal Visual Stimuli," *Journal of Psychology,* 1938, *6,* 187-199.
31. Same citation, p. 193.
32. Same citation.
33. J. G. Miller, "Discrimination without Awareness," *American Journal of Psychology,* 1939, *52,* 562-578. J. G. Miller, "The Role of Motivation in Learning without Awareness," *American Journal of Psychology,* 1940, *53,* 229-239.
34. J. W. Coyne, H. E. King, J. Zubin, and C. Landis, "Accuracy of Recognition of Subliminal Auditory Stimuli," *Journal of Experimental Psychology,* 1943, *33,* 508-513.
35. H. E. King, C. Landis, and J. Zubin, "Visual Subliminal Perception Where a Figure Is Obscured by the Illumination of the Ground," *Journal of Experimental Psychology,* 1944, *34,* 60-69.
36. W. E. Vinacke, "The Discrimination of Color and Form at Levels of Illumination below Conscious Awareness," *Archives of Psychology,* 1942, No. 267, pp. 53.
37. D. A. Laird, "How the Consumer Estimates Quality by Subconscious Sensory Impressions," *Journal of Applied Psychology,* 1932, *16,* 241-246.
38. Murphy, Murphy, and Newcomb, same citation as note 7, p. 163; by permission of Harper & Brothers, copyright, 1931, 1937, Harper & Brothers.
39. Same citation, pp. 163-164; by permission of Harper & Brothers.
40. R. M. Collier, "An Experimental Study of the Effects of Subliminal Stimuli," *Psychological Monographs,* 1940, *52,* No. 236, p. 3.

41. Hon. M. Maverick of Texas, *Congressional Record,* 75th Congress, 2d Session, Dec. 13, 1937, *82,* No. 24, p. 1407.
42. W. Lippmann, *Public Opinion.* New York: The Macmillan Company, 1922, Part III.
43. C. E. Skinner (editor), *Readings in Psychology.* New York: Rinehart & Company, Inc., 1935, p. 545.
44. R. Pintner, "Intelligence as Estimated from Photographs," *Psychological Review,* 1918, *25,* 286-296.
45. Same citation, p. 296.
46. D. A. Laird and H. Remmers, "A Study of Estimates of Intelligence from Photographs," *Journal of Experimental Psychology,* 1924, *7,* 429-446.
47. F. V. Markey, "Variations in Judgment," *Journal of Applied Psychology,* 1934, *18,* 297-303. A. W. Kornhauser and R. N. McMurry, "Rating from Photographs," *The Personnel Journal,* 1938, *17,* 20-24. R. W. Husband, "The Photograph on the Application Blank," *The Personnel Journal,* 1934, *13,* 69-72.
48. S. W. Cook, "The Judgment of Intelligence from Photographs," *Journal of Abnormal and Social Psychology,* 1939, *3,* 384-389.
49. M. S. Viteles and K. R. Smith, "The Prediction of Vocational Aptitude and Success from Photographs," *Journal of Experimental Psychology,* 1932, *15,* 615-629.
50. *The New York Times,* May 21, 1933.
51. "Speaking of Pictures," *Life,* March 10, 1947, *22,* 20-22; photos, Courtesy of Wide World Photos, Inc.; Acme Newspictures, Inc.; K. Chester; International News Photos; Eric Schaal; Associated Press; and New York *Daily News;* and *Life,* copyright Time, Inc.
52. G. W. Allport, *Personality: A Psychological Interpretation.* New York: Henry Holt and Company, Inc., 1937, p. 14.
53. A. L. Lowell, *Public Opinion in War and Peace.* Cambridge: Harvard University Press, 1923, p. 24; reprinted by permission of the President and Fellows of Harvard College, copyright, 1923, Harvard University.
54. E. Kretschmer, *Körperbau und Charakter* (10th ed.). Berlin: Verlag Julius Springer, 1931.
55. C. R. Garvey, "Comparative Body Build of Manic-Depressive and Schizophrenic Patients," *Psychological Bulletin,* 1933, *30,* 567 and 739.
56. E. F. Wells, "The Relation between Psychosis and Physical Type: A Statistical Study," *American Journal of Psychology,* 1938, *51,* 136-145. P. S. deQ. Cabot, "The Relationship between Characteristics of Personality and Physique in Adolescents," *Genetic Psychology Monographs,* 1938, No. 1, *20,* 3-120.

57. M. L. Farber, "A Critique and an Investigation of Kretschmer's Theory," *Journal of Abnormal and Social Psychology*, 1938, *33*, 398-404.
58. W. H. Sheldon, with the collaboration of S. S. Stevens, and W. B. Tucker, *The Varieties of Human Physique: An Introduction to Constitutional Psychology*. New York: Harper & Brothers, 1940. Also, W. H. Sheldon and S. S. Stevens, *The Varieties of Temperament; A Psychology of Constitutional Differences*. New York: Harper & Brothers, 1942.
59. Lippmann, same citation as note 42, Chap. 7.
60. S. A. Rice, "'Stereotypes': A Source of Error in Judging Human Character," *Journal of Personnel Research*, 1926, *5*, 267-276.
61. O. F. Litterer, "Stereotypes," *Journal of Social Psychology*, 1933, *4*, 59-69.
62. D. Katz and K. Braly, "Racial Stereotypes of 100 College Undergraduates," *Journal of Abnormal and Social Psychology*, 1933, *28*, 280-290.
63. M. Meenes, "A Comparison of Racial Stereotypes of Negro College Students in 1935 and in 1942," *Psychological Bulletin*, 1942, *39*, 467-468.
64. K. Fink and H. Cantril, "The Collegiate Stereotype as Frame of Reference," *Journal of Abnormal and Social Psychology*, 1937, *32*, 352-356.
65. H. Cantril, "Request for Cooperative Research," *Journal of Social Psychology*, 1939, *18*, 153-154.
66. G. B. Vetter, "The Measurement of Social and Political Attitudes and the Related Personality Factors," *Journal of Abnormal and Social Psychology*, 1930, *25*, 149-189.
67. A. W. Kornhauser, "Analysis of 'Class' Structure of Contemporary American Society—Psychological Bases of Class Divisions." In G. W. Hartmann and T. Newcomb (editors), *Industrial Conflict: A Psychological Interpretation*. New York: The Cordon Company, 1939, pp. 248-249.
68. Lowell, same citation as note 53, p. 48.
69. Lippmann, same citation as note 42, p. 45; by permission of The Macmillan Company, copyright, 1922, Walter Lippmann.
70. Quoted by A. Lipsky, *Man the Puppet*. New York: Frank-Maurice, 1925, p. 52.
71. M. Sherif, "The Psychology of Slogans," *Journal of Abnormal and Social Psychology*, 1937, *32*, 450-461.
72. J. E. Hulett, Jr., "Propaganda and the Proposed Child Labor Amendment," *Public Opinion Quarterly*, 1938, *2*, 105-116, p. 114.
73. F. E. Lumley, "Slogans as a Means of Social Control," *Proceedings of the American Sociological Society*, 1921, *16*, 121-134, p. 127.

74. S. S. Sargent, "Emotional Stereotypes in the Chicago Tribune," *Sociometry,* 1939, *2,* 69-75, compare p. 74.

75. Compare A. L. Edwards, "Studies of Stereotypes: I. The Directionality and Uniformity of Responses to Stereotypes," *Journal of Social Psychology,* 1940, *12,* 357-366, pp. 357-358.

Chapter Eleven THE INFLUENCE OF OTHER PERSONS

(*Pages 239-278*)

1. G. J. Hoffman, "An Experiment in Self-estimation," *Journal of Abnormal and Social Psychology,* 1923, *18,* 43-49.
2. *Time,* April 13, 1942, *39,* 78.
3. G. V. Hamilton, *A Research in Marriage.* New York: Albert & Charles Boni, Inc., 1929, pp. 258-259.
4. *Superman,* Nov. 5, 1939.
5. R. S. Lynd and H. M. Lynd, *Middletown: A Study in Contemporary American Culture.* New York: Harcourt, Brace and Company, Inc., 1929, p. 265, copyright, 1929, Harcourt, Brace and Company, Inc.
6. C. Bühler, *From Birth to Maturity.* London: Paul, Trench, Trubner, 1935, pp. 11-12.
7. A. Gesell, *Mental Growth of the Pre-school Child.* New York: The Macmillan Company, 1925. A. Gesell, *An Atlas of Infant Behavior* (2 vols.). New Haven: Yale University Press, 1934.
8. R. Barker, T. Dembo, and K. Lewin, "Experiments on Frustration and Regression in Children," *Psychological Bulletin,* 1937, *34,* 754-755; R. Barker, T. Dembo, and K. Lewin, *Frustration and Regression: An Experiment with Young Children.* Iowa City, Iowa: University of Iowa Press, 1941.
9. M. E. Wright, "The Constructiveness of Play as Affected by Group Play and Frustration," *Psychological Bulletin,* 1941, *38,* 562; M. E. Wright, "Constructiveness of Play as Affected by Group Organization and Frustration," *Character and Personality,* 1942, *11,* 40-49.
10. R. R. Sears, "Experimental Studies of Projection: I. Attribution of Traits," *Journal of Social Psychology,* 1936, *6,* 151-163.
11. R. R. Sears, "Experimental Studies of Projection: II. Ideas of Reference," *Journal of Social Psychology,* 1937, *8,* 389-400.
12. L. Bellak, "An Experimental Investigation of Projection," *Psychological Bulletin,* 1942, *39,* 489-490; L. Bellak, "The Concept of Projection: An Experimental Investigation and Study of the Concept," *Psychiatry,* 1944, *7,* 353-370.

13. F. W. Finger, "Sex Beliefs and Practices among Male College Students," *The Journal of Abnormal and Social Psychology*, 1947, *42*, 57-67.
14. Compare L. L. Bernard, *An Introduction to Social Psychology*. New York: Henry Holt and Company, Inc., 1926, p. 282.
15. G. W. Allport, *Personality: A Psychological Interpretation*. New York: Henry Holt and Company, Inc., 1937, p. 167.
16. H. A. Murray, "Visceral Manifestations of Personality," *Journal of Abnormal and Social Psychology*, 1937, *32*, 161-184, p. 167.
17. F. Aveling and H. L. Hargreaves, "Suggestibility with and without Prestige in Children," *British Journal of Psychology*, 1921, *18*, 362-388.
18. G. H. Estabrooks, "Experimental Studies in Suggestion," *Journal of Genetic Psychology*, 1929, *36*, 120-139.
19. G. Murphy, L. B. Murphy, and T. M. Newcomb, *Experimental Social Psychology* (revised edition). New York: Harper & Brothers, 1937, pp. 168-169.
20. H. T. Moore, "The Comparative Influence of Majority and Expert Opinion," *American Journal of Psychology*, 1921, *32*, 16-20.
21. J. W. Boldyreff and P. A. Sorokin, "An Experimental Study of the Influence of Suggestion on the Discrimination and the Valuation of People," *American Journal of Sociology*, 1932, *37*, 720-737.
22. Also compare O. W. Eagleson and E. J. Lipford, "A Study of Number Choices," *The Journal of General Psychology*, 1944, *31*, 129-133.
23. L. D. Goodfellow, "A Psychological Interpretation of the Results of the Zenith Radio Experiments in Telepathy," *Journal of Experimental Psychology*, 1938, *23*, 601-623.
24. H. Cantril, *The Psychology of Social Movements*. New York: John Wiley & Sons, Inc., 1941.
25. Same citation, p. 65.
26. H. Cantril, with the assistance of H. Gaudet and H. Herzog, *The Invasion from Mars: A Study in the Psychology of Panic*. Princeton: Princeton University Press, 1940.
27. Compare Cantril, same citation as note 24, pp. 72-73.
28. R. M. Simmons, "A Study of a Group of Children of Exceptionally High Intelligence Quotient in Situations Partaking of the Nature of Suggestion," *Teachers College, Contributions to Education*, 1940, No. 788.
29. R. M. Collier, "The Effect of Propaganda upon Attitude Following a Critical Examination of the Propaganda Itself," *The Journal of Social Psychology*, 1944, *20*, 3-17.
30. Murphy, Murphy, and Newcomb, same citation as note 19, p. 181. Compare E. Faris, "The Concept of Imitation," *American Journal of Sociology*, 1926, *32*, 367-378.

31. D. Starch, "Unconscious Imitation in Handwriting," *Psychological Review,* 1911, *18,* 223-228.
32. Private communication from Professor E. Dale of Ohio State University.
33. H. Blumer, *Movies and Conduct.* New York: By permission of The Macmillan Company, 1933, p. 38, copyright, 1933, The Macmillan Company.
34. Compare J. Peterson, "Imitation and Mental Adjustment," *Journal of Abnormal and Social Psychology,* 1922, *17,* 1-15.
35. S. B. Leacock, *Humor: Its Theory and Technique.* New York: Dodd, Mead & Company, 1935.
36. L. Omwake, "A Study of Sense of Humor: Its Relation to Sex, Age, and Personal Characteristics," *Journal of Applied Psychology,* 1937, *21,* 688-704.
37. L. Omwake, "Humor in the Making," *The Journal of Social Psychology,* 1942, *15,* 265-279.
38. T. G. Andrews, "A Factorial Analysis of Responses to the Comic as a Study in Personality," *The Journal of General Psychology,* 1943, *28,* 209-224.
39. W. McDougall, *Outline of Psychology,* New York: Charles Scribner's Sons, 1923, pp. 165-170.
40. S. Freud, *Wit and Its Relation to the Unconscious.* New York: Moffat Yard & Co., 1916.
41. C. W. Kimmins, *The Springs of Laughter.* London: Methuen & Co., Ltd., 1928. A. M. Ludovici, *The Secret of Laughter.* London: Constable & Company, Ltd., 1932. S. B. Leacock, same citation as note 35. M. Eastman, *Enjoyment of Laughter.* New York: Simon and Schuster, 1936.
42. J. H. Burma, "Humor as a Technique in Race Conflict," *American Sociological Review,* 1946, *11,* 710-715.
43. Quoted by Kimmins, same citation as note 41, p. 10.
44. Eastman, same citation as note 41.
45. Ludovici, same citation as note 41.
46. R. M. Washburn, "A Study of the Smiling and Laughing of Infants in the First Year of Life," *Genetic Psychology Monographs,* 1929, *6,* Nos. 5 and 6, 403-537.
47. J. M. Willmann, "An Analysis of Humor and Laughter," *American Journal of Psychology,* 1940, *53,* 70-85.
48. P. Kambouropoulou, "Individual Differences in the Sense of Humor and Their Relation to Temperamental Differences," *Archives of Psychology,* 1930, *19,* No. 121, pp. 83.
49. M. St. C. Hester, *Variation in Humor According to Age and Mental Condition,* Master's Thesis in Columbia University Library, 1924; described by Murphy, Murphy, and Newcomb, same citation as note 19, p. 285.

50. H. A. Wolff, C. E. Smith, and H. A. Murray, "The Psychology of Humor," *Journal of Abnormal and Social Psychology,* 1934, *28,* 341-365.

51. L. Omwake, "Factors Influencing the Sense of Humor," *Journal of Social Psychology,* 1939, *10,* 95-104.

52. But compare J. M. Willmann, same citation as note 47.

53. These cartoons are taken from *The New Yorker* of Feb. 3, 1940, *15,* p. 23, Richard Taylor; Feb. 24, 1940, *15,* p. 66, O. Soglow; Feb. 10, 1940, *15,* p. 28, Ned Hilton; June 29, 1940, *15,* p. 13, Whitney Darrow, Jr.; Jan. 13, 1940, *15,* p. 13, Charles Addams.

54. This section is based to a large extent upon J. F. Dashiell, "Experimental Studies of the Influence of Social Situations on the Behavior of Individual Human Adults." In C. Murchison (editor), *A Handbook of Social Psychology.* Worcester: Clark University Press, 1935, Chap. 23.

55. L. E. Travis, "The Effect of a Small Audience upon Eye-Hand Coordination," *Journal of Abnormal and Social Psychology,* 1925, *20,* 142-146.

56. G. S. Gates, "The Effect of an Audience upon Performance," *Journal of Abnormal and Social Psychology,* 1924, *18,* 334-342.

56-A. Dashiell, same citation as note 54, p. 1106.

57. N. G. Hanawalt and K. F. Ruttiger, "The Effect of an Audience on Remembering," *The Journal of Social Psychology,* 1944, *19,* 259-272.

58. F. H. Allport, "The Influence of the Group upon Association and Thought," *Journal of Experimental Psychology,* 1920, *3,* 159-182. F. H. Allport, *Social Psychology.* Boston: Houghton Mifflin Company, 1924, Chap. 11.

59. J. F. Dashiell, "An Experimental Analysis of Some Group Effects," *Journal of Abnormal and Social Psychology,* 1930, *25,* 190-199.

60. S. B. Weston and H. B. English, "The Influence of the Group on Psychological Test Scores," *American Journal of Psychology,* 1926, *37,* 600-601. P. R. Farnsworth, "Concerning So-called Group Effects," *Journal of Genetic Psychology,* 1928, *35,* 587-594.

61. F. J. Roethlisberger and W. J. Dickson, *Management and the Worker.* Cambridge: Harvard University Press, 1939.

62. Dashiell, same citation as note 54, p. 1115.

63. I. C. Whittemore, "The Influence of Competition on Performance: An Experimental Study," *Journal of Abnormal and Social Psychology,* 1924, *19,* 236-253. I. C. Whittemore, "The Competitive Consciousness," *Journal of Abnormal and Social Psychology,* 1925, *20,* 17-33.

64. Dashiell, same citation as note 59.

65. H. F. Whiting and H. B. English, "Fatigue Tests and Incentives," *Journal of Experimental Psychology,* 1925, *8,* 33-49.

66. Compare C. J. Leuba, "A Preliminary Experiment to Quantify an Incentive and Its Effects," *Journal of Abnormal and Social Psychology,* 1930, *25,* 275-288.

67. J. B. Maller, "Cooperation and Competition," *Teachers College Contributions to Education,* 1929, No. 384, pp. 176.

68. E. B. Hurlock, "The Value of Praise and Reproof as Incentives for Children," *Archives of Psychology,* 1924, *11,* No. 71, pp. 78.

69. E. P. Gilchrist, "Extent to Which Praise and Reproof Affect a Pupil's Work," *School and Society,* 1916, *4,* 872-874. D. A. Laird, "How the College Student Responds to Different Incentives to Work," *Pedagogical Seminary,* 1923, *30,* 366-370. T. H. Briggs, "Praise and Censure as Incentives," *School and Society,* 1927, *26,* 596-598.

70. A. Jenness, "Social Influences in the Change of Opinion: The Role of Discussion in Changing Opinion Regarding a Matter of Fact," *Journal of Abnormal and Social Psychology,* 1932, *27,* 29-34, 279-296.

71. H. Gurnee, "Maze Learning in the Collective Situation," *Journal of Psychology,* 1937, *3,* 437-443. H. Gurnee, "A Comparison of Collective and Individual Judgments of Fact," *Journal of Experimental Psychology,* 1937, *21,* 106-112. H. Gurnee, "Effect of Collective Learning upon the Individual Participants," *Journal of Abnormal and Social Psychology,* 1939, *34,* 529-532.

72. E. B. South, "Some Psychological Aspects of Committee Work," *Journal of Applied Psychology,* 1927, *11,* 348-368, 437-464.

73. J. F. Dashiell, "Experiments in the Sifting of Testimony," *Psychological Bulletin,* 1933, *30,* 720. Dashiell, same citation as note 54, pp. 1135-1140.

74. R. L. Thorndike, "The Effect of Discussion upon the Correctness of Group Decisions, When the Factor of Majority Influence is Allowed For," *Journal of Social Psychology,* 1938, *9,* 343-362.

75. Murphy, Murphy, and Newcomb, same citation as note 19, p. 738.

76. Dashiell, same citation as note 54, p. 1144.

77. Also compare D. Wheeler and H. Jordan, "Change of Individual Opinion to Accord with Group Opinion," *Journal of Abnormal and Social Psychology,* 1929, *24,* 203-206.

78. M. Sherif, "An Experimental Study of Stereotypes," *Journal of Abnormal and Social Psychology,* 1935, *29,* 371-375; M. Saadi and P. R. Farnsworth, "The Degrees of Acceptance of Dogmatic Statements and Preference for Their Supposed Makers," *Journal of Abnormal and Social Psychology,* 1934, *29,* 143-150; M. Sherif, *The Psychology of Social Norms.* New York: Harper & Brothers, 1936.

79. C. H. Marple, "The Comparative Susceptibility of Three Age Levels to the Suggestion of Group versus Expert Opinion," *Journal of Social Psychology,* 1933, *4,* 176-186.

▶ *Chapter Twelve* GROUP BEHAVIOR

(*Pages 279-307*)

1. R. T. LaPiere and P. R. Farnsworth, *Social Psychology.* New York: McGraw-Hill Book Company, Inc., 1936, p. 481, note 5.
2. K. Young, *Social Psychology: An Analysis of Social Behavior.* New York: Appleton-Century-Crofts, Inc., 1930, p. 503.
3. G. Le Bon, *The Crowd: A Study of the Popular Mind.* London: T. Fisher Unwin, 1925.
4. S. Freud, *Group Psychology and the Analysis of the Ego.* (Transl. by J. Strachey.) London: The International Psycho-Analytical Press, 1922, p. 15.
5. W. McDougall, *The Group Mind* (revised edition). New York: G. P. Putnam's Sons, 1928, Chap. 3.
6. F. H. Allport, *Social Psychology.* Boston: Houghton Mifflin Company, 1924, Chap. 1.
7. N. C. Meier, G. H. Mennenga, and H. J. Stoltz, "An Experimental Approach to the Study of Mob Behavior," *The Journal of Abnormal and Social Psychology,* 1941, *36,* 506-524.
8. Courtesy of *Time* magazine, copyright Time, Inc., Oct. 7, 1940, *46,* p. 19.
9. Written by S. Q. Janus.
10. F. L. Schuman, *The Nazi Dictatorship: A Study in Social Pathology and the Politics of Fascism* (second ed. revised). New York: Alfred A. Knopf, Inc., 1936, pp. 91-93, copyright, 1936, Alfred A. Knopf, Inc.
11. C. R. Griffith, "A Comment upon the Psychology of the Audience," *Psychological Monographs,* 1921, *30,* No. 136, 36-47.
12. H. L. Hollingworth, *The Psychology of the Audience.* New York: American Book Company, 1935, Chap. 3.
13. Same citation.
14. L. L. Bernard, *An Introduction to Social Psychology.* New York: Henry Holt and Company, Inc., 1926, pp. 461-462, copyright, 1926, Henry Holt and Company.
15. Compare W. D. Scott, *Psychology and Public Speaking.* New York: Noble and Noble, 1928, pp. 173-184.
16. M. C. Harriman, "Dear Mrs. Post," *The Saturday Evening Post,* May 15, 1937, *209,* 18-19, 52, and 57-58, p. 57.

17. Quoted by permission of Ted Malone and the National Broadcasting Company from broadcast of June 20, 1940.
18. Compare F. Kent, *Political Behavior: The Heretofore Unwritten Laws, Customs, and Principles of Politics as Practiced in the United States.* New York: William Morrow & Co., 1928.
19. R. K. White, "A Quantitative Analysis of Hitler's Speeches," *Psychological Bulletin,* 1942, *39,* 486-487.
20. Mrs. W. A. Becker, *Living for the Ages.* Washington, D. C.: D.A.R., Apr. 19, 1937, pamphlet.
21. Quoted from *The Spoken Word,* Aug. 18, 1936, p. 17, by H. Cantril and M. Sherif, "The Kingdom of Father Divine," *Journal of Abnormal and Social Psychology,* 1938, *33,* 147-167, p. 156.
22. *Life* magazine, Dec. 11, 1939, *7,* 32; photo, courtesy of Wilburn Davis, Fort Worth Press.
23. *Life* magazine, Oct. 20, 1947, *23,* 146; photo by Bob Miller.
24. H. M. Stephens, *A History of the French Revolution* (3 vols.). New York: Charles Scribner's Sons, Inc., 1902, vol. 1, p. 178, copyright, 1902, Charles Scribner's Sons, Inc.
25. Young, same citation as note 2, p. 677.
26. From *Life* magazine, Feb. 26, 1940, *8,* pp. 76 and 77. Photos of "Walkathon" by Fred P. Peele; sit-down strike by William Vandivert; "Big Apple," "hot-foot," and goldfish swallowing by Associated Press; tree-sitting by Keystone View Co.
27. P. Wylie, *Generation of Vipers,* New York: Rinehart & Company, Inc., 1942, pp. 162-163, copyright, 1942, Philip Wylie.
28. D. Katz and R. L. Schanck, *Social Psychology.* New York: John Wiley & Sons, Inc., 1938, p. 285.
29. M. Bracker, "Get Yer Soov-neers!," *The New York Times Magazine,* Oct. 1, 1939, p. 11.
30. Same citation.
31. M. Berger, "Many Delight in Gimcracks," *The New York Times,* Oct. 15, 1939.
32. E. S. Bogardus, *Fundamentals of Social Psychology* (third ed.). New York: Appleton-Century-Crofts, Inc., 1942, pp. 306-309.
33. T. Veblen, *The Theory of the Leisure Class,* New York: Modern Library, Inc., 1934, pp. 131-132.
34. E. B. Hurlock, "Motivation in Fashion," *Archives of Psychology,* 1929, *17,* No. 111, pp. 71.
35. S. H. Britt, unpublished study.
36. E. L. Thorndike, "Science and Values," *Science,* Jan. 3, 1936, *83,* 1-8, p. 5.
37. Veblen, same citation as note 33.
38. *Life* magazine, Feb. 26, 1940, *8,* p. 68. Photos of "windblown" bob

and knitted cardigan suit by Wide World Photos, Inc.; beach pajamas by Acme Photo; evening dress by Keystone View Co.

39. G. W. Allport, *Personality: A Psychological Interpretation.* New York: Henry Holt and Company, Inc., 1937, p. 176.
40. P. H. Nystrom, *Economics of Fashion.* New York: The Ronald Press Company, 1928, p. 36.
41. J. E. Janney, "Fad and Fashion among Undergraduate Women," *The Journal of Abnormal and Social Psychology,* 1941, *36,* 275-278.
42. Compare P. M. Gregory, "Fashion and Monopolistic Competition," *The Journal of Political Economy,* 1948, *56,* 69-75.
43. A. L. Kroeber, "On the Principle of Order in Civilization as Exemplified by Change in Fashion," *American Anthropologist, New Series,* 1919, *21,* 235-263.
44. Pictures reproduced through the courtesy of B. Kuppenheimer & Co., Inc., Chicago, Illinois.
45. Dr. F. L. Thomsen, U. S. Department of Agriculture, as reported in *Washington Post,* December 23, 1939.

▶ *Chapter Thirteen* SEX, DOMINANCE, AND PRESTIGE

(*Pages 308-330*)

1. Aristotle, *History of Animals* (transl. by Taylor), Book 9, Chap. 1, as given by C. C. Miles, "Sex in Social Psychology." In C. A. Murchison (editor), *A Handbook of Social Psychology.* Worcester: Clark University Press, 1935, Chap. 16, copyright, 1935, Clark University.
2. Compare Miles, same citation, p. 748.
3. W. B. Johnson and L. M. Terman, "Some Highlights in the Literature of Psychological Sex Differences Published since 1920," *Journal of Psychology,* 1940, *9,* 327-336, p. 328.
4. M. Mead, *Sex and Temperament.* New York: William Morrow & Company, 1935.
5. K. M. Bowman, "The Challenge of Sex Offenders: Psychiatric Aspects of the Problem," *Mental Hygiene,* 1938, *22,* 10-20, p. 17.
6. L. M. Terman and C. C. Miles, *Sex and Personality.* New York: McGraw-Hill Book Company, Inc., 1936.
7. Ferguson, L. W., "The Cultural Genesis of Masculinity-Femininity," *Psychological Bulletin,* 1941, *38,* 584-585.
8. Bowman, same citation as note 5, p. 15.
9. A. C. Kinsey, W. B. Pomeroy, and C. E. Martin, *Sexual Behavior in the Human Male.* Philadelphia: W. B. Saunders Company, 1948, pp. 21-34.
10. Same citation.

11. Same citation, p. 218.
12. Same citation, p. 335.
13. Same citation, p. 369, copyright, 1948, W. B. Saunders Company.
14. Same citation.
15. Same citation, p. 219.
16. Same citation, Table 136 on p. 550.
17. Same citation, and also p. 347.
18. Same citation, p. 263.
19. Same citation, p. 224.
20. Same citation, p. 392.
21. H. C. Bingham, "Sex Development in Apes," *Comparative Psychology Monographs,* 1928, *5,* No. 1, pp. 165.
22. S. Zuckerman, *The Social Life of Monkeys and Apes.* London: Paul, Trench, Trubner, 1932.
23. A. H. Maslow, "The Rôle of Dominance in the Social and Sexual Behavior of Infra-human Primates: I. Observations at Vilas Park Zoo," *Journal of Genetic Psychology,* 1936, *48,* 261-277, p. 264.
24. T. Schjelderup-Ebbe, "Social Behavior of Birds." In C. Murchison (editor), *A Handbook of Social Psychology.* Worcester: Clark University Press, 1935, Chap. 20.
25. C. Murchison, "The Experimental Measurement of a Social Hierarchy in *Gallus Domesticus:* I. The Direct Identification and Direct Measurement of Social Reflex No. 1 and Social Reflex No. 2," *Journal of General Psychology,* 1935, *12,* 3-39. C. Murchison, "II. The Identification and Inferential Measurement of Social Reflex No. 1 and Social Reflex No. 2 by Means of Social Discrimination," *Journal of Social Psychology,* 1935, *6,* 3-30. C. Murchison, "III. The Direct and Inferential Measurement of Social Reflex No. 3," *Journal of Genetic Psychology,* 1935, *46,* 76-102. C. Murchison, "IV. Loss of Body Weight under Conditions of Mild Starvation as a Function of Social Dominance," *Journal of General Psychology,* 1935, *12,* 296-312. C. Murchison, C. M. Pomerat, and M. X. Zarrow, "V. The Postmortem Measurement of Anatomical Features," *Journal of Social Psychology,* 1935, *6,* 172-181. C. Murchison, "VI. Preliminary Identification of Social Law," *Journal of General Psychology,* 1935, *13,* 227-248. C. Murchison, "The Time Function in the Experimental Formation of Social Hierarchies of Different Sizes in *Gallus Domesticus,*" *Journal of Social Psychology,* 1936, *7,* 3-18.
26. W. C. Allee, "Group Organization Among Vertebrates," *Science,* March 20, 1942, *95,* 289-293.
27. *Time* magazine, Sept. 4, 1939, *34,* p. 31, citing G. K. Noble in *Collecting Net.*
28. R. H. Brown, "Stability of Conditioning and Sexual Dominance in the Rabbit," *Science,* Dec. 3, 1937, *86,* 520.

29. Maslow, same citation as note 23, p. 263.
30. Same citation, p. 269.
31. Same citation, p. 273.
32. A. H. Maslow, "The Rôle of Dominance in the Social and Sexual Behavior of Infra-human Primates: II. An Experimental Determination of the Behavior Syndrome of Dominance," *Journal of Genetic Psychology,* 1936, *48,* 278-309.
33. A. H. Maslow, "The Rôle of Dominance in the Social and Sexual Behavior of Infra-human Primates: IV. The Determination of Hierarchy in Pairs and in a Group," *Journal of Genetic Psychology,* 1936, *49,* 161-198.
34. Same citation, p. 197.
35. R. M. Yerkes, "Social Dominance and Sexual Status in the Chimpanzee," *The Quarterly Review of Biology,* 1939, *14,* 115-136, p. 134.
36. M. P. Crawford, "Dominance and the Behavior of Pairs of Female Chimpanzees When They Meet after Varying Intervals of Separation," *The Journal of Comparative Psychology,* 1942, *33,* 259-265.
37. A. H. Maslow, "The Rôle of Dominance in the Social and Sexual Behavior of Infra-human Primates: III. A Theory of Sexual Behavior of Infra-human Primates," *Journal of Genetic Psychology,* 1936, *48,* 310-338, p. 310.
38. Same citation, p. 323.
39. W. Waller, "The Rating and Dating Complex," *American Sociological Review,* 1937, *2,* 727-734.
40. A. H. Maslow, "Dominance Feeling, Behavior, and Status," *Psychological Review,* 1937, *44,* 404-429.
41. H. H. Anderson, "The Measurement of Domination and Socially Integrative Behavior in Teachers' Contacts with Children," *Child Development,* 1939, *10,* 73-89, p. 89. Also, H. H. Anderson, "An Examination of the Concepts of Domination and Integration in Relation to Dominance and Ascendance," *Psychological Review,* 1940, *47,* 21-37.
42. C. H. Judd, *The Psychology of Social Institutions.* New York: By permission of The Macmillan Company, 1926, p. 61, copyright, 1926, The Macmillan Company.
43. F. L. Goodenough and J. E. Anderson, *Experimental Child Study.* New York: Appleton-Century-Crofts, Inc., 1931, Chap. 29.
44. M. Walker. In W. I. Thomas and D. S. Thomas, *The Child in America.* New York: Alfred A. Knopf, Inc., 1928, pp. 519-520.
45. E. Hanfmann, "Social Structure of a Group of Kindergarten Children," *American Journal of Orthopsychiatry,* 1935, *5,* 407-410.
46. M. Maudry and M. Nekula, "Social Relations between Children of the Same Age during the First Two Years of Life," *Journal of Genetic Psychology,* 1939, *54,* 193-215.

47. P. J. Greenberg, "Competition in Children: An Experimental Study," *American Journal of Psychology,* 1932, *44,* 221-248.
48. M. B. Parten. In Thomas and Thomas, same citation as note 44, p. 521.
49. M. B. Parten, "Leadership among Preschool Children," *Journal of Abnormal and Social Psychology,* 1933, *27,* 430-440, p. 440.
50. W. Moede, *Experimentelle Massenpsychologie.* Leipzig: S. Hirzel, 1920.
51. J. B. Maller, "Cooperation and Competition: An Experimental Study in Motivation," *Teachers College Contributions to Education,* 1929, No. 184, pp. 176.
52. A. H. Maslow, "Dominance, Personality, and Social Behavior in Women," *Journal of Social Psychology,* 1939, *10,* 3-39.
53. A. H. Maslow, "Self-Esteem (Dominance-Feeling) and Sexuality in Women," *The Journal of Social Psychology,* 1942, *16,* 259-294, p. 294.
54. J. Carpenter and P. Eisenberg, "Some Relations between Family Background and Personality," *Journal of Psychology,* 1938, *6,* 115-136.

▶ *Chapter Fourteen* THE PSYCHOLOGY OF LEADERSHIP AND INVENTION

(*Pages 331-369*)

1. G. Murphy, L. B. Murphy, and T. M. Newcomb, *Experimental Social Psychology* (revised edition). New York: By permission of Harper & Brothers, 1937, pp. 757-758.
2. K. Young, *Personality and Problems of Adjustment.* New York: Appleton-Century-Crofts, Inc., 1940, p. 117.
3. A. F. J., "Cooperation and Competition," *Journal of Abnormal and Social Psychology,* 1939, *34,* 415.
4. P. J. W. Pigors, *Leadership or Domination.* Boston: Houghton Mifflin Company, 1935, p. 16.
5. E. B. Gowin, *The Executive and His Control of Men.* New York: The Macmillan Company, 1915, p. 29.
6. E. D. Partridge, "Leadership among Adolescent Boys," *Teachers College Contributions to Education,* 1934, No. 608, pp. 109.
7. L. M. Terman, "A Preliminary Study in the Psychology and Pedagogy of Leadership," *Pedagogical Seminary,* 1904, *11,* 413-451.
8. R. H. Simpson, "A Study of Those Who Influence and of Those Who Are Influenced in Discussion," *Teachers College Contributions to Education,* 1938, No. 748, pp. 89.
9. W. H. Cowley, "The Traits of Face-to-Face Leaders," *Journal of Abnormal and Social Psychology,* 1931, *26,* 304-313.

10. H. B. Carlson and W. Harrell, "An Analysis of *Life's* 'Ablest Congressmen' Poll," *Journal of Social Psychology,* 1942, *15,* 153-158.
11. E. C. Hunter and A. M. Jordan, "An Analysis of Qualities Associated with Leadership among College Students," *Journal of Educational Psychology,* 1939, *30,* 497-509.
12. F. H. Allport, *Social Psychology.* Boston: Houghton Mifflin Company, 1924, pp. 419-424.
13. L. L. Bernard, *Introduction to Social Psychology.* New York: Henry Holt and Company, Inc., 1926, Chap. 34.
14. O. Tead, *The Art of Leadership.* New York: McGraw-Hill Book Company, Inc., 1935, p. 83.
15. T. E. Coffin, "A Three-Component Theory of Leadership," *Journal of Abnormal and Social Psychology,* 1944, *39,* 63-83, pp. 67-68.
16. Same citation, p. 64.
17. R. M. Stogdill, "Personal Factors Associated with Leadership: A Survey of the Literature," *The Journal of Psychology,* 1948, *25,* 35-71.
18. Same citation, pp. 63-64.
19. Compare W. O. Jenkins, "A Review of Leadership Studies with Particular Reference to Military Problems," *Psychological Bulletin,* 1947, *44,* 54-79, p. 75.
20. D. Starch, *How to Develop Your Executive Ability.* New York: Harper & Brothers, 1943.
21. S. B. Williams and H. J. Leavitt, "Group Opinion As A Predictor of Military Leadership," *Journal of Consulting Psychology,* 1947, *11,* 283-291.
22. OSS Assessment Staff, *Assessment of Men: Selection of Personnel for the Office of Strategic Services.* New York: Rinehart & Company, Inc., 1948.
23. B. P. Beckwith, "Philanthropic Gifts and Givers," *Social Forces,* 1938, *16,* 510-522.
24. S. H. Britt, "The Significance of the Last Will and Testament," *Journal of Social Psychology,* 1937, *8,* 347-353. E. C. Lindeman, *Wealth and Culture.* New York: Harcourt, Brace and Company, 1936, Chap. 6.
25. Beckwith, same citation as note 23, p. 512.
26. Same citation, pp. 515-516.
27. Compare D. Sanderson and R. W. Nafe, "Studies in Rural Leadership," *Publications of the American Sociological Society,* 1929, *23,* 163-175.
28. Tead, same citation as note 14, p. 20.
29. Pigors, same citation as note 4, p. 16.
30. Quoted by A. Lipsky, *Man the Puppet.* New York: Frank-Maurice, 1925, p. 52.

31. Hon. C. Blease in *Congressional Record,* 69th Congress, 1st Session, Jan. 27, 1926, vol. 67, Part 3, p. 2819.
32. J. F. Brown, *Psychology and the Social Order: An Introduction to the Dynamic Study of Social Fields.* New York: McGraw-Hill Book Company, Inc., 1936, p. 342.
33. Same citation, p. 344.
34. D. Katz and R. L. Schanck, *Social Psychology.* New York: John Wiley & Sons, Inc., 1938, pp. 173-174, copyright, 1938, Daniel Katz and Richard L. Schanck.
35. Gowin, same citation as note 5, pp. 264-270.
36. H. C. Lehman, "The Age of Eminent Leaders: Then and Now," *American Journal of Sociology,* 1947, *52,* 342-356.
37. H. C. Lehman, "Optimum Ages for Eminent Leadership," *The Scientific Monthly,* 1942, *54,* 162-175.
38. P. A. Sorokin, "Leaders of Labor and Radical Movements in the United States and Foreign Countries," *American Journal of Sociology,* 1927, *33,* 382-411.
39. Same citation, p. 410.
40. F. W. Taussig and C. S. Joslyn, *American Business Leaders.* New York: The Macmillan Company, 1932, p. 241.
41. J. M. Cattell, "Families of American Men of Science," *The Popular Science Monthly,* 1915, *86,* 504-515.
42. E. Klein, "The Relation between One's Attitude to His Father and His Social Attitudes," Master's Thesis, Columbia University, 1925. Cited by Murphy, Murphy, and Newcomb, same citation as note 1, p. 941.
43. H. T. Moore, "Innate Factors in Radicalism and Conservatism," *Journal of Abnormal and Social Psychology,* 1929, *35,* 220-238.
44. T. H. Howells, "A Comparative Study of Those Who Accept as against Those Who Reject Religious Authority," *University of Iowa Studies: Studies in Character,* 1928, *2,* No. 2, pp. 80.
45. Murphy, Murphy, and Newcomb, same citation as note 1, p. 930, copyright, 1931, 1937, Harper & Brothers, citing: P. M. Symonds, "A Social Attitude Questionnaire," *Journal of Educational Psychology,* 1925, *16,* 316-322. H. B. Carlson, "Attitudes of Undergraduate Students," *Journal of Social Psychology,* 1934, *5,* 202-213. R. E. Eckert and H. C. Mills, "International Attitudes and Related Academic and Social Factors," *Journal of Educational Psychology,* 1935, *9,* 142-153. A Kolstad, "A Study of Opinions on Some International Problems," *Teachers College Contributions to Education,* 1933, No. 555, pp. 95.
46. Hunter and Jordan, same citation as note 11.
47. Same citation, p. 509.

48. P. Odegard, *The American Public Mind.* New York: Columbia University Press, 1931, p. 149.
49. G. Moore and K. C. Garrison, "A Comparative Study of Social and Political Attitudes of College Students," *Journal of Abnormal and Social Psychology,* 1932, *27,* 195-208.
50. D. Katz and F. H. Allport, *Students' Attitudes: A Report of the Syracuse University Reaction Study.* Syracuse: Craftsman Press, Inc., 1931.
51. C. R. Pace, "The Relationship between Liberalism and Knowledge of Current Affairs," *Journal of Social Psychology,* 1939, *10,* 247-258.
52. F. H. Allport and D. A. Hartmann, "The Measurement and Motivation of Atypical Opinion in a Certain Group," *American Political Science Review,* 1925, *19,* 735-760.
53. H. Cantril, "The Prediction of Social Events," *Journal of Abnormal and Social Psychology,* 1938, *33,* 364-389.
54. R. S. Lynd and H. M. Lynd, *Middletown: A Study in Contemporary American Culture.* New York: Harcourt, Brace and Company, 1929, p. 498, footnote 1.
55. W. I. Thomas, *Primitive Behavior: An Introduction to the Social Sciences.* New York: McGraw-Hill Book Company, Inc., 1937, pp. 726-727, copyright, 1937, McGraw-Hill Book Company, Inc., quoting C. M. Fassett, *Proceedings of Pacific Northwest Municipalities,* 1912.
56. K. Young, *Social Psychology: An Analysis of Social Behavior.* New York: Appleton-Century-Crofts, Inc., 1930, p. 390.
57. H. Cantril, "A Psychological Reason for the Lag of 'Non-material' Culture Traits," *Social Forces,* 1935, *13,* 376-379.
58. J. K. Folsom, *Social Psychology.* New York: By permission of Harper & Brothers, 1931, p. 593, copyright, 1931, Harper & Brothers.
59. Compare Bernard, same citation as note 13, p. 165.
60. C. Patrick, "Creative Thought in Poets," *Archives of Psychology,* 1935, *26,* No. 178, pp. 74. C. Patrick, "Creative Thought in Artists," *Journal of Psychology,* 1937, *4,* 35-73. C. Patrick, "Scientific Thought," *Journal of Psychology,* 1938, *5,* 55-83. C. Patrick, "Whole and Part Relationship in Creative Thought," *American Journal of Psychology,* 1941, *54,* 128-131.
61. The cartoon by Ned Hilton is from *The New Yorker,* Feb. 10, 1940, *15,* p. 28; the one by O. Soglow is from *The New Yorker,* Nov. 1, 1947, *23,* p. 58; and the one by Lester Colin is from *The Saturday Evening Post,* June 5, 1948, *220,* p. 102.
62. C. Patrick, "Creative Thought in Artists," *Journal of Psychology,* 1937, *4,* 35-73, p. 53.
63. E. D. Hutchinson, "The Technique of Creative Thought," *The American Scholar,* 1932, *1,* 296-306.

64. Hutchinson, same citation, p. 297.
65. A. L. Kroeber, "The Superorganic," *American Anthropologist, New Series,* 1917, *19,* 163-213.
66. W. F. Ogburn, *Social Change with Respect to Culture and Original Nature.* New York: B. W. Huebsch, 1922.
67. The first pair of cartoons are by Edwin Marcus in *The New York Times,* April 13, 1941; and by Gene Elderman in the *Washington Post,* April 13, 1941. The second pair are by Ben Roth in *The Saturday Review of Literature,* Aug. 24, 1946, *29,* p. 18; and by Richard Decker in *The New Yorker,* Aug. 24, 1946, *22,* p. 25.
68. Folsom, same citation as note 58, pp. 577-578.
69. F. S. Chapin, *Cultural Change.* New York: Appleton-Century-Crofts, Inc., 1928, pp. 334-337.
70. H. G. Wells, *The New and Revised Outline of History,* quoting James Harvey Robinson. New York: Garden City Publishing Co., Inc., 1931, p. 1171, copyright, H. G. Wells.
71. *Technological Trends and Public Policy, Including the Social Implications of New Inventions.* Washington, D. C.: Report of Subcommittee on Technology of U. S. National Resources Committee, 1937.
72. *Post* cover by Constantin Alajálov reproduced by special permission of *The Saturday Evening Post* and Constantin Alajálov, copyright 1948 by the Curtis Publishing Company. *Esquire* cover by Barbara Shermund reprinted from August, 1948, *Esquire.*
73. A. Flexner, "The Usefulness of Useless Knowledge," *Harper's Magazine,* 1939, *179,* 544-552, p. 545, copyright, Harper & Brothers.
74. W. F. Ogburn, "The Influence of Inventions on American Social Institutions in the Future," *American Journal of Sociology,* 1937, *43,* 365-376.
75. R. K. White, "Note on the Psychopathology of Genius," *Journal of Social Psychology,* 1930, *1,* 311-315.
76. C. R. Griffith, *An Introduction to Applied Psychology.* New York: The Macmillan Company, 1934, p. 175.
77. I. Langmuir, "Unforeseeable Results of Research," address during the intermission of the New York Philharmonic Symphony United States Rubber Company broadcast of Sunday, Jan. 21, 1945, copyright, United States Rubber Company.
78. H. Hart and others, "Preliminary Conclusions from a Study of Inventors," *Publications of the American Sociological Society,* 1926, *21,* 191-194.
79. H. C. Lehman, "The Creative Years: Oil Paintings, Etchings, and Architectural Works," *Psychological Review,* 1942, *49,* 19-42, p. 19.
80. J. B. Heidler and H. C. Lehman, "Chronological Age and Productivity in Various Types of Literature," *The English Journal,* 1937,

26, 294-304. H. C. Lehman, "The Creative Years in Science and Literature," *The Scientific Monthly,* 1936, *43,* 151-162. H. C. Lehman, "The Creative Years: 'Best Books,'" *The Scientific Monthly,* 1937, *45,* 65-75. H. C. Lehman, "The Most Proficient Years at Sports and Games," *Research Quarterly of the American Association for Health, Physical Education and Recreation,* 1938, *9,* 3-19. H. C. Lehman, "The Chronological Ages of Some Recipients of Large Annual Incomes," *Social Forces,* 1941, *20,* 196-206. H. C. Lehman and W. S. Gamertsfelder, "Man's Creative Years in Philosophy," *Psychological Review,* 1942, *49,* 319-343. H. C. Lehman, "Optimum Ages for Leadership," *The Scientific Monthly,* 1942, *54,* 162-175. H. C. Lehman, "The Creative Years: Oil Paintings, Etchings, and Architectural Works," *Psychological Review,* 1942, *49,* 19-42. H. C. Lehman, "Man's Most Creative Years: Then and Now," *Science,* Nov. 5, 1943, *98,* 393-399. H. C. Lehman, "Man's Most Creative Years: Quality versus Quantity of Output," *The Scientific Monthly,* 1944, *59,* 384-393. H. C. Lehman, "'Intellectual' versus 'Physical' Peak Performance: The Age Factor," *The Scientific Monthly,* 1945, *61,* 127-137. H. C. Lehman, "Age of Starting to Contribute versus Total Creative Output," *Journal of Applied Psychology,* 1946, *30,* 460-480. H. C. Lehman, "The Age of Eminent Leaders: Then and Now," *American Journal of Sociology,* 1947, *52,* 342-356. (Also, note H. C. Lehman, "The Longevity of the Eminent," *Science,* 1943, *98,* 270-273.)

81. J. B. Heidler and H. C. Lehman, "Chronological Age and Productivity in Various Types of Literature," *The English Journal,* 1937, *26,* 294-304, p. 304.
82. H. C. Lehman, "Age of Starting to Contribute versus Total Creative Output," *Journal of Applied Psychology,* 1946, *30,* 460-480, p. 479.
83. H. C. Lehman, "The Creative Years: 'Best Books,'" *The Scientific Monthly,* 1937, *45,* 65-75.
84. E. L. Thorndike, E. O. Bregman, J. W. Tilton, and E. Woodyard, *Adult Learning.* New York: The Macmillan Company, 1928.
85. E. Raskin, "Comparison of Scientific and Literary Ability: A Biographical Study of Eminent Scientists and Men of Letters of the Nineteenth Century," *Journal of Abnormal and Social Psychology,* 1936, *31,* 20-35.
86. Compare H. C. Lehman, "The Most Proficient Years at Sports and Games," *Research Quarterly of the American Association for Health, Physical Education and Recreation,* 1938, *9,* 3-19.
87. H. C. Lehman, "Man's Most Creative Years: Quality versus Quantity of Output," *The Scientific Monthly,* 1944, *59,* 384-393, p. 392.

88. H. C. Lehman, "'Intellectual' versus 'Physical' Peak Performance: The Age Factor," *The Scientific Monthly,* 1945, *61,* 127-137, p. 130.
89. Same citation, p. 135.
90. H. C. Lehman, "The Chronological Ages of Some Recipients of Large Annual Incomes," *Social Forces,* 1941, *20,* 196-206.
91. H. C. Lehman, "Man's Most Creative Years: Then and Now," *Science,* Nov. 5, 1943, *98,* 393-399.

▶ *Chapter Fifteen* GROUPS AND INSTITUTIONS

(*Pages 373-382*)

1. C. H. Cooley, *Social Organization.* New York: Charles Scribner's Sons, 1909, p. 23.
2. K. Young, *Personality and Problems of Adjustment.* New York: Appleton-Century-Crofts, Inc., 1940, p. 129, copyright, 1940, Appleton-Century-Crofts, Inc.
3. J. O. Hertzler, *Social Institutions.* New York: McGraw-Hill Book Company, Inc., 1929.
4. K. Young, *Social Psychology: An Analysis of Social Behavior.* New York: Appleton-Century-Crofts, Inc., 1930, p. 677.
5. D. Katz and R. L. Schanck, *Social Psychology.* New York: John Wiley & Sons, Inc., 1938, pp. 169 *ff.*
6. J. Frank, *Law and the Modern Mind.* New York: Brentano's, 1930.
7. E. D. Starbuck, *Psychology of Religion.* New York: Charles Scribner's Sons, 1907. W. James, *The Varieties of Religious Experience.* New York: Longmans, Green & Co., 1902. E. M. Ligon, *The Psychology of Christian Personality.* New York: The Macmillan Company, 1935. E. M. Ligon, *Their Future Is Now: The Growth and Development of Christian Personality.* New York: The Macmillan Company, 1939.
8. S. A. Rice, *Quantitative Methods in Politics.* New York: Alfred A. Knopf, Inc., 1928.
9. A. Smith, *Wealth of Nations.* New York: E. P. Dutton & Company, Inc., 1933.
10. E. Beaglehole, *Property: A Study in Social Psychology.* London: George Allen and Unwin, Ltd., 1931.
11. Katz and Schanck, same citation as note 5, p. 171.
12. Same citation, pp. 179-186.
13. D. Katz and F. H. Allport, *Students' Attitudes.* Syracuse: Craftsman Press, Inc., 1931.
14. F. H. Allport, "The J-curve Hypothesis of Conforming Behavior," *Journal of Social Psychology,* 1934, *5,* 141-183.

15. F. H. Allport and R. S. Solomon, "Lengths of Conversation: A Conformity Situation, Analyzed by the Telic Continuum and J-curve Hypothesis," *Journal of Abnormal and Social Psychology,* 1939, *34,* 419-464, p. 422.
16. Allport, same citation as note 14.
17. O. L. Harvey, "The Institutionalization of Human Sexual Behavior: A Study of Frequency Distributions," *Journal of Abnormal and Social Psychology,* 1935, *29,* 427-433.
18. S. H. Britt, "Pedestrian Conformity to a Traffic Regulation," *Journal of Abnormal and Social Psychology,* 1940, *35,* 114-119.
19. Same citation, p. 115.
20. Compare N. Frederiksen, G. Frank, and H. Freeman, "A Study of Conformity to a Traffic Regulation," *Journal of Abnormal and Social Psychology,* 1939, *34,* 118-123.
21. G. W. Allport, "The Psychology of Participation," *Psychological Review,* 1945, *53,* 117-132, pp. 121-122.

▶ *Chapter Sixteen* THE FAMILY

(*Pages 383-415*)

1. Unpublished data. Also compare K. Dunlap, *Civilized Life.* Baltimore: The Williams and Wilkins Company, 1935, pp. 207-208. F. L. Wells, "Attitude Measurement and the Dunlap Dilemma," *Science,* March 1, 1935, *81,* p. 227.
2. M. Shirley, *The First Two Years.* Minneapolis: University of Minnesota Press, 1933, Vol. 3.
3. G. W. Allport, *Personality: A Psychological Interpretation.* New York: Henry Holt and Company, Inc., 1937, pp. 122 *ff.*
4. Allport, same citation, p. 124.
5. Same citation, p. 125.
6. Same citation.
7. H. E. Burtt, "An Experimental Study of Early Childhood Memory," *Journal of Genetic Psychology,* 1932, *40,* 287-295. H. E. Burtt, "A Further Study of Early Childhood Memory," *Journal of Genetic Psychology,* 1937, *50,* 187-192.
8. W. H. Burnham, *The Wholesome Personality.* New York: Appleton-Century-Crofts, Inc., 1932, p. 35, copyright, 1932, William H. Burnham.
9. A. T. Jersild, *Child Psychology.* New York: Prentice-Hall, Inc., 1933, p. 426.
10. K. Young, *Social Psychology: An Analysis of Social Behavior.* New York: Appleton-Century-Crofts, Inc., 1930, pp. 246-247, copyright, 1930, Kimball Young.

11. A. T. Jersild, F. V. Markey, and C. L. Jersild, "Children's Fears, Dreams, Wishes, Daydreams, Dislikes, Pleasant and Unpleasant Memories," *Child Development Monographs,* 1933, No. 12, pp. 172, especially p. 153.
12. S. H. Britt, "Technique for Improving Reading Interests," *Psychological Techniques,* 1940, *1,* 4.
13. G. Murphy, L. B. Murphy, and T. M. Newcomb, *Experimental Social Psychology* (revised edition). New York: By permission of Harper & Brothers, 1937, p. 588, copyright, 1931, 1937, Harper & Brothers.
14. E. R. Guthrie, *The Psychology of Learning.* New York: Harper & Brothers, 1935, p. 22.
15. W. James, *Talks to Teachers on Psychology: And to Students on Some of Life's Ideals.* New York: Henry Holt and Company, Inc., 1925, pp. 68-69, copyright, 1899, 1900, William James.
16. E. B. Hurlock, "The Value of Praise and Reproof as Incentives for Children," *Archives of Psychology,* 1924, *11,* No. 71, pp. 78.
17. G. S. Gates and L. Q. Rissland, "The Effect of Encouragement and of Discouragement upon Performance," *Journal of Educational Psychology,* 1923, *14,* 21-26. R. R. Sears, "An Experimental Test of One Phase of the Hypothecated Repression Sequence," *Psychological Bulletin,* 1936, *33,* 744.
18. G. Forlano and H. C. Axelrod, "The Effect of Repeated Praise or Blame on the Performance of Introverts and Extroverts," *Journal of Educational Psychology,* 1937, *28,* 92-100.
19. E. S. Conklin, "The Foster-Child Fantasy," *American Journal of Psychology,* 1920, *31,* 59-76.
20. M. Svendsen, "Children's Imaginary Companions," *Archives of Neurology and Psychiatry,* 1934, *32,* 985-999.
21. L. B. Ames and J. Learned, "Imaginary Companions and Related Phenomena," *The Journal of Genetic Psychology,* 1946, *69,* 147-167, p. 166.
22. E. R. Groves, *The Drifting Home.* Boston: Houghton Mifflin Company, 1926, pp. 161 and 165, copyright, 1926, Houghton Mifflin Company.
23. K. Young, "Parent-Child Relationship: Projection of Ambition," *The Family,* 1927, *8,* 67-73, p. 70.
24. L. M. Gilbreth, *Living with Our Children.* New York: W. W. Norton & Company, 1928, p. 66.
25. S. H. Britt, "Let Your Child Grow Up," *Think,* 1940, *6,* 11 and 30.
26. Compare D. M. Levy, "Maternal Overprotection," *Psychiatry,* 1938, *1,* 561-591; 1939, *2,* 99-128; 1939, *2,* 563-597; 1941, *4,* 393-431; 1941, *4,* 567-626.
27. D. M. Levy, *Maternal Overprotection.* New York: Columbia University Press, 1943.

28. G. S. Hall, "The Early Sense of Self," *American Journal of Psychology,* 1898, *9,* 351-395.
29. B. Russell, *Conquest of Happiness.* New York: Liveright Publishing Corporation, 1930, p. 203.
30. A. Adler, *Problems in Neurosis.* New York: Cosmopolitan Book Corporation, 1930.
31. Compare Murphy, Murphy, and Newcomb, same citation as note 13, pp. 348-363.
32. J. W. Macfarlane, "Family Influences on Children's Personality Development," *Childhood Education,* 1938, *15,* 55-59, p. 56.
33. Same citation, p. 57.
34. Compare K. Young, *Personality and Problems of Adjustment.* New York: Appleton-Century-Crofts, Inc., 1940, pp. 410-411.
35. R. S. Lynd and H. M. Lynd, *Middletown: A Study in Contemporary American Culture.* New York: Harcourt, Brace and Company, 1929, p. 522.
36. J. K. Folsom, *Social Psychology.* New York: By permission of Harper & Brothers, 1931, p. 631, copyright, 1931, J. K. Folsom.
37. K. Davis, "Adolescence and the Social Structure," *The Annals of the American Academy of Political and Social Science,* 1944, *236,* 8-16, p. 12.
38. H. V. Gaskill, *Personality.* New York: Prentice-Hall, Inc., 1936, pp. 1-2.
39. E. L. Kelly, "Psychological Factors in Assortative Mating," *Psychological Bulletin,* 1940, *37,* 473.
40. M. R. Davie and R. J. Reeves, "Propinquity of Residence before Marriage," *American Journal of Sociology,* 1939, *44,* 510-517. Compare J. H. S. Bossard, "Ecological Areas and Marriage Rates," *American Journal of Sociology,* 1938, *44,* 70-96.
41. R. H. Abrams, "Residential Propinquity as a Factor in Marriage Selection," *American Sociological Review,* 1943, *8,* 288-294.
42. K. Young, same citation as note 34, pp. 507 and 513, copyright, 1940, Appleton-Century-Crofts, Inc.
43. Lynd and Lynd, same citation as note 35, p. 117.
44. Same citation, p. 118.
45. E. Westermarck, *The Future of Marriage in Western Civilisation.* New York: The Macmillan Company, 1936.
46. Lynd and Lynd, same citation as note 35, p. 112.
47. J. T. Landis, "Length of Time Required to Achieve Adjustment in Marriage," *American Sociological Review,* 1946, *11,* 666-677.
48. E. W. Burgess and L. S. Cottrell, Jr., *Predicting Success or Failure in Marriage.* New York: Prentice-Hall, Inc., 1939.
49. Same citation, pp. 229-230, copyright, 1939, Prentice-Hall, Inc.
50. Compare *Problems of a Changing Population.* Washington, D. C.:

U. S. Government Printing Office, National Resources Committee, 1938.

51. *Fifteenth Census of the United States.* Washington, D. C., 1933, Vol. 2, p. 566.

52. K. B. Davis, *Factors in the Sex Life of Twenty-two Hundred Women.* New York: Harper & Brothers, 1929.

53. S. A. Rice, "Undergraduate Attitudes Toward Marriage and Children," *Mental Hygiene,* 1929, *13,* 788-793.

54. G. Gallup, survey by American Institute of Public Opinion, as reported in *Washington Post,* April 5, 1941, p. 9.

55. R. Reed, "Changing Conceptions of the Maternal Instinct," *Journal of Abnormal and Social Psychology,* 1923, *18,* 78-87.

56. D. E. Hall and G. J. Mohr, "Prenatal Attitudes of Primiparae. A Contribution to the Mental Hygiene of Pregnancy," *Mental Hygiene,* 1933, *17,* 226-234.

57. E. R. Mowrer, "The Family in the Machine Age," *Living,* 1939, *1,* 67-68 and 86, p. 67.

58. Same citation.

59. P. Popenoe and R. H. Johnson, *Applied Eugenics.* New York: By permission of The Macmillan Company, 1933, pp. 182-183, copyright, 1933, The Macmillan Company.

60. C. Kirkpatrick, "A Methodological Analysis of Feminism in Relation to Marital Maladjustment," *American Sociological Review,* 1939, *4,* 325-334.

61. C. Kirkpatrick, "The Measurement of Ethical Inconsistency in Marriage," *The International Journal of Ethics,* 1936, *46,* 444-460.

62. L. M. Terman and P. Buttenwieser, "Personality Factors in Marital Compatibility," *Journal of Social Psychology,* 1935, *6,* 143-171 and 267-289.

63. Burgess and Cottrell, same citation as note 48.

64. E. W. Burgess, "National Organization Plans," *Proceedings of the First Southern Regional Conference and Louisiana State Conference on Family Relations,* Feb. 24-25, 1939, edited by H. S. Daggett, Louisiana State University, 1939. Also compare E. W. Burgess, "Predictive Factors in the Success or Failure of Marriage," *Living,* 1939, *1,* 1-3.

65. L. M. Terman, P. Buttenwieser, L. W. Ferguson, W. B. Johnson, and D. P. Wilson, *Psychological Factors in Marital Happiness.* New York: McGraw-Hill Book Company, Inc., 1938.

66. Burgess and Cottrell, same citation as note 48, p. 344, copyright, 1939, Prentice-Hall, Inc.

67. A. C. Kinsey, W. B. Pomeroy, and C. E. Martin, *Sexual Behavior in the Human Male.* Philadelphia: W. B. Saunders Co., 1948, p. 544.

68. H. J. Locke, "Predicting Marital Adjustment by Comparing a Di-

vorced and a Happily Married Group," *American Sociological Review*, 1947, *12*, 187-191.
69. Same citation, p. 190.
70. B. B. Lindsey, *The Companionate Marriage*. New York: Boni and Liveright, 1927.
71. M. M. Knight, "The Companionate and the Family," *Journal of Social Hygiene*, 1924, *10*, 257-267.
72. J. C. Flanagan, "A Study of Psychological Factors Related to Fertility," *Proceedings of the American Philosophical Society*, 1939, *4*, 513-523.
73. E. R. Mowrer, *Family Disorganization*. Chicago: University of Chicago Press, 1927, p. 156.

▶ *Chapter Seventeen* EDUCATION—THE SCHOOL

(*Pages 416-443*)

1. "Is An Eighth-Grade Education Enough?" *The Journal of The National Education Association*, 1942, *31*, 206.
2. W. S. Deffenbaugh and T. Covert, *School Administrative Units*. Washington, D. C.: U. S. Government Printing Office, 1933, Office of Education Pamphlet No. 34. *Educational Directory, 1939*. Washington, D. C.: U. S. Government Printing Office, 1938, Office of Education Bulletin, 1939, No. 1.
3. R. S. Lynd and H. M. Lynd, *Middletown in Transition: A Study in Cultural Conflicts*. New York: Harcourt, Brace and Company, 1937, p. 411, copyright, 1937, Harcourt, Brace and Company.
4. R. S. Lynd and H. M. Lynd, *Middletown: A Study in Contemporary American Culture*. New York: Harcourt, Brace and Company, 1929, p. 186.
5. Compare E. D. Martin, *The Meaning of a Liberal Education*. New York: W. W. Norton & Company, 1926, pp. vii-viii.
6. J. R. Tunis, "New Leaven on the Campus," *Survey Graphic*, 1939, *28*, 595-597 and 655, p. 597.
7. Compare M. McConn, *College or Kindergarten?* New York: The New Republic, 1928, Chap. 2.
8. J. R. Tunis, *Was College Worth While?* New York: Harcourt, Brace and Company, 1936, p. 16.
9. Same citation, p. 68.
10. W. S. Learned and B. D. Wood, *The Student and His Knowledge, A Report to the Carnegie Foundation on the Results of the High School and College Examinations of 1928, 1930, and 1932*. New

York: Carnegie Foundation for the Advancement of Teaching, 1938.

11. R. M. Hutchins, "We Are Getting No Brighter," *The Saturday Evening Post,* Dec. 11, 1937, *210,* 5-7 and 98, p. 6.
12. E. Horn, *Methods of Instruction in the Social Studies.* Report of the Commission on the Social Studies, American Historical Association, Part XV. New York: Charles Scribner's Sons, 1937, pp. 142-143, copyright, 1937, Charles Scribner's Sons, citing H. K. Newburn, "The Relative Effect of Two Methods of Vocabulary Drill on Achievement in American History," *University of Iowa Studies in Education,* 1934, *9,* No. 3, p. 25; and F. Scott and G. C. Myers, "Children's Empty and Erroneous Concepts of the Commonplace," *Journal of Educational Research,* 1923, *8,* 327-334, p. 327.
13. Olsen, E. G., Chap. XXVII, "School Affairs," in Robinson, T. H., and others, *A Survey in the Social Sciences: Men, Groups, and the Community.* New York: Harper & Brothers, 1940, p. 732, copyright, 1940, Harper & Brothers.
14. Horn, same citation as note 12, pp. 96-97.
15. E. E. Bayles, "An Unemphasized Factor in Current Theories regarding the Transfer of Training," *Journal of Educational Psychology,* 1936, *27,* 425-430, p. 429.
16. W. James, *Talks to Teachers on Psychology: And to Students on Some of Life's Ideals.* New York: Henry Holt and Company, Inc., 1925, p. 150, copyright, 1899, 1900, William James.
17. E. Freeman, *Social Psychology.* New York: Henry Holt and Company, Inc., 1936, pp. 263-265.
18. Courtesy of *Time,* copyright Time, Inc., Feb. 5, 1945, *45,* 87.
19. *The New Republic,* Apr. 26, 1939, *98,* p. 337.
20. Hutchins, same citation as note 11.
21. Survey by *The New York Times,* reported by Benjamin Fine, Apr. 4, 1943, pp. 1 and 32-33.
22. H. H. Anderson, J. E. Brewer, and M. F. Reed, "Studies of Teachers' Classroom Personalities: III. Follow-Up Studies of the Effects of Dominative and Integrative Contacts on Children's Behavior," *Applied Psychology Monographs,* 1946, No. 11, pp. 156.
23. G. G. Thompson, "The Social and Emotional Development of Pre-School Children under Two Types of Educational Program," *Psychological Monographs,* 1944, *56,* pp. 29.
24. *Knighthood of Youth Club Guide.* Lincoln, Nebraska: State Department of Public Instruction, 1933, pp. 36-37.
25. H. Hartshorne, M. A. May, J. B. Maller, and F. K. Shuttleworth, *Studies in the Nature of Character.* (3 vols.) New York: The Macmillan Company, 1928-1930.
26. Same citation as note 24, p. 49.

27. F. Astor, "Application of Mental Hygiene Principles to the Classroom," *Twenty-five Years of Progress in Education,* Proceedings of the Fifth Conference on Education and the Exceptional Child, The Woods Schools, Langhorne, Pa., 1939, 16-24, p. 22.
28. G. W. Allport, *Personality: A Psychological Interpretation.* New York: Henry Holt and Company, Inc., 1937, pp. 250-252.
29. Same citation, pp. 251-252.
30. G. B. Watson, "Next Steps in Personality Measurement," *Character and Personality,* 1933, *2,* 66-73, p. 69.
31. W. G. Campbell, *An Objective Study of Student Honesty.* Austin: University of Texas, 1928, unpublished thesis. Reported in V. Jones, *Character and Citizenship Training in the Public School.* Chicago: University of Chicago Press, 1936, pp. 16-17.
32. Jones, same citation.
33. W. Richmond, *An Introduction to Sex Education.* New York: Rinehart & Company, Inc., 1934, p. 79.
34. C. R. Griffith, *Psychology Applied to Teaching and Learning.* New York: Rinehart & Company, Inc., 1939, pp. 592-593.
35. J. H. Conn, "Sex Attitudes and Sex Awareness in Young Children," *Child Study,* 1939, *16,* 86-87 and 106-107, p. 86; quoted with the permission of the Child Study Association of America.
36. A. C. Kinsey, W. B. Pomeroy, and C. E. Martin, *Sexual Behavior in the Human Male.* Philadelphia: W. B. Saunders Co., 1948, p. 223.
37. "The State and Sectarian Education," *National Education Association Research Bulletin,* 1946, *24,* 1-44.
38. A. W. Johnson, "Bible Reading in the Public Schools," *Education,* 1939, *59,* 274-280, p. 277.
39. *The New York Times,* March 9, 1948, p. 1.
40. E. K. Wickman, *Children's Behavior and Teacher's Attitudes.* New York: Commonwealth Fund, 1928.
41. N. M. Campbell, "The Elementary School Teacher's Treatment of Classroom Behavior Problems," *Columbia University, Teachers College Contributions to Education,* 1935, No. 668, pp. 71.
42. Wickman, same citation as note 40.
43. Lynd and Lynd, same citation as note 4, p. 209, copyright, 1929, Harcourt, Brace and Company.
44. Data on pay of teachers are taken from: "Education—An Investment in People," published by the Committee on Education 1944-45 of the U. S. Chamber of Commerce, and summarized in *The Journal of the National Education Association,* 1945, *34,* 77-80; also, "Federal Aid for Education: A Review of Pertinent Facts," *National Education Association Research Bulletin,* 1942, *20,* 119-147, especially p. 126.
45. "Federal Aid for Education: A Review of Pertinent Facts," same citation as note 44, p. 129.

46. Compare *The New York Times,* Feb. 14, 1947, pp. 23-24.
47. Lynd and Lynd, same citation as note 4, p. 221, copyright, 1929, Harcourt, Brace and Company.
48. *Administrative Practices Affecting Classroom Teachers, Part I: The Selection and Appointment of Teachers.* Washington, D. C.: National Education Association, Research Bulletin, Jan., 1932, *10,* pp. 55, p. 19.
49. G. Counts, *Social Composition of Boards of Education.* Chicago: University of Chicago Press, 1927.
50. D. DuShane, Chairman of Committee on Tenure, *Teachers' Contracts: With Special Reference to Adverse Conditions of Employment.* Washington, D. C.: National Education Association, 1936, p. 22.
51. E. O. Melby, "Rules, Regulations, and Written Instructions as Administrative Controls," *American School Board Journal,* May, 1927, *74,* 43-45, p. 45.
52. DuShane, same citation as note 50, p. 24.
53. Anonymous, in *Bulletin of the American Association of University Professors,* 1938, *24,* 380-382, p. 381.
54. L. A. Cook, R. B. Almack, and F. Greenhoe, "Teacher and Community Relations," *American Sociological Review,* 1938, *3,* 167-174, p. 171.
55. Cook, Almack, and Greenhoe, same citation. Also compare L. A. Cook and F. Greenhoe, "Community Contacts of 9,122 Teachers," *Social Forces,* 1940, *19,* 63-72.

▶ *Chapter Eighteen* RELIGION—THE CHURCH

(*Pages 444-461*)

1. H. Höffding, *The Philosophy of Religion.* London: By permission of Macmillan and Co., Ltd., copyright, 1914, p. 90.
2. H. C. Link, *The Return to Religion.* New York: The Macmillan Company, 1936.
3. *Washington Post,* Sept. 11, 1940.
4. L. du Noüy, *Human Destiny.* New York: Longmans, Green and Co., 1947.
5. E. A. Ross, *Social Psychology: An Outline and Source Book.* New York: By permission of The Macmillan Company, 1908, p. 313.
6. E. T. Bell, *Man and His Lifebelts.* New York: Reynal & Hitchcock, Inc., 1938, pp. 34-35, copyright, 1938, The Williams & Wilkins Company.

7. "The Circulation of the Bible," *Information Service of Federal Council of the Churches of Christ in America,* Oct. 4, 1941, *20,* No. 31.
8. J. L. Liebman, *Peace of Mind.* New York: Simon & Schuster, 1946.
9. P. Popenoe and R. H. Johnson, *Applied Eugenics.* New York: The Macmillan Company, 1933, pp. 213-214.
10. F. H. Hankins, *An Introduction to the Study of Society.* New York: The Macmillan Company, 1935, p. 480.
11. Bell, same citation as note 6, p. 31.
12. R. S. Lynd and H. M. Lynd, *Middletown: A Study in Contemporary American Culture.* New York: Harcourt, Brace and Company, 1929, p. 355.
13. E. S. Conklin, *The Psychology of Religious Adjustment.* New York: The Macmillan Company, 1929.
14. D. Starch, H. M. Stanton, and W. Koerth, *Controlling Human Behavior.* New York: The Macmillan Company, 1936, p. 57.
15. D. Katz and F. H. Allport, *Students' Attitudes.* Syracuse: Craftsman Press, Inc., 1931.
16. Compare T. D. Eliot, "A Psychoanalytic Interpretation of Group Formation and Behavior," *American Journal of Sociology,* 1920, *26,* 333-352.
17. S. H. Britt, unpublished material.
18. K. Young, "The Psychology of Hymns," *Journal of Abnormal and Social Psychology,* 1926, *20,* 391-406.
19. E. L. Thorndike, *Your City.* New York: Harcourt, Brace and Company, 1939, p. 99.
20. Bell, same citation as note 6, p. 58.
21. R. L. Schanck, "A Study of a Community and Its Groups and Institutions Conceived of as Behaviors of Individuals," *Psychological Monographs,* 1932, *43,* No. 195, pp. 133.
22. Compare C. R. Griffith, *An Introduction to Applied Psychology.* New York: The Macmillan Company, 1934.
23. H. Gurnee, *Elements of Social Psychology.* New York: Rinehart & Company, Inc., 1936, pp. 449-454.
24. Same citation, p. 452, copyright, 1936, Herbert Gurnee.
25. F. M. Ligon, *The Psychology of Christian Personality.* New York: The Macmillan Company, 1935.
26. Gurnee, same citation as note 23, p. 454, copyright, 1936, Herbert Gurnee.
27. L. L. Thurstone and E. J. Chave, *The Measurement of Attitude: A Psychophysical Method and Some Experiments with a Scale for Measuring Attitude toward the Church.* Chicago: University of Chicago Press, 1929.
28. G. J. Dudycha, "The Religious Beliefs of College Students," *Journal of Applied Psychology,* 1933, *17,* 585-603.

29. E. Nelson, "Student Attitudes toward Religion," *Genetic Psychology Monographs,* 1940, *22,* 323-423.
30. G. W. Allport, J. M. Gillespie, and J. Young, "The Religion of the Post-War College Student," *The Journal of Psychology,* 1948, *25,* 3-33, p. 30.
31. H. C. Lehman and P. A. Witty, "Scientific Eminence and Church Membership," *Scientific Monthly,* 1931, *33,* 544-549.
32. J. S. Leuba, "Religious Beliefs of American Scientists," *Harper's Magazine,* 1934, *169,* 291-300.
33. Lynd and Lynd, same citation as note 12, p. 315.
34. Same citation, pp. 316-323.
35. R. S. Lynd and H. M. Lynd, *Middletown in Transition: A Study in Cultural Conflict.* New York: Harcourt, Brace and Company, 1937, pp. 416-417, copyright, 1937, Harcourt, Brace and Company.
36. J. Davis, *Capitalism and Its Culture.* New York: Rinehart & Company, Inc., 1935, pp. 373-374.
37. Same citation, p. 516.
38. F. Paulsen, *A System of Ethics* (transl. by F. Thilly). New York: copyright, Charles Scribner's Sons, 1899, pp. 94-95.
39. Davis, same citation as note 36, pp. 395-400.
40. E. A. Ross, *Principles of Sociology.* New York: Century Company, 1920, p. 541, footnote 17.
41. R. H. Abrams, *Preachers Present Arms.* New York: Round Table Press, Inc., 1933.
42. *Time* magazine, May 27, 1940, *35,* pp. 69-71.
43. "Religious Propaganda against the War," *Bulletin of Institute for Propaganda Analysis, Inc.,* Jan. 25, 1941, *4,* pp. 12.
44. R. H. Abrams, "The Churches and the Clergy in World War II," *The Annals of the American Academy of Political and Social Science,* 1948, *256,* 110-119, p. 111.
45. Same citation, p. 114.
46. Same citation, pp. 116-118.
47. Paulsen, same citation as note 38, p. 95.
48. W. A. Brown, M. A. May, and F. K. Shuttleworth, *The Education of American Ministers.* New York: Institute of Social and Religious Research, 1934.
49. K. Sward, "The Johnstown Strike of 1937: A Case Study of Large-Scale Conflict." In G. W. Hartmann and T. Newcomb (editors), *Industrial Conflict: A Psychological Interpretation.* New York: The Cordon Company, 1939, Chap. 4.
50. Davis, same citation as note 36, p. 396, copyright, 1935, Jerome Davis.

Chapter Nineteen FRATERNITIES AND POLITICAL PARTIES

(*Pages 462-480*)

1. *Ritual—Second Temple, Fraternity Sons of Osiris.* Quakertown, Pennsylvania: Fraternity of Osiris, Rosicrucian Foundation, 1909, pp. 4 and 69-70.
2. W. R. Baird, *Baird's Manual, American College Fraternities* (13th edition), (edited by F. W. Shepardson). Menasha, Wisconsin: George Banta, 1935.
3. *Life* magazine, May 20, 1940, *8,* p. 109; photo by Paul Dorsey.
4. Same citation, p. 113; photo by Paul Dorsey.
5. N. P. Gist, "Structure and Process in Secret Societies," *Social Forces,* 1938, *16,* 349-357, p. 350.
6. Same citation, p. 351.
7. C. W. Ferguson, *Fifty Million Brothers: A Panorama of American Lodges and Clubs.* New York: Rinehart & Company, Inc., 1937.
8. C. Merz, *The Great American Band-Wagon.* New York: The John Day Company, 1928, p. 24, copyright, 1928, Charles Merz, copyright, 1925, 1926, 1927, 1928, Harper & Brothers.
9. Same citation, pp. 25-26.
10. L. Montross and L. Montross, *Fraternity Row.* New York: George H. Doran Company, 1926, p. vii.
11. D. Katz and R. L. Schanck, *Social Psychology.* New York: John Wiley & Sons, Inc., 1938, pp. 179-186.
12. D. Katz and F. H. Allport, *Students' Attitudes.* Syracuse: Craftsman Press, Inc., 1931.
13. N. P. Gist, "Dogma and Doctrine in Secret Societies," *Sociology and Social Research,* 1939, *23,* 121-130.
14. V. Sheean, *Personal History.* New York: Modern Library, Inc., 1934, Chap. 1.
15. Gist, same citation as note 13, p. 128.
16. Ferguson, same citation as note 7, p. 104.
17. R. S. Lynd and H. M. Lynd, *Middletown: A Study in Contemporary American Culture.* New York: Harcourt, Brace and Company, 1929, p. 289.
18. Merz, same citation as note 8, pp. 32-33.
19. K. Young, *Social Psychology: An Analysis of Social Behavior.* New York: Appleton-Century-Crofts, Inc., 1930, p. 309, copyright, 1930, Kimball Young.
20. S. H. Britt, "Newspaper Circulation and National Elections," *Social Science,* 1941, *16,* 254-257.

21. L. D. White, *The Prestige Value of Public Employment in Chicago.* Chicago: University of Chicago Press, 1929.
22. "The Fortune Survey: XXVII. The People of the U.S.A.—A Self-Portrait," *Fortune,* 1940, *21,* 14, 20, 28, 133-134, 136, p. 133.
23. F. Kent, "The Psychology of Voting," *Forum,* 1924, *72,* 804-810, p. 805.
24. W. F. Vaughan, "An Experimental Study in Political Prejudice," *Journal of Abnormal and Social Psychology,* 1930, *25,* 268-274.
25. R. H. Gundlach, "Confusion among Undergraduates in Political and Economic Ideas," *Journal of Abnormal and Social Psychology,* 1937, *32,* 357-367.
26. N. C. Meier, "Motives in Voting: A Study in Political Opinion," *American Journal of Sociology,* 1925, *31,* 199-212.
27. G. W. Hartmann, "A Field Experiment on Comparative Effectiveness of 'Emotional' and 'Rational' Political Leaflets in Determining Election Results," *Journal of Abnormal and Social Psychology,* 1936, *31,* 99-114.
28. S. C. Menefee and A. G. Granneberg, "Propaganda and Opinions on Foreign Policies," *Journal of Social Psychology,* 1940, *11,* 393-404.
29. P. F. Lazarsfeld, B. Berelson, and H. Gaudet, *The People's Choice: How the Voter Makes Up His Mind in a Presidential Campaign.* New York: Duell, Sloan and Pearce, 1944, copyright, 1944, Duell, Sloan and Pearce.
30. Same citation, p. 73.
31. Same citation, p. 87.
32. Same citation, p. 95.
33. G. W. Allport, "The Composition of Political Attitudes," *American Journal of Sociology,* 1929, *35,* 220-238.
34. W. F. Ogburn and A. J. Jaffe, "Independent Voting in Presidential Elections," *American Journal of Sociology,* 1936, *42,* 186-201.
35. W. A. Kerr, "A Quantitative Study of Political Behavior," *The Journal of Social Psychology,* 1944, *19,* 273-281.
36. H. G. Gosnell and N. N. Gill, "Analysis of 1932 Vote in Chicago," *American Political Science Review,* 1935, *29,* 967-984.
37. Ogburn and Jaffe, same citation as note 34.
38. C. Tibbits, "Majority Votes and the Business Cycle," *American Journal of Sociology,* 1931, *36,* 596-606.
39. S. P. Hayes, Jr., "The Inter-relations of Political Attitudes: IV. Political Attitudes and Party Regularity," *Journal of Social Psychology,* 1939, *10,* 503-552.
40. S. A. Rice, *Quantitative Methods in Politics.* New York: Alfred A. Knopf, Inc., 1928, p. 278.
41. Allport, same citation as note 33.
42. G. W. Hartmann, "The Contradiction between the Feeling-tone of

Political Party Names and Public Response to Their Platforms," *Journal of Social Psychology,* 1936, *7,* 336-355.

43. R. Stagner, "Fascist Attitudes: An Exploratory Study," *Journal of Social Psychology,* 1936, *7,* 309-319. R. Stagner, "Fascist Attitudes: Their Determining Conditions," *Journal of Social Psychology,* 1936, *7,* 438-454.
44. S. C. Menefee, "The Effect of Stereotyped Words on Political Judgments," *American Sociological Review,* 1936, *1,* 614-621.
45. E. Raskin and S. W. Cook, "A Further Investigation of the Measurement of an Attitude toward Fascism," *Journal of Social Psychology,* 1936, *9,* 201-206.
46. S. P. Hayes, Jr., "The Inter-relations of Political Attitudes: II. Consistency in Voters' Attitudes," *Journal of Social Psychology,* 1939, *10,* 359-378.
47. S. P. Hayes, Jr., "The Inter-relations of Political Attitudes: III. General Factors in Political Attitudes," *Journal of Social Psychology,* 1939, *10,* 379-398.
48. Lynd and Lynd, same citation as note 17, Chap. 24.

▶ *Chapter Twenty* OCCUPATIONAL GROUPS

(*Pages 481-495*)

1. I. Lippincott, *Economic Development of the United States.* New York: Appleton-Century-Crofts, Inc., 1925, p. 20.
2. W. James, *Principles of Psychology* (2 vols.) . New York: Henry Holt and Company, Inc., 1890, Vol. 1, p. 121, copyright, 1890, Henry Holt and Company.
3. A. E. Briggs, "Social Distance Between Lawyers and Doctors," *Sociology and Social Research,* 1928, *13,* 156-163, p. 160.
4. E. S. Robinson, *Law and the Lawyers.* New York: The Macmillan Company, 1935, pp. 3-7.
5. Compare S. H. Britt, "The Lawyer and the Psychologist," *Illinois Law Review,* 1942, *36,* 621-627.
6. S. H. Britt, "Blood-grouping Tests and the Law: The Problem of 'Cultural Lag,'" *Minnesota Law Review,* 1937, *21,* 671-702, pp. 700-701.
7. J. B. Schwabb, "Occupational Attitudes of Lawyers," *Sociology and Social Research,* 1939, *24,* 53-62.
8. From *The Law and Mr. Smith,* by Max Radin, copyright, 1938, p. 305; used by special permission of the Publishers, The Bobbs-Merrill Company, Indianapolis.
9. A. W. Kornhauser, "Analysis of 'Class' Structure of Contemporary

American Society—Psychological Bases of Class Divisions." In G. W. Hartmann and T. Newcomb (editors), *Industrial Conflict: A Psychological Interpretation*. New York: The Cordon Company, 1939, Chap. 11, pp. 199-200.

10. W. Lippmann, *Public Opinion*. New York: By permission of The Macmillan Company, 1934, p. 51, copyright, 1922, Walter Lippmann.
11. W. Williams, *Mainsprings of Men*. New York: Charles Scribner's Sons, 1925, p. 67.
12. W. M. Proctor, *Educational and Vocational Guidance*. Boston: Houghton Mifflin Company, 1925, pp. 4-5.
13. Compare J. W. Gardner, "The Use of the Term 'Level of Aspiration,'" *Psychological Review*, 1940, *47*, 59-68.
14. D. Katz and R. L. Schanck, *Social Psychology*. New York: John Wiley & Sons, Inc., 1938, p. 498.
15. J. Davis, "Testing the Social Attitudes of Children in the Government Schools in Russia," *American Journal of Sociology*, 1927, *32*, 947-952.
16. F. Wilkinson, "Social Distance between Occupations," *Sociology and Social Research*, 1929, *13*, 234-244.
17. R. S. Lynd and H. M. Lynd, *Middletown: A Study in Contemporary American Culture*. New York: Harcourt, Brace and Company, 1929, p. 22, footnote 2.
18. Same citation, pp. 23-24, copyright, 1929, Harcourt, Brace and Company.
19. "The Fortune Survey: XXVII. The People of the U.S.A.—A Self-Portrait," *Fortune*, 1940, *21*, 14, 20, 28, 133-134, 136, p. 28.
20. H. Cantril, "Identification with Social and Economic Class," *The Journal of Abnormal and Social Psychology*, 1943, *38*, 74-80.
21. Lynd and Lynd, same citation as note 17, p. 49.
22. A. Thomsen, "Expectation in Relation to Achievement and Happiness," *The Journal of Abnormal and Social Psychology*, 1943, *38*, 58-73.
23. Compare H. M. Bell, *Matching Youth and Jobs*. Washington, D. C.: American Youth Commission, 1940.
24. A. W. Jones, *Life, Liberty, and Property*. Philadelphia: J. B. Lippincott Company, 1941.
25. Lynd and Lynd, same citation as note 17, pp. 53-54, copyright, 1929, Harcourt, Brace and Company.
26. S. A. Raube, *Factors Affecting Employee Morale*, Studies in Personnel Policy No. 85. New York: National Industrial Conference Board, Inc., 1947.
27. F. J. Roethlisberger and W. J. Dickson, *Management and the Worker*. Cambridge: Harvard University Press, 1939.

28. C. M. Arensberg and D. McGregor, "Determination of Morale in an Industrial Company," *Applied Anthropology,* 1942, *1,* 12-34.
29. Lippincott, same citation as note 1, pp. 491-492.
30. *Violations of Free Speech and Rights of Labor.* Preliminary Report of the Committee on Education and Labor, pursuant to Senate Resolution 266, 74th Congress. Report No. 46, 75th Congress, 1st Session, Feb. 8, 1937, p. 8.
31. *Violations of Free Speech and Rights of Labor.* Report of the Committee on Education and Labor, pursuant to Senate Resolution 266, 74th Congress. Report No. 46, Part 3, 75th Congress, 2nd Session, pp. 80-121.
32. Same citation as note 30, p. 6.
33. B. Minton and J. Stuart, *Men Who Lead Labor.* New York: Modern Age Books, Inc., 1937.
34. S. H. Britt and R. L. Lowry, "Conformity Behavior of Labor Newspapers with Respect to the A.F.L.-C.I.O. Conflict," *The Journal of Social Psychology,* 1941, *14,* 375-387.
35. C. Daugherty, *Labor Problems in American Industry* (revised edition). Boston: Houghton Mifflin Company, 1938.
36. V. Hamren, "Social Farness between the A.F. of L. and the C.I.O.," *Sociology and Social Research,* 1940, *24,* 442-452; V. Hamren, "Social Nearness between the A.F. of L. and the C.I.O.," *Sociology and Social Research,* 1942, *26,* 232-240.
37. Compare *Advertising Age,* Apr. 28, 1947, p. 32.

▶ *Chapter Twenty-One* DELINQUENCY PATTERNS

(*Pages 499-514*)

1. W. I. Thomas, *The Unadjusted Girl.* Boston: Little, Brown & Company, 1923, p. 43, copyright, 1923, Little, Brown & Company.
2. J. G. Patrick, "The Role of Intimate Groups in the Personality Development of Selected College Men," *University of Southern California School of Research Studies,* 1935, No. 6, pp. 43.
3. H. C. Lehman and P. A. Witty, *The Psychology of Play Activities.* New York: A. S. Barnes & Company, 1927, Chap. 8.
4. L. Mumford, *The Culture of Cities.* New York: Harcourt, Brace and Company, 1938.
5. *The Leisure Hours of 5,000 People.* New York: National Recreation Association, 1934. Also, compare E. S. Bogardus and M. Flad, "Leisure Time Activities of Four Hundred Persons," *Sociology and Social Research,* 1934, *18,* 265-274.

6. "Behind the Marble Mask," *Collier's National Weekly*, Sept. 3, 1938, 11-14, p. 11, copyright, Crowell-Collier Company.

7. *Questions and Answers: The Program of the United States Housing Authority—Its Record to Date.* Washington, D. C.: U. S. Government Printing Office, Federal Works Agency, U. S. Housing Authority, April, 1940, p. 16; photo by Oliver.

8. F. M. Thrasher, *The Gang: A Study of 1,313 Gangs in Chicago.* Chicago: University of Chicago Press, 1927.

9. S. H. Britt and S. Q. Janus, "Toward a Social Psychology of Play," *Journal of Social Psychology,* 1941, *13,* 351-384.

10. J. A. Puffer, *The Boy and His Gang.* Boston: Houghton Mifflin Company, 1912. P. H. Furfey, *Gang Age: A Study of the Preadolescent Boy and His Recreational Needs.* New York: The Macmillan Company, 1926. Thrasher, same citation as note 8.

11. J. McV. Hunt, "An Instance of the Social Origin of Conflict Resulting in Psychosis," *American Journal of Orthopsychiatry,* 1938, *8,* 158-164, p. 159.

12. *Report on Crime and the Foreign Born.* Washington, D. C.: U. S. Government Printing Office, Publication No. 10 of The National Commission on Law Observance and Enforcement, 1931. Part II by A. C. Bowler, pp. 83-196. Also, compare S. Glueck and E. Glueck, *Juvenile Delinquents Grown Up.* New York: Commonwealth Fund, 1940.

13. Same citation as note 7, p. 20, taken from *Survey Graphic;* prepared by Pictorial Statistics, Inc.

14. H. Hartshorne and M. A. May, *Studies in the Nature of Character* (3 vol.). Vol. 1. *Studies in Deceit.* New York: The Macmillan Company, 1928. R. Stagner, "Economic Status and Personality," *School and Society,* 1935, *42,* 551-552.

15. R. E. L. Faris and H. W. Dunham, *Mental Disorders in Urban Areas: An Ecological Study of Schizophrenia and Other Psychoses.* Chicago: University of Chicago Press, 1939. C. W. Schroeder, "Mental Disorders in Cities," *American Journal of Sociology,* 1942, *8,* 40-47.

16. C. R. Shaw, with the collaboration of F. M. Zorbaugh, H. D. McKay, and L. S. Cottrell, *Delinquency Areas: A Study of the Geographic Distribution of School Truants, Juvenile Delinquents, and Adult Offenders in Chicago.* Chicago: University of Chicago Press, 1929.

17. C. R. Shaw, H. D. McKay, and others, *Juvenile Delinquency and Urban Areas.* Chicago: University of Chicago Press, 1942. Also, compare C. R. Shaw and H. D. McKay, *Social Factors in Juvenile Delinquency.* The National Commission on Law Observance and Enforcement—Report on the Causes of Crime, 1931, Vol. 2, No. 13.

18. *Facts about Juvenile Delinquency; Its Prevention and Treatment.* Washington, D. C.: U. S. Government Printing Office, Publication

No. 215 of Children's Bureau of U. S. Department of Labor, 1935, p. 6.
19. C. R. Shaw, *The Jack-Roller.* Chicago: University of Chicago Press, 1930, p. 10.
20. Compare S. Glueck and E. T. Glueck, *500 Criminal Careers.* New York: Alfred A. Knopf, Inc., 1930. S. Glueck and E. T. Glueck, *One Thousand Juvenile Delinquents.* Cambridge: Harvard University Press, 1934.
21. S. Glueck and E. Glueck, same citation as note 12.
22. Same citation, p. 103, copyright, 1940, Commonwealth Fund.
23. Compare R. T. LaPiere and P. R. Farnsworth, *Social Psychology.* New York: McGraw-Hill Book Company, Inc., 1936, p. 317.
24. Compare H. Oppenheimer, *Rationale of Punishment.* London: University of London Press, 1913.
25. A. G. Caldwell, "The Deterrent Influence of Corporal Punishment upon Prisoners Who Have Been Whipped," *American Sociological Review,* 1944, *9,* 171-177.
26. Judge P. N. Schaeffer, "The Responsibility of the Community for Crime," *American Journal of Psychiatry,* 1938, *95,* 23-33, p. 32. Compare A. L. Gausewitz, "Considerations Basic to a New Penal Code," *Wisconsin Law Review,* 1936, *11,* 346-400 and 480-540.
27. Compare A. J. Harno, "Rationale of a Criminal Code," *University of Pennsylvania Law Review,* 1937, *85,* 549-563, p. 555.
28. Same citation, pp. 560-561.
29. W. Healy, "A New Program for Treatment of Youthful Offenders," *American Sociological Review,* 1940, *5,* 610-617; W. Healy, "The Program of the American Law Institute for Dealing with Youthful Offenders," *American Journal of Orthopsychiatry,* 1941, *11,* 175-177.

▶ *Chapter Twenty-Two* RACE DIFFERENCES

(*Pages 515-527*)

1. G. Wallas, *Human Nature in Politics* (third ed.). London: copyright, Constable & Company, Ltd., 1914, p. 55.
2. O. Klineberg, *Race Differences.* New York: Harper & Brothers, 1935, p. 18.
3. *Life* magazine, Nov. 13, 1939, *7,* p. 38. Photo, center left, by Associated Press Photo; top right, by Wide World Photos, Inc.; other five by Dever from Black Star.
4. J. Deniker, *The Races of Man.* New York: Charles Scribner's Sons, 1900.

5. Klineberg, same citation as note 2, p. 21.
6. A. Hrdlička, *The Old Americans.* Baltimore: The Williams and Wilkins Company, 1925.
7. H. A. Wallace, in *The Genetic Basis for Democracy.* New York: American Committee for Democracy and Intellectual Freedom, 1939, 1-7, p. 6.
8. Compare K. Dunlap, "The Average Animal," *Journal of Comparative Psychology,* 1935, *19,* 1-3.
9. J. S. Huxley and A. C. Haddon, *We Europeans.* New York: By permission of Harper & Brothers, 1936, p. 128, copyright, 1936, Harper & Brothers.
10. Klineberg, same citation as note 2, p. 24.
11. Same citation, p. 18; by permission of Harper & Brothers, copyright, 1935, Harper & Brothers.
12. Huxley and Haddon, same citation as note 9, p. 224; by permission of Harper & Brothers, copyright, 1936, Harper & Brothers.
13. Klineberg, same citation as note 2, p. 28.
14. Same citation, p. 34.
15. *The Nazi Primer: Official Handbook for Schooling the Hitler Youth* (translated by H. L. Childs). New York: Harper & Brothers, 1938. A. Hitler, *Mein Kampf.* New York: Reynal & Hitchcock, Inc., 1939.
16. W. I. Thomas, *Primitive Behavior, An Introduction to the Social Sciences.* New York: McGraw-Hill Book Company, Inc., 1937, p. 774, quoting C. P. Steinmetz, *New York World,* Aug. 20, 1923.
17. Same citation, pp. 772-773, copyright, 1937, McGraw-Hill Book Company.
18. O. Klineberg, "A Study of Psychological Differences Between 'Racial' and National Groups in Europe," *Archives of Psychology,* 1931, *20,* No. 132, pp. 57.
19. Klineberg, same citation as note 2, p. 155.
20. Same citation, p. 157; by permission of Harper & Brothers, copyright, 1935, Harper & Brothers.
21. Same citation, pp. 158-159.
22. Same citation, p. 160, by permission of Harper & Brothers; citing O. Klineberg, "An Experimental Study of Speed and Other Factors in 'Racial' Differences," *Archives of Psychology,* 1928, *15,* No. 93, pp. 111.
23. Same citation, p. 175, citing T. L. Kelley, *Interpretation of Educational Measurements.* Chicago: World Book Company, 1927.
24. H. E. Jones, H. S. Conrad, and M. B. Blanchard, "Environmental Handicap in Mental Test Performance," *University of California Publications in Psychology,* 1932, *5,* 63-99, p. 80.
25. O. Klineberg, *Negro Intelligence and Selective Migration.* New York: Columbia University Press, 1935.

26. Boas, "An Anthropologist's Credo," *The Nation,* Aug. 27, 1938, *147,* 201-204, p. 203.

▶ *Chapter Twenty-Three* PREJUDICES AGAINST MINORITY GROUPS

(*Pages 528-555*)

1. H. C. Brearley, "Race as a Sociological Concept," *Sociology and Social Research,* 1939, *23,* 514-518, p. 515.
2. D. Young, *American Minority Peoples.* New York: Harper & Brothers, 1932.
3. R. Benedict, "Our Last Minority: Youth," *The New Republic,* Feb. 24, 1941, *104,* 271-272, p. 271, copyright, 1941, New Republic.
4. S. H. Britt and S. Q. Janus, "Criteria of Frustration," *Psychological Review,* 1940, *47,* 451-470. Also, compare S. S. Sargent, "Reaction to Frustration—A Critique and Hypothesis," *Psychological Review,* 1948, *55,* 108-114.
5. J. Dollard, L. W. Doob, N. E. Miller, O. H. Mowrer, R. R. Sears, C. S. Ford, C. I. Hovland, and R. T. Sollenberger, *Frustration and Aggression.* New Haven: Yale University Press, 1939.
6. K. Lewin, R. Lippitt, and R. K. White, "Patterns of Behavior in Experimentally Created 'Social Climates,'" *Journal of Social Psychology,* 1939, *10,* 271-299. Also compare R. Lippitt, "Field Theory and Experiment in Social Psychology: Autocratic and Democratic Group Atmospheres," *American Journal of Sociology,* 1939, *45,* 26-49; R. Lippitt, "An Experimental Study of the Effect of Democratic and Authoritarian Group Atmospheres," *University of Iowa Studies: Studies in Child Welfare,* 1940, *16,* No. 3, 43-195. Also, compare O. H. Mowrer, "Authoritarianism vs. 'Self-Government' in the Management of Children's Aggressive (Anti-Social) Reactions as a Preparation for Citizenship in a Democracy," *The Journal of Social Psychology,* 1939, *10,* 121-126.
7. H. Meltzer, "Hostility and Tolerance in Children's Nationality and Race Attitudes," *The American Journal of Orthopsychiatry,* 1941, *11,* 662-675.
8. E. L. Horowitz, "The Development of Attitude toward the Negro," *Archives of Psychology,* 1936, *28,* No. 194, pp. 47.
9. D. Young, "Some Effects of a Course in American Race Problems on the Race Prejudice of 450 Undergraduates at the University of Pennsylvania," *Journal of Abnormal and Social Psychology,* 1927, *22,* 235-242. D. D. Droba, "Education and Negro Attitudes," *Sociology and Social Research,* 1932, *17,* 137-141.

10. F. T. Smith, *An Experiment in Modifying Attitudes toward the Negro.* Ph.D. Thesis, Teachers College, Columbia University, 1933. Cited by G. Murphy, L. B. Murphy, and T. M. Newcomb, *Experimental Social Psychology* (revised edition). New York: Harper & Brothers, 1937, pp. 972-973.

11. P. S. Buck, "A Protest against Racial Arrogance," *The Christian,* Feb. 18, 1933, 233-234, p. 233.

12. *The Negro in Chicago,* edited by the Chicago Commission on Race Relations. Chicago: University of Chicago Press, 1922, pp. 438 *ff.*

13. G. J. Nathan and H. L. Mencken, *The American Credo.* New York: Alfred A. Knopf, Inc., 1921, in pp. 111-191.

14. F. A. Moss, *Applications of Psychology.* Boston: Houghton Mifflin Company, 1929, pp. 101-104, copyright, 1929, Fred A. Moss.

15. C. S. Johnson, *The Negro College Graduate.* Chapel Hill: University of North Carolina Press, 1938.

16. *Racial Inequalities in Education.* New York: Bulletin of the National Association for the Advancement of Colored People, October, 1938. Also, G. Beech, "Schools for a Minority," *Survey Graphic,* 1939, *28,* 615-618 and 640-641.

17. R. S. Lynd and H. M. Lynd, *Middletown in Transition: A Study in Cultural Conflicts.* New York: Harcourt, Brace and Company, 1937, p. 463, copyright, 1937, Harcourt, Brace and Company.

18. E. F. Frazier, *The Negro Family in the United States.* Chicago: University of Chicago Press, 1939. E. F. Frazier, *Negro Youth at the Crossways.* Washington, D. C.: American Council on Education, 1940.

19. C. S. Johnson, *Growing Up in the Black Belt: Negro Youth in the Rural South.* Washington, D. C.: American Council on Education, 1941.

20. H. W. Odum, *Race and Rumors of Race: Challenge to American Crisis.* Chapel Hill: University of North Carolina Press, 1943.

21. Compare H. G. Canady, "The Problem of Equating the Environment of Negro-White Groups for Intelligence Testing in Comparative Studies," *The Journal of Social Psychology,* 1943, *17,* 3-15.

22. C. W. Hunter, *A Comparative Study of the Relationship Existing between the White Race and the Negro Race in the State of North Carolina and in the City of New York,* Master's Thesis, Columbia University, 1927. Cited by R. T. LaPiere and P. R. Farnsworth, *Social Psychology.* New York: McGraw-Hill Book Company, Inc., 1936, p. 278, note 3.

23. O. Klineberg, *Race Differences.* New York: Harper & Brothers, 1935, Chap. 8.

24. Same citation, p. 189; by permission of Harper & Brothers, copyright, 1935, Harper & Brothers.

25. O. Klineberg, *Negro Intelligence and Selective Migration.* New York: Columbia University Press, 1935.
26. Murphy, Murphy, and Newcomb, same citation as note 10, p. 65; by permission of Harper & Brothers, copyright, 1931, 1937, Harper & Brothers.
27. Compare Klineberg, same citation as note 23, p. 23.
28. M. J. Herskovits, *The Negro and the Intelligence Tests.* Hanover: The Sociological Press, 1928.
29. E. B. Reuter, *The Mulatto in the United States.* Boston: Richard G. Badger, 1918, p. 202.
30. W. L. Warner, B. H. Junker, and W. A. Adams, *Color and Human Nature: Negro Personality Development in a Northern City.* Washington, D. C.: American Council on Education, 1941. Also, R. I. Sutherland, *Color, Class,* and *Personality.* Washington, D. C.: American Council on Education, 1942.
31. B. Lasker, *Race Attitudes in Children.* New York: Henry Holt and Company, Inc., 1929.
32. R. Blake and W. Dennis, "The Development of Stereotypes concerning the Negro," *The Journal of Abnormal and Social Psychology,* 1943, *38,* 525-531.
33. Horowitz, same citation as note 8.
34. Lynd and Lynd, same citation as note 17, p. 425, footnote 27.
35. St. C. Drake and H. R. Cayton, *Black Metropolis.* New York: Harcourt, Brace and Company, 1945.
36. A. T. Raper, *The Tragedy of Lynching.* Chapel Hill: University of North Carolina Press, 1933.
37. *Lynchings and What They Mean.* Atlanta: Southern Commission on the Study of Lynching, 1931, p. 31.
38. F. L. Allen, *Only Yesterday: An Informal History of the Nineteen-Twenties.* New York: Harper & Brothers, 1931, pp. 63-64, copyright, 1931, Frederick Lewis Allen.
39. A. M. Lee and N. D. Humphrey, *Race Riot.* New York: Dryden Press, 1943.
40. H. Orlansky, "The Harlem Riot: A Study in Mass Frustration," *Social Analysis,* 1943, No. 1, pp. 29.
41. G. Myrdal, and others, *An American Dilemma: The Negro Problem and Modern Democracy.* New York: Harper & Brothers, 1944.
42. *Life* magazine, Apr. 24, 1944, *16,* 32.
43. H. M. Vinacke, *A History of the Far East in Modern Times.* New York: Alfred A. Knopf, Inc., 1928, p. 55.
44. P. J. Treat, *The Far East: A Political and Diplomatic History* (revised edition). New York: Harper & Brothers, 1935, pp. 526-531. Vinacke, same citation as note 43, p. 374.

45. C. R. Miller, *How to Detect and Analyze Propaganda.* New York: Town Hall, 1939, pp. 11-12.

46. A. L. Severson, "Nationality and Religious Preferences as Reflected in Newspaper Advertisements," *American Journal of Sociology,* 1939, *44,* 540-545.

47. *The Nazi Primer* (translated by H. L. Childs). New York: Harper & Brothers, 1938, p. 56.

48. "Current Manifestations of Organized Anti-Semitism," *Information Service of Federal Council of the Churches of Christ in America,* June 10, 1939, *18,* pp. 6, p. 1.

49. M. Meenes, "American Jews and Anti-Semitism," *Journal of Negro Education,* 1941, *10,* 557-566.

50. E. Frenkel-Brunswik and R. N. Sanford, "Some Personality Factors in Anti-Semitism," *The Journal of Psychology,* 1945, *20,* 271-291.

51. D. J. Levinson and R. N. Sanford, "A Scale for the Measurement of Anti-Semitism," *The Journal of Psychology,* 1944, *17,* 339-370.

52. S. H. Flowerman and M. Jahoda, "The Study of Man—Polls on Anti-Semitism. How Much Do They Tell Us?," *Commentary,* 1946, *1,* 82-86.

53. M. Jahoda and N. W. Ackerman, "Some Remarks on the Motivation for Anti-Semitic Attitudes," *The American Psychologist,* 1942, *2,* 322-323. Also, N. W. Ackerman and M. Jahoda, "Toward a Dynamic Interpretation of Anti-Semitic Attitudes," *American Journal of Orthopsychiatry,* 1948, *18,* 163-173.

54. Professor Daniel Katz aided greatly in this analysis of anti-Semitism.

55. D. S. Strong, *Organized Anti-Semitism in America: The Rise of Group Prejudice during the Decade 1930-40.* Washington, D. C.: American Council on Public Affairs, 1941.

56. Survey by Anti-Defamation League of B'nai B'rith, as reported in *The New York Times,* Mar. 29, 1948, p. 23.

57. Compare E. Freeman, "The Motivation of Jew-Gentile Relationships," in I. Graeber and S. H. Britt (editors), *Jews in a Gentile World: The Problem of Anti-Semitism.* New York: The Macmillan Company, 1942, Chap. 6, pp. 149-178.

58. "Jews in America," *Fortune* magazine, February, 1936, *13,* 79-85, 128, 130, 133-134, 136, 141-142, 144.

59. P. S. Bernstein, "Some Facts about Jews," *Harper's Magazine,* 1939, *178,* 501-506, p. 502.

60. For a fuller discussion of anti-Semitism, see I. Graeber and S. H. Britt, same citation as note 57.

▶ *Chapter Twenty-Four* NATIONALISM AND WAR

(*Pages 556-594*)

1. W. D. Wallis, "Prejudices of Men," *American Journal of Sociology,* 1929, *34,* 804-821. Also C. J. H. Hayes, *Essays on Nationalism.* New York: The Macmillan Company, 1926.
2. H. C. Lehman, "National Differences in Creativity," *American Journal of Sociology,* 1947, *52,* 475-488.
3. W. B. Pillsbury, *The Psychology of Nationality and Internationalism,* New York: Appleton-Century-Crofts, Inc., 1919, p. 20.
4. E. Diggins, *A Statistical Study of National Prejudices,* Master's Thesis, Columbia University, 1927. Described by G. Murphy, L. B. Murphy, T. M. Newcomb, *Experimental Social Psychology* (revised edition). New York: Harper & Brothers, 1937, pp. 993-995.
5. Compare N. Carpenter and D. Katz, "The Cultural Adjustment of the Polish Group in the City of Buffalo," *Social Forces,* 1927, *6,* 76-90. Also W. I. Thomas and F. Znaniecki, *The Polish Peasant in Europe and America* (second ed.). (2 vol.) Chicago: University of Chicago Press, 1927.
6. *Time* magazine, copyright, Time, Inc., July 15, 1935, *26,* p. 26, quoting H. Nicolson.
7. "Americans and Britons Appraise Each Other," *Opinion News* (of National Opinion Research Center), Oct. 15, 1947, *9,* 3-13 and 16, p. 5.
8. H. Herring, "The Unconquerable Mexican," *Harper's Magazine,* June, 1937, *175,* 46-56, p. 46, copyright, Harper & Brothers.
9. E. S. Bogardus, "Causes of Race Antagonism: An Outline," *Sociology and Social Research,* 1939, *24,* 166-170, p. 168.
10. Compare R. S. Lynd and H. M. Lynd, *Middletown: A Study in Contemporary American Culture.* New York: Harcourt, Brace and Company, 1929, p. 201.
11. Same citation, p. 487, copyright, 1929, Harcourt, Brace and Company.
12. Compare C. E. Merriam, *The Making of Citizens: A Comparative Study of Methods of Civic Training.* Chicago: University of Chicago Press, 1931.
13. Compare H. U. Faulkner, "Perverted American History," *Harper's Magazine,* February, 1926, *152,* 337-346. Also compare "Propaganda over the Schools," *Bulletin of Institute for Propaganda Analysis, Inc.,* Feb. 25, 1941, *4,* pp. 16.
14. *Can You Name Them?* New York: American Committee for Democracy and Intellectual Freedom, 1939, p. 5.

15. K. Young, *Social Psychology: An Analysis of Social Behavior.* New York: Appleton-Century-Crofts, Inc., 1930, p. 487.
16. D. Katz and R. L. Schanck, *Social Psychology.* New York: John Wiley & Sons, Inc., 1938, pp. 680-681.
17. W. Millis, "The Faith of an American." In Stephen Vincent Benét (editor), *Zero Hour: A Summons to the Free.* New York: Rinehart & Company, Inc., copyright, 1940, 215-244, p. 235, and reprinted by permission of the publishers, Rinehart & Company, Inc.
18. D. V. McGranahan, "A Comparison of Social Attitudes among American and German Youth," *The Journal of Abnormal and Social Psychology,* 1946, *41,* 245-257.
19. "Propaganda Techniques of German Fascism," *Bulletin of Institute for Propaganda Analysis, Inc.,* May, 1938, *1,* No. 8, 37-53.
20. Same citation, p. 41.
21. J. S. Huxley and A. C. Haddon, *We Europeans.* New York: Harper & Brothers, 1936, p. 13.
22. E. R. Jaensch, "Der Hühnerhof als Forschungs—und Aufklärungsmittel in menschlichen Rassenfragen," *Zeitschrift für Tierpsychologie,* 1939, *2,* 223-258.
23. H. Stölting, "Blutreinheit und Blutmischungen in ihrer tieferen Bedeutung," *Zeitschrift für pädagogische Psychologie,* 1938, *39,* 99-105.
24. H. E. Salisbury, "Russian Fallacies about Us—and Vice Versa," *The New York Times Magazine,* Apr. 6, 1947, pp. 12-13, 56, 58.
25. A. Campbell, "The American Concept of Russia," *The Journal of Social Issues,* 1948, *4,* 15-20, p. 16.
26. Same citation.
27. *The New York Times,* May 29, 1948, p. 1.
28. E. Krehbiel, *Nationalism, War and Society.* New York: The Macmillan Company, 1916, pp. 16-17.
29. J. S. Huxley, "Science, War and Reconstruction," *Science,* Feb. 16, 1940, *91,* 151-158, p. 151.
30. K. Dunlap, "The Causes and the Prevention of War," *Journal of Abnormal and Social Psychology,* 1940, *35,* 479-497, p. 481.
31. M. A. May, *A Social Psychology of War and Peace.* New Haven: Yale University Press, 1943.
32. J. T. Shotwell. In C. S. Marsh (editor), *Educational Broadcasting 1936.* Chicago: University of Chicago Press, 1937, 130-136, p. 131.
33. S. Raushenbush and J. Raushenbush, *War Madness.* Washington, D. C.: National Home Library Foundation, 1937.
34. E. Staley, *War and the Private Investor.* New York: Doubleday & Company, Inc., 1935.
35. Q. Wright, "The Causation and Control of War," *American Sociological Review,* 1938, *3,* 461-474, p. 462.

36. P. A. Sorokin, "A Neglected Factor of War," *American Sociological Review,* 1938, *3,* 475-486, p. 475.
37. L. C. Rosten, "Men Like War," *Harper's Magazine,* July, 1935, *171,* 189-197, p. 192, copyright, Harper & Brothers.
38. *The New York Times,* Oct. 8, 1936.
39. Compare "Propaganda for Blitzkrieg," *Bulletin of Institute for Propaganda Analysis, Inc.,* Aug. 1, 1940, *3,* pp. 7.
40. Same citation, p. 7.
41. P. M. A. Linebarger, *Psychological Warfare.* Washington: Infantry Journal Press, 1948, p. 39.
42. Compare H. Lasswell, *Propaganda Technique in the World War.* New York: Alfred A. Knopf, Inc., 1927, p. 195.
43. G. Creel, *How We Advertised America: The First Telling of the Amazing Story of the Committee on Public Information That Carried the Gospel of Americanism to Every Corner of the Globe.* New York: Harper & Brothers, 1920.
44. Linebarger, same citation as note 41.
45. Compare R. H. Gundlach, "The Psychology of Nationalism as a Major Factor for War," *Psychological Bulletin,* 1940, *37,* 590.
46. N. Angell, *The Public Mind: Its Disorders: Its Exploitations.* New York: E. P. Dutton & Company, Inc., 1927, p. 51, copyright, 1927, E. P. Dutton & Company, Inc.
47. "Soldiers of the Lord," *Bulletin of Institute for Propaganda Analysis, Inc.,* Apr. 1, 1940, *3,* pp. 12, p. 1.
48. S. Rogerson, *Propaganda in the Next War.* London: Geoffrey Bles, 1938, p. 149.
49. *The New York Times,* Apr. 11, 1939.
50. Compare "We Are Content with Hitler . . . ," Special Bulletin on War Propaganda, *Institute for Propaganda Analysis, Inc.,* No. 3, Dec. 5, 1939, pp. 2.
51. "The Fotune Survey: XXVI," *Fortune* magazine, 1940, *21,* 56-57, 86, 88, 90, 92, p. 88.
52. H. Cantril, D. Rugg, and F. Williams, "America Faces the War: Shifts in Opinion," *The Public Opinion Quarterly,* 1940, *4,* 651-656.
53. Polls of American Institute of Public Opinion, *Washington Post,* Jan. 22, 1941; Feb. 9, 1941; Feb. 14, 1941; Feb. 28, 1941.
54. Poll of American Institute of Public Opinion, *Washington Post,* Mar. 21, 1941.
55. Poll of American Institute of Public Opinion, *Washington Post,* Apr. 20, 1941.
56. Poll of American Institute of Public Opinion, *Washington Post,* May 2, 1941.

57. B. Lasker and A. Roman, *Propaganda from China and Japan: A Case Study in Propaganda Analysis.* American Council, Institute of Pacific Relations, 1938 (printed in Camden, N. J.), pp. 41-45.
58. *Washington Post,* Aug. 15, 1945, p. 6.
59. Quoted by H. L. Stimson, "The Decision to Use the Atomic Bomb," *Harper's Magazine,* 1947, *194,* 97-107, p. 106.
60. W. A. Higinbotham, "Foreword by an Atomic Scientist," *The Journal of Social Issues,* 1948, *4,* 2-4.
61. P. Woodward, "How Do the American People Feel about the Atomic Bomb?" *The Journal of Social Issues,* 1948, *4,* 7-14.
62. Same citation, p. 8.
63. Same citation, p. 14.
64. "Spain: A Case Study," *Bulletin of Institute for Propaganda Analysis, Inc.,* July 1, 1939, 2, pp. 8, p. 1.
65. W. Miller, *I Found No Peace.* New York: Simon and Schuster, 1936, p. 165.
66. *The New York Times,* Nov. 14, 1937.
67. W. B. Knight, *How to Run a War.* New York: Alfred A. Knopf, Inc., 1936, pp. 231-232, copyright, 1936, Alfred A. Knopf, Inc., quoting excerpt from a circular letter of World Peaceways, Jan. 25, 1936.
68. J. S. Huxley, "Science, War and Reconstruction," *Science,* Feb. 16, 1940, *91,* 151-158, p. 152.
69. *Washington Star,* May 7, 1945, p. A-4.
70. "Cost of War and War Threats since 1915," ***U. S. News and World Report,*** May 28, 1948, *24,* 34-35.
71. Same citation.
72. E. Maccoby and B. Willerman (editors), "Citizen Participation in World Affairs," *The Journal of Social Issues,* 1948, *4,* 1-63: "Introduction," 5-6, p. 5.
73. Same citation, "Summary of Discussions," 57-59, p. 57.
74. M. A. May, "The Psychological Foundations of Peace," *The Annals of the American Academy of Political and Social Science,* 1944, *235,* 128-134, p. 128.
75. G. A. Lundberg, *Can Science Save Us?* New York: Longmans, Green and Co., 1947, p. 107.
76. Millis, same citation as note 17, p. 237.
77. May, same citation as note 74, p. 131.
78. G. W. Allport, "Human Nature and the Peace," *Psychological Bulletin,* 1945, *42,* 376-378. Also published as "The Psychologists' Manifesto," Chapter 26 in G. Murphy (editor), *Human Nature and Enduring Peace.* Boston: Houghton Mifflin Company, 1945, pp. 454-460.

▶ *Chapter Twenty-Five* KNOWLEDGE FOR WHAT?

(*Pages 595-601*)

1. From *The Miracle of America,* reprinted by *Look* magazine from materials from the Advertising Council.
2. P. Wylie, *Generation of Vipers.* New York: Rinehart & Company, Inc., 1942, p. 21.
3. Data from Bureau of Agricultural Economics, and Federal Reserve Board.
4. A. T. Vanderbilt, "Public Opinion and the Professions," *American Bar Association Journal,* 1939, *25,* 999-1002, p. 1001.
5. *Philadelphia Record,* Nov. 8, 1936.
6. S. H. Britt, "Time Lag in the Law: Blood-Grouping Tests in the Courts," *The American Scholar,* 1940, *9,* 201-213.
7. R. S. Lynd and H. M. Lynd, *Middletown in Transition: A Study in Cultural Conflicts.* New York: Harcourt, Brace and Company, 1937, p. 492.
8. R. Bain, "Our Schizoid Culture," *Sociology and Social Research,* 1935, *19,* 266-276.
9. Same citation, p. 268.
10. R. Bain, "Cultural Integration and Social Conflict," *American Journal of Sociology,* 1939, *44,* 499-509, p. 509.
11. R. B. Fosdick, *The Rockefeller Foundation: A Review for 1939.* New York: The Rockefeller Foundation, p. 39.
12. Compare Hearings on Nomination of Thurman W. Arnold to be Assistant Attorney General, Mar. 11, 1938, Washington, D. C.: U. S. Government Printing Office, p. 5.
13. G. A. Lundberg, *Can Science Save Us?* New York: Longmans, Green & Co., 1947, p. 88.
14. Same citation, p. 4, copyright, 1947, George A. Lundberg.
15. Same citation, pp. 23-24.
16. R. S. Lynd, *Knowledge for What? The Place of Social Science in American Culture.* Princeton: Princeton University Press, 1939.

APPENDIX B

LIST OF TEXTBOOKS ON SOCIAL PSYCHOLOGY

1. F. H. Allport, *Social Psychology*. Boston: Houghton Mifflin Company, 1924.
2. J. M. Baldwin, *The Individual and Society*. Boston: Richard G. Badger, 1911.
3. L. L. Bernard, *An Introduction to Social Psychology*. New York: Henry Holt and Company, Inc., 1926.
4. C. Bird, *Social Psychology*. New York: Appleton-Century-Crofts, Inc., 1940.
5. E. S. Bogardus, *Essentials of Social Psychology*. Los Angeles: University of Southern California Press, 1920.
6. E. S. Bogardus, *Fundamentals of Social Psychology* (third ed.). New York: Appleton-Century-Crofts, Inc., 1942.
7. A. O. Bowden and I. R. Melbo, *Social Psychology of Education: Applications of Social Psychology to Educational Problems*. New York: McGraw-Hill Book Company, Inc., 1937.
8. S. H. Britt, *Social Psychology of Modern Life* (revised edition). New York: Rinehart & Company, Inc., 1949.
9. J. F. Brown, *Psychology and the Social Order: An Introduction to the Dynamic Study of Social Fields*. New York: McGraw-Hill Book Company, Inc., 1936.
10. L. G. Brown, *Social Psychology: The Natural History of Human Nature*. New York: McGraw-Hill Book Company, Inc., 1934.
11. C. H. Cooley, *Human Nature and the Social Order*. New York: Charles Scribner's Sons, 1902.
12. K. Dunlap, *Social Psychology*. Baltimore: The Williams and Wilkins Company, 1927.
13. K. Dunlap, *Civilized Life: The Principles and Applications of Social Psychology*. Baltimore: The Williams and Wilkins Company, 1935.
14. C. A. Ellwood, *An Introduction to Social Psychology*. New York: Appleton-Century-Crofts, Inc., 1917.
15. C. A. Ellwood, *The Psychology of Human Society*. New York: Appleton-Century-Crofts, Inc., 1925.
16. B. C. Ewer, *Social Psychology*. New York: The Macmillan Company, 1935.
17. E. Faris, *The Nature of Human Nature and Other Essays in Social Psychology*. New York: McGraw-Hill Book Company, Inc., 1937.
18. J. K. Folsom, *Social Psychology*. New York: Harper & Brothers, 1931.

19. E. Freeman, *Social Psychology*. New York: Henry Holt and Company, Inc., 1936.
20. R. H. Gault, *Social Psychology: The Bases of Behavior Called Social*. New York: Henry Holt and Company, 1923.
21. H. Gurnee, *Elements of Social Psychology*. New York: Rinehart & Company, Inc., 1936.
22. C. H. Judd, *The Psychology of Social Institutions*. New York: The Macmillan Company, 1926.
23. J. R. Kantor, *An Outline of Social Psychology*. Chicago: Follett Publishing Company, 1929.
24. F. B. Karpf, *American Social Psychology: Its Origins, Development, and European Background*. New York: McGraw-Hill Book Company, Inc., 1932.
25. D. Katz and R. L. Schanck, *Social Psychology*. New York: John Wiley & Sons, Inc., 1938.
26. O. Klineberg, *Social Psychology*. New York: Harper & Brothers, 1940.
27. D. Krech and R. S. Crutchfield, *Theory and Problems of Social Psychology*. New York: McGraw-Hill Book Company, Inc., 1948.
28. M. H. Krout, *Introduction to Social Psychology*. New York: Harper & Brothers, 1942.
29. E. T. Krueger and W. C. Reckless, *Social Psychology*. New York: Longmans, Green & Co., 1934.
30. R. T. LaPiere and P. R. Farnsworth, *Social Psychology* (second ed.). New York: McGraw-Hill Book Company, Inc., 1942.
31. R. T. LaPiere, *Collective Behavior*. New York: McGraw-Hill Book Company, Inc., 1938.
32. W. McDougall, *Introduction to Social Psychology* (revised edition). Boston: John W. Luce & Company, 1926.
33. R. Mujkerji and N. Sen-Gupta, *Introduction to Social Psychology: Mind in Society*. Boston: D. C. Heath and Company, 1928.
34. C. Murchison, *Social Psychology: The Psychology of Political Domination*. Worcester: Clark University Press, 1927.
35. C. Murchison (editor), *A Handbook of Social Psychology*. Worcester: Clark University Press, 1935.
36. G. Murphy and L. B. Murphy, *Experimental Social Psychology*. New York: Harper & Brothers, 1931.
37. G. Murphy, L. B. Murphy, and T. M. Newcomb, *Experimental Social Psychology* (revised edition). New York: Harper & Brothers, 1937.
38. A. Myerson, *Social Psychology: An Introduction to the Study of Personality and the Environment*. New York: Prentice-Hall, Inc., 1934.
39. T. M. Newcomb, E. L. Hartley, and others (editors), *Readings in Social Psychology*. New York: Henry Holt and Company, 1947.
40. E. D. Partridge, *Social Psychology of Adolescence*. New York: Prentice-Hall, Inc., 1938.

41. J. M. Reinhardt, *Social Psychology.* Philadelphia: J. B. Lippincott Company, 1938.

42. E. A. Ross, *Social Psychology: An Outline and Source Book.* New York: The Macmillan Company, 1908.

43. M. Sherif, *Outline of Social Psychology.* New York: Harper & Brothers, 1948.

44. J. J. Smith, *Social Psychology: The Psychology of Attraction and Repulsion.* Boston: Richard G. Badger, 1930.

45. J. W. Sprowls, *Social Psychology Interpreted.* Baltimore: The Williams and Wilkins Company, 1927.

46. E. L. Thorndike, *Human Nature and the Social Order.* New York: The Macmillan Company, 1940.

47. R. H. Thouless, *General and Social Psychology* (revised edition). London: University Tutorial Press, 1937.

48. W. F. Vaughan, *Social Psychology.* New York: The Odyssey Press, 1948.

49. J. M. Williams, *Principles of Social Psychology.* New York: Alfred A. Knopf, Inc., 1922.

50. K. Young, *Source Book for Social Psychology.* New York: Appleton-Century-Crofts, Inc., 1927.

51. K. Young, *Social Psychology* (second ed.). New York: Appleton-Century-Crofts, Inc., 1944.

52. F. Znaniecki, *The Laws of Social Psychology.* Chicago: University of Chicago Press, 1925.

APPENDIX C

OTHER BIBLIOGRAPHICAL SOURCES

▶ GENERAL BIBLIOGRAPHICAL SOURCES:

1. *American Journal of Psychology,* Index to Volumes 1-30 (1887-1919). (Subject and author indices.)
2. J. M. Baldwin, *Dictionary of Philosophy and Psychology* (3 vol.). New York: The Macmillan Company, 1901-1905. Vol. 3, Parts 1 and 2 (Bibliography of philosophy, psychology, and cognate subjects, prior to 1905, by B. Rand.)
3. C. M. Louttit, *Bibliography of Bibliographies on Psychology, 1900-1927.* Washington, D. C.: Bulletin of the National Research Council, 1928, No. 65. (Many bibliographies of special fields and special topics.)
4. *Biological Abstracts* (1926-present).
5. *Child Development Abstracts* (1927-present).
6. *Education Abstracts* (1936-present).
7. *Education Index* (1929-present).
8. *Philosophic Abstracts* (1940-present).
9. *Psychological Abstracts* (1927-present). (A monthly issue with a detailed subject index at the end of each yearly volume.)
10. *Psychological Bulletin* (1903-present). (Reviews—and abstracts until 1927—of special fields and topics, with bibliographies.)
11. *Psychological Index* (1894-1935). (Yearly bibliography.)
12. *Social Science Abstracts* (1929-1932).
13. *Vocational Guidance Digest* (1936-present).

▶ CHECK LISTS OF SOCIOLOGICAL, PSYCHOLOGICAL, AND ALLIED JOURNALS:

1. E. S. Conklin, "A Volume-Year Check List of Psychological and Allied Journals," *University of Oregon Publications, Psychology Series,* 1931, *2,* 105-128.
2. *Psychological Abstracts,* 1929, *3,* 724-731. (Directory of periodicals—compare additions in subsequent volumes.)
3. *Psychological Abstracts,* 1947, *21,* 558-563. (Directory of periodicals.)
4. *Social Science Abstracts,* 1929, *1,* 1556-1573. (Directory of periodicals—compare more complete list in *Index,* 1933, *5,* 681-725.)

▶ IMPORTANT SOCIOLOGICAL, PSYCHOLOGICAL, AND ALLIED JOURNALS:

(PUBLISHED IN ENGLISH)

1. *American Journal of Orthopsychiatry*
2. *American Journal of Psychiatry*
3. *American Journal of Psychology*
4. *American Journal of Sociology*
5. *American Psychologist*
6. *American Sociological Review*
7. *Applied Psychology Monographs* (see *Psychological Monographs: General and Applied*)
8. *Archives of Neurology and Psychiatry*
9. *Archives of Psychology* (see *Psychological Monographs: General and Applied*)
10. *Biological Abstracts*
11. *British Journal of Educational Psychology*
12. *British Journal of Medical Psychology*
13. *British Journal of Psychology*
14. *British Journal of Psychology—Monograph Supplement*
15. *Canadian Journal of Psychology*
16. *Character and Personality* (see *Journal of Personality*)
17. *Child Development*
18. *Child Development Monographs*
19. *Child Study*
20. *Comparative Psychology Monographs*
21. *Education*
22. *Education Abstracts*
23. *Education Index*
24. *Educational and Psychological Measurement*
25. *Educational Research Bulletin*
26. *Educational Review*
27. *Genetic Psychology Monographs*
28. *Human Relations*
29. *International Journal of Opinion and Attitude Research*
30. *Journal of Abnormal and Social Psychology*
31. *Journal of Aesthetics and Art Criticism*
32. *Journal of Applied Psychology*
33. *Journal of Child Psychiatry*
34. *Journal of Clinical Psychology*
35. *Journal of Comparative and Physiological Psychology* (formerly published as *Journal of Comparative Psychology*)

36. *Journal of Consulting Psychology*
37. *Journal of Criminal Law and Criminology*
38. *Journal of Educational Method*
39. *Journal of Educational Psychology*
40. *Journal of Educational Research*
41. *Journal of Educational Sociology*
42. *Journal of the Exceptional Child*
43. *Journal of Experimental Education*
44. *Journal of Experimental Psychology*
45. *Journal of General Psychology*
46. *Journal of Genetic Psychology* (*Pedagogical Seminary*)
47. *Journal of Higher Education*
48. *Journal of Nervous and Mental Diseases*
49. *Journal of Parapsychology*
50. *Journal of Personality* (formerly published as *Character and Personality*)
51. *Journal of Personnel Research* (see *Personnel Journal*)
52. *Journal of Psychology*
53. *Journal of Social Issues*
54. *Journal of Social Philosophy*
55. *Journal of Social Psychology*
56. *Marriage and Family Living* (formerly published as *Living*)
57. *Mental Hygiene*
58. *Nervous Child*
59. *Occupational Psychology*
60. *Personnel*
61. *Personnel Journal*
62. *Personnel Psychology*
63. *Philosophic Abstracts*
64. *Philosophical Review*
65. *Psychiatric Quarterly*
66. *Psychiatry*
67. *Psychoanalytic Quarterly*
68. *Psychoanalytic Review*
69. *Psychological Abstracts*
70. *Psychological Bulletin*
71. *Psychological Clinic* (no longer published)
72. *Psychological Exchange* (no longer published)
73. *Psychological Index* (no longer published)
74. *Psychological Monographs: General and Applied* (formerly published as *Psychological Monographs*)
75. *Psychological Record*
76. *Psychological Review*
77. *Psychologists League Journal* (no longer published)

78. *Psychometrika*
79. *Psychosomatic Medicine*
80. *Public Opinion Quarterly*
81. *Review of Educational Research*
82. *School and Society*
83. *Science*
84. *Social Forces*
85. *Social Science*
86. *Social Science Abstracts* (no longer published)
87. *Sociology and Social Research*
88. *Sociometry*
89. *Sociometry Monographs*
90. *Vocational Guidance Digest*

(PUBLISHED IN FOREIGN LANGUAGES)

*91. *Acta Psychologica*
*92. *Archiv. für die gesamte Psychologie*
93. *(L') Anneé Psychologique*
94. *Archives de Psychologie*
95. *Journal de Psychologie normale et pathologique*
*96. *Journal für Psychologie und Neurologie*
*97. *Psychologische Forschung*
98. *Rivista di Psicologia*
*99. *Zeitschrift für angewandte Psychologie*
*100. *Zeitschrift für pädagogische Psychologie*
*101. *Zeitschrift für Psychologie: I. Zeitschrift für Psychologie*
*102. *Zeitschrift für Psychologie: II. Zeitschrift für Sinnephysiologie*

(PUBLISHED IN VARIOUS LANGUAGES)

*103. *Studies in Philosophy and Social Science* (formerly published as *Zeitschrift für Sozial-Forschung*)

* Not available during latter part of World War II and immediately following.

APPENDIX D

TERMINOLOGY

The following dictionaries, vocabularies, and encyclopedias may prove useful:

1. J. M. Baldwin, *Dictionary of Philosophy and Psychology* (3 vol.). New York: The Macmillan Company, 1901-1905. Vol. 1 and 2 reprinted—New York: Peter Smith, 1940.
2. H. B. English, *A Student's Dictionary of Psychological Terms* (fourth edition). New York: Harper & Brothers, 1934.
3. M. Erdélyi and F. Grossman, *Dictionary of Terms and Expressions of Industrial Psychology ("Psychotechnics"), in German, English, French, Hungarian.* New York: Pitman Publishing Corporation, 1939.
4. H. P. Fairchild (editor), *Dictionary of Sociology.* New York: Philosophical Library, 1944.
5. P. L. Harriman (editor), *Encyclopedia of Psychology.* New York: Philosophical Library, 1946.
6. P. L. Harriman (editor), *The New Dictionary of Psychology.* New York: Philosophical Library, 1947.
7. L. E. Hinsie and J. Shatzky, *Psychiatric Dictionary, with Encyclopedic Treatment of Modern Terms.* New York: Oxford University Press, 1940.
8. R. H. Hutchings, *Psychiatric Word Book.* Utica, New York: The State Hospitals Press, 1932.
9. A. K. Kurtz and H. A. Edgerton, *Statistical Dictionary of Terms and Symbols.* New York: John Wiley & Sons, Inc., 1939.
10. W. S. Monroe (editor), *Encyclopedia of Educational Research: A Critical Inventory of the Accomplishments of Research.* New York: The Macmillan Company, 1941.
11. C. A. Ruckmick, *German-English Dictionary of Psychological Terms.* Iowa City: Athens Press, 1928.
12. D. D. Runes (editor), *The Dictionary of Philosophy.* New York: Philosophical Library, 1942.
13. E. R. A. Seligman (editor), *Encyclopaedia of the Social Sciences* (15 vols.). New York: The Macmillan Company, 1930.
14. H. C. Warren (editor), *Dictionary of Psychology.* Boston: Houghton Mifflin Company, 1934.

AUTHOR INDEX

SUBJECT INDEX